Truth

Prometheus's Literary Classics Series

Truth

Émile Zola

Translated by Ernest A. Vizetelly

LITERARY CLASSICS

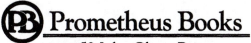 Prometheus Books

59 John Glenn Drive
Amherst, New York 14228-2197

Published 2002 by Prometheus Books
59 John Glenn Drive, Amherst, New York 14228–2197
VOICE: 716–691–0133, ext. 207. FAX: 716–564–2711
WWW.PROMETHEUSBOOKS.COM

Truth originally published: New York: John Lane, 1903

Library of Congress Cataloging-in-Publication Data

Zola, Emile, 1840–1902.
    [Vérité. English]
    Truth / Emile Zola ; translated by Ernest A. Vizetelly.
        p. cm. — (Literary classics)
    ISBN 1–57392–938–7 (pbk. : alk. paper)
    I. Vizetelly, Ernest Alfred, 1853–1922. II. Title. III. Literary
classics (Amherst, N.Y.)

PQ2521.V4 E5 2001
843'.8—dc21   2001049201
                                                            CIP

Printed in the United States of America on acid-free paper

ÉMILE ZOLA was born in Paris on April 2, 1840, the son of an Italian-Greek engineer father and a French mother. When Zola was two, his family moved to Aix-en-Provence. His father died soon thereafter, leaving his mother struggling to support herself and the boy. In 1860, after two years of study at the Lycée St-Louis, Zola returned to Paris, where he became a clerk and journalist, and began his writing career. He published a collection of short stories, *Contes à Ninon* (Stories for Ninon), in 1864, followed by *La Confession de Claude* (1865), *Thérèse Raquin* (1867), and *Madeleine Férat* (1868).

In 1871 Zola commenced the long series called *Les Rougon-Macquart*, a sequence of twenty books described in the subtitle as "the natural and social history of a family under the Second Empire." The series included such acclaimed works as *Nana* (1880), *Germinal* (1885), *La Terre* (1887, Earth), *La Bête humaine* (1890, The Beast in Man), and *Docteur Pascal* (1893).

Zola's novel *Lourdes* was published in 1894 as part of the trilogy *Les Trois Villes*, which included *Rome* (1896) and *Paris* (1898).

With Gustave Flaubert and others, Zola helped found the Naturalist school of French literature. Its concentration on misery and misfortune swung public taste away from nineteenth-century Romanticism to a middle road of balanced taste.

In 1898 Zola espoused the cause of Alfred Dreyfus, a French Jewish army officer convicted of treason in 1894. Convinced of Dreyfus's innocence and believing him to be a victim of anti-Semitism, Zola published his open letter "J'accuse" in the newspaper *L'Aurore* (January 13, 1898), denouncing the French general staff. This led to Zola's own trial on charges of offending the French government, which reopened the Dreyfus case to public review. Sentenced to imprisonment, Zola escaped to England. Both Dreyfus and Zola were eventually vindicated, and Zola returned to France in 1899.

Zola died on September 28, 1902, a victim of asphyxiation.

PREFACE

CONSPICUOUS among the writings which influenced the great changes witnessed by the world at the end of the eighteenth century were the 'Nouvelle Héloise,' the 'Contrat Social,' the 'Émile ou l'Éducation' of Jean-Jacques Rousseau. At the close of the nineteenth, the advent of the twentieth century, one finds three books, 'Fécondité,' 'Travail,' and 'Vérité,' the works of Émile Zola, Rousseau's foremost descendant. It is too soon by far to attempt to gauge the extent of the influence which these works may exercise; but, disseminated in French and in many other languages to the uttermost ends of the earth, they are works which will certainly have to be reckoned with in a social as well as a literary sense. The writings of Rousseau, violently assailed by some, enthusiastically praised by others, ended by leaving their mark on the world at large. Very few may read them nowadays, but in certain essential respects their spirit pervaded the nineteenth century, and their influence is not dead yet, for the influence which springs from the eternal truths of nature cannot die. As for the critics who will undoubtedly arise to dispute the likelihood of any great influence being exercised by the last writings of Émile Zola, I adjourn them to some twenty years hence. Rome was not built in a day, many long years elapsed before the spirit of Rousseau's writings became fully disseminated, and, although the world moves more quickly now than it did then, time remains a factor of the greatest importance.

Moreover, the future alone can decide the fate of Émile Zola's last books; for, while dealing with problems of the present time, they are essentially books which appeal to the future for their justification. Each of those three volumes, ' Fécondité,' ' Travail,' and ' Vérité,' takes as its text an existing state of things, and then suggests alterations and remedies which can only be applied gradually, long years being required to bring about any substantial result. It is known that the series was to have comprised a fourth and concluding volume, which would have been entitled ' Justice '; and indeed the actual writing of that volume would have been begun on September 29 last if, at an early hour on that very day, the hand of Émile Zola had not been stayed for ever by a tragic death, which a few precautions would undoubtedly have prevented. At an earlier stage it was surmised—on many sides I see by the newspaper cuttings before me—that this unwritten book, ' Justice,' would deal chiefly with the Dreyfus case, in which Zola played so commanding and well-remembered a part. But that was a mistake, a misconception of his intentions. Though his work would have embraced the justice dispensed in courts of law, his chief thought was social justice, equity as between class and class, man and man. And thus the hand of death at least robbed those who are in any way oppressed of a powerful statement of their rights.

As for the Dreyfus case, it figures in the present volume, or rather it serves as the basis of one of the narratives unfolded in it. The Dreyfus case certainly revealed injustice; but it even more particularly revealed falsehood, the most unblushing and the most egregious mendacity, the elevation of the *suppressio veri* and the *suggestio falsi* to the dignity of a fine art. The world has known greater deeds of injustice than the Dreyfus case, but never has it known—and may it never again know—such a widespread exhibition of mendacity, both so unscrupulous and so persevering, attended too by the most amazing credulity on the part of nine-tenths of the French nation—for small indeed (at the beginning, at all events) was the heroic band which championed the truth. Behind all the mendacity and credulity, beyond the personages directly implicated in the case, stood one of the great forces of the world, the Roman Catholic Church. Of all the ministers of that Church in France, only one raised his voice in favour of the truth, all the others were tacitly or actively accomplices in the great iniquity. And that will explain much which will be found in Émile Zola's last book.

The horrible crime on which he bases a part of his narrative is not ascribed to any military man (in fact the army scarcely figures in 'Vérité'); it is one of the crimes springing from the unnatural lives led by those who have taken vows in the Roman Church, of which some record will be found in the reports on criminality in France, which the Keeper of the Seals issues every ten years. Many such crimes, particularly those which are not carried to the point of murder, are more or less hushed up, the offenders being helped to escape by their friends in the Church; but sufficient cases have been legally investigated during the last thirty years to enable one to say that the crime set forth in 'Vérité' is not to be regarded as altogether exceptional in its nature. The scene of the book is laid in the French school world, and by the intriguing of clericalist teachers the crime referred to is imputed to a Jew schoolmaster. Forthwith there comes an explosion of that anti-Semitism —cruelly and cowardly spurred on by the Roman Church —which was the very *fons et origo* of the Dreyfus case.

On the dogmas of the Roman Church, and on her teaching methods with the young, falls the entire responsibility of such fanaticism and such credulity. Republican France, fully enlightened respecting the Church's aims by many circumstances and occurrences—the Dreyfus case, the treasonable monarchical spirit shown by her officers when educated in Jesuit colleges, the whole Nationalist agitation, and the very educational exhibits sent by the Religious Orders to the last great world-show in Paris, exhibits which proved peremptorily that 1,600,000 children were being reared by Brothers and Sisters in hatred and contempt of the government of the country—France is now driving the Church from both the elementary and the superior schools. Those who merely glance with indifference at the Paris letters and telegrams appearing in the newspapers may be told that a great revolution is now taking place in France, a revolution partaking of some of the features of the Reformation, a change such as England, for instance, has not witnessed since Henry VIII. and James II. The effects of that change upon the world at large may be tremendous; Rome knows it, and resists with the tenacity of despair; but faith in her dogmas and belief in her protestations have departed from the great majority of the French electorate; and, driven from the schools, unable in particular to continue moulding the women by whom hitherto she has so largely exercised her influence, the Church already finds herself in sore straits, at a loss almost how to proceed. By hook or crook she will resist, undoubtedly, to the last gasp; but with the secularisation of the whole educational system it will be difficult for her to recruit adherents in the future, and poison the national life as she did poison it throughout the years of the Dreyfus unrest. She sowed the storm and now she is reaping the whirlwind.

Besides the powerful ' story of a crime ' which is unfolded in the pages of ' Vérité,' besides the discussion of political and religious methods and prospects, and the exposition of educational views which will be found in the book, it has other very interesting features. The whole story of Marc Froment and his struggle with his wife Geneviève is admirable. It has appealed to me intensely, for personal reasons, though happily my home never knew so fierce a conflict. Yet experience has taught me what may happen when man and woman do not share the same faith, and how, over the most passionate love, the sincerest affection, there may for that reason fall a blighting shadow, difficult indeed to dispel. And though Marc Froment at last found his remedy, as I found mine, living to enjoy long after-years of perfect agreement with the chosen helpmate, it is certain that a difference of religious belief is a most serious danger for all who enter the married state, and that it leads to the greatest misery, the absolute wrecking of many homes. In ' Vérité ' the subject is treated with admirable insight, force, and pathos; and I feel confident that this portion of the book will be read with the keenest interest.

Of the rest of the work I need hardly speak further; for I should merely be paraphrasing things which will be found in it. Some of the personages who figure in its pages will doubtless be recognised. Nobody acquainted with the Dreyfus case can doubt, I think, the identity of the scoundrel who served as the basis of Brother Gorgias. Father Crabot also is a celebrity, and Simon, David, Delbos, and Baron Nathan are drawn from life. There are several striking scenes—the discovery of the crime, the arrest and the first trial of the Jew schoolmaster, the parting of Marc from his wife, and subsequently from his daughter Louise, the deaths of Madame Berthereau and Madame Duparque, and the last public appearance of the impudent Gorgias. But amid all the matter woven into the narrative one never loses sight of the chief theme—the ignominy and even the futility of falsehood, the debasing effects of credulity and ignorance, the health and power that come from knowledge—this being the stepping-stone to truth, which ends by triumphing over all things.

Let me add that the book is the longest as well as the last of my dear master's writings. While translating it I have pruned it slightly here and there in order to get rid of sundry repetitions. In so long a work some repetition is perhaps necessary; and it must be remembered that with Émile Zola repetition was more or less a method. One blow seldom, if ever, sufficed him; he was bent on hammering his points into his reader's skull. With the last part of ' Vérité ' I have had some little difficulty, the proofs from which my translation has been made containing some scarcely intelligible passages, as well as various errors in names and facts, which I have rectified as best I could. These, however, are matters of little moment, and can hardly affect the work as a whole, though, of course, it is unfortunate that Zola should not have been spared to correct his last proofs.

And now as this is, in all likelihood, the last occasion on which I shall be privileged to present one of his works in an English dress, may I tender to all whom my translations have reached—the hundreds of reviewers and the many thousands of readers in the lands where the English language is spoken—my heartfelt thanks for the courtesy, the leniency, the patience, the encouragement, the favour they have shown to me for several years ? As I said in a previous preface, I am conscious of many imperfections in these renderings of mine. I can only regret that they should not have been better; but, like others, I have my limitations. At the same time I may say that I have never undertaken any of these translations in a perfunctory or a mere mercantile spirit. Such as they are, they have been to me essentially a labour of love. And now that I am about to lay down my pen, that I see a whole period of my life closing, I think it only right to express my gratitude to all whose support has helped me to accomplish my self-chosen task of placing the great bulk of Émile Zola's writings within the reach of those Anglo-Saxons who, unfortunately, are unable to read French. My good friend once remarked that it was a great honour and privilege to be, if only for one single hour, the spokesman of one's generation. I feel that the great honour and privilege of my life will consist in having been—imperfectly no doubt, yet not I hope without some fidelity—his spokesman for ten years among many thousands of my race.

E. A. V.

Merton, Surrey, England
January, 1903

TRUTH

BOOK I

I

ON the previous evening, that of Wednesday, Marc Froment, the Jonville schoolmaster, with Geneviève his wife and Louise his little girl, had arrived at Maillebois, where he was in the habit of spending a month of his vacation, in the company of his wife's grandmother and mother, Madame Duparque and Madame Berthereau— 'those ladies,' as folk called them in the district. Maillebois, which counted two thousand inhabitants and ranked as the chief place of a canton, was only six miles distant from the village of Jonville, and less than four from Beaumont, the large old university town.

The first days of August were oppressively hot that year. There had been a frightful storm on the previous Sunday, during the distribution of prizes; and again that night, about two o'clock, a deluge of rain had fallen, without, however, clearing the sky, which remained cloudy, lowering, and oppressively heavy. The ladies, who had risen at six in order to be ready for seven o'clock Mass, were already in their little dining-room awaiting the younger folk, who evinced no alacrity to come down. Four cups were set out on the white oilcloth table-cover, and at last Pélagie appeared with the coffee-pot. Small of build and red-haired, with a large nose and thin lips, she had been twenty years in Madame Duparque's service, and was accustomed to speak her mind.

'Ah! well,' said she, 'the coffee will be quite cold, but it will not be my fault.'

When she had returned, grumbling, to her kitchen, Madame Duparque also vented her displeasure. 'It is

unbearable,' she said; 'one might think that Marc took
pleasure in making us late for Mass whenever he stays
here.'

Madame Berthereau, who was more indulgent, ventured
to suggest an excuse. 'The storm must have prevented
them from sleeping,' she replied; 'but I heard them hastening overhead just now.'

Three and sixty years of age, very tall, with hair still very
dark, and a frigid, symmetrically wrinkled face, severe
eyes, and a domineering nose, Madame Duparque had long
kept a draper's shop, known by the sign of 'The Guardian
Angel,' on the Place St. Maxence, in front of the cathedral
of Beaumont. But after the sudden death of her husband,
caused, it was said, by the collapse of a Catholic banking-
house, she had sensibly disposed of the business, and retired, with an income of some six thousand francs a year,
to Maillebois, where she owned a little house. This had
taken place about twelve years previously, and her daughter, Madame Berthereau, being also left a widow, had joined
her with her daughter Geneviève, who was then entering
her eleventh year. To Madame Duparque, the sudden
death of her son-in-law, a State revenue *employé*, in whose
future she had foolishly believed but who died poor, leaving
his wife and child on her hands, proved another bitter blow.
Since that time the two widows had resided together in the
dismal little house at Maillebois, leading a confined, almost
claustral, life, limited in an increasing degree by the most
rigid religious practices. Nevertheless Madame Berthereau,
who had been fondly adored by her husband, retained, as a
memento of that awakening to love and life, an affectionate
gentleness of manner. Tall and dark, like her mother, she
had a sorrowful, worn, and faded countenance, with submissive eyes and tired lips, on which occasionally appeared
her secret despair at the thought of the happiness she had
lost.

It was by one of Berthereau's friends, Salvan, who, after
being a schoolmaster at Beaumont, became an Inspector of
Elementary Schools and, subsequently, Director of the
Training College, that the marriage of Marc and Geneviève
was brought about. He was the girl's surrogate-guardian.
Berthereau, a liberal-minded man, did not follow the observances of the Church, but he allowed his wife to do so; and
with affectionate weakness he had even ended by accompanying her to Mass. In a similarly affectionate way,

Salvan, whose freedom of thought was yet greater than his friend's, for he relied exclusively on experimental certainty, was imprudent enough to foist Marc into a pious family without troubling himself about any possibility of conflict. The young people were very fond of each other, and in Salvan's opinion they would assuredly arrange matters between them. Indeed, during her three years of married life, Geneviève, who had been one of the best pupils of the Convent of the Visitation at Beaumont, had gradually neglected her religious observances, absorbed as she was in her love for her husband. At this Madame Duparque evinced deep affliction, although the young woman, in her desire to please her, made it a duty to follow her to church whenever she stayed at Maillebois. But this was not sufficient for the terrible old grandmother, who in the first instance had tried to prevent the marriage, and who now harboured a feeling of dark rancour against Marc, accusing him of robbing her of her grandchild's soul.

'A quarter to seven!' she muttered as she heard the neighbouring church clock strike. 'We shall never be ready!'

Then, approaching the window, she glanced at the adjacent Place des Capucins. The little house was built at a corner of that square and the Rue de l'Église. On its ground floor, to the right and the left of the central passage, were the dining and drawing rooms, and in the rear came the kitchen and the scullery, which looked into a dark and mouldy yard. Then, on the first floor, on the right hand were two rooms set apart for Madame Duparque, and, on the left, two others occupied by Madame Berthereau; whilst under the tiles, in front of Pélagie's bed-chamber and some store places, were two more little rooms, which had been furnished for Geneviève during her girlhood, and of which she gaily resumed possession whenever she now came to Maillebois with her husband. But how dark was the gloom, how heavy the silence, how tomblike the chill which fell from the dim ceilings! The Rue de l'Église, starting from the apse of the parish church of St. Martin, was too narrow for vehicular traffic; twilight reigned there even at noontide; the house-fronts were leprous, the little paving-stones were mossy, the atmosphere stank of slops. And on the northern side the Place des Capucins spread out treeless, but darkened by the lofty front of an old convent, which had been divided between the Capuchins, who there had a large and handsome chapel, and the Brothers of the Christian Schools, who had installed a very prosperous educational establishment in some of the conventual dependencies.

Madame Duparque remained for a moment in contemplation of that deserted space, across which flitted merely the shadowy figures of the devout; its priestly quietude being enlivened at intervals only by the children attending the Brothers' school. A bell rang slowly in the lifeless air, and the old lady was turning round impatiently, when the door of the room opened and Geneviève came in.

'At last!' the grandmother exclaimed. 'We must breakfast quickly: the first bell is ringing.'

Fair, tall, and slender, with splendid hair, and a face all life and gaiety inherited from her father, Geneviève, childlike still, though two and twenty, was laughing with a laugh which showed all her white teeth. But Madame Duparque, on perceiving that she was alone, began to protest: 'What! is not Marc ready?'

'He's following me, grandmother; he is coming down with Louise.'

Then, after kissing her silent mother, Geneviève gave expression to the amusement she felt at finding herself once more, as a married woman, in the quiet home of her youth. Ah! she knew each paving-stone of that Place des Capucins; she found old friends in the smallest tufts of weeds. And by way of evincing amiability and gaining time, she was going into raptures over the scene she viewed from the window, when all at once, on seeing two black figures pass, she recognised them.

'Why, there are Father Philibin and Brother Fulgence!' she said. 'Where can they be going at this early hour?'

The two clerics were slowly crossing the little square, which, under the lowering sky, the shadows of their cassocks seemed to fill. Father Philibin, forty years of age and of peasant origin, displayed square shoulders and a course, round, freckled face, with big eyes, a large mouth, and strong jaws. He was prefect of the studies at the College of Valmarie, a magnificent property which the Jesuits owned in the environs of Maillebois. Brother Fulgence, likewise a man of forty, but little, dark, and lean, was the superior of the three Brothers with whom he carried on the neighbouring Christian School. The son of a servant girl and a mad doctor, who had died a patient in a madhouse, he was of a nervous, irritable temperament, with a disorderly overweening mind; and it was he who was now speaking to his companion in a very loud voice and with sweeping gestures.

'The prizes are to be given at the Brothers' school this afternoon,' said Madame Duparque by way of explanation. 'Father Philibin, who is very fond of our good Brothers, has consented to preside at the distribution. He must have just arrived from Valmarie; and I suppose he is going with Brother Fulgence to settle certain details.'

But she was interrupted, for Marc had at last made his appearance, carrying his little Louise, who, scarcely two years old, hung about his neck, playing and laughing blissfully.

'Puff, puff, puff!' the young man exclaimed as he entered the room. 'Here we are in the railway train. One can't come quicker than by train, eh?'

Shorter than his three brothers, Mathieu, Luc, and Jean, Marc Froment had a longer and a thinner face, with the lofty towerlike family forehead greatly developed. But his particular characteristics were his spell-working eyes and voice, soft clear eyes which dived into one's soul, and an engaging conquering voice which won both mind and heart. Though he wore moustaches and a slight beard, one could see his rather large, firm, and kindly mouth. Like all the sons of Pierre and Marie Froment,[1] he had learned a manual calling, that of a lithographer, and, securing his bachelor's degree when seventeen years of age, he had come to Beaumont to complete his apprenticeship with the Papon-Laroches, the great firm which supplied maps and diagrams to almost every school in France. It was at this time that his passion for teaching declared itself, impelling him to enter the Training College of Beaumont, which he had quitted in his twentieth year as an assistant-master, provided with a superior certificate. Having subsequently secured that of Teaching Capacity, he was, when seven and twenty, about to be appointed schoolmaster at Jonville when he married Geneviève Berthereau, thanks to his good friend Salvan, who introduced him to the ladies, and who was moved by the sight of the love which drew the young folk together. And now, for three years past, Marc and Geneviève, though their means were scanty and they experienced all manner of pecuniary straits and administrative worries, had been leading a delightful life of love in their secluded village, which numbered barely eight hundred souls.

[1] See M. Zola's novel, *Paris.*

But the happy laughter of the father and the little girl did not dissipate the displeasure of Madame Duparque. 'That railway train is not worth the coaches of my youth,' said she. 'Come, let us breakfast quickly, we shall never get there.'

She had seated herself, and was already pouring some milk into the cups. While Geneviève placed little Louise's baby-chair between herself and her mother, in order to keep a good watch over the child, Marc, who was in a conciliatory mood, tried to secure the old lady's forgiveness.

'Yes, I have delayed you, eh?' he said. 'But it is your fault, grandmother; one sleeps too soundly in your house, it is so very quiet.'

Madame Duparque, who was hurrying over her breakfast, with her nose in her cup, did not condescend to answer. But a pale smile appeared on the face of Madame Berthereau after she had directed a long look at Geneviève, who seemed so happy between her husband and her child. And in a low voice, as if speaking involuntarily, the younger widow murmured, glancing slowly around her: 'Yes, very quiet, so quiet that one cannot even feel that one is living.'

'All the same, there was some noise on the square at ten o'clock,' Marc retorted. 'Geneviève was amazed. The idea of a disturbance at night on the Place des Capucins!'

He had blundered badly in his desire to make the others laugh. This time it was the grandmother who, with an offended air, replied: 'It was the worshippers leaving the Capuchin Chapel. The offices of the Adoration of the Holy Sacrament were celebrated yesterday evening at nine o'clock. The Brothers took with them those of their pupils who attended their first Communion this year, and the children were rather free in talking and laughing as they crossed the square. But that is far better than the abominable pastimes of the children who are brought up without moral or religious guidance!'

Silence, deep and embarrassing, fell immediately. Only the rattle of the spoons in the cups was to be heard. That accusation of abominable pastimes was directed against Marc's school, with its system of secular education. But, as Geneviève turned on him a little glance of entreaty, he did not lose his temper. Before long he even resumed the conversation, speaking to Madame Berthereau of his life at Jonville, and also of his pupils, like a master who was attached to them and who derived from them pleasure and satisfaction. Three, said he, had just obtained the certificate awarded for successful elementary studies.

But at this moment the church bell again rang out slowly, sending a wail through the heavy atmosphere above the mournful, deserted district.

'The last bell!' cried Madame Duparque. 'I said that we should never get there in time!'

She rose, and had already begun to hustle her daughter and her granddaughter, who were finishing their coffee, when Pélagie, the servant, again appeared, this time trembling, almost beside herself, and with a copy of *Le Petit Beaumontais* in her hand.

'Ah! madame, madame, how horrible! The newspaper boy has just told me——'

'What? Make haste!'

The servant was stifling.

'That little Zéphirin, the schoolmaster's nephew, has just been found murdered, there, quite near, in his room.'

'Murdered!'

'Yes, madame; strangled in his nightdress. It is an abominable affair!'

A terrible shudder swept through the room; even Madame Duparque quivered.

'Little Zéphirin?' said she. 'Ah! yes, the nephew of Simon, the Jew schoolmaster, a child with a pretty face but infirm. For his part the lad was a Catholic; he went to the Brothers' school, and he must have been at the ceremony last night, for he took his first Communion lately. . . . But what can you expect? Some families are accursed!'

Marc had listened, chilled and indignant. And careless now whether he gave offence or not, he answered: 'Simon, I know Simon! He was at the Training College with me; he is only two years older than myself. I know nobody with a firmer intellect, a more affectionate heart. He had given shelter to that poor child, that Catholic nephew, and allowed him to attend the Brothers' school, from conscientious scruples which are seldom found. What a frightful blow has fallen on him!'

Then the young man rose, quivering: 'I am going to him,' he added; 'I want to hear everything, I want to sustain him in his grief.'

But Madame Duparque no longer listened. She was pushing Madame Berthereau and Geneviève outside, scarcely allowing them time to put on their hats. The ringing of the last bell had just ceased, and the ladies hastened towards the church, amidst the heavy, storm-laden silence of the deserted square. And Marc, after entrusting little Louise to Pélagie, in his turn went out.

The elementary schools of Maillebois, newly built and divided into two pavilions, one for boys and one for girls, stood on the Place de la République, in front of the town hall, which was also a new building of corresponding architecture, and only the High Street, really a section of the road from Beaumont to Jonville running across the square, separated the two edifices, which with their chalky whiteness were the pride of the district. The High Street, which the parish church of St. Martin likewise faced, a little further down, was, as became a centre of trade, a populous thoroughfare, animated by the constant coming and going of pedestrians and vehicles. But silence and solitude were found again behind the schools, and weeds sprouted there between the little paving-stones. A street, the Rue Courte, in which one found but the parsonage and a stationer's shop kept by Mesdames Milhomme, connected the sleepy end of the Place de la République with the Place des Capucins, in such wise that Marc had few steps to take.

The school playgrounds faced the Rue Courte, and were separated by two little gardens set apart for the schoolmaster and the schoolmistress. On the ground floor of the boys' pavilion, at a corner of the playground, was a tiny room, which Simon had been able to give to little Zéphirin on taking charge of him. The boy was a nephew of his wife, Rachel Lehmann, and a grandson of the old Lehmanns, who were poor Jew tailors, dwelling in the Rue du Trou, the most wretched street of Maillebois. Zéphirin's father, Daniel Lehmann, a mechanician, had contracted a love-match with a Catholic girl, an orphan named Marie Prunier, who had been reared by the Sisters, and was a dressmaker. The young couple adored each other, and at first their son Zéphirin was not baptised nor indeed brought up in any religious faith, neither parent desiring to grieve the other by rearing the child according to his or her particular creed. But after the lapse of six years a thunderbolt fell: Daniel met with a frightful death, being caught and crushed to pieces in some machinery before the very eyes of his wife, who had come to the works, bringing his lunch with her. And Marie, terrified by the sight, won back to the religion of her youth, picturing the catastrophe as the chastisement of Heaven, which thereby punished her for her guilt in having loved a Jew, soon caused her son to be baptised, and sent him to the Brothers' school. Unhappily, through some hereditary taint or flaw, the lad's frame became distorted, he grew gradually humpbacked; in which misfortune the mother imagined she could trace the implacable wrath of God pursuing her relentlessly, because she was unable to pluck from her heart the fond memory of the husband she had adored. That anguish, combined with excessive toil, ended by killing her about the time when little Zéphirin, having reached his eleventh birthday, was ready to take his first Communion. It was then that Simon, though poor himself, gave the boy shelter, in order that he might not become a charge on his wife's relations. At the same time the schoolmaster, who was tolerant as well as kindhearted, contented himself with lodging and feeding his nephew, allowing him to communicate as a Catholic and to complete his studies at the Brothers' school.

The little room in which Zéphirin slept—formerly a kind of lumber-room, but tidily arranged for him—had a window opening almost on a level with the ground, behind the school, the spot being the most secluded of the square. And that morning, about seven o'clock, as young Mignot, the assistant-master, who slept on the first floor of the building, went out, he noticed that Zéphirin's window was wide open. Mignot was passionately fond of fishing, and, profiting by the arrival of the vacation, he was about to start, in a straw hat and a linen jacket, and with his rod on his shoulder, for the banks of the Verpille, a streamlet which ran through the industrial quarter of Maillebois. A peasant by birth, he had entered the Beaumont Training College, even as he might have entered a seminary, in order to escape the hard labour of the fields. Fair, with close-cut hair, he had a massive pock-marked face, which gave him an appearance of sternness, though he was not hard-hearted, being indeed rather kindly disposed; but his chief care was to do nothing which might impede his advancement. He was five and twenty years of age, but showed no haste to get married, waiting in that respect as in others, and destined to become such as circumstances might decree. That morning he was greatly struck by the sight of Zéphirin's open window, although there was nothing very extraordinary in such a thing, for the lad usually rose at an early hour. However, the young master drew near and glanced into the room. Then stupefaction rooted him to the spot, and his horror found vent in cries.

'O God, the poor boy! O God, God, what can have happened? What a terrible misfortune!'

The tiny room, with its light wall paper, retained its wonted quietude, its suggestion of happy boyhood. On the table was a coloured statuette of the Virgin with a few books and little prints of a religious character, carefully arranged and classified. The small white bed was in no wise disarranged, the lad had not slept in it that night. The only sign of disorder was an overturned chair. But on the rug beside the bed Zéphirin was lying strangled, his face livid, his bare neck showing the imprint of his murderer's cruel fingers. His rent garment allowed a glimpse of his misshapen spine, the hump, that jutted out below his left arm, which was thrown back across his head. In spite of its bluish pallor his face retained its charm; it was the face of a fair curly-haired angel, delicately girlish, with blue eyes, a slender nose, and a small sweet mouth, whose gentle laugh in happy hours had brought delightful dimples to the child's cheeks.

But Mignot, quite beside himself, did not cease to cry his horror aloud. 'Ah! God, God, how frightful! For God's sake help, help! Come quickly!'

Then Mademoiselle Rouzaire the schoolmistress, who heard the cries, hastened to the spot. She had been paying an early visit to her garden, being anxious about some lettuces which the stormy weather was helping to go to seed. She was a red-haired woman of two and thirty, tall and strongly built, with a round freckled face, big grey eyes, pale lips, and a pointed nose, which denoted cunning and avaricious harshness. Ugly though she was, her name had been associated with that of the handsome Mauraisin, the Elementary Inspector, whose support ensured her advancement. Moreover she was devoted to Abbé Quandieu, the parish priest, the Capuchins, and even the Christian Brothers, and personally conducted her pupils to the catechism classes and the church ceremonies.

As soon as she beheld the horrid sight, she also raised an outcry: 'Good Lord, take pity on us! It is a massacre; it is the devil's work, O God of Mercy!'

Then, as Mignot was about to spring over the window-bar, she prevented him: 'No, no, don't go in, one must ascertain, one must call——'

As she turned round, as if seeking somebody, she perceived Father Philibin and Brother Fulgence emerging from the Rue Courte, on their way from the Place des Capucins, across which Geneviève had seen them pass. She recognised them, and raised her arms to heaven, as if at the sight of Providence.

'Oh, Father! oh, Brother! come, come at once, the devil has been here!'

The two clerics drew near and experienced a terrible shock. But Father Philibin, who was energetic and of a thoughtful bent, remained silent, whereas impulsive Brother Fulgence, ever prompt to throw himself forward, burst into exclamations: 'Ah! the poor child, ah! what a horrid crime! So gentle and so good a lad, the best of our pupils, so pious and fervent too! Come, we must investigate this matter, we cannot leave things as they are.'

This time Mademoiselle Rouzaire did not dare to protest as the Brother sprang over the window-bar followed by Father Philibin, who, having perceived a ball of paper lying near the boy, at once picked it up. From fear or rather prudence the schoolmistress did not join the others; indeed, she even detained Mignot outside for another moment. That which the ministers of the Deity might venture to do was not fit perhaps for mere teachers. Meantime, while Brother Fulgence bent over the victim without touching him, but again raising tumultuous exclamations, Father Philibin, still silent, unrolled the paper ball, and, to all appearance, examined it carefully. He was turning his back to the window, and one could only see the play of his elbows, without distinguishing the paper, the rustling of which could be heard. This went on for a few moments; and when Mignot, in his turn, sprang into the room he saw that the ball which Father Philibin had picked up had been formed of a newspaper, in the midst of which a narrow, crumpled, and stained slip of white paper appeared.

The Jesuit looked at the assistant-master, and quietly and slowly remarked: 'It is a number of *Le Petit Beaumontais* dated yesterday, August 2; but the singular thing is that, crumpled up in it, there should be this copy-slip for a writing lesson. Just look at it.'

As the slip had been noticed by Mignot already, Father Philibin could not do otherwise than show it; but he kept it between his big fingers so that the other only distinguished the words, *'Aimez vous les uns les autres'* ('Love one another ') lithographed in a well-formed 'English' round-hand. Rents and stains made this copy-slip a mere rag of paper, and the assistant-master gave it only a brief glance, for fresh exclamations now arose at the window.

They came from Marc, who had just arrived, and who was filled with horror and indignation at the sight of the poor little victim. Without listening to the schoolmistress's explanations, he brushed her aside and vaulted over the window-bar. The presence of the two clerics astonished him; but he learnt from Mignot that he and Mademoiselle Rouzaire had summoned them as they were passing, immediately after the discovery of the crime.

'Don't touch or disturb anything!' Marc exclaimed. 'One must at once send to the mayor and the gendarmerie.'

People were collecting already; and a young man, who undertook the suggested commission, set off at a run, while Marc continued to inspect the room. In front of the body he saw Brother Fulgence distracted with compassion, with his eyes full of tears, like a man of nervous temperament unable to control emotion. Marc was really touched by the Brother's demeanour. He himself shuddered at the sight of what he beheld, for the abominable nature of the crime was quite evident. And a thought, which was to return later on as a conviction, suddenly flitted through his mind, then left him, in such wise that he was only conscious of the presence of Father Philibin, who, full of deep distressful calm, still held the newspaper and the writing-copy. For a moment the Jesuit had turned round as if to look under the bed; then, however, he had stepped back.

'You see,' he said, without waiting to be questioned, 'this is what I found on the floor, rolled into a ball, which the murderer certainly tried to thrust into the child's mouth as a gag, in order to stifle his cries. As he did not succeed he strangled him. On this writing-copy, soiled by saliva, one can see the marks left by the poor little fellow's teeth. The ball was lying yonder, near that leg of the table. Is that not so, Monsieur Mignot? You saw it?'

'Oh! quite so,' replied the assistant-master, 'I noticed it at once.'

As he drew near again and examined the copy, he felt vaguely surprised on noticing that the right-hand corner of the slip of paper was torn off. It seemed to him that he had not remarked that deficiency when the Jesuit had first shown him the slip; but perhaps it had then been hidden by Father Philibin's big fingers. However, Mignot's memory grew confused; it would have been impossible for him to say whether that corner had been torn away in the first instance or not.

Marc, however, having taken the slip from the Jesuit, was studying it and expressing his thoughts aloud: 'Yes, yes, it has been bitten. But it won't be much of an indication, for such slips are sold currently; one can find them everywhere. Oh! but there is a kind of flourish down here, I see, some initialling which one cannot well decipher.'

Without any haste, Father Philibin stepped up to him. 'Some initialling? Do you think so? It seemed to me a mere blot, half effaced by saliva and by the bite which pierced the slip, close by.'

'A blot, no! These marks are certainly initials, but they are quite illegible.' Then, noticing that a corner of the slip was deficient, Marc added: 'That, no doubt, was done by another bite. Have you found the missing piece?'

Father Philibin answered that he had not looked for it; and he again unfolded the newspaper and examined it carefully, while Mignot, stooping, searched the floor. Nothing was found. Besides, the matter was regarded as being of no importance. Marc agreed with the two clerics that the murderer, seized with terror, must have strangled the boy after vainly endeavouring to stifle his cries by stuffing the paper gag into his mouth. The extraordinary circumstance was that the copy-slip should have been found rolled up with the newspaper. The presence of a number of *Le Petit Beaumontais* could be understood, for anybody might have one in his pocket. But whence had that slip come, how did it happen to be crumpled, almost kneaded, with the newspaper? All sorts of suppositions were allowable, and the officers of the law would have to open an investigation in order to discover the truth.

To Marc it seemed as if a calamitous gust had just swept through the dim tragedy, suddenly steeping everything in horrid night. 'Ah!' he murmured involuntarily, 'it is Crime, the monster, in the depths of his dark pit.'

Meantime people continued to assemble before the window. On perceiving the throng the Mesdames Milhomme, who kept the neighbouring stationery business, had hastened from their shop. Madame Alexandre, who was tall, fair, and gentle in appearance, and Madame Edouard, who was also tall but dark and somewhat rough, felt the more concerned as Victor, the latter's son, went to the Brothers' school, while Sébastien, the former's boy, attended Simon's. Thus they listened eagerly to Mademoiselle Rouzaire, who, standing in the middle of the group, was giving various particulars, pending the arrival of the mayor and the gendarmes.

'I went myself,' she said, 'to that touching Adoration of the Holy Sacrament at the Capuchin Chapel last evening, and poor Zéphirin was there with a few schoolfellows—those who took their first Communion this year. He edified us all, he looked a little angel.'

'My son Victor did not go, for he is only nine years old,' Madame Edouard answered. 'But did Zéphirin go alone? Did nobody bring him back?'

'Oh! the chapel is only a few yards distant,' the schoolmistress explained. 'I know that Brother Gorgias had orders to escort the children whose parents could not attend, and whose homes are rather distant. But Madame Simon asked me to watch over Zéphirin, and it was I who brought him back. He was very gay; he opened the shutters, which were simply pushed to, and sprang into his room through the open window, laughing and saying that it was the easiest and shortest way. I stayed outside for a moment, waiting until he had lighted his candle.'

Marc, drawing near, had listened attentively. 'What time was it?' he now inquired.

'Exactly ten,' Mademoiselle Rouzaire replied. 'St. Martin's clock was striking.'

The others shuddered, moved by that account of the lad springing so gaily into the room where he was to meet such a tragic death. And Madame Alexandre gently gave expression to a thought which suggested itself to all: 'It was hardly prudent to let the lad sleep by himself in this lonely room, so easily reached from the square. The shutters ought to have been barred at night.'

'Oh! he fastened them,' said Mademoiselle Rouzaire.

'Did he do so last night while you were here?' inquired Marc, intervening once more.

'No, when I left him to go to my rooms he had lighted his candle and was arranging some pictures on his table, with the window wide open.'

Mignot, the assistant-master, now joined in the conversation. 'This window made Monsieur Simon anxious,' he said; 'he wished he could have given the lad another room.

He often recommended him to fasten the shutters carefully. But I fear that the child paid little heed.'

The two clerics in their turn had now decided to quit the room. Father Philibin, after laying the number of *Le Petit Beaumontais* and the copy-slip on the table, had ceased speaking, preferring to look and listen; and he followed very attentively each word and gesture that came from Marc, while Brother Fulgence, for his part, continued to relieve himself with lamentations. Eventually the Jesuit, who seemed to read the young schoolmaster's thoughts in his eyes, remarked to him: 'So you think that some tramp, some night prowler, seeing the boy alone in this room, may have got in by the window?'

From prudence Marc would express no positive opinion. 'Oh! I think nothing,' said he; 'it is for the law to seek and find the murderer. However, the bed has not been opened, the boy was certainly about to get into it, and this seems to show that the crime must have been committed shortly after ten o'clock. Suppose that he busied himself for half an hour at the utmost with his pictures, and that he then saw a stranger spring into his room. In that case he would have raised a cry, which would certainly have been heard. You heard nothing, did you, mademoiselle?'

'No, nothing,' the schoolmistress replied. 'I myself went to bed about half-past ten. The neighbourhood was very quiet. The storm did not awaken me until about one o'clock this morning.'

'Very little of the candle has been burnt,' Mignot now observed. 'The murderer must have blown it out as he went off by the window, which he left wide open, as I found it just now.'

These remarks, which lent some weight to the theory of a prowler springing into the room, ill-using and murdering the boy, increased the horror-fraught embarrassment of the bystanders. All wished to avoid being compromised, and therefore kept to themselves their thoughts respecting the impossibilities or improbabilities of the theory which had been propounded. After a pause, however, as the mayor and the gendarmes did not appear, Father Philibin inquired: 'Is not Monsieur Simon at Maillebois?'

Mignot, who had not recovered from the shock of his discovery, gazed at the Jesuit with haggard eyes. To bring the assistant-master to his senses, Marc himself had to express his astonishment: 'But Simon is surely in his rooms! Has he not been told?'

'Why no!' the assistant answered, 'I must have lost my head. Monsieur Simon went to attend a banquet at Beaumont yesterday evening, but he certainly came home during the night. His wife is rather poorly; they must be still in bed.'

It was now already half-past seven, but the stormy sky remained so dark and heavy that one might have thought dawn was only just appearing in that secluded corner of the square. However, the assistant-master made up his mind and ascended the stairs to fetch Simon. What a happy awakening it would be for the latter, he muttered sarcastically, and what an agreeable commission for himself was that which he had to fulfil with his chief!

Simon was the younger son of a Jew clockmaker of Beaumont; he had a brother, David, who was his elder by three years. When he was fifteen and David eighteen their father, ruined by lawsuits, succumbed to a sudden attack of apoplexy; and three years later their mother died in very straitened circumstances. Simon had then just entered the Training College, while David joined the army. The former, quitting the college at an early age, became assistant-master at Dherbecourt, a large *bourg* of the district, where he remained nearly ten years. There also, in his twenty-sixth year, he married Rachel Lehmann, the daughter of the little tailor of the Rue du Trou, who had a fair number of customers at Maillebois. Rachel, a brunette with magnificent hair and large caressing eyes, was very beautiful. Her husband adored her, encompassed her with passionate worship. Two children had been born to them, a boy, Joseph, now four, and a girl, Sarah, two years of age. And Simon, duly provided with a certificate of Teaching Capacity, was proud of the fact that at two and thirty he should be schoolmaster at Maillebois—where he had now dwelt a couple of years—for this was an instance of rapid advancement.

Marc, though he disliked the Jews by reason of a sort of hereditary antipathy and distrust, the causes of which he had never troubled to analyse, retained a friendly recollection of Simon, whom he had known at the Training College. He declared him to be extremely intelligent, a very good teacher, full of a sense of duty. But he found him too attentive to petty details, too slavishly observant of regulations, which he followed to the very letter, ever bending low before discipline, as if fearful of a bad report and the dissatisfaction of his superiors. In this Marc traced the terror and humility of the Jewish race, persecuted for so many centuries, and ever retaining a dread of outrage and iniquity. Moreover, Simon had good cause for prudence, for his appointment at Maillebois, that clerical little town with its powerful Capuchin community and its Brothers' school, had caused almost a scandal. It was only by dint of correctitude and particularly of ardent patriotism among his pupils, such as the glorification of France as a military power, the foretelling of national glory and a supreme position among the nations, that Simon obtained forgiveness for being a Jew.

He now suddenly made his appearance, accompanied by Mignot. Short, thin, and sinewy, he had red, closely-cropped hair and a sparse beard. His blue eyes were soft, his mouth was well shaped, his nose of the racial type, long and slender; yet his physiognomy was scarcely prepossessing, it remained vague, confused, paltry; and at that moment he was so terribly upset by the dreadful tidings that, as he appeared before the others, staggering and stammering, one might have thought him intoxicated.

'Great God! is it possible?' he gasped. 'Such villainy, such monstrosity!'

But he reached the window, where he remained like one overwhelmed, unable to speak another word, and shuddering from head to foot, his glance fixed meanwhile on the little victim. Those who were present, the two clerics, the lady stationers, and the schoolmasters, watched him in silence, astonished that he did not weep.

Marc, stirred by compassion, took hold of his hands and embraced him: 'Come, you must muster your courage; you need all your strength,' he said to him.

But Simon, without listening, turned to his assistant. 'Pray go back to my wife, Mignot,' he said; 'I do not want her to see this. She was very fond of her nephew, and she is too poorly to be able to bear such a horrible sight.'

Then, as the young man went off, he continued in broken accents: 'Ah! what an awakening! For once in a while we were lying late in bed. My poor Rachel was still asleep, and, as I did not wish to disturb her, I remained by her side, thinking of our holiday pleasures. I roused her late last night when I came home, and she did not get to sleep again till three in the morning, for the storm upset her.'

'What time was it when you came home?' Marc inquired.

'Exactly twenty minutes to twelve. My wife asked me the time and I looked at the clock.'

This seemed to surprise Mademoiselle Rouzaire, who remarked: 'But there is no train from Beaumont at that hour.'

'I did n't come back by train,' Simon explained. 'The banquet lasted till late, I missed the 10.30 train, and rather than wait for the one at midnight I decided to walk the distance. I was anxious to join my wife.'

Father Philibin still preserved silence and calmness; but Brother Fulgence, unable to restrain himself any longer, began to question Simon.

'Twenty minutes to twelve! Then the crime must have been committed already. You saw nothing? You heard nothing?'

'Nothing at all. The square was deserted, the storm was beginning to rumble in the distance. I did not meet a soul. All was quiet in the house.'

'Then it did not occur to you to go to see if poor Zéphirin had returned safely from the chapel, and if he were sleeping soundly? Did you not pay him a visit every evening?'

'No, he was already a very shrewd little man, and we left him as much liberty as possible. Besides, the place was so quiet, there was nothing to suggest any reason for disturbing his sleep. I went straight upstairs to my room, making the least possible noise. I kissed my children, who were asleep, then I went to bed; and, well pleased to find my wife rather better, I chatted with her in an undertone.'

Father Philibin nodded as if approvingly, and then remarked: 'Evidently everything can be accounted for.'

The bystanders seemed convinced; the theory of a prowler committing the crime about half-past ten o'clock, entering and leaving the room by the window, seemed more and more probable. Simon's statement confirmed the information given by Mignot and Mademoiselle Rouzaire. Moreover, the Mesdames Milhomme, the stationers, asserted that they had seen an evil-looking man roaming about the square at nightfall.

'There are so many rascals on the roads!' said the Jesuit Father by way of conclusion. 'We must hope that the police will set hands on the murderer, though such a task is not always an easy one.'

Marc alone experienced a feeling of uncertainty. Although he had been the first to think it possible that some stranger might have sprung on Zéphirin, he had gradually realised that there was little probability of such an occurrence. Was it not more likely that the man had been acquainted with the boy and had at first approached him as a friend? Then, however, had come the abominable impulse, horror and murder, strangulation as a last resource to stifle the victim's cries, followed by flight amidst a gust of terror. But all this remained very involved; and after some brief perception of its probability Marc relapsed into darkness, into the anxiety born of contradictory suppositions. He contented himself with saying to Simon, by way of calming him: 'All the evidence agrees: the truth will soon be made manifest.'

At that moment, just as Mignot returned after prevailing on Madame Simon to remain in her room, Darras, the Mayor of Maillebois, arrived with three gendarmes. A building contractor, on the high road to a considerable fortune, Darras was a stout man of forty-two, with a fair, round, pinky, clean-shaven face. He immediately ordered the shutters to be closed and placed two gendarmes outside the window, while the third, entering the house passage, went to guard the door of the room, which Zéphirin never locked. From this moment the orders were that nothing should be touched, and that nobody should even approach the scene of the crime. On hearing of it the mayor had immediately telegraphed to the Public Prosecution Office at Beaumont, and the magistrates would surely arrive by the first train.

Father Philibin and Brother Fulgence now spoke of having to attend to various matters connected with the distribution of prizes which was to take place in the afternoon, and Darras advised them to make haste and then return, for, said he, the Procureur de la République, otherwise the Public Prosecutor, would certainly wish to question them about the number of *Le Petit Beaumontais* and the copy-slip found near the body. So the two clerics took their departure; and while the gendarmes, stationed on the square outside the window, with difficulty restrained the now increasing crowd, which became violent and raised threatening cries, demanding the execution of the unknown murderer, Simon again went into the building with Darras, Marc, Mademoiselle Rouzaire, and Mignot, the whole party waiting in a large classroom lighted by broad windows which faced the playground.

It was now eight o'clock, and after a sudden stormy rainfall, the sky cleared, and the day became a splendid one. An hour elapsed before the magistrates arrived. The Procureur de la République, Raoul de La Bissonnière, came in person, accompanied by Daix, the Investigating Magistrate. Both were moved by the magnitude of the crime and foresaw a great trial. La Bissonnière, a dapper little man with a doll-like face, and whiskers of a correct legal cut, was very ambitious. Not content with his rapid advancement to the post he held—he was only forty-five—he was ever on the watch for some resounding case which would launch him in Paris, where, thanks to his suppleness and address, his complaisant respect for the powers of the day, whatever they might be, he relied on securing a high position. On the other hand, Daix, tall and lean, with a sharp-cut face, was a type of the punctilious Investigating Magistrate, devoted to his professional duties. But he was also of an anxious and timid nature, for his ugly but coquettish and extravagant wife, exasperated by the poverty of their home, terrorised and distressed him with her bitter reproaches respecting his lack of ambition.

On reaching the schools the legal functionaries, before taking any evidence, desired to visit the scene of the crime. Simon and Darras accompanied them to Zéphirin's bedchamber while the others, who were soon joined by Father Philibin and Brother Fulgence, waited in the large classroom. When the magistrates returned thither, they had verified all the material features of the crime, and were acquainted with the various circumstances already known to the others. They brought with them the number of *Le Petit Beaumontais* and the copy-slip, to which they seemed to attach extreme importance. At once seating themselves at Simon's table, they examined those two pieces of evidence, exchanging impressions concerning them, and then showing the copy-slip to the two schoolmasters, Simon and Marc, as well as to the schoolmistress and the clerics. But this was only done by way of eliciting some general information, for no clerk was present to record a formal interrogatory.

'Oh! those copies,' Marc replied, 'are used currently in all the schools, in the secular ones as well as in those of the religious orders.'

This was confirmed by Brother Fulgence. 'Quite so,' said he; 'similar ones would be found at our school, even as there must be some here.'

La Bissonnière, however, desired more precise information. 'But do you remember having placed this one in the hands of any of your pupils?' he asked Simon. 'Those words "Love one another" must have struck you.'

'That copy was never used here,' Simon answered flatly. 'As you point out, monsieur, I should have recollected it.'

The same question was then addressed to Brother Fulgence, who at first evinced some little hesitation. 'I have three Brothers with me—Brothers Isidore, Lazarus, and Gorgias,' he replied, 'and it is difficult for me to avouch anything.'

Then, in the deep silence which was falling, he added: 'But no, no, that copy was never used at our school, for it would have come before me.'

The magistrates did not insist on the point. For the time being they did not wish the importance which they attached to the slip to become too manifest. They expressed their surprise, however, that the missing corner of it had not been found.

'Do not these slips sometimes bear in one corner a stamp of the school to which they belong?' Daix inquired. Brother Fulgence had to admit that it was so, but Marc protested that he had never stamped any copy-slips used in his school.

'Excuse me,' declared Simon in his tranquil way, 'I have some slips here on which a stamp would be found. But I stamp them down below—here!'

Perceiving the perplexity of the magistrates, Father Philibin, hitherto silent and attentive, indulged in a light laugh. 'This shows,' he said, 'how difficult it is to arrive at the truth. . . . By the way, Monsieur le Procureur de la République, matters are much the same with the stain which you are now examining. One of us fancied it to be some initialling, a kind of flourish. But, for my part, I believe it to be a blot which some pupil tried to efface with his finger.'

'Is it usual for the masters to initial the copy-slips?' asked Daix.

'Yes,' Brother Fulgence acknowledged, 'that is done at our school.'

'Ah! no,' cried Simon and Marc in unison, 'we never do it in the Communal schools.'

'You are mistaken,' said Mademoiselle Rouzaire, 'although I do not stamp my copies, I have sometimes initialled them.'

With a wave of the hand La Bissonnière stopped the discussion, for he knew by experience what a muddle is reached when one enters into secondary questions of personal habits. The copy-slip, the missing corner of it, the possible existence of a stamp and a paraph would all have to be studied in the course of the investigation. For the moment he now contented himself with asking the witnesses to relate how the crime had been discovered. Mignot had to say that the open window had attracted his attention and that he had raised an outcry on perceiving the victim's body. Mademoiselle Rouzaire explained how she had hastened to the spot and how, on the previous evening, she had brought Zéphirin home from the Capuchin Chapel, when he had sprung into the room by the window. Father Philibin and Brother Fulgence in their turn related how chance had connected them with the tragedy, in what condition they had found the room, and in what particular spot they had discovered the paper gag, which they had merely unfolded before placing it on the table. Finally, Marc indicated a few observations which he had made on his arrival, subsequent to that of the others.

La Bissonnière thereupon turned to Simon and began to question him: 'You have told us that you came home at twenty minutes to twelve, and that the whole house then seemed to you to be perfectly quiet. Your wife was asleep——'

At this point Daix interrupted his superior: 'Monsieur le Procureur,' said he, 'is it not advisable that Madame Simon should be present? Could she not come down here a moment?'

La Bissonnière nodded assent, and Simon went to fetch his wife, who soon made her appearance.

Rachel, attired in a plain morning wrap of unbleached linen, looked so beautiful as she entered the room amidst the deep silence, that a little quiver of admiration and tender sympathy sped by. Hers was the Jewish beauty in its flower, a delightfully oval face, splendid black hair, a gilded skin, large caressing eyes, and a red mouth with speckless, dazzling teeth. And one could tell that she was all love, a trifle indolent, living in seclusion in her home, with her husband and her children, like a woman of the East in her little secret garden. Simon was about to close the door behind her, when the two children, Joseph and Sarah, four and two years old respectively, and both of them strong and flourishing, ran in, although they had been forbidden to come downstairs. And they sought refuge in the folds of their mother's wrap, where the magistrates, by a gesture, intimated they might remain.

The gallant La Bissonnière, moved by the sight of such great beauty, imparted a flute-like accent to his voice as he asked Rachel a few questions: 'It was twenty minutes to twelve, madame, was it not, when your husband came home?'

'Yes, monsieur, he looked at the clock. And he was in bed and we were still chatting in an undertone and with the light out, in order that the children might not be roused, when we heard midnight strike.'

'But before your husband's arrival, madame, between half-past ten and half-past eleven, did you hear nothing, no footsteps nor talking, no sounds of struggling, nor stifled cries?'

'No, absolutely nothing, monsieur. I was asleep. It was my husband's entry into our room which awoke me. He had left me feeling poorly, and he was so pleased to find me better that he began to laugh as he kissed me, and I made him keep quiet for fear lest the others should be disturbed, so deep was the silence around us. Ah! how could we have imagined that such a frightful misfortune had fallen on the house!'

She was thoroughly upset, and tears coursed down her cheeks, while she turned towards her husband as if for consolation and support. And he, weeping now at the sight of her grief, and forgetting where he was, caught her passionately in his arms, and kissed her with infinite tenderness. The two children raised their heads anxiously. There was a moment of deep emotion and compassionate kindliness, in which all participated.

'I was rather surprised at the time because there is no train at that hour,' resumed Madame Simon of her own accord. 'But when my husband was in bed he told me how it happened.'

'Yes,' Simon explained, 'I could not do otherwise than attend that banquet; but when, on reaching the station at Beaumont, I saw the half-past ten o'clock train steaming away before my eyes, I felt so annoyed that I would not

wait for the train at midnight, but set out on foot at once.
A walk of less than four miles is nothing to speak of.   The
night was very beautiful, very warm.   .   .   .   About one
o'clock, when the storm burst, I was still talking softly to
my wife, telling her how I had spent my evening, for she
could not get to sleep again.   It was that which kept us
late in bed this morning, ignorant of the dreadful blow that
had fallen on us.'

Then, as Rachel began to weep again, he once more
kissed her, like a lover and like a father.   'Come, my darling, calm yourself.   We loved the poor little fellow with
all our hearts, and we have no cause for self-reproach in
this abominable catastrophe.'

That was also the opinion of the onlookers.   Darras, the
mayor, professed great esteem for the zealous and honest
schoolmaster Simon.   Mignot and Mademoiselle Rouzaire,
although by no means fond of the Jews, shared the opinion
that this one at all events strove by irreproachable conduct
to obtain forgiveness for his birth.   Father Philibin and
Brother Fulgence on their side, in presence of the general
sentiment of the others, affected neutrality, remaining apart
and preserving silence, while with keen eyes they scrutinised
people and things.   The magistrates, thrown back on the
theory of some stranger who must have entered and left the
boy's room by the window, had to rest content with this
first verification of the facts.   Only one point as yet was
clearly established, the hour of the crime, which must have
been perpetrated between half-past ten and eleven o'clock.
As for the crime itself it remained engulfed in darkness.

Leaving the authorities, who had certain details to settle,
Marc, after embracing Simon in brotherly fashion, was desirous of going home to lunch.   The scene between the
husband and the wife had taught him nothing, for he well
knew how tenderly they loved each other.   But tears had
come to his eyes, he had been deeply stirred by the sight of
such dolorous affection.

Noon was about to strike at St. Martin's Church when he
again found himself on the square, which was now blocked
by such an increasing crowd that it was difficult for him to
open a way.   As the news of the crime spread, folk arrived
from all directions, pressing towards the closed window,
which the two gendarmes could hardly defend; and the
horribly exaggerated accounts of the affair which circulated
through the crowd raised its indignation to fever heat and

made it growl wrathfully. Marc had just freed himself from the throng when a priest approached him and inquired:

'Have you come from the school, Monsieur Froment? Are all these horrible things which people are repeating true?'

The questioner was Abbé Quandieu, priest of St. Martin's, the parish church. Forty-three years old, tall and robust, the Abbé had a gentle, kindly face, with light blue eyes, round cheeks, and a soft chin. Marc had met him at Madame Duparque's, for he was the old lady's confessor and friend. And though the schoolmaster was not fond of priests he felt some esteem for this one, knowing that he was tolerant and reasonable—possessed, too, of more feeling than real mental ability.

In a few words Marc recounted the facts of the case, which were already sufficiently horrid.

'Ah, poor Monsieur Simon!' said the priest compassionately, 'how deeply grieved he must be, for he was very much attached to his nephew and behaved very well in regard to him! I have had proof of it.'

This spontaneous testimony pleased Marc, who remained conversing with the priest for another minute. But a Capuchin Father drew near, Father Théodose, the Superior of the little community attached to the neighbouring chapel. Superbly built, having also a handsome face with large ardent eyes, and a splendid dark beard, which rendered him quite majestic, Father Théodose was a confessor of repute, and a preacher of a mystical turn, whose glowing accents attracted all the devout women of Maillebois. Though he was covertly waging war against Abbé Quandieu, he affected in his presence the deferential manner of a younger and more humbly situated servant of Providence. He immediately gave expression to his emotion and his grief, for he had noticed the poor child, he said, at the chapel on the previous evening. So pious a child he was, a little angel with a cherub's fair curly locks. But Marc did not tarry to listen, for the Capuchin inspired him with unconquerable distrust and antipathy. So he turned his steps homeward; but all at once he was again stopped, this time by a friendly tap on the shoulder.

'What! Férou, are you at Maillebois?' he exclaimed. The man whom he addressed by the name of Férou was schoolmaster at Le Moreau, a lonely hamlet, some two and a half miles from Jonville. The little place had not even a priest of its own, but was looked after, from the religious standpoint, by the Jonville priest, Abbé Cognasse. Férou there led a life of black misery with his wife and his children, three girls. He was a big loosely-built fellow of thirty, whose clothes always seemed too short for him. His dark hair bristled on his long and bony head, he had a bumpy nose, a wide mouth, and a projecting chin, and knew not what to do with his big feet and his big hands.

'You know very well that my wife's aunt keeps a grocery shop here,' he answered. 'We came over to see her. But, I say, what an abominable business this is about the poor little hunchback! Won't it just enable those dirty priests to belabour us and say that we pervert and poison the young!'

Marc regarded Férou as a very intelligent, well-read man, whom a confined life full of privations had embittered to the point of violence and inspired with ideas of revenge. The virulence of the remark he had just made disturbed Marc, who rejoined: 'Belabour us? I don't see what we have to do with it.'

'Then you are a simpleton,' Férou retorted. 'You don't understand that species, but you will soon see the good Fathers and the dear Brothers, all the black gowns, hard at work. Have n't they already allowed it to be surmised that Simon himself strangled his nephew?'

At this Marc lost his temper. Férou's hatred of the Church led him too far.

'You are out of your senses,' said Marc. 'Nobody suspects, nobody for one moment would dare to suspect, Simon. All acknowledge his integrity and kindliness. Even Abbé Quandieu told me a moment ago that he had had proof of his fatherly treatment of the poor victim.'

Férou's lean and lanky figure was shaken by a convulsive laugh, his hair seemed to bristle yet higher on his equine head. 'Ah! it 's too amusing,' he replied. 'So you fancy they will restrain themselves when a dirty Jew is in question? Does a dirty Jew deserve to have the truth told about him? Your friend Quandieu and all the others will say whatever may be desirable if it is necessary that the dirty Jew should be found guilty, thanks to the complicity of us others, the scamps who know neither God nor country, and who corrupt the children of France. For that is what the priests say of us—you know it well!'

Then as Marc, chilled to the heart, continued to protest,

Férou resumed yet more vehemently: 'But you know what goes on at Le Moreux! I starve there, I 'm treated with contempt, pressed down even lower than the wretched road-menders. When Abbé Cognasse comes over to say Mass he 'd spit on me if he met me. And if I don't eat bread every day it 's simply because I refused to sing in the choir and ring the church bell! You know Abbé Cognasse yourself. You have managed to check him at Jonville, since you contrived to get the mayor over to your side; but, none the less, you are always at war; he would devour you if you only gave him the chance. A village schoolmaster indeed! Why, he 's everybody's beast of burden, everybody's lackey, a man without caste, an arrant failure; and the peasants distrust him, and the priests would like to burn him alive in order to ensure the undivided reign of the Church Catechism throughout the country!'

He went on bitterly, enumerating the sufferings of those damned ones, as he called the elementary teachers. He himself, a shepherd's son, successful at the village school which he had attended, and afterwards a student at the Training College, which he had quitted with excellent certificates, had always suffered from lack of means; for in a spirit of rectitude after some trouble with a shop girl at Maillebois, when he was assistant-master there, he had foolishly married her, although she was as poor as himself. But was Marc any happier at Jonville, even though his wife received frequent presents from her grandmother? Was he not always struggling with indebtedness, struggling too with the priest, in order to retain dignity and independence? True, he was seconded by Mademoiselle Mazeline, the mistress of the girls' school, a woman of firm sense, with an inexhaustible heart, who had helped him to win over the parish council and gradually the whole commune. But circumstances had been in his favour, and the example was perhaps unique in the department. On the other hand, the state of affairs at Maillebois completed the picture. There, on one side, one found Mademoiselle Rouzaire won over to the cause of the priests and the monks, learning to take her pupils to church, and fulfilling so well the office of the nuns that it had been considered unnecessary to install a nuns' school in the little town. Then, on the other hand, there was that poor fellow Simon, an honest man certainly, but one who, from fear of being treated as a dirty Jew, tried circumspection with everybody, allowing his nephew

to be educated by the dear Brothers, and bowing down to
the ground before all the rooks who infested the country.

'A dirty Jew!' cried Férou with emphasis, by way of
conclusion. 'He is, and always will be, a dirty Jew. And
to be both a schoolmaster and a Jew beats everything.
. . . Ah! well, you 'll see, you 'll see!'

Then, with impetuous gestures which shook the whole
of his big loose frame he took himself off and mingled with
the crowd.

Marc had remained on the kerb of the footway, shrugging
his shoulders and regarding Férou as a semi-lunatic, for the
picture which he had drawn seemed to him full of exaggeration. But of what use was it to answer that poor fellow
whose brain would soon be turned by ill luck? Yet Marc
was haunted by what he had heard, and grew vaguely
anxious as he resumed his walk towards the Place des
Capucins.

It was a quarter past twelve when he reached the little
house, and for a quarter of an hour the ladies had been
awaiting him in the dining-room, where the table was already laid. This fresh delay had quite upset Madame
Duparque. She said nothing, but the brusqueness with
which she sat down and nervously unfolded her napkin denoted how culpable she considered this lack of punctuality.

'I must apologise,' the young man explained, 'but I had
to wait for the magistrates, and there was such a crowd on
the square afterwards that I could not pass.'

At this, although the grandmother was resolved on silence,
she could not restrain an exclamation: 'I hope that you are
not going to busy yourself with that abominable affair!'

'Oh!' Marc merely answered, 'I certainly hope I sha'n't
have to do so—unless it be as a matter of duty.'

When Pélagie had served an omelet and some slices of
grilled mutton with mashed potatoes, the young man related all that he had learnt. Geneviève listened to his
story, quivering with horror and pity, while Madame Berthereau, who was also greatly moved, battled with her tears
and glanced furtively at Madame Duparque, as if to ascertain how far she might allow her sensibility to go. But the
old lady had relapsed into silent disapproval of everything
which seemed to her contrary to her rule of life. She ate
steadily, and it was only after a time that she remarked, 'I
remember very well that a child disappeared at Beaumont
during my youth. It was found under the porch of St.

Maxence. The body was cut in quarters, and there was only the heart missing. It was said that the Jews required the heart for the unleavened bread of their Passover.'

Marc looked at her in amazement. 'You are not serious, grandmother: you surely don't believe such a stupid and infamous charge?'

She turned her cold, clear eyes on him, and, instead of giving a direct answer, she said: 'It is simply an old recollection which came back to me. . . . Of course I accuse nobody.'

At this Pélagie, who had just brought the dessert, ventured to join in the conversation with the familiarity of an old servant: 'It is quite right of madame to accuse nobody, and others ought to follow madame's example. The neighbourhood has been in a state of revolution since this morning. You can have no idea of the frightful stories which are being told. Just now, too, I heard a workman say that the Brothers' school ought to be burnt down.'

Deep silence followed those words. Marc, struck by them, made a gesture, then restrained himself, like one who prefers to keep his thoughts to himself. And Pélagie continued: 'Madame will let me go to the distribution of prizes this afternoon, I hope? I don't think my nephew Polydor will have a prize; but it would please me to be present. Those good Brothers! It won't be a happy festival for them, falling on the very day when one of their best pupils has been killed!'

Madame Duparque nodded assent to the servant's request, and the conversation was then turned into another channel. Indeed the end of the meal was brightened somewhat by the laughter of little Louise, who gazed in astonishment at the grave faces of her father and her mother, who usually smiled so brightly. This led to some relaxation of the tension, and for a moment they all chatted in a cordial, intimate way.

The distribution of prizes at the Brothers' school that afternoon roused great emotion. Never before had the ceremony attracted such a throng. True, the circumstance that it was presided over by Father Philibin, the prefect of the studies at the College of Valmarie, made it particularly notable. The rector of that College, Father Crabot, who was famous for his society influence and the powerful part he was said to play in contemporary politics, also attended, desirous as he was of giving the Brothers a public mark of

his esteem.   Further, there was a reactionary deputy of the
department, Count Hector de Sanglebœuf, the owner of La
Désirade, a splendid estate of the environs, which, with a
few millions, had formed the marriage portion of his wife,
a daughter of Baron Nathan, the great Jew banker.   However, that which excited everybody, and which drew to the
usually quiet and deserted Place des Capucins such a feverish crowd, was the monstrous crime discovered in the morning, the murder of one of the Brothers' pupils under the
most abominable circumstances.

And it seemed as if the murdered boy were present, as if
only he were there, in the shady courtyard where the platform was set up beyond the serried rows of chairs, while
Father Philibin spoke in praise of the school, of its director,
the distinguished Brother Fulgence, and of his three assistants, Brothers Isidore, Lazarus, and Gorgias.   The haunting sensation became yet more intense when the prize-list
was read by the last-named, a thin, knotty man, showing a
low, harsh brow under his frizzy black hair, a big nose
projecting like an eagle's beak between his prominent
cheek-bones, and thin lips which in parting revealed wolf-
like teeth.   Zéphirin had been the best scholar of his class,
every prize of which he had won.   Thus his name recurred
incessantly, and Brother Gorgias, in his long black cassock,
on which the ends of his neck-band showed like a splotch
of white, let that name fall from his lips in such slow lugubrious fashion that on each occasion a quiver of growing
intensity sped through the assembled throng.   Every time
the poor little dead boy was called he seemed to rise up to
receive his crown and his gilt-edged book.   But, alas!
crowns and books alike formed an increasing pile on the
table; and nothing could be more poignant than the silence
and the void to which so many prizes were cast, the prizes
of that model pupil who had vanished so tragically, and
whose lamentable remains were lying only a few doors away.
At last the emotion of the onlookers became too great to be
restrained; sobs burst forth while Brother Gorgias continued
to call that name with a twitching of the upper-lip, habitual
to him, which disclosed some of the teeth on the left side of
his mouth amid an involuntary grimace-like grin, suggestive
of both scorn and cruelty.

The function ended amid general uneasiness.   However
fine might be the assembly which had hastened thither to
exalt the Brothers, anxiety increased, disquietude swept

over all, as if some menace had come from afar. But the worst was the departure amid the murmurs and the covert curses of numerous groups of artisans and peasants gathered on the square. The abominable stories of which Pélagie had spoken circulated through that quivering crowd. A horrid story which had been stifled the previous year, the story of a Brother whom his superiors had conjured away to save him from the Assize Court, was repeated. All sorts of rumours had been current since that time, rumours of abominations, of terrified children who dared not speak out. Naturally there had been much enlargement of those mysterious rumours as they passed from mouth to mouth; and the indignation of the folk assembled on the square came from the revival of them which was prompted by the murder of one of the Brothers' pupils. Accusations were already taking shape, words of vengeance spread around. Would the guilty one again be allowed to escape? Would that vile and bloody den never be closed? Thus, as the fine folk departed, and particularly when the robes of the monks and the cassocks of the priests were seen, fists were stretched out, and menaces of death arose: the whole of one group of onlookers pursuing with hisses Fathers Crabot and Philibin as they hurried away, pale and anxious; while Brother Fulgence ordered the school-gates to be strongly bolted.

Marc, out of curiosity, had watched the scene from a window of Madame Duparque's little house, and, becoming keenly interested in it, he had even gone for a moment to the threshold, in order that he might see and hear the better. How ridiculous had been Férou's prophecy that the Jew would be saddled with the crime, that the rancorous black gowns would make a scapegoat of the secular schoolmaster! Far from things taking that course, it seemed as though they might turn out very badly for the good Brothers. The rising wrath of the crowd, those menaces of death, indicated that matters might go very far indeed, that the popular anger might spread from the one guilty man to the whole of his congregation, and shake the very Church itself in the region, if indeed the guilty man were one of its ministers. Marc questioned himself on that point but could form no absolute conviction; indeed, even suspicion seemed to him hazardous and wrong. The demeanour of Father Philibin and Brother Fulgence had appeared quite natural, full of perfect tranquillity. And he strove to be very tolerant and just, for fear lest he might yield to his impulses as a freethinker delivered from belief in dogmas.   All was dark in that terrible tragedy, and he resolved to wait until he should learn more.

But while he stood there he saw Pélagie returning in her Sunday-best, accompanied by her nephew, Polydor Souquet, a lad of eleven, who carried a handsomely bound book under his arm.

'It's the good conduct prize, monsieur!' exclaimed the servant proudly.   'That is even better than a prize for reading or writing, is it not?'

The truth was that Polydor, sly but torpid, astonished even the Brothers by his prodigious idleness.   He was a pale, sturdy boy, with very light hair and a long dull face. The son of a road-mender addicted to drink, he had lost his mother at an early age, and lived chancewise nowadays while his father broke stones on the roads.   Hating every kind of work, terrified particularly by the idea of having to break stones in his turn, he allowed his aunt to indulge in the dream of seeing him become a Brother, invariably agreeing with everything she said, and often visiting her in her kitchen, in the hope thereby of securing some dainty morsel.

Pélagie, however, in spite of her delight, was affected by the uproar on the square.   She at last looked round, quivering, and cast a glance of fury and defiance at the crowd. 'You hear them, monsieur!' she exclaimed.   'You hear those anarchists!   The idea of it!   Such devoted Brothers, who are so fond of their pupils, who look after them with such motherly care!   For instance, there's Polydor.   He lives with his father on the road to Jonville, nearly a mile away.   Well, last night, after that ceremony, for fear of a mishap, Brother Gorgias accompanied him to his very door. Is that not so, Polydor?'

'Yes,' the boy answered laconically in his husky voice.

'Yet folk insult and threaten the Brothers!' the servant resumed.   'How wicked!   You can picture poor Brother Gorgias taking that long walk in the dark night, in order that nothing might befall this little man!   Ah! it's enough to disgust one of being prudent and kind!'

Marc, who had been scrutinising the boy, was struck by his resolute taciturnity, by the hypocritical somnolence in which he seemed to find a pleasant refuge.   He listened no further to Pélagie, to whose chatter he never accorded much attention.   But on returning to the little drawing-room, where he had left his wife reading while Madame Duparque and Madame Berthereau turned to their everlasting knitting for some religious charities, he felt anxious, for he perceived that Geneviève had laid her book aside, and was gazing with much emotion at the tumult on the square. She came to him, and with an affectionate impulse, fraught with alarm, looking extremely pretty in her agitation, she almost threw herself upon his neck.

'What is happening?' she asked. 'Are they going to fight?'

He began to reassure her; and all at once Madame Duparque, raising her eyes from her work, sternly gave expression to her will: 'Marc, I hope that you will not mix yourself up in that horrid affair. What madness it is to suspect and insult the Brothers! God will end by avenging His ministers!'

II

MARC was unable to get to sleep that night, for he was haunted by the events of the day—by that monstrous, mysterious, puzzling crime. Thus, while Geneviève, his wife, reposed quietly beside him, he dwelt in thought upon each incident of the affair, classified each detail, striving to pierce the darkness and establish the truth.

Marc's mind was one that sought logic and light. His clear and firm judgment demanded in all things a basis of certainty. Thence came his absolute passion for truth. In his eyes no rest of mind, no real happiness, was possible without complete, decisive certainty. He was not very learned, but such things as he knew he wished to know completely, in order that he might have no doubt of the possession of the truth, experimental truth, established for ever. All unrest came to an end when doubt ceased; he then fully recovered his spirits, and to his passion for the acquirement of truth was added one for imparting it to others, for driving it into the brains and hearts of all. His marvellous gifts then became manifest; he brought with him a methodical power which simplified, classified, illumined everything. His quiet conviction imposed itself on his hearers, light was shed on dim notions, things seemed easy and simple. He instilled life into the driest subjects. He succeeded in imparting a passionate interest even to grammar and arithmetic, rendering them as interesting as stories to his pupils. In him one really found the born teacher.

He had discovered that he possessed that teaching gift at the time when, already possessed of a bachelor's degree, he had come to Beaumont to finish his apprenticeship as a lithographic draughtsman in the establishment of Messrs. Papon-Laroche. Entrusted with the execution of many school diagrams, he had exercised his ingenuity in simplifying them, creating perfect masterpieces of clearness and

precision, which had revealed to him his true vocation, the
happiness that he found in teaching the young.

It was at Papon-Laroche's establishment also that he had
first met Salvan, now Director of the Training College, who,
observing his bent, had approved of the course he took in
yielding to it completely, and becoming what he was to-day
—a humble elementary schoolmaster who, convinced of the
noble usefulness of his duties, was happy to discharge them
even in a small and lonely village.   Marc's affection for
those whose narrow and slumbering minds required awakening and expansion had decided his career.   And, in the
discharge of his modest functions, his passion for truth increased, becoming a more and more imperious craving.   It
ended indeed by constituting the *ratio* of his health, his very
life, for it was only by satisfying it that he enjoyed normal
life.   When it escaped him, he fell into anguish of spirit,
consumed by his desire to acquire and possess it wholly, in
order that he might communicate it to others, failing which
he spent his days in intolerable suffering, often physical as
well as mental.

From this passion assuredly sprang the torment which
kept Marc awake that night by the side of his sleeping wife.
He suffered from his ignorance, his failure to penetrate the
truth respecting the murder of that child.   He was not confronted merely by an ignoble crime; he divined behind it
the existence of dark and threatening depths, some dim but
yawning abyss.   Would his sufferings continue then as long
as he should not know the truth, which perchance he might
never know ? for the shadows seemed to increase at each
effort that he made to dissipate them.   Mastered by uncertainty and fear, he ended by longing for daybreak, in
order that he might resume his investigations.   But his wife
laughed lightly in her sleep; some happy dream, no doubt,
had come to her; and then the terrible old grandmother
seemed to rise up before the young man's eyes, and repeat
that he must on no account meddle in that horrible affair.
At this the certainty of a conflict with his wife's relations
appeared to him, and brought his hesitation and unhappiness to a climax.

Hitherto he had experienced no serious trouble with that
devout family whence he, who held no religious belief whatever, had taken the young girl who had become his wife,
his life's companion.   He did not carry tolerance so far as
to follow his wife to Mass, as Berthereau had done, but he

had allowed his daughter Louise to be baptised, in order that he might have some peace with the ladies. Besides, as his wife in her adoration for him had ceased to follow the religious observances of her Church soon after the marriage, no quarrel had yet arisen between them. Occasionally he remarked in Geneviève some revival of her long Catholic training, ideas of the absolute which clashed with his own, superstitions which sent a chill to his heart. But these were merely passing incidents; he believed that the love which bound him to his wife was strong enough to triumph over such divergencies; for did they not soon find themselves in each other's arms again, even when they had momentarily felt themselves to be strangers, belonging to different worlds?

Geneviève had been one of the best pupils of the Sisters of the Visitation; she had quitted their establishment with a superior certificate, in such wise that her first idea had been to become a teacher herself. But there was no place for her at Jonville, where the excellent Mademoiselle Mazeline managed the girls' school without assistance; and, naturally enough, she had been unwilling to quit her husband. Then household duties had taken possession of her; now, also, she had to attend to her little girl; and thus all thought of realising her early desire was postponed, perhaps for ever. But did not this very circumstance make their life all happiness and perfect agreement, far from the reach of storms?

If, from concern for their future happiness, the worthy Salvan, Berthereau's faithful friend, to whom the marriage was due, had for a moment thought of trying to check the irresistible love by which the young people were transported, he must have felt reassured on finding them still tenderly united after three years of matrimony. It was only now while the wife dreamt happily in her slumber that the husband for the first time experienced anxiety at the thought of the case of conscience before him, foreseeing, as he did, that a quarrel might well arise with his wife's relations, and that all sorts of unpleasant consequences might ensue in his home, should he yield to his imperative craving for truth.

At last, however, he dozed off and ended by sleeping soundly. In the morning, when his eyes opened to the clear bright light, he felt astonished at having passed through such a nightmare-like vigil. It had assuredly been caused by the haunting influence of that frightful crime, to

which, as it happened, Geneviève, still full of emotion and
pity, was the first to refer again.

'Poor Simon must be in great distress,' she said. 'You
cannot abandon him. I think that you ought to see him this
morning and place yourself at his disposal.'

Marc embraced her, delighted to find her so kind-hearted
and brave. 'But grandmother will get angry again,' he replied, 'and our life here will become unbearable.'

Geneviève laughed lightly, and gently shrugged her
shoulders. 'Oh! grandmother would quarrel with the very
angels,' she retorted. 'When one does half what she desires, one does quite enough.'

This sally enlivened them both, and, Louise having awoke,
they spent a few delightful moments in playing with her in
her little cot.

Then Marc resolved to go out and resume his inquiry
directly after breakfast. While he was dressing, he thought
the matter over quietly and sensibly. He was well acquainted with Maillebois and the characteristics of its two
thousand inhabitants, divided into petty *bourgeois*, petty
shopkeepers, and workmen; the latter, some eight hundred
in number, being distributed through the workshops of
some four or five firms, all of which were prosperous,
thanks to the vicinity of Beaumont. Being nearly equally
divided, the two sections of the population fought strenu-
ously for authority, and the Municipal Council was a faithful
picture of their differences, one half of it being Clerical
and Reactionary, while the other was Republican and Progressive. As yet only a very few Socialists figured in the
population, lost among all the folk of other views, and they
were quite without influence. Darras, the Mayor and
building contractor, was certainly a declared Republican,
and even made a profession of anti-clericalism. But, owing
to the almost equal strength of the two parties in the council, it was only by a majority of two votes that he, rich and
active, with about a hundred workpeople under his orders,
had been preferred to Philis, a retired tilt and awning
maker, with an income of from ten to twelve thousand
francs a year, who led the stern confined life of a militant
Clerical, interested in nothing beyond the observance of the
narrowest piety. Thus Darras was compelled to observe
extreme prudence, for the displacement of a few votes
would unseat him. Ah! if there had been only a substantial Republican majority behind him, how bravely he would

have supported the cause of liberty, truth, and justice, instead of practising, as he was reduced to do, the most diplomatic ' opportunism.'

Another thing known to Marc was the increasing power of the Clerical party, which seemed likely to conquer the whole region.   For ten years the little community of Capuchins established in the old convent, a part of which it had surrendered to the Brothers of the Christian Schools, had carried on the worship of St. Antony of Padua with ever-increasing audacity, and also with such great success that the profits were enormous.[1]   While the Brothers, on their side, derived advantage from this success, which brought them many pupils and thus increased the prosperity of the schools, the Capuchins worked their chapel as one may work a distillery, and sent forth from it every kind of moral poison.   The Saint stood on a golden altar, ever decked with flowers and ablaze with lights, collection boxes appeared on all sides, and a commercial office was permanently installed in the sacristy, where the procession of clients lasted from morn till night.   The Saint did not merely find lost things,—his specialty in the early days of his *cultus*,—he had extended his business.   For a few francs he undertook to enable the dullest youths to pass their examinations, to render doubtful business affairs excellent, to exonerate the rich scions of patriotic families from military service, to say nothing of performing a multitude of other equally genuine miracles, such as healing the sick and the maimed, and according a positive protection against ruin and death, in the last respect going indeed so far as to resuscitate a young girl who had expired two days previously.   Naturally enough, as each new story circulated, more and more money flowed in, and the business spread from the *bourgeois* and shopkeepers of Reactionary Maillebois to the workmen of Republican Maillebois, whom the poison ended by infecting.

It is true that, in his Sunday sermons, Abbé Quandieu, priest of St. Martin's, the parish church, forcibly pointed out the danger of low superstition; but few people listened to him.   Possessed of a more enlightened faith than that of

[1] The Protestant reader may be informed that this Saint (1195–1231) was a Portuguese Franciscan, famous for the eloquence of his sermons. The practices of which M. Zola speaks are not inventions.   The so-called worship of St. Antony has become widespread in France of recent years. Such is superstition !—*Trans.*

many priests, he deplored the harm which the rapacity of the Capuchins was doing to religion. In the first place they were ruining him; the parish church was losing many sources of revenue, all the alms and offerings now going to the convent chapel. But his grief came largely from a higher cause; he experienced the sorrow of an intelligent priest who was not disposed to bow to Rome in all things, but who still believed in the possible evolution amid the great modern democratic movement of an independent and liberal Church of France. Thus he waged war against those ' dealers of the Temple ' who betrayed the cause of Jesus; and it was said that Monseigneur Bergerot,[1] the Bishop of Beaumont, shared his views. But this did not prevent the Capuchins from increasing their triumphs, subjugating Maillebois and transforming it into a holy spot, by dint of their spurious miracles.

Marc also knew that, if Monseigneur Bergerot was behind Abbé Quandieu, the Capuchins and the Brothers possessed the support of Father Crabot, the all-powerful Rector of the College of Valmarie. If Father Philibin, the Prefect of the Studies there, had presided at the recent prize-giving at the Brothers' school, it had been by way of according to the latter a public mark of esteem and protection. The Jesuits had the affair in hand, as folk of evil mind were wont to say. And Simon, the Jew schoolmaster, found himself caught amid those inextricable quarrels, alone in a region swept by religious passion, at a dangerous moment, when the victory would be won by the most impudent. Men's hearts were perturbed; a spark would suffice to fire and devastate all minds. Nevertheless the Communal school had not lost a pupil as yet; its attendances and successes equalled those of the Brothers' school; and this comparative victory was undoubtedly due to the prudent skill displayed by Simon, who behaved cautiously with everybody, and who moreover was supported openly by Darras, and covertly by Abbé Quandieu. But the rivalry of the two schools would undoubtedly lead to the real battle, the decisive assault which must come sooner or later; for these two schools could not possibly live side by side, one must end by devouring the other. And the Church would be unable to subsist should she lose the privilege of teaching and enslaving the humble.

[1] Frequently referred to in M. Zola's *Lourdes* and *Rome* as a liberal prelate at variance with the Vatican.— *Trans.*

That morning, during breakfast with the ladies in the dismal little dining-room, Marc, already oppressed by his reflections, felt his discomfort increase. Madame Duparque quietly related that if Polydor had secured a prize the previous day, he owed it to a pious precaution taken by his aunt Pélagie, who had thoughtfully given a franc to St. Antony of Padua. On hearing this, Madame Berthereau nodded as if approvingly, and even Geneviève did not venture to smile, but seemed interested in the marvellous stories related by her grandmother. The old lady recounted a number of extraordinary incidents, how lives and fortunes had been saved, thanks to presents of two and three francs bestowed on the Saint by the medium of the Capuchins' Agency. And one realised how — one little sum being added to another—rivers of gold ended by flowing to their chapel, like so much tribute levied on public suffering and imbecility.

However, that morning's number of *Le Petit Beaumontais*, printed during the night, had arrived, and Marc was well pleased when, at the end of a long article on the crime of Maillebois, he found a paragraph containing a very favourable mention of Simon. The schoolmaster, who was esteemed by everybody, had received, it was said, the most touching assurances of sympathy in the great misfortune which had befallen him. This note had evidently been penned by some correspondent the previous evening, after the tumultuous departure from the distribution of prizes which had indicated in which direction the wind was likely to blow. Indeed, nobody could have mistaken the public hostility against the Brothers; and all the vague rumours, all the horrid stories hushed up in the past, aggravated that hostility, in such wise that one was threatened with some abominable scandal in which the whole Catholic and Reactionary party might collapse.

Thus Marc was surprised at the lively and even triumphant demeanour of Pélagie when she came in to clear the breakfast table. He lingered there on purpose to draw her out.

'Ah! there 's good news, monsieur,' said she; 'I learnt something, and no mistake, when I went on my errands this morning! I knew very well that those anarchists who insulted the Brothers yesterday were liars.'

Then she recounted all the tittle-tattle of the shops, all the gossip she had picked up on the foot-pavements whilst

going from door to door. Amid the oppressive horror, the
disturbing mystery that had weighed upon the town for four
and twenty hours, the wildest fancies had been gradually
germinating. It seemed as if some poisonous vegetation
had sprung up during the night. At first there were only
the vaguest suppositions; then explanations, suggested
chancewise, became certainties, and doubtful coincidences
were transformed into irrefutable proofs. And a point to
be remarked was that all these stealthy developments,
originating nobody knew how or where, but spreading hour
by hour, and diffusing doubt and uneasiness, turned in
favour of the Brothers and against Simon.

'It is quite certain, you know, monsieur,' said Pélagie,
'that the schoolmaster cared very little for his nephew.
He ill-treated him; he was seen doing so by people who
will say it. Besides, he was vexed at not having him in his
school. He was in no end of a passion when the lad took
his first Communion; he shook his fist at him and blas-
phemed. . . . And, at all events, it is very extraordinary
that the little angel should have been killed only a little
while after he had left the Holy Table, and when God was
still within him.'

A pang came to Marc's heart; he listened to the servant
with stupefaction. 'What do you mean?' he at last exclaimed. 'Are people accusing Simon of having killed his
nephew?'

'Well, some don't scruple to think it. That story of
going to enjoy himself at Beaumont, then missing the train
at half-past ten, and coming back on foot seems a strange
one. He reached home at twenty minutes to twelve, he
says. But nobody saw him, and he may very well have
returned by train an hour earlier, at the very moment when
the crime was committed. And when it was over he only
had to blow out the candle, and leave the window wide open
in order to make people suppose that the murderer had
come from outside. At about a quarter to eleven Mademoiselle Rouzaire, the schoolmistress, distinctly heard a
sound of footsteps in the school, moans and calls too, and
the opening and shutting of doors——'

'Mademoiselle Rouzaire!' cried Marc. 'Why, she did
not say a word of that in her first evidence. I was present!'

'Excuse me, monsieur, but at the butcher's just now
Mademoiselle Rouzaire was telling it to everybody, and I
heard her.'

The young man, quite aghast, allowed the servant to continue:

'Monsieur Mignot, the assistant-master, also says that he was greatly surprised at the head-master's sound sleep in the morning. And, indeed, it is extraordinary that one should have to go and awaken a man on the day when a murder is committed in his house. It seems too that he was n't the least bit touched; he merely trembled like a leaf, when he saw the little body.'

Marc again wished to protest; but Pélagie, in a stubborn, malicious way, went on: 'Besides, it was surely he, for a copy-slip which came from his class was found in the child's mouth. Only the master could have had that slip in his pocket—is that not so? It is said that it was even signed by him. At the greengrocer's too I heard a lady say that the police officials had found a number of similar slips in his cupboard.'

This time Marc retorted by stating the facts, speaking of the illegible initials on the slip, which Simon declared had never been in his hands; though, as it was of a pattern in common use, one might have found it in any school. However, when Pélagie declared that overwhelming proofs had been discovered that very morning during the search made by the officials in Simon's rooms, the young man began to feel exceedingly disturbed, and ceased to protest, for he realised that in the frightful confusion which was spreading through people's minds all arguments would be futile.

'You see, monsieur,' Pélagie continued, 'one can expect anything when one has to deal with a Jew. As the milkman said to me just now, those folk have no real family ties, no real country; they carry on dealings with the devil, they pillage people, and kill just for the pleasure of doing evil. And you may say what you like, you won't prevent people from believing that that Jew needed a child's life for some dirty business with the devil, and cunningly waited till his nephew had taken his first Communion in order that he might pollute and murder him while he was stainless and full of perfume from the presence of the Host.'

It was the charge of ritual murder reappearing, that haunting charge transmitted through the ages and reviving at each catastrophe, relentlessly pursuing those hateful Jews who poisoned wells and butchered little children.

On two occasions Geneviève, who suffered when she saw how Marc was quivering, had felt desirous of interrupting

and joining in his protests.   But she had restrained herself
from fear of irritating her grandmother, who was evidently
well pleased with the servant's gossip, for she nodded
approval of it.   In fact, Madame Duparque regarded it as
a victory; and, disdaining to lecture her son-in-law, whom
she deemed already vanquished, she contented herself with
saying to the ever-silent Madame Berthereau: 'It is just
like that dead child who was found many years ago in the
porch of St. Maxence.   A woman in the service of some
Jews narrowly escaped being sentenced in their place, for
only a Jew could have been the murderer.   When one fre-
quents such folk one is always exposed to the wrath of
God.'

Marc preferred to make no rejoinder; and almost immediately afterwards he went out.   But his perturbation was
extreme, and a doubt came to him.   Could Simon really be
guilty ?   The suspicion attacked him like some evil fever
contracted in a pernicious spot; and he felt a need of reflecting and recovering his equilibrium before he called
upon his colleague.   So he went off along the deserted
road to Valmarie, picturing, as he walked, all the incidents
of the previous day, and weighing men and things.   No,
no! Simon could not be reasonably suspected.   Certainties
presented themselves on all sides.   First of all, such a horrible crime on his part was utterly illogical, impossible.
He was assuredly healthy in body and mind, he had no
physiological flaws, his gentle gaiety denoted the regularity
of his life.   And he had a wife of resplendent beauty whom
he adored, beside whom he lived in loving ecstasy, grateful
to her for the handsome children who had sprung from
their affection and had become their living love and worship.   How was it possible to imagine that such a man
had yielded to a fit of abominable madness a few moments
before rejoining his well-loved spouse and his little children
slumbering in their cots ?   Again, how simple and truthful
on the previous day had been the accents of that man who
was exposed to the scrutiny of so many enemies, who loved
his calling to the point of heroism, who made the best of his
poverty without ever uttering a word of complaint!

The account he had given of his evening had been very
clear, his wife had confirmed his statements respecting the
time of his return, none of the information that he had furnished seemed open to doubt.   And if some obscure points
remained, if that crumpled copy-slip found with a number

of *Le Petit Beaumontais* constituted an enigma as yet un-
ravelled, reason at least indicated that the culprit must be
sought elsewhere; for Simon's nature and life, the very
conditions in which he lived, showed that he could have
had nothing to do with the crime.   On that point Marc
experienced a feeling of certainty, based on reason, on truth
itself, which remains unshakable when once it is established
by observation and the deductions that facts supply.

Thus the young man's conviction was formed; there were
certain ascertained facts to which he would bring everything else back, and, although every error and falsehood
might be launched, he would brush all assertions aside if
they did not agree with such truths as were already known
and demonstrated.

Serene once more, relieved of the burden of his doubts,
Marc returned to Maillebois, passing the railway station at
the moment when some passengers were alighting from a
train which had just arrived.   Among those who emerged
from the station he perceived the Elementary Education
Inspector of the *arrondissement*, handsome Mauraisin, as he
was called, a very dark, foppish little man of thirty-eight,
whose thin lips and whose chin were hidden by a carefully
kept moustache and beard, while glasses screened his eager
eyes.   Formerly a professor at the Beaumont Training
College, Mauraisin belonged to that new generation, the
Arrivistes, who are ever on the lookout for advancement,
and who always place themselves on the stronger side.
He, it was said, had coveted the directorship of the Training College, which had fallen to Salvan, whom he pursued
with covert hatred, but very prudently, for he was aware of
Salvan's great credit with Le Barazer, the Academy Inspector,[1] on whom he himself depended.   Besides, in presence
of the equality of the forces which were contending for
supremacy in his *arrondissement*, Mauraisin, in spite of his

[1] In matters of education the French territory is apportioned among
a number of 'Academies,' such as those of Paris, Caen, Rennes, Bor-
deaux, Dijon, &c., which are each governed by Rectors, and which,
combined, constitute the University of France, of which the Minister
of Public Instruction for the time being is the grand-master.   The
Rectors communicate with him ; under them, in each territorial department within their jurisdiction, they have an ' Inspecteur d'Académie,'
who is provided with a general secretary, and who in turn has under him
several subordinate inspectors called ' Inspecteurs de l'Instruction
primaire.'   There is one of these for each *arrondissement* into which
the departments are divided.— *Trans.*

personal preferences for the clericals, the priests, and
monks, whom he regarded as 'devilish clever,' had been
skilful enough to refrain from declaring himself too openly.
Thus, when Marc perceived the Elementary Inspector, it
was allowable for him to fancy that Le Barazer, with whose
good nature he was acquainted, had despatched his subordinate to the assistance of Simon in the terrible catastrophe which threatened to sweep the schoolmaster of
Maillebois and his school away.

The young man therefore hastened his steps, desirous of
paying his respects to the Inspector, but all at once an unexpected incident restrained him. A cassock had emerged
from a neighbouring street, and he recognised in its wearer
Father Crabot, the Rector of the Jesuit College of Valmarie.
A tall, finely-built man, without a white hair at five and
forty, Father Crabot had a broad and regular face, with a
somewhat large nose, amiable eyes, and thick, caressing lips.
The only failing with which he was reproached was a tend-
ency to become a fashionable cleric as a result of the many
aristocratic connections which he was always eager to form.
But those connections simply increased the sphere of his
power, and some people said, with good reason, that he was
the secret master of the department, and that the victory of
the Church, which was assuredly approaching, depended
solely on him.

Marc felt surprised and disquieted on seeing the Jesuit at
Maillebois at that hour. Had he quitted Valmarie very
early in the morning then? What urgent business, what
pressing visits had brought him there? Whence had he
come, whither was he going, distributing bows and smiles as
he passed through the streets full of the fever born by
rumour and tittle-tattle? And all at once Marc saw Father
Crabot stop at the sight of Mauraisin and offer the latter
his hand with charming cordiality. Their conversation was
not a long one; it consisted, no doubt, of the usual com-
monplaces, but they seemed to be on excellent terms, as if
indeed they discreetly understood each other. When the
Elementary Inspector quitted the Jesuit, he drew his little
figure erect, evidently feeling very proud of that hand-
shake, which had inspired him with an opinion, a resolution, which perhaps he had hitherto hesitated to form. But
Father Crabot, going his way, also caught sight of Marc,
and recognising him, from having seen him at Madame Duparque's, where he occasionally condescended to call, made

a great show of doffing his hat by way of salutation.   The
young man, who stood on the kerb of the footway, was
compelled to respond by a similar act of politeness, and
then watched the Jesuit as the latter, filling the streets with
the sweep of his cassock, betook himself through Maillebois,
which felt very honoured, flattered, and subjugated by his
presence.

Marc, for his part, slowly resumed his walk towards the
school.   The current of his thoughts had changed, he was
growing gloomy again, as if he were returning to some contaminated spot where slow poison had diffused hostility.
The houses did not seem to be the same as on the previous
day; and, in particular, the faces of the people appeared to
have changed.   Thus, when he reached Simon's rooms, he
was quite surprised to find his friend quietly sorting some
papers in the midst of his family.   Rachel was seated near
the window, the two children were playing in a corner, and
if it had not been for the sadness of the parents one would
have thought that nothing unusual had occurred in the
house.

Simon, however, stepped forward and pressed Marc's
hands with keen emotion, like one who felt how friendly
and bravely sympathetic was the visit.   The perquisition
early that morning was at once spoken of.

'Have the police been here?' Marc inquired.

'Yes, it was quite natural they should come: I expected
it.   Of course they found nothing, and went off with empty
hands.'

Marc restrained a gesture of astonishment.   What had
Pélagie told him?   Why had people spread rumours of
crushing proofs, of the discovery among other things of
copy-slips identical with the one found in the room of the
crime?   Were lies being told then?

'And you see,' Simon continued, 'I am setting my papers
in order, for they mixed them up.   What a frightful affair,
my friend!   We no longer know if we exist.'

Then he mentioned that the post-mortem examination of
Zéphirin's remains was to take place that very day.   Indeed, they were then expecting the medical officer of the
Public Prosecution service.   But doubtless it would only
be possible to bury the body on the morrow.

'For my part,' Simon added, 'as you will well understand,
I seem to be living in a nightmare.   I ask myself if such a
catastrophe is possible.   I have been thinking of nothing

else since yesterday morning; I am always beginning the same story afresh, my return on foot, so late but in great quietude, my arrival at the house which was fast asleep, and then that frightful awakening in the morning.'

These remarks gave Marc an opportunity to ask a few questions. 'Did you meet nobody on the road?' he inquired. 'Did nobody see you arrive here at the hour you named?'

'Why, no! I met nobody, and I think nobody saw me come in. At that late hour nobody is about in Maillebois.'

Silence fell. Then Marc resumed: 'But as you did not take the train back you did not use your return ticket. Have you still got it?'

'My return ticket? No! I was so furious when I saw the half-past ten o'clock train going off without me, that I threw the ticket away, in the station yard, directly I decided to return on foot.'

Silence fell again, and Simon gazed fixedly at his friend, saying: 'Why do you put these questions to me?'

Marc affectionately grasped his hands once more, and retained them for a moment in his own, whilst resolving to warn him of impending danger, indeed to tell him everything. 'I regret,' he said, 'that nobody saw you, and I regret still more that you did not keep your return ticket. There are so many fools and malicious folks about! It is being reported that this morning the police found overwhelming proofs here, copies of the writing-slip, initialled in the same way as the one which formed part of the gag. Mignot, it seems, is astonished that he should have found you so sound asleep yesterday morning; and Mademoiselle Rouzaire now remembers that about a quarter to eleven o'clock on the night of the crime, she heard voices and footsteps, as if somebody were entering the house.'

Very pale but very calm, Simon smiled and shrugged his shoulders: 'Ah! that 's it, is it? They are suspecting me. Well, I now understand the expressions I have seen on the faces of the folk who have been passing the school since early this morning! Mignot, who is a good fellow at heart, will of course say as everybody else says, for fear of compromising himself with a Jew like me. As for Mademoiselle Rouzaire, she will sacrifice me ten times over, if her confessor has suggested it to her, and if she finds a chance of advancement or merely additional consideration in such a fine deed. Ah! they are suspecting me, are they? and the whole pack of clerical hounds has been let loose!'

He almost laughed as he spoke. But Rachel, whose customary indolence seemed to have been increased by her deep grief, had now suddenly risen, her beautiful countenance all aglow with dolorous revolt.

'You, you! They suspect you of such ignominy!' she exclaimed; 'you who were so kind and gentle when you came home, and clasped me in your arms, and spoke such loving words to me! They must be mad! Is it not sufficient that I should speak the truth, tell of your return, and of the night we spent together?'

Then she flung herself upon his neck, weeping and relapsing into the weakness of an adored and caressed woman. Pressing her to his heart her husband strove to reassure and calm her.

'Don't be distressed, my darling! Those stories are idiotic, they stand on nothing. I am quite at ease; the authorities may turn everything here upside down; they may search all my past life, they will find no guilt in it. I have only to speak the truth, and, do you know, nothing can stand against the truth; it is the great, the eternal victor.'

Then, turning to his friend, he added: 'Is it not so, my good Marc? is one not invincible when one has truth on one's side?'

If Marc had not been convinced already of Simon's innocence his last doubts would have fled amid the emotion of that scene. Yielding to an impulse of his heart he embraced both husband and wife, as if giving himself to them entirely, in order to help them in the grave crisis which he foresaw. Desirous as he was of taking immediate action, he again spoke of the copy-slip, for he felt that it was the one important piece of evidence on which the elucidation of the whole affair must be reared. But how puzzling was that crumpled, bitten slip of paper, soiled by saliva, with its initialling or its blot half effaced, and with one of its corners carried away, no doubt, by the victim's teeth! The very words 'Love one another,' lithographed in a fine English round-hand, seemed fraught with a terrible irony. Whence had that slip come? Who had brought it to that room—the boy or his murderer? And how could one ascertain the truth when the Mesdames Milhomme, the neighbouring stationers, sold such slips almost daily?

Simon, for his part, could only repeat that he had never had that particular one in his school. 'All my boys would say so. That copy never entered the school, never passed under their eyes.'

Marc regarded this as valuable information. 'Then they could testify to that effect!' he exclaimed. 'As it is being falsely rumoured that the police found similar copies in your rooms, one must re-establish the truth immediately,—call on your pupils at their homes, and demand their evidence before anybody tries to tamper with their memory. Give me the names of a few of them; I will take the matter in hand, and carry it through this afternoon.'

Simon, strong in the consciousness of his innocence, at first refused to do so. But eventually, among his pupils' parents, he named Bongard, a farmer on the road to La Désirade, Masson Doloir, a workman living in the Rue Plaisir, and Savin, a clerk in the Rue Fauche. Those three would suffice unless Marc should also like to call on the Mesdames Milhomme. Thus everything was settled, and Marc went off to lunch, promising that he would return in the evening to acquaint Simon with the result of his inquiries.

Once outside on the square, however, he again caught sight of handsome Mauraisin. This time the Elementary Inspector was deep in conference with Mademoiselle Rouzaire. He was usually most punctilious and prudent with the schoolmistresses, in consequence of his narrow escape from trouble, a few years previously, in connection with a young assistant-teacher who had shrieked like a little booby when he had simply wished to kiss her. Malicious people said that Mademoiselle Rouzaire did not shriek, although she was so ugly, and that this explained both the favourable reports she secured and her prospects of rapid advancement.

Standing at the gate of her little garden, she was now speaking to Mauraisin with great volubility, making sweeping gestures in the direction of the boys' school; while the Inspector, wagging his head, listened to her attentively. At last they entered the garden together, gently closing the gate behind them. It was evident to Marc that the woman was telling Mauraisin about the crime and the sounds of footsteps and voices which she now declared she had heard. At the thought of this the quiver of the early morning returned to Marc; he again experienced discomfort—a discomfort arising from his hostile surroundings, from the dark, stealthy plot which was brewing, gathering like a storm, rendering the atmosphere more and more oppressive. Singular indeed was the fashion in which that Elementary

Inspector went to the help of a threatened master: he began by taking the opinions of all the surrounding folk whom jealousy or hatred inspired!

At two o'clock in the afternoon Marc found himself on the road to La Désirade, just outside Maillebois. Bongard, whose name had been given him by Simon, there owned a little farm of a few fields, which he cultivated himself with difficulty, securing, as he put it, no more than was needed to provide daily bread. Marc luckily met him just as he had returned home with a cartload of hay. He was a strong, square-shouldered, and stoutish man, with round eyes and placid silent face, beardless but seldom fresh shaven. On her side La Bongard, a long bony *blonde*, who was also present, preparing some mash for her cow, showed an extremely plain countenance, outrageously freckled, with a patch of colour on each cheek-bone, and an expression of close reserve. Both looked suspiciously at the strange gentleman whom they saw entering their yard.

'I am the Jonville schoolmaster,' said Marc. 'You have a little boy who attends the Communal school at Maillebois, have you not?'

At that moment Fernand, the boy in question, who had been playing on the road, ran up. He was a sturdy lad of nine years, fashioned, one might have thought, with a bill-hook, and showing a low brow and a dull, heavy countenance. He was followed by his sister Angèle, a lass of seven, with a similarly massive but more knowing face, for in her quick eyes one espied some dawning intelligence which was striving to escape from its fleshy prison. She had heard Marc's question, and she cried in a shrill voice: 'I go to Mademoiselle Rouzaire's, I do; Fernand goes to Monsieur Simon's.'

Bongard had sent his children to the Communal schools, first because the teaching cost him nothing, and secondly because, as a matter of mere instinct,—for he had never reasoned the question,—he was not on the side of the priests. He practised no religion, and if La Bongard went to church it was simply from habit and by way of diversion. All that the husband, who was scarce able to read or write, appreciated in his wife, who was still more ignorant than himself, was her powers of endurance, which, similar to those of a beast of burden, enabled her to toil from morn till night without complaining. And the farmer showed little or no anxiety whether his children made progress at school.   As a matter of fact little Fernand was industrious and took no end of pains, but could get nothing into his head; whereas little Angèle, who proved yet more pains-taking and stubborn, at last seemed likely to become a passable pupil.   She was like so much human matter in the rough, lately fashioned of clay, and awaking to intelligence by a slow and dolorous effort.

'I am Monsieur Simon's friend,' Marc resumed, 'and I have come on his behalf about what has happened.   You have heard of the crime, have you not?'

Most certainly they had heard of it.   Their anxious faces suddenly became impenetrable, in such wise that one could read on them neither feeling nor thought.   Why had that stranger come to question them in this fashion?   Their ideas about things concerned nobody.   Besides, it was necessary to be prudent in matters in which a word too much often suffices to bring about a man's sentence.

'And so,' Marc continued, 'I should like to know if your little boy ever saw in his class a copy-slip like this.'

Marc himself on a slip of paper had written the words *'Aimez vous les uns les autres'* in a fine round-hand of the proper size.   Having explained matters, he showed the paper to Fernand, who looked at it in a dazed fashion, for his mind worked slowly and he did not yet understand what was asked him.

'Look well at it, my little friend,' said Marc; 'did you ever see such a copy at the school?'

But before the lad had made up his mind, Bongard, in his circumspect manner, intervened: 'The child does n't know, how can he know?'

And La Bongard, like her husband's shadow, added: 'Why of course a child, it can never know.'

Without listening to them, however, Marc insisted, and placed the copy in the hands of Fernand, who, fearing that he might be punished, made an effort, and at last responded: 'No, monsieur, I never saw it.'

As he spoke he raised his head, and his eyes met his father's, which were fixed on him so sternly that he hast-ened to add, stammering as he did so: 'Unless all the same I did see it; I don't know.'

That was all that could be got out of him.   When Marc pressed him, his answers became incoherent, while his parents themselves said yes or no chancewise, according to what they deemed to be their interest.   It was Bongard's prudent habit to jog his head in approval of every opinion expressed by those who spoke to him, for fear of compromising himself. Yes, yes, it was a frightful crime, and if the culprit should be caught it would be quite right to cut off his head. Each man to his trade, the gendarmes knew theirs, there were rascals everywhere. As for the priests, there was some good in them, but all the same one had a right to follow one's own ideas. And at last, as Marc could learn nothing positive, he had to take himself off, watched inquisitively by the children, and pursued by the shrill voice of little Angèle, who began chattering with her brother as soon as the gentleman could no longer detect what she said.

The young man gave way to some sad reflections as he returned to Maillebois. He had just come in contact with the thick layer of human ignorance, the huge blind, deaf multitude still enwrapped in the slumber of the earth. Behind the Bongards the whole mass of country folk remained stubbornly, dimly vegetating, ever slow to awaken to a true perception of things. There was a whole nation to be educated if one desired that it should be born to truth and justice. But how colossal would be the labour! How could it be raised from the clay in which it lingered, how many generations perhaps would be needed to free the race from darkness! Even at the present time the vast majority of the social body remained in infancy, in primitive imbecility. In the case of Bongard one descended to mere brute matter, which was incapable of being just because it knew nothing and would learn nothing.

Marc turned to the left, and after crossing the High Street found himself in the poor quarter of Maillebois. Various industrial establishments there polluted the waters of the Verpille, and the sordid houses of the narrow streets were the homes of many workpeople. Doloir the mason tenanted four fairly large rooms on a first floor over a wineshop in the Rue Plaisir. Marc, imperfectly informed respecting the address, was seeking it when he came upon a party of masons who had just quitted their work to drink a glass together at the bar of the wineshop. They were discussing the crime in violent language.

'A Jew's capable of anything,' one big fair fellow exclaimed. ' There was one in my regiment who was a thief, but that did not prevent him from being a corporal, for a Jew always gets out of difficulties.'

Another mason, short and dark, shrugged his shoulders.
' I quite agree,' said he, ' that the Jews are not worth much,
but all the same the priests are no better.'

' Oh! as for the priests,' the other retorted, ' some are
good, some are bad. At all events the priests are Frenchmen, whereas those dirty beasts, the Jews, have sold France
to the foreigners twice already.' Then, as his comrade,
somewhat shaken in his views, asked him if he had read
that in *Le Petit Beaumontais*, ' No, I did n't,' he added;
' those newspapers give me too much of a headache. But
some of my mates told me, and, besides, everybody knows
it well.'

The others, thereupon feeling convinced, became silent,
and slowly drained their glasses. They were just quitting
the wineshop when Marc, approaching, asked the tall fair
one if he knew where Doloir the mason lived. The workman laughed. ' Doloir, monsieur? that 's me,' he said;
' I live here; those are my three windows.'

The adventure quite enlivened this tall sturdy fellow of
somewhat military bearing. As he laughed his big moustaches rose, disclosing his teeth, which looked very white in
his highly coloured face, with large, good- natured blue
eyes.

' You could not have asked anybody more likely to know,
could you, monsieur?' he continued. ' What do you wish
of me?'

Marc looked at him with a feeling of some sympathy in
spite of the hateful words he had heard. Doloir, who had
been for several years in the employment of Darras, the
Mayor and building contractor, was a fairly good workman
—one who occasionally drank a drop too much, but who
took his pay home to his wife regularly. He certainly
growled about the employers, referred to them as a dirty
gang, and called himself a socialist, though he had only a
vague idea what socialism might be. At the same time he
had some esteem for Darras, who, while making a great
deal of money, tried to remain a comrade with his men.
But above everything else three years of barrack-life had
left an ineffaceable mark on Doloir. He had quitted the
army in a transport of delight at his deliverance, freely
cursing the disgusting and hateful calling in which one
ceased to be a man. But ever since that time he had been
continually living his three years' service afresh; not a day
passed but some recollection of it came to him. With his

hand spoilt as it were by the rifle he had carried, he had
found his trowel heavy, and had returned to work in a
spiritless fashion, like one who was no longer accustomed to
toil, but whose will was broken and whose body had become
used to long spells of idleness, such as those which intervened between the hours of military exercise.   To become
once more the excellent workman that he had been previously was impossible.   Besides, he was haunted by military matters, to which he was always referring apropos of
any subject that presented itself.   But he chattered in a
confused way, he had no information, he read nothing, he
knew nothing, being simply firm and stubborn on the
patriotic question, which, to his mind, consisted in preventing the Jews from handing France over to the foreigners.

'You have two children at the Communal school,' Marc
said to him, ' and I have come from the master, my friend
Simon, for some information.   But I see that you are
hardly a friend of the Jews.'

Doloir still laughed.   ' It 's true,' said he, ' that Monsieur
Simon is a Jew; but hitherto I always thought him a worthy
man.   What information do you want, monsieur ? '

When he learnt that the question was merely one of showing his children a writing copy in order to ascertain whether
they had ever used it in their class, he responded: 'Nothing
can be easier, monsieur, if it will do you a service.   Come
upstairs with me, the children must be at home.'

The door was opened by Madame Doloir, a dark, short
but robust woman, having a serious, energetic face with a
low brow, frank eyes, and a square-shaped chin.   Although
she was barely nine and twenty she was already the mother
of three children, and it was evident that she was expecting
a fourth.   But this did not prevent her from being always
the first to rise and the last to go to bed in the home, for
she was very industrious, very thrifty, always busy, scrubbing
and cleaning.   She had quitted her employment as a seamstress about the time of the birth of her third child, and
nowadays she only attended to her home, but she did so
like a woman who fully earned her bread.

'This gentleman is a friend of the schoolmaster, and
wishes to speak to the children,' her husband explained to
her.

Marc entered a very clean dining or living room.   The
little kitchen was on the left, with its door wide open.   In
front were the bedrooms of the parents and the children.

'Auguste! Charles!' the father called.

Auguste and Charles, one eight, the other six years old, hastened forward, followed by their little sister Lucille, who was four. They were handsome, well-fed children in whom one found the characteristics of the father and the mother combined; the younger boy appearing more intelligent than the elder one, and the little girl, a *blondine* with a soft laugh, already looking quite pretty.

When, Marc, however, showed the copy to the boys and questioned them, Madame Doloir, who hitherto had not spoken a word, hastily intervened: 'Excuse me, monsieur, but I do not wish my children to answer you.'

She said this very politely, without the slightest sign of temper, like a good mother, indeed, who was merely fulfilling her duty.

'But why?' Marc asked in his amazement.

'Why, because there is no need for us, monsieur, to meddle in an affair which seems likely to turn out very badly. I have had it dinned into my ears ever since yesterday morning; and I won't have anything to do with it, that 's all.'

Then, as Marc insisted and began to defend Simon, she retorted: 'I say nothing against Monsieur Simon, the children have never had to complain of him. If he is accused, let him defend himself: that is his business. For my part I have always tried to prevent my husband from meddling in politics, and if he listens to me he will hold his tongue, and take up his trowel without paying any attention either to the Jews or to the priests. All this, at bottom, is politics again.'

She never went to church, although she had caused her children to be baptised and had decided to let them take their first Communion. Those, however, were things one had to do. For the rest, she simply and instinctively held conservative views, accepting things as they were, accommodating herself to her narrow life, for she was terrified by the thought of catastrophes which might diminish their daily bread. With an expression of stubborn resolve she repeated: 'I do not wish any of us to be compromised.'

Those words were decisive: Doloir himself bowed to them. Although he usually allowed his wife to lead him, he did not like her to exercise her power before others. But this time he submitted.

'I did not reflect, monsieur,' he said. 'My wife is right.

It is best for poor devils like us to keep quiet. One of the men in my regiment knew all sorts of things about the Captain. Ah! they did not stand on ceremony with him. You should have seen what a number of times he was sent to the cells!'

Marc, like the husband, had to accept the position; and so, renouncing all further inquiry there, he merely said: ' It is possible that the judicial authorities may ask your boys what I desired to ask them. In that case they will have to answer.'

'Very good,' Madame Doloir answered quietly, 'if the judicial authorities question them we shall see what they ought to do. They will answer or not, it will all depend; my children are mine, and it is my business.'

Marc withdrew, escorted by Doloir, who was in a hurry to return to his work. When they reached the street, the mason almost apologised. His wife was not always easy to deal with, he remarked; but when she said the right thing, it was right and no mistake.

Such was Marc's discouragement that he now wondered whether it would be worth his while to carry the inquiry further by visiting Savin the clerk. In the Doloirs' home he had not found the same dense ignorance as at the Bon-gards'. The former were a step higher in the social scale, and if both husband and wife were still virtually illiterate, they at least came in contact with other classes, and knew a little of life. But how vague was still the dawn which they typified, how dim was the groping through idiotic egotism, in what disastrous errors did lack of solidarity maintain the poor folk of that class! If they were not happier it was because they were ignorant of every right condition of civic life, of the necessity that others should be happy in order that one might be happy oneself. Marc thought of that human house, the doors and windows of which people have striven to keep closed for ages, whereas they ought to be opened widely in order to allow air and warmth and light to enter in torrents freely.

While he was thus reflecting, he turned the corner of the Rue Plaisir, and reached the Rue Fauche, where the Savins dwelt. He thereupon felt ashamed of his discouragement, so he climbed the stairs to their flat, and speedily found himself in the presence of Madame Savin, who had hastened to answer his ring.

'My husband, monsieur? Yes, as it happens, he is at

home, for he was rather feverish this morning and could not go to his office. Please follow me.'

She was charming was Madame Savin, dark, refined and gay, with a pretty laugh, and so young-looking also, though her twenty-eighth year was already past, that she seemed to be the elder sister of her four children. The firstborn was a girl, Hortense; followed by twin boys, Achille and Philippe, and then by another boy, Jules, whom the young mother was still nursing. It was said that her husband was terribly jealous, that he suspected her, and watched her, ever full of ill-natured disquietude, although she gave him no cause for it. A bead-worker by trade, and an orphan, she had been sought by him in marriage for her beauty's sake, after her aunt's death, when she was quite alone in the world; and on this account she retained a feeling of gratitude towards him, and conducted herself very uprightly like a good wife and a good mother.

Just as she was about to usher Marc into the adjoining room, some embarrassment came over her. Perhaps she feared the bad temper of her husband, who was ever ready to pick a quarrel, and to whom she preferred to yield for the sake of domestic peace.

'What name am I to give, monsieur?' she asked.

Marc told her his name and the object of his visit, whereupon with graceful suppleness she glided away, leaving the young man in the little ante-chamber, which he began to scrutinise. The flat was composed of five rooms, occupying the whole of that floor of the house. Savin, a petty *employé* of the Revenue service, clerk to the local tax-collector, had to keep up his rank, which in his opinion necessitated a certain amount of outward show. Thus his wife wore bonnets, and he himself never went out otherwise than in a frock coat. But how painful were the straits of the life which he led behind that façade so mendaciously suggestive of class superiority and easy circumstances! The bitterness of his feelings came from his consciousness that he was bound fast to his humble duties, that he had no prospect whatever of advancement, but was condemned for life to never-changing toil and a contemptible salary, which only just saved him from starvation. Poor in health and soured, humble and irritable at one and the same time, feeling as much terror as rage in his everlasting anxiety lest he might displease his superiors, he showed himself obsequious and cowardly at his office, whilst at home he terror-

ised his wife with his fits of passion, which suggested those
of a sickly child.   She smiled at them in her pretty, gentle
way, and after attending to the children and the household
she found a means to work bead-flowers for a firm at Beaumont, very delicate and well-paid work, which provided the
family with little luxuries.   But her husband, vexed at
heart, such was his middle-class pride, would not have it
said that his wife was forced to work, and so it was necessary for her to shut herself up with her beads, and deliver
her work by stealth.

For a moment Marc heard a sharp voice speaking angrily.
Then, after a gentle murmur, silence fell, and Madame
Savin reappeared: ' Please follow me, monsieur.'

Savin scarcely rose from the arm-chair in which he was
nursing his attack of fever.   A village schoolmaster was of
no consequence.   Short, lean, and puny, quite bald already, although he was only thirty-one years old, the clerk
had a poor, cadaverous countenance, with slight, tired
features, light eyes, and a very scanty beard of a dirty
yellowish tinge.   He finished wearing out his old frock coats
at home, and that day the coloured scarf he had fastened
about his neck helped to make him look like a little old man,
burdened with complaints and quite neglectful of his person.

' My wife tells me, monsieur,' he said, 'that you have
called about that abominable affair, in which Simon the
schoolmaster, according to some accounts, is likely to be
compromised; and my first impulse, I confess it, was to
refuse to see you.'

Then he stopped short, for he had just noticed on the
table some bead-work flowers which his wife had been
making as she sat beside him, while he perused *Le Petit
Beaumontais*.   He gave her a terrible glance which she
understood, for she hastened to cover her work with the
newspaper.

' But don't regard me as a Reactionary, monsieur,' Savin
resumed.   ' I am a Republican—in fact a very advanced
Republican; I do not hide it, my superiors are well aware
of it.   When one serves the Republic it is only honest to be
a Republican, is it not ?   Briefly, I am on the side of the
Government for and in all things.'

Compelled to listen politely, Marc contented himself with
nodding his assent.

' My views on the religious question are very simple,'
Savin continued.   ' The priests ought to remain in their

own sphere. I am an anti-clerical as I am a Republican. But I hasten to add that in my opinion a religion is neces- sary for women and children, and that as long as the Catholic religion is that of the country, why, we may as well have that one as another! Thus, with respect to my wife, I have made her understand that it is fitting and necessary for a woman of her age and position to follow the observances of religion in order that she may have a rule and a *morale* in the eyes of the world. She goes to the Capuchins!'

Madame Savin became embarrassed, her face turned pink, and she cast down her eyes. That question of relig- ious practices had long been a great source of unpleasant- ness in her home. She, with all her charming delicacy, her gentle, upright, heart, had always regarded those prac- tices with repugnance. As for her husband, he, wild with jealousy, ever picking quarrels with her respecting what he called her unfaithfulness of thought, looked upon Confes- sion and Communion solely as police measures, moral curbs, excellently suited to restrain women from descending the slope which leads to betrayal. And his wife had been obliged to yield to him in the matter, and accept the con- fessor whom he selected, the bearded Father Théodose, though with her woman's instinct she divined the latter to be a man of a horrid nature. But if she was wounded at heart and blushed with offended delicacy, she none the less shrugged her shoulders and continued to obey her husband for the sake of domestic quietude.

'As for my children, monsieur,' Savin was now saying, ' my resources have not enabled me to send Achille and Philippe, my twin sons, to college; so, naturally enough, I have sent them to the secular school in accordance with my duty as a functionary and a Republican. In the same way my daughter Hortense goes to Mademoiselle Rouzaire's; but, at bottom, I am well pleased to find that that lady has religious sentiments, and conducts her pupils to church— for, after all, such is her duty, and I should complain if she did not do so. Boys always pull through. And yet if I did not owe an account of my actions to my superiors, would it not have been more advantageous for my sons if I had sent them to a Church school? Later in life they would have been helped on, placed in good situations, sup- ported, whereas now they will simply vegetate, as I myself have vegetated.'

His bitter rancour was overflowing; and, seized with a

secret dread, he added in a lower tone: 'The priests, you see, are the stronger, and in spite of everything one ought always to be with them.'

A feeling of compassion came over Marc; that poor, puny, trembling being, driven desperate by mediocrity of circumstances and foolishness of nature, seemed to him in sore need of pity. Foreseeing the conclusion of all his speeches the young man had already risen. 'And so, monsieur,' he said, 'the information which I desired to obtain from your children——'

'The children are not here,' Savin answered; 'a lady, a neighbour, has taken them for a walk. But, even if they were here, ought I to allow them to answer you? Judge for yourself. A functionary can in no case take sides. And I already have quite enough worries at my office without incurring any responsibility in this vile affair.'

Then, as Marc hastily bowed, he added: 'Although the Jews prey on our land of France I have nothing to say against that Monsieur Simon, unless it be that a Jew ought never to be allowed to be a schoolmaster. I hope that *Le Petit Beaumontais* will start a campaign on that subject. . . . Liberty and justice for all—such ought to be the watchwords of a good Republican. But the country must be put first, the country alone must be considered, when it is in danger! Is that not so?'

Madame Savin, who since Marc's entry into the room had not spoken a word, escorted the young man to the door of the flat, where, while still retaining an air of embarrassment amid her submissiveness—that of a slave-wife superior to her harsh master—she contented herself with smiling divinely. Then at the bottom of the stairs Marc encountered the children whom the neighbour was bringing home. Hortense, the girl, now nine years old, was already a pretty and coquettish little person, with artful eyes which gleamed with maliciousness when she did not veil them with the expression of hypocritical piety which she had learnt to acquire at Mademoiselle Rouzaire's. But Marc was more interested in the twin boys, Achille and Philippe, two thin pale lads, sickly like their father, and very unruly and sly for their seven years. They pushed their sister against the banister, and almost made her fall; and when they had climbed the stairs, and the door of the flat opened, an infant's wail was heard, that of little Jules, who had awoke and was already in the arms of his mother, eager for her breast.

As Marc walked down the street, he caught himself talking aloud. So they were all agreed, from the ignorant peasant to the timid and idiotic clerk, passing by way of the brutified workman, the spoilt fruit of barrack life and the salary system. In ascending the social scale one merely found error aggravated by narrow egotism and base cowardice. Men's minds remained steeped in darkness; the semi-education which was nowadays acquired without method, and which reposed on no serious scientific foundation, led simply to a poisoning of the brain, to a state of disquieting corruption. There must be education certainly, but complete education, whence hypocrisy and falsehood would be banished — education which would free the mind by acquainting it with truth in its entirety. Marc trembled at the thought of the abyss of ignorance, error, and hatred which opened before him. What an awful bankruptcy there would be if those folk were needed some day for some work of truth and justice! And those folk typified France; they were the multitude, the heavy, inert mass, many of them worthy people no doubt, but none the less a mass of lead, which weighed the nation down to the ground, incapable as they were of leading a better life, of becoming free, just, and truly happy, because they were steeped in ignorance and poison.

As Marc went slowly towards the school to acquaint his friend Simon with the sad result of his visits, he suddenly remembered that he had not yet called on the Mesdames Milhomme, the stationers of the Rue Courte; and although he anticipated no better result with them than with the others he resolved to fulfil his commission to the very end.

The Milhommes, the ladies' husbands, had been two brothers, born at Maillebois. Edouard, the elder, had inherited a little stationery business from an uncle, and, being of a stay-at-home and unaspiring disposition, had made a shift to live on it with his wife; while his younger, more active, and ambitious brother Alexandre laid the foundations of a fortune while hurrying about the country as a commercial traveller. But death swooped down on both: the elder brother was the first to die, as the result of a tragic accident, a fall into a cellar; the second succumbing six months later to an attack of pulmonary congestion while he was at the other end of France. Their widows remained —one with her humble shop, the other with a capital of some twenty thousand francs, the first savings on which her

husband had hoped to rear a fortune.   It was to Madame
Edouard, a woman of decision and diplomatic skill, that the
idea occurred of inducing her sister-in-law, Madame Alexandre, to enter into a partnership, and invest her twenty
thousand francs in the little business at Maillebois, which
might be increased by selling books, stationery, and other
articles for the schools.   Each of the two widows had a son,
and from that time forward the Mesdames Milhomme, as
they were called, Madame Edouard with her little Victor,
and Madame Alexandre with her little Sébastien, had kept
house together, living in the close intimacy which their interests required, although their natures were radically
different.

Madame Edouard followed the observances of the
Church, but this did not mean that her faith was firm.   She
simply placed the requirements of her business before everything else.   Her customers were chiefly pious folk whom
she did not wish to displease.   Madame Alexandre, on the
contrary, had given up church-going at the time of her
marriage, for her husband had been a gay companion and
freethinker, and she refused to take up religion again.   It
was Madame Edouard, the clever diplomatist, who ingeniously indicated that these divergencies might become a
source of profit.   Their business was spreading; their shop,
situated midway between the Brothers' school and the Communal school, supplied articles suitable for both—lesson
books, copybooks, diagrams, and drawing copies, without
speaking of pens, pencils, and similar things.   Thus it was
decided that each of the two women should retain her views
and ways, the one with the priests, the other with the
freethinkers, in such wise as to satisfy both sides.   And in
order that nobody might remain ignorant of the understanding, Sébastien was sent to the secular Communal school,
where Simon the Jew was master, while Victor remained at
the Brothers' school.   Matters being thus settled, engineered
with superior skill, the partnership prospered, and Mesdames Milhomme now owned one of the most thriving
shops in Maillebois.

Marc, on reaching the Rue Courte, in which there were
only two houses, the Milhommes' and the parsonage, slackened his steps, and for a moment examined the windows of
the stationery shop, in which religious prints were mingled
with school pictures glorifying the Republic, whilst illus-
trated newspapers, hanging from strings, almost barred the

doorway. He was about to enter when Madame Alexandre —a tall and gentle-looking blonde, whose face, faded already, though she was only thirty, was still lighted by a faint smile—appeared upon the threshold. Close beside her was her little Sébastien, of whom she was very fond: a child of seven, fair and gentle like his mother, very handsome also, with blue eyes, a delicately shaped nose, and a mouth bespeaking amiability.

Madame Alexandre was acquainted with Marc, and she at once referred to the abominable crime which seemed to haunt her. ' How dreadful, Monsieur Froment! ' said she. ' To think also that it occurred so near to us! I frequently saw poor little Zéphirin go by, either on his way to school or returning home. And he often came here to buy copybooks and pens. I can no longer sleep since I saw him dead! '

Then she spoke compassionately of Simon and his grief. She considered him to be very kind-hearted and upright, particularly as he took a great interest in her little Sébastien, who was one of his most intelligent and docile pupils. Whatever other people might say, she would never be able to think the master capable of such a frightful deed as that crime. As for the copy-slip of which people talked so much, nothing would have been proved even if similar ones had been found in the school.

' We sell such slips, you know, Monsieur Froment,' she continued, ' and I have already searched through those which we have in stock. It is true that none bear those particular words, " Love one another "——'

At this moment Sébastien, who had been listening attentively, raised his head. ' I saw one like that,' said he. ' My cousin Victor brought one home from the Brothers' school—there were those words on it! '

His mother appeared stupefied: ' What are you saying ? ' she exclaimed. ' You never mentioned that to me! '

' But you did not ask. Besides, Victor forbade me to tell, because it 's forbidden to take the copy-slips from school.'

' Then where is that one ? '

'Ah! I don't know. Victor hid it somewhere, so that he might not be scolded.'

Marc was following the scene, astonished, delighted, his heart beating fast with hope. Was the truth about to come forth from the mouth of that child ? Perchance this would

prove the feeble ray which spreads little by little until it
finally expands into a great blaze of light.   And the young
man was already putting precise and decisive questions to
Sébastien, when Madame Edouard, accompanied by Victor, appeared upon the scene.   She was returning from a
visit which she had just made to Brother Fulgence, under
the pretext of applying for the payment of a stationery
account.

Taller than her sister-in-law, Madame Edouard was dark,
with a massive square-shaped face and a masculine appearance.   Her gestures were quick, her speech was loud.   A
good and honest woman in her way, she would not have
wronged her partner of a *sou*, though she never hesitated to
domineer over her.   She indeed was the man in the household, and the other as a means of defence only possessed
her force of inertia, her very gentleness, of which she availed
herself at times for weeks and months together, thereby often
securing the victory.   As for Victor, Madame Edouard's
son, he was a sturdy, squarely-set lad, nine years of age,
with a big dark head and massive face, quite a contrast
indeed to his cousin Sébastien.

Directly Madame Edouard was apprised of the situation,
she looked at her son severely: 'What! a copy?   You stole
a copy from the Brothers and brought it here?'

Victor had already turned a glance of despair and fury
upon Sébastien.   'No, no, mamma,' he answered.

'But you did, for your cousin saw it.   He does not
usually tell falsehoods.'

The boy ceased answering, but he still cast terrible
glances at his cousin.   And the latter was by no means at
his ease, for he well knew the physical strength of his play-
mate, and commonly represented the vanquished, beaten
enemy whenever they had a game at war together.   Under
the elder's guidance, there were endless noisy gallops
through the house; the younger, so gentle by nature, letting
himself be led into them with a kind of rapturous terror.

'No doubt he did not steal it,' Madame Alexandre observed indulgently.   'Perhaps he only brought it home by
mistake.'

In order that his cousin might the more readily forgive
his indiscretion, Sébastien at once confirmed this suggestion:
'Of course, it was like that.   I did not say he stole it.'

Madame Edouard, having now calmed down, ceased to
exact an immediate answer from Victor, who remained

silent as if stubbornly resolved upon making no confession.
His mother, for her part, doubtless reflected that it would
be scarcely prudent to investigate the matter in a stranger's
presence without weighing the gravity of the consequences.
She pictured herself taking one or the other side in the
affair, and setting either the Brothers' school or the Communal school against her, thereby losing one set of customers.
So, after casting a domineering glance at Madame Alexandre, she contented herself with saying to her son: 'That
will do. Go indoors, monsieur; we will settle all this by
and by. Just reflect, and if you do not tell me the real
truth, I shall know what to do to you.'

Then, turning to Marc, she added: 'We will tell you
what he says, monsieur; and you may depend upon it that
he will soon speak unless he desires such a whipping as he
is not likely to forget.'

Marc could not insist any further, however ardent might
be his desire to learn the whole truth immediately, in order
that he might convey it to Simon like tidings of deliverance.
But he no longer felt a doubt respecting the genuineness of
the decisive fact, the triumphant proof which chance had
placed in his hands; so he at once hastened to his friend's,
to tell him of his successive repulses with the Bongards, the
Doloirs, and the Savins, and of the unhoped-for discovery
which he made at the Milhommes'. Simon listened
quietly, showing no sign of the delight which Marc had
anticipated. Ah! there were similar copies at the Brothers'
school? Well, he was not astonished to hear it. For his
own part, why should he worry, as he was innocent?

'I thank you very much for all the trouble you have taken,
my good friend,' he added, 'and I fully understand the importance of that child's statement. But I cannot accustom
myself to the idea that my fate depends on what may be
said, or what may not be said, considering that I am guilty
of nothing. To my thinking, that is as evident as the sun
in the skies.'

Marc, who felt quite enlivened, began to laugh. He now
shared his friend's confidence. And after they had chatted
for a moment, he took his leave, but suddenly returned to
ask: 'Has handsome Mauraisin been to see you?'

'No, I have not seen him,' Simon answered.

'In that case, my friend, he must have wished to ascertain the opinions of all Maillebois before coming. I caught
sight of him this morning, first with Father Crabot, and

afterwards with Mademoiselle Rouzaire.   While I was running about this afternoon, too, I fancied I saw him twice—
once slipping into the Ruelle des Capucins, and then, as it
seemed to me, on his way to the mayor's.   He must have
been making inquiries in order to be sure of taking the
stronger side.'

Simon, hitherto so calm, made a nervous gesture; for,
timid by nature, he regarded his superiors with respect and
fear.   Indeed, his sole personal worry in the catastrophe
was the possibility of a great scandal which might cost him
his situation, or at least cause him to be regarded very unfavourably by the officials of his department.   And he was
about to confess this apprehension to Marc when, as it
happened, Mauraisin presented himself, looking frigid and
thoughtful.

'Yes, Monsieur Simon, I have hastened here on account
of that horrible affair.   I am in despair for the school, for
all of you, and for ourselves.   It is very serious—very
serious—very serious.'

As he spoke the Elementary Inspector drew up his little
figure, and his words fell from his lips with increasing severity.   In a formal way he had shaken hands with Marc,
knowing that Le Barazer, the Academy Inspector, his superior, was partial to the young man.   But he looked at
him askance through his glasses as if to invite him to withdraw.   And Marc could not linger, although it worried him
to leave Simon alone with that man, on whom his position
depended, and before whom he now trembled—he who had
shown so much courage ever since the morning.   But there
was no help for it; so Marc went home full of the new impression that had come to him, the covert hostility of that
man Mauraisin, whom he divined to be a traitor.

The evening, spent with the ladies, proved very quiet.
Neither Madame Duparque nor Madame Berthereau referred to the crime, and the little house fell asleep peacefully, as if nought of the tragedy in progress elsewhere had
ever entered it.   Marc had thought it prudent to say nothing
about his busy afternoon.   On going to bed he contented
himself with telling his wife that he felt quite at ease with
reference to his friend Simon.   The news pleased Geneviève; and they then continued chatting until rather late,
for in the daytime they were never alone together, never
able to speak freely, in such wise that they seemed to be
strangers.   When they fell asleep in each other's arms, it

was as if they had been blissfully reunited after a positive separation.

But, in the morning, Marc was painfully astonished to find an abominable article against Simon in *Le Petit Beau-montais*. He remembered the paragraph of the previous day which had expressed so much sympathy with the schoolmaster and had covered him with praise. Twenty-four hours had sufficed to effect a complete change, and now, with a wonderful show of perfidious suppositions and false interpretations of the facts, the Jew was savagely sac-rificed, plainly accused of the ignoble crime. What could have happened then ? What powerful influence could have been at work ? Whence came that poisoned article, drafted so carefully in order that the Jew might be for ever con-demned by the ignorant populace athirst for falsehood ? That newspaper melodrama with its mysterious intrica-cies, its extraordinary fairy-tale improbabilities, would prove, Marc felt it, a legend changing into truth, positive truth, from which people henceforth would refuse to depart. And when the young man had finished his perusal he again be-came conscious of some secret working in the gloom, some immense work which mysterious forces had been accom-plishing since the previous day in order to ruin the innocent and thereby save the unknown culprit.

Yet no fresh incident had occurred, the magistrates had not returned to Maillebois, there was still only the gen-darmes guarding the chamber of the crime, where lay the remains of the poor little victim, awaiting burial. The post-mortem examination on the previous day had merely confirmed the facts which were already known: After a scene of horror Zéphirin had been killed by strangulation, as was indicated by the deep violet finger-marks around his neck. It had been settled that the funeral should take place that afternoon, and, according to report, preparations were being made to invest it with avenging solemnity. The authorities were to be present as well as all the victim's school-fellows.

Marc, whom anxiety assailed once more, spent a gloomy morning. He did not go to see Simon, for he thought it best to do so in the evening after the funeral. He contented himself with strolling through Maillebois, which he found drowsy, as if gorged with horrors, while waiting for the promised spectacle. After his walk the young man's spirits revived, and he was finishing lunch with the ladies, amused by the prattle of little Louise, who was very lively that day, when Pélagie, on entering the room with a fine plum tart, found herself unable to restrain her rapturous delight.

'Ah! madame,' she exclaimed, 'they are arresting that brigand of a Jew! At last! It 's none too soon!'

'They are arresting Simon? How do you know it?' exclaimed Marc, who had turned very pale.

'Why, everybody says so, monsieur. The butcher across the road has just gone off to see it.'

Marc flung down his napkin, rose, and went out without touching any tart. The ladies were aghast, deeply offended by such a breach of good manners. Even Geneviève seemed to be displeased.

'He is losing his senses,' said Madame Duparque dryly. 'Ah! my dear girl, I warned you. Without religion no happiness is possible.'

When Marc reached the street he immediately realised that something extraordinary was taking place. All the shopkeepers were at their doors, some people were running, while an ever-increasing uproar of shouts and jeers was to be heard. Hastening his steps Marc turned into the Rue Courte, and there he at once perceived the Mesdames Milhomme and their children assembled on the threshold of the stationery shop. They also were deeply interested in the great event. And Marc then remembered that there was some good evidence to be obtained there, of which he had better make sure immediately.

'Is it true?' he asked. 'Is Monsieur Simon being arrested?'

'Why, yes, Monsieur Froment,' Madame Alexandre replied in her gentle way. 'We have just seen the Commissary pass.'

'And it is certain, you know,' said Madame Edouard in her turn, looking him straight in the face, and anticipating the question which she had already read in his eyes, 'it is quite certain that Victor never had that pretended copy-slip. I have questioned him, and I am convinced that he is telling no falsehood.'

The boy raised his face, with its square chin and large eyes full of quiet impudence. 'No, of course I am not telling a falsehood,' he said.

Amazed, chilled to the heart, Marc turned to Madame Alexandre: 'But what was it your son said, madame? He saw that copy in his cousin's hands—he declared it!'

The mother appeared ill at ease and did not immediately answer. Her little Sébastien had already taken refuge in her skirts as if to hide his face, and she with a quivering hand fondled his hair, covered his head anxiously and protectingly.

'No doubt, Monsieur Froment,' she at last responded, 'he saw it, or rather he fancied he saw it. At present he is not very sure: he thinks he may have been mistaken. And so, you see, there is nothing more to be said.'

Unwilling to insist with the women, Marc addressed himself to the little boy. 'Is it true that you did not see the copy? There is nothing so wicked as a lie, my child.'

Sébastien, instead of answering, pressed his face more closely to his mother's skirt, and burst into sobs. It was evident that Madame Edouard, like a good trader, who feared that by taking any particular side in the conflict she might lose a part of her custom, had imposed her will upon the others. She was as firm as a rock, and it would be impossible to move her. However, she condescended to indicate the reasons by which she was guided.

'*Mon Dieu*, Monsieur Froment,' she said, 'we are against nobody, you know; we need everybody's help in our business. Only it must be admitted that all the appearances are against Monsieur Simon. Take, for instance, that train which he says he missed, that return ticket which he threw away in the station yard, that four-mile walk when he met nobody. Besides, Mademoiselle Rouzaire is positive that she heard a noise about twenty minutes to eleven o'clock, whereas he pretends that he did not return till an hour later. Explain, too, how it happened that Monsieur Mignot had to go and wake him when it was nearly eight o'clock in the morning—he who is usually up so early. . . . Well, perhaps he will justify himself. For his sake, let us hope so——'

Marc stopped her with a gesture. She was repeating what he had read in *Le Petit Beaumontais*, and he was terrified by it. He cast a keen glance on both women—the one who so resolutely silenced her conscience, the other who trembled from head to foot; and he himself shuddered at the thought of their sudden falsehood which might lead to such disastrous consequences. Then he left them and hastened to Simon's.

A closed vehicle, guarded by two plain-clothes officers, was waiting at the door. The orders were stringent, but

Marc at last contrived to enter. While two other officers guarded Simon in the classroom, the Commissary of Police, who had arrived with a warrant signed by Investigating Magistrate Daix, conducted a fresh and very minute perquisition through the whole house, seeking, no doubt, for copies of the famous writing slip. But he found nothing; and when Marc ventured to ask one of the officers if a similar perquisition had taken place at the school kept by the Brothers of the Christian Doctrine, the man looked at him in amazement. A perquisition at the good Brothers' school? What for, indeed? But Marc was already shrugging his shoulders at his own simplicity, for, even supposing that the officers had gone to the Brothers', the latter had been allowed ample time to burn and destroy everything likely to compromise them.

The young man had to exert all his powers of restraint to prevent himself from expressing his feelings of revolt. His powerlessness to demonstrate the truth filled him with despair. For yet another hour he had to remain in the hall, waiting for the finish of the Commissary's search. At last, just as the officers were about to remove Simon, he was able to see him for a moment. Madame Simon and her two children were there also, and she flung herself, sobbing, about her husband's neck, while the Commissary, a rough but not hard-hearted man, made a pretence of giving some last orders. There came a most heart-rending scene.

Simon, livid, crushed by the downfall of his life, strove to preserve great calmness.

'Do not grieve, my darling,' he said. 'It can only be an error, an abominable error. Everything will certainly be explained as soon as I am interrogated, and I shall soon return to you.'

But Rachel sobbed yet more violently, with a wild expression on her tear-drenched face, while she raised the poor little ones, Joseph and Sarah, in order that their father might kiss them once again.

'Yes, yes, the poor children; love them well; take good care of them until my return. And I beg you do not weep so; you will deprive me of all my courage.'

He tore himself from her clasp, and then, at the sight of Marc, his eyes sparkled with infinite joy. He quickly grasped the hand which the young man offered him: 'Ah! comrade, thank you! Let my brother David be warned at once; be sure to tell him I am innocent. He will seek

everywhere, he will find the culprit, it is to him that I confide my honour and my children's.'

'Be easy,' replied Marc, half-choking with emotion, 'I
will help him.'

But the Commissary now returned and put an end to the
leave-taking. It was necessary that Madame Simon, wild
with grief, should be removed at the moment when Simon
was led away by the two officers. What followed was
monstrous. The hour fixed for the funeral of little Zéphirin was three, and, in order to prevent any regrettable collision, it had been decided to arrest Simon at one o'clock.
But the perquisition had lasted so long that the very thing
which the authorities had wished to prevent took place.
When Simon appeared outside, on the little flight of steps,
the square was already crowded with people who had come
to see the funeral procession. And this crowd, which had
gorged itself with the tales of *Le Petit Beaumontais*, and
which was still stirred by the horror of the crime, raised
angry shouts as soon as it perceived the schoolmaster, that
accursed Jew, that slayer of little children, who for his
abominable witchery needed their virgin blood, whilst it
was yet sanctified by the presence of the Host. That was
the legend, never to be destroyed, which sped from mouth
to mouth, maddening the tumultuous and menacing crowd.

'To death! To death with the murderer and sacrilegist!
To death, to death with the Jew!'

Chilled to his bones, paler and yet more rigid than before,
Simon, from the top of the steps, responded by a cry which
henceforth came without cessation from his lips as if it were
the very voice of his conscience: 'I am innocent, I am
innocent!'

Then rage transported the throng, the hoots ascended
tempestuously, a huge human wave bounded forward to
seize the accursed wretch and throw him down and tear him
into shreds.

'To death! to death with the Jew!'

But the officers had quickly pushed Simon into the waiting vehicle, and the driver urged his horse into a fast trot,
while the prisoner, never tiring, repeated his cry in accents
which rose above the tempest:

'I am innocent! I am innocent! I am innocent!'

All the way down the High Street the crowd rushed,
howling louder and louder, behind the vehicle. And Marc,
who had remained in the square, dazed and full of anguish,

began to think of the other demonstration, the indignant
murmurs, the explosion of revolt which had attended the
end of the prize-giving at the Brothers' school two days
previously.   Barely forty-eight hours had sufficed for a
complete revulsion of public opinion, and he was terrified
by the abominable skill, the cruel promptitude displayed by
the mysterious hands which had gathered so much darkness
together.   His hopes had crumbled, he felt that truth was
obscured, defeated, in peril of death.   Never before had he
experienced such intense distress of mind.

But the procession for little Zéphirin's funeral was already
being formed.   Marc saw the devout Mademoiselle Rouzaire bringing up the girls of her class, after witnessing
Simon's Calvary without making even a gesture of sympathy.   Nor had Mignot, who was surrounded by some of
the boys, gone to press his superior's hand.   He stood there
sullen and embarrassed, suffering no doubt from the struggle between his good nature and his interests.   At last the
procession started, directing its steps towards St. Martin's
amidst extraordinary pomp.   Again one realised how carefully artful hands had organised everything in order to
move the people, excite its pity, and its desire for vengeance.
On either side of the little coffin walked those of Zéphirin's
school-fellows who had taken their first Communion at the
same time as himself.   Next appeared Darras, the Mayor,
attended by the other authorities and acting as chief
mourner.   Then came all the pupils of the Brothers'
school, led by Brother Fulgence with his three assistants,
Brothers Isidore, Lazarus, and Gorgias.   The important
airs which Brother Fulgence gave himself were much remarked; he came, went, and commanded on all sides,
going even so far in his agitation as to meddle with Mademoiselle Rouzaire's pupils as though they were under his
orders.   And several Capuchins were also present with
their superior, Father Théodose, and there were Jesuits
from the College of Valmarie, headed by their rector,
Father Crabot, together with priests who had come from
all the surrounding districts—such a gathering of gowns and
cassocks, indeed, that the whole Church of the region
seemed to have been mobilised in order to ensure itself a
triumph by claiming as its own the poor little body which,
amid that splendid procession, was now being carried to
the grave.

Sobs burst forth along the whole line of route, and furious

cries resounded: ' Death to the Jews! Death to the dirty
Jews! '

A final incident completed Marc's enlightenment while,
with his heart full of bitterness, he continued to watch the
scene. He caught sight of Inspector Mauraisin, who, as on
the previous day, had come from Beaumont to ascertain, no
doubt, what might be his best line of conduct. And when
Father Crabot passed, Marc saw that he and Mauraisin
exchanged a smile and a discreet salutation, like men who
understood each other and regarded each other's conduct
with approval. All the monstrous iniquity, woven in the
gloom during the last two days, then appeared to Marc
under the clear sky, while the bells of St. Martin's rang
out in honour of the poor little boy whose tragic fate was
about to be so impudently exploited.

But a rough hand was laid on Marc's shoulder, and some
words addressed to him in a tone of bitter irony caused him
to look round.

' Well, what did I tell you, my worthy and simple colleague? The dirty Jew is convicted of villainy and murder.
And while he travels to Beaumont gaol, all the good Brothers
are triumphing! '

It was Férou who spoke—Férou the rebellious, starveling
schoolmaster, looking more gawky than ever, with his hair
all in disorder, his long bony head, and his big sneering
mouth.

' How can they be accused,' he continued, 'since the little
victim belongs to them, to them alone ? Ah! it 's certain
that nobody will dare to accuse them, for all Maillebois has
seen them take him to the grave in grand procession! The
amusing thing is the buzzing of that ridiculous black fly,
that idiotic Brother Fulgence, who knocks up against everybody. He 's over zealous. But you must have also seen
Father Crabot with his shrewd smile, which doubtless hides
no little stupidity, whatever may be his reputation for skil-
fulness. At all events, remember what I tell you, the
cleverest, the only really clever one among them all, is
certainly Father Philibin, who pretends to look like a big
booby. You may search for him, but you won't find him
there. It was n't likely that he would come to Maillebois
to-day. He 's keeping himself in the background, and you
may be sure that he 's doing some fine work. Ah! I don't
know exactly who the culprit may be—he is certainly none
of those—but he belongs to their shop, that 's as plain as a

pikestaff, and they will overturn everything rather than give him up.'

Then as Marc, still overcome, remained silent, merely nodding, Férou went on: 'Ah! they regard it as a fine opportunity to crush the freethinkers. A Communal schoolmaster guilty of abomination and murder! What a splendid battle-cry! They will soon settle our hash, rogues that we are, without God or country! Yes, death to the traitors who 've sold themselves! Death to the dirty Jews!'

Waving his long arms, Férou went off into the crowd. As he was wont to say with his excessive jeering bitterness, it mattered little to him at bottom whether he ended by being burnt at the stake, in a shirt dipped in brimstone, or whether he starved to death in his wretched school at Le Moreux.

That evening, when, after a silent dinner in the ladies' company, Marc found himself alone again with Geneviève, she, observing his despair, lovingly passed her arms about him, and burst into tears. He felt deeply moved, for it had seemed to him that day as if their bond of union had been slightly shaken, as if severance were beginning. He pressed her to his heart, and for a long time they both wept without exchanging a word.

At last, hesitating somewhat, she said to him: ' Listen, my dear Marc, I think we should do well to shorten our stay with grandmother. We might go away to-morrow.'

Surprised by these words, he questioned her: 'Has she had enough of us then? Were you told to signify it to me ?'

' Oh! no, no! On the contrary, it would grieve mamma. We should have to invent a pretext, get somebody to send us a telegram.'

' But in that case, why should we not spend our full month here as usual? We have some little differences together, no doubt; but I don't complain.'

For a moment Geneviève remained embarrassed. She did not dare to confess her anxiety at the thought that something had seemed to be detaching her from her husband that evening, in the atmosphere of devout hostility in which she lived at her grandmother's. She had felt indeed as if the ideas and feelings of her girlhood were returning and clashing with the life which she led as wife and mother. But all that was merely the faint touch of the past, and her gaiety and confidence soon returned amid Marc's caresses.

Near her, in the cradle, she could hear the gentle and regular breathing of her little Louise.

'You are right,' she said. 'Let us stay—and do your duty as you understand it. We love each other too well to be otherwise than happy, always.'

III

FROM that time forward, in order to avoid painful quarrels, nothing more was said of the Affaire Simon in the ladies' little house. At meals they spoke merely of the fine weather, as if they were a thousand leagues from Maillebois, where the popular passions raged more and more tempestuously, old friends of thirty years' standing, and even relatives quarrelling, threatening one another and exchanging blows. Marc, who in the home of Geneviève's family displayed such silence and lack of interest, became elsewhere one of the most ardent combatants, an heroic worker in the cause of truth and justice.

On the evening of the day when Simon was arrested he had persuaded his colleague's wife to seek an asylum with her parents, the Lehmanns, those tailors who dwelt in a little dark house of the Rue du Trou. It was holiday-time, the school was closed; and, besides, Mignot the assistant-master, remained to guard the building—that is, when he was not fishing in the Verpille. Moreover, Mademoiselle Rouzaire, who wished to take part in the affair, in which her evidence was likely to prove important, had also remained at her post, renouncing on this occasion the holiday visit which she usually paid to an aunt dwelling at a distance. Thus Madame Simon, leaving her furniture behind, in order that folk might not regard her departure as terrified flight and a tacit acknowledgment of guilt, had taken Joseph and Sarah to the Rue du Trou, with a single trunk of clothes, as if she merely intended to stay with her parents for a few weeks.

From that moment Marc visited the Lehmanns almost daily. The Rue du Trou, which opened into the Rue du Plaisir, was one of the most sordid streets of the poor quarter of Maillebois, and the Lehmanns' house was composed merely of a dark shop and a still darker shop parlour on the ground floor, then three first-floor rooms, reached by a black staircase, at the very top of which was a spacious

76

garret, this last being the only part of the house which the
sunrays occasionally entered. The damp, greenish, cellar-
like shop parlour served as a kitchen and living room.
Rachel took possession of the dismal bedroom of her girlhood; and the old people contented themselves with one
chamber, the third being given to the children, who were
also allowed the run of the garret, which made them a gay
and spacious playroom.

Marc constantly felt surprised that such an admirable
woman as Rachel, one of so rare a beauty, should have
sprung in such a horrid den from needy parents, weighed
down by a long heredity of anxious penury. Lehmann,
her father, was, at five and fifty, a Jew of the classic type,
short and insignificant, with a large nose, blinking eyes, and
a thick grey beard which hid his mouth. His calling
had distorted him; he had one shoulder higher than the
other, and a kind of anxious discomfort of body was thus
added to his humility. His wife, who plied her needle from
morning till night, hid herself away in his shadow, being yet
more retiring in her humility and silent disquietude. They
led a narrow life full of difficulties, earning a scanty subsistence by dint of hard work for slowly-acquired customers, such as the few Israelites of the region who were in
easy circumstances, and certain Christians who did not
spend much money on their clothes. The gold of France,
with which the Jews were said to gorge themselves, was
certainly not piled up there. Indeed, a feeling of great
compassion came to one at the sight of those poor weary old
people, who were ever trembling lest somebody should deprive them of the bread which cost them so much toil.

At the Lehmanns', however, Marc became acquainted
with Simon's brother David, whom a telegram had summoned on the day of the arrest. Taller and stronger than
Simon, whose senior he was by three years, David had a
full firm face with bright and energetic eyes. After his
father's death he had entered the army, in which he had
served for twelve years, rising from the ranks to a lieuten-
ancy, and after innumerable struggles and rebuffs being, it
seemed, near promotion to the rank of captain, when he
suddenly sent in his papers, lacking the courage to contend
any longer against the affronts to which his comrades and
superiors subjected him because he was a Jew. This had
taken place some five years before the crime of Maillebois,
at the time when Simon was about to marry Rachel

David, who remained a bachelor, looked round him for occupation, and, like a man of initiative and energy, embarked in an enterprise of which nobody had previously thought. This was the working of some very extensive sand and gravel pits on the estate of La Désirade, which then still belonged to the millionaire banker, Baron Nathan. The latter, taken with the young man's energy and sense, granted him a thirty years' lease on fairly low terms, and thus David was soon on the high road to fortune; for in three years he earned a hundred thousand francs in this enterprise, which steadily increased in magnitude and at last absorbed every hour of his time.

But, on hearing of the charge brought against his brother, he did not hesitate; he placed his business in the hands of a foreman on whom he could rely, and hurried to Maillebois. He did not for a moment doubt his brother's innocence. It was materially impossible, he felt, that such a deed could be the act of such a man, the one whom he knew best in all the world, who was indeed the counterpart of himself. But he evinced great prudence, for he desired to do nothing that might harm his brother, and he knew, too, that all Jews were unpopular. Thus, when Marc in his impassioned way spoke to him of his suspicions, declaring that the real culprit must certainly be one of the Brothers of the Christian Doctrine, David, though at heart of the same opinion, strove to calm his friend, saying that one must not lose sight of the theory of a prowling tramp, a chance murderer, who might have entered and left by the window. As a matter of fact, he felt that he would increase the popular prejudice against Simon by bringing any random charge against the Brothers; he foresaw, too, that all efforts would be vain against the coalition of the interested parties unless he were possessed of decisive proofs. Meantime, in order that Simon might benefit by an element of doubt, would it not be best to revert to the theory of that prowler, which everybody had admitted as possible at the moment of the discovery of the crime? It would serve as an excellent basis for provisional operations; whereas a campaign at that moment against the well-informed and powerfully supported Brothers could only turn against the prisoner.

David was able to see Simon in the presence of Investigating Magistrate Daix, and by the long hand-shake which they then exchanged they fully understood that each was possessed by the same feelings. Later, David also saw his brother at the prison, and, on returning to the Lehmanns, he described Simon as being still in great despair, ever straining his mind in endeavouring to unravel the enigma, but displaying extraordinary energy in defending his honour and that of his children. When David recounted all this, seated in the dim little shop where Marc also was present, the latter was profoundly stirred by the silent tears of Madame Simon, who looked so beautiful and dolorous in her self-abandonment, like a woman of weak loving nature cruelly struck down by destiny. The Lehmanns also could only sigh and display the shrinking despair of poor folk who were resigned to contumely. They still plied their needles, and, though they were convinced of their son-in-law's innocence, they dared not proclaim it before their customers for fear lest they should aggravate his position and lose their own means of livelihood. The public effervescence at Maillebois was unhappily increasing, and one evening a band of brawlers smashed the shop windows. It was necessary to put up the shutters at once. Then little manuscript notices were posted in various parts of the town, calling upon patriots to assemble and burn down the shop. For some days indeed—particularly one Sunday, after a pompous religious ceremony at the Capuchin Chapel—the explosion of anti-semite passion became so intense that Darras, the Mayor, had to send to Beaumont for police, deeming it necessary to have guards posted in the Rue du Trou lest the house of the Lehmanns should be sacked.

From hour to hour the affair expanded, and grew more virulent, becoming a social battlefield on which rival parties contended hotly. Magistrate Daix had doubtless received orders to conduct his investigations with all possible speed. In less than a month he interrogated all the witnesses— Mignot, Mademoiselle Rouzaire, Father Philibin, Brother Fulgence, several schoolchildren and railway employés. Brother Fulgence, with his usual exuberance, demanded that his three assistants, Brothers Isidore, Lazarus, and Gorgias, should also be interrogated; he likewise insisted that a search should be made at his school, and this was done; but naturally nothing was found. Daix thought it his duty, however, to inquire minutely into the suggestion that the crime might have been committed by a tramp. By his orders the entire gendarmerie of the department scoured the roads, and some fifty tramps were arrested, and then released, without the slightest clue being arrived at. In one instance a pedlar remained three days under lock and key, but to no purpose. Then Daix, setting aside the theory of a prowler, remained in presence of the copy-slip, the one tangible piece of evidence at his disposal, the only thing on which he could rear his charge.

When this reached the ears of Marc and David, they became calm again, for it seemed to them impossible that a serious accusation could be based on that slip of paper, the importance of which was so open to discussion. As David repeated, although no guilty tramp had been found, the hypothesis that one existed, or at least an element of doubt, still remained. And if thereto one added the lack of proof against Simon, the moral improbability of his guilt, his never-varying protests of innocence, it was purely impossible for an Investigating Magistrate, possessed of any conscience, to come to the conclusion that he was the culprit. A *non-lieu*, otherwise a decision that there was no ground to proceed further against the prisoner, seemed a certainty on which one might rely.

There came days, however, when Marc and David, who co-operated in brotherly fashion, began to lose some of their fine assurance. Bad rumours reached them. The Congregations were bestirring themselves frantically. Father Crabot was for ever visiting Beaumont, availing himself of his society connections to dine with government officials, members of the judicial and even the university world. As the Jew prisoner seemed more and more likely to secure release, so, on all sides, the battle grew fiercer. At last, then, it occurred to David to endeavour to obtain the support of Baron Nathan, the great banker and former proprietor of La Désirade, who was staying there as the guest of his daughter, the Countess de Sanglebœuf, whose marriage portion had consisted of that royal domain and a sum of ten millions of francs [1] in hard cash. Thus, one bright afternoon in August, David and Marc, who also had a slight acquaintance with the Baron, set out on foot for La Désirade, a very pleasant walk, for the distance from Maillebois was not much more than a mile.

Count Hector de Sanglebœuf, the last scion of his house, one of the early members of which had been squire to St. Louis, had found himself completely ruined when he was only thirty-six years of age. His father had devoured the

---

[1] About $1,940,000.

greater part of the family fortune and he himself had consumed the remnants. After holding a commission in the
Cuirassiers, he had resigned it, feeling tired of garrison life;
and for a time he had remained living with a widow, the
Marchioness de Boise, who was ten years his senior, and far
too intent on her own comfort to marry him, for her penury,
added to his own, would only have conduced to a disastrous future. People related that it was this mistress who
had ingeniously arranged the Count's marriage with Baron
Nathan's daughter Lia, a young person of four and twenty,
very beautiful and all ablaze with millions. Nathan had
negotiated the transaction with his eyes open, knowing perfectly well what he gave and what he was to receive in exchange, adding his daughter to the millions which left his
safe in order that he might have as son-in-law a Count of
very old and authentic nobility, which circumstance would
open to him the portals of a sphere from which he had been
hitherto excluded.

He himself had lately acquired the title of Baron, and he
was at last escaping from the ancient ' ghetto,' that universal
contumely of which the haunting thought made him shudder. A dealer in money, he had filled his cellars with gold,
and his one frantic craving nowadays, like that of the
Christian moneymongers, whose appetites were fully as
keen, was to gratify his pride and his instincts of domination, to be saluted, honoured and worshipped upon all
sides, and in particular to be delivered from the ever-
pursuing dread of being kicked and spat upon like a mere
dirty Jew. Thus he quite enjoyed staying with his son-in-
law at La Désirade, deriving no little consideration from
the connections of his daughter the Countess, and remaining
in so small a degree a Jew that, like many other renegades
of his class, he had enrolled himself among the anti-semites,
and professed the most fervent royalism and patriotism.
Indeed, the dexterous, smiling Marchioness de Boise, who
had derived from her lover's marriage all the profit she had
anticipated for him and for herself, was often obliged to
moderate the Baron's ardour. That marriage, it should be
mentioned, had scarcely changed the position of the
Marchioness and Count Hector. The former, a beautiful
ripening blonde, was doubtless devoid of jealousy in the
strict sense of the word, besides being intelligent enough to
combine such worldly enjoyment as money may procure
with the happiness of a long and peaceful *liaison*. Besides,

she knew the beautiful Lia to be an admirable piece of
statuary, an idol full of narrow egotism, who found it blissful
to be installed in a sanctuary, where attendant worshippers
adored but did not unduly tire her.   She did not even read,
for reading soon brought her fatigue; she was quite content
to remain seated for hours together in the midst of general
attentions, with never a thought for anybody but herself.

Doubtless she did not long remain ignorant of the real
position of the Marchioness and her husband, but she dismissed the thought of it, not wishing to be worried, and
indeed she was at last unable to dispense with that caressing
friend, who was ever in admiration before her, and who
lavished on her such loving and pleasing expressions as ' my
pussy,' ' my beautiful darling,' ' my dear treasure.'   A more
touching friendship was never seen, and the Marchioness
soon had her room and her place at table at La Désirade.
Then another idea of genius came to her.   She undertook
to convert Lia to the Catholic faith.   The young wife was
at first terrified by the idea, for she feared that she might be
overwhelmed with religious exercises and observances.   But,
directly Father Crabot was brought into the affair, he, with
his worldly graciousness, made the path quite easy.   Yet
the Countess was most won over by the enthusiasm which
her father displayed for the Marchioness's idea.   It was as
if the Baron hoped that he would cleanse himself of some
of his own horrid Jewry in the water of the young woman's
baptism.   When the ceremony took place it quite upset society in Beaumont, and it was always spoken of as a great
triumph of the Church.

As a final achievement, the motherly Marchioness de
Boise, who directed the steps of Hector de Sanglebœuf as
if he were her big, dull-witted, obedient child, had with the
help of his wife's fortune caused him to be elected as one of
the deputies of Beaumont, insisting too that he should join
the little parliamentary group of Opportunist Reactionaries,
who gave out that they had ' rallied ' to the Republic; for
by this course she hoped to raise him to some high political
position.   The amusing part of the affair was that Baron
Nathan, who, scarce freed from the stigma of his Jewish
ancestry, had become an uncompromising Royalist, now
found himself a far more fervent partisan of the monarchy
than his son-in-law, and this in spite of the latter's descent
from a squire of St. Louis.   The Baron, who had found an
opportunity for personal triumph in the baptism of his

daughter — on which occasion he had chosen her new
'Christian' name, Marie, by which he always addressed her
with a kind of pious affectation — triumphed also in the
election of his son-in-law as deputy, for he felt that he might
be able to make use of him in the political world.   But,
apart from questions of interest, he quite enjoyed himself at
La Désirade, which was now full of priests, and where all
the talk was about the various pious works in which the
Marchioness de Boise associated her friend Marie, with
whom she became yet more intimate and loving.

David and Marc slackened their steps when, admitted by
the lodge-keeper of La Désirade, they at last found themselves in the grounds.   It was a splendid and enjoyable
August day, and the beauty of the great trees, the infinite
placidity of the lawns, the delightful freshness of the waters
filled them with admiration.   A king might have dwelt
there.   At the end of the enchanting avenues of verdure
extending on all sides, one invariably perceived the château,
a sumptuous Renaissance château, rising like lace-work of
pinkish stone against the azure of the sky.   And at the sight
of that paradise acquired by Jew wealth, at the thought of
the splendid fortune amassed by Nathan the Jew money-
monger, Marc instinctively recalled the gloomy little shop
in the Rue du Trou, the dismal hovel without air or sunshine,
where Lehmann, that other Jew, had been plying his needle
for thirty years, and earning only enough to provide himself
with bread.   And, ah! how many other Jews there were,
yet more wretched than he — Jews who starved in filthy
dens.   They were the immense majority, and their existence
demonstrated all the idiotic falsity of anti-semitism, that
proscription *en masse* of a race which was charged with the
monopolisation of all wealth, when it numbered so many
poor working-folk, so many victims, crushed down by the
almightiness of money, whether it were Jew, or Catholic, or
Protestant.   As soon as ever a French Jew became a great
capitalist, he bought a title of Baron, married his daughter
to a Count of ancient stock, made a pretence of showing
himself more royalist than the king, and ended by becoming the worst of renegades, a fierce anti-semite, who not
only denied, but helped to slaughter, his kith and kin.
There was really no Jew question at all, there was only a
Capitalist question—a question of money heaped up in the
hands of a certain number of gluttons, and thereby poisoning
and rotting the world.

As David and Marc reached the château they perceived Baron Nathan, his daughter, and his son-in-law seated under a large oak tree in the company of the Marchioness de Boise and a cleric, in whom they recognised Father Crabot. Doubtless the Rector of the College of Valmarie had been invited to a quiet family lunch, in neighbourly fashion—for a distance of less than two miles separated the two estates; and doubtless, also, some serious question had been discussed at dessert. Then, to enjoy the fine weather, they had seated themselves in some garden chairs, under that oak and near a marble basin, into which ever fell the crystal of a source which an indelicate nymph was pouring from her urn.

On recognising the visitors, who discreetly halted a short distance away, the Baron came forward and conducted them to some other seats, set out on the opposite side of the basin. Short and somewhat bent, quite bald at fifty, with a yellow face, a fleshy nose, and black eyes—the eyes of a bird of prey set deeply under projecting brows—Nathan had assumed for the nonce an expression of grievous sympathy as if he were receiving folk in deep mourning who had just lost a relative. It was plain that the visit did not surprise him. He must have been expecting it.

'Ah! how I pity you, my poor David,' he said. 'I have often thought of you since that misfortune. You know how highly I esteem your intelligence, enterprise, and industry. But what an affair, what an abominable affair your brother Simon has put on your shoulders! He is compromising you, he is ruining you, my poor David!'

And with an impulse of sincere despair the Baron raised his quivering hands and added, as if he feared he might see the persecutions of olden time begin afresh: 'The unhappy man! He is compromising all of us!'

Then David with his quiet bravery began to plead his brother's cause, expressing his absolute conviction of his innocence, enumerating the moral and material proofs which in his estimation were irrefutable, while Nathan curtly jogged his head.

'Yes, yes, it is only natural,' the Baron at last replied, 'you believe him to be innocent; I myself still wish to do so. Unfortunately it is not a question of convincing me, you must convince the officers of the law, and also the exasperated masses who are capable of doing harm to all of us if he is not condemned. . . . No, I shall never forgive your brother for having saddled us with such a dreadful affair.'

Then, on David explaining that he had come to him, knowing his influence, and relying on his help to make the truth manifest, the Baron became colder, more and more reserved, and listened in silence.

'You always showed me so much kindness, Monsieur le Baron,' said David, 'and as you used to invite the judicial authorities of Beaumont here, I thought that you might perhaps be able to give me some information. For instance, you are acquainted with Monsieur Daix, the Investigating Magistrate who has the affair in hand, and who, I hope, will soon stay further proceedings. Perhaps you may have some news on that subject; besides which, if a decision has not yet been reached, a word from you might prove valuable——'

'No, no,' Nathan protested, 'I know nothing, I desire to know nothing. I have no official connections, no influence. Besides, my position as a co-religionist prevents me from doing anything; I should merely compromise myself without rendering you any service. But wait a moment, I will call my son-in-law.'

Marc had remained silent, contenting himself with listening. He had accompanied David merely to give him the support of his presence as one of Simon's colleagues. But while he listened he glanced in the direction of the oak tree, at the ladies sitting there—Countess Marie, as the beautiful Lia was now called, and the Marchioness de Boise, between whom Father Crabot was reposing in a rustic arm-chair, while Count Hector de Sanglebœuf, who had remained erect, finished chewing a cigar. The Marchioness, still slim and still pretty under her fair hair, which she powdered, was expressing great anxiety respecting a sunbeam which darted on the nape of the Countess's neck; and although the beautiful Jewess, indolent and superb, declared that she was in no way inconvenienced, her friend, lavishing on her all the usual pet names, 'my pussy,' 'my jewel,' and 'my treasure,' at last compelled her to change places. The Jesuit Crabot, who was evidently at his ease, smiled at both of them with the air of a very tolerant father-confessor. And meantime a never-ending flute-like strain came from the crystalline water which the indelicate nymph was pouring from her urn into the marble basin.

Sanglebœuf, on being called by his father-in-law, came

forward slowly. With a big body and a full and highly-
coloured face, a low forehead and short-cropped, ruddy,
bristling hair, he had eyes of a dim blue, a small flabby
nose, and a large voracious mouth, half-hidden by thick
moustaches. As soon as the Baron had told him of the
help which David solicited, he became quite angry, though
he affected a kind of military plain-speaking.

'What! mix myself up in that affair! Ah, no!' he exclaimed. 'You must excuse me, monsieur, if I employ my
credit as a deputy in clearer and cleaner affairs. I am
quite willing to believe that you personally are an honourable man. But you will really have a great deal to do if
you wish to defend your brother. Besides, as all those who
support you say, we are the enemy. Why do you apply to
us ?'

Then, turning his big, blurred, wrathful eyes on Marc, he
began to hold forth against the godless and unpatriotic folk
who dared to insult the army. Too young to have fought
in 1870, he had merely served as a garrison soldier, taking
part in no campaign whatever. Nevertheless he had remained a cuirassier to his very marrow, to cite one of his
own expressions. And he boasted that he had set two
emblems at his bedside, two emblems which summed up his
religion—a crucifix and a flag, his flag—for which, unfortunately for a good many people, he had not died.

'When you have restored the Cross to the schools, monsieur,' he continued, 'when your schoolmasters decide to
make Christians and not citizens of their pupils, then, and
only then, will you have any claim on us should you ask us
to render you a service.'

David, pale and frigid, allowed him to run on without
attempting any interruption. It was only when he had
finished that he quietly rejoined: 'But I have asked you for
nothing, monsieur. It was to Monsieur le Baron that I
ventured to apply.'

Nathan, fearing a scene, then intervened, and led David
and Marc away, as if to escort them through a part of the
grounds. Father Crabot, on hearing the Count's loud
voice, had for a moment raised his head; then had returned
to his worldly chat with his two dear lady penitents. And
when Sangleboeuf had joined the others again, one could
distinctly hear them laughing at the good lesson which, in
their opinion, had just been administered to a couple of
dirty Jews.

'What can you expect? They are all like that,' said
Nathan to David and Marc, lowering his voice, when they
were some thirty paces distant. 'I summoned my son-in-
law in order that you might see for yourselves what are the
views of the department—I mean of the upper classes, the
deputies, functionaries, and magistrates. And so, how
could I be of any use to you? Nobody would listen to me.'

This hypocritical affectation of good nature, in which one
detected a quiver of the old hereditary racial dread, must
have seemed cowardly even to the Baron himself, for he
presently added: 'Besides, they are right; I am with them;
France before everything else, with her glorious past, and
the *ensemble* of her firm traditions. We cannot hand her
over to the Freemasons and the cosmopolites! And I cannot let you go, my dear David, without offering you a word
of advice. Have nothing to do with that affair; you would
lose everything in it, you would be wrecked for ever.
Your brother will get out of the mess by himself if he is
innocent.'

Those were his last words; he shook hands with them,
and quietly walked back, while they in silence quitted the
grounds. But on the high road they exchanged glances
almost of amusement, however much they might be disappointed, for the scene in which they had participated seemed
to them quite typical, perfect of its kind.

'Death to the Jews!' exclaimed Marc facetiously.

'Ah! the dirty Jews!' David responded in the same jesting way, tinged with bitterness. 'He advised me to forsake
my brother; and for his part he would not hesitate. He
has thrown his brothers over plenty of times already, and
he will do so again. I certainly must not knock for help at
the doors of my famous and powerful co-religionists. They
shiver with fear.'

Several more days now went by, and, however prompt
Magistrate Daix might have been with his investigations, he
still delayed his decision. It was said that he was a prey
to increasing perplexity, having a very keen professional
mind, and too much intelligence to have failed to divine the
truth; but, on the other hand, being worried by public
opinion and browbeaten at home by his terrible wife.
Madame Daix, ugly, coquettish, and very pious—indeed,
another of Father Crabot's dearly-loved penitents—was
consumed by ambition, tortured by penurious circumstances, haunted by dreams of life in Paris, finery, and a

social position, as the outcome of some great sensational 'affair.' Such an 'affair' was within her reach now, and she never ceased repeating to her husband that it would be idiotic not to profit by the opportunity; for if he were so simple as to release that dirty Jew they would end by dying in a garret. Yet Daix struggled, honest still, but perturbed and no longer hurrying, clinging in fact to a last hope that something would happen to enable him to reconcile his interests with his duty. This fresh delay seemed of good augury to Marc, who was well aware of the magistrate's torments, but who still remained optimistically convinced that truth possessed an irresistible power, to which all ended by submitting.

Since the beginning of the affair he often went to Beaumont of a morning to see his old friend Salvan, the Director of the Training College. He found him well posted with information, and derived also a good deal of faith and courage from what he said. Besides, that college where he had lived three years, full of apostolic enthusiasm, had remained dear to him. It stood on a lonely little square at the end of the Rue de la République; and when in those vacation days he reached the director's quiet private room, which looked into a little garden, he felt himself in a spot where peace and happy confidence prevailed. One morning, however, when he called, he found Salvan full of grief and irritation. At first he had to wait in the ante-chamber, for the director was engaged with another visitor; but the latter, a fellow-schoolmaster named Doutrequin—a man with a low stubborn brow, broad clean-shaven cheeks, and the expression of a magistrate conscious of the importance of his functions—soon quitted the private room, and Marc bowed to him as he passed. Then, his turn having come, he was astonished by the agitation of Salvan, who, raising his arms to the ceiling, greeted him with the exclamation: 'Well, my friend, you know the abominable news, don't you?'

Of medium height, unassuming but energetic, with a good round face, all gaiety and frankness, Salvan, as a rule, turned laughing eyes upon those to whom he spoke. But now his glance was ablaze with generous anger.

'What is it?' Marc inquired anxiously.

'Ah, so you do not know yet? Well, my friend, those blackguards have dared to do it. Last night Daix signed an *ordonnance* sending Simon for trial!'

Marc turned pale, but remained silent, while Salvan, pointing to a number of *Le Petit Beaumontais* which lay open on his table, added: 'Doutrequin, who just went out, left me that filthy rag which gives the news, and he confirmed its accuracy, on the authority of one of the clerks at the Palace of Justice whom he knows.'

Then, taking up the paper, crumpling it, and flinging it into a corner of the room with a gesture of disgust, Salvan continued: 'Ah! the filthy rag! If iniquity becomes possible it is because that paper poisons the poor and lowly with its lies. They are still so ignorant, so credulous, so ready to believe the stories that flatter their base passions. And to think that paper first acquired a circulation, first found its way into all hands, by belonging to no party, by remaining neutral, by merely printing serial stories, matter-of-fact accounts of current events, and pleasant articles popularising general knowledge. By that means, in the course of years, it became the friend, the oracle, the daily pabulum of the simple-minded and the poor who cannot think for themselves. But now, abusing its unique position, its immense connection, it places itself in the pay of the parties of error and reaction, makes money out of every piece of financial roguery, and every underhand political plot. It is of secondary importance if lies and insults come from the fighting journals which are openly reactionary. They support a faction, they are known, and when one reads them one is prepared for what they may say. Thus *La Croix de Beaumont*, the Church party's organ, has started an abominable campaign against our friend Simon, "the Jew schoolmaster who poisoned and murdered little children," as it calls him; but all that has scarcely moved me. When, however, *Le Petit Beaumontais* publishes the ignoble and cowardly articles with which you are acquainted, those charges and slanders picked up in the gutter, it is a crime. To penetrate among the simple by affecting bluff good nature, and then to mingle arsenic with every dish, to drive the masses to delirium and to the most monstrous actions in order to increase one's sales, I know of no greater crime! And make no mistake, if Daix did not stay further proceedings it was because public opinion weighed on him, poor wretched man that he is, afraid to be honest, and afflicted too with a wife who rots everything. And public opinion, you know, is such as it is made by *Le Petit Beaumontais*, which is the prime mover in the iniquity, for it sows imbecility and cruelty in the minds of the multitude, whence now, I fear, we shall see a detestable harvest rise!'

Salvan sank into his arm-chair in front of his writing-table with an expression of despairing anguish on his countenance. And silence fell while Marc walked slowly to and fro, overwhelmed by that recapitulation of opinions which he himself fully shared. At last, however, he stopped, saying: 'All the same, we must come to a decision, and what shall we do? Let us suppose that this iniquitous trial takes place: Simon cannot be condemned, it would be too monstrous! And, surely, we shall not remain with our arms folded. When this terrible blow falls on poor David he will want to act. What do you advise us to do?'

'Ah, my friend!' cried Salvan, 'how willingly I would be the first to act, if you could give me the means! You readily understand—do you not?—that in the person of that unfortunate Simon, it is the secular schoolmaster whom they are pursuing and whom they want to crush. They regard our dear training school as a nursery of godless, unpatriotic men, and they are eager to destroy it. For them I am a kind of Satan, engendering atheist missionaries, to ruin whom has long been their dream. What a triumph for the Church gang if one of our former pupils should ascend the scaffold, convicted of an infamous crime! Ah, my dear college, my poor house, which I should like to see so useful, so great, so necessary for the destinies of the country, through what a terrible time will it now have to pass!'

All Salvan's ardent faith in the good work he did was manifest in his fervid words. Originally a schoolmaster, then an Elementary Inspector, a militant with a clear mind devoted to knowledge and progress, he had given himself, on his appointment as Director of the Training College, to one sole mission—that of preparing efficient schoolmasters ready to champion experimental science and freed from the bonds of Rome—men who would at last teach Truth to the people and make it capable of practising Liberty, Justice, and Peace. Therein lay the whole future of the nation—the future indeed of all mankind.

'We shall all group ourselves around you,' said Marc, quivering; 'we will not suffer you to be stopped in your work, the most urgent and loftiest of all at the present time!'

Salvan smiled sadly. 'Oh, all, my friend! How many are there around me then? There is yourself, and there

was also that unfortunate fellow, Simon, on whom I greatly
relied. Again, there is Mademoiselle Mazeline, the schoolmistress at your village, Jonville. If we had a few dozen
teachers like her we might expect that the next generation
would at last see women, wives and mothers, delivered
from the priests! As for Férou, wretchedness and revolt
are driving him crazy, bitterness of feeling is poisoning his
mind. And after him comes the mere flock of indifferent,
egotistical folk, stagnating in the observance of routine, and
having only one concern, that of flattering their superiors in
order to secure good reports. Then too there are the renegades, those who have gone over to the enemy, as, for instance, that Mademoiselle Rouzaire, who alone does the
work of ten nuns, and who behaves so shamefully in the
Simon affair. I was forgetting another, Mignot, one of our
best pupils, who is certainly not a bad fellow, but whose
mind requires forming, liable as it is to turn out good or
bad, according to influence.'

Salvan was growing excited, and it was with increased
force that he continued: 'But a case that one may well
despair of is that of Doutrequin, whom you saw leaving me
just now. A schoolmaster himself, he is the son of one; in
'70 he was fifteen, and three years later he entered the college still shuddering at the thought of the invasion, and
dreaming of revenge. At that time considerations of
patriotism influenced the whole of our educational system
in France. The country asked us merely for soldiers; the
army was like a temple, a sanctuary, that army which has
remained waiting with arms grounded for thirty years, and
which has devoured thousands upon thousands of millions
of francs! And thus we have been turned into a warrior
France instead of becoming a France of progress, truth,
justice, and peace, such as alone could have helped to save
the world. And now one sees so-called patriotism changing
Doutrequin, once a good Republican, a supporter of Gambetta, and still quite recently an anti-clerical, into an anti-
semite, even as it will end by changing him into a clerical
altogether. A few minutes ago he favoured me with an
extraordinary speech, an echo of the articles in *Le Petit
Beaumontais*: '' France before everything else,'' said he; it
was necessary to drive out the Jews, to make a fundamen-
tal dogma of respect for the army, and to allow more liberty
in education, by which he meant to allow the religious Congregations full freedom to keep the masses ignorant. He

typifies the bankruptcy of the earlier patriotic Republicans. Yet he is a worthy man, an excellent teacher, with five assistants under him, and the best-kept school in Beaumont. Two of his sons are already assistant-teachers in other schools of the department, and I know that they share their father's views and even exaggerate them as young men are wont to do. What will become of us if such sentiments should continue to animate our elementary masters? Ah! it is high time to provide others, to send a legion of men of free intelligence to teach the people truth, which is the one sole source of equity, kindliness, and happiness!'

He spoke these last words with such fervour that Marc smiled! 'Ah! my dear master, now I recognise you,' he said. 'You are not going to give up the battle! You will end by winning it, for you have truth on your side.'

Salvan gaily admitted that he had previously given way to a fit of discouragment. The infamous proceedings with which Simon was threatened had unnerved him. 'Advice?' he repeated, ' you asked me for advice as to how you should act. Let us see; let us examine the situation together.'

There was Forbes, the Academy Rector,[1] gentle and affable, a very able man of letters, and a very intelligent man also. But he was deep in historical studies, covertly disdainful of the present age, and he acted as a mere go-between for the intercourse of the Minister of Public Instruction and the university staff. Then, however, came Le Barazer, the Academy Inspector; and Salvan's hope of future victory was centred in that sensible and courageous man, who was also a skilful politician. The experience of Le Barazer, who was now barely fifty years of age, dated back to the heroic days of the Republic, when the necessity of secular and compulsory education had imposed itself as the one sole possible basis of a free and just democracy. A worker for the good cause from the very outset, Le Barazer had retained all his hatred of clericalism, convinced that it was absolutely necessary to drive the priests from the schools, and to free people's minds from all mendacious superstitions, if one desired that the nation should be strong, well-instructed, and capable of acting in the plenitude of its intelligence. But age, the obstacles he had encountered, the ever tenacious resistance of the Church, had added great prudence and tactical skill to his Republican zeal.

[1] See foot-note, p. 44, *ante.*

Nobody knew better than he how to utilise the little ground
which he gained each day, and to oppose inertia to the assaults of his adversaries, when forcible resistance was
impossible. He exerted the power he held as Academy
Inspector without ever entering into a direct contest with
anybody, either the Prefect or the Deputies or the Senators
of the department, though, on the other hand, he refused
to yield so long as his views were not adopted.

It was thanks to him that Salvan, although violently attacked by the clerical faction, was able to continue his work
of regeneration, the renewing of the *personnel* of the elementary schoolmasters; and doubtless he alone could in a
measure defend Simon against his subordinate, Inspector
Mauraisin. For that handsome gentleman also had to be
reckoned with, and he was likely to prove ferocious, a traitor
to the university cause, and an accomplice of the Congregations, since he had come to the conclusion that the
Church would prove victorious in the affair, and pay a
higher reward than the other side for the services rendered
to it.

'Have you heard of his evidence?' Salvan continued.
'It appears that he said everything he could against Simon
to Daix. To think that the inspection of our schools is
confided to Jesuits of his stamp! It is the same with that
fellow, Depinvilliers, the principal of the Lycée [1] of Beaumont, who attends Mass at St. Maxence every Sunday with
his wife and his two ugly daughters. Opinions are free, of
course; but if Depinvilliers is free to go to Mass, he ought
not to be free to hand one of our establishments of secondary education over to the Jesuits. Father Crabot reigns at
our Lycée as he reigns at the College of Valmarie. Ah!
the bitter irony of it when one thinks that this secular
Lycée, this Republican Lycée, which I sometimes hear
called the rival of the Jesuit College, is in reality a mere
branch of it! Ah! our Republic does fine work, it places
its interests in very trusty and loyal hands! I can well
understand Mauraisin working for the other side, which is
ever active and which pays its supporters well!'

Then, coming to the point, Salvan added: 'I tell you
what I will do. I will see Le Barazer. Do not go to him
yourself. It is better that any application should come
from me, whom he supports so bravely. And it is useless

---

[1] A government secondary college.

to hustle him, he will act at the moment he thinks fit, and with such means as are at his disposal.　He will certainly keep Mauraisin quiet, if he can render Simon no more direct service.　.　.　.　But what I advise you to do is to see Lemarrois, our Mayor and Deputy.　You know him well, do you not ?　He was a friend of Berthereau, your wife's father.　He may be useful to you.'

Marc then took leave, and on reaching the street decided to call on Lemarrois at once.　Eleven o'clock was striking, and he would doubtless find him at home.　Turning, therefore, into the Rue Gambetta, a thoroughfare running from the Lycée to the Hôtel de Ville, and thus cutting Beaumont in halves, he made his way to the Avenue des Jaffres, the famous promenade of the town, which also traversed it, but from the Préfecture to the Cathedral.　In that very avenue, in the midst of the aristocratic quarter, Lemarrois owned a luxurious house, where his beautiful wife, a Parisienne, often gave entertainments.　Wealthy and already of repute in his profession, he had brought her from Paris at the time when he had returned to his native place to practise there and satisfy his political ambition.　While he was yet a medical student, he had made the acquaintance of Gambetta, with whom intimacy had followed, for he showed much enthusiasm and firm Republicanism, and became indeed one of the great man's favourite disciples.　Thus he was regarded at Beaumont as a pillar of the middle-class Republic.　And not only was he the husband of an amiable wife, but, intelligent and good-hearted, he was personally very popular with the poor, whom he attended gratuitously.　His political advancement had been rapid; first he had become municipal councillor, then a departmental councillor, then deputy and mayor.　For twelve years now he had been installed in the latter functions, and was still the uncontested master of the town and the chief of the departmental parliamentary contingent, though the latter included some reactionary deputies.

Directly he saw Marc enter his study, a spacious room furnished with chastened luxury, he went towards him with both hands outstretched, and an expression of smiling sympathy on his face.　Dark, with scarcely a grey hair, though he was nearly fifty, he had a big head, with quick, bright eyes, and a profile fit for a medal.

'Ah! my good fellow, I was astonished not to see you, and I can guess what motive has brought you to-day!

What an abominable business, is it not ?   That unfortunate
Simon is innocent, that is certain from the frantic way in
which he is being charged.   I am on your side, you know
—on your side with all my heart!'

Pleased by this reception, cheered at meeting a just man,
Marc quickly explained to him that he came to solicit his
influential help.   There was surely something to be done.
One could not allow an innocent man to be tried and perhaps condemned.

But Lemarrois was already raising his arms to heaven.
'Do something, no doubt, no doubt!' said he.   'Only,
what can one do against public opinion when the whole
department is already stirred up ?   As you must know, the
political situation is becoming more and more difficult.
And the general elections will take place next May—that
is, in scarcely nine months' time!   Do you not understand
to what extreme prudence we are reduced ? for we must not
expose the Republic to the risk of a check.'

He had seated himself and his face became anxious while,
toying with a large paper-knife, he expressed his fears about
the agitated condition of the department, in which the
Socialists were actively bestirring themselves, and gaining
ground.   He did not fear the election of any of them as yet,
for none could command a sufficient majority; but if two
Reactionaries, one of whom was Sanglebœuf, the so-called
rallié, had been returned at the last elections, it was by
reason of a diversion created by the Socialists.   Each time
that he pronounced that word ' Socialists ' it was with a kind
of aggressive bitterness, in which one could detect the fear
and anger of the middle-class Republic, which now possessed power, in presence of the slow but irresistible use of
the Socialist Republic which wished to possess it.

' So how can I help you, my good fellow ? ' he continued;
' I am bound hand and foot, for we have to reckon with
public opinion.   I don't refer to myself,—I am certain of re-
election,—but I have to think of my colleagues whom I must
not leave wounded on the battle-field.   If it were merely a
question of my own seat I would sacrifice it at once so as to
act solely in accordance with my conscience; but the Republic is at stake and we must not allow it to be defeated.'

Then he complained of the Prefect of the department,
that handsome, well-groomed Hennebise, who sported
glasses and arranged his hair so carefully.   He gave no
help whatever; for being perpetually afraid of getting into

difficulties with his Minister or the Jesuits, he was careful to offend neither. He probably had secret leanings towards the priests and the military set, and it would be necessary to watch him, while pursuing, however, a course of diplomacy and compromise similar to his own.

'Briefly,' said Lemarrois, 'you see me in despair, reduced to measure every step and weigh every word for the next nine months under penalty of being hissed by the readers of *Le Petit Beaumontais*, to the great delight of the clerical faction. This Simon affair falls on us at a most unfavourable moment. If the elections were not so near, I would march with you at once.'

Then, quite abruptly, he, usually so calm, lost his temper: 'To make matters worse, Simon not only saddles us with this business at a difficult moment, but he chooses Delbos as his advocate, Delbos the Socialist, who is the *bête noire* of all right-thinking people. Frankly, that is the climax; Simon must be really desirous of seeing himself condemned.'

Marc had remained listening, pained at heart, feeling that another of his illusions was taking flight. Yet he knew Lemarrois to be honest, and he had seen him give many proofs of firm Republican faith.

'But Delbos is very talented,' the young man answered, 'and if poor Simon chose him, it was because, like all of us, he considered him to be the man of the situation. Besides, it is not certain that another advocate would have accepted the brief. It is a frightful moment; people are becoming cowards.'

That word must have seemed to Lemarrois like a smack. He made a quick gesture, but he evinced no anger—indeed, he began to smile. 'You consider me very cautious, do you not, my young friend?' he said. 'When you get older you will see that it is not always easy in politics to behave in accordance with one's own convictions. But why do you not apply to my colleague Marcilly, your young deputy, the favourite and the hope of all the young intellectuals of the department? I have become an old, spent, prudent hack—that 's understood. But Marcilly, whose mind is so free and broad, will certainly place himself at your head. Go to see him, go to see him.'

Then, having escorted Marc to the landing, he again pressed his hands, promising that he would help him with all his power, when circumstances should permit it.

Indeed, thought Marc, why should he not go to Marcilly ?
The latter also lived in the Avenue des Jaffres, and it was
not yet noon.   The young schoolmaster was entitled to call
on him, as he had acted, very discreetly, as one of his electoral canvassers, being full of enthusiasm for a candidate
who was so sympathetic and possessed of such high literary
culture.   Born at Jonville, Marcilly had distinguished himself as a pupil of the Training College, and had subsequently
held a professorship at the Faculty of Beaumont, which
post he had resigned in order to become a parliamentary
candidate.   Short, fair, and refined in appearance, with an
amiable and ever-smiling face, he played havoc with women's hearts, and even won the partiality of men, thanks to
his rare skill in saying the right word to each, and in evincing all necessary obligingness.   To the younger members of
the electorate he endeared himself by his own comparative
youth, for he was only thirty-two, and by the happy and
elegant form of his speeches, in which he displayed much
broadness of mind and knowledge of men and things.   It
was felt at the time of his election that one would at last
have a really young deputy on whom one might rely.   He
would renew the science of politics, infuse into it the blood
of the rising generations, and adorn it with faultless language, all the delightful bloom of sound literature.   Indeed,
for three years past Marcilly had been acquiring a more
and more important position in the Chamber.   His credit
constantly increased, and, in spite of the fact that he was
only two and thirty, he had already been spoken of for a
ministerial portfolio.   It was certain also that if he attended
to his constituents' affairs with untiring complaisance, he
pushed on his own still more successfully, profiting by every
circumstance to rise a little higher, but doing so in such a
natural and easy way that nobody had yet regarded him as
a mere *Arriviste*, one of those representatives of hot, impatient youth, eager for enjoyment and power in every
form.   His rooms were furnished and ornamented in a
delicate style, and he received Marc like a comrade.   He
spoke of Simon, too, immediately, in a voice full of emotion, saying how deeply he was affected by the poor man's
fate.   Of course he did not refuse to help him, he would
speak in his favour, he would see people who might be useful.   But whatever might be his graciousness, he ended by
recommending extreme prudence on account of the proximity of the elections.   If his manners were more caressing,

his answer was much the same as Lemarrois'; he was secretly resolved to do nothing for fear of compromising the Republican party. The two schools might differ in outward appearance — that of Lemarrois being older and rougher in its ways; that of Marcilly, younger and more prodigal of compliments — but both were determined to abandon no shred of the power they held. And now, for the first time, Marc felt that Marcilly might be merely an *Arriviste* in his flower, resolved to follow his own course and bear his fruit. Nevertheless, on taking leave, it became necessary to thank him, for with a flow of gentle words the young deputy repeated that he was at his visitor's disposal and would assuredly give some help.

Marc was full of fear and anxiety when he returned to Maillebois that day. Calling on the Lehmanns in the afternoon, he found the family in desolation. They had so confidently expected that further proceedings would be abandoned. David, who was present, quite upset by the bad news, still tried to believe in the possibility of some miracle which would prevent that iniquitous trial from taking place. But, on the morrow, things began to move quickly. The Indictment Chamber[1] seemed to be in a singular hurry, for, the case was set down for hearing at the earliest assizes, those of October. In presence of the inevitable, David, with his ardent faith in his brother's innocence, recovered all his courage, all that strength and firmness of mind which were to make him a hero. The trial would have to take place; it could not be avoided; but where was the jury that would dare to convict Simon when no proofs were forthcoming? The prisoner never varied in his cry of innocence; and the calmness with which he waited, the confidence in speedy release which he expressed to his brother at each visit, greatly fortified the latter. At the Lehmanns' house, as the expectations of acquittal grew stronger, plans were formed, and Madame Simon talked of a month's rest which she, her husband, and the children would afterwards take in Provence, where they had some friends. It was in the midst of this fresh spell of hopefulness that David one morning asked Marc to go with him to Beaumont in order that they might discuss the affair with Delbos, Simon's counsel.

The young advocate resided in the Rue Fontanier, in the

---

[1] A tribunal discharging the duties of a grand jury.— *Trans.*

popular trading quarter of the town. The son of a peasant of the environs, he had studied law in Paris, where for a short time he had frequented many young men of Socialist views. But hitherto, for lack of one of those great causes which class a man, he had not bound himself to any party. In accepting a brief in Simon's case, that case which made his colleagues of the bar tremble, he had decided his future. He studied it and became impassioned on finding himself in presence of all the public powers, all the forces of reaction, which, in order to save the old rotten framework of society from destruction, were coalescing and striving to ruin a poor and guiltless man. And the rise of militant Socialism was at the end of it all, the salvation of the country by the new force of which the freed masses now disposed.

'Well, so there is to be a battle!' Delbos exclaimed gaily, when he received his visitors in his little study, littered with books and papers. 'Ah! I cannot tell if we shall conquer, but at all events we shall do the others some harm.'

Short, dark, and wiry, with eyes of fire and tongue of flame, he possessed an admirable voice and an extraordinary gift of eloquence, at once enthusiastic, logical, and precise. David, however, was struck by his apparent doubt of victory and repeated what he had been saying for a week past: 'Conquer? Oh! we shall certainly do so. Where can a jury be found that would dare to convict my brother without proofs?'

Delbos looked at him, and then began to laugh, saying: 'Let us go down into the street, my poor friend, and the first twelve citizens we get together will spit in your face and call you a dirty Jew. You don't read *Le Petit Beaumontais*, and you are ignorant of the beautiful souls and minds of your contemporaries. But all allusions would be dangerous and culpable: is that not so, Monsieur Froment?'

Then, as Marc spoke of the disappointment he had experienced when visiting influential persons, Delbos, wishing to free his client's brother of his erroneous views, insisted on the subject. No doubt they had a friend in Salvan, but he was sorely threatened, and, instead of defending others, needed to be defended himself. Then Le Barazer would sacrifice something to the fire, suffering Simon to go to his fate and reserving all his authority and influence for the defence of secular education. Next Lemarrois, the once incorruptible Republican, was unknowingly on that path of disquietude which leads straight to reaction.

Then came Marcilly, at the mention of whose name Delbos
was all afire. No trust whatever was to be placed in him,
he had always lied, and to-morrow he would become a renegade and a traitor. Indeed, one would obtain only fair
words from all those folks; nothing in the way of deeds was
to be expected, neither an act of frankness nor one of
courage.

Having thus judged the university men and the politicians,
Delbos passed to the judicial world. He was convinced
that Magistrate Daix had suspected the truth, but had set it
on one side, terrified as he was by the perpetual quarrels
which his wife stirred up in order to prevent him from releas-
ing the dirty Jew. And in acting as he had done he had
surely experienced great perturbation of conscience, for at
bottom he was honest. But, apart from him, one had to
fear the Procureur de la République, the frisky Raoul de
La Bissonière, whose speech to the jury would certainly
prove ferocious. Vain of his petty *noblesse*, it seemed to La
Bissonière great condescension on his part to serve the Republic, and he meant to be rewarded for doing so by rapid
advancement, which he hastened as best he could, fawning
on both the Government and the Congregations, zealous
too as a patriot and an anti-semite. As for President Gragnon, in him one would have a jovial judge, a hard drinker,
a keen sportsman, fond of petticoats, addicted to witticisms,
affecting brusqueness, not certainly sceptical, without soul
or faith, and at the mercy of the stronger side. Finally,
there would be the jury, the composition of which it was
easy to foresee. One might expect a few representatives of
the manufacturing and trading classes, some professional
men, clerks, and retired officers, and all would have
poisoned minds, all would tremble for their skins, and
yield to the general dementia.

' So, you see,' Delbos concluded bitterly, ' your brother,
forsaken by everybody since he so awkwardly requires help
when fear respecting the result of the elections paralyses
even the friends of truth and justice, will have a fine collection of stupidity, egotism, and cowardice to judge him.'
And, as David preserved dolorous silence, he added: ' Oh!
we shall not allow ourselves to be devoured without raising
an outcry. But I prefer to show you things as they are.
And now let us examine the position with respect to the
case itself.'

He could tell what views would be set forth by the prosecution. Pressure had been brought to bear on the witnesses from all sides. Quite apart from public opinion in the midst of whose vitiated atmosphere they lived, they were certainly being worked upon by occult powers, caught in a skilfully contrived skein of daily exhortations which dictated to them the statements they were to make. Mademoiselle Rouzaire now declared peremptorily that she had heard Simon come home at a quarter to eleven o'clock on the night of the crime. Even Mignot now fancied that he had heard footsteps and voices about the same hour. Then influence must have been exercised on Simon's pupils, the Bongard, Doloir, Savin, and Milhomme children, with the object of extracting from them statements unfavourable to the prisoner. Little Sébastien Milhomme, for instance, had now declared, while sobbing distressfully, that he had never seen his cousin Victor with any copy-slip coming from the Brothers' school; and apropos of that affair, people spoke of an unexpected visit that Madame Edouard Milhomme had lately received from a distant cousin, General Jarousse, who commanded the division garrisoned at Beaumont. He had never previously confessed his relationship to the lady stationer, but had suddenly remembered it, and paid her that friendly call.

Moreover, the prosecution insisted on the failure of all efforts to find any tramp who might have committed the crime, as had been originally suspected. It also asserted that it had vainly sought any witness, guard, or wayfarer, who had seen Simon returning from Beaumont to Maillebois on foot. On the other hand, it had failed to establish that he had returned by train, for no railway employé remembered having seen him; besides which several return tickets had not been given up on the night of the crime. But it seemed that the evidence of Brother Fulgence and Father Philibin would be very grave, particularly that of the latter, who would prove that the copy-slip connected with the crime had really belonged to Simon's school. And to make things complete, two handwriting experts of the prosecution, Masters Badoche and Trabut, had declared that they fully recognised Simon's initials, an E and an S intertwined, in the faint and virtually illegible paraph on the slip.

Thus one could divine the form which the ' act of accusation ' or indictment would take. It would set forth that Simon lied, and that he had assuredly returned from Beaumont by train, and must have reached his home at the very

time when Mademoiselle Rouzaire declared that she had
heard him.   On the other hand it seemed certain that little
Zéphirin, after returning from the Capuchin Chapel at ten
o'clock, had not gone to bed immediately, but had amused
himself by arranging some religious pictures on his table, in
such wise that one might say the crime had been committed
between a quarter to eleven and eleven o'clock.

It was easy to picture the scene.   Simon, seeing a light,
had entered his nephew's room, and found him there, about
to get into bed.   Arriving from a banquet, heated by wine,
he had yielded to a fit of abominable madness.   Moreover,
he hated the child, he was infuriated by the fact that he
was a Catholic, and thus it was allowable to hint at the possibility of ritual crime, at the horrible legend fixed in the
minds of the masses.   But, at all events, there certainly
had been abomination; and the maddened criminal, after
thrusting the first thing he had at hand into the victim's
mouth in order to stifle his cries, had lost his head, and,
frantic with terror, had strangled the lad when the impro-
vised gag fell out and the cries began afresh, more terrible
than ever.   It was not so easy to explain how it happened
that the number of *Le Petit Beaumontais* and the copy-slip
had been mingled together.   Doubtless the newspaper had
been in Simon's pocket, for the boy would not have had
one in his possession.   As for the copy-slip, the prosecution,
after hesitating slightly, had adopted the view that this also
must have been in Simon's pocket, for the report of the
handwriting experts identifying the initials showed that it
belonged to him.

The crime accomplished, the rest was easily explained.
Simon left the body on the floor, touched nothing in the
room, but contented himself with opening the window
widely in order to make it appear that the murderer had
come from outside.   In one respect he had blundered
badly, he had not thought of picking up and destroying the
newspaper and the copy-slip, which had rolled to the foot
of the bed.   This showed how great had been his perturbation.   And, doubtless, he had not immediately joined his
wife, as she fixed the hour of his return at twenty minutes
to twelve.   In all probability he had spent some time seated
on the stairs, trying to recover his calmness.   The prosecution did not go so far as to charge Madame Simon with
complicity; nevertheless, it gave out that she did not tell
the truth when she spoke of the smiling quietude, the gay

affection displayed by her husband that night; and a proof of her disregard for veracity was to be found in the evidence of Mignot, who was astonished that his principal should have risen so late the next morning, and who asserted that he had found him pale and shivering, scarce able to walk, when he went to tell him the dreadful tidings. Mademoiselle Rouzaire, Brother Fulgence, and Father Philibin agreed that Simon had almost fainted at the sight of the little body, although in other respects he showed the most revolting dryness of heart. And in this again was there not an overwhelming proof of culpability? The wretched man's guilt could be doubted by none.

Having thus explained the views of the prosecution, Delbos resumed: 'The moral impossibilities are gross; no man of good sense will think Simon guilty, and, besides, there are several material improbabilities. But this frightful tale is sufficiently well constructed to seize hold of the masses and to become one of those legendary fables which acquire the force of truth. Our weakness proceeds from the fact that, not knowing the real story, we cannot set it up in opposition to the legend now being forged. The theory of a night prowler, to which you seem to cling, can only serve to cast a little doubt into the minds of the jury; for there are serious objections to it. And so whom can we accuse, and what shall my system of defence be?'

At this Marc, hitherto very attentive and silent, could not restrain himself from giving expression to the conviction which had slowly gathered in his mind: 'But there is no doubt at all for me; the criminal was one of the Brothers!'

Delbos, well pleased with the answer, and signifying his approval by an energetic gesture, then exclaimed: 'Quite so. My own conviction is the same. The more I study the case the more I am led to that conclusion as being the only one possible.' And as David anxiously shook his head, he added: 'Yes, I know; it seems to you that your brother's position would be very dangerous if one of those Ignorantines were accused without decisive proof. And you are certainly right. Nevertheless, I have to plead, and the best way to prove your brother's innocence is to demonstrate who the guilty man must be. Is it not so? You will tell me that the question becomes one of ascertaining who that man is, and for that very reason I wish to go into the matter with you thoroughly.'

The discussion continued, and Marc recapitulated the

reasons which made him believe the murderer to be one of
the Brothers.   First, the copy-slip had come from this
school; that was virtually proved by what had occurred at
the Milhommes.   Then there was the initialling of the slip,
and the corner of it which had been torn away, in which clue
the solution of the enigma probably lurked.   A decisive
moral proof was the extraordinary zeal the Congregations
displayed in denouncing Simon.   They would not have
stirred up heaven and earth in this fashion if they had not
found it necessary to save some black sheep; though of
course they also hoped to crush the secular schools and to
insure the triumph of the Church.   Moreover, there were
features in the crime which suggested that it could only
have been perpetrated by some sly, cruel, bestial frock-
wearer.   But unfortunately arguments did not suffice, and
Marc was in despair that his investigations had been
thwarted by a combination of obscurity, confusion, and dread
which artful, invisible hands seemed to increase each day.

' Come,' interrupted Delbos, ' you suspect neither Brother
Fulgence nor Father Philibin, eh ? '

' Oh no!' Marc answered, ' I saw them near the body
when the crime was discovered.   Brother Fulgence certainly returned to his school on quitting the Capuchin
Chapel on the Thursday evening.   Besides, though he is
vain and crazy, I do not think him capable of such a
dreadful deed.   As for Father Philibin, he did not quit
Valmerie that evening.   Moreover, he also seems to me
honest, a worthy man at bottom.'

Silence fell.   Then Marc, with a dreamy expression in
his eyes, resumed: ' Yet something had certainly happened
that morning just as I arrived at the school.   Father Philibin had picked up the newspaper and the copy-slip, and I
now ask myself whether he profited by that brief opportunity to tear off and do away with that corner of the slip,
on which, perhaps, there may have been some indication.
. . .   But Mignot, though he hesitated at first, now declares the corner must have been missing when he first saw
the slip.'

' And what about the assistant Brothers, Isidore, Lazarus,
and Gorgias ? ' asked Delbos.

David, who on his side had prosecuted unremitting inquiries with admirable zeal, intelligence, and patience, shook
his head.   ' All three have *alibis* which a dozen of their set
will establish in court,' he replied.   ' Isidore and Lazarus,

it seems, returned to the school from the Capuchin Chapel with their principal, Brother Fulgence. Brother Gorgias for his part saw a child home, but he also had returned to the school by half-past ten, according to all the members of the staff and various lay witnesses—friends of the Brothers, it is true—who perceived him going in.'

Again did Marc intervene in his pensive manner, his eyes wandering afar like those of a man in quest of truth. 'That Brother Gorgias is not to my liking; I thought of him,' he said. 'The child he escorted home was Polydor, the nephew of a woman named Pélagie, who is cook to my wife's relatives. I tried to question the boy, but he is sly, idle, addicted to falsehoods, and I got nothing out of him except a little more confusion. All the same, Brother Gorgias haunts me. He is said to be brutal, sensual, cynical, displaying excessive piety, professing a stern, uncompromising, exterminating creed. I have been told also that he formerly had some connection with Father Philibin and even with Father Crabot. . . . Brother Gorgias, yes, I certainly thought for a moment that he might be our man. But then I found I had nothing to go upon except suppositions.'

'Certainly, Brother Gorgias is not a pleasant customer,' declared David, 'and my feelings are akin to yours. But can we denounce him when we have only arguments to bring against him? No witness would support us; all would stand up for the Brother and whitewash him in reply to our impious charges.'

Delbos had listened attentively. 'At all events,' said he, 'I cannot defend Simon without carrying the battle into the enemy's camp. Bear in mind, too, that the only help from which you may derive some advantage will perhaps come to you from the Church itself. The old quarrel between our Bishop, Monseigneur Bergerot, and Father Crabot, the Rector of Valmarie, is taking a very serious turn, by reason, precisely, of the Simon affair. My own belief is that the crafty mind and the invisible hand, which seem to you to be directing the whole business, are those of Father Crabot. I certainly do not accuse him of the crime, but it is he who is protecting the culprit. And if we attack him we shall strike the head of the band, besides which the Bishop will be on our side—not openly, of course; but is not such assistance something, even if it be secret ? '

A smile of doubt appeared on Marc's face, as if he felt

that one never had the Church on one's side when human
truth and justice were at stake.   However, he likewise regarded Father Crabot as the enemy, and to trace the
developments of the case back to him and to endeavour to
destroy him was the right course.   So they spoke of Father
Crabot and of his past life, which a somewhat mysterious
legend poetised.   He was thought to be the illegitimate
grandson of a famous general, a prince of the First Empire,
which relationship, in the estimation of patriotic souls, en-
dued his pious ministry with some of the resounding glory
of battle and conquest.   But the romantic circumstances in
which he had taken orders touched people more deeply.
At thirty years of age he had been a rich, handsome, gallant
cavalier, on the point of marrying a beautiful widow, a
Duchess with a great name and a great fortune; but brutal
death had struck her down in her flower.   That blow, as
Father Crabot often said, had shown him the bitter nothingness of human joys, and cast him into the arms of religion.
He had gained thereby the tremulous tenderness of all women's hearts; they were well pleased, indeed, that he
should have sought a refuge in heaven, for love of the one
woman whom he had adored.

Then another legend, that of the foundation of the College of Valmarie, endeared him to the devotees of the
region.   The Valmarie estate had previously belonged to
the old Countess de Quédeville, who, after notorious
amours, had retired thither to sanctify her last years by the
practice of extreme piety.   Her son and daughter-in-law
having perished in an accident while travelling, she remained alone with her grandson and sole heir, Gaston, a
boy of nine years, who was most aggressively turbulent,
violent in speech, and wild in his play.   Not knowing how
to subdue him, and not daring to trust him to school life,
the Countess had engaged as tutor a young Jesuit of six and
twenty, Father Philibin, whose manners suggested his
peasant origin, but who was recommended to her for his
extreme firmness.   He, no doubt, made the Countess acquainted with Father Crabot, who was some five or six
years his senior, and who was then at the height of his celebrity, radiant with the halo of his great passion and its
tragic, divine ending.   Six months later, as friend and confessor, he reigned at Valmarie, evil-minded people asserting
that he was the lover of the Countess.

As that turbulent boy Gaston seemed to disturb the

happy quietude of the domain, a truly royal one with its
grand old trees, its running waters, its great stretches of
green velvet, there was at one moment some thought of
sending him to the Jesuit Fathers in Paris. He climbed
the loftiest poplars for rooks' nests, took to the river in his
clothes to fish for eels, came home in rags, with arms and
legs bruised, and his face bleeding, giving his grandmother
no rest whatever from anxiety, in spite of Father Philibin's
reputed firmness. But all at once the situation was tragically altered: Gaston was drowned one day while walking
out, under the nominal supervision of his tutor. The latter
related that the boy had fallen into a dangerous hole full of
water, whence it had been impossible to extricate him, in
spite of the efforts of a young fellow of fifteen, Georges
Plumet—the son of one of the gardeners and sometimes
Gaston's companion in his escapades—who had run up on
seeing the accident from a distance. The Countess, profoundly grieved, died during the following year, bequeath-
ing Valmarie and all her fortune to Father Crabot—or, to
be exact, to a petty clerical banker of Beaumont, who lent
his name in such matters—with directions to establish a
Jesuit College on the estate. Crabot, for a time, had taken
himself elsewhere, then had returned with the rank of
Rector, and for ten years now the College had been pros-
pering under his control.

He reigned there from his austere and retired little cell,
whose walls were bare, and whose furniture was limited to
a little pallet, a table, and two chairs. He made the bed,
he swept the floor himself; and though he heard the confessions of his female penitents in the chapel, it was in that
cell that he listened to those of the men, as if he were
proud of the poverty and solitude into which he withdrew
like some redoubtable divinity, leaving to Father Philibin,
the Prefect of the Studies, all usual daily intercourse with
the pupils of the establishment. But, although he rarely
showed himself to them in the class-rooms, he reserved
'parlour-days' to himself, lavished attentions on his pupils'
relations, particularly on the ladies and young girls of the
local aristocracy, busying himself with the future of his
dear sons and dear daughters, arranging their marriages,
insuring them good positions, in fact disposing of all those
fine folk for the greater glory of God and of his particular
Order. And it was thus that he had become an all-powerful personage.

'To tell the truth,' Delbos resumed, 'Father Crabot strikes me as being a mediocrity, whose entire strength proceeds from the stupidity of those among whom he works. I am more distrustful of Father Philibin, whom you think a worthy man. I am impressed by his affected roughness and frankness. Suspicion clings to his doings and to Crabot's in the time of the Countess de Quédeville, such as the drowning of that child Gaston, and all the more or less lawful manœuvring to acquire the estate and the fortune. It happens that the only witness of Gaston's death, Georges Plumet, the gardener's son, is precisely Brother Gorgias, for whom Philibin assumed great affection and of whom he made an Ignorantine, when, of course, he changed his name. And now we find those three men together again, and the solution of the present mystery is to be found, perhaps, in that circumstance; for, if Brother Gorgias be guilty, the efforts of the others to save him might be explained by strong personal motives, the existence of some skeleton in their cupboard, and the dread lest he should speak out if he were abandoned. Unfortunately, as you said just now, we can only form suppositions, whereas we need substantial, authentic facts. However, let us keep on searching. Defence, I repeat it, will only be possible if I am armed sufficiently to be an accuser and an avenger.'

That conversation with Delbos inspirited David and Marc. And, even as had been foreseen, they tasted for a moment the pleasure of witnessing a quarrel in the clerical camp. At the outset of the affair Abbé Quandieu, the parish priest of Maillebois, had not concealed his belief in the innocence of Simon. He did not go so far as to accuse one of the Brothers; but he allowed it to be seen that he disapproved of the frantic campaign which the Brothers and the Capuchins were carrying on with the object of gaining the whole district for themselves; for, apart from his own loss of parishioners, it distressed him, for religion's sake, to see the basest superstitions triumphing. When he found public opinion suddenly poisoned with respect to Simon's case, he became neutral, never speaking of the affair, but dreading, in his sincere piety, lest his dear gentle Lord of charity and love should be slain and replaced by a God of falsehood and iniquity. His only consolation was that his views coincided with those of Monseigneur Bergerot, the Bishop, who was fond of him and whom he often visited. Like the priest himself, the Bishop was accused of Gallicanism, which simply meant that he did not invariably bow to Rome, and that the idolatrous worship of images and the impudent trafficking of those who contracted to perform spurious miracles were repugnant to his pure faith. For instance, he observed with saddened eyes the invading tendencies of the Maillebois Capuchins, who so openly traded on the shrine of St. Antony of Padua which they had set up in their chapel, thus competing disloyally with the church of St. Martin, where Abbé Quandieu officiated. The Bishop's anxiety increased when behind the Capuchins he divined the presence of the Jesuits, all the disciplined troops of his enemy Father Crabot, who was always employing his influence to thwart him, and who dreamt of becoming master of the diocese.

The Bishop reproached the Jesuits with compelling God to go to men, instead of forcing men to go to God, and he also saw in them the artisans of the society compromise, of the falling off both in faith and in observances, which in his opinion was destroying the Church. In the Simon affair, on finding them so intent upon ruining the unhappy prisoner, he became suspicious and studied the case very carefully with Abbé Quandieu, who was well informed. He must then have arrived at a decisive opinion. Perhaps indeed he learnt who was really the culprit. But what course could he take, how could he give up a member of the religious Orders, without risk of doing harm to religion? He lacked the courage to go as far as that. Yet certainly his silence was full of bitterness, and he felt anxious as to the consequences of the monstrous adventure into which others were forcing the Church, which he would have liked to see all peace, equity, and kindliness.

Thus Monseigneur Bergerot's resignation was not absolute. The idea of abandoning his dear Abbé Quandieu, of allowing those whom he called ' the dealers of the Temple' to consummate his ruin, was unbearable to him. On coming, then, to Maillebois in the course of a pastoral round of inspection, he officiated personally in the ancient church of St. Martin, and delivered an address in which he blamed all gross superstition, referring plainly to the commerce carried on by the Capuchins in their chapel, which was now driving as much trade as a bazaar. Nobody was mistaken as to the Bishop's meaning; moreover, everyone felt that the blow was directed not only against Father Théodose, but against Father Crabot who was behind him. And as Monseigneur ended by expressing the hope that the Church of France

would remain the pure source of all truth and justice, the
scandal became the greater, for in those words an allusion
to the Simon affair was detected, and the Bishop was accused of casting the Brothers of the Christian Doctrine to
the Jews, the bribe-takers, and the traitors.   On returning
to his episcopal palace Monseigneur Bergerot must have
trembled at the thought of the courage he had shown, particularly as everything was done to embitter his position still
more.   Some intimates, in recounting the visit of thanks
which Abbé Quandieu paid him, mentioned that the Bishop
and the poor priest had wept together.

The agitation at Beaumont increased as the assizes drew
near; the Indictment Chamber having returned the papers
in Simon's case to the Prosecution Office, the first hearing
had been fixed for Monday, October 20.   Meantime the
position taken up by the Bishop brought popular passions to
a climax.   He was attacked even more violently by *Le Petit
Beaumontais* than by *La Croix de Beaumont*, though the latter journal was in the hands of the Jesuits.   The Simonists
had plucked up a little courage at the advent of his unhoped-for help; but the anti-Simonists poisoned public
opinion with fresh romances, among others an extraordinary
invention to the effect that a Jew syndicate had been formed
to buy up all the powers of the world by dint of millions.
And three millions, it was said, had gone to Monseigneur
Bergerot as his share.

From that moment dementia and violence reigned throughout the town.   From Le Mauviot, the working-class *faubourg*,
to the Avenue des Jaffres, the aristocratic quarter, passing
by way of the Rue Fontanier and the adjoining narrow
streets where the smaller shopkeepers congregated, the contest became more and more bitter, the Simonists, who were
few in number, being crushed by the ever-growing hordes of
their adversaries.   On one occasion a crowd went to hoot
Salvan, the Director of the Training College, as he was suspected of Simonism; and in a like spirit, Depinvilliers, the
Jew-hating and patriotic principal of the Lycée, was acclaimed.   Paid brawlers, recruited on the pavements and
reinforced by clerical young men of position, swept the
streets and threatened the Jew-shops.   The saddest was
that the Republican and even some of the Socialist working
men either disinterested themselves from the contest or took
up positions against right and truth.   Then terror reigned,
cowardice became widespread, all the social forces coalesced

against the unhappy prisoner. The University, headed by
Forbes, its Rector, did not stir for fear of compromising
itself. The official Administration, personified by Prefect
Hennebise, had disinterested itself from the question at the
outset, desirous as it was of incurring no worries. The
politicians, the Senators as well as the Deputies, remained
silent for fear they might lose their seats if they spoke otherwise than the electors did. The Church, in which the
Bishop had ceased to count, Father Crabot becoming its
real chief, demanded the setting up of piles and stakes, and
the extermination of all Jews, Protestants, and Freemasons.
The army, by the voice of General Jarousse, also called for
the cleansing of the country, and the enthronement of an
emperor or a king as soon as all the rogues without God or
fatherland should be sabred. And there remained the Judicial Bench, towards which every hope went forth, for did
it not hold in its hands the necessary *dénouement*, the condemnation of the dirty Jew, by which alone the salvation of
France might be assured? Thus Gragnon, the presiding
judge, and Raoul de La Bissonnière, the Public Prosecutor,
had become great personages, of whom nobody doubted, for
their anti-Simonism was as notorious as were their desire for
advancement and their passion for popularity.

When the names inscribed on the general roll of jurors
for the coming assizes were made public, there was a fresh
outburst of violence and intrigue. The most terrible pressure was brought to bear on the persons who were likely to
serve; so that nobody might remain ignorant of their names
and addresses *Le Petit Beaumontais* printed them, thus de-
signating them to the fury of the crowd in the event of their
failing to convict the prisoner. They received anonymous
letters, they were upset by strange visitors, they were begged
to think of their wives and children. In the drawing-rooms
of the Avenue des Jaffres people amused themselves with
elaborate calculations, passing in review the more or less
certain opinions of each individual juror. Would such a
one convict or would he not? The question became a
society pastime.

At beautiful Madame Lemarrois' house each Saturday,
her day, nothing else was spoken of. All the ladies came:
Générale Jarousse, who, although lean, ugly, and dusky,
was said to be abominably unfaithful to the general, her
husband; Présidente Gragnon, who, still superb and languishing, fascinated the young Assessors of the Public

Prosecution Service; Préfete Hennebise, who, like an artful and prudent Parisienne, spoke little and listened a great deal; together with the eager Madame Daix, the Investigating Magistrate's wife, and at times even Madame de La Bissonnière, the Prosecutor's spouse, though she, gentle and retiring in her ways, seldom went into society.   The ladies had all attended a great fête given at La Désirade by the Sanglebœufs in accordance with the advice of Baron Nathan, who had prevailed on his daughter to shake off her indolence and place herself, like others of her sex, at the service of the good cause.   The part which women played in the affair was indeed an influential one: they were worth an army, said young Deputy Marcilly, who, waiting to see on which side victory would rest, comported himself as a Simonist with some and as an anti-Simonist with others.

But a last quarrel maddened everybody.   One morning *Le Petit Beaumontais* formally suggested that at least some part of the case should be heard *in camera*.   This idea had certainly not originated with the newspaper itself; one divined in it a deep knowledge of the sentiments of the multitude, a hope that mystery would make the charges appear yet more monstrous than they were, and a desire for some convenient means by which one might subsequently justify the condemnation of an innocent man, as for instance by asserting that facts had come out *in camera* with which the general public was not acquainted.   The Simonists detected the danger, protested, appealed for full light, the hearing of the whole case in open court; whereupon the anti-Simonists, fired with indignation, shrieked that the appeal was scandalous, and demanded to know whether the ears of respectable people were to be soiled by being compelled to listen to the most abominable particulars.   Thus, during the last week, a furious *mêlée* raged in Beaumont.

At last the great day, October 20, arrived.   The school term having begun, Marc had been obliged to reinstall himself at Jonville, with Geneviève and little Louise, whom Madame Duparque and Madame Berthereau had insisted on keeping with them throughout the whole vacation that year.   Marc had assented the more readily as his sojourn at Maillebois permitted him to carry on his investigations, which, alas! led to nothing.   But at the same time he had felt so uncomfortable in the ladies' house, where never a word was said of the great affair, that he was happy to find himself once more in his school, among his troop of playful boys, some of whom were so dear to him. On the other hand, at his own request, he had been cited as a witness in the case in order that he might testify to Simon's good character; and he awaited the trial with a quiver of emotion, again possessed by tenacious reliance in truth and justice, for it seemed to him impossible that a man could be condemned without proofs, in these days and in France, a land of liberty and generosity.

When he arrived at Beaumont on the Monday morning the town appeared to be in a state of siege. Most of the troops were kept under arms in their barracks, but gendarmes and infantrymen guarded the approaches of the Palace of Justice; and in order to reach it Marc had to overcome all sorts of obstacles, although he was duly provided with a witness's summons. Again, he found the staircases and passages likewise barred by troops. The Assize Court, a new and very spacious hall, glittered with gilding and imitation marble, in the crude light entering by six large windows. The place was already crowded two hours before the opening of the proceedings. All the fine folk of Beaumont were assembled behind the judges' arm-chairs. There were ladies in full dress everywhere, even on the benches usually reserved for witnesses. And the 'pit,' where only standing room was provided, was already tumultuous. A picked throng was gathered there; one recognised the church beadles and the hired ' demonstrators ' of the streets, with whom mingled some of the ranters of the Young Catholic set. There was a long delay, and thus Marc had ample time to examine the faces around him and to realise amid what hostile passions the proceedings would take their course.

The Court appeared: first Gragnon and his Assessors, then the Procureur de la République, La Bissonnière. The first formalities were accomplished rapidly; but it was rumoured that a 'panel' had not been formed without difficulty, several jurors on the roll having applied to be excused, so great was their dread of incurring any responsibility in Simon's case. At last the twelve chosen men entered the court in a file, and took their seats morosely, like condemned criminals. There were five shopkeepers, two manufacturers, two individuals living on their means, a doctor, an architect, and a retired army captain. The architect, a pious man, named Jacquin, who worked for the bishopric, happened to be the foreman, his name having come first at the drawing of lots. If the counsel for the defence had not challenged him by reason of his connections, it was because he enjoyed a well-deserved reputation for loyalty, uprightness, and honesty. Moreover, something like disappointment became manifest among the anti-Simonists on the arrival of the jurymen, whose names were repeated here and there, as each in succession was identified. Some of them appeared to be doubtful customers; and there had been hopes of a more reliable jury, one absolutely determined to convict the prisoner.

Deep silence fell; then the examination of Simon began. Looking puny and awkward as he entered the court, he had created an unfavourable impression. But he had drawn himself up, and now, by reason of the quiet and easy way in which he answered the questions addressed to him, he appeared to be impudent. Gragnon, the presiding judge, had put on the scoffing air which he assumed on great occasions, while keeping his little grey eyes fixed upon the advocate, Maître Delbos, the anarchist, as he called him, whom he had undertaken to suppress with a thumb-stroke. Meantime he indulged in witticisms, striving to provoke laughter, but growing gradually irritated by the calmness of Simon, who, as he did not lie, was unable to contradict himself and thus give himself away. The judge therefore became insolent, vainly endeavouring to provoke a protest from Delbos; but the latter, knowing his man, held his tongue and smiled. On the whole, the first day's proceedings, while rejoicing the Simonists, rendered the anti-Simonists extremely anxious, for the prisoner had clearly set forth the hour of his return to Maillebois, and the manner in which he had immediately joined his wife, without it being possible for the judge to produce a single certain, ascertained fact in opposition to his declarations. At the rising of the Court, when the crowd retired, the witnesses for the defence were hooted, and there was almost a fight on the steps of the Palace of Justice.

On the Tuesday the hearing of the witnesses began amid a yet greater concourse of people. First came assistant-master Mignot, whose statements were now less assertive than they had been during the magisterial inquiry. He no longer spoke positively of the hour at which he had heard sounds of footsteps and voices. Simple and worthy fellow as he was at bottom, he doubtless felt disturbed when he thought of the terrible consequences of such evidence as the judge tried to extract from him. But Mademoiselle Rouzaire was pitilessly precise. She specified the exact time, a quarter to eleven o'clock, adding even that she had fully recognised Simon's voice and footfall. Then came a long procession of railway employés, *octroi* officials,[1] and mere wayfarers, whose evidence was taken to solve the question whether the prisoner had travelled by the 10.30 train, as the prosecution asserted, or whether he had returned home on foot, as he himself claimed to have done. The depositions on the subject were interminable, full of confusion and contradictions. The impression they left, however, was somewhat favourable to the defence. But next came the much awaited evidence of Father Philibin and Brother Fulgence. The former, which was very brief, proved a disappointment, for the Jesuit merely recounted in a few husky sentences how he had found the little body on the floor near the bed. But Brother Fulgence amused the whole assembly by the vehemence he imparted to his narrative, throughout the whole of which he gesticulated as wildly as a jumping-jack. Nevertheless, he seemed quite pleased with the effect he produced. From the very outset of the affair he had not ceased to muddle and spoil things.

At last the three assistant Brothers, Isidore, Lazarus, and Gorgias, who had been specially cited by the defence, were called. Delbos allowed the two former to retire after a few insignificant questions, but he rose and remained erect while Gorgias was at the bar. That former little peasant, the son of a gardener at Valmarie, Georges Plumet as he was called in the days of the Countess de Quédeville, and now Brother Gorgias of the Ignorantine Order, was a strong, thin, dark and knotty man, with a low stern forehead, projecting cheek-bones, and thick lips under a big nose shaped like an eagle's beak. As formerly mentioned, he was afflicted with a tic, a convulsive twitching of his upper lip on its left side, which thus disclosed his strong teeth, and formed a kind of involuntary rictus, having a violent and scoffing expression. When he stepped forward in his old black frock and with his white band of doubtful cleanliness, a quiver, which had come nobody knew whence, sped through the assembly. And immediately a duel, with questions as keen as sword thrusts and answers as cutting as parries, began

---

[1] Those who collect municipal dues at the gates or outskirts of French towns.— *Trans.*

between the advocate and the Brother on the subject of the evening of the crime, on the time which the witness had taken to escort little Polydor to his home, and the precise hour at which he had returned to the school. The public listened in perplexity, failing to understand the decisive importance of this examination, for the witness was a stranger to most of the people present. As it happened, Brother Gorgias, in his violent scoffing way, found an answer for every question, produced proofs, and established the fact that at half-past ten o'clock he had been in bed in his cell. Brothers Isidore and Lazarus were recalled, the doorkeeper of the Brothers' school was fetched, together with two inhabitants of Maillebois, belated promenaders, and all swore and confirmed the Ignorantine's assertions.

Of course this duel was not fought without considerable intervention on the part of President Gragnon, who thought the opportunity favourable to silence Delbos, on the ground that he addressed insulting questions to the Brother. Delbos retorted by submitting 'conclusions,' and there was quite a to-do, amidst which Brother Gorgias seemed triumphant, turning on the advocate sly glances of disdain, as if to imply that he feared nothing whatever, protected as he was by his God of anger and extermination, who proved so terrible to infidels. But if the incident yielded no result that Delbos could immediately put to use, it wrought great perturbation; and some folk felt terribly alarmed lest Simon should escape as the result of such attempts to cast doubt into the minds of the jurors. That alarm must have spread to the Congregations, for a fresh incident occurred after the evidence of the handwriting experts, Masters Badoche and Trabut, who, amidst general stupefaction, explained how they detected Simon's initials, an E and an S interlaced, in the paraph on the copy-slip, when nobody else could see them there. That copy-slip was the one document in the case, everything depended on it; thus the evidence of those extraordinary experts was extremely grave: it meant the condemnation of Simon.

It was then that Father Philibin, who had followed the proceedings most attentively, asked the judge's permission to return to the bar. There, in a ringing voice, he, who had first shown himself so spiritless and retiring, recounted a brief story of a certain letter he had seen—a letter written by Simon to a friend, and signed with the same flourishes. And when Gragnon pressed him, asked for precise particulars, the Jesuit raised his hand towards the picture of the Crucifixion above the judgment seat, and declared theatrically that it was a secret of the confessional, and that he would say no more. Thus the second day's proceedings came to an end amid a paroxysm of feverishness and tumult.

On the Wednesday the question of hearing the report on the post-mortem examination and the evidence of the school children *in camera* was dealt with. The presiding judge had the right to take such a course; but Delbos, without contesting it, set forth all the danger of wrapping the affair in mystery, and submitted fresh ' conclusions ' to the effect that all evidence should be heard in open court. None the less Gragnon quietly pronounced a judgment, which the numerous gendarmes who were present immediately put into execution by pushing the public outside. There was an extraordinary outburst of emotion, a perfect scramble, followed by passionate discussions in the passages. During the two hours occupied by the proceedings *in camera* the excitement kept on increasing. Frightful rumours and statements circulated as if what was being said in court filtered through the walls. At first the chatterers dealt with the report on the post-mortem examination, discussing in turn every expression said to be contained in it, and adding horrible particulars, hitherto unknown to anybody, but absolutely proving Simon's guilt. Then came the evidence of the Bongard, Doloir, Savin, and Milhomme children, who were pictured saying things they had never said. However, people were convinced that all had been corrupted, and, in spite of Delbos's protest, which indeed was regarded as a mere comedy, it was declared that the Simonists themselves had desired proceedings *in camera* in order to save the secular school of Maillebois from utter disgrace. Thus, was not condemnation certain? Besides, those who might be disturbed by the lack of sufficient proof respecting the death of Zéphirin would be told that certain things had been stated *in camera*—things they would be unable to control, knowing nothing of them.

When the doors were reopened there came a rush, people swept in tumultuously, searching and sniffing for some trace of the monstrosities they had imagined. But during the remainder of the sitting they heard little beyond the evidence of a few witnesses for the defence, witnesses as to character, among whom Marc figured, and who all declared

Simon to be a very kind and gentle man, fondly attached to
his wife and children.　Only one witness attracted any attention, this being Mauraisin, the Elementary Inspector,
who had felt greatly annoyed by the citation which Delbos
had intentionally sent to him.　At a loss between his desire
to please the anti-Simonists and his fear of displeasing his
immediate superior, Le Barazer, whom he knew to be discreetly a Simonist, Mauraisin was in the first instance
obliged to admit that he had reported most favourably on
Simon and his school, and subsequently he could only
qualify those reports by vague insinuations respecting the
prisoner's sly character and the sectarian violence of his
religious passions.

The speeches of La Bissonnière and Delbos occupied the
Court throughout the Thursday and the Friday.　During
the earlier proceedings La Bissonnière had intervened as
little as possible, spending most of his time in taking notes
and contemplating his finger-nails.　At heart he was not
free from uneasiness, and he must have asked himself if he
would not do well to relinquish certain charges as some of
the so-called proofs were so very fragile.　Thus his address
was rather spiritless.　He contented himself with pointing
out the various probabilities of guilt, and ended by asking
merely for the application of the law.　His speech had
lasted barely two hours, its success was meagre, and the
anxiety of the anti-Simonists again became acute.

Not enough time was left that day for Delbos, who only
finished his speech on the morrow.　He began by drawing
a portrait of Simon, showing him in his school, esteemed
and loved, having an adorable wife and beautiful children
at his fireside.　Then, after setting forth the horrible and
ignoble circumstances of the crime, the advocate asked if
such a man could be guilty of it.　He took the so-called
proofs of the prosecution one by one, and demonstrated
their nothingness.　On the subject of the copy-slip, and the
report of the hand-writing experts, he waxed terrible; he
showed that the ownership of the one document in the case
could not be attributed to Simon, and he exposed the arrant
stupidity of the report drawn up by Masters Badoche and
Trabut.　He discussed and destroyed every item of evidence, even that which had been taken *in camera*, thereby
drawing on himself all the thunders of President Gragnon.
Quite a violent quarrel arose, and, indeed, from that moment Delbos spoke under the constant threat of being arbi-

trarily silenced. Nevertheless, from a defender he became
an accuser; he cast before the Court the Brothers and the
Capuchins, and the Jesuits also. He carried the case back
to Father Crabot in order that he might strike the chief of
the coalition, as he desired to do. Only a Brother, he said,
could have committed the crime, and, although he did not
name Brother Gorgias, he designated him; he gave all the
reasons on which his conviction was based, he pointed out
all the underhand devices which had been adopted by the
other side, the formation of a great clerical conspiracy of
which Simon was the victim, and the necessity for the plotters that an innocent man should be condemned in order
that the real culprit might be saved. In conclusion he
cried to the jury that it was not the murderer of little
Zéphirin, but the secular schoolmaster, the Jew, whom they
were really asked to condemn. The end of his speech,
though rent by the interruptions of the presiding judge and
the hooting of the audience, was, on the whole, regarded as
an oratorical triumph, which placed Delbos in the front
rank, but for which his client, no doubt, would pay heavily.

La Bissonnière immediately rose to reply to it, his countenance assuming an expression of grief and indignation.
An unqualifiable scandal had taken place; the counsel for
the defence had dared to accuse a Brother without producing any serious proof in support of his monstrous allegation.
He had done worse: he had denounced as that Brother's
accomplices both his superiors and other members of the religious Orders, including even one of high personality, before whom all honest folk bowed with respect. Religion
was outraged, anarchist passions were let loose, those who
acknowledged neither God nor patriotic feeling would fain
precipitate the country into an abyss. For three hours La
Bissonnière went on denouncing the enemies of society in
flowery language, drawing his little figure erect, as if he
felt he were at last rising to the high destiny to which his
ambition aspired. As he finished he became ironical; he
wished to know if the fact of being a Jew sufficed to make
a man innocent; and then he asked the jury for all its
severity, for the head of the wretch who had degraded and
murdered a little child. Frantic applause burst forth, and
Delbos, by his vehement rejoinder full of exasperation, only
drew on himself a fresh tempest of insults and threats.

It was seven o'clock in the evening when the jurors retired
to consider their verdict. As the questions put to them by

the Court were few in number, it was hoped that matters
would be finished in less than an hour, and that one might
then go off to dine.   Night had fallen, and the few big
lamps placed on the tables did not suffice to illumine the
great hall.   Candles, which looked like church tapers, had
been set up in front of the newspaper reporters, who were
still working.   The atmosphere was hot and murky, but not
a lady quitted her seat, the crowd stubbornly remained
there, phantom-like in places according to the play of the
lights, which threw great tragic shadows around.   All gave
full rein to their passions, there was a deafening uproar of
voices, with an agitation, a seething and bubbling, as in
some fermenting vat.   The few Simonists were triumphant;
they declared it would be impossible for the jury to convict.
And, in spite of the noisy applause bestowed on La Bissonnière's reply, the anti-Simonists, who crowded the hall,
showed themselves nervous, trembling lest the expiatory victim should escape them.   It was asserted that Jacquin, the
foreman of the jury, had spoken to somebody of the anguish
he felt in presence of the absolute lack of proofs.   And
three other jurymen were mentioned as having appeared
favourable to the prisoner.   Acquittal became possible.
Thus there was angry waiting, waiting which lasted and
lasted, contrary to all previous expectations.   Eight o'clock
struck, nine o'clock struck, and still the jurors did not return.   They had been shut up for two hours, unable, no
doubt, to come to an agreement.   This only increased the
general uncertainty, and, although the door of the jury's
retiring room was carefully closed, rumours came from it,
nobody knew how, raising the agitation of the ravenous,
extenuated, impatient throng to a climax.

All at once it was learnt that the foreman, acting for himself and his colleagues, had begged the presiding judge to
go to them.   According to another version it was the judge
who had placed himself at their disposal, insisting to see
them, which seemed a scarcely correct proceeding.   However, the waiting began once more, long minutes went by.
What could the judge be doing with the jurors?   Legally he
might only acquaint them with the dispositions of the law,
should they be ignorant of the consequences of their decision.   But the delay which was taking place appeared very
long for a simple explanation of that kind; and, indeed, a
fresh rumour suddenly spread among Gragnon's intimates,
who did not seem at all struck by the enormity of such a

story. It was to the effect that a document had reached the judge after the close of the proceedings, and that he had found it absolutely necessary to lay it before the jurymen, though the prisoner and his counsel were not present. However, ten o'clock struck, and at last the jury reappeared.

Then, in the anxious and suddenly silent hall, when the judges had returned and taken their seats, their robes setting red blotches against the background of shifting darkness, architect Jacquin, the foreman, arose. His face, distinctly seen, for the light of a lamp fell on it, was very pale. And it was in a somewhat weak voice that he pronounced the customary formula. The jury's answer was 'yes' to all the questions, but it granted the admission of extenuating circumstances, illogically of course, and with the sole object of avoiding the capital penalty. The penalty, in the circumstances, was penal servitude for life, and sentence was pronounced by President Gragnon with the air of a well-satisfied jolly dog and the jeering nasal accent habitual to him. The Procureur de la République, La Bissonnière, picked up his papers with a quick gesture, like a man relieved and delighted at having secured his desire. From the audience frantic applause had risen immediately—the loud baying of hungry hounds, to whom the long-pursued quarry was at last flung. It was like the delirium of cannibals gorging themselves with human flesh. And yet amid that tumult, fraught with horrid savagery, above all the ferocious baying, there rose a cry—Simon's unceasing cry, ' I am innocent! I am innocent! '—a loud and stubborn call which sowed truth in worthy hearts, whilst Advocate Delbos, with tears springing to his eyes, leant towards the condemned man and embraced him like a brother.

David, who had abstained from appearing in court, in order that he might give no occasion for an increase of anti-Semite hatred, awaited the result at Delbos's rooms in the Rue Fontanier. Until ten o'clock he remained counting the minutes, consumed by the most torturing fever, knowing not whether he ought to rejoice or despair at such delay. He continually went to the window to lean out, and listen to the sounds in the distance. And the very atmosphere of the street, and the exclamations of a few people passing, had already imparted to him the fatal tidings, when Marc arrived, sobbing, exhausted, and confirmed them. Salvan accompanied Marc—Salvan, whom the young man had met on quitting the court, and who was also beside himself.

There came an hour of tragic despair, of utter collapse, when all that was good and just seemed to be engulfed for ever; and when Delbos, after an interview with Simon, whom he had found stricken yet still erect, arrived in his turn, he could only cast himself on David's neck and embrace him, even as he had embraced his brother yonder.

'Ah! weep, my friend!' he cried. 'It is the greatest iniquity of the century!'

IV

ON his return to Jonville after the vacation that year, Marc had found himself engaged in another struggle, one having no connection with Simon's case. His adversary, Abbé Cognasse, the parish priest, anxious to get him into difficulties, had decided to make an effort to win over the village Mayor, one Martineau, a peasant, through the latter's wife, 'the beautiful Martineau,' as she was called.

Abbé Cognasse was a terrible man, tall, lean, and angular, with a determined chin, and a sharp nose under a low brow and a thick mane of dark hair. His eyes glowed with aggressive fire; his knotty hands, which he seldom washed, seemed made expressly for the purpose of throttling those who dared to resist him. Forty years of age, he kept one servant, Palmyre, an old maid of sixty, who was inclined to be humpbacked and who was yet more terrible than her master, so miserly and harsh indeed that she was regarded as the terror of the district. The priest was said to lead a chaste life, but he ate a great deal and he drank very copiously, though without intoxicating himself. A peasant's son, and therefore narrow and stubborn in his opinions, he always insisted upon his rights and his dues, never foregoing a single copper of the latter, even when the poorest of his parishioners was in question. Thus he was very anxious to hold Mayor Martineau in his power in order to become the real master of the commune, and thereby increase his own profits as well as assure the triumph of religion. As for his quarrel with Marc, this had arisen over a sum of thirty francs a year which the parish had arranged to pay the schoolmaster for ringing the church bell, and which Marc, for a time, duly received, although he absolutely refused to put his hands to the bell-rope.

Martineau was not easily won over when he found himself supported. Of the same age as the priest, square of face and sturdy of build, ruddy and bright-eyed, he spoke little

and evinced great caution.   He was said to be the wealthiest
cultivator of the commune, and, his extensive property gaining him the favour of his fellow parishioners, he had been
Mayor of Jonville for ten years past.   Scarcely knowing how
to read and write, he did not care to pronounce openly between the Church and the school; he thought it best to
affect neutrality, though he always ended by siding with
one or the other, according whether he felt the priest or the
schoolmaster to be the stronger.   In the depths of his heart
he was inclined to favour the latter, for in his veins coursed
some of that ancient rancour which animates the French
peasant against the priest, whom he regards as an idle man
bent on enjoying life, one indeed who does nothing and yet
requires to be paid, and who captures the wives and daughters of his parishioners in the name of an invisible, jealous
and ever-threatening Deity.   But if Martineau did not follow the Church observances, he had never opposed his *curé*
without assistance, for he held that the black-gowns were
extremely clever, whatever else might be said about them.
Thus it was largely because Marc displayed so much quiet
energy and intelligence that Martineau had joined his side,
allowing him to go forward without pledging himself too
much.
But it occurred to Abbé Cognasse to make use of the
Mayor's wife, the beautiful Martineau, who, although she
was not one of his penitents, attended church very regularly
on Sundays and festivals.   Very dark, with large eyes, a
fresh mouth, and a buxom figure, she was coquettishly inclined, fond of exhibiting a new gown, of airing a lace cap,
of arraying herself in her gold jewellery.   Her assiduity at
Mass was due to that alone.   Church-going had become her
diversion.   There was no other spot whither she could repair in full dress, to show herself, and pass her neighbours
in review.   Indeed, in that village of less than eight hundred souls, for lack of any other meeting place and occasion for ceremony and festival, the damp little nave of the
church, where Mass was so hastily celebrated, became the
drawing-room, the theatre, the one general parade and recreation ground of the women who were desirous of pleasing.
Those who went thither were influenced very little by faith;
their craving was to wear their Sunday finery and to show
themselves.   Their mothers had done it, their daughters
would do it also; it was the general custom.   As for Madame Martineau, on being approached and flattered by

Abbé Cognasse, she endeavoured to convince her husband
that the priest was right in the matter of the thirty francs.
But Martineau sharply bade her hold her tongue and return to her cows, for he belonged to the old school, and did
not allow women to meddle in matters which concerned men.

In itself the story of the thirty francs was very simple. Ever
since there had been a schoolmaster at Jonville he had been
paid that sum annually to ring the church bell. But Marc,
being unwilling to do so, ended by persuading the parish
council to devote the money to another purpose. If the
priest needed a bellringer he could surely pay for one himself.
But the old clock in the church steeple was in a sad condition, constantly losing time, and a former clockmaker, dwelling in the vicinity, was willing to repair it and keep it in
working order for that very sum of thirty francs a year. It
was with some little malice that Marc suggested the acceptance of the offer, while the peasants reflected and sounded
themselves, wondering whether their interests would be
best served by having the bell rung for Mass, or by having
a clock to tell them the correct time. As for ensuring both
services by voting an additional thirty francs, they never
gave that point a moment's thought, for their policy was to
burden the parish with no useless expense whatever. Nevertheless, there was a fine tussle, in which the influence of the
priest and that of the schoolmaster came into collision, the
latter finally remaining victorious, in spite of the maledictions which Abbé Cognasse, in his sermons, heaped on the
impious folk who, by silencing the bell, wished to silence
the call of religion. One fine Sunday morning, however,
after a month's quietude, a succession of furious peals resounded from the church steeple; and people then discovered that the priest's old servant, the terrible Palmyre, was
ringing the bell with all the furious strength of her wiry little
arms.

Abbé Cognasse understood that the Mayor was escaping
him, and, though inwardly aglow with anger, he henceforth
became prudent, displaying all the flexible craft of his cloth.
Then, as Martineau grew conscious of the firmness of the
hands to which he had confided himself, he more and more
frequently consulted Marc, who at last felt that he was
master. As parish clerk the young man ended by discreetly
guiding the council, duly respecting the self-esteem of its
members and remaining in the background, content to inspire those peasants, whose chief desire was for quietude

and prosperity, with intelligence, sense, and healthy determination.   Under the young man's auspices education
spread, casting light upon all things, destroying foolish superstitions, and driving not only mental poverty but also the
poverty of homes away; for wealth comes with knowledge.
Never indeed had Jonville made so much progress; it was
becoming the most prosperous and the happiest parish of
the department.

It must be said that Marc was greatly assisted in his work
by Mademoiselle Mazeline, the mistress of the girls' school,
which a wall alone separated from the boys' school, where
the young man was master.   Short and dark, quite destitute
of beauty, but very charming, with a broad face, a full
kindly mouth, fine black eyes glowing with tenderness and
abnegation beneath a lofty and bossy brow, Mademoiselle
Mazeline was all intelligence, sense, healthy and upright
determination, like one born to educate and emancipate the
little girls confided to her.   She came from that Training
School of Fontenay-aux-Roses which, thanks to the heart
and mind of an illustrious master, has already sent forth a
whole cohort of able pioneers, whose mission it is to form
the wives and mothers of to-morrow.   And if, at six and
twenty years of age, the young woman was already mistress
of a school, it was thanks to her intelligent superiors, Salvan
and Le Barazer, who were giving her a trial in that lonely
village in order to ascertain if she would turn out the good
work which they awaited.   At heart they felt some anxiety
on account of her advanced opinions, fearing that she might
indispose her pupils' parents by her anti-clerical views, her
conviction that woman would only bring happiness to the
world when she was at last delivered from the priests.   But
Mademoiselle Mazeline behaved with great sense and good
humour, and if she did not take her girls to Mass, she
treated them in such a motherly fashion, taught them and
cared for them so affectionately, that the peasants became
deeply attached to her.   Thus she greatly helped Marc in
his work by proving that, although one may not go to Mass,
and although one may set one's belief more particularly in
human work and conscientiousness, one may nevertheless
become the most intelligent, most upright, and kindly
woman in the world.

But Abbé Cognasse, whatever his repulse at Jonville, fully
revenged himself at Le Moreux, a little parish some two
and a half miles distant, which, having no priest of its own,

was dependent upon him. If, however, there were less than two hundred inhabitants at Le Moreux, and if the village was hidden away among the hills, the difficult roads cutting it off from frequent intercourse with the rest of the world, on the other hand it was by no means a wretched spot. Its only poor family was that of its schoolmaster; all the others possessed fertile lands, and lived with hardly a care amid the sleepy quietude of routine. Saleur, the Mayor, a short stout man with a bovine muzzle and little or no neck, had been a grazier, and had suddenly made a fortune by selling his meadow lands, herds, and flocks at a high price to a company, which wished to syndicate all the stock-raising in the department. Since then he had transformed his house into a coquettish villa, and had become a *bourgeois*, sending his son Honoré to the Beaumont Lycée before letting him go as a student to Paris. Although the people of Moreux were jealous of Saleur, they reappointed him Mayor at each election, for the all-sufficient reason that, having to do nothing for a living, he was well able to attend to the parish affairs. He, however, cast them upon the shoulders of Férou, the schoolmaster, who as parish clerk received an annual salary of one hundred and eighty francs,[1] in return for which he had to perform no little work, keep the registers, draw up reports, write letters, and attend to something or other at almost every moment.

Saleur was dense and heavy, crassly ignorant, scarce able to sign his name, and, though not harsh at bottom, he treated Férou as if the latter were a mere writing machine, regarding him indeed with the quiet contempt of a man who had needed nothing like so much learning to make his fortune and live at his ease. Moreover, the Mayor bore the schoolmaster a grudge for having quarrelled with Abbé Cognasse by refusing to take his pupils to church, and sing as a choirman. It was not that Saleur himself followed the observances of the Church; for it was merely as a supporter of the cause of order that he went to Mass with his wife, a lean, insignificant, red-haired woman, who was neither devout nor coquettish, but who also regarded attendance at church on Sundays as a social duty. Thus Saleur's grudge against Férou arose simply from the circumstance that the schoolmaster's rebellious attitude aggravated the quarrels which were perpetually occurring between the priest of Jonville and the inhabitants of Le Moreux.

[1] About $35.

For instance, the latter complained that the priest treated
them with little or no respect, that they only obtained from
him some scraps of Masses, bestowed on them like alms,
that they were compelled to send their children to Jonville
for the catechism classes and the first Communion, and that
all sorts of difficulties were placed in their way with respect
to weddings, baptisms, and churchings; whereupon the infuriated Abbé retorted that when folk wished to obtain
favours from Heaven their first duty was to provide themselves with a priest of their own.   On weekdays, when it
was invariably closed, the church of Le Moreux looked like
a dismal empty barn; but for half an hour every Sunday
Abbé Cognasse swept down on it like a tempest, feared by
everybody and terrorising the parish with his capriciousness
and his violence.

Marc, who was acquainted with the situation, could not
think of Férou without feeling much compassionate sympathy.   In that well-to-do village of Le Moreux, he, the
schoolmaster, alone was unable to satisfy his hunger.   The
horrible misery which assails so many poor schoolmasters
became in his case most tragically acute.   He had made his
début at Maillebois as an assistant teacher, with a salary of
nine hundred francs,[1] when he was twenty-four years of age.
And now, after six years' work, exiled to Le Moreux on account of his bitter disposition, he still only received a thousand francs a year, or, allowing for the amount deducted for
the pension fund, sixty-five francs a month—that is to say,
fifty-two sous a day.[2]   Yet he had a wife and three little
girls to keep!   Black misery reigned in the damp old hovel
which served as a school, the food was often such as dogs
would have scorned to touch, the girls went about shoeless,
the wife did not possess a decent gown.   And indebtedness
was always increasing, the threatening, deadly indebtedness
in which so many humble servants of the State become engulfed, while those at the head of affairs are often wickedly
paid six times as much as their services deserve.

How great was the courage, the heroism which Férou
needed to try to hide that misery, to remain erect in his
threadbare frock-coat, to hold his rank as a man of letters, a monsieur who by the regulations was forbidden to
carry on any commercial calling whatever.   Morning after
morning the struggle began afresh, night was only reached
by force of energy and will.   That shepherd's son, whose

---

[1] About $175 per annum.   [2] About 50 cents.

keenly intelligent mind had retained great independence, discharged his duties passionately, as often as not without any show of resignation. His wife, a stout and pleasant blonde, formerly assistant to her aunt, who kept a shop at Maillebois, where Férou had met and married her honestly enough, after getting her into trouble, gave him it is true some little help, attending for instance to the girls, teaching them to read and sew, while he had on his hands the ill-bred, dense, and malicious boys. Under all the circumstances was it surprising that he sometimes yielded to the discouragement which comes from ungrateful toil, to the sudden rebellion of his suffering heart? Born poor, he had always suffered from poverty, ill fed and ill clad, and now that he was a monsieur his poverty became the more frightfully bitter. Around him he saw only happy folk, peasants possessed of lands, able to eat their fill, proud of the crown-pieces they had put by. Most of them were brutish, scarcely able to write. They invariably needed his help when a letter had to be drafted. Yet he, the only man of intellect, education, and culture among them, often lacked a franc to buy himself a couple of new collars or to pay for the repair of his old shoes. And the others treated him as a lackey, overwhelmed him with scorn, jeered at his ragged coat, of which, at heart, they were jealous.

But the comparison which they drew between him, the schoolmaster, and Abbé Cognasse, the priest, was particularly unfavourable to Férou. The schoolmaster was so poorly paid and so wretched, he was treated impertinently by his pupils, and disdainfully by their parents; he was destitute, too, of all authority, unsupported by his superiors; whereas the priest, far more liberally remunerated, receiving moreover all sorts of presents in addition to his stipend, was backed up by his bishop and petted by the devout, whilst as for authority he spoke like one who had only to address himself to his Master to bring as he pleased thunder, or rain, or sunshine on the crops. Thus, although Abbé Cognasse was always quarrelling with the folk of Le Moreux, and although they had lost their faith and had almost ceased to follow the observances of religion, he still reigned over them. And thus, on the other hand, schoolmaster Férou, tortured by his life of indigence, gorged with bitterness, turned into a Socialist by sheer force of circumstances, drew bad reports upon himself by expressing subversive views with respect to that social system which condemned him,

the representative of intelligence and knowledge, to starve,
whilst all around him stupidity and ignorance possessed and
enjoyed.

The winter proved very severe that year. Already in
November Jonville and Le Moreux were buried in snow and
ice.   Marc heard that two of Férou's little girls were ill and
that their father was scarcely able to provide them with
broth.   He strove to assist him, but he himself was very
poor, and had to obtain Mademoiselle Mazeline's help in
the good work.   Like Férou indeed, Marc, as schoolmaster,
only received a salary of one thousand francs a year, but
his duties as parish clerk were better remunerated than his
colleague's.   Again, the building in which the Jonville boys'
and girls' schools were lodged—the former village parsonage, restored and enlarged—was more healthy than that of
Le Moreux.   Nevertheless, the young man hitherto had
only made both ends meet by the liberality of Madame Duparque, his wife's grandmother, who sent frocks for Louise,
linen for Geneviève, besides little presents in money at certain seasons of the year.   Since the Simon case, however,
she had given nothing, and Marc was almost relieved, for
the harsh words accompanying each of her presents had
often hurt his feelings.   But how straitened did the home
now become, and what toil, courage, and economy were
needed to live and discharge one's office with dignity!

Marc, who loved his profession, had returned to it with a
kind of dolorous ardour, and nobody, on seeing him at
work, punctually discharging each duty through those first
winter months so hard to the poor, had any suspicion of the
sombre grief, the bitter despair, which he hid so jealously
beneath a brave assumption of tranquillity.   He had remained sorely hurt ever since the condemnation of Simon;
the wound dealt him by that monstrous iniquity would not
heal.   In moments of privacy he lapsed into black reveries,
and Geneviève often heard him exclaim: 'It is frightful!
I thought I knew my country, and I did not know it!'

Yes, how had it been possible for such an infamous thing
to take place in France, the France of the Great Revolution, which Marc had regarded hitherto as the deliverer and
justiciar promised to the world?   He loved his country
dearly for its generosity, for its independent courage, for all
the noble and great work which he thought it was destined
to accomplish.   And now it allowed—nay, actually demanded—the condemnation of an innocent man!   And it

reverted to the old-time imbecility, the barbarity of ancient days! Had it been changed, had it been poisoned to bring about that dementia? Grief and shame haunted him; it was as if he himself had had a share in that crime. And with his eager passion for truth and his craving to impose it upon all, he felt intolerable discomfort when he saw false-hood triumph, and found himself powerless to fight and de-stroy it by shouting aloud the truth which he had sought so zealously. He lived through the affair again, he still sought and sought, without discovering anything more, so great was the tangle created by invisible hands. And after his long hours of teaching, such despair at times came over him in the evening that Geneviève gently cast her arms about him and kissed him tenderly, desirous of giving him a little comfort.

'You will make yourself ill, my poor friend,' she said. 'Don't think of those sad things any more.'

Tears came to his eyes, so deeply was he touched. In his turn, he kissed her tenderly. 'Yes, yes,' he answered, 'you are right, one must be brave. But how can I help it? I cannot prevent myself from thinking, and it is great torment.'

Then smiling, and raising a finger to her lips, she led him to the cot where little Louise was already fast asleep. 'You must only think of our darling; you must say to yourself that we are working for her. She will be happy if we are.'

'Yes, that would be the more sensible course. But, then, is not our happiness to come from the happiness of all?'

Geneviève had evinced much sense and affection through-out the affair. She had been grieved by the demeanour of her grandmother towards her husband, to whom, during the last days spent at Maillebois, even Pélagie, with spiteful affection, had never spoken. Thus, when the young peo-ple had quitted the house on the Place des Capucins, the parting had been a very cold one; and since that time Gen-eviève had contented herself with calling on her relations at long intervals, by way of avoiding a complete rupture. Now that she was back at Jonville she had again ceased to attend Mass, for she did not wish to give Abbé Cognasse any op-portunity to approach her and endeavour to undermine her affection for her husband. Evincing no interest in the quarrel between the Church and the school, she was content to cling to Marc's neck; and, like a woman who has given herself entirely to the loved one, it was in his arms that she sought a refuge, even when heredity and the effects of a Catholic education prevented her from fully approving his actions.   Perhaps in the Simon affair she did not think as he did, but she knew how loyal, generous, and just he was, and she could not blame him for acting according to his conscience.   Nevertheless, like a sensible woman, she occasionally recalled him to prudence.   What would have become of them and their child if he had compromised himself so far as to lose his position?   At the same time, they loved each other so much, they were still so full of passion one for the other, that no quarrel between them had a chance of becoming serious.   The slightest disagreement ended in an embrace, a great quiver, and a rain of ardent kisses.

'Ah, my dear, dear Geneviève, when one has given oneself, one can never take oneself back!'

'Yes, yes, my dear Marc, I am yours; I know how good you are; do with me as you please.'

He allowed her all freedom.   Had she gone to Mass he would not have tried to prevent her.   Whatever might be his own views, he wished to respect her liberty of conscience. And, as christening was a usual thing, he had not thought of opposing the baptism of little Louise.   When at times he felt worried by the divergence of religious views, he asked himself if love did not suffice as a remedy for everything, if one did not always end by agreeing, whatever catastrophe might befall, when every evening there came the closest union, husband and wife having but one heart and one being.

If the Simon affair continued to haunt Marc, it was because he was unable to cease occupying himself with it.   He had vowed that he would never rest until he should discover the real culprit; and he kept his word, influenced more by passion than by strict duty.   On Thursdays, when his afternoons were free, he hastened to Maillebois to call at the Lehmanns' dark and dismal shop in the Rue du Trou.   The condemnation of Simon had fallen on that wretched dwelling like a thunderbolt.   Public execration seemed to cast the convict's family, his friends, and even the few acquaintances who remained faithful to him, out of the pale of humanity.   Lehmann and his wife, who evinced such wretched resignation to their lot, were forsaken by their customers, and would have starved had they not secured some poorly-paid piecework for Parisian clothiers.   But it was particularly Madame Simon, the mournful Rachel, and her little children, Joseph and Sarah, who suffered from the savage hatred assailing their name. It had been impossible for the children to return to school. The town-lads hooted them, pelted them with stones, and one day the little boy came home with his lip badly cut by a missile. As for the mother, who had assumed mourning and whose beauty became the more dazzling in the plain black gown which she always wore, she spent her days in weeping, relying only on some prodigy for salvation. Alone among the inmates of the desolate house, amid the yielding grief of the others, did David remain erect, silent and active, still seeking and still hoping.

He had allotted to himself a superhuman task—that of saving and rehabilitating his brother. He had sworn to him at their last interview that he would dedicate his life to the work of penetrating the frightful mystery, of discovering the real murderer, and of dragging the truth into the broad light of day. Thus he had definitively placed the working of his sand and gravel pits in the hands of a reliable manager, knowing that if he should lack money he would from the outset find his efforts crippled. Personally, he devoted himself entirely to his search for the truth, ever following up the slightest clues, ever deep in the quest for new facts. If it had been possible for his zeal to weaken, the letters from Cayenne, which his sister-in-law at long intervals received from his brother, would have sufficed to inflame his courage. Simon's departure, his embarkation with other unhappy beings, the awful voyage, the arrival yonder amid all the horrors of the penal settlement—those were scorching memories which threw David into indescribable agitation, which returned amid dreadful shudders at each and every hour. And now came letters, doctored and amputated by the officials, yet allowing one to detect beneath each phrase the cry of one who was enduring intolerable torture, the revolt of an innocent man for ever brooding over his pretended crime, and at a loss to understand why it was that he should expiate another's deed. Was not madness at the end of that devouring anguish? Simon alluded gently to the thieves and assassins, his companions; and one could divine that his hatred was directed against the keepers, the torturers, who, uncontrolled, far removed from the civilised world, became like the wild men of primeval caverns, gloating over the sufferings they inflicted upon other men. It was a sphere of mire and blood; and

one evening a pardoned convict recounted such horrible particulars to David, in Marc's presence, that the two friends,
their bleeding hearts wrung by terror and compassion, were
stirred to furious protest and cried their pain aloud.

Unfortunately the ceaseless inquiries, which both David
and Marc prosecuted with discreet stubbornness, yielded no
great result.   They had resolved to keep a watch on the
Brothers' school at Maillebois, and particularly on Brother
Gorgias, whom they still suspected.   But a month after the
trial all three of the assistant Brothers, Isidore, Lazarus,
and Gorgias, disappeared together, being sent to some other
community at the other end of France.   Brother Fulgence,
the director, alone remained at Maillebois, where three new
Ignorantines joined him.   David and Marc could draw no
positive conclusions from this incident, for the Brothers
often went from one establishment to another.   Besides, as
all three assistants had been removed, it was impossible to
tell to which one of them that removal was really due.

So far as Maillebois was concerned the worst result of
Simon's condemnation had been the terrible blow dealt to
the Communal school, from which several families had
withdrawn their children in order to confide them to the
Brothers, who had never previously known such great prosperity.   Nowadays the victorious faces of priests, monks,
and Brothers were met on all sides in the town; and the new
master appointed to succeed Simon, a pale and puny little
fellow named Méchain, seemed scarcely the man to resist
that invading tide.   He was said to be consumptive, and he
certainly suffered a great deal from the severity of the winter, when he left his boys largely in the charge of Mignot,
who, always at a loss when he was not guided, now took the
advice of Mademoiselle Rouzaire.   She was more than ever
on the side of the clerical faction which at present reigned
over the region; and thus she persuaded Mignot to take the
boys to Mass, and even set up a large wooden crucifix in
the class-room.   These things were tolerated in official
spheres, where it was thought, perhaps, that they might
have a good effect on certain families and facilitate the return of children to the Communal school.   But, as a matter of fact, all Maillebois was going over to the Clericals,
and the crisis had become extremely serious.

Marc's desolation increased as he observed the spirit of
ignorance enthroned over the region.   Simon's name had
become a bogie name; one could not mention it without

driving people wild with rage and fear. They regarded it as an accursed name which brought misfortune—a name that summed up all human iniquity. Silence ought to be observed; no allusion, however slight, ought to be made to it, for otherwise one might draw the most dreadful catastrophes upon the country. A few men of sensible upright minds had certainly felt greatly disturbed since the trial, and had even admitted the possibility of the condemned man's innocence; but in presence of the furious wave of public opinion they no longer spoke; they even advised their friends to remain silent. What would be the use of protesting, of endeavouring to secure justice? Why should one expose oneself to utter ruin without rendering any practical help to anybody? At each indication furnished by circumstances Marc felt stupefied at finding everybody crouching in falsehood and error, as in some ever-growing pond of filthy, slimy, poisonous water. On various occasions he happened to meet Bongard the farmer, Doloir the mason, and Savin the clerk, and he quite understood that all three had been minded to withdraw their children from the Communal school and send them to the Brothers', and that if they had abstained from doing so it was only from some dim fear that they might thereby harm themselves with the authorities.

Bongard, who kept very quiet, at a loss whether to side with the priests or the government, ended, however, by relating that the Jews spread the cattle plague through the country, for his two children had seen a man throwing some white powder into a well. Doloir on his side talked of an international Jew syndicate which had been formed to sell France to Germany, and threatened to box the ears of Méchain, the new schoolmaster, if his boys, Auguste and Charles, should learn anything wrong at that Communal school where children were corrupted. Then Savin became more bitter than ever, haunted at times by the idea that if he vegetated it was because he had not joined the Freemasons, and at others covertly regretting that he had not openly become a partisan of the Church. At one moment also he declared the Simon affair to have been a comedy. One culprit had been sacrificed to save all the others and to hide what went on in every school of France, whether it were secular or religious. Thus, to save his children, Hortense, Achille, and Philippe, from perdition, he thought of removing them from school altogether, and allowing them to grow up as nature might direct.

Marc listened to it all, feeling quite upset and at a loss to understand how people of any sense could reach such a degree of aberration. There was something more than innate ignorance in such mentality. It had been created by the continuous working of all the stupid things which were currently said, by the growth of popular prejudices through the ages, by the virus of all the superstitions and legends which destroyed men's reason. And how was purification possible, how could one cure those poor ailing, intoxicated people and endow them with good health, intellectually and morally?

Marc experienced deep emotion one day when he went to buy a schoolbook of the Mesdames Milhomme, the stationers in the Rue Courte. Both of them were in the shop with their sons, Madame Alexander with Sébastien, and Madame Edouard with Victor. Marc was served by the latter lady, who, though she seemed taken aback when he suddenly entered, promptly recovered her assurance and frowned with an expression of harsh and egotistical determination. But Madame Alexandre had risen quivering, and under the pretence of making Sébastien wash his hands, she at once led him away. Marc was deeply stirred by that flight. It was a proof of what he suspected—the great perturbation that had reigned in that home ever since Simon, the innocent man, had been condemned. Would the truth ever come from that little shop then? He knew not, and, feeling more distressed than ever, he withdrew, after allowing Madame Edouard to tell him some extraordinary tales by way of masking her sister-in-law's weakness. An old lady customer of hers, she said, often dreamt of poor little Zéphirin, Simon's victim, who appeared to her, bearing a martyr's palm. And since the Brothers' school had been suspected by the freethinkers it had been granted the visible protection of Heaven, for on three different occasions surrounding buildings had been struck by lightning whereas the school had remained unharmed.

Finally, apropos of some administrative affair, Marc had occasion to call on Darras, the Mayor, who had always been regarded as a Simonist, having openly displayed his sympathy with the prisoner at the time of the trial. But, after all, he was a functionary, and did not his position now compel him to observe complete neutrality? His discretion was increased by some little cowardice, a fear of coming into collision with the majority of the electors and of losing his

position of mayor, of which he was so proud. So, when
Marc's business was settled and the young man ventured to
question him, he raised his arms to the ceiling despairingly.
He could do nothing, he was bound by his position, particularly as the Clericals would certainly secure a majority
in the municipal council at the next elections if the population were irritated any further. That disastrous Simon
affair had given the Church a wonderfully favourable battlefield, where it gained the easiest victories over the poor
ignorant multitude, poisoned with errors and lies. As long
as that blast of dementia should continue blowing, one
could attempt nothing, one must bow the head, and let the
storm sweep on. Darras even exacted from Marc a promise
that he would not repeat what he said to him. Then he
escorted him to the door as a proof of his secret sympathy,
and again implored him to remain silent and motionless until
the advent of better times.

When Marc, as the result of such incidents, felt overcome
with despair and disgust, there was only one spot where he
found any comfort. That was the private room of Salvan,
the Director of the Beaumont Training College. He visited
Salvan frequently during the trying winter months, when his
colleague Férou was starving at Le Moreux and contending
against Abbé Cognasse. He spoke to his friend of the revolting wretchedness of the poor ill-paid schoolmaster, beside the prosperity of the fatly-kept priest. And Salvan
admitted that such wretchedness was the cause of the discredit into which the position of elementary schoolmaster
was fast falling. If students for the Training Colleges were
only recruited with difficulty, it was because the paltry
stipend of fifty-two sous a day, allowed a man when he became a titular head-master at thirty years of age, no longer
tempted anybody. The peasants' sons who were anxious
to escape the plough, and among whom both the Training
Colleges and the Seminaries found most of their pupils, now
preferred to go to the towns in search of fortune, to engage
in commerce there, and even to become mere clerks. It was
only exoneration from military service, obtained by signing
a contract to follow the teaching profession for at least ten
years, that still induced some of them to enter that calling,
in which so little money and so few honours were to be won,
whereas a deal of worry and a deal of scorn were to be expected by all.

Yet the recruiting of the Training Colleges was the great

question, on which the education of the country, its very
strength and salvation, depended.   Co-equal with it in importance was that of the exact training to be given in those
colleges to the schoolmasters of the future.   It was necessary to animate them with the flame of reason and logic, to
warm their hearts with the love of truth and justice.   The
recruiting depended entirely on the grant of higher remuneration to the profession, such reasonable remuneration as
would enable a schoolmaster to lead a life of quiet dignity;
whilst as for the training of the future teachers an entirely
new programme was needed.   As Salvan rightly said, on
the value of the elementary master depended the value of
elementary education, the mentality of the poorer classes,
who formed the immense majority of the community.   And
beyond that matter there was that of the future of France.
Thus the question became one of life or death for the
nation.

Salvan's mission was to prepare masters for the liberating
work which would be entrusted to them.   But hitherto it had
been impossible to create apostles such as were needed, men
who based themselves solely on experimental methods, who
rejected dogmas and mendacious legends, the whole huge
fabric of error by which the humble of the world have been
held in misery and bondage for ages.   The existing masters
were mostly worthy folk, Republicans even, quite capable
of teaching reading, writing, arithmetic, and a little history,
but absolutely incapable of forming citizens and men.   In
the disastrous Simon affair they had been seen passing almost entirely to the side of falsehood, because they lacked
reasoning powers, method, and logic.   They did not know
how truth ought to be loved; it had sufficed them to hear
that the Jews had sold France to Germany, and at once
they had become delirious!   Where then, ah! where was
that sacred battalion of elementary schoolmasters which was
to have taught the whole people of France by the sole light
of certainties scientifically established, in order that it might
be delivered from the darkness of centuries, and rendered
capable, at last, of practising truth, and liberty, and justice?

One morning Marc received a letter in which Salvan
begged him to call at the first opportunity.   On the following Thursday afternoon the young man therefore repaired
to Beaumont, to that Training College which he could never
enter without a feeling of emotion, without memories and
hopes arising in his mind.   The director was awaiting him

in his private room, a door of which opened into a little garden brightened already by the warm April sunshine.

'My dear friend,' said Salvan, 'this is why I sent for you. You are acquainted with the deplorable state of affairs at Maillebois. Méchain, the new master, whose appointment in such grave circumstances was a mistake, is not badly disposed; I even think that he is on our side; but he is weak, and in a few months' time he has allowed himself to be outflanked. Moreover, he is ill, and has applied for a change of appointment, wishing, if possible, to go to the south. What we need at Maillebois is a master of sterling good sense and strong will, one possessed of all the intelligence and energy necessitated by the present situation. And so there have been thoughts of you——'

'Of me!' cried Marc, taken aback by so sudden and unexpected an announcement.

'Yes; you alone are thoroughly acquainted with the district and the frightful crisis to which it is now a prey. Since the condemnation of poor Simon, the elementary school has been, so to say, accursed; it loses pupils every month, while the Brothers' school tends to take its place. Maillebois is now becoming a centre of Clericalism, low superstition, and reactionary stupidity, which will end by devouring everything if we do not resist. The population is already relapsing into the hateful passions, the foolish imaginings of nine hundred years ago, and we need an artisan of the future, a sower of the good crop to restore the Communal school to prosperity. So, as I said before, you were thought of——'

'But is it merely a personal desire that you are expressing, or have you been asked to consult me?' asked Marc, again interrupting.

Salvan smiled: 'Oh! I am a functionary of no great importance; I can hardly hope to see all my personal desires accomplished. The truth is that I have been requested to sound you. It is known that I am a friend of yours. Le Barazer, our Academy Inspector, sent for me last Monday, and from our conversation sprang the idea of offering you the Maillebois school.'

Marc could not refrain from shrugging his shoulders.

'Oh! Le Barazer did not behave very bravely in Simon's case, I am aware of it,' Salvan continued. 'He might have done something. But we have to take men as they are. One thing which I can promise you is that if you do not find him exactly on your side, hereafter he will at least prove the hidden prop, the inert substance on which you may lean for support without fear. He always ends by getting the better of Prefect Hennebise, who is so dreadfully afraid of worries; and Forbes, the Rector, good man, is content to reign without governing. The dangerous party is that lay Jesuit Mauraisin, your Elementary Inspector, Father Crabot's friend, with whom Le Barazer thinks it more politic to behave gently. But come, surely the idea of battle does not frighten you!'

Marc remained silent, with downcast eyes, absorbed in anxious thoughts, assailed by doubt and hesitation. Then Salvan, who could read his mind and who, moreover, was acquainted with the drama of his home life, stepped forward and took his hands, saying with great feeling: 'I know what I am asking of you, my friend. I was a great friend of Berthereau, Geneviève's father, a man with a very free, broad mind, but at the same time a sentimental man who ended by accompanying his wife to Mass in order to please her. Later I acted as surrogate-guardian to his daughter, your wife, and I often visited the little house on the Place des Capucins, where Madame Duparque already reigned so despotically over her daughter, Madame Berthereau, and over her grandchild, Geneviève. Perhaps I ought to have warned you more than I did at the time of your marriage, for there is always some danger when a man like you marries a young girl who ever since infancy has been steeped in the most idolatrous of religions. But, so far, I have had no great occasion for self-reproach, for you are happy. Nevertheless, it is quite true that, if you accept the Maillebois appointment, you will find yourself in continual conflict with those ladies. That is what you are thinking of, is it not?'

Marc raised his head. 'Yes, I confess it, I fear for my happiness. As you know, I have no ambition. To be appointed at Maillebois would doubtless be desirable advancement; but I am perfectly content with my position at Jonville, where I am delighted to have succeeded and to have rendered some services to our cause. Yet now you wish me to quit that certainty, and jeopardise my peace elsewhere!'

A pause followed; then Salvan gently asked: 'Do you doubt Geneviève's affection?'

'Oh! no,' cried Marc; and after another pause and some

little embarrassment: 'How could I doubt her, loving as she is, so happy in my arms? . . . But you can have no notion of the life we led with those ladies during the vacation, while I was busy with Simon's case. It became unbearable. I was treated as a stranger there; even the servant would not speak to me. And I felt as if I had been carried thousands of leagues away, to some other planet, with whose inhabitants I had nothing in common. Worst of all, the ladies began to spoil my Geneviève; she was relapsing into the ideas of her convent days, and she herself ended by growing frightened, and felt very happy when we found ourselves once more in our little nest at Jonville.'

He paused, quivering, and then concluded: 'No! no! Leave me where I am. I do my duty there: I carry out a work which I regard as good. It is sufficient for each workman to bring his stone for the edifice.'

Salvan, who had been pacing the room slowly, halted in front of the young man. 'I do not wish you to sacrifice yourself, my friend,' he said; 'I should regret it all my life if your happiness should be compromised, if the bitterness born of conflict should infect your hearth. But you are of the metal out of which heroes are wrought. . . . Do not give me an answer now. Take a week to think the matter over. Come again next Thursday; we will then have another chat, and arrive at a decision.'

Marc returned to Jonville that evening, feeling very worried. Ought he to silence his fears, which he scarcely dared to acknowledge to himself, and engage in a struggle with his wife's relations—a struggle in which all the joy of his life might be annihilated? He had decided at first that he would have a frank explanation with Geneviève; but afterwards his courage failed him, he foresaw only too well that she would simply tell him to act in accordance with his opinions and as his duty directed. Thus, assailed by increasing anguish of mind, discontented with himself, the young man did not speak to his wife of Salvan's offer. Two days went by amid hesitation and doubt; and then he ended by reviewing the situation and weighing the various reasons which might induce him to accept or refuse the Maillebois appointment.

He pictured the little town. There was Darras the Mayor, who, although a good-natured man and one of advanced views, no longer dared to be openly just for fear of losing his official position, and placing his fortune in

jeopardy.   There were also all the Bongards, the Doloirs, the
Savins, the Milhommes, all those folk of average intellect
and morality who had favoured him with such strange dis-
courses, in which cruelty was blended with imbecility;
while behind them came the multitude, a prey to even more
ridiculous fancies and capable of more immediate ferocity.
The superstitions of savages prevailed among the masses,
their mentality was that of a nation of barbarians, adoring
fetiches, setting its glory in massacre and rapine, and displaying neither a shred of tolerance, nor of sense, nor of
kindliness.   But why did they remain steeped—at their
ease, as it were—in all the dense filth of error and falsehood?   Why did they reject logic, even mere reason, with
a kind of instinctive hatred, as if they were terrified by
everything that was pure, simple, and clear ?   And why, in
the Simon case, had they given to the world the extraordinary and deplorable spectacle of a people paralysed in its
sensibility and intelligence, determined neither to see nor to
understand, but bent on enveloping itself in all possible
darkness, in order that it might be unable to see, and free
to clamour for death amid the black night of its superstitions and its prejudices?   Those folk had assuredly been
contaminated, poisoned; day by day newspapers like *Le
Petit Beaumontais* and *La Croix de Beaumont* had poured
forth the hateful beverage which corrupts and brings delirium.   Poor childish minds, hearts deficient in courage,
all the suffering and humble ones, brutified by bondage and
misery, become an easy prey for forgers and liars, for those
who batten upon public credulity.   And ever since the beginning of time every Church and Empire and Monarchy in
the world has only reigned over the multitude by poisoning
it, after robbing and maintaining it in the terror and slavery
of false beliefs.

But if the people had been poisoned so easily it must have
been because it possessed no power of resistance.   Poison,
moral poison, acts particularly on the ignorant, on those
who know nothing, those who are incapable of criticising,
examining, and reasoning.   Thus, beneath all the anguish,
iniquity, and shame, one found ignorance—ignorance, the
first and the only cause of mankind's long Calvary, its slow
and laborious ascent towards the light through all the filth
and the crimes of history.   And assuredly, if nations were
to be freed, one must go to the root of things—that root of
ignorance; for once again it had been demonstrated that an

ignorant people could not practise equity, that truth alone could endow it with the power of dispensing justice.

At that point of his reflections Marc felt very much astonished. How came it that the mentality of the masses was no higher than that of mere savages ? Had not the Republic reigned for thirty years, and had not its founders shown themselves conscious of the necessities of the times by basing the state edifice on scholastic laws, restoring the elementary schools to honour and strength, and decreeing that education thenceforth should be gratuitous, compulsory, and secular ? They must have fancied at that time that the good work was virtually done, that a real democracy, delivered from old-time errors and falsehoods, would at last sprout from the soil of France. But thirty years had elapsed, and any forward step that might be achieved seemed to be cancelled by the slightest public disturbance. The people of to-day relapsed into the brutish degradation, the dementia of the people of yesterday, amidst a sudden return of ancestral darkness. What had happened then? What covert resistance, what subterranean force was it that had thus paralysed the immense efforts which had been attempted to extricate all the humble and suffering ones from their slavery and obscurity ? As Marc put this question to himself he at once saw the enemy arise—the enemy, the creator of ignorance and death, the Roman Catholic Church.

It was that Church which, with the patient tactics of a tenacious worker, had barred the roads, and gradually seized on all those poor dense minds which others had tried to wrest from its domination. She had always fully understood that she must remain the master of the educational system in order that she might create night and falsehood as she listed, if she desired to keep the bodies and souls of the masses in subjection. Thus it was on the battlefield of the schools that she had once again waged hostilities, displaying marvellous suppleness in her hypocritical craft, pretending even to be Republican, and availing herself of the laws of freedom to keep within the prison house of her dogmas and superstitions the millions of children whom those same laws had been devised to liberate. And all those children were young brains won over to error, future soldiers for the religion of spoliation and cruelty which reigned over the hateful society of the era.

The crafty old Pope was seen leading the campaign, that turning movement which was to drive the Revolution from

its own land of France, and, in the name of liberty, filch
and appropriate all its conquests.   The founders of the existing *régime*, the early Republicans, in presence of the
feigned disarming of the Church, had been simple-minded
enough to regard themselves as victors, to lapse into tranquillity, and even to smile upon the priests.   They celebrated a new spirit of concord and pacification, the union
of all beliefs in one sole national and patriotic faith.   As
the Republic was triumphant, why should it not welcome all
its children, even those who, again and again, had tried to
throttle it?   But, thanks to that benevolent grandeur of
views, the Church went on prosecuting her subterranean
march, the Congregations which had been expelled[1] came
back one by one, the everlasting work of invasion and enthralment was pursued without an hour's rest.   Little by
little the colleges of the Jesuits, the Dominicans, and other
Congregations peopled the civil service, the magistrature,
and the army with their pupils and creatures, while the
secular schools were dispossessed by those of the Brothers
and Sisters.   Thus, on suddenly awaking with a great start,
the country had found itself once more in the hands of the
Church, the best posts of its governmental organisation being held by the Church's men, while its future was pledged,
since the children of the masses, the peasants, artisans, and
soldiers of to-morrow were held beneath the rods of the
Ignorantines.

Marc, as it happened, witnessed on the Sunday an extraordinary spectacle which fully confirmed his impressions.
He was still deep in thought, still unable to make up his
mind to accept Salvan's offer.   And having gone to Maillebois that Sunday in order to see David, he afterwards came
upon a remarkable religious ceremony, which *Le Croix de
Beaumont* and *Le Petit Beaumontais* had been announcing
in flamboyant articles for a fortnight past, in such wise that
all the devotees of the region were in a fever of excitement
over it.   The question was one of a superb reliquary, containing a fragment of the skull of St. Antony of Padua, a
perfect treasure, for the purchase of which as much as
ten thousand francs, it was said, had been subscribed by
some of the faithful, who had presented it to the Capuchin Chapel.   For the inauguration of the reliquary at the
feet of the statue of the Saint there was to be a grand

[1] This is not an allusion to the recent expulsions of the religious
Orders, but to those carried out a score of years ago.— *Trans.*

solemnity, which Monseigneur Begerot had consented to
adorn with his presence. It was the Bishop's graciousness
in this respect which impassioned everybody; for none had
forgotten how he had formerly supported Abbé Quandieu,
the parish priest, against the efforts of the Capuchins to gain
all the faithful and all the money of the region to themselves. Besides, he had always been regarded as a thorough
Simonist. Yet he had now consented to bestow on the
Capuchins and their trade a public mark of his sympathy;
and it followed that he must have submitted to very powerful influences, for it was extraordinary that after an interval
of only a few months he should give the lie to all his previous actions, and resign himself to a course which must
have been painful indeed to a man of so much culture and
gentle good sense.

Attracted by curiosity, Marc repaired with the crowd to
the chapel, where during the next two hours he beheld the
strangest things possible. The trade which the Maillebois
Capuchins carried on with their St. Antony of Padua had
become very considerable, amounting to some hundreds of
thousands of francs every year, collected in little sums, vary-
ing from one franc to ten. Father Théodose, the superior,
whose fine apostolic head sent all the lady devotees into raptures, had proved himself to be an inventor and manager of
great genius. He had devised and organised the democratic
miracle, the domestic, every-day miracle such as was within
the reach of the humblest purses. At the outset St. Antony's
statue in the chapel had been a somewhat paltry one, and
the Saint had busied himself with little else than the finding
of lost things, his old-time specialty. But after a few successes of this kind, as money began to flow in, Father Théodose by a stroke of genius extended the sphere of the Saint's
miraculous action, applying it to all the needs and desires
of his steadily increasing customers. The sick who were
afflicted with incurable maladies, those also who merely
suffered from head or stomach ache; the petty shopkeepers
who were in embarrassed circumstances, who lacked the
money to honour their acceptances, or who did not know
how to get rid of damaged goods; the speculators who had
embarked in shady undertakings and who feared the loss of
their fortunes and their liberty; the mothers who were in
despair at finding no husbands for their plain and dowerless
daughters; the poor devils out of work, who were weary of
seeking employment, and who felt that only a prodigy could

enable them to earn their bread; the heirs who were anxious with respect to the sentiments of an ailing grand-
parent, and who desired the help of Heaven to ensure them
a bequest; the idle schoolboys, the hare-brained school girls,
all the dunces who were certain to fail at their examinations if Providence did not come to their assistance: all
the sorry weaklings, destitute of will, incapable of effort,
who, regardless of work and common sense, awaited some
undeserved success from a superior power—all these might
address themselves to St. Antony, confide their case to him,
and secure his all-powerful intercession with the Deity, the
chances of success in their favour being six to four, according to careful statistics which had been prepared!

So everything was organised in a lavish way. The old
statue was replaced by a new one, very much larger and
gilded far more profusely; and collection boxes were set up
on all sides—collection boxes of a new pattern, each having
two compartments, one for money gifts and the other for
letters which were addressed to the Saint, and which specified the nature of the applications. It was of course allowable to give no money; but it was remarked that the Saint
granted only the prayers of those who bestowed at least
some small alms. In the result a tariff was established,
based on experience—so Father Théodose asserted—one
franc and two frances given being for little favours, five
francs and ten francs when one was more ambitiously inclined. Besides, if the applicant did not give enough, the
Saint soon made it known by failing to intervene, and it
then became necessary to double and treble one's alms.
Those customers who desired to delay payment until the
miracle was accomplished ran the risk of never securing a
favour at all. Moreover, the Saint retained all freedom of
action, choosing the elect as he pleased, and rendering accounts to none. Thus the whole affair was a gamble, a kind
of divine lottery, in which one might draw a good or a bad
number ; and it was this very circumstance which impassioned the masses among whom the gambling instinct is so
keen. They rushed upon the collection boxes and gave
their franc, their two francs, or their five francs, all aflame
with the hope that they would perhaps secure a big prize,
some illicit and unhoped-for gain, some fine marriage, some
diploma, some huge bequest. Never had there been a more
impudent attempt to brutify the public, a more shameless
speculation on human stupidity and the instincts of idleness

and covetousness, one which destroyed all self-reliance and spread broadcast the idea of achieving success by chance alone without the slightest show of merit.[1]

Marc understood by the feverish enthusiasm of the groups around him that the business would spread still further and contaminate the whole region, thanks to that chiselled, gilded, silver reliquary, in which a fragment of St. Antony's skull was enshrined. This was Father Théodose's last device in response to the competition which other religious Orders had started at Beaumont, with a great swarming of statues and collection boxes, in order that the public might try their luck with other miracle-working saints. Mistakes would now be impossible, he alone possessed the sacred fragment of bone, and he alone would be able to supply the miracle gamblers with the very best chances of success. Posters covered the walls of the chapel, a new prospectus guaranteed the absolute authenticity of the relic, set forth that the tariffs would not be increased in spite of the new advantages offered, and carefully regulated operations in order that no recrimination might ensue between the Saint and his customers. The first thing, however, which struck Marc painfully was the presence of Mademoiselle Rouzaire, who had brought the girls of the Communal school to the ceremony as if their attendance were a part of the curriculum. And he was stupefied when at the head of the girls he saw the tallest of them carrying a religious banner of white silk embroidered with gold. But Mademoiselle Rouzaire made no secret of her sentiments. Whenever one of her pupils competed for a certificate she sent her not only to take Communion, but to place two francs in one of St. Antony's collection boxes, in order that the Deity might facilitate her examination. When the pupil was more stupid than usual she even advised her to put five francs into the box, as the Saint would assuredly have extra trouble in her case. She also made her pupils keep diaries in which they had to record their sins day by day, and distributed good

[1] M. Zola's account of the worship of St. Antony is strictly accurate. Can one wonder that the Government of the Republic should have decided to expel from France some of the bandits who, masquerading under the guise of monks, initiated this colossal fraud? The idea of it sprang from their keen jealousy of the wealth of the Assumptionist Fathers whom they found raking in money at Lourdes by the aid of bogus miracles. They carried the miracle craze further by diffusing the worship of St. Antony throughout France, preying on all the credulous with the most astounding impudence.—*Trans.*

marks to them for attendance at Mass. Singular indeed
was the secular Communal school kept by Mademoiselle
Rouzaire!

The little girls ranged themselves on the left side of the
nave, while the little boys of the Brothers' school installed
themselves on the right, in the charge of Brother Fulgence,
who, as usual, made no end of fuss. Father Crabot and
Father Philibin, who had wished to honour the ceremony
with their presence, were already in the choir.   Perhaps
they were further desirous of enjoying their victory over
Monseigneur Bergerot, for everybody knew how the Rector
of Valmarie had helped to glorify the worship of St. Antony
of Padua, in such wise that it was a triumph to have compelled the Bishop to make due amends for his severity of
language respecting 'base superstition.' When Monseigneur
Bergerot entered the chapel, followed by Abbé Quandieu,
Marc felt confused, almost ashamed for them, such dolorous
submission, such enforced relinquishment did he detect beneath their grave pale countenances.

The young man easily guessed what had happened, how
the dementia, the irresistible onrush of the devout, had
ended by sweeping the Bishop and the priest from the positions they had originally taken up. Abbé Quandieu had
long resisted, unwilling as he was to lend himself to what
he regarded as idolatry. But at sight of the scandal occasioned by his demeanour and the solitude growing around
him, he had been seized with anguish, wondering if religion
would not suffer from his uncompromising attitude, and at
last resigning himself to the painful duty of casting the holy
mantle of his ministry over the new and pestilential sore.
One day he had carried the story of his doubts, his struggles,
his defeat to Monseigneur Bergerot, who like him was vanquished, who like him feared some diminution of the power
of the Church if it should confess its follies and its flaws.
And the weeping Bishop had embraced the priest and
promised to attend the ceremony which was to seal the reconciliation with the Capuchins and their allies. Keen suffering must have come to them from their powerlessness,
from their enforced cowardice; and they must have suffered
yet more bitterly at seeing their ideal soiled, their faith
made a mere matter of barter. Ah! that Christianity, so
pure at its advent, a great cause of brotherhood and deliverance, and even that Catholicism which had winged its flight
so boldly and proved itself so powerful an instrument of

civilisation, in what mud would both expire, if they must be thus allowed to sink to the vilest trading, to become the prey of the basest passions, mere things to be bought and sold, instruments for the diffusion of brutishness and falsehood! Worms were gathering in them, as in all old things, and soon would come rottenness, final decomposition, which would leave nought save a little dust and mouldiness behind.

The ceremony proved a triumphal one. A constellation of candles glittered around the reliquary which was blessed and censed. There were orisons and addresses, and canticles chanted amid the mighty strains of the organ. Several ladies were taken ill, one of Mademoiselle Rouzaire's little girls had to be led away, so oppressive became the atmosphere. But the delirium of the congregation reached a climax when Father Théodose, having ascended the pulpit, recited the Saint's miracles: one hundred and twenty-eight lost objects duly found; fifty doubtful commercial transactions brought to a good issue; thirty tradespeople saved from bankruptcy by the sudden sale of old goods stored away in their shops; ninety-three sick people, paralytic, consumptive, affected with cancer or with gout, restored to health; twenty-six young girls married although they were portionless; thirty married women becoming the mothers of boys or girls, according to their choice; three hundred clerks placed in good offices with the salaries they desired; six inheritances acquired suddenly and against all hopes; seventy-seven pupils, girls and boys, successful at their examinations, although their teachers had foretold the contrary; and all sorts of other favours and graces, conversions, illicit unions transformed into lawful ones, unbelievers dying converted, lawsuits gained, unsaleable lands suddenly disposed of, houses let after remaining tenantless for ten years! And ardent covetousness convulsed the throng at each fresh announcement of a miracle, till at last a clamour of satisfied passion greeted the enumeration of each favour, which Father Théodose announced from the pulpit in a thundering voice. It all ended in an attack of veritable dementia, the whole congregation rising and howling, stretching forth convulsive hands as if to catch one or another of those great lottery prizes that rained down from heaven.

Angered and disgusted, Marc was unable to remain there any longer. He had seen Father Crabot await a benevolent smile from Monseigneur Bergerot, then hold with him a friendly conversation, which everybody remarked. Meantime Abbé Quandieu was smiling also, though a twitch of pain lurked round his lips. The sacrifice was consummated. The victory of the Brothers and the monks, the triumph of the Catholicism of idolatry, servitude, and annihilation would prove complete. The young man felt stifled in that atmosphere, so he left the chapel to seek the sunshine and the pure air.

But St. Antony of Padua pursued him even across the square outside. Groups of female devotees were chattering together, even as the women gamblers had chattered in the old days while loitering near the doors of the lottery offices.

'As for me,' said one very fat and doleful woman, 'I never have any luck; I never win at any game. And perhaps that 's why St. Antony does not listen to me. I gave forty sous on three occasions, once for my goat which was ailing, but all the same it died; the next time for a ring I lost, and which I never found; and then, the third time, for some potatoes which were rotting, but it was no good, I could n't find a buyer for them. Ah! I am really unlucky and no mistake!'

'You are too patient, my dear,' a little dark wizened old woman answered. 'As for me, when St. Antony won't lend ear, I make him listen.'

'But how, my dear?'

'Oh! I punish him. For instance, there was that little house of mine which I could n't let because people complain that it 's too damp and that children get ill and die there. Well, I gave three francs, and then I waited. Nothing, not a sign of a tenant! I gave three francs a second time, and still there was no result. That made me cross and I hustled the statuette of the Saint which stands on the chest of drawers in my bedroom. As he still did nothing for me, I turned his face to the wall to let him reflect. He spent a week like that, but still nothing came of it, for it did not humiliate him sufficiently. I had to think of something else ; I felt quite furious, and I ended by tying him to a cord and lowering him into my well, head downwards. Ah! my dear, he then understood that I was bound to have the last word with him; for he had n't been in the well two hours when some people called and I let them my little house.'

'But you pulled him out of the well?'

'Oh! at once.   I set him on the drawers again, after
wiping him quite clean and apologising to him.   . . .
We are not on bad terms together on account of that affair,
oh! dear no; only, do you see, when one has paid one's
money, one ought to be energetic.'

'All right, my dear, I 'll try.   . . .   I have some worries with the Justice of the Peace, so I will go inside and
give two francs.   And if the Saint does n't help me to win
the suit, I will show him my displeasure.'

'That 's it, my dear!   Tie a stone to his neck, or wrap
him up in some dirty linen.   He does n't like that at all.
It will make him do the right thing.'

Marc could not help smiling in spite of his bitter feelings.   He continued listening, and heard a group of serious
looking men—among whom he recognised Philis, the Municipal Councillor and clerical rival of Mayor Darras—deploring the fact that not a parish of the arrondissement had yet
consecrated itself to the Sacred Heart of Jesus.   That was
another clever invention, more dangerous still than the base
trafficking in St. Antony of Padua.   True, the poorer
classes as yet remained indifferent to it, as it lacked the attraction of a miraculous and a gambling element.   None the
less, there was a grave peril in that idolatrous worship of the
Sacred Heart, a real, red, bleeding heart torn away amid a
last palpitation, and portrayed like the heart of some animal
in a butcher's shop.   The endeavour was to make that gory
picture the emblem of modern France, to print it in purple,
to embroider it in silk and gold on the national flag, so that
the whole country might become a mere dependency of the
Church which invented that repulsive fetich worship.   Here
again one found the same manœuvre, the same attempt to
lay the grip of priestcraft on the nation, to win over the multitude by means of superstition and legend, in the hope of
steeping it once more in ignorance and bondage.   And in
the case of the Sacred Heart, as in that of St. Antony of
Padua, it was particularly the Jesuits who were at work, disorganising the olden Catholicism with their evil power, and
reducing religion to a level with the carnal practices of savage tribes.

Marc hurried away.   He again felt suffocated, he longed
for solitude and space.   Geneviève, desirous of spending an
afternoon with her parents, had accompanied him to Mail-
elbois that Sunday.   Madame Duparque, being attacked by
gout, was confined to her arm-chair, and had been prevented

therefore from attending the ceremony at the chapel.   As
Marc no longer visited his wife's relations, he had agreed
with Geneviève that he would meet her outside the railway
station in time for the four o'clock train.   It was now
scarcely more than three, and so he walked mechanically to
the tree-planted square where the railway station stood, and
sank upon a bench there amid the solitude.   He was still
pondering, still absorbed in a great, decisive, mental battle.

All at once light flashed upon his mind.   The extraordinary spectacle he had just beheld, the things he had seen
and heard, filled him with glowing certainty.   If the nation
were passing through such a frightful crisis; if it were becoming divided into two hostile Frances, ready to devour
one another, it was simply because Rome had carried her
battle into French territory.   France was the last great
Roman Catholic power that remained;[1] she alone still possessed the men and the money, the strength needed to impose Roman Catholicism on the world.   It was logical,
therefore, that her territory should have been chosen for the
supreme battle of Rome, who was so frantically desirous of
recovering her temporal power, as that alone could lead her
to the realisation of her ancient dream of universal domination.   Thus all France had become like those frontier plains,
those fertile ploughlands, vineyards, and orchards where two
armies meet and contend to decide some mighty quarrel.
The crops are ravaged by cavalry charges, the vineyards
and orchards are ripped open by galloping batteries of artillery; shells blow up the villages, grape-shot cuts down the
trees, and changes the plain into a lifeless desert.   And, in
like way, the France of to-day is devastated and ruined by
the warfare which the Church there wages against the Revolution, an exterminating warfare without truce or mercy, for
the Church well understands that, if she does not slay the
Revolution, by which is symbolised the spirit of liberty and
justice, the Revolution will slay her.   Thence comes the
desperate struggle on every field, among every class — a
struggle poisoning every question that arises, fomenting civil
war, transforming the motherland into a field of massacre,

---

[1] Austria, the reader may be reminded, is in great straits, held
together merely by the prestige of its reigning monarch ; Italy is hostile
to the temporal claims of the papacy ; Spain has been killed by its
priests ; Portugal slumbers in insignificance ; even the prosperity of
Belgium has been largely affected by the blighting influence of its
religious Orders.— *Trans.*

where perhaps only ruins will soon remain. And therein lies the mortal danger, a certainty of death if the Church should triumph and cast France once more into the darkness and wretchedness of the past, making of her also one of those fallen nations which expire in the misery and nothingness with which Roman Catholicism has stricken every land where she has reigned.

Reflections, which previously had filled Marc with much perplexity, now came to him afresh, illumined by new light. He pictured the subterranean work of the Church during the last fifty years: the clever manœuvres of the Teaching Orders to win future power by influencing the children; and the policy followed by Leo XIII., his crafty acceptance of the Republic for the sole purpose of worming his way into it and subduing it. But if the France of Voltaire and Diderot, the France of the Revolution and the Three Republics, had become the poor, misled, distracted France of to-day, which almost reverted to the past instead of marching towards the future, it was more particularly because the Jesuits and the other teaching Orders had set their grip on the children, trebling the number of their pupils in thirty years, spreading their powerful establishments over the entire land. And, all at once, impelled thereto by events, and compelled moreover to take up position, the triumphant Church unmasked her work, and defiantly acknowledged that she meant to be the sovereign of the nation.

All the various conquests hitherto achieved arose before the scared eyes of the onlookers: The high positions in the army, the magistrature, the civil and political services were in the hands of men formed by the Church; the once liberal, unbelieving, railing middle class had been won back to the retrograde Church-spirit from the fear of being dispossessed by the rising tide of the masses; the latter themselves were poisoned with gross superstitions, held in crass ignorance and falsehood in order that they might remain the human cattle whom the master fleeces and slaughters. And the Church, no longer hiding her designs, impudently pursued her work of conquest, setting up St. Antony's collection boxes with a great display of puffery on all sides, distributing flags adorned with the gory emblem of the Sacred Heart to the villages, opening congregational schools in competition to every secular one, and even seizing on the latter, where the teachers often became creatures of her own, and did her work either from cowardice or interest.

She, the Roman Catholic Church, was now openly at war with civil society. She raised money expressly to carry on her work of conquest; many of the religious congregations had taken to industry and trade; one alone, that of the Good Pastor, realising some twelve millions of francs profit[1] every year by exploiting the forty-seven thousand work-girls who slaved in its two hundred and seven establishments. And the Church sold all kinds of things: alcoholic liqueurs and shoes, medicines and furniture, miraculous waters and embroidered nightgowns for women of bad character. She turned everything into money, she levied the heaviest tribute on public stupidity and credulity by her spurious miracles and her everlasting exploitation of religion. Her wealth amounted to thousands of millions of francs, her estates were immense, and she disposed of enough ready cash to buy parties, hurl them one upon the other, and triumph amid the blood and ruin of civil war. The struggle appeared terrible and immediate to Marc, who had never previously felt how very necessary it was that France should slay that Church if she did not wish to be slain by her.

All at once the Bongards, the Doloirs, the Savins, the Milhommes seemed to appear before him; he could hear them stammering the paltry excuses that came from cowardly hearts and poisoned minds, seeking refuge in ignorance and fear-fraught egotism. They represented France, the scared, brutified masses, handed over to prejudice and clerical imbecility. To rot the people more quickly anti-Semitism had been invented, that revival of religious hate by which too it was hoped to win over even unbelievers who had deserted the Church. But to hurl the people against the Jews and to exploit its ancestral passions was only a beginning; at the end lay a return to slavery, a plunge into darkness and ancient bondage. And to-morrow there would be Bongards, Doloirs, Savins, and Milhommes of a still lower type, more stupefied, more steeped in darkness and falsehood than those of to-day, if the children should still be left in the hands of the Brothers and the Jesuits, on the forms of the many Congregational schools.

It would not be sufficient to close those schools; it was also necessary to purify the Communal schools, which the stealthy work of the Church had ended by affecting, paralysing secular education, and installing reactionary masters

[1] $2,316,000.

and mistresses among the teachers, who by their lessons and
their examples perpetuated error. For one man like Férou,
so intelligent and brave, even if maddened by misery, for
one woman like Mademoiselle Mazeline, all heart and
reason, how many disturbingly worthless ones there were—
how many, too, who were badly disposed, who went over to
the enemy and did the greatest harm! There were Mademoiselle Rouzaires, who from ambition sided with the
stronger party and carried their interested clericalism to excess; there were Mignots drifting, allowing themselves to be
impelled hither and thither by those around them; there
were Doutrequins, honest old Republicans, who had become
anti-Semites and reactionaries from an error of patriotism;
and behind all these appeared the entire elementary staff
of the country, disturbed, spoilt, losing its way, and liable
to lead the children confided to it, the generations of which
the future would be compounded, to the bottomless pit.
Marc felt a chill at his heart as he thought of it. Never
before had the peril threatening the nation seemed to him
so imminent and so redoubtable.

It was certain that the elementary schools would prove
the battle-ground of the social contest; for the one real
question was to decide what education should be given to
those masses which, little by little, would assuredly dispossess the middle class of its usurped power. Victorious over
the expiring nobility in 1789, the *bourgeoisie* had replaced
it, and for a whole century it had kept possession of the entire spoils, refusing to the masses their equitable share. At
present the *rôle* of the *bourgeoisie* was finished; it acknowledged it, by going over to reaction, desperate as it felt at
the idea of having to part with power, terrified by the rise
of the democracy which was certain to dispossess it. Voltairean when it had thought itself in full and peaceful enjoyment of its conquests, clerical now that in its anxious
need it found it had to summon reaction to its help, it was
worn out, rotted by abuse of power, and the ever advancing
social forces would eliminate it from the system. The energy of to-morrow would be found in the masses, in them
slumbered humanity's huge reserve force of intelligence and
will. Marc's only hope now was in those children of the
people who frequented the elementary schools from one to
the other end of France. They constituted the raw material out of which the future nation would be fashioned,
and it was necessary to educate them in such wise that they

might discharge their duty as freed citizens, possessed of knowledge and will power, released from all the absurd dogmas, errors, and superstitions which destroy human liberty and dignity.

No happiness was possible, whether moral or material, save in the possession of knowledge. The view inspired by the Gospel dictum, 'Happy the poor in spirit,'[1] had held mankind in a quagmire of wretchedness and bondage for ages. No, no! The poor in spirit are perforce mere cattle, fit flesh for slavery and for suffering. As long as there shall be a multitude of the poor in spirit, so will there be a multitude of wretched beings, mere beasts of burden, exploited, preyed upon by an infinitesimal minority of thieves and bandits. The happy people will one day be that which is possessed of knowledge and will. It is from the black pessimism based on sundry passages of the Bible that the world must be delivered—the world, terrified, crushed down for more than two thousand years, living solely for the sake of death. Nothing could be more dangerous than to take the old Semite doctrine as the only moral and social code. Happy, on the contrary, are those who know—happy the intelligent, the men of will and action, for the kingdom of the world shall belong to them! That was the cry which now arose to Marc's lips, from his whole being, in a great transport of faith and enthusiasm.

And all at once he arrived at a decision: he would accept Salvan's offer, he would come to Maillebois as elementary master, and he would contend against the Church, against that contamination of the people, of which he had witnessed one of the delirious fits at the ridiculous ceremony held that afternoon. He would work for the liberation of the humble, he would strive to make them free citizens. To win back those masses whom he saw weighed down by ignorance and falsehood, incapable of justice, he would go to the children and to the children's children, instruct them, and, little by little, create a people of truth who, then alone, would become a people of justice. That was the loftiest duty, the most pressing good work, that on which depended the

---

[1] This is how the French render the well-known words of the Sermon on the Mount, as given in Matthew v. 2. It will be remembered that in Luke vi. 20, only the word 'poor' is given, 'in spirit' being omitted. I must confess that I do not know what the 'higher criticism' has to say of this inconsistency, and I am not learned enough to express an opinion of any value on the Greek texts.—*Trans.*

country's very salvation, its strength and glory in its liberating and justice-bringing mission through the ages and through the other nations. And if, after three days' hesitation and anguish at the idea of imperilling the happiness he enjoyed in Geneviève's arms, a moment had sufficed for Marc to arrive at that weighty decision, was it not that he had also found himself confronted by the serious problem of the position of woman, whom the Church had turned into a mere stupefied serf, an instrument of falsity and destruction?

What would they become as wives and mothers, those little girls whom Mademoiselle Rouzaire now led to the Capuchins ? When the Church had seized them and held them by their senses, their weakness, and their sufferings, it would never release them; it would employ them as terrible engines of warfare, to demolish men and pervert children. So long as woman, in her ancient contest with man, with respect to unjust laws and iniquitous moral customs, should thus remain the property and the weapon of the Church, social happiness would remain impossible, war would be perpetuated between the disunited sexes. And woman would only at last be a free creature, a free companion for man, disposing of herself and of her happiness for the happiness of her husband and her child, on the day when she should cease to belong to the priest, her present master—he who disorganised and corrupted her.

With respect to Marc himself, was it not an unacknowledged fear, the dread of some drama, which might ravage his own household, that had made him tremble and recoil from the prospect of doing his duty ? The sudden decision he had taken might mean a struggle at his own hearth, the necessity of doing his duty to those of his own home, even though his heart might bleed cruelly the while. He knew that now; thus there was some heroism in the course he chose with all simplicity, with all enthusiasm for the good work which he hoped to prosecute. The highest *rôle* and the noblest in a nascent democracy is that of the poor and scorned elementary schoolmaster, appointed to teach the humble, to train them to be happy citizens, the builders of the future City of Justice and Peace. Marc felt it was so, and he suddenly realised the exact sense of his mission, his apostleship of Truth, that fervent passion to acquire Truth, certain and positive, then cry it aloud and teach it to all, which had ever possessed him.

Raising his eyes to the railway station, the young man

suddenly perceived that it was past four o'clock.   The train
which he and his wife were to have taken had gone, and it
would be necessary to wait till six, when the next one
started.   Almost immediately afterwards he saw Geneviève
approaching, looking much distressed, and carrying little
Louise in her arms in order to get over the ground more
rapidly.   'Ah! my friend, you must forgive me, I quite forgot the time,' she exclaimed.   'Grandmother detained me,
and seemed so annoyed by my impatience to join you that
I ended by no longer noticing how time slipped by.'

She had seated herself on the bench beside him, with
Louise on her lap.   He smilingly inclined his head and
kissed the child, who had raised her little hands to pull his
beard.   And he quietly answered: 'Well, we will wait till
six o'clock, my dear.   There is nobody to interfere with us,
we can remain here.   Besides, I have something to tell you.'

But Louise wanted to play, and, stamping on her father's
thighs, she cast her arms about his neck.

'Has she been good?' he asked.

'Oh! she always is at grandmother's; she's afraid of being
scolded.   But now, you see, she wants to have her revenge.'

When the young woman had managed to reseat the child
on her lap again, she inquired of her husband: 'What is it
you want to tell me?'

'Something which I did not previously speak to you
about, as I had not made up my mind.   I am offered the
post of schoolmaster here, at Maillebois, and I am going to
accept it.   What do you think of it?'

She looked at him in amazement, at first unable to reply.
And for a moment in her eyes he plainly detected a gleam
of joyous surprise, followed, however, by increasing anxiety.

'Yes, what do you think of it?' he repeated.

'I think, my friend, that it is advancement, such as you
did not expect so soon—only, the position will not be an
easy one here, amid such exasperated passions — your
opinions, too, being known to everybody.'

'No doubt.   I thought of that, but it would be cowardly
to refuse the fight.'

'But to speak quite plainly, my friend, I very much fear
that if you accept the post it will lead to a complete rupture
with grandmother.   With mother we might still get on.   But,
as you know, grandmother is intractable ; she will imagine
that you have come here to do the work of Antichrist.   It
means certain rupture.'

A pause, full of embarrassment, followed. Then Marc resumed: 'So you advise me to refuse? You also would disapprove of it: you would not be pleased if I came here?'

She again raised her eyes to his, and with an impulse of great sincerity replied: 'Disapprove of what you do? You grieve me, my friend: why do you say that? Act as your conscience bids, do your duty as you understand it. You are the only good judge, and whatever you do will be well done.'

But, though she spoke those words, he could detect that her voice was trembling, as if with fear of some unconfessed peril which she felt to be near at hand. There came a fresh pause, during which her husband took hold of her hands and caressed them lovingly in order to reassure her.

'So you have quite made up your mind?' she asked.

'Yes, quite: I feel that I should be acting wrongly if I acted otherwise.'

'Well, as we still have an hour and a half to wait for our train, I think we ought to return to grandmother's at once, to acquaint her with your decision.   .   .   I want you to behave frankly with her, not as if you were hiding things.'

The young woman was still looking at her husband, and at that moment all that he read in her glance was a great deal of loyalty mingled with a little sadness.

'You are right, my darling,' he answered; 'let us go to grandmother's at once.'

They walked slowly towards the Place des Capucins, delayed somewhat by the little legs of Louise, whom her mother held by the hand. But the close of that fine April day was delightful, and they covered the short distance in a kind of reverie, without exchanging a word. The square had become deserted again, the ladies' house seemed to be wrapped in its wonted somnolence. They found Madame Duparque seated in the little drawing-room, resting her ailing leg on a chair, while she knitted stockings for some charity. Madame Berthereau was embroidering near the window.

Greatly astonished by Geneviève's return, and particularly by the presence of Marc, the grandmother dropped her knitting, and, without even telling them to sit down, waited for them to speak. When Marc had acquainted her with the position, the offer made to him, his decision to accept it, and his desire to inform her of it in a deferential way, she gave a sudden start, then shrugged her shoulders.

'But it is madness, my boy,' said she ; 'you won't keep the appointment a month.'

'Why not?'

'Why? Because you are not the schoolmaster we require. You are well aware of the good spirit of the district, where religion is securing such splendid triumphs. And with your revolutionary ideas your position would be untenable, you would soon be at war with the whole population.'

'Well, I should be at war. Unfortunately one has to fight in order to be victorious.'

Thereupon the old lady became angry: 'Don't speak foolishly!' she exclaimed. 'There seems to be no end to your pride and rebellion against religion! But you are only a grain of sand, my poor boy, and I really pity you when I see you imagining yourself strong enough to conquer in a battle in which both Heaven and man will annihilate you!'

'It is not I who am strong, it is reason, it is truth.'

'Yes, I know. . . . But it is of no consequence! Just listen to me! I will not have you here as schoolmaster. I am anxious for my tranquillity and honourability. It would be too much grief and shame for me to see our Geneviève here, in Maillebois, as the wife of a man denying both God and country, and scandalising all pious souls by his actions. It is madness, I tell you! You will immediately refuse.'

Madame Berthereau, sorely grieved by this sudden dispute, lowered her head over her embroidery in order that she might not have to intervene. Geneviève remained erect, but had become very pale, while little Louise, whose hand she still held, felt so frightened that she hid her face in the folds of her mother's skirt. But Marc was determined to remain calm, and without even raising his voice he answered:

'No, I cannot refuse. I have come to a decision, and I merely desired to inform you of it.'

At this Madame Duparque, although she was scarcely able to move, by reason of her attack of gout, lost all self-control. As a rule nobody dared to resist her, and she was exasperated at now finding herself confronted by such quiet determination. A wave of terrible anger rose within her, and words she would rather have left unspoken rushed from her lips: 'Come! say everything,' she cried; 'confess it, you are only coming here in order that you may busy yourself on the spot with that abominable Simon case! Yes! you are on the side of those ignoble Jews; you still think of stirring

up all that filth, and pouncing upon some innocent to send
him yonder, in the place of the vile assassin who was so
justly condemned! And that innocent, you are still stubbornly seeking him among the worthiest of God's servants!
Is that not so? Confess it! Why don't you confess it?'

Marc could not help smiling; for he fully understood that
the real cause of all the anger with which he was assailed
was indeed the Simon case, the dread lest he should take
it in hand again, and at last discover the real culprit. He
could divine that behind Madame Duparque there stood her
confessor, Father Crabot, and that the Jesuits and their
allies, in order to prevent him from carrying on a campaign
at Maillebois, were determined to tolerate there no schoolmaster who was not virtually in their hands.

'Why, certainly,' he answered in his quiet way, 'I am
still convinced of my comrade Simon's innocence, and I
shall do everything I can to demonstrate it.'

Madame Duparque in her rage jerked herself first towards
Madame Berthereau and then towards Geneviève. 'You
hear him, and you say nothing! Our name will be brought
into that campaign of ignominy. Our daughter will be seen
in the camp of the enemies of society and religion! . . .
Come, come, you who are her mother ought to tell her that
such a thing is out of question, that she must prevent such
infamy for the honour of herself and that of all of us.'

The old lady's last words were addressed to Madame
Berthereau, who, utterly scared by the quarrel, had now let
her embroidery fall from her hands. For a moment she
remained silent, for it cost her an effort to emerge from the
gloomy self-effacement in which she usually lived. At last,
making up her mind, she said: 'Your grandmother is right,
my girl. Your duty requires that you should not tolerate
actions in which you would have your share of responsibility
before God. Your husband will listen to you if he loves
you. Indeed, you are the only one who can speak to his
heart. Your father never went against my desires in matters of conscience.'

Geneviève turned towards Marc, at the same time pressing
little Louise to her side. She was stirred to the depths of
her being: all her girlhood at the Convent of the Visitation,
all her pious training and education, seemed to revive,
filling her with vertigo. And yet she repeated what she had
already said to her husband: 'Marc is the only good judge;
he will do what he deems to be his duty.'

Despite her ailing leg, Madame Duparque had managed to struggle to her feet. 'Is that your answer?' she cried wrathfully. 'You, whom we brought up in a Christian manner—you who were well beloved by God—you already deny Him, and live religionless, like some beast of the fields? And you choose Satan without making even an effort to overcome him? Ah, well, your husband is only the more guilty, and he shall be punished for that also; you will be punished both of you, and God's curse shall extend even to your child!'

She stretched forth her arms, and stood there in such a threatening posture that little Louise, who was terror-stricken, began to sob. Marc quickly caught up the child and pressed her to his heart, while she, as if eager for his protection, flung her arms around his neck. And Geneviève likewise drew near and leant against the shoulder of the man to whom she had given her life.

'Be gone! be gone! all three of you!' cried Madame Duparque. 'Go to your folly and your pride, they will work your ruin! You hear me, Geneviève: there shall be no more intercourse between us until you come back here in all humility. For you will come back some day; you belonged to God too long for it to be otherwise; besides, I shall pray to Him so well that He will know how to win you back entirely. . . . But now be gone, be gone, I will have nothing more to do with you!'

Torn by anguish, her eyes full of tears, Geneviève looked at her distracted mother, who was weeping silently. So heartrending was the scene that the young woman again seemed to hesitate; but Marc gently took her hand and led her away. Madame Duparque had already sunk into her arm-chair, and the little house relapsed into its frigid gloom and dismal silence.

On the following Thursday Marc repaired to Beaumont to inform Salvan that he accepted his offer. And early in May he received the appointment, quitted Jonville, and installed himself at Maillebois as head-master of the Boys' Elementary School.

BOOK II

I

ONE sunny morning in May Marc, for the first time, took his class at Maillebois. On the side facing the square, the large schoolroom had three lofty windows, through whose panes of ground glass streamed a gay, white, and vivid light. In front of the master's desk, which stood on a small platform reached by three steps, the boys' little double desks were set out, four in each of the eight rows.

Loud laughter, in fact quite an uproar, burst forth when one of the lads, on proceeding to his seat, stumbled and fell intentionally.

'Now, boys,' Marc quietly said, 'you must behave yourselves. I am not going to punish you, but you will find it more beneficial and pleasant to behave yourselves with me. . . . Monsieur Mignot, please call the register.'

Marc had wished to have Mignot's assistance on this first occasion, and the other's demeanour plainly indicated his hostility and the surprise he felt at having as his principal a man who had compromised himself so greatly in the recent scandals. Mignot had even joined in the boys' laughter when one of them had stumbled and fallen by way of amusing the others. However, the calling of the register began.

'Auguste Doloir!'

'Present!' exclaimed a merry-looking lad in so gruff a voice that the whole class again exploded.

Auguste was the mason's elder son, and it was he who had stumbled a few minutes previously. Nine years of age, he looked vigorous and intelligent, but he was wrong-headed, and his pranks often revolutionised the school.

'Charles Doloir!' called Mignot.

'Present!' And this time Auguste's brother, two years his junior, answered in so shrill a voice that the storm of laughter began afresh. Though Charles was of a more refined and gentle nature than Auguste, he invariably seconded him.

But Marc let the matter pass. He wished to be patient and to inflict no punishments that first day. While the calling of the register proceeded he glanced round the large room where he would have to deal with all those turbulent lads. At Jonville there had been no such lavish provision of blackboards—one behind his desk for himself, and two others, right and left, for the boys—nor such a display of coloured prints representing weights and measures, the mineral, vegetable, and animal kingdoms, useful and harmful insects, mushrooms and toadstools, without counting the large and numerous maps. There, too, in a cabinet was a collection of the 'solid bodies,' as well as various instruments for the teaching of physics and chemistry. But Marc did not find among his new pupils the good understanding and cordiality which had prevailed among those whom he had left at Jonville. The neglect of his weak and ailing predecessor, Méchain, had evidently helped to disorganise the school, which, after numbering nearly sixty pupils, could now muster scarcely forty. Thus its position was sorely compromised, and the hard task of restoring it to prosperity and orderliness lay before him.

'Achille Savin!' Mignot called.

There was no answer, and he therefore repeated the name. Yet both the Savins, the twin sons of the tax-collector's clerk, sat at one of the double desks, with their heads lowered and a sly expression on their faces. Though they were only eight years of age they seemed already proficient in prudent hypocrisy.

'Achille and Philippe Savin!' Mignot repeated, glancing at them.

Thereupon, making up their minds, they answered leisurely but in unison, 'Present!'

Marc, who felt surprised, inquired why they had previously remained silent; but he could obtain no answer from them; they looked at him distrustfully as if they had to defend themselves from him.

'Fernand Bongard!' Mignot continued.

Again nobody answered. Fernand, the peasant farmer's son, a sturdy boy of ten, sat there huddled up, leaning on his elbows, with a stupefied expression on his face. He seemed to be sleeping with his eyes open. But one of his schoolfellows gave him a nudge, and then in a scared way he shouted 'Present!'

This time none of the others dared to laugh, for they

feared Fernand's fists. And, silence continuing, Mignot
was able to call the last name: 'Sébastien Milhomme!'

Marc had already recognised Madame Alexandre's son.
Eight years of age, with a face all gentleness, refinement,
and intelligence, he sat at the first desk on the right hand.
And the young man smiled at the lad, charmed by his can-
did eyes, in which he fancied he could detect the early
sparkle of a young mind, such as he desired to awaken.

'Present!' Sébastien answered in a clear gay voice, which
to Marc seemed like music compared with all the full or
mocking voices of the others.

The calling of the register was finished; and at a sign
from Mignot all the boys now rose for prayers. Since
Simon's departure, Méchain had allowed prayers to be said
at the beginning and the end of each class, yielding, in this
respect, to the stealthy persuasion of Mademoiselle Rouzaire, who, citing her own practice as an example, asserted
that the fear of hell greatly helped to keep her pupils quiet.
Moreover, parents were pleased with the prayer-saying, and
Mauraisin, the Elementary Inspector, regarded it with
favour, although it in no wise figured in the regulations.
That morning, however, Marc swiftly intervened, saying in
his quiet and resolute way: 'Sit down, boys. You are not
here to say prayers. You may say them at home if your
fathers and mothers desire it.'

Mignot, nonplussed, looked at him inquisitively. Ah!
well, he would not exercise much authority at Maillebois if
he began by suppressing prayers! Marc fully understood
the meaning of his assistant's glance, for ever since his arrival in the little town he had been conscious of the general
feeling, the conviction that he was destined to encounter
rapid and complete defeat. Besides, Salvan had warned
him, and had recommended extreme prudence, a course of
skilful tolerance during the first months. If Marc, after
due reflection, ventured to suppress prayers, it was as a first
step, the result of which would enable him to feel his way.
He would have liked to remove the big crucifix which
Méchain, exhausted by the pressure brought to bear on
him, had allowed to be hung over the blackboard behind
the master's desk. But the young man felt that he could
hardly do that immediately; it was necessary that he should
establish himself firmly in his position and know his ground
thoroughly before he engaged in a real battle. Apart from
the crucifix he was also irritated by four glaring chromo-

lithographs which hung from the walls, one of them representing the fable of St. Geneviève delivering Paris, another Joan of Arc listening to the voices from heaven, another St. Louis healing the sick by the touch of his hands, and another Napoleon riding across a battlefield. Miracle and force, religious lie and military violence were ever given as examples, ever sown as seed in the minds of the children who would become the citizens of to-morrow. Marc asked himself if all that ought not to be changed, if education ought not to be begun afresh at the very beginning, with lessons of truth and solidarity, if one was to create free and intelligent men, capable of practising justice.

The first class was duly held, Marc gently yet firmly taking possession of his post among his new pupils, whose curiosity he found tinged with rebellion. The pacific conquest of their minds and hearts which the young master desired to effect proceeded patiently day by day. At the outset he occasionally experienced some secret bitterness, for his mind wandered back to the well-loved pupils, the children of his brain, whom he had left at Jonville, and whom he knew to be now in the hands of one of his former colleagues, Jauffre, with whose spirit of intrigue and thirst for immediate success he was well acquainted. He felt some remorse at the thought that he had abandoned his work yonder to one who would surely destroy it, and his only consolation lay in the circumstance that he had taken up yet more pressing and necessary work at Maillebois. To that work he became more and more passionately attached, devoting himself to it with enthusiastic faith as the days flew by and lesson followed lesson.

On the morrow of the General Elections, which took place during that month of May, quietude fell upon the region. Prior to those elections silence and restraint with respect to Simon's case had been declared imperative, in order that the result of the polling might not prove disastrous for the Republic; and directly those elections were over—the new Chamber of Deputies being composed of virtually the same men as the previous one—silence was again declared to be necessary, lest, by raising inopportune questions, one should retard the realisation of promised reforms. The truth was that after all the battling of the electoral campaign the successful candidates desired to enjoy the dearly-bought fruits of victory in peace. Thus, at Beaumont, neither Lemarrois nor Marcilly, on being re-elected, was willing to mention Simon's name, although each had promised to act as soon as his mandate should be renewed and he should no longer have to fear the blindness of universal suffrage. But at present it was held that Simon had been judged and well judged; in fact the slightest allusion to his affair was deemed contrary to patriotism. Naturally enough the same views prevailed at Maillebois. Darras, the Mayor, even begged Marc, in the interest of the unhappy prisoner and his relatives, to do nothing whatever, but to wait for some wakening of public opinion. Meantime absolute forgetfulness was effected, perfect silence was enjoined, as if there were no Simonists or anti-Simonists left.

Marc had to resign himself to the position, particularly as he was entreated in that sense by the ever humble and anxious Lehmanns, and even by David, who, with all his heroic tenacity, understood the necessity of patience. Yet Simon's brother was now following up a serious clue. Indirectly and without positive proof thereof, he had heard of the illegal communication which President Gragnon had made to the jury in their retiring room prior to the verdict; and if he could only establish the fact that this communication had been really made, the annulment of all the proceedings would necessarily follow. But David was conscious of the difficulties of the times, and prosecuted his inquiries with the greatest secrecy for fear of warning his adversaries. Marc, though of a more feverish spirit, at last consented to follow the same tactics and feign forgetfulness. Thus the Simon affair began to slumber as if it were ended and forgotten, whereas, in reality, it remained the secret sore, the poisoned, incurable wound of which the social body—ever exposed to the danger of some sudden and mortal outburst of delirium—was dying. For, be it remembered, one single act of injustice may suffice for a whole nation to be stricken with dementia and slowly die.

In this position of affairs Marc for a time was able to devote himself entirely to his school duties, and he did so with the conviction that he was contributing to the only work by which iniquity may be destroyed and its renewal prevented—that work which consists in diffusing knowledge and sowing the seeds of truth among the rising generations. Never before had he understood so fully the terrible difficulties of the task. He found himself utterly alone. He felt that his pupils and their parents, his assistant Mignot, and his neighbour Mademoiselle Rouzaire were all against him. And the times were disastrous; the Brothers' school recruited five more pupils from the Communal school during Marc's first month. A blast of unpopularity threatened to sweep the young man away. Parents went to the Ignorantines in order to save their children from the abominations of that new secular master who had suppressed prayers on the very day he had entered upon his functions. Thus Brother Fulgence was quite triumphant. He was again assisted by Brothers Gorgias and Isidore, who had disappeared for a while after Simon's trial, and who now had been recalled, by way of showing, no doubt, that the community deemed itself to be above suspicion. If Brother Lazarus, the third assistant, had not returned to Maillebois with the others, the reason was that he had died during his absence. The others remained the masters of the town, whose streets were always full of cassocks.

For Marc the worst was the mocking contempt with which all those folk seemed to regard him. They did not condescend to make any violent attack on him, they waited for him to commit suicide by some act of stupendous folly. Mignot's demeanour on the first day had become that of the whole district. As Mademoiselle Rouzaire said, it was expected that Marc would render his position untenable in less than two months. The young man detected the hopes of his adversaries by the manner in which Inspector Mauraisin spoke to him on the occasion of his first visit. Mauraisin, knowing that Marc was covered by Salvan and Le Barazer, displayed a kind of ironical indulgence, allowing the young man to follow his own course, but watching stealthily for some serious blunder which would enable him to apply for his removal to another part. He said nothing about the suppression of prayers, he desired something more decisive, an *ensemble* of crushing facts. The Inspector was seen laughing over the matter with Mademoiselle Rouzaire, one of his favourites, and from that moment Marc was surrounded by spies, eager to denounce both his expressions of opinion and his actions.

Every time that Marc called upon Salvan in search of a little comfort, his protector repeated to him: ' Be prudent, my friend. . . . Yesterday Le Barazer received another anonymous letter denouncing you as a poisoner and a henchman of hell. You know that I wish all success to the good work, but I also think that it may be compromised by precipitate action. As a beginning, render yourself necessary, bring back affluence to the school, get yourself liked.'

At this Marc, however bitter his feelings, ended by smiling: 'You are right, I feel it is so,' he answered; 'it is by force of wisdom and affection that one must conquer.'

He, Geneviève, and little Louise were now dwelling in the quarters formerly allotted to Simon. The lodging was larger and more comfortable than that of Jonville. There were two bedrooms and two sitting-rooms, besides a kitchen and dependencies. And the whole was very clean and very bright, full of sunshine, and overlooked a fairly large garden in which vegetables and flowers grew. But the young couple's furniture was scanty; and since their quarrel with Madame Duparque, it was difficult for them to make both ends meet, for Marc's meagre salary was all they had to depend upon. That salary now amounted to twelve hundred francs a year, but it really represented no more than the thousand francs allowed at Jonville, for there Marc had also received payment as parish clerk, which post was not to be thought of at Maillebois. And how were they to manage on a hundred francs a month in that little town where living was more expensive than in the village? How were they to maintain some little appearance of dignity and comfort? How was Marc to wear fairly respectable frock coats, such as usage demanded? It was a grave problem, the solution of which required prodigies of thrift, continuous secret heroism in all the petty details of life. They often ate dry bread in order that they might have clean linen.

But, in Geneviève, Marc found a valuable, an admirable helpmate. She renewed the exploits she had accomplished at Jonville, she managed to provide for all the requirements of the home, without allowing much of its penury to be seen. She had to attend to everything—cooking, washing, and mending—and Louise was ever all smiles and smartness in her light-hued little frocks. If Mignot, according to usage, had taken his meals with his principal, the money paid for his board might have helped Geneviève slightly. But the young bachelor, who had his own quarters on the other side of the landing, preferred to patronise a neighbouring eating-house, perhaps in order to mark his hostility and to avoid compromising himself by any companionship with a man for whom Mademoiselle Rouzaire predicted the worst catastrophes. He, Mignot, with his paltry monthly salary of

seventy-one francs and twenty-five centimes,[1] led the usual
wretched life of a young assistant-master, ill clad and ill
fed, with no other diversion within his reach than that of
fishing on Thursdays and Sundays.   This rendered him all
the more ill-tempered and distrustful, as though indeed it
were Marc's fault if he partook of such sorry messes at
the eating-house.   Yet Geneviève displayed solicitude for
his welfare.   She offered to mend his linen, and one
evening, when he was suffering from a cold, she hastened to
make him some herb-drink.   As she and her husband said,
the young fellow was not bad-hearted, he was badly advised.
Perhaps, by showing him some kindness and equity, they
might at last win him over to better sentiments.

That which Geneviève dared not say, for fear of grieving
Marc, was that the home suffered particularly from the
quarrel with Madame Duparque.   In former days the grandmother had provided Louise with clothes, made presents,
and rendered assistance at difficult times.   Now that the
young people were at Maillebois, only a few doors distant
from the old lady, she might often have helped them.
Under the circumstances it was very embarrassing to live
so near, and to be obliged to turn one's head aside every
time one met her.   On two occasions little Louise, who,
being only three years of age, could not understand the
situation, held out her arms and called when the old lady
passed, in such wise that the fated reconciliation ended by
taking place.   Geneviève, on returning home one day, in
a state of great emotion, related that she had yielded to
circumstances and had embraced her grandmother and
mother on meeting them on the Place des Capucins, where
Louise, in all innocence, had run forward and cast herself
into their arms.

At this confession Marc, in his turn, kissed his wife, saying with a good-natured smile: 'But that is all right, my
darling.   For your sake and Louise's I am well pleased
with the reconciliation.   It was bound to come, and if I am
on bad terms with those ladies you surely don't imagine that
I am such a barbarian as to demand the same of you.'

'No, my friend,' Geneviève replied, 'only it is very embarrassing in a family when the wife visits a place where her
husband cannot go.'

'Why should it be embarrassing?   For the sake of peace

[1] A little less than $14.

it is best that I should not call on your grandmother again, for I cannot possibly agree with her. But there is nothing to prevent you and the little one from visiting her and your mother also, from time to time.'

Geneviève had become grave, her eyes fell, and while she reflected she quivered.

'I should have preferred not to go to grandmother's without you,' she said. 'I feel firmer when we are together. . . . But you are right, I understand that it would be painful for you to accompany me, and, on the other hand, it is difficult for me to break off now.'

Thus the question was settled. At first Geneviève went but once a week to the little house on the Place des Capucins, taking Louise with her, and spending an hour there during the school work of Marc, who contented himself with bowing to the ladies when he met them.

And now, for a period of two years, with infinite patience and good nature, Marc prosecuted the conquest of his pupils amid hostile surroundings and innumerable worries. He was a born teacher, one who knew how to become a child again in order that children might understand him. And, in particular, he strove to be gay; he willingly joined in his pupils' play, behaving as if he were simply a companion, an elder brother. And in the school work his strength lay in his power to cast his science aside, to place himself within the reach of young and imperfectly awakened minds, by finding easy explanatory words suited to each occasion. It was as if he himself were still somewhat ignorant, and participated in the delight of learning. Heavily laden as the curriculum might be, what with reading, writing, grammar, orthography, composition, arithmetic, history, geography, elementary science, singing, gymnastics, notions of agriculture, manual work, morals and civic instruction, he passed nothing by until the lads had understood it. All his first efforts indeed were concentrated on method, in order that nothing taught might be lost, but that everything might be positively and fully assimilated.

Ah! how fervently did Marc devote himself to that sowing and cultivation of truth! He strove to plan things in such wise that truth might impose itself on his pupils by its own power, nourish their expanding minds, and become both their flesh and their brains. And what truth it was! It so happens that every error claims to be truth. Does not even the Roman Catholic Church, though based on

absurd dogmas, pretend that it is the sole truth?   Thus Marc
began by teaching that there is no truth outside the pale of
reason, logic, and particularly experiment.   When the son
of a peasant or a workman is told by his schoolmaster that
the world is round and revolves in space, he accepts the
statement upon trust just as he accepts the statements made
to him by the priest on matters of religion at the Catechism
class.   In order that he may appreciate the difference, experiment must show him the scientific certainty of the former
statement.   All so-called revealed truth is falsehood; experimental truth alone is accurate — one, entire, eternal.
Marc therefore at the outset found it necessary to rebut the
Catholic catechism by the scientific catechism.   He took
the world and mankind as they were explained by science,
and set them forth in their living reality and their march
towards a continual and ever more and more perfect future.
There was no possibility of real amelioration, liberation, and
happiness otherwise than by truth—that is, by knowledge of
the conditions in which mankind exists and progresses.   All
the craving for knowledge as a means for rapid attainment
to health and peace bore within itself its method of free expansion, science ceasing to be a dead letter, and becoming
a source of life, an excitant of temperament and character.

But knowledge was not sufficient—a social bond, a spirit-
ual link of perpetual solidarity was required.   And this
Marc found in Justice.   He had often noticed with what a
flash of rebellion a boy, molested in his rights, would exclaim: ' That is n't fair! '   Indeed, any act of injustice
raises a tempest in the depths of those young minds, and

brings them frightful suffering. This is because the idea
of justice in them is absolute. Mark turned to good use
the candour of equity, the innate need of truth and
justice, that one finds in children when life has not yet
inclined them to mendacious and iniquitous compromises.
By way of Truth towards Justice—such was the road along
which he strove to direct his pupils, as often as possible requiring them to judge themselves when they happened to be
in fault. If they had told a falsehood, he made them admit
the wrong they had done both to their schoolfellows and to
themselves. If they were disorderly and delayed lessons,
he showed them that they were the first to suffer. At times
a culprit spontaneously admitted his offence, thus earning
forgiveness. Emulation in equity ended by animating those
young people; they learnt to rival one another in frankness.
At times, of course, there was trouble, conflict, catastrophe,
for all this was only a beginning, and several generations of
schoolboys would be needed for schools to become the real
abodes of healthy and happy life. Marc, however, rejoiced
over the slightest results that he obtained, convinced as he
was that if knowledge were primarily essential for all progress, nothing definitive with respect to the happiness of
mankind could be achieved without the assistance of the
spirit of justice. Why did the *bourgeois* class, which was
the best educated, become rotten so soon? Was it not by
reason of its iniquities, its denial of justice, its refusal to
restore what it had stolen, to give to the humble and the
suffering their legitimate share of the world's good things?
Some folk, in condemning education, cited the ignominious
downfall of the *bourgeoisie* as an example, and accused
science of producing a multitude of casteless individuals,
thereby increasing the sum of evil and tribulation. And
yes, so long as the passion for knowledge merely for its own
sake should become keener and keener in a social system
which was all falsehood and injustice, it would only add to
existing ruins. It was necessary that science should tend
towards justice, and bring to the future city of fraternity a
moral system of liberty and peace.

Even to be just did not suffice; Marc also required
kindliness and affection of his pupils. Nothing could
germinate, nothing could flower, unless it were by love
and for it. In the universal flame of desire and union
one found the focus of the world. Within each human
being was implanted an imperious need to mingle with

all others; and personal action, liberty, and individuality
were like the play of different organs, all dependent on
the universal Being.   If each individual man, even when
isolated, represented so much will and power, his actions,
at all events, only began to count when they exercised
an influence on the community.   To love, to make oneself loved, to make all others love: the teacher's *rôle*
was found entire in those three propositions, those three
degrees of human instruction.   To love—Marc loved his
pupils with his whole heart, giving himself to them unre-
servedly, knowing full well that one must indeed love if one
would teach, for only love has the power of touching and
convincing.   To make oneself loved—that was a task to
which he devoted every hour, fraternising with his boys,
never seeking to make them fear him, but, on the contrary,
striving to win them over by persuasion, affection, the good-
fellowship of an elder brother still growing up among his
juniors.   To make all others love—that again was his constant thought; he was ever recalling the true saying that the
happiness of each is compounded of the happiness of all;
and he brought forward the daily example of the progress
and pleasure of each boy when the whole class had worked
well.

Schooling, no doubt, should have as its objects the culture
of energy, the liberation and exaltation of each individuality;
a child must judge and act by himself alone in order that
as a man he may yield the sum-total of his personal value.
But, as Marc put it, would not the crop resulting from such
intensive culture increase the common harvest of all?   Could
a man create true glory for himself without contributing in
one or another form to the happiness of others?   Education
necessarily tended to solidarity, to the universal attraction
which was gradually blending mankind into one family.
And Marc's mind and heart were set on sympathy and
affection, on a joyous, brotherly school, full of sunshine,
song, and laughter, where happiness was taught, where the
pupils learnt to live the life of science, truth, and justice,
which would come in all its fulness when the way for it
should have been sufficiently prepared by generations of
children taught as they ought to be.

From the very outset Marc combated the system by
which violence, terror, and folly were inculcated in so many
children.   The right of the stronger, massacre, carnage,
the devastation and razing of cities—all those things were

set before the young, glorified in books, pictures, and constant, almost hourly, lessons. Great was the display of the
bloody pages of history, the wars, the conquests, the names
of the captains who had butchered their fellow-beings.
The minds of children were enfevered by the crash of arms,
by nightmares of slaughter steeping the plains in blood. In
the prize books given to them, in the little papers published
for their perusal, on the very covers of their copy-books,
their eyes encountered the savagery of armies, the burning
of fleets, the everlasting calamity of man sinking to the
level of a wolf. And when a battle was not depicted there
came a miracle, some absurd legend, some source of darkness: a saint delivering a country by his or her prayers, an
intervention of Jesus or Mary ensuring the ownership of the
world to the wealthy, a Churchman solving political and
social difficulties by a mere sign of the Cross. The humble
were invariably warned that they must show obedience and
resignation. To impress it on their minds in childhood's
hour, stormy skies were shown them, illumined by the lightning of an irritated and cruel Deity. Terror reigned, terror
of that Deity, terror too of the devil, a base and hideous
terror, which seized on man in his infancy and kept him
cowering until he reached the grave after a life which was
all dense night, ignorance, and falsehood. In that manner
one fashioned only slaves, flesh fit to serve the master's
capricious purposes. And indeed that education of blind
faith and perpetual extermination was based on the necessity
of ever having soldiers ready to defend the established and
iniquitous order of things.

Yet what an antiquated idea it was to cultivate human
energy by lessons of warfare! It corresponded with the
times when the sword alone decided questions between
nation and nation, and between kings and their subjects.
But nowadays, if nations still guard themselves—as they do,
in formidable fashion, full of anxious dread lest everything
should collapse—who will dare to say that victory will rest
with the warlike nations? Who, on the contrary, cannot see
that the triumphant nation of to-morrow will be that which
defeats the others on the economic field, by reorganising
the conditions of human toil, and by bringing more justice
and happiness to mankind?

To Marc it seemed that the only worthy *rôle* for France
was that of completing the Revolution and becoming the
great emancipator. The narrow doctrine that one's sole

purpose should be to make soldiers of Frenchmen filled him
with grief and anger. On the morrow of the disasters of
1870 such a programme may have had its excuse; and yet
all the unrest of years and years, the whole abominable
crisis of the present times has proceeded from that programme, from having placed one's supreme hope in the
army, from having abandoned the democracy to military
leaders. If it be still necessary to guard oneself, surrounded
as one is by neighbours in arms, it is yet more necessary to
become workers, free and just citizens, such as those to
whom to-morrow will belong. On the day when France
knows it and wills it, on the day when she becomes a nation
freed from error, the armour-plated empires around her will
crumble beneath the breath of truth and justice emanating
from her lips—a breath which will achieve that which can
never be accomplished by all her armies and her guns.
Nations awaken nations, and on the day when, one by one,
the nations rise, enlightened, instructed by example, the
world will witness the victory of peace, the end of war.
Marc could imagine for his country no more splendid *rôle*
than that of hastening the day when all countries would
mingle in one. Thus he kept a strict watch over his pupils'
books, replacing as far as possible all pictures and descrip-
tions of spurious miracles and bloody battles by others which
dealt with the truths of science and the fruitful labours of
mankind. The one true source of energy lies in work for
happiness' sake.

In the course of the second year some good results were
already manifest. Dividing his school into two classes,
Marc took charge of the first, composed of boys from nine
to thirteen years of age, while Mignot attended to the
second, in which the lads were from six to nine years old.
The young principal also adopted the system of appointing
monitors, whence he derived certain advantages, a saving
of time in some matters, and an increase of emulation among
his boys. Not a moment was lost during school hours, yet
he allowed the lads as much independence as possible,
chatting with them, provoking objections from them, and
imposing nothing on them by dint of authority, desirous as
he was that all feeling of certainty should come from their
own minds. Thus gaiety prevailed, and the lessons in which
those young minds passed from discovery to discovery were
full of attractiveness.

On one matter only did Marc insist, and that was great

cleanliness. Under his guidance the lads took pleasure in
washing their hands at the water taps, and the class-room
windows were opened widely at each interval between lessons, as well as afterwards. Before Marc's time it had been
the practice (a usual one in French elementary schools) for
the boys to sweep the schoolroom floor, whereby they raised
a terrible amount of dust,—a redoubtable means of spreading contagion,—but he taught them to wash the floor with
sponges, a duty which they soon regarded as a pastime.

One sunshiny day in May, two years after Marc's appointment to Maillebois, Inspector Mauraisin paid the school a
surprise visit during the interval between morning lessons.
It was in vain that he had hitherto kept a watch on Marc.
He was disconcerted by the young man's prudence, infuriated by his inability to send in a bad report such as would
have justified removal. That clumsy revolutionary dreamer,
whom nobody had expected to see six months in office, was
becoming a perfect fixture, to the amazement and scandal
of all right-thinking people. By devising that surprise visit,
however, the Inspector hoped to catch him in fault.

As it happened, the boys had just been washing the
class-room floor, and handsome little Mauraisin, sprucely
buttoned up in his frock coat, raised a cry of alarm:
'What! are you flooded?'

When Marc explained that he had replaced sweeping by
washing, for reasons of hygiene, the Inspector shrugged his
shoulders: 'Another novelty!' said he. 'You might at
least have warned the Administration. Besides, all this
water cannot be healthy, it must tend to rheumatism. You
will please content yourself with the broom so long as you
are not authorised to use sponges.'

Then, as the interval between lessons was not quite over,
he began to rummage everywhere, even opening the cupboards to see if their contents were in order. Perhaps he
hoped to find some bad books, some Anarchist pamphlets.
At all events he criticised everything, laid stress on the
slightest sign of negligence, passing censure in a loud voice,
in the very midst of the boys, by way of humiliating Marc
in their presence. At last, the boys having resumed their
seats, the usual questioning began.

Mauraisin's first attack fell upon Mignot because little
Charles Doloir, eight years of age, and therefore in the
second class, was unable to answer a question on a subject
which he had not yet studied.

'So you are behindhand with the programme!' said the
Inspector. 'Why, your pupils ought to have reached that
lesson two months ago.'

Mignot, who, though he stood there in a respectful attitude, was plainly irritated by the other's aggressive tone,
turned towards his principal. It was indeed at the latter
that Mauraisin had really aimed his remark. And so the
young head-master replied: 'Excuse me, Monsieur l'Inspecteur, it was I who thought it right to intervert certain
parts of the programme in order to make some of the lessons clearer. Besides, is it not better to attend less to the
exact order of the lessons as given in the books than to their
spirit, in such wise, however, that all may be taught to the
boys in the course of the year?'

Mauraisin affected great indignation: 'What! you interfere with the programme, monsieur? You, yourself, decide
what to take of it and what to leave out? You substitute
your fancy for the wisdom of your superiors? Well, they
shall know that this class is behindhand.'

Then, his glance falling on the elder Doloir, Auguste,
who was ten years old, he told him to stand up, and began
to question him about the Reign of Terror, asking him
to name the leaders of the period, Robespierre, Danton,
Marat.

'Was Marat handsome, my boy?' he inquired.

Now Auguste Doloir, though Marc had succeeded in obtaining a little better behaviour from him, was still the rebel
and trickster of the school. Either from ignorance or
roguishness, it was hard to say, he now made answer: 'Oh!
very handsome, monsieur.'

His schoolfellows, vastly amused, laughed and wriggled
on their seats.

'No, no, my boy!' exclaimed Mauraisin, 'Marat was
hideous, with every vice and every crime stamped upon his
countenance!' And, turning towards Marc, he added
clumsily enough: 'You do not teach them that Marat was
handsome, I imagine!'

'No, Monsieur l'Inspecteur,' the master answered with a
smile.

Laughter arose once more, and Mignot had to step
between the desks to restore order, while Mauraisin,
clinging to the subject of Marat, began to refer to Charlotte Corday. As luck would have it, he addressed himself to Fernand Bongard, now a tall boy of eleven, whom

he probably imagined to be one of the most advanced pupils.

'Here! you big fellow yonder, can you tell me how Marat died?'

He could not have been more unlucky. It was only with the greatest difficulty that Marc taught Fernand anything. The lad was not merely thick-headed, he did not try to learn, and as for the names and dates of history he was on the worst possible terms with them. He rose with a scared expression in his dilated eyes.

'Come, compose yourself, my boy,' said Mauraisin. 'Did not Marat die under peculiar circumstances?'

Fernand remained silent, with his mouth wide open. But a compassionate schoolfellow behind him whispered: 'In a bath'; whereupon in a very loud voice he answered: 'Marat drowned himself while taking a bath.'

This time the laughter became delirium, and Mauraisin flew into a temper: 'These boys are really stupid!' he exclaimed. 'Marat was killed in his bath by Charlotte Corday, a young girl of high-strung nature, who sacrificed herself in order to save France from a monster thirsting for blood. . . . Are you taught nothing, then, as you cannot answer the simplest questions?'

However, he interrogated the twin brothers Savin, Achille and Philippe, respecting the religious wars, and obtained fairly satisfactory answers from them. They were scarcely popular in the school, for not only were they sly and addicted to falsehoods, but they denounced those of their schoolfellows whom they saw in fault, besides telling their father of everything that occurred. Nevertheless the Inspector, won over by their hypocritical ways, cited them as examples: 'These boys know at least something,' said he. And again addressing himself to Philippe he inquired: 'Now, can you tell me what one ought to do to follow one's religion properly?'

'One ought to go to Mass, monsieur.'

'No doubt, but that is not sufficient; one ought to do everything that religion teaches. You hear, my boy— everything that religion teaches.'

Marc looked at Mauraisin in stupefaction, still he did not intervene, for he guessed that the Inspector in putting that singular question had been prompted by a desire to make him compromise himself by some imprudent remark. Indeed, that was so fully the other's object that he continued aggressively, addressing himself this time to Sébastien Milhomme: 'You, the little boy yonder with the fair hair, tell me what religion teaches?'

Sébastien, who stood erect, with an expression of consternation on his face, made no answer. He was the best pupil of the class, with a quick, intelligent mind, and an affectionate and gentle disposition. His inability to answer the Inspector brought tears to his eyes. As he received no lessons in religion, he did not even understand what he was asked.

'Well, you need not look at me like that, you little stupid!' exclaimed Mauraisin; 'my question is clear enough.'

But Marc was unable to restrain himself any longer. The embarrassment of his best pupil, to whom he was growing extremely attached, proved unbearable to him. So he came to his help: 'Excuse me, Monsieur l'Inspecteur, the teachings of religion are contained in the Church Catechism, and the Catechism is not included in our programme. So how can the lad answer you?'

This answer, no doubt, was what Mauraisin had expected. 'I have no lessons to receive from you, Monsieur le Maître,' he responded, feigning anger once more, 'I know what I am about. There is no properly conducted school in which a child cannot give a general answer to a question about the religion of his country.'

'I repeat, Monsieur l'Inspecteur,' rejoined Marc in a firm voice, in which a little rising anger became apparent, 'I repeat that it is not for me to teach the Catechism. You are mistaken, you are not at the school of the Brothers of the Christian Doctrine, who make the Catechism the basis of all their teaching. You are in a secular Republican school, expressly set apart from all the churches — one where the teaching is based solely on reason and science. If it be necessary, I shall appeal on the subject to my superiors.'

Mauraisin understood that he had gone too far. Each time that he had endeavoured to shake Marc's position he had found his superior, Academy Inspector Le Barazer, tacitly, passively supporting the young man, refusing to take any action against him unless grave and well-proven charges were brought forward. Moreover, Mauraisin knew Le Barazer's opinions respecting the absolute neutrality of the schools in religious matters. And so, without insisting

on the subject, he curtailed his inspection, soon bringing it
to an end, though not without again indulging in criticisms,
for he was determined to find nothing satisfactory. The
boys themselves deemed him ridiculous, and covertly made
merry over the bad temper of that vain little fop whose hair
and beard were so sprucely kept. When he withdrew,
Mignot went so far as to shrug his shoulders, and whisper
to Marc: 'We shall have a bad report, but you were quite
right. That man is becoming altogether too stupid.'

For some time now, Mignot, gained upon by Marc's firm
yet gentle behaviour, had been coming over to his side. It
was not that he as yet shared his opinions in all things, for
he was still anxious respecting his own advancement; but
he had a sound mind at bottom, and was gradually yielding
to the other's good guidance.

'Oh! a bad report!' Marc repeated gaily; 'he won't dare
to venture beyond hypocritical and venomous attacks.
. . . Ah! do you see him going into Mademoiselle
Rouzaire's? He's with his divinity now. The worst is
that his behaviour is not dictated by principle, but merely
by personal policy, a desire to make his way in the world.'

At each inspection Mauraisin lavished very favourable
reports upon Mademoiselle Rouzaire. She, at all events,
took her girls to church, compelled them to recite the Catechism in school hours, and allowed the Inspector to question
them about religion as much as he desired. One of her
pupils, little Hortense Savin, who was being prepared for
her first Communion, quite astonished Mauraisin by her
extensive knowledge of Bible history. And if Angèle Bongard, thick-skulled like her brother, showed less proficiency
in spite of her painfully stubborn efforts to learn, on the
other hand Lucile Doloir, a little lass six years of age, who
had joined the school only recently, gave promise of great
intelligence, and would make, later on, a very charming
'Handmaiden of the Virgin.'

When morning lessons were over, Marc again caught
sight of Mauraisin, whom Mademoiselle Rouzaire was escorting to the threshold of her school. They lingered there
together, chatting in an intimate way and making gestures
suggestive of great distress of mind. They were undoubtedly deploring what went on in the neighbouring boys'
school, which was still in the hands of the disgraceful master
of whom, for two years, they had been vainly trying to rid
the town.

After long expecting the sudden removal of Marc, Maillebois was now growing accustomed to his presence.　At a
sitting of the Municipal Council, Mayor Darras had even
found an opportunity to praise him; and his position had
been strengthened recently by an incident of considerable
significance: the return of two boys who had been previously transferred to the Brothers' school.　This indicated
that parents felt tranquillised, and were disposed to accept
the young man, and it was also a check for the Congregational school, hitherto so prosperous and victorious.　Was
Marc about to succeed, then, in restoring the secular school
to honour, by dint of wisdom and affection, as he had said
to Salvan?　Anxiety must have arisen among the Ignorantines and the monks, the whole clerical faction, for the
young man suddenly found himself attacked in so singular
a fashion that he was quite surprised.　Mauraisin, on calling upon the Mayor and others, had left the Catechism
question on one side, speaking only of Marc's new system
of washing the schoolroom floor, and in this connection
affecting much alarm for the children's health.　A great
controversy arose: ought the floor to be washed or ought it
to be swept?　Before long Maillebois was divided into two
camps, which became quite impassioned and hurled all sorts
of arguments at one another.　The children's parents were
consulted, and Savin, the clerk, denounced the washing
system so bitterly that for a moment it was thought he would
remove his twin boys from the school.　But Marc carried
the question to a higher court, soliciting the opinion of his
superiors, and requesting them to appoint a commission of
medical men and hygienists.　Then came a serious investigation, and victory rested with the washing system.　For
the master this was quite a triumph; the children's parents
became more and more disposed to support him; even
Savin, with whom it was so difficult to deal, had to retract,
and another boy came back from the Brothers' school,
which, people began to say, was horribly dirty.

But, in spite of this dawning sympathy, Marc harboured
no illusions.　He felt that years would be necessary to free
the region from the poison of Clericalism.　Gaining a little
more ground every now and then, he practised the greatest
prudence, well pleased with the result, however slight it
might be.　At the instance of Geneviève, he had carried
his desire for peace so far as to renew his intercourse with
her relations.　This, as it happened, took place in connec-

tion with the famous washing controversy, in which, contrary to custom, the ladies shared his views. So now, from time to time, accompanying his wife and daughter, he again visited the little house on the Place des Capucins. The two old ladies remained ceremonious and carefully avoided all dangerous subjects of conversation. Thus there was no pleasant intimacy. Nevertheless the reconciliation delighted Geneviève, for it freed her from the embarrassment she had felt when calling alone on her grandmother and mother. At present she saw them almost daily, and sometimes left Louise with them, coming and going from one house to the other, Marc evincing no anxiety, but feeling, indeed, well pleased with the gaiety displayed by his wife, on whom the ladies again lavished caresses, services, and little presents.

One Sunday, on going to lunch with a friend at Jonville, Marc—by the force of contrast—suddenly realised how much ground he had already gained at Maillebois. He had never previously understood how decisive a schoolmaster's influence might prove. Whilst Maillebois was slowly reverting to justice, health, and prosperity, he found Jonville relapsing into darkness, poverty, and stagnation. It grieved him to find that little or nothing remained of the good work he had done there in former years. And this was due solely to the deplorable action of the new schoolmaster, Jauffre, who cared for nothing save his own personal success. Short, dark, quick and cunning, with narrow prying eyes, Jauffre owed his success in life to the priest of his native village, who had taken him from his father, a blacksmith, to teach him his first lessons. Later on another priest had enriched him by negotiating his marriage with a butcher's daughter, who was short and dark like himself, and who brought him as dowry an income of two thousand francs a year. Jauffre was convinced, therefore, that if he desired to become a personage he ought to remain on the side of the priests, who some day doubtless would provide him with a splendid position. The income he owed to his wife already rendered him respectable, and his superiors treated him with consideration, for a man who was not dependent on the administration for his living could hardly be hustled about as if he were a mere starveling like Férou. In the school world, as elsewhere, favours go to the rich, never to the poor.

Besides, exaggerated reports were spread respecting

Jauffre's fortune, in such wise that all the peasants took off
their hats to him, he completing his conquest of them by
his greed for gain, his wonderful skill in extracting as much
profit as possible from everybody and everything.   He was
not troubled with any sincere belief; if he were a Republican, a good patriot, and a good Catholic, it was only so far
as his interests required.   Thus, although he called upon
Abbé Cognasse as soon as he was appointed to Jonville, he
did not immediately hand the school over to him, for he
detected the anti-clerical spirit then prevalent in the village.
But he gradually allowed the priest to become all-powerful
by intentional relinquishment of his own privileges, and by
covert resistance to the express desires of the Mayor and the
parish council.   Mayor Martineau, so strong and firm when
he had leant on Marc, became quite lost on having to contend single-handed against the new schoolmaster, who soon
became the real ruler of the parish, and ended by relinquish-
ing his authority to Abbé Cognasse in such wise that, at the
expiration of six months, Jonville was in the priest's hands.

Jauffre's line of conduct interested Marc particularly, because it was a masterpiece of Jesuitry.   He obtained precise
information about it from the schoolmistress, Mademoiselle
Mazeline, on whom he called.   She was sincerely grieved
at being unable to effect anything useful now that she remained alone in a parish where all was rotting.   She told
Marc of the comedy played by Jauffre in the earlier days
when Mayor Martineau complained of one or another en-
croachment on the part of the priest, which the schoolmaster
himself had stealthily provoked.   The latter pretended to
be as indignant as the Mayor, and accused his wife, Madame
Jauffre, who was very devout, of assisting Abbé Cognasse.
As it happened, the husband and the wife were in full agreement, and had devised this plan in order to escape responsibility.   And so Martineau was speedily vanquished,
particularly as his coquettish wife became the great friend
of Madame Jauffre, who, on the strength of her dower,
affected the manners of a born lady.   Before long Jauffre
began to ring the bell for Mass, a duty which Marc had
always refused to discharge.   It brought in only thirty
francs a year, but then, in Jauffre's opinion, thirty francs
were not to be sneezed at.   At Marc's instigation the
money had been devoted for a time to the repair of the old
church clock, and now the latter, being neglected as in
former days, got out of order once more, in such wise that

the peasants never again knew the correct time, for the clock went by fits and starts, being one day too fast and another too slow. As Mademoiselle Mazeline remarked, with a sad smile, that clock was the image of the parish, where nothing was now done in accordance with sense and logic.

The worst was that Abbé Cognasse's triumph extended to Le Moreux, whose Mayor, Saleur, the ex-grazier, impressed by the turn which things were taking at Jonville, and fearing for the fat life which he led, thanks to his new wealth, went back to the Church, however little he might really like the priests. And it was on that wretched rebel schoolmaster, Férou, that the effects of the reconciliation fell. Whenever Abbé Cognasse now came to Le Moreux, he displayed a most insolent sense of victory, and inflicted on the schoolmaster all sorts of humiliations, with which the other had to put up, abandoned as he was by the Mayor and the parish council. Never did a poor man lead a more rageful life. Possessed of a broad, quick mind, but condemned to live among so much ignorance and malice, Férou was impelled to the most extreme views by his ever-increasing misery. His wife, worn out by hard toil, and his three poor, pale, and puny daughters were starving. Yet, although indebtedness was consuming his last resources, he did not submit. Looking more of a scarecrow than ever in his old whitening frock coat, he evinced greater and greater bitterness, not only refusing to take his pupils to Mass, but even growling insults when the priest went by on Sundays. A catastrophe was imminent, dismissal was inevitable, and, to make matters worse, as the unlucky man had served only eight of his ten years as a teacher,[1] he would be seized by the military authorities immediately after his dismissal. What would become of the mournful wife and little girls, when the husband, the father, should be lodged in some barracks?

On leaving Jonville that day, Marc and Mademoiselle Mazeline, who accompanied him as far as the railway station, passed the church at the moment when vespers were ending. Palmyre, Abbé Cognasse's terrible old servant, stood on the threshold, taking stock of those who showed themselves good Christians. Jauffre came out, and two of his pupils saluted him in military fashion, a mark of

---

[1] See page 137, *ante.*

deference which he exacted, and which flattered his patriotic
feelings.   Then appeared Madame Jauffre and Madame
Martineau, Martineau himself, and a stream of peasants of
both sexes.   Marc hastened his steps in order to avoid
recognition and an impulse to express his grief aloud.   He
was struck by the fact that Jonville was less well kept than
formerly; signs of abandonment, of a diminution of prosperity were already apparent.   But then was not that the
law?   Did not intellectual poverty engender material poverty?   Filth and vermin have invaded every country where
Roman Catholicism has triumphed.   Wherever it has passed
it has proved a blast of death, striking the soil with sterility,
casting men into idleness and imbecility, for it is the very
negation of life, and it kills nations like a slow but deadly
poison.

Marc felt relieved when, on the morrow, he once more
found himself in his school at Maillebois among the children
whose minds and hearts he was striving to awaken.   Doubtless his work progressed very slowly, but the result achieved
lent him the strength to persevere.   Unfortunately, the
parents of his boys gave him no help.   His advance would
have been more rapid if the lads had found in their homes
some continuance of the principles inculcated during their
school hours.   But the contrary happened at times.   In
Achille and Philippe Savin, Marc detected the sullen,
jealous bitterness of their father, and he could only endeavour to check their propensity for falsehood, slyness,
and tale-bearing.   Again, though the Doloirs were intelligent enough if they had only been minded to learn, they
showed little real improvement.   Auguste was very inatten-
tive and quarrelsome, and Charles followed in his elder
brother's footsteps.   With Fernand Bongard the difficulty
was different; he was exceptionally obtuse, and it was only
with an incredible amount of trouble that one could make
him understand and remember the slightest thing.   Yet
there was some improvement among the boys in their *ensemble* since Marc had brought them under a regimen of
reason and truth.

Besides, the young man did not hope to change the world
with one generation of schoolboys.   The elementary master's
task requires the greatest patience and abnegation; and
Marc's one desire was to furnish an example by giving his
whole life to the obscure work of preparing the future.   If
others would only perform their duty one might hope that

in three or four generations a new liberating France might be created, such as might emancipate the world. And the young man was ambitious of no immediate reward, no personal success, though to his great delight he did receive a recompense for his efforts in the satisfaction which one of his pupils, little Sébastien Milhomme, gave him. That gentle and remarkably intelligent lad had become passionately attached to truth. Not only was he the first of his class, but he also displayed much sincerity and uprightness, at once boyishly and charmingly uncompromising in character. His schoolfellows often chose him as umpire in a difficulty, and when he had pronounced judgment he would not admit that any should free themselves from the effects of his decision. Marc always felt happy when he saw Sébastien at his desk, with his long and somewhat pensive face crowned by fair and curly hair, and lighted by fine blue eyes, which, fixed on the master with an ardent desire to learn, drank in every lesson. And it was not only Sébastien's rapid progress which won Marc's heart; he was still fonder of the boy on account of all the good and generous qualities which he divined in him. Indeed, Sébastien's was an exquisite little nature which Marc took pleasure in wakening, one of those child-natures in which all the florescence of noble thoughts and noble deeds was beginning to bud.

A painful scene occurred one day towards the close of the afternoon lessons. Fernand Bongard, whom others were fond of teasing on account of his dense stupidity, had discovered that the peak of his cap had been torn off. Forthwith he had burst into tears, declaring that his mother would surely beat him. Marc wished to discover the author of this malicious act, but all the boys laughingly denied their guilt, Auguste Doloir more impudently even than the others, though there was reason to suspect that the misdeed was his work. And, indeed, as it was proposed to keep the whole school in after lessons, until the culprit should confess, Achille Savin betrayed Auguste by pulling the peak of Fernand's cap out of his pocket. This gave Marc an opportunity to denounce falsehood, and he did so with so much warmth that the culprit himself shed tears and asked forgiveness. But Sébastien Milhomme's emotion was extraordinary, and when the others departed he lingered in the empty schoolroom, looking at his master with a desperate expression in his eyes.

' Have you something to say to me, my boy? ' Marc asked him.

' Yes, monsieur,' Sébastien replied.   Yet he became silent, his lips trembling, and his handsome face flushing with confusion.

' Is it very difficult to say, then? ' Marc inquired.

' Yes, monsieur, it 's a falsehood which I told you, and which makes me feel very unhappy.'

The young master smiled, anticipating some peccadillo, some childishly exaggerated scruple of conscience.   ' Well, tell me the truth,' he said, ' it will relieve you.'

Another pause of some length followed.   Signs of a fresh mental battle became apparent in Sébastien's limpid blue eyes and even on his pure lips.   But at last the boy made up his mind and said: ' Well, monsieur, I told you a false-hood a long time ago, when I was quite little and ignorant —I told you a falsehood by saying what was not true, that I had never seen my cousin Victor with that writing copy —you remember, monsieur—the copy which people talked about so much.   He had given it to me as he did not want to keep it himself, for he felt anxious about it as he had taken it from the Brothers'.   And on that very day when I told you I did not remember anything about it, I had hidden it in a copybook of my own.'

Marc listened, thunderstruck.   Once more the whole Si-mon case seemed to arise before him, emerging from its appa-rent slumber.   But he did not wish the lad to see how deeply he was stirred by the unexpected shock, and so he asked him: 'Are you sure that you are not again mistaken ? Did the copy bear the words "*Aimez vous les uns les autres*" ? '

' Yes, monsieur.'

' And there was a paraph down below?   I have taught you what a paraph is, have I not? '

' Yes, monsieur.'

For a moment Marc relapsed into silence.   His heart was beating violently, he feared lest the cry which was rising to his lips might escape him.   Then, wishing to make quite sure, he continued: ' But why did you keep silent till now, my lad?   And what induced you to tell me the truth this evening? '

Sébastien, already relieved, looked his master straight in the face with an expression of charming candour.   His delicate smile returned, and he explained the wakening of his conscience in the simplest way.

'Oh! if I did not tell you the truth sooner, monsieur, it was because I felt no need of doing so. I no longer remembered that I had told you a falsehood, it was so long ago. But one day, here, you explained to us how wrong it was to tell falsehoods, and then I remembered it, and began to feel worried. Afterwards, every time you spoke of the happiness one found in always saying the truth, I felt the more worried because I had not said it to you. . . . And to-day it pained me so I could n't bear it any longer, and I had to tell you.'

Emotion brought tears to Marc's eyes. So his lessons were already flowering in that little mind, and it was he who garnered that first harvest—a harvest of truth—such precious truth, too, which would perhaps enable him to bring about a little justice. Never had he hoped for so prompt and so sweet a reward. The emotion he felt was exquisite. With an impulse of tender affection he stooped and kissed the lad.

'Thank you, my little Sébastien, you have given me great pleasure, and I love you with all my heart.'

Emotion had come upon the boy also. 'Oh! I love you very much, monsieur,' he answered, 'for otherwise I should not have dared to tell you everything.'

Marc resisted his desire to question the boy fully, for he feared lest he might be accused of having abused his authority as master to aggravate the confession. He merely ascertained that Madame Alexandre had taken the copy-slip from her son, who did not know what she had done with it, for she had never again mentioned it to him. For the rest, the young man preferred to see the mother. She alone could produce the slip—if it were still in her possession— and what a precious document it would prove, for would it not constitute the long-sought 'new fact,' which might enable Simon's family to apply for the revision of his iniquitous trial?

On remaining alone, Marc felt full of joy. He wished it were possible for him to hasten to the Lehmanns immediately, to tell them the good news, and impart a little happiness to their sad, mourning home, which was the object of so much popular execration. At last! at last! a sunray had flashed upon the black night of iniquity.

Going upstairs to join his wife, he cried to her as he reached the threshold, such was his excitement, his craving to relieve his heart: 'Geneviève, do you know, I now have

proof of Simon's innocence   .   .   .   Ah! justice is wakening; we shall be able to go forward now!'

He had not noticed the presence, in a shadowy corner,
of Madame Duparque, who, since the reconciliation, condescended to visit her granddaughter occasionally.   She, on
hearing him, gave a start and exclaimed in her harsh voice:
'What?   Simon's innocence!   Do you still persevere in
your folly, then?   A proof indeed!   What proof do you
mean?'

Then, after he had related his conversation with little
Milhomme, the old lady again flew into a temper: 'The
evidence of a child!   That is n't of much value!   He now
pretends that he formerly lied; but what proof is there that
he is not lying now?   .   .   .   So the culprit would be a
Brother, eh?   Oh! speak your mind plainly, acknowledge
it; your only object is to accuse one of the Brothers, is that
not so?   It is always the same rageful impiety with you!'

Somewhat disconcerted at having thus come upon the old
lady, and wishing to spare his wife the grief of any fresh
rupture, Marc contented himself with saying: 'I won't discuss things with you, grandmother.   I merely wished to inform Geneviève of some news which was likely to please
her.'

'But your news does not please her!' cried Madame Duparque.   'Look at her!'

Marc turned towards his wife, who stood there in the
fading light which fell from the window.   And indeed, to
his surprise, he saw that she was grave, that her beautiful
eyes had darkened, as if the night, now slowly approaching,
had filled them with shadows.

'Is it true, Geneviève?' he asked her; 'does a work of
justice no longer please you?'

She did not answer him at once.   She had become pale
and embarrassed, as if tortured by painful hesitation.   And
just as he, likewise feeling very uneasy, was repeating his
question, she was saved the distress of answering him by the
sudden appearance of Madame Alexandre.

Sébastien, on returning home, had bravely told his mother
of his confession respecting the copy-slip.   She had lacked
the strength to scold him for his good action; but full of
fear at the thought that the schoolmaster would call, question her, and demand the document in the presence of her
terrible sister-in-law, Madame Edouard, who was so anxious
for the prosperity of their little stationery business, she had

preferred to go to the school and do what she could to bury
the affair at once.

Yet now she was there her discomfort became great indeed.   Like a gust of wind she had darted out of her shop,
hardly knowing what she would say, and at present she remained stammering, full of embarrassment, particularly as
she perceived Geneviève and Madame Duparque with Marc,
whom she had hoped to see privately, alone.

'Monsieur Froment,' she began, ' Sébastien has just told
me, yes, of that confession he thought fit to make to you.
.   .   .   So I deemed it best to give you the reasons of my
conduct.   You understand—do you not?—all the worry
which such a story would bring us with the difficulties that
already beset us in our business.   Well, the fact is, it 's
true; I did have that paper, but it no longer exists; I destroyed it.'

She breathed again as if relieved, having contrived to
say what she considered necessary in order to be freed from
trouble.

'You destroyed it!' Marc exclaimed with a pang.   'Oh!
Madame Alexandre!'

Some slight embarrassment returned to her and she once
more sought her words: ' I did wrong, perhaps.   .   .   .   But
think of our position!   We are two poor women with nobody to assist us.   And, besides, it was so sad to have our
children mixed up in that abominable affair.   .   .   .   I
could not keep a paper which prevented me from sleeping:
I burnt it   .   .   .'

She was still quivering so perceptibly that Marc looked
at her as she stood there, tall and fair, with the gentle face
of a woman of loving nature.   And it seemed to him that
she was experiencing some secret torment.   For a moment
he felt suspicious—wondered if she were lying—and it occurred to him to test her sincerity.

'By destroying that paper, Madame Alexandre,' he said,
'you condemned an innocent man a second time.   .   .   .
Think of all that he is suffering yonder.   You would weep
if I read his letters to you.   There can be no worse torture
than his—the deadly climate, the harshness of his keepers,
and, above all else, the consciousness of his innocence and
the fearful obscurity as to the truth, amid which he is struggling.   .   .   .   And what a frightful nightmare for you,
should you remember that all this is your work!'

She had become quite white, and her hands moved

involuntarily as if to ward off some horrible vision. There was kindness and weakness in her nature, but Marc could not tell whether it were a quiver of remorse, or some desperate struggle that he detected in her. For a moment, as if imploring help, she stammered wildly: ' My poor child! my poor child!'

And that child, that little Sébastien, to whom she was so fondly, so passionately attached, to whom she would have sacrificed everything, must have suddenly appeared before her, and have restored some little of her strength. ' Oh! you are cruel, Monsieur Froment!' she said; ' you make me terribly unhappy. . . . But how can it be helped, since it 's done? I cannot find that paper again among the ashes.'

' So you burnt it, Madame Alexandre—you are sure of it?'

' Certainly, I told you so. . . . I burnt it for fear lest my little man should be compromised, and suffer from it all his life.'

She spoke those last words in an ardent voice, as if with fierce resolution. Marc was convinced, and made a gesture of despair. Once again the triumph of truth was delayed, prevented. Without a word he escorted Madame Alexandre to the door, she again becoming all embarrassment, at a loss indeed how to take leave of the ladies who were present. Bowing and stammering excuses, she disappeared, and, when she was gone, deep silence reigned in the room.

Neither Geneviève nor Madame Duparque had intervened. Both had remained frigid and motionless. And they still preserved silence while Marc, absorbed in his grief, his head bowed, walked slowly to and fro. At last, however, Madame Duparque rose to take her departure, and on reaching the threshold she turned and said: ' That woman is a lunatic! Her story of a destroyed paper appears to me to be a fairy tale which nobody would believe. You would do wrong to relate it, for it would not help on your affairs. . . . Good-night: be sensible.'

Marc did not even answer. With a heavy tread he long continued walking up and down. Night had gathered round, and Geneviève lighted the lamp. And when by its pale glow she began to lay the table in silence, her husband did not even try to confess her. One sorrow was enough, and he did not wish to hasten the advent of another, such as would come should he learn, as he might, that she, his wife, was no longer in communion with him in respect to many things.

But during the following days he was haunted by Madame Duparque's last words. Supposing indeed that he should try to make use of the new fact which had come to his knowledge, what credit would his statement obtain among the public ? Doubtless he would secure the testimony of Sébastien; the boy would repeat that he had seen the copy-slip which his cousin Victor had brought from the Brothers' school. But it would be the testimony of a child barely ten years old, and his mother would strive to weaken its importance. It was the paper itself that ought to be produced; and the statement that it had been burnt would merely lead to the affair being buried once again.

The more Marc reflected, the more he understood the necessity of waiting. The new fact could not be put to use, given the conditions in which he had discovered it. And yet for him how precious it was, how fertile in decisive proof! It rendered his faith in Simon's innocence unshakable, it confirmed all his deductions, materialised the conviction to which reasoning had brought him. One of the Brothers was the real culprit; a legally conducted inquiry would soon have shown which of them it was. Yet the young man again had to resign himself to patience, and rely on the strength of truth, which was now at last on the march, and which would never more be stopped until full light should be cast upon everything.

At the same time Marc's anguish increased, the torture of his conscience became more tragical day by day. It was frightful to know that an innocent man was suffering abominable martyrdom in a penal settlement, and that the real culprit was free, near at hand, impudent and triumphant, still pursuing his vile work as a corrupter of children; and it was still more frightful that one should be unable to cry all that aloud and prove it, confronted as one was by the base complicity of all the social forces banded together by egotistical interest to perpetuate the monstrous iniquity. Marc no longer slept, he carried his secret with him like a sharp goad which incessantly reminded him that it was his duty to ensure justice. Never for an hour did he cease to think of his mission, and his heart bled despairingly because he knew not what to do to hasten its success.

Even at the Lehmanns he said nothing of Sébastien's confession. What good would it have done to give these

poor folk a vague uncertain hope ?   Life still treated them
very harshly, overwhelmed them with opprobrium and grief
—grief for the prisoner yonder, whose letters rent their
hearts, and whose name was cast in their teeth as a supreme
insult.   Old Lehmann's trade had declined yet more;
Rachel, always gowned in mourning like a widow, distressed by the rapid growth of her children, who would
learn everything before long, scarcely dared to go out.
Thus Marc only confided in David, in whom glowed the
stubborn determination to make everybody recognise and
acclaim his brother's innocence at some future time.   He
lived apart, ignored, carefully avoiding all appearance on
the scene, but never, not for an hour, did he pause in the
task of rehabilitation which had become the sole object of
his life.   He reflected, studied, followed clues which he too
often had to abandon after a few steps.   Despite two years
of constant research, he had discovered nothing decisive.
His suspicion of an illegal communication made by President Gragnon to the jurors had become a moral certainty,
only he had failed in all his efforts to procure proof, and
could not tell how to obtain it.   Nevertheless he was not
discouraged; he had resolved to devote ten, twenty years
of his life even, to reach the real culprit.   Marc's revelation
inspired him with additional courage and patience.   He
likewise held that it was best to keep Sébastien's confession
secret, so long as it was not strengthened by some material
proof.   For the moment it merely supplied the hope of an
additional triumph.   And that said, David again turned,
calmly and firmly, to his investigations, pursuing them
with no haste, but ever in the same prudent, continuous
manner.

One morning, before lessons began, Marc at last made up
his mind to remove the large crucifix which hitherto he had
left hanging from the wall behind his desk.   He had been
waiting for two years to be sufficiently master of the situation before expressing in this manner the independence of
the secular school—such as he understood and desired it—
in matters of religion.   Until now he had willingly yielded
to Salvan's prudent advice, for he understood that he must
assure himself of his position before making it a position of
combat.   But he now felt strong enough to begin the battle.
Had he not restored prosperity to the Communal school by
winning back to it numerous pupils who had been transferred to the Brothers'?   Had he not gradually gained per-

sonal respect, the affection of the children, the favour of
their parents ?   Besides, he was impelled to take action first
by his recent visit to Jonville, which he had left on the high
road to knowledge, and which Abbé Cognasse was once
more transforming into an abode of darkness, and secondly
by all the anxiety and anger stirred up within him by Sébastien's confession—anger with the ignominy that he divined
around him in Maillebois, which was enslaved and poisoned
by the clerical faction.

That morning, then, he had already climbed upon a stool
to remove the crucifix, when Geneviève, holding little
Louise by the hand, entered the classroom to inform him
of her intention to take the child to spend the day with her
grandmother.   At the sight of Marc on the stool the young
woman was quite surprised.   'What are you doing there ?'
she asked him.

'Can't you see ?' he answered.   'I am taking down this
crucifix, which I intend to give to Abbé Quandieu myself,
in order that he may restore it to the church which it ought
never to have left.   .   .   .   Here! help me—take it!'

But she did not hold out her arms.   She did not move.
Turning extremely pale, she watched him as if she were
witnessing some forbidden and dangerous deed which filled
her with fear.   And he had to descend from the stool un-
helped by her, encumbered with the big crucifix, which he
immediately locked up in one of the cupboards.

'You would n't help me,' he exclaimed.   'What is the
matter ?   Do you disapprove of what I have done ?'

In spite of her emotion, Geneviève answered plainly:
'Yes, I disapprove of it.'

Her answer amazed Marc.   Like her he began to quiver.
It was the first time that she assumed such an aggressive and
angry tone with him.   He felt a little shock, a slight rending, such as presages rupture.   And he looked at her with
astonishment and anxiety, as if he had heard a voice he did
not know, as if a stranger had just spoken to him.

'What! you disapprove of what I do ?   Was it really you
who said that ?'

'Yes, it was I.   It is wrong of you to do what you have
done.'

She it was indeed; for she stood before him, tall and
slender, with her fair amiable face, and her glance gleaming
with some of her father's sensual passion.   Yes, it was she,
and yet in the expression of those large blue eyes there was

already something different, a shadow, a little of the mystical dimness of the *au-delà*.   And Marc in his astonishment
felt a chill come to his heart as he suddenly observed that
change.   What had happened, then?   Why was she no
longer the same?   But he recoiled from an immediate explanation, and contented himself with adding: 'Hitherto,
even when you did not think perhaps as I did, you always
told me to act in accordance with my conscience, and that
is what I have now done.   And so your blame surprised me
painfully.   We shall have to talk of it.'

She did not disarm, she preserved her angry frigidity of
manner.   'We will talk of it if you so desire,' she replied;
'meantime I am going to take Louise to grandmother, who
will not bring her back till this evening.'

Sudden enlightenment dawned upon Marc.   It was Madame Duparque who was taking Geneviève from him, and
who, doubtless, would take Louise also.   He had acted
wrongly in disinteresting himself from his wife's doings, in
allowing her and the child to spend so much time in that
pious house, where the dimness and atmosphere of a chapel
prevailed.   He had failed to notice the stealthy change
which had been taking place in his wife during the last two
years, that revival of her pious youth, of the indelible education of other days, which, little by little, had been bringing her back to the dogmas which he imagined had been
overcome by the efforts of his intellect and the embrace of
his love.   As yet she had not begun to follow her religion
again by attendance at Mass, Communion, and Confession,
but he felt that she was already parting from him, reverting
to the past with slow but certain steps, each of which would
place them farther and farther asunder.

'Are we no longer in agreement, then, my darling?' he
asked her sadly.

With great frankness she replied: 'No.   And grandmother
was right, Marc; all the trouble has come from that horrible
affair.   Since you have been defending that man, who was
transported and who deserved his punishment, misfortune
has entered our home, and we shall end by agreeing no
more in anything.'

He raised a cry of despair.   'Is it you,' he repeated,
'you who speak like that?   You are against truth, against
justice now!'

'I am against the deluded and malicious ones whose evil
passions attack religion.   They wish to destroy God; but,

even if one quits the Church, one should at least respect its ministers, who do so much good.'

This time Marc made no rejoinder. A quarrel was out of place at that moment when he was expecting the arrival of the boys. But was the evil so deep already? His grief arose chiefly from the fact that at the root of the dissentiment parting him from his wife he found the Simon affair, the mission of equity which he had imposed on himself. No concession in that matter was possible on his part, and thus no agreement could be arrived at. For two years past that monstrous affair had been mingled with every incident; it was like a poisoned source which would continue to rot both people and things, so long as justice was not done. And now his own home was poisoned by it.

Seeing that he preserved silence, Geneviève went towards the door, repeating quietly: 'Well, I am going to grandmother's with Louise.'

Marc thereupon caught up the child as if anxious to kiss her. Would he also allow that little one, the flesh of his flesh, to be taken from him? Ought he not to keep her in his arms to save her from imbecile and deadly contagion? For a moment he looked at her. Already at five years of age, she showed signs of becoming tall and slender like her mother, her grandmother, and her great-grandmother. But she lacked their pale fair hair, and she had the lofty brow of the Froments, the brow that suggested an impregnable tower of sense and knowledge. Laughing loudly, she cast her arms prettily about her father's neck.

'You know, papa, I will repeat my fable to you when I come home; I know it quite well.'

Yielding to a sentiment of tolerance, Marc, for the second time, resolved that he would have no dispute. He restored the little one to her mother, who led her away. Moreover, the boys were now arriving, and the classroom soon became full. But anxiety remained in the master's heart at the thought of the struggle which he had resolved to wage when he removed the crucifix from the wall. That struggle, it was now certain, would reach his own hearth. His tears and the tears of his loved ones would flow. Nevertheless, by an heroic effort, he mastered his suffering; and summoning little Sébastien, the monitor, he bade him watch over the reading class, while for his part he gaily proceeded with some demonstrations on the blackboard, amidst the joyous brightness with which the sunshine flooded the schoolroom.

II

THREE days later, in the evening, while Marc was undressing in the bedroom, Geneviève being already in bed, he told her that he had received an urgent letter from Salvan, who wished to see him on the morrow, Sunday.

'No doubt it is about that crucifix which I removed from the classroom,' the young man added. ' Some parents have complained, it seems; and very likely there will be a great to-do. But I anticipated it.'

Geneviève, whose head lay deep in her pillow, returned no answer. But when Marc was in bed and the light was extinguished, he was delightfully surprised to find her casting her arms about him, and whispering in his ear: 'I spoke to you harshly the other day; and, it 's true, I don't think as you do about religion or about the affair; but I still love you very dearly, I love you with all my heart.'

Marc felt the more moved by these words as, since the recent dispute, his wife had turned her back upon him, as though in token of conjugal rupture.

'And as you are going to have trouble,' she continued softly, ' I don't want you to think me angry. One's ideas may differ, but all the same one may love one another very much—is it not so ? And if you are mine, I am still yours, my dear, dear husband.'

On hearing her speak like that he clasped her to him with passionate eagerness. 'Ah! my dear wife, as long as you love me, as long as you are mine,' said he, 'I shall fear nought of the terrible threats around us.'

She yielded to his embrace, quivering, transported by the joy of love which was essential to her being. And there came a moment of perfect communion, irresistible reconciliation. The good understanding of a young couple, united by love, is only seriously threatened when some divergency of that love arises. As long as they are swayed by passion one for the other, they remain in agreement athwart the worst mishaps. He who would part them must first of all destroy their mutual passion.

When Marc gave Geneviève a last kiss before both fell
asleep, he thought it well to reassure her: 'I shall act very
prudently in this affair, I promise you,' said he. 'You know
too that I am moderate and reasonable at bottom.'

'Ah! do as you please,' she answered prettily. 'All I
ask is that you should come back to me, and that we should
still love each other.'

On the morrow the young man repaired to Beaumont,
quite enlivened by his wife's ardent affection. He derived
fresh courage from it, and thus it was with a smiling face
and the demeanour of a combatant that he entered Salvan's
private room at the Training College. But the first words
spoken by the director, after they had shaken hands in a
friendly way, surprised and embarrassed him.

'I say, my good fellow,' Salvan began, 'so it seems that
you have at last discovered the new fact, the long-sought
proof of our poor Simon's innocence, which will enable one
to apply for the revision of his trial?'

Marc, who had anticipated an immediate explanation on
the subject of the crucifix, remained for a moment silent,
wondering whether he ought to tell the truth even to Salvan. At last, seeking his words, he said slowly: 'The new
fact . . . no, I have nothing decisive as yet.'

But Salvan did not notice his hesitation. 'That is what
I thought,' he rejoined, 'for you would have warned me,
eh? Nevertheless, there is a rumour of some discovery
made by you, a document of capital importance, placed in
your hands by chance, something like a sword of Damocles
which you are said to hold over the heads of the real culprit and his accomplices, the whole clerical gang of the
region.'

Marc listened, full of stupefaction. Who could have
spoken? How was it that Sébastien's confession and his
mother's visit had become known? How was it that particulars had been spread abroad, modified and exaggerated
as they passed from mouth to mouth? The young man
suddenly made up his mind to tell the truth to Salvan; he
felt it necessary to confide in that worthy and sensible friend
and adviser, on whom he placed so much reliance. So he
told him how he knew that a copy-slip, similar to the one
brought forward in evidence against Simon, had been taken
from the Brothers' school, and how it had been destroyed.

Salvan, who was deeply moved, rose from his chair. 'It
was the proof we needed!' he exclaimed. 'But you act

rightly in remaining silent since we hold no material evidence. One must wait. . . . At present, however, I understand the disquietude, the covert alarm, which for some days past I have detected among our adversaries. Some words may have escaped you or the boy, or his mother, and chance words often go far; or else some mysterious agency may have placed the secret in circulation, misrepresenting the facts. In any case the culprit and his accomplices have certainly felt the ground quaking beneath them; and, naturally, they are alarmed, for they will have to defend their crime.'

Then, passing to the subject which had prompted his urgent letter, he resumed: 'But I wished to speak to you of another incident, which everybody is talking about—your removal of that crucifix from your classroom. You know my views: our schools ought to be purely and simply secular, therefore all religious symbols are out of place in them. But you can have no idea of the tempest which your action will raise. Unfortunately, it is now the interest of the good Brothers and their supporters, the Jesuits, to ruin you absolutely, alarmed as they are by the weapons which they believe to be in your hands. By your action in the matter of the crucifix you have laid yourself open to attack, and so they are naturally rushing forward to the onslaught.'

Marc understood, and made a gesture of defiance, like a man fully prepared for battle. ' But have I not acted prudently, in accordance with your advice ? ' he responded. ' Did I not wait two long years before removing that cross which was hung up after Simon's trial to indicate that the clerical faction had virtually taken possession of the Communal school ? I have set that poor school on its legs again; it was suspected and discredited, and I have made it prosperous and free. So was it not legitimate that my first independent act as schoolmaster, after winning acceptance and then victory, should be to rid the school of all emblems, and restore it to that neutrality in matters of religion, from which it ought never to have departed ? '

Salvan interrupted him: ' Once again, I do not blame you. You showed great patience and tolerance. Nevertheless, your action has taken place at a terrible moment, and, feeling alarmed for you, I wished to discuss matters in order to provide, if possible, for all dangerous contingencies.'

They sat down and talked at length. The political situation of the department was still very bad. Fresh elections had taken place recently, and the result had been another step in the direction of clerical reaction. An extraordinary thing had happened: Lemarrois, the Mayor of Beaumont, Gambetta's former friend, whose position as deputy had been deemed unassailable, had found himself obliged to submit to a second ballot,[1] through the advent of a Socialist candidate, none other than Advocate Delbos, whose address at Simon's trial had marked him out for the support of the revolutionary *faubourgs ;* and, at the second polling, Lemarrois had only won by a majority of about a thousand votes. Meanwhile, the Royalist and Catholic reactionaries had gained a seat, the handsome Hector de Sanglebœuf having secured the return of a friend, a general officer, thanks to the entertainments which he gave at La Désirade, and the lavish manner in which he distributed Jew gold, derived from his father-in-law, Baron Nathan. Then, too, in order to secure re-election, the amiable Marcilly, once the hope of all the young men of culture, had skilfully completed his evolution towards the welcoming Church, which was very desirous of concluding a new pact with the *bourgeoisie*, whom the progress of Socialism terrified.

Though it had accepted political equality the *bourgeoisie* indeed was unwilling to concede equality in the economic field, for it desired to restore nothing of what it had stolen. And to resist the onslaught from below, it preferred to ally itself with its old enemies. It again began to think that religion had some good features, that it was useful as a kind of police institution, a barrier, which alone might check the growing appetite of the masses. And as a first step the *bourgeoisie* was gradually garbing itself in militarism, nationalism, anti-semitism, and all the other hypocritical disguises under which invading Clericalism pursued its road.

The army became merely the emblem of brute force upholding the thefts of ages, an impregnable wall of bayonets within whose shelter property and capital, duly gorged, might digest in security. The nation, the country, was the *ensemble* of abuses and iniquities which it was criminal to

---

[1] In French elections, when several nominees contest some particular seat, a candidate, to be successful, must obtain one half, *plus* one, of the total number of votes recorded. If no candidate secures that number a second ballot ensues a fortnight later. On the second occasion a relative majority suffices for election.— *Trans.*

touch, the monstrous social edifice, not one beam of which
must be changed for dread lest all should fall.   The Jews,
even as in the Middle Ages, served as a pretext to instil
fresh warmth into cooling beliefs, to exploit ancestral hatred,
and sow the horrid seeds of civil war.   And beneath that
all-embracing movement of reaction there was nought save
the stealthy labour of the Church, seeking to regain the
ground she had formerly lost when the old world broke up
beneath the liberating breath of the French Revolution.   It
was the Revolution that the Church strove to kill by regaining ascendency over the *bourgeoisie*, which the Revolution
had raised to power, and which had decided to betray it in
order to retain that power, of which it owed account to the
masses.   And the return of the *bourgeoisie* to the bosom of
the Church would lead to the reconquest of the people, for
the Church's vast design was to subjugate men by the influence of women, and particularly to lay hold of the children in their schools and confine their minds in the dim
prison of dogmas.   If the France of Voltaire were again becoming the France of Rome it was because the teaching
Congregations had set their grip on the young.   And the
position was becoming worse and worse, the Church was
already shrieking victory—victory over the democracy, victory over science—full of the hope that she would prevent
the inevitable, the completion of the Revolution, the junc-
tion of the masses with the *bourgeoisie* in the seat of power,
and the final liberation of the entire people.

'The situation grows worse daily,' said Salvan; 'you
know what a frantic campaign is being carried on against
our system of elementary education.   Last Sunday, at
Beaumont, a priest went so far as to say in the pulpit that a
secular schoolmaster was Satan disguised as a pedagogue.
"Fathers and mothers!" he cried, "you should wish your
children to be dead rather than in such hells as those
schools!"   .   .   .   As for secondary education, that also
is a prey to clerical reaction.   Apart from the ever-increasing prosperity of such Congregational establishments
as the College of Valmarie, where the Jesuits finish poisoning the sons of the *bourgeoisie*, the officers, functionaries,
and magistrates of the future, our Lycées, even, remain in
the power of the priests.   Here at Beaumont, for instance,
the director, the devout Depinvilliers, openly receives
Father Crabot, who is, I think, the confessor of his wife and
daughters.   Lately, as he felt discontented with Abbé

Leriche, a worthy but very aged man who had fallen asleep
in his post, he secured a thoroughly militant chaplain. At
the Lycées, no doubt, religious exercises are optional; but
for a boy to be exempted from them a request from his
parents is required. And naturally the pupil about whom
a fuss is made in that respect is badly noted, set upon one
side, and even subjected to all sorts of petty persecutions.
. . . Briefly, after thirty years of Republican rule, a
century of active free thought, the Church still trains and
educates our children, still remains paramount, intent on
retaining her domination over the world by moulding in the
same old moulds as formerly the men of bondage and error
that she needs to govern on her behalf. And all the
wretchedness of the times comes from that cause.'

'But what do you advise me to do, my friend?' Marc inquired. 'After acting as I have done, am I to retreat?'

' No, certainly not. Perhaps, if you had warned me, I
might have begged you to wait a little longer. But as you
have removed that crucifix you must defend yourself.
After writing to you I saw Le Barazer, our Academy Inspector, and I now feel somewhat easier in mind. You
know him, and you are aware how difficult it is to guess his
thoughts. Yet I believe that he is at heart on our side,
and I should be greatly surprised if he were to play into the
hands of our enemies. But everything will depend on you,
on your power of resistance, on the firmness of the position
you have acquired at Maillebois. I foresee a frantic campaign on the part of the Brothers, the Capuchins, and the
Jesuits, for you are not merely a secular schoolmaster, otherwise an incarnation of Satan, but you are, particularly, the
defender of Simon—that is, the torchbearer, the soldier of
truth and justice, whose light must be extinguished and
whose lips must be sealed. In any case, be prudent and
sensible and keep up your courage.'

Salvan, who had risen, grasped the young man's hands,
and for a moment they remained thus, smiling as they gazed
at each other, their eyes shining with courage and faith.

'At least you do not despair of the final result, my friend?'

' Despair, my boy? Ah! never! Victory is certain; I
do not know when it will come, but it is certain. Besides,
there is more cowardice and egotism than actual malice
among some of our adversaries. How many of our university men are neither really good nor really bad, though on
striking an average one finds perhaps rather more goodness

than evil among them. The worst is that they are functionaries, and as such are wedded to routine, apart from
which their one concern is their advancement, as is natural.
Forbes, our Rector, harbours, I fancy, the contempt of a
philosopher for these wretched times, and on that account
is content to play the part of a piece of administrative me-
chanism connecting the Minister with the university staff.
Then, too, if Depinvilliers sets himself on the side of the
Church, it is merely because he has two ugly daughters on
his hands, and relies on Father Crabot to supply them with
rich husbands.   As for the terrible Mauraisin—whom you
will do well to beware of, for he has an ugly soul—he would
like to be in my shoes; and he would go over to your side
to-morrow if he thought you in a position to give him my
berth.   .   .   .   Yes, yes, many of them are merely poor
hungry devils, while others are men of weak intellect—they
will come over to our side and even help us when we have
won the battle.'

He laughed indulgently.   Then, becoming grave once
more, he added: 'Besides, the good work I do here prevents me from despairing.   As you know, I hide myself
away in my little corner; but, day by day, I strive to hasten
the future.   And things move—they move.   I am very well
satisfied with my young men.   No doubt it is still rather
difficult to recruit students, for the profession appears so
thankless, so poorly paid, leading to nothing but contumely
and a life of certain wretchedness.   All the same, we had
more competitors than usual this year.   It is hoped that
the Chambers will end by voting reasonable salaries, such
as may enable the humblest masters to live in some little
dignity.   And you will see, you will see what will happen
when properly trained masters leave this college and spread
through the villages and the towns, carrying words of deliverance with them, destroying error, superstition, and
falsehood on all sides, like the missionaries of a new humanity!   The Church will be vanquished then, for it can only
subsist and triumph amid ignorance, and when it is swept
away the whole nation will march unchecked towards solidarity and peace.'

'Ah! my old friend, that is the great hope!' cried Marc;
'that is what lends all of us the strength and cheerfulness
we need to do our work.   Thanks for inspiriting me; I will
try to be sensible and courageous.'

They once more shook hands energetically, and Marc

returned to Maillebois, where the fiercest battle, war to the knife, awaited him.

There, as at Beaumont, the political situation had become worse. The last municipal elections, following those for the Chamber of Deputies, had also given disastrous results. Darras had found his party in a minority in the new Municipal Council; and Philis, the clerical councillor, the leader of the reactionary cause, had now been elected Mayor. Before everything else, Marc wished to see Darras in order to ascertain how far the latter might yet be able to support him. So he presented himself, one evening, in the comfortable drawing-room of the handsome house which the contractor had built himself. Darras, as soon as he perceived him, raised his arms to the ceiling.

'Ah! my dear schoolmaster, so now you have the whole pack at your heels! Oh! I shall be on your side, you may rely on me now that I am beaten, reduced to opposition. . . . It was difficult for me to be always on your side when I was Mayor; for, as you know, the majority I disposed of was only one of two votes. But even when I had to act contrary to your desires, I repeated to myself that you were a thousand times right. At present we shall be able to go forward, since the only course open to me is to fight and try to upset Philis, and take the mayoralty from him. You did quite right when you removed that crucifix from the schoolroom; it wasn't there in Simon's time, and it ought never to have been there at all.'

Marc made bold to smile. 'Why, every time I spoke to you of removing it,' said he, 'you protested. You talked of the necessity of prudence, of the danger of frightening the children's parents, and giving our adversaries a weapon against us.'

'But I have just admitted to you how embarrassed I was! Ah! it is by no means easy to manage a town like Maillebois, where the forces of the different parties have always balanced, and where nobody has ever been able to tell whether the freethinkers or the priests would win the day. At this moment we are certainly not in a brilliant position, but we must keep up our courage. We shall end by giving them a good licking, which will make us masters of the town for good.'

'That's certain,' replied Marc, delighted with the fine valour displayed by the ambitious contractor, who, at heart, was a worthy man.

'Particularly,' continued Darras, 'as Philis won't dare to take any serious step, for, in his turn, he has only a majority of two, such as rendered me so timid.　He is condemned to mark time, and will live in constant fear of some slight change which may place him in a minority.　I know by experience what that means!'

He made merry over it in a noisy way.　He harboured against Philis the hatred of a big and healthy man with a sound stomach and a sound brain, who was chagrined by the sight of the new Mayor's lean little figure, dark, hard face, pointed nose and thin lips.　Philis had retired from business as a tilt and awning maker, at the time of his wife's death, and, though possessed of an income of some ten thousand francs a year, the real origin of which remained somewhat obscure, he lived in great retirement, attended by a single servant, a huge fair creature of whom evil tongues spoke very badly.　Her master had a daughter named Octavie, twelve years of age, now with the nuns of the Visitation at Beaumont, and a son, Raymond, ten years old, who was a boarder at the Jesuit College of Valmarie, pending the time when he might enter the military school of St. Cyr.　Having thus rid himself of his children, the new Mayor led a close, narrow life, most careful in all his religious observances, ever in conference with the black frocks, and really acting as the executor of the Congregations' decisions.　His election as Mayor was sufficient proof of the acute stage which the religious crisis had reached in that town of Maillebois, which the struggle between the Republic and the Church was ravaging.

'And so I may go forward,' said Marc; 'you will support me with the minority of the Council?'

'Why, certainly!' cried Darras.　'Only, be reasonable, don't give us too big an affair to deal with.'

On the very morrow the contest began; and apparently it was Savin, the clerk, the father of the twin boys, Achille and Philippe, who was chosen to strike the first blow.　At all events, on leaving his office in the evening, he came to the school to pick a quarrel with the master.

'You know what I am—is that not so, Monsieur Froment?' said he.　'I am a radical Republican, and nobody can suspect me of conspiring with the priests.　Nevertheless, on behalf of a number of parents I have come to ask you to replace that crucifix which you removed, for religion is necessary for children as well as for women. . . . No

priests in the school, I agree to that; but Christ, remember
it, was the first of Republicans and revolutionaries!'

Marc, however, desired to know the names of the other
parents whom Savin represented. 'If you have not come
merely on your own behalf,' said he, 'will you tell me what
families have delegated you?'

'Oh! "delegated"—that is not quite correct. I have
seen Doloir the mason, and Bongard the farmer, and have
found that they blame you as I myself do. Only, it is
always compromising to protest and give one's signature—
is that not so? I myself risk a good deal by coming forward, on account of my superiors. But the voice of my
conscience as the father of a family speaks too loudly for
me to act otherwise. How shall I ever manage those two
scapegraces of mine, Achille and Philippe, if you do not
frighten them a little with fear of the punishment of God
and the torments of hell? Look at my big girl, Hortense,
who is so good in every respect, and who was admired by
all Maillebois when she took her first Communion this year!
By taking her to church, Mademoiselle Rouzaire has made
her really perfect. Compare your work with Mademoiselle
Rouzaire's, compare my two boys with my daughter. By that
comparison alone you stand condemned, Monsieur Froment.'

Marc smiled in his quiet way. The amiable Hortense, a
pretty and precocious girl of thirteen, one of Mademoiselle
Rouzaire's favourites, occasionally contrived to climb over
the wall separating the playgrounds of the two schools, in
order that she might hide away in corners with lads of her
own age. Even as Savin had suggested, the young man
had often compared his pupils, from whom by degrees he
obtained a little more reason and truth, with the pupils of
the schoolmistress, his neighbour—the affectedly prim and
gentle little girls who were fed on clerical pap, falsehood, and
hypocrisy, and perturbed, even secretly spoilt, by the corrupting influence of the mysterious. Marc would have liked
to have seen his boys and those girls together—those girls
who were now reared and educated apart, from whom
everything was hidden, whose minds and whose senses were
heated by all the fires of mysticism. They would then have
ceased to climb over walls to go in search of so-called sin,
the forbidden fruit of damnation and delight. Yes, only a
system of mixed schools could ensure the health and
strength of the free and happy nation of to-morrow.[1]

[1] This problem seems to have been solved in the United States,

To Savin, however, Marc merely said: ' Mademoiselle
Rouzaire does her duty as she understands it; and I do
mine in the same way. . . . If families would only help
me, the good work of training and education would progress
more rapidly.'

At this Savin lost his temper. Lean and puny, buttoned
up in his shabby frock coat, he drew himself erect on his
little legs: ' Do you insinuate that I give bad examples to
my children ? ' he asked.

' Oh! certainly not. Only everything that I teach them
here is afterwards contradicted by what they see in the
world around them. They find truthfulness regarded as
dangerous audacity, and reason condemned as being insufficient, incapable of forming honest men.'

Marc indeed was greatly grieved that he should be
thwarted so often by his pupils' parents, when he dreamt of
obtaining from them the necessary help to hasten the emancipation of the humble. If on leaving school every day the
children had only found in their homes some realisation of
their lessons, some practice of the social duties and rights
in which they were instructed, how much easier and swifter
would have been the march of improvement! Such col-
laboration was even indispensable; the schoolmaster could
not suffice for many things, the most delicate, the most useful, when his pupils' parents did not continue his work in
the same spirit and complete it. The master and the
parents ought to have gone hand in hand towards the same
goal of truth and justice. And how sad it was when, instead of obtaining the parents' help, the master saw them
destroying the little good he effected, unconscious for the
most part of what they were doing, yielding simply to the
incoherence of their ideas and their lives.

But Savin was again speaking. ' Briefly,' said he, ' you
will hang up that cross again, Monsieur Froment, if you
wish to please us all, and live on good terms with us, which
is what we desire, for you are not a bad schoolmaster.'

where, judging by official reports, the mingling of the sexes in the
schools is extensive. Thence (I judge the matter as an European) must
have come the very great and distinctly beneficial influence exercised
by American women on the national character. Perhaps it is not too
much to say that, apart from such incentives as a mere desire to gain
money, the women of the United States have largely helped to make
their race the most enterprising and progressive in the world. As for
the influence of mixed schools on morals, Americans have repeatedly
assured me that it has been the best possible.—*Trans.*

Marc smiled again. 'Thank you,' he said. 'But why did not Madame Savin accompany you? She, at any rate, would have been playing her proper part, for she follows the observances of the Church—I know it.'

'She is religious, as all respectable women ought to be,' the clerk answered dryly. 'I would rather have her go to Mass than take a lover.'

He looked at Marc suspiciously, consumed as he was by sickly jealousy, regarding every man as a possible rival. Why did the schoolmaster regret that his wife had not accompanied him? Had she not twice called at the school recently under the pretext of explaining to the master why Achille and Philippe had been absent on sundry occasions? For some time past he, Savin, had compelled her to confess regularly once a week to Father Théodose, the Superior of the Capuchins, for it had occurred to him that the shame of avowal might stay her in her course along the road to infidelity. On her side, if in earlier times she had followed the Church observances merely in order to secure peace at home—for she was quite destitute of faith—she now repaired with some alacrity to the tribunal of penitence, for, like the other young devotees who dreamt of Father Théodose, she had rid herself of earlier prejudices, and begun to regard him as a superb and most delightful man.

'As it happens,' said Marc, with some little maliciousness, in response to Savin's declaration, 'I had the pleasure of meeting Madame Savin last Thursday. She was leaving the chapel on the Place des Capucins, and we had a brief chat. As all her words to me were most gracious, I thought I might express my regret at not seeing her with you to-day.'

The husband made a doleful gesture. His everlasting suspicions had reached such a point that he himself now went to Beaumont to deliver the bead work which he allowed his wife to do in secret in order to add a few indispensable coppers to his meagre salary. Their case was one of hidden wretchedness, with all the torments that make hells of the homes of needy employés, burdened with children, the embittered husband becoming an unbearable despot, and the gentle and pretty wife resigning herself in silence until she at last discovers some consolation.

'My wife neither has nor ought to have any opinion but mine,' Savin ended by declaring. 'It is in her name as well as my own, and in the names of many other parents—

I repeat it — that I have made this application to you.
. . . It is now for you to decide if you will act upon it.
You will think the matter over.'

'I have thought it over, Monsieur Savin,' replied Marc,
who had become grave again. 'Before removing that
crucifix I understood fully what I was going to do; and
since it is no longer there, I shall certainly not put it up
again.'

On the following day a report spread through Maillebois
that a deputation of parents, fathers and mothers, had
called upon the schoolmaster, and that there had been a
stormy explanation, a frightful scandal. But Marc soon
understood whence the attack had really come, for chance
acquainted him with the circumstances which had led to
Savin's visit. Though pretty Madame Savin took no real
interest in the affair, absorbed as she was in her desire for a
little more personal happiness, she had none the less served
as an instrument in the hands of Father Théodose; for it
was on being approached by her, on the Capuchin's behalf,
that her husband had repaired to a secret interview with the
latter, which interview had prompted him to call on Marc
and endeavour to check a state of things which was so prejudicial to family morality and good order. No crucifixes
in the schools indeed! Would that not mean indiscipline
among the boys, and shamelessness among the girls and
their mothers also ? So the lean and little Savin, the Republican and anti-clerical, unhinged by his wretched spoilt
life and his idiotic jealousy, had set forth to champion the
cause of virtue, like an authoritarian, a topsy-turvy Catholic, who pictured the human paradise as a gaol, in which
everything human ought to be subdued and crushed.

Besides, behind Father Théodose, Marc readily divined
Brother Fulgence and his assistants, Brothers Gorgias and
Isidore, who hated the secular school more than ever since
it had been taking pupils from them. And behind the
Brothers came Fathers Philibin and Crabot of the College
of Valmarie, those powerful personages whose skilful unseen
hands had been directing the whole campaign ever since the
monstrous Simon affair. The accomplices in that slumbering crime seemed determined to defend it by other deeds
of iniquity. At the outset Marc had guessed where the
whole band, from the lowest to the highest, was crouching.
But how could one seize and convict them ? If Father
Crabot, amiable and worldly, still showed himself constantly

among the fine society of Beaumont, busily directing the
steps of his penitents and ensuring the rapid fortune of his
former pupils, his assistant, Father Philibin, had virtually
disappeared, restricting himself entirely, so it seemed, to
his absorbing duties as manager at Valmarie. Nothing
transpired of the stealthy work which was so ardently pursued in the darkness, every moment being employed to
ensure the triumph of the good cause. All that Marc himself could detect was the espionage attending his own movements. He was tracked with priestly caution, black figures
were constantly prowling around him. None of his visits
to the Lehmanns, none of his conversations with David
could have remained unknown. And, as Salvan had said,
the others tracked him because he was an impassioned
soldier of truth and justice, because he was a witness who
already possessed certain proofs, and whose avenging cry
must be thrust back into his throat, even by extermination
if necessary. To that task the frock and cassock wearers
devoted themselves with increasing audacity, joined even
by poor Abbé Quandieu, who felt grieved at having to place
religion at the service of such iniquitous work, but who resigned himself to it in obedience to the behests of his
Bishop, the mournful Monseigneur Bergerot, whom he
visited every week at Beaumont to take his orders and
console him in his defeat. Bishop and priest cast the cloak
of their ministry over the sore devouring the Church whose
respectful sons they were, hiding meantime their tears and
their fears, unwilling to acknowledge the mortal danger into
which they saw religion sinking.

One evening Mignot, on coming into the school from the
playground, said to Marc in a fury:

'It 's getting quite disgusting, monsieur! I 've again
caught Mademoiselle Rouzaire spying on us from the top of
a ladder!'

Indeed, whenever the schoolmistress fancied that she
would not be detected, she set a ladder against the wall
dividing the two playgrounds, in order that she might ascertain what was going on in the boys' school. And Mignot
accused her of sending secret reports on the subject to
Mauraisin every week.

'Oh! let her pry,' Marc answered gaily. 'But there is
no occasion for her to tire herself by climbing a ladder.
I 'll set the door wide open for her, if she desires it.'

'Ah! no, not that!' cried the assistant. 'Let her keep

her place! If she tries it on again, I shall go round and pull her down by the legs!'

Marc, to his great satisfaction, was now gradually completing the conquest of Mignot. The latter, like a peasant's son whose one desire was to escape the plough, a man of average mind and character, who like so many others thought solely of his immediate interests, had always shown himself distrustful with Simon. Indeed, nothing good could come from a Jew, and so he had deemed it prudent to keep aloof from him. At the time of the trial, therefore, though he was sufficiently honest to refrain from overwhelming the innocent prisoner, he had not given the good and truthful evidence which might have saved him. At a later stage he had likewise placed himself on the defensive with Marc, with whom he thought it would be foolish to ally himself if he desired advancement. For nearly a whole year, therefore, he had displayed hostility, taking his meals at an eating-house, grudging the help he gave in the school work, and freely blaming his principal's attitude. At that time indeed he had been very thick with Mademoiselle Rouzaire, and willing, it seemed, to place himself at the orders of the Congregations. But Marc, instead of evincing any perturbation, had treated his assistant with unremitting kindness, as if he were desirous of giving him all necessary time to reflect and understand that his real interest lay on the side of truth and equity.

Indeed, in Marc's opinion, that big, calm young fellow, whose only passion was angling, offered an interesting subject for experiment. Though he became cowardly when he thought of the future, and was somewhat spoilt by the environment of ferocious egotism in which he found himself, there was nothing absolutely evil in his nature. In fact, he might be made an excellent school teacher and even a man of most upright mind if he were helped, sustained by one of energy and intelligence. The idea of experimenting in that sense attracted Marc, who felt well pleased as, little by little, he gained the confidence and affection of this wanderer, thereby proving the truth of the axiom in which he set all his hopes of future deliverance — that there is no man, even one on the road to perdition, who may not be made an artisan of progress. Mignot had been won over by the active gaiety, the beneficent glow of truth and justice which Marc set around him. He now took his meals with his principal, and had become, as it were, a member of the family.

'It is wrong of you not to distrust Mademoiselle Rouzaire,' he resumed. 'You have no idea, monsieur, of what
she is capable. She would betray you a dozen times over
in order to obtain good reports from her friend Mauraisin.'

Then, being in a confidential mood, he related how she
had repeatedly urged him to listen at keyholes and report
to her. He knew her well; she was a terrible woman,
harsh and avaricious, despite all her varnish of exaggerated
courtesy; and though she was big and bony, with a flat,
freckled face, quite destitute of any charm, she ended by
seducing everybody. As she herself boasted, she knew how
to act. To the anti-clericals who angrily reproached her
for taking her girls so often to church, she replied that she
was compelled to comply with the desires of the parents
under penalty of losing her pupils. To the clericals she
gave the most substantial pledges, convinced as she was
that they were the stronger party and that on their influence
depended the best appointments even in the secular school
world. In reality she was guided solely by her own interests, as she understood them, having inherited the instincts
of a petty trader from her parents, who had kept a fruiterer's
shop at Beaumont. She had not married, because she preferred to live as she listed, and, although she did not carry
on with the priests, as was maliciously rumoured by evil
tongues, it seemed certain that she had a soft spot in her
heart for handsome Mauraisin, who, like the little man he
was, admired women built after the fashion of gendarmes.
Again, it was not true that she got drunk, though she was
very fond of sweet liqueurs. If she occasionally looked
very red when afternoon lessons began, it was simply because she ate abundantly and her digestive organs were out
of order.

Marc made an indulgent gesture. 'She does not keep
her school badly,' said he; 'the only thing that grieves me
is the spirit of narrow pietism which she introduces into all
her teaching. My boys and her girls are separated by an
abyss, not merely by a wall. And when they meet one
another, later, and think of marrying, they will belong to
different worlds. But is not that the traditional custom?
The warfare of the sexes largely arises from it.'

The young man did not mention the chief cause of his
rancour against Mademoiselle Rouzaire, the reason which
had impelled him to keep aloof from her. This was her
abominable conduct in Simon's case. He remembered the

quiet effrontery with which she had played the game of the
Congregations at the trial at Beaumont, how she had heaped
impudent falsehoods on the innocent prisoner, how she had
accused him of giving immoral and anti-patriotic lessons to
his pupils.   And so Marc's intercourse with her since his
appointment to Maillebois had never gone beyond the limits
of strict politeness, such as the proximity of their homes
required.   She, however, having seen the young man
strengthen his position, in such wise that his sudden downfall could now hardly be anticipated, had made attempts at
reconciliation; for, in her anxiety to be always on the
stronger side, she was not the woman to turn her back on
the victorious.   She had manœuvred particularly with the
object of ingratiating herself with Geneviève, but the latter
in this matter had hitherto shared Marc's opinions and
kept her at a distance.

'At all events, monsieur,' Mignot concluded, 'I advise
you to keep your eyes open.   If I had listened to La Rouzaire I should have betrayed you a score of times.   She
never ceased questioning me about you, repeating to me
that I was a stupid and would never succeed in getting into
a decent position. . . .   But you showed me great kindness, and you don't know what horrid things you saved me
from; for one soon listens to those creatures when they
promise you every kind of success.   And, as I am on this
subject, I hope you will excuse me if I venture to give you
some advice.   You ought to warn Madame Froment.'

'Warn her ?   What do you mean ?'

'Yes, yes, I don't keep my eyes in my pockets.   For
some time past I have seen La Rouzaire prowling around
your wife.   It is "dear madame" here, a smile or a caress
there, all kinds of advances, which would make me tremble
if I were in your shoes.'

Marc, who felt greatly astonished, made a pretence of
smiling: 'Oh! my wife has nothing to fear, she is warned,'
said he.   'It is difficult for her to behave impolitely with
a neighbour, particularly when one is connected by similar
duties.'

Mignot did not insist, but he shook his head doubtfully,
for his intercourse with the Froments had acquainted him
with the secret drama which was slowly gathering in their
home.   However, it seemed as if he were unwilling to say
all he knew.   And Marc, on his side also, became silent,
again mastered by the covert dread, the unacknowledged

weakness which assailed and paralysed him whenever the possibility of a struggle between Geneviève and himself presented itself to his mind.

All at once the attack of the Congregations, which he had been anticipating ever since his visit to Salvan, took place. The campaign began with a virulent report from Mauraisin on the subject of the removal of the crucifix, and the scandal caused among the boys' parents by that act of religious intolerance. Savin's protest was duly recorded, and the Doloir and Bongard families were cited among those who blamed the proceeding. The incident was one of exceptional gravity, according to the Inspector, for it had occurred in a clerical-minded town, reputed for its frequent and numerously attended pilgrimages—a town indeed where it was necessary for the secular school to make concessions if it was to escape defeat from its Congregational rival. Mauraisin concluded, therefore, in favour of the removal of the schoolmaster, a sectarian of the worst kind, who had thus incautiously compromised the university cause. And his indictment was completed by the recital of a number of little facts, the harvest of all the daily espionage carried on by Mademoiselle Rouzaire, whose docile little girls, ever at Mass or at the Catechism classes, were contrasted with the idle, rebellious, unbelieving lads trained by that anarchist master, Froment.

Three days later Marc learnt that Count Hector de Sanglebœuf, the Catholic deputy, accompanied by two of his colleagues, had made an application on the subject to Prefect Hennebise. Sanglebœuf was evidently acquainted with Mauraisin's report, even if he had not helped to draft it in conjunction with his friend Father Crabot, who so frequently visited La Désirade; and the idea undoubtedly was to take that report as a basis in demanding the dismissal of Marc.

Hennebise, whose policy was to live at peace with everybody, and who constantly urged his subordinates to refrain from stirring up trouble, must have felt very worried by the incident, which might lead to disastrous complications. The Prefect's feelings were with Sanglebœuf, but it was dangerous to adhere publicly to the reactionary cause; so, while sympathising with the fiery anti-Semite deputy, he explained that he was not master of the situation, for the law was precise and prevented him from removing a schoolmaster unless that step were proposed to him by Academy

Inspector Le Barazer. With some relief, therefore, the Prefect referred the gentlemen to the Inspector, to whose office, which was also in the Prefecture buildings, they immediately repaired.

Le Barazer, an ex-professor who had become a prudent diplomatist, listened to them with a great show of attentive deference. He was a man of fifty, with a broad full-coloured face, and as yet scarcely a grey hair. He had grown up hating the Empire, and as he regarded secular education as one of the foundation stones of the Republic, he pursued by all available means the task of crushing the Congregational schools, whose triumph in his estimation would have killed France. But experience had shown him the danger of violent action, and he adhered to a long meditated and prudent course, which led some extremists to regard him as a very lukewarm Republican. Yet he was associated with some extraordinary victories achieved by long years of discreet and patient action. At Sangleboeuf's first words he made a show of disapproving Marc's removal of the crucifix, which, said he, was a useless demonstration, though he pointed out that nothing in the laws compelled the schoolmasters to allow religious emblems in the schools. It was all a mere question of usage, and he discreetly allowed it to be seen that this usage scarcely had his approval. Then, as Sangleboeuf, losing his temper, proclaimed himself a defender of the Church, and described the schoolmaster of Maillebois as a shameless individual who had stirred up the entire population against him, the Inspector placidly promised that he would study the question with all the care it deserved.

But Sangleboeuf wished to know if he had not received a report from his subordinate, Mauraisin; and whether that report did not suffice to show the gravity of the evil, the demoralisation, which could only be arrested by the immediate removal of the schoolmaster. At this question Le Barazer feigned great surprise. What report? Ah! yes, the quarterly report from the Elementary Inspector! Were its contents known, then? In any case, those reports were purely administrative, and merely supplied certain elements of appreciation for the Academy Inspector, whose duty it was to make personal inquiries. And thereupon Le Barazer dismissed the gentlemen, after again promising to take their application into full account.

A month went by, and nothing reached Marc, who **daily**

expected a summons to the Prefecture. Le Barazer was doubtless following his usual tactics in order to gain time and exhaust the determination of the other side. Even as his friend Salvan had foretold, he was covertly supporting the young schoolmaster. But it was essential that the affair should not be aggravated, that increasing scandal should not compel his intervention; for assuredly he would not defend Marc beyond certain limits, but would end by sacrificing him if he thought that course expedient in order that the rest of his slow and opportunist campaign against the Congregational schools might not be interfered with. Unfortunately, things went from bad to worse at Maillebois. *Le Petit Beaumontais*, yielding to an inspiration which could be easily identified, started a vile campaign against Marc. As usual, it began with brief and vague paragraphs: Abominations were taking place in a neighbouring little town, and if necessary precise information would be given. Then schoolmaster Froment was plainly named, and under the headline ' The Scandal of Maillebois,' which was repeated almost daily, the paper published an extraordinary collection of tittle-tattle, the results of a pretended inquiry among the pupils and their parents, in which the schoolmaster was accused of the blackest crimes.

People were quite upset by these so-called revelations; the good Brothers and the Capuchins helped to spread terror abroad, and devotees never passed the Communal school without crossing themselves. Marc became conscious that he was in great peril; and Mignot bravely began to pack up his belongings, feeling certain that he would be swept away with his principal, whose side he had taken. Meantime Mademoiselle Rouzaire affected the most victorious airs when she conducted her girls to Mass; Father Théodose in his chapel, and even Curé Quandieu in his pulpit at St. Martin's, foretold the approaching restoration of God among the infidels, by which they meant that the crucifix would be soon set up again, with all solemnity, in the secular school; and, as a last blow, Marc, on meeting Darras, found him very cold, resolved to abandon him, for fear of losing the support of the minority of the Municipal Council.

' What can you expect, my dear fellow,' said the ex-Mayor; ' you have gone too far; we cannot follow you, at present at all events. . . . That blackbeetle Philis is watching me, and I should merely share your fate, which would be useless.'

In his despair Marc hastened to Salvan, whom he regarded as the only faithful supporter remaining to him.
And he found him thoughtful, gloomy, almost embarrassed.

'Things are going badly,' said he. 'Le Barazer remains
silent, seemingly anxious, and such a furious campaign is
being waged around him that I fear he may abandon you.
. . . Perhaps you acted too hastily.'

Marc's heart was wrung by a pang of grief, for he inter-
preted those last words as signifying that even Salvan abandoned him. 'You, you as well, my master!' he exclaimed.

But Salvan, full of emotion, caught hold of his hands.
'No, no, my lad, you must not doubt me; I remain on your
side with all my heart. Only you can have no idea of the
difficulties in which all of us have been placed by your
action, simple and logical though it was. This Training
College is suspected, denounced as a hot-bed of irreligion.
Depinvilliers profits by it to exalt the services which the
chaplain of his Lycée renders to the cause of national pacification, the reconcilement of all parties in the bosom of the
Church. Even our Rector, the peaceable Forbes, is full of
concern, fearing lest his tranquillity should be destroyed.
Le Barazer, no doubt, is skilful, but does he possess the
necessary strength of resistance?'

'What is to be done, then?'

'Nothing: one must wait. I can only repeat to you that
you must show yourself prudent and courageous. For the
rest we must rely on the force of truth and justice.'

During the next two months Marc displayed much brave
serenity amid the outrages by which he was assailed each
day. As if ignorant of the muddy tide beating against his
door, he pursued his duties with wondrous gaiety and uprightness. Never had he accomplished more important or
more useful work, devoting himself to his pupils, and teaching them, as much by example as by words, how necessary
it was to continue working and to retain one's love for
truth and justice amid the very worst events. To the filth,
the bitter insults flung at him by his fellow townsmen, he
replied with gentleness, kindliness, and sacrifice. He strove
to make the children better than their fathers, he sowed the
happy future in the furrows of the hateful present, he redeemed the crime of others at the cost of his own happiness.
It was the thought of the young ones around him, the duty
of helping to save them a little more each day from error and
falsehood, that lent him so much calmness and enabled him

to await the blow he expected with a quiet smile, like one who, every evening, felt well satisfied with the work accomplished during the day.

At last, one morning, *Le Petit Beaumontais* announced that the revocation of 'the ignoble poisoner of Maillebois' was signed. On the previous day Marc had heard of a fresh visit which the Count de Sanglebœuf had paid to the Prefecture, and he ceased to hope; his ruin was about to be consummated. The evening proved a very trying one. Whenever he quitted his classroom, and his boys, with their smiling faces and their fair and their dark little pates, were no longer near to remind him of the good time coming, he sank into sadness, and only after a struggle recovered the courage which he needed for the morrow. And so that particular evening proved particularly bitter. He thought of his work, destined to be so brutally interrupted—of those dearly-loved boys, whom he had taught perhaps for the last time, and whom he would not be allowed to save. They would be taken from him, handed over to some deformer of intellect and character, and it was the wreck of his ministry that made his heart bleed. He went to bed in such a gloomy mood that Geneviève gently, silently, cast her arms about him, as she still did occasionally from an impulse of wifely affection.

'You are worried, are you not, my poor darling?' she whispered.

He did not answer immediately. He knew that she shared his views less than ever, and he always avoided painful explanations in spite of his secret remorse at allowing her to drift away from him without attempting an effort to make her wholly his own. Indeed, if he himself had again ceased to call on her mother and grandmother, he lacked the courage to forbid her visits to that icy little house, though he well divined that their happiness was greatly endangered there. Each time that Geneviève returned from the Place des Capucins he felt that she belonged to him a little less than before. Recently, while the whole clerical pack was barking at his heels, he had learnt that the ladies had denied him on every side, blushing for their connection as if it were some unmerited shame that soiled their family.

'Why don't you answer me, dear?' Geneviève began again. 'Don't you think that I share your sorrow?'

He felt touched, and, returning her embrace, replied:

'Yes, I am grieved.   But it is about matters in which you
do not feel as I do, and, as I don't wish to reproach you,
what is the use of confiding them to you?   Still I may say
I fear that in a few days we shall be here no longer.'

'How is that ?'

'Oh! I shall certainly be sent elsewhere if I am not dismissed altogether.   It is all over . . . and we shall
have to go away, I know not whither.'

She raised a cry of delight: 'Oh, my dear! so much the
better!   That is the best thing that can happen to us.'

He felt astonished, for her meaning at first escaped him.
And when he questioned her she seemed somewhat embarrassed, and endeavoured to recall her words: 'Oh, I say
that because, of course, it would be all the same to me if I
did have to go away with you and our Louise.   One may
be happy anywhere.'   But when he pressed her she added:
'Besides, if we went elsewhere we should no longer be worried by all the horrid things which go on here, and which
might end by making us quarrel.   I should be so happy if
we could be alone in some little nook where nobody would
come between us, where nothing from outside would try to
separate us.   Oh! let us go away to-morrow, dear!'

Several times already, in moments of affectionate self-
abandonment, Marc had noticed in his wife that same dread
of rupture, that desire, that need to remain wholly his.   It
was as if she said to him: 'Keep me on your heart, carry
me away, so that none may tear me from your arms.   I
feel that I am being parted from you a little more each day,
I shiver with the great chill which comes over me when I
am no longer in your embrace.'   And, with his dread of the
inevitable, nothing could have upset him more.

'Go away, my love?' he answered; 'it is not enough to
go away.   But what joy you give me, and how grateful I
feel to you for comforting me like that!'

Several more days elapsed and still the terrible letter expected from the Prefecture did not arrive.   No doubt this
was due to the fact that a fresh incident began to impassion
the district and divert public attention from the secular
school of Maillebois.   For some time past Abbé Cognasse of
Jonville, whose triumph was complete, had been meditating
a great stroke, striving to induce Mayor Martineau to allow
the parish to be consecrated to the Sacred Heart of Jesus.
In all likelihood the idea had not come from the Abbé himself for every Thursday morning during the previous month

he had been seen going to the College of Valmarie, where he had long conferences with Father Crabot. And a remark made by Férou, the schoolmaster at Le Moreux, was circulating, filling some folk with indignation and amusing others.

'If those dirty Jesuits bring their bullock's heart here, I will spit in their faces,' he had said.

Henceforth the worship of the Sacred Heart was absorbing the whole Christian faith, developing into a new Incarnation, a new Catholicism. The sickly vision of a poor creature stricken with hysteria—the sad and ardent Marie Alacoque—that real, gory heart half wrenched from an open bosom, was becoming the symbol of a baser faith, degraded, lowered to supply a need of carnal satisfaction. The ancient and pure worship of an immaterial Jesus, who had risen on high to join the Father, seemed to have become too delicate for modern souls lusting for terrestrial enjoyment; and it had been resolved to serve the very flesh of Jesus, His heart of flesh, to devotees, by way of daily sustenance, such as superstition and brutishness required. It was like a premeditated onslaught on human reason, an intentional degradation of the religion of former times in order that the mass of believers, bowed beneath the weight of falsehood, might become yet more stupefied and more servile. With the religion of the Sacred Heart only tribes of idolaters were left, fetichists who adored offal from a slaughter-house, and carried it, banner-wise, on a pike-head. And all the genius of the Jesuits was found therein—the humanisation of religion, God coming to man since centuries of effort had failed to lead man to God. It was necessary to give the ignorant multitude the only deity it understood, one made in its own image, gory and dolorous like itself, an idol of violent hues, whose brutish materiality would complete the transformation of the faithful into a herd of fat beasts, fit for slaughter. All conquests effected on reason are conquests effected on liberty, and it had become necessary to reduce France to that savage worship of the Sacred Heart, fit for the aborigines of some undiscovered continent, in order to hold it in submission beneath the imbecility of the Church's dogmas.

The first attempts had been made on the very morrow of the great defeats, amid the grief arising from the loss of the two provinces. Then already the Church had availed herself of the public confusion to endeavour to consecrate France to the Sacred Heart—France, which after being chastised so heavily by the hand of God, repented of her sins. And at

last, on the highest summit of that great revolutionary city
of Paris, the Church had reared that Sacred Heart, palpi-
tating and gory red like the hearts which one sees hanging
from hooks in butchers' shops.   From that summit it bled
over the entire land, to the farthest depths of the country
districts.   And if at Montmartre it kindled the adoration
of the gentility, of ladies and gentlemen belonging to the
administrative services, the magistracy and the army, with
what emotion must it not infect the simple, the ignorant,
and the devout of the villages and hamlets!   It became the
national emblem of repentance, of the country's self-relin-
quishment in the hands of the Church.   It was embroidered
in the centre of the tricolor flag, whose three colours became
mere symbols of the azure of heaven, the lilies of the Virgin,
and the blood of the martyrs.   And huge, swollen, and
streaming with gore, it hung thus like the new Deity of degenerate Catholicism, offered to the base superstition of enslaved France.

At first it had been Father Crabot's idea to triumph at
Maillebois, the chief place in the canton, by consecrating
that little town to the Sacred Heart.   But he had become
anxious, for at Maillebois there was a manufacturing suburb
inhabited by some hundreds of working men who were beginning to send Socialist representatives to the Municipal
Council.   Thus, in spite of the Brothers and the Capuchins,
he had feared some sensational repulse.   All considered, it
was better to act at Jonville, where the ground appeared
well prepared.   If successful there, one might always repeat
the experiment on a larger stage, some other time.

Abbé Cognasse now reigned at Jonville, which schoolmaster Jauffre had gradually handed over to him.   Jauffre's
guiding principle was a very simple one.   As Clericalism
was sweeping through the region, why should he not allow
it to waft him to the headmastership of some important
school at Beaumont?   Thus, after prompting his wife to
make advances to the parish priest, he himself had openly
gone over to the Church, ringing the bell, chanting at the
offices, taking his pupils to Mass every Sunday.   Mayor
Martineau, who, following Marc, had been an anti-clerical
in former times, was at first upset by the new schoolmaster's
doings.   But what could he say to a man who was so well
off and who explained so plausibly that it was wrong to be
against the priests?   Thus Martineau was shaken in his ideas
and allowed the other to follow his course, till, at last,

prompted thereto by the beautiful Madame Martineau, he himself declared to the parish council that it was best to live in agreement with the curé. After that, a year sufficed for Abbé Cognasse to become the absolute master of the parish, his influence no longer being counterbalanced by that of the schoolmaster, who, indeed, willingly walked behind him, confident that he would derive a handsome profit from his submissiveness.

Nevertheless, when the idea of consecrating Jonville to the Sacred Heart was propounded, some dismay and resistance arose. Nobody knew whence that idea had come, nobody could have said by whom it had been first mooted. However, Abbé Cognasse, with his eager militant nature, immediately made it his business in the hope of gaining great personal glory should he be the first priest of the region to win an entire parish over to God. He made such a stir, indeed, that Monseigneur Bergerot, in despair at the threat of a new superstition, and grieved by its base idolatry, summoned him to Beaumont, where, however, after a scene which proved, it was rumoured, both terrible and pathetic, the Bishop once again was compelled to give way. But, on two occasions, the parish council of Jonville held tumultuous meetings, several members angrily desiring to know what profit they would all derive from the consecration of the parish to the Sacred Heart. For a moment it seemed as if the affair were condemned and buried. But Jauffre also made a trip to Beaumont, and, though nobody guessed exactly what personage he saw there, he no sooner came back than, in a gentle, insidious manner, he resumed the negotiations with the parish council.

The question was what the parish would gain by consecrating itself to the Sacred Heart. Well, first of all, several ladies of Beaumont promised presents to the church, a silver chalice, an altar cloth, some flower vases, and a big statue of the Saviour, with a huge, flaming, bleeding heart painted on it. Then, too, said Jauffre, there was talk of giving a dowry of five hundred francs to the most deserving Maiden of the Virgin when she married. But the council seemed to be most impressed by the promise of setting up a branch establishment of the Order of the Good Shepherd, where two hundred girls would work at fine linen, chemises, petticoats, and knickers, for some of the great Parisian shops. The peasants at once pictured all their daughters working for the good Sisters, and speculated on the large amount of

money which such an establishment would probably bring
into the district.

At last it was decided that the ceremony should take
place on June 10 (a Sunday), and, as Abbé Cognasse
pointed out, never was festival favoured by brighter sunshine.   For three days his servant, the terrible Palmyre,
with the help of Madame Jauffre and the beautiful Madame
Martineau, had been decorating the church with evergreens
and hangings, lent by the inhabitants.   The ladies of Beaumont, Présidente Gragnon, Générale Jarousse, Préfete
Hennebise—and even, so it was said, Madame Lemarrois,
the wife of the radical mayor and deputy,—had presented
the parish with a superb tricolor flag on which the Sacred
Heart was embroidered, with the motto: 'God and Country.'
And Jauffre himself was to carry that flag, walking on the
right hand of the Mayor of Jonville.   An extraordinary
concourse of important personages arrived during the morning: many notabilities of Beaumont, with the ladies who
had presented the flag; Philis, the Mayor of Maillebois,
with the clerical majority of his council, as well as a shoal
of cassocks and frocks; a grand-vicar, delegated by Monseigneur the Bishop, Father Théodose and other Capuchins,
Brother Fulgence and his assistant Brothers, Father Philibin
and even Father Crabot, both of whom were surrounded
and saluted with the greatest deference.   But people noticed
the absence of Abbé Quandieu, who, according to his own
account, had been laid up by a violent attack of gout at the
last moment.

At three o'clock in the afternoon a band of music, which
had come from the chief town, struck up an heroic march
on the Place de l'Église.   Then appeared the parish coun-
cillors, all wearing their scarves, and headed by Mayor
Martineau and schoolmaster Jauffre, the latter of whom
grasped the staff of his flag with both hands.   A halt ensued until the band had finished playing.   A dense crowd
of peasant families in their Sunday best, and ladies in full
dress, had gathered round, waiting.   Then, all at once, the
principal door of the church was thrown wide open, and
Curé Cognasse appeared in rich sacerdotal vestments, followed by numerous members of the clergy, the many priests
who had hastened to Jonville from surrounding spots.
Chants arose, and all the people prostrated themselves devoutly during the solemn blessing of the flag.   The pathetic
moment came when Mayor Martineau and the members of

the council knelt beneath the folds of the symbolic standard, which Jauffre held slantwise above them in order that one might the better see the gory heart embroidered amid the three colours. And then in a loud voice the Mayor read the deed officially consecrating the parish of Jonville to that heart.

Women wept and men applauded. A gust of blissful insanity arose into the clear sunlight, above the blare of the brass instruments and the beating of the drums which had again struck up a triumphal march. And the procession entered the church, the clergy, the Mayor, and the council, still and ever attended by the schoolmaster and the flag. Then came the benediction of the Holy Sacrament; the monstrance glittering like a great star on the altar, amid all the lighted candles, while the municipality again knelt down most devoutly. And afterwards Abbé Cognasse began to speak with fiery eloquence, exulting at the sight of the representatives of civil authority sheltering themselves beneath the banner of the Sacred Heart, prostrating themselves before the Holy Sacrament, abdicating all pride and rebellion in the hands of the Deity, relying on Him alone to govern and save France. Did not this signify the end of impiety, the Church mistress of men's souls and bodies, sole representative of power and authority on earth? Ah! she would not long delay to restore happiness to her well-beloved eldest Daughter, who at last repented of her errors, submitted, and sought nothing but salvation. Every parish would end by following the example of Jonville, the whole country would give itself to the Sacred Heart, France would recover her empire over the world by the worship of the national flag now transformed into the flag of Jesus! Cries of ecstatic intoxication burst forth, and the splendid ceremony came to an end in the sacristy, whither the council, headed by the Mayor, repaired to sign the deed on parchment which set forth that the whole parish of Jonville had for ever consecrated itself to the Divine Heart, the civil power piously renouncing its claims in favour of the religious power.

But when the party quitted the church a scandalous scene occurred. Among the crowd was Férou, the schoolmaster at Le Moreux, clad in a wretched, tattered frock coat and looking more emaciated, more ardent than ever. He had sunk to the worst tortures of indebtedness, he was pursued for francs and half francs which he had borrowed, for he could no longer obtain on credit the six pounds of bread

which he needed daily to feed his exhausted wife and his
three lean and ailing daughters.　Even before it was due,
his paltry salary of a hundred francs a month disappeared
in that ever-widening gulf, and the little sum which he received as parish clerk was constantly being attached by
creditors.　His growing and incurable misery had increased
the contempt of the peasants who were all at their ease, and
who looked askance at knowledge as it did not even feed
the master appointed to teach it.　And Férou, the only
man of intelligence and culture in that abode of dense
ignorance, grew more and more exasperated at the thought
that he, the man who knew, should be the poor one, whereas
the ignorant were rich.　Feverish rebellion against such
social iniquity came upon him, he was maddened by the
sufferings of those who were dear to him, and dreamt of
destroying this abominable world by violence.

As he stood there he caught sight of Saleur, the Mayor
of Le Moreux, who, wishing to make himself agreeable to
the triumphant Abbé Cognasse, had come over to Jonville,
arrayed in a fine new frock coat.　Peace now reigned
between his parish and the priest, though the latter still
grumbled at having to walk several miles to say Mass for
people who might very well have kept a priest of their own.
However, all the esteem which had departed from the thin,
ghastly, ill-paid, penniless, and deeply indebted schoolmaster
had now gone to the sturdy and flourishing priest who was so
much better off, and who turned every baptism, wedding, and
burial into so much money.　Beaten, as was only natural, in
that unequal duel, Férou was no longer able to control his rage.

' Well, Monsieur Saleur,' he exclaimed, ' here 's a carnival
and no mistake!　Are n't you ashamed to lend yourself to
such ignominy? '

Though Saleur was not at heart with the priests, this remark vexed him.　He construed it as an attack upon his
own *bourgeois* position as an enriched grazier, living on
his income in a pretty house, repainted and decorated at his
own expense.　So he sought for dignified words of repri-
mand: 'You would do better to keep quiet, Monsieur
Férou.　The shame belongs to those who can't even succeed sufficiently to lead respectable lives.'

Irritated by this rejoinder, which smacked of the low
standard of morality that brought him so much suffering,
Férou was about to reply when his anger was diverted by
the sight of Jauffre.

' Ah! colleague,' said he, ' so it 's you who carry their banner of falsehood and imbecility! That 's a fine action for an educator of the lowly and humble ones of our democracy! You know very well that the priest's gain is the schoolmaster's loss.'

Jauffre, like a man who had an income of his own, and who, moreover, was well pleased with what he had done, replied with compassionate yet crushing contempt: ' Before judging others, my poor comrade, you would do well to provide your daughters with shifts to hide their nakedness! '

At this Férou lost all self-control. With his unkempt hair bristling on his head, and a savage gleam in his wild eyes, he waved his long arms and cried: ' You gang of bigots! you pack of Jesuits! Carry your bullock's heart about, worship it, eat it raw, and become, if you can, even more bestial and imbecile than you are already! '

A crowd gathered around the blasphemer, hoots and threats arose, and things would have turned out badly for him if Saleur, like a prudent Mayor, alarmed for the good name of his commune, had not extricated him from the hostile throng and led him away by the arm.

On the morrow the incident was greatly exaggerated; on all sides people talked of execrable sacrilege. Indeed, *Le Petit Beaumontais* related that the schoolmaster of Le Moreux had spat on the national flag of the Sacred Heart at the very moment when worthy Abbé Cognasse was blessing that divine emblem of repentant and rescued France. And in its ensuing number it announced that the revocation of schoolmaster Férou was a certainty. If that were so, the consequences would be serious, for as Férou had not completed his term of ten years' duty as a teacher he would have to perform some years' military service. And, again, while he was in barracks, what would become of his wife and daughters, those woeful creatures for whom he was already unable to provide? He gone, would they not utterly starve to death?

When Marc heard of what had happened he went to see Salvan at Beaumont. This time the newspaper's information was correct, the revocation of Férou was about to be signed, Le Barazer was resolved on it. And as Marc nevertheless begged his old friend to attempt some intervention, the other sadly refused to do so.

' No, no, it would be useless,' he said; ' I should simply encounter inflexible determination. Le Barazer cannot act otherwise; at least, such is his conviction. Opportunist as he is, he finds in that course a means of ridding himself of the other difficulties of the present time. . . . And you must not complain too much; for if his severity falls on Férou it is in order that he may spare you.'

At this Marc burst into protest, saying how much he was upset and grieved by such a *dénouement*.

'But you are not responsible, my dear fellow,' Salvan replied. 'He is casting that prey to the clericals because they require one, and because he thus hopes to save a good workman like yourself. It is a very *distinguée* solution, as somebody said to me yesterday. . . . Ah! how many tears and how much blood must necessarily flow for the slightest progress to be accomplished, how many poor corpses must fill up the ditches in order that the heroes may pass on!'

Salvan's forecast was fulfilled to the very letter. Two days afterwards Férou was dismissed, and, rather than resign himself to military service, he fled to Belgium, full of exasperation at the thought that justice should be denied him. He hoped to find some petty situation at Brussels, which would enable him to send for his wife and children, and make himself a new home abroad. He even ended by declaring that he felt relieved at having escaped from the university galleys, and that he now breathed freely, like a man who was at last at liberty to think and act as he listed.

Meantime his wife installed herself with her three little girls in two small, sordid rooms at Maillebois, where, with all bravery, she at once began to ply her needle as a seamstress, though she found herself unable to earn enough for daily bread. Marc visited her and helped her as far as he could, feeling quite heartbroken at the sight of her pitiable wretchedness. And a remorseful feeling clung to him, for the affair of the crucifix appeared to be forgotten amid the keen emotion roused by the sacrilege of Jonville and the revocation which had followed it. *Le Petit Beaumontais* triumphed noisily, and the Count de Sanglebœuf promenaded the town with victorious airs as if his friends, the Brothers, the Capuchins, and the Jesuits, had now become the absolute masters of the department. And then life followed its course, pending the time when the struggle would begin again, on another field.

One Sunday Marc was surprised to see his wife come home

carrying a Mass-book. 'What! have you been to church?' he asked her.

'Yes,' she answered,' I have just taken the Communion.'

He looked at her, turning pale the while, penetrated by a sudden chill, a quiver, which he strove to hide. 'You do that now, and you did not tell me of it?' said he.

On her side she feigned astonishment, though, according to her wont, she remained very calm and gentle: 'Tell you of it—why?' she asked. 'It is a matter of conscience. I leave you free to act according to your views, so I suppose I may act according to mine.'

'No doubt; all the same, for the sake of a good understanding between us, I should have liked to have known.'

'Well, you know now. I do not hide it, as you may see. But we shall, none the less, remain good friends, I hope.'

She added nothing more, and he lacked the strength to tell her of all that he felt seething within him, to provoke the explanation which he knew to be imperative. But the day remained heavy with silence. This time some connecting link had certainly snapped and sundered them.

III

SOME months elapsed, and day by day Marc found himself confronted by the redoubtable question: Why had he married a woman whose belief was contrary to his own? Did not he and Geneviève belong to two hostile spheres, divided by an abyss, and would not their disagreement bring them the most frightful torture? Some scientists were suggesting that when people desired to marry they should undergo proper examination, and provide themselves with certificates setting forth that they were free from all physical flaws. The young man for his part felt convinced that all such certificates ought also to state that the holder's heart and mind were free from every form of inherited or acquired imbecility. Two beings, ignorant one of the other, coming from different worlds, as it were, with contradictory and hostile notions, could only torture and destroy each other. And yet how great an excuse was, at the outset, furnished by the imperious blindness of love, and how difficult it was to solve the question in some particular cases, which were often those instinct with most charm and tenderness!

Marc did not yet accuse Geneviève—he merely dreaded lest she should become a deadly weapon in the hands of those priests and monks against whom he was waging war. As the Church had failed to strike him down by intriguing with his superiors, it must now be thinking of dealing him a blow in the heart by destroying his domestic happiness. That was essentially the device of the Jesuits, the everlasting manœuvre of the father-confessor, who helps on the work of Catholic domination in stealthy fashion, like a worldly psychologist well acquainted with the passions and the means they offer for triumphing over the human beast, who, fondled and satiated, may then be strangled. To glide into a home, to set oneself between husband and wife, to capture the latter and thereby destroy the man whom the Church wishes to get rid of, no easier and more widely adopted stratagem than this is known to the black whisperers of the confessional.

The Church, having taken possession of woman, has used her as its most powerful weapon of propaganda and enthralment. At the first moment an obstacle certainly arose. Was not woman all shame and perdition, a creature of sin, and terror, before whom the very saints trembled? Vile nature had set its trap in her, she was the source of life, she was life itself, the contempt of which was taught by the Church. And so for a moment the latter denied a soul to woman, the creature from whom men of purity fled to the desert, in danger of succumbing if the evening breeze wafted to them merely the odour of her hair. Beauty and passion being cast out of the religious system, she became the mere embodiment of all that was condemned, all that was regarded as diabolical, denounced as the craft of Satan, all against which prayer, mortification, and strict and perpetual chastity were enjoined. And in the desire to crush sexuality in woman, the ideal woman was shown sexless, and a virgin was enthroned as queen of heaven.

But the Church ended by understanding the irresistible sexual power of woman over man, and in spite of its repugnance, in spite of its terror, decided to employ it as a means to conquer and enchain man. That great flock of women, weakened by an abasing system of education, terrorised by the fear of hell, degraded to the status of serfs by the hatred and harshness of priests, might serve as an army. And as man was ceasing to believe and turning aside from the altars, an effort to bring him back to them might be attempted with the help of woman's Satanic but ever victorious charm. She need only withhold herself from man, and he would follow her to the very foot of the shrines. In this, no doubt, there was much immoral inconsistency; but had not the Church lost much of its primitive sternness, and had not the Jesuits appeared upon the scene to fight the great fight on the new field of casuistry and accommodation with the world? From that time, then, the Church handled woman more gently and skilfully than before. It still refused to take her to wife, for it feared and loathed her as the embodiment of sin, but it employed her to ensure its triumph. Its policy was to keep her to itself, by stupefying her as formerly, by holding her in a state of perpetual mental infancy. That much ensured, it turned her into a weapon of war, confident that it would vanquish incredulous man by setting pious woman before him. And in woman the Church always had a witness at the family hearth, and was able to exert its influence even in the most intimate moments of conjugal life, whenever it desired to plunge resisting men into the worst despair. Thus, at bottom, woman still remained the human animal, and the priests merely made use of her in order to ensure the triumph of their creed.

Marc easily reconstituted the early phases of Geneviève's life: in childhood, the pleasant convent of the Sisters of the Visitation, with all sorts of devout attractions; the evening prayer on one's knees beside the little white bed; the providential protection promised to those who were obedient; the lovely stories of Christians saved from lions, of guardian angels watching over children, and carrying the pure souls of the well-beloved to heaven, such indeed as Monsieur le Curé related in the dazzling chapel. Afterwards came years of skilful preparation for the first Communion, with the extraordinary mysteries of the Catechism enshrouded in fearsome obscurity, for ever disturbing the reason, and kindling all the perverse fever of mystical curiosity. Then in the first troublous hour of maidenhood the young girl, enraptured with her white gown, her first bridal gown, was affianced to Jesus, united to the divine lover, whose gentle sway she accepted for ever; and man might come afterwards, he would find himself forestalled by an influence which would dispute his possession of her with all the haunting force of remembrance. Again and again throughout her life woman would see the candles sparkling, feel the incense filling her with languor, hark back to the wakening of her senses amid the mysterious whispering of the confessional and the languishing rapture of the Holy Table. She would spend her youth encompassed by the worst prejudices, nourished with the errors and falsehoods of ages, and, above all things, kept in close captivity in order that nothing of the real world might reach her. Thus the girl of sixteen or seventeen, on quitting the good Sisters of the Visitation, was a miracle of perversion and stultification, one whose natural vision had been dimmed, one who knew nothing of herself nor of others, and who in the part she would play in love and wifehood would bring, apart from her beauty, nought save religious poison, the evil ferment of every disorder and every suffering.

Marc pictured Geneviève, somewhat later, in the devout little house on the Place des Capucins. It was there that

he had first seen her in the charge of her grandmother and
mother, the chief care of whose vigilant affection had been
to complete the convent work by setting on one side everything that might have made the girl a creature of truth and
reason. It was enough that she should follow the Church's
observances like an obedient worshipper; she was told that
she need take no interest in other things; she was prepared
for life by being kept quite blind to it. Some effort on
Marc's part was already necessary to enable him to recall her
such as she had been at the time of their first interviews—
delightfully fair, with a refined and gentle face, so desirable
too with the flush of her youth, the penetrating perfume of
her blond beauty, that he only vaguely remembered whether
she had then shown much intelligence and sense. A gust
of passion had transported them both; he had felt that she
shared his flame; for, however chilling might have been her
education, she had inherited from her father a real craving
for love.

In matters of intellect she was doubtless no fool; he must
have deemed her similar to other young girls, of whom one
knows nothing; and certainly he had resolved to look into
all that after their marriage. But when he now recalled
their first years at Jonville he perceived how slight had been
his efforts to know her better and make her more wholly his
own. They had spent those years in mutual rapture, in
such passionate intoxication that they had remained unconscious even of their moral differences. She showed real intelligence in many things, and he had not cared to worry
her about the singular gaps which he had occasionally discovered in her understanding. As she ceased to follow the
observances of the Church he imagined that he had won
her over to his views, though he had not even taken the
trouble to instruct her in them. He now suspected that
there must have been some little cowardice on his part, some
dislike of the bother of re-educating her entirely, and also
some fear of encountering obstacles, and spoiling the adorable quietude of their love. Indeed, as their life was all
happiness, why should he have sought a cause of strife,
particularly as he had felt convinced that their great love
would suffice to ensure their good understanding whatever
might arise?

But now the crisis was at hand, heavy with menace.
When Salvan had interested himself in the marriage he
had pointed out to Marc that if husband and wife were

ill-assorted there was always some fear for the future; and
to tranquillise his own conscience with respect to the young
man's case it had been necessary that he should accept the
view adopted by Marc, that when a young couple adored
one another it was possible for the husband to make his
wife such as he desired her to be.   Indeed, when an ignorant young girl is handed over to a man whom she loves, is
it not in his power to re-create her in his own image ?   He
is her god, and may mould her afresh by the sovereign
might of love.   Such is the theory, but how often is it put
into practice ?   Languor, blindness, come upon the man
himself; and in Marc's case it was only long afterwards
that he had realised how ignorant he had really remained of
Geneviève's mind—a mind which, awaking according to the
play of circumstances, revealed itself at last as that of an
unknown, antagonistic woman.

The effects of the warm bath of religiosity in which Geneviève had grown up were still there.   The adored woman,
whom Marc had imagined to be wholly his own, was possessed by the indelible, indestructible past, in which he had
no share whatever.   He perceived with stupefaction that
they had nothing in common, that though he had made her
wife and mother, he had in no degree modified her brain,
fashioned from her cradle days by skilful hands.   Ah! how
bitterly he now regretted that, in the first months of their
married life, he had not striven to conquer the mind that
existed behind the charming face which he had covered
with his kisses!   He ought not to have abandoned himself
to his happiness, he ought to have striven to re-educate the
big child who hung so amorously about his neck.   As it
had been his desire to make her entirely his own, why had
he not shown himself a prudent, sensible man, whose reason
remained undisturbed by the joys of love ?   If he suffered
now it was by reason of his vain illusions, his idleness, and
his egotism in refraining from action, from the fear of spoiling the felicity of his dalliance.

But the danger had now become so serious that he resolved to contend with it.   A last excuse for avoiding
anything like rough intervention remained to him: respect
for another's freedom, tolerance of whatever might be the
sincere faith of his life's companion.   With amorous weakness he had consented to a religious marriage, and subsequently to the baptism of his daughter Louise, and, in the
same way, he now lacked the strength to forbid his wife's

attendance at Mass, Communion, and Confession, if her
belief lay in such observances. Yet times had changed;
he might have pleaded that at the date of his wedding,
and again at the period of his daughter's birth, he had been
quite indifferent to Church matters, whereas things were
very different now that he had formally rejected the Church
and its creed. He had imposed a duty on himself, he ought
to set an example, he ought not to allow in his own home
that which he condemned in the homes of others. If he,
the secular schoolmaster, who showed such marked hostility
to the interference of priests in the education of the young,
should suffer his wife to go to Mass and take little Louise
with her, would he not render himself liable to reproach?
Nevertheless, he did not feel that he had the right to prevent
those things, so great was his innate respect for liberty of
conscience. Thus, confronted as he was by the imperious
necessity of defending his happiness, he perceived no other
available weapons, particularly in his own home, than discussion, persuasion, and the daily teaching of life in all that
it has of a logical and healthful nature. That which he
ought to have done at the outset, he must attempt now, not
only in order to win his Geneviève over to healthy human
truth, but also to prevent their dear Louise from following
her into the deadly errors of Roman Catholicism.

For the moment, however, the case of Louise, now seven
years of age, seemed less urgent. Moreover, though Marc
was convinced that a child's first impressions are the keenest
and the most tenacious, circumstances compelled a waiting
policy with respect to his little girl. He had been obliged
to let her attend the neighbouring school, where Mademoiselle Rouzaire was already filling her mind with Bible history. There were also prayers at the beginning and at the
end of lessons, Sunday attendance at Mass, benedictions and
processions. The schoolmistress had certainly bowed assent
with a sharp smile when Marc had exacted from her a
promise that his daughter should not be required to follow
any religious exercises. But the girl was still so young that
it seemed ridiculous to insist on preserving her from contamination in this fashion; besides which, Marc was not
always at hand to make sure whether she said prayers with
the other children or not. That which disgusted him with
Mademoiselle Rouzaire was less the clerical zeal which
seemed to consume her than her hypocrisy, the keen personal interest which guided all her actions. The woman's

lack of real faith, her mere exploitation of religious senti-
mentality for her own advantage, was so apparent that even
Geneviève, whose uprightness still remained entire, was
wounded by it, and for this reason had repulsed the other's
advances.

The schoolmistress, indeed, wishing to worm her way
into Marc's home and scenting the possibility of a drama
there, had suddenly manifested great friendship for her
neighbour. What delight and glory it would be if she could
render the Church a service in that direction, separate the
wife from the husband, and strike the secular schoolmaster
down at his own fireside! She therefore showed herself
very amiable and insinuating, ever keeping on the watch
behind the party-wall, hoping for some opportunity which
would enable her to intervene and console the ' poor persecuted little wife.' At times she risked allusions, expressions
of sympathy, words of advice: ' It was so sad when husband
and wife were not of the same faith! And assuredly one
must not wreck one's soul, so it was best to offer some
gentle resistance.' On two occasions Mademoiselle Rouzaire had the pleasure of seeing Geneviève shed tears. But
afterwards the young wife, feeling very uneasy, drew away
from her, and avoided all further confidential chats. That
mealy-mouthed woman, with her ' gendarme ' build, her
fondness for anisette, and her chatter about the priests,—
' who, after all, were not different from other men, and of
whom it was wrong to speak badly,'—inspired her with
unconquerable repugnance. Thus repulsed, Mademoiselle Rouzaire felt her hatred for her neighbours increase,
and visited her spite on little Louise by instructing her
most carefully in religious matters, in spite of the paternal
prohibition.

If Marc was not seriously concerned as yet about his
daughter, he understood that it was urgent he should act in
order to prevent his beloved Geneviève from being wrested
from him. It was now plain to him that her religious views
had revived at her grandmother's house. The pious little
home on the Place des Capucins was like a hotbed of mystical contagion, where a faith, which had not been extinguished, but which had died down amid the first joys of
human love, was bound to be fanned into flame once more.
Had they remained at Jonville in loving solitude, he, Marc,
might have sufficed for Geneviève's yearning passion. But
at Maillebois foreign elements had intervened between them.

That terrible Simon case had brought about the first snap, and then had come its consequences, the struggle between himself and the Congregations, and the liberating mission which he had undertaken. Besides, they had no longer remained alone; a stream of people and things now flowed between them, growing ever wider and wider, and they could already foresee the day when they would be utter strangers, one to the other.

At present Geneviève met some of Marc's bitterest enemies at Madame Duparque's. The young man learnt at last that the terrible grandmother, after years of humble solicitation, had obtained the favour of being included among Father Crabot's penitents. The Rector of Valmarie usually reserved his services as confessor for the fine ladies of Beaumont, and only some very powerful reasons could have induced him to confess that old *bourgeoise*, who, socially, was of no account whatever. And not only did he receive her at the chapel of Valmarie, but he did her the honour to repair to the Place des Capucins whenever an attack of gout confined her to her armchair. He there met other personages of the cloth, Abbé Quandieu, Father Théodose, and Brother Fulgence, who became partial to that pious nook all shadows and silence, that well-closed little house where their conclaves, it seemed, might pass unperceived. Nevertheless, rumours circulated, some evil-minded people saying that the house was indeed the clerical faction's secret headquarters, the hidden laboratory, where its most important resolutions were prepared. Yet how could one seriously suspect the modest dwelling of two old ladies, who certainly had every right to receive their friends? The latter's shadows were scarcely seen; Pélagie, the servant, swiftly and softly closed the door upon them; not a face ever appeared at the windows, not a murmur filtered through the sleepy little façade. Everything was very dignified—great deference was shown for that highly respectable dwelling.

But Marc regretted that he had not gone there more frequently. Assuredly he had made a great mistake in abandoning Geneviève to the two old ladies, allowing her to spend whole days in their company with little Louise. His presence would have counteracted the contagion of that sphere; had he been there the others would have restrained the stealthy attacks which, as he well realised, they made upon his ideas and his person. Geneviève, as if conscious

of the danger with which the peace of her home was threatened, occasionally offered some resistance, struggling to
avoid hostilities with the husband whom she still loved.
For instance, on returning to the observances of the Church,
she had chosen Abbé Quandieu as her confessor instead of
Father Théodose, whom Madame Duparque had sought to
impose on her. The young woman was conscious of the
warlike ardour that lurked behind the Capuchin's handsome
face, his beautifully-kept black beard, and his glowing eyes,
which filled his penitents with dreams of rapture; whereas
the Abbé was a prudent and gentle man, a fatherly confessor, whose frequent silence was full of sadness—one, too, in
whom she vaguely divined a friend, one who suffered from
the fratricidal warfare of the times, and longed for peace
among all workers of good will. Geneviève, indeed, was
yet at a stage of loving tenderness, when her mind, though
gradually becoming clouded, still manifested some anxiety
before it finally sank into mystical passion. But day by
day she was confronted by more serious assaults, and yielded
more and more to the disturbing influence of her relatives,
whose unctuous gestures and caressing words slowly be-
numbed her. In vain did Marc now repair more frequently
to the Place des Capucins; he could no longer arrest the
poison's deadly work.

As yet, however, there was no attempt to enforce authority, no brutal roughness. Geneviève was merely enticed,
flattered, cajoled, with gentle hands. And no violent words
were spoken of her husband; on the contrary, he was said
to be a man deserving of all pity, a sinner whose salvation
was most desirable. The unhappy being! He knew not
what incalculable harm he was doing to his country, how
many children's souls he was wrecking, sending to hell,
through his obstinate rebellion and pride! Then, at first
vaguely, and afterwards more and more plainly, a desire
was expressed in Geneviève's presence that she might devote
herself to the most praiseworthy task of converting that
sinner, redeeming that guilty man, whom, in her weakness,
she still loved. What joy and glory would be hers if she
should lead him back to religion, arrest his rageful work of
destruction, save him, and thereby save his innocent victims
from eternal damnation! For several months, with infinite
craft, the young woman was in this wise worked upon, prepared for the enterprise expected of her, with the evident
hope of bringing about conjugal rupture by fomenting a col-

lision between the two irreconcilable principles which she and her husband represented—she a woman of the past, full of the errors of the ages—he a man of free thought, marching towards the future. And in time the much-sought, inevitable developments appeared.

The conjugal life of Marc and Geneviève grew sadder every day—that life so gay and loving once, when their kisses had perpetually mingled with their merry laughter. They had not yet reached the quarrelling stage; but, as soon as they found themselves alone together and unoccupied, they felt embarrassed. Something of which they never spoke seemed to be growing up between them, chilling them more and more, prompting them to enmity. On Marc's side there was a growing consciousness that she who was bound up with every hour of his life, she whom he embraced at night, was a woman foreign to him, one whose ideas and sentiments he reprobated. And on Geneviève's side there was a similar feeling, an exasperating conviction that she was regarded as an ignorant, unreasonable child, one who was still adored but with a love laden with much dolorous compassion. Thus their first wounds were imminent.

One night, when they were in bed, encompassed by the warm darkness, while Marc held Geneviève in a mute embrace as if she were some sulking child, she suddenly burst into bitter sobs, exclaiming: 'Ah! you love me no longer!'

'No longer love you, my darling!' he replied; 'why do you say that?'

'If you loved me you would not leave me in such dreadful sorrow! You turn away from me more and more each day. You treat me as if I were some ailing creature, sickly or insane. Nothing that I may say seems of any account to you. You shrug your shoulders at it. Ah! I feel it plainly, you are growing more and more impatient; I am becoming a worry, a burden to you.'

Though Marc's heart contracted, he did not interrupt her, for he wished to learn everything.

'Yes,' she resumed, 'unhappily for me I can see things quite plainly. You take more interest in the last of your boys than you do in me. When you are downstairs with the boys, in the classroom, you become impassioned, you pour out your whole soul, you exert yourself to explain the slightest things to them, and laugh and play with them like an elder brother. But directly you come upstairs you get gloomy again; you can think of nothing to say to me, you look ill at ease, like a man who 's worried by his wife and tired of her. . . . Ah! God, God, how unhappy I am!'

Again she burst into sobs.

Then Marc, making up his mind, gently responded: 'I dared not tell you the cause of my sadness, darling, but if I suffer it is precisely because I find in you all that you reproach me with. You are never with me now. You spend whole days elsewhere, and when you come home you bring with you an air of unreason and death, which ravages our poor home. It is you who no longer speak to me. Your mind is always wandering, deep in some dim dream, even while you are sewing, or serving the meals, or attending to our little Louise. It is you who treat me with indulgent pity, as if I were a guilty man, perhaps one unconscious of his crime; and it is you who will soon have ceased to love me, if you refuse to open your eyes to a little reasonable truth.'

But she would not admit it; she interrupted each sentence that came from him with protests full of vehemence and stupefaction: 'I! I! It is I whom you accuse! I tell you that you no longer love me, and you dare to assert that I am losing my love for you!' Then, casting aside all restraint, revealing the innermost thoughts that haunted her day by day, she continued: 'Ah! how happy are the women whose husbands share their faith! I see some in church who are always accompanied by their husbands. How delightful it must be for husband and wife to place themselves conjointly in the hands of God! Those homes are blessed, they indeed have but one soul, and there is no felicity that heaven does not shower on them!'

Marc could not restrain a slight laugh, at once very gentle and distressful. 'So now, my poor wife,' he said, 'you think of trying to convert me?'

'What harm would there be in that?' she answered eagerly. 'Do you imagine I do not love you enough to feel frightful grief at the thought of the deadly peril you are in? You do not believe in future punishment, you brave the wrath of heaven; but for my part I pray heaven every day to enlighten you, and I would give — ah! willingly — ten years of my life to be able to open your eyes, and save you from the terrible catastrophes which threaten you. Ah! if you would only love me, and listen to me, and follow me to the land of eternal delight!'

She trembled in his embrace, she glowed with such a fever of superhuman desire that he was thunderstruck, for he had not imagined the evil to be so deep. It was she who catechised him now, who tried to win him to her faith, and he felt ashamed, for was she not doing what he himself ought to have done the very first day—that is, strive to convert her to his own views? He could not help expressing his thoughts aloud, and unluckily he said: 'It is not you yourself who is speaking; you have been given a task full of danger for the happiness of both of us.'

At this she began to lose her temper: 'Why do you wound me like that?' she asked. 'Do you think I am incapable of acting for myself—from personal conviction and affection? Am I senseless, then—so stupid and docile that I can only serve as an instrument? Besides, even if people —who are worthy of all respect, and whose sacred character you disregard—do speak to me about you in a brotherly way which would surprise you—ought you not rather to be moved by it, ought you not to yield to such loving-kindness? . . . God, who might strike you down, holds out His arms to you . . . yet when He makes use of me and my love to lead you back to Him you can only jest and treat me as if I were a foolish little girl repeating a lesson! . . . Ah! we understand each other no longer, and it is that which grieves me so much!'

While she spoke he felt his fear and desolation increasing. 'That is true,' he repeated slowly, 'we no longer understand one another. Words no longer have the same meaning for us, and every reproach that I address to you, you address to me. Which of us will break away from the other? Which of us loves the other and works for the other's happiness? . . . Ah! I am the guilty one and I greatly fear that it is too late for me to repair my fault. I ought to have taught you where to find truth and equity.'

At these words, so suggestive of his profession, her rebellion became complete. 'Yes, for you I am always a foolish pupil who knows nothing and whose eyes require to be opened. But it is I who know where truth and justice are to be found. You have not the right to speak those words.'

'Not the right!'

'No; you have plunged into that monstrous error, that ignoble Simon affair, in which your hatred of the Church blinds you and urges you to the worst iniquity. When a man like you goes so far as to override all truth and justice in order to strike and befoul the ministers of religion, it is better to believe that he has lost his senses.'

This time Marc reached the root of the quarrel which Geneviève was picking with him. The Simon case lay beneath everything else, it was that alone which had inspired all the discreet and skilful manœuvring of which he beheld the effects. If his wife were enticed away from him at her relatives' home, if she were employed as a weapon to strike him a deadly blow, it was especially in order that an artisan of truth, a possible justiciary, might be smitten in his person. It was necessary to suppress him, for his destruction alone could ensure the impunity of the real culprits.

His voice trembled with deep grief as he answered: 'Ah! Geneviève, this is more serious. There will be an end to our home if we can no longer agree on so clear and so simple a question. Are you no longer on my side, then, in that painful affair?'

'No, certainly not.'

'You think poor Simon guilty?'

'Why, there is no doubt of it! The reasons you give for asserting his innocence repose on no foundation whatever! I should like you to hear the persons whose purity of life you dare to suspect! And as you fall into such gross error respecting a case in which everything is so evident, a case which is settled beyond possibility of appeal, how can I place the slightest faith in your other notions, your fanciful social system, in which you begin by suppressing religion?'

He had taken her in his arms again, and was holding her in a tight embrace. Ah! she was right. Their slowly increasing rupture had originated in their divergence of views on that question of truth and justice, in reference to which others had managed to poison her understanding. 'Listen, Geneviève,' he said; 'there is only one truth, one justice. You must listen to me, and our agreement will restore our peace.'

'No, no!'

'But, Geneviève, you must not remain in such darkness when I see light all around me; it would mean separation forever.'

'No, no, let me be! You tire me; I won't even listen.'

She wrenched herself from his embrace and turned her back upon him. He vainly sought to clasp her again, kissing her and whispering gentle words; she would not move, she would not even answer. A chill swept down on the

conjugal couch, and the room seemed black as ink, dolor-
ously lifeless, as if the misfortune which was coming had
already annihilated everything.

From that time forward Geneviève became more nervous
and ill-tempered. Much less consideration was now shown
for her husband at her grandmother's house; he was attacked in her presence in an artfully graduated manner, as
by degrees her affection for him was seen to decline. Little
by little he became a public malefactor, one of the damned,
a slayer of the God she worshipped. And the rebellion to
which she was thus urged re-echoed in her home in bitter
words, in an increase of discomfort and coldness. Fresh
quarrels arose at intervals, usually at night, when they retired to rest, for in the daytime they saw little of each other,
Marc then being busy with his boys and Geneviève being
constantly absent, now at church, now at her grandmother's.
Thus their life was gradually quite spoilt. The young woman showed herself more and more aggressive, while her
husband, so tolerant by nature, in his turn ended by mani-
festing irritation.

'My darling, I shall want you to-morrow during afternoon
lessons,' he said one evening.

'To-morrow? I can't come,' she replied; 'Abbé Quandieu will be expecting me. Besides, you need not rely on
me for anything.'

'Won't you help me, then?'

'No, I detest everything you do. Damn yourself if you
choose; but I have to think of my salvation.'

'Then each is to go his own way?'

'As you please.'

'Oh! darling, darling, is it you who speak like that?
Are they going to change your heart after fogging your
mind? So now you are altogether on the side of the cor-
rupters and poisoners?'

'Be quiet, be quiet, you unhappy man! It is your work
which is all falsehood and poison. You blaspheme; your
justice and your truth are filthy; and it is the devil—yes,
the devil—who teaches those wretched children of yours,
whom I no longer even pity, for they must be stupid indeed
to remain here!'

'My poor darling, how is it possible that you, once so intelligent, can say such foolish things?'

'When a man finds women foolish he leaves them to
themselves.'

Thereupon, in his turn losing his temper, Marc, indeed, left her to herself, making no effort to win her back by a loving caress as in former days. It often happened that they were unable to get to sleep; they lay in bed, side by side, with their eyes wide open in the darkness, silent and motionless, as if the little space which separated them had become an abyss.

Marc was particularly afflicted by the growing hatred which Geneviève manifested against his school, against the dear children whom he so passionately strove to teach. At each fresh dispute she expressed herself so bitterly that it seemed as if she became jealous of the little ones when she saw him treat them so affectionately, endeavour so zealously to make them sensible and peaceable. At bottom, indeed, Geneviève's quarrel with Marc had no other cause; for she herself was but a child, one of those who needed to be taught and freed, but who rebelled and clung stubbornly to the errors of the ages. And in her estimation all the affection which her husband lavished on his boys was diverted from herself. As long as he should busy himself with them in such a fatherly fashion, she would be unable to conquer him, carry him away into the divine and rapturous stultification, in which she would fain have seen him fall asleep in her arms. The struggle at last became concentrated on that one point. Geneviève no longer passed the classroom without feeling an inclination to cross herself, like one who was utterly upset by the diabolical work accomplished there, who was irritated by her powerlessness to wrest from such impious courses the man whose bed she still shared.

Months, even years went by, and the battle between Marc and Geneviève grew fiercer. But no imprudent haste was displayed at the home of her relatives, for the Church has all eternity before her to achieve her ends. Besides, leaving on one side that vain marplot, Brother Fulgence, Father Théodose and Father Crabot were too skilled in the manipulation of souls to overlook the necessity of proceeding slowly with a woman of passionate nature, whose mind was an upright one when mysticism did not obscure and pervert it. As long as she should love her husband, as long as there should be no conjugal rupture, the work they had undertaken would not be complete. And it required a long time to uproot and extirpate a great love from a woman's heart and flesh in such wise that it might never grow again. Thus Geneviève was left in the hands of Abbé Quandieu,

so that he might gently rock her to sleep before more energetic action was attempted.   Meantime, the others contented themselves with watching her.   It was a masterpiece
of delicate, gradual, but certain spell working.

Another affair helped to disturb Marc's home.   He took
a great deal of interest in Madame Férou, who had installed
herself with her three daughters in a wretched lodging at
Maillebois, where she had sought work as a seamstress while
awaiting a summons from her husband, the dismissed schoolmaster, who had fled to Brussels to seek employment there.
But the wretched man's endeavours had proved fruitless.
He had found himself unable even to provide for his own
wants; and tortured by separation, exasperated by exile, he
had lost his head and returned to Maillebois with the bravado of one whom misery pursues and who can know no
worse misfortune than that already befalling him.   Denounced on the very next day, he was seized by the military
authorities as a deserter, and Salvan had to intervene
actively to save him from being incorporated at once in
some disciplinary company.   He was now in garrison in a
little Alpine town, at the other end of France, while his
wife and daughters, scarcely possessed of shelter and
clothes, often found themselves without bread.

Marc also had exerted himself on Férou's behalf at the
time of his arrest.   He had then seen him for a few minutes
and was unable to forget him.   That poor, big, haggard
fellow lingered in his mind like the victim, *par excellence*, of
social abomination.   Doubtless he had made his retention
in office impossible, even as Mauraisin said; but how many
excuses there were for this shepherd's son who had become
a schoolmaster, who had been starved for years, who had
been treated with so much scorn on account of his poverty,
who had been cast to the most extreme views by his circumstances: he, a man of intelligence and learning, who found
himself possessing nothing, knowing not one joy of life,
whereas ignorant brutes possessed and enjoyed all around
him.   And the long iniquity had ended in brutal barrack-
life far away from those who were dear to him, and who
were perishing of misery.

' Is it not enough to goad one into turning everything upside down? ' he had cried to Marc at their brief interview,
his eyes flashing while he waved his long bony arms.   ' I
signed, it 's true, a ten years' engagement which exempted
me from barrack-life if I gave those ten years to teaching.

And it 's true also that I gave only eight years, as I was revoked for having said what I thought about the black-frocks'
revolting idolatry! But was it I who cancelled my engagement? And after casting me brutally adrift, without any
means of subsistence, is n't it monstrous to seize me and
claim payment of my old debt to the army, in such wise that
my wife and children must remain with nobody to earn a
living for them? The eight years I spent in the university
penitentiary, where a man who believes in truth is allowed
neither freedom of speech nor freedom of action, were not
enough for them! They insist on robbing me of two more
years, on shutting me up in their gaol of blood and iron,
and reducing me to that life of passive obedience which is
the necessary apprenticeship for devastation and massacre,
the mere thought of which exasperates me! Ah! it 's too
much. I 've given them quite enough of my life, and they
will end by maddening me if they ask me for more.'

Alarmed at finding him so excited, Marc tried to calm
him by promising to do all he could for his wife and daughters. In two years' time he would be released, and then
some position might be found for him, and he would be able
to begin his life afresh. But Férou remained gloomy, and
growled angry words: 'No, no, I 'm done for. I shall
never get through those two years quietly. They know it
well, and it 's to get the chance of killing me like a mad
dog that they are sending me yonder.'

Then he inquired who had replaced him at Le Moreux,
and on hearing that it was a man named Chagnat, an ex-
assistant teacher at Brévannes, a large parish of the region,
he began to laugh bitterly. Chagnat, a dusky little man
with a low brow and retreating mouth and chin, was the
personification of the perfect beadle—not a hypocrite like
Jauffre, who made use of religion as a means to advancement, but a shallow-brained bigot, such a dolt indeed as to
believe in any nonsensical trash that fell from the priest's
lips. His wife, a huge carroty creature, was yet more stupid
than himself. And Férou's bitter gaiety increased when he
learnt that Mayor Saleur had completely abdicated in favour
of that idiot Chagnat, whom Abbé Cognasse employed as
a kind of sacristan-delegate to rule the parish on his behalf.

'When I told you long ago,' said Férou, 'that all that
dirty gang, the priests, the good Brothers, and the good
Sisters, would eat us up and reign here, you would n't believe me; you declared that my mind was diseased! Well,

now it has come to pass; they are your masters, and you 'll
see into what a fine mess they will lead you. It disgusts
one to be a man: a stray dog is less to be pitied. And as
for myself I 've had quite enough of it all. I 'll bring things
to an end if they plague me.'

Nevertheless Férou was sent off to join his regiment, and
another three months went by, the wretchedness of his unhappy wife steadily increasing. She, once so fair and
pleasant with her bright and fresh round face, now looked
twice as old as she really was, aged betimes by hard toil and
want. She still found very little work, and spent an entire
winter month fireless, almost without bread. To make
matters worse, her eldest daughter fell ill with typhoid
fever, and lay perishing in the icy garret into which the
wind swept through every chink in the door and window.
Marc, who in a discreet way had already given alms to the
poor woman, at last begged his wife to entrust her with
some work.

Although Geneviève spoke of Férou even as those whom
she met at her grandmother's house spoke of him, saying
that he had blasphemously insulted the Sacred Heart and
was a sacrilegist, she felt stirred by the story of his wife's
bitter want. ' Yes,' she said to her husband, ' Louise needs
a new frock; I have the stuff, and I will take it to that
woman.'

' Thank you for her. I will go with you,' Marc replied.

On the following day they repaired together to Madame
Férou's sordid lodging, whence her landlord threatened to
expel her as she was in arrears with her rent. Her eldest
daughter was now near her death; and when the Froments
arrived she herself and her two younger girls were sobbing
in heartrending fashion amid the fearful disorder of the
place. For a moment Marc and Geneviève remained standing there, amazed and unable to understand the situation.

' You have n't heard it, you have n't heard it, have you? '
Madame Férou at last exclaimed. ' Well, it 's done now;
they are going to kill him. Ah! he guessed it; he said that
those brigands would end by having his skin.'

She went on speaking in a disjointed fashion amid her
sobs, and Marc was thus able to extract from her the distressful story. Férou, as was inevitable, had turned out a
very bad soldier, and unfavourably noted by his superiors,
treated with the utmost harshness as a revolutionary, he
had carried a quarrel with his corporal so far as to rush on

the latter and kick and pommel him. For this he had been
court-martialled, and they were now about to send him to
a military *bagnio* in Algeria, where he would be drafted into
one of those disciplinary companies, among which the
abominable tortures of the old ages are still practised.

' He will never come back, they will murder him! ' his
wife continued in a fury. ' He wrote to bid me good-bye;
he knows that he will soon be killed. . . . And what
shall I do? What will become of my poor children? Ah!
the brigands, the brigands! '

Marc listened, sorely grieved, unable to think of a word
of consolation, whereas Geneviève began to show signs of
impatience. ' But, my dear Madame Férou,' she exclaimed,
' why should they kill your husband? The officers of our
army are not in the habit of killing their men. You increase
your own distress by your unjust thoughts.'

' They are brigands, I tell you! ' the unhappy woman repeated with growing violence. ' What! my poor Férou
starved for eight years, discharging the most ungrateful
duties, and he is taken for another two years and treated
like a brute beast, simply because he spoke like a sensible
man! And now what was bound to happen has happened;
he is sent to the galleys, where they 'll end by murdering
him after dragging him from agony to agony! No, no, I
won't have it! I 'll go and tell them that they are all a band
of brigands—brigands! '

Marc endeavoured to calm her. He, all kindliness and
equity, was shocked by such excessive social iniquity. But
what could those on whom it recoiled, the wife and children,
do, crushed as they were beneath the millstone of tragic
fate? ' Be reasonable,' said he. ' We will try to do something; we will not forsake you.'

But Geneviève had become icy cold. That wretched
home where the mother was wringing her hands, where the
poor puny girls were sobbing and lamenting, no longer inspired her with any pity. She no longer even saw the eldest
daughter, wrapped in the shreds of a blanket and looking
so ghastly as she gazed at the scene with dilated, expres-
sionless eyes, unable even to weep, such was her weakness.
Erect and rigid, still carrying the little parcel formed of the
stuff for Louise's new frock, the young woman slowly said:
' You must place yourself in the hands of God. Cease to
offend Him, for He might punish you still more.'

A laugh of terrible scorn came from Madame Férou: 'Oh!

God is too busy with the rich to pay attention to the poor!'
she cried. 'It was in His name that we were reduced to
this misery, it is in His name that they are going to murder my poor husband!'

At this Geneviève was carried away by anger: 'You blaspheme! You deserve no help!' said she. 'If you had only
shown a little religious feeling, I know persons who would
have helped you already.'

'But I ask you for nothing, madame,' the poor woman
answered. 'Yes, I know that help has been refused me because I do not go to confession. Even Abbé Quandieu,
who is so charitable, does not dare to include me among his
poor. . . . But I am not a hypocrite, I simply endeavour to earn my bread by work.'

'Well, then, apply for work to the wretched madmen who
regard the priests and the officers as brigands!'

And thereupon Geneviève hurried away in a passion, carrying with her the stuff for her daughter's frock. Marc was
obliged to follow her, though he quivered with indignation.
And halfway down the stairs he could restrain himself no
longer. 'You have just done a bad action!' he exclaimed.

'How?'

'How? A God of kindness would be charitable to all.
Your God of wrath and punishment is but a monstrous
phantasy. . . . It is not necessary that one should
humble oneself to deserve assistance, it is sufficient that one
should suffer.'

'No, no! Those who sin deserve their sufferings! Let
them suffer if they persist in impiety. My duty is to do
nothing for them.'

That same evening, when they were alone, the quarrel
began afresh, and Marc, on his side, for the first time became violent, unable as he was to forgive Geneviève's lack
of charity. Hitherto he had fancied that her mind alone
was threatened, but was it not evident now that her heart
also would be spoilt? And that night irreparable words
were spoken, husband and wife realised what an abyss had
been dug between them by invisible hands. Then both relapsed into silence in the black room full of grief and pain,
and on the morrow they did not exchange a word.

Moreover, a source of constant disputes, one which was
bound to make rupture inevitable, had now sprung up.
Louise would be soon ten years old, and the question of
sending her to Abbé Quandieu's Catechism classes, in order

that she might be prepared for her first Communion, presented itself.   Marc, after begging Mademoiselle Rouzaire
to exempt his daughter from all religious exercises, had noticed that the schoolmistress took no account of his request,
but crammed the child with orisons and canticles as she did
with her other pupils.   But he was obliged to close his eyes
to it, for he realised that the schoolmistress was only too
anxious to have a chance of appealing to Geneviève on the
subject in order to create trouble in his home.   When the
Catechism question arose, however, he desired to act firmly,
and watched for an opportunity to have a decisive explanation with Geneviève.   That opportunity presented itself
naturally enough on the day when Louise, returning from
her lessons, said to her mother in her father's presence:
'Mamma, Mademoiselle Rouzaire told me to ask you to see
Abbé Quandieu, so that he may put my name down for his
Catechism class.'

"All right, my dear, I will go to see him to-morrow.'

Marc, who was reading, quickly raised his head: 'Excuse
me, my dear, but you will not go to Abbé Quandieu.'

'Why not ? '

'It is simple enough.   I do not wish Louise to follow the
Catechism lessons because I do not wish her to make her
first Communion.'

Geneviève did not immediately lose her temper, but
laughed as if with ironical compassion: 'You are out of your
senses, my friend,' said she.   'Not make her first Communion indeed!   Why in that case how would you find a
husband for her?   What a casteless, shameless position you
would give her throughout her life!   Besides, you allowed
her to be baptised, you allowed her to learn her Bible history and prayers, so it is illogical on your part to forbid the
Catechism and the Communion.'

Marc also kept his temper for the moment, and answered
quietly: 'You are right, I was weak, and for that very reason
I am resolved to be weak no longer.   I showed all tolerance
for your belief as long as the child remained quite young,
and hung about your skirts.   A daughter, it is said, ought
to belong more particularly to her mother, and I am willing
that it should be so until the time comes when the question
of the girl's moral life, her whole future, presents itself.
Surely the father then has a right to intervene ? '

Geneviève waved her hand impatiently and her voice began to tremble as she answered: ' I wish Louise to follow

the Catechism lessons, you don't wish her to do so. If we have equal rights over the child we may go on disputing for ever without reaching a solution. What I desire seems to you idiotic, and what you desire appears to me abominable.'

'Oh! what I desire, what I desire! My desire simply is that my daughter shall not be prevented from exercising her own free will later on. . . . The question now is to profit by her childishness in order to deform her mind and heart, poison her with lies, and render her for ever incapable of becoming human and sensible. And that is what I desire to prevent. But I do not wish to impose my will on her, I simply wish to ensure her the free exercise of her will at a later date.'

'But how do you provide for that? What is to be done with this big girl?'

'It is only necessary to let her grow up and to open her eyes to every truth. When she is twenty she will decide who is right—you or I; and if she should then think it sensible and logical she will revert to the Catechism and make her first Communion.'

At this Geneviève exploded: 'You are really mad! You say such absurd things before the child that I feel ashamed of you!'

Marc also lost patience. 'Absurd, my poor wife? It is your notions that are absurd! And I won't have my child's mind perverted with such absurdities.'

'Be quiet! be quiet!' she cried. 'You don't know what you wrench from me when you speak like that! Yes, you tear away all my love for you, all our happiness, which I should still like to save! . . . But how are we to agree if words no longer have the same meaning for us, if what you declare to be absurd is for me the divine and the eternal? . . . And is not your fine logic at fault? How can Louise choose between your ideas and mine if you now prevent me from having her instructed as I desire? . . . I do not prevent you from telling her whatever you wish, but I must be free to take her to the Catechism class.'

Marc was already weakening: 'I know the theory,' said he. 'The child enlightened by both the father and the mother, with the right of choosing between their views later on. But is that right left intact when a full course of religious training, aggravating the child's long Catholic heredity, deprives her of all power of thinking and acting freely? The father, who is so imperfectly armed, can do little when he talks truth and sense to a girl whose senses and whose heart are disturbed by others. And when she has grown up amid the pomps of the Church, its terrifying mysteries and its mystical absurdities, it is too late for her to revert to a little sense—her mind has been warped for ever.'

'If you have your right as a father,' Geneviève retorted violently, 'I have my right as a mother. You are not going to take my daughter from me when she is only ten years old and still has so much need of me. It would be monstrous! I am an honest woman, and I mean to make Louise an honest woman too. . . . She shall go to the Catechism class, and, if necessary, I myself will take her!'

Marc, who had risen from his chair, made a furious gesture of protest, but he had strength enough to restrain the violent, the supreme words which would have precipitated immediate rupture. What could he say, what could he do? As usual, he recoiled from the fearful prospect of seeing his home destroyed, his happiness changed into hourly torture. He still loved that woman who showed herself so narrow-minded and particularly so stubborn; there still lingered on his lips the taste of hers; and he could not forget, he could not obliterate, the happy days of their early married life, the powerful bond then formed between them, that child who was the flesh of their flesh, and now the cause of their quarrels. Like many others before him he felt he was driven into a corner, whence he could not extricate himself unless he took to brutal courses—tore the child from her mother's arms, and plunged the house into desolation and commotion every day. And there was too much gentleness, too much kindness, in his nature; he lacked the cold energy that was requisite for a struggle in which his own heart and the hearts of those he loved must bleed. On that field then he was foredoomed to defeat.

Louise had listened in silence, without moving, to the dispute between her father and mother. For some time past, whenever she had seen them thus at variance, her large brown eyes had glanced from one to the other with an expression of sad and increasing surprise.

'But, papa,' she now said, amid the painful silence which had fallen, 'why don't you wish me to go to the Catechism class?'

She was very tall for her age, and had a calm and gentle face, in which the features of the Duparques and the Froments were blended. Though she was still only a child, she displayed keen intelligence, and a thirst for information which constantly impelled her to ply her father with questions. And she worshipped him, and showed also great affection for her mother, who attended to all her wants with a kind of loving passion.

'So you think, papa,' she resumed, 'that if things which are not reasonable are told me at the Catechism class I shall accept them ? '

Marc, in spite of his emotion, could not help smiling. ' Reasonable or not,' said he, ' you must of necessity accept them.'

' But you will explain them to me ? '

' No, my dear; they are, and must remain, unexplainable.'

' But you explain to me everything I ask you when I come back from Mademoiselle Rouzaire's and have n't understood some lesson. . . . It is thanks to you that I am often the first of my class.'

' If you came back from Abbé Quandieu's there would be nothing for me to explain to you,' Marc answered, ' for the essential characteristic of the pretended truths of the Catechism is that they are not accessible to our reason.'

' Ah! how funny!'

For a moment Louise remained silent, in meditation, her glance wandering far away. Then, still with a pensive expression on her face, she slowly gave utterance to her thoughts. ' It 's funny; when things have n't been explained to me and I don't understand them I recollect nothing about them, it is as if they did n't exist. I close my eyes and see nothing. Everything is black. And then, however much I may try, I 'm the last of the class.'

She looked charming with her serious little face, well balanced as she already was, going instinctively towards all that was good, clear, and sensible. Whenever an attempt was made to force into her head things whose sense escaped her, or which seemed to her to be wrong, she smiled in a quiet way and passed them by.

But Geneviève now intervened, saying with some irritation, ' If your father cannot explain the Catechism to you I will do so.'

At this Louise immediately ran to kiss her mother as if she feared she had offended her: ' That 's it, mamma, you will hear me my lessons. You know that I always try my best to understand.' And, turning towards her father, she gaily resumed, ' You see, papa, you may as well let me go to the Catechism, particularly as you say yourself that one ought to learn everything, so that one may be the better able to judge and choose.'

Then, once again, Marc gave way, having neither the strength nor the means to act otherwise. He reproached himself with his weakness; but such was his craving for affection that it was impossible for him to be otherwise than weak when he thought of his devastated home where the struggle each day became more painful.

The rupture was soon to be precipitated, however, by a final incident. Years had elapsed since Marc's arrival at Maillebois, and there had been all sorts of changes among his pupils. Sébastien Milhomme, his favourite, now fifteen years of age, was by his advice preparing himself for admission into the Training College of Beaumont, having secured his elementary certificate already in his twelfth year. Four other boys had left the school with similar certificates—the two Doloirs and the twin Savins. Auguste Doloir had now embraced his father's calling as a mason, while his brother Charles had been apprenticed to a locksmith. As for Savin, he had declined to follow Marc's advice and make schoolmasters of his sons, for he did not wish to see them starve, said he, in an ungrateful calling which everybody held in contempt. So he had proudly placed Achille with a process-server and was looking about him for some petty employment which would suit Philippe.

Meantime, the hard-headed Fernand Bongard had quietly returned to his father's farm to till the ground, having failed to gain a certificate, though in Marc's hands he had acquired more understanding than his parents possessed. As for the girls who had quitted Mademoiselle Rouzaire, Angèle Bongard, who was more intelligent than her brother, had duly carried a certificate to the farm, where, like the shrewd ambitious young person she was, quite capable of keeping accounts, she dreamt of improving her position. Then Hortense Savin, still without a certificate at sixteen years of age, had become a very pretty brunette, extremely devout and sly. She had remained a Handmaiden of the Virgin, and her father dreamt of a fine marriage for her, though there were rumours of a mysterious seduction, the consequences of which she each day found it more difficult to hide.

Of course several new boys had come to Marc's school, replacing their elders there. There was another little Savin,

Jules, whom Marc remembered having seen as an infant at the time of the Simon case; and there was another little Doloir, Léon, born subsequent to the affair, and now nearly seven years old. Later on the children's children would be coming to the school, and if Marc were left at his post perhaps he would teach them also, thus facilitating another step to humanity, ever on the march towards increase of knowledge.

But Marc was particularly concerned about one of his new boys, one whom he had greatly desired to have at the school. This was little Joseph, Simon's son, who had now almost completed his eleventh year. For a long time Marc had not dared to expose him to the taunts and blows of the other boys. Then, thinking that their passions had calmed down sufficiently, he had made the venture, applying to Madame Simon and the Lehmanns, and promising them that he would keep a good watch over the lad. For three years now he had had Joseph in the school, and, after defending him against all sorts of vexations, had prevailed on the other boys to treat him with some good fellowship. Indeed, he even made use of the lad as a living example when seeking to inculcate principles of tolerance, dignity, and kindness.

Joseph was a very handsome boy, in whom his mother's beauty was blended with his father's intelligence; and the dreadful story of his father's fate, with which it had been necessary to acquaint him, seemed to have ripened him before his time. Usually grave and reserved, he studied with a sombre ardour, intent on being always the first of his class, as if, by that triumph, to raise himself above all outrage. His dream, his express desire, which Marc encouraged, was to become a schoolmaster, for in this he boyishly pictured a kind of *revanche* and rehabilitation. No doubt it was Joseph's fervour, the passionate gravity of that clever and handsome boy, which the more particularly struck little Louise, whose senior he was by nearly three years. At all events she became his great friend, and they were well pleased whenever they found themselves together.

At times Marc kept Joseph after lessons, and at times also his sister Sarah came to fetch him. Then, if Sébastien Milhomme, as was sometimes the case, happened to be at Marc's, a delightful hour was spent. The four children agreed so well that they never quarrelled. Sarah, whom her mother feared to confide to others as she did her boy, was, at ten years of age, a most charming child, gentle and

loving; and Sébastien, five years her elder, treated her with
the playful affection of an elder brother.   Geneviéve alone
manifested violent displeasure when the four children happened to meet in her rooms.   She found in this another
cause for anger with her husband.   Why had he brought
those Jews into their home ?   There was no need for her
daughter to compromise herself by associating with the children of that horrid criminal who had been sent to the galleys!   Thus this also helped to bring about quarrels in the
home.

At last came the fated catastrophe.   One evening, when
the four young people were playing together after lessons,
Sébastien suddenly felt ill.   He staggered as if intoxicated,
and Marc had to take him to his mother's.   On the morrow the boy was unable to leave his bed, a terrible attack
of typhoid fever prostrated him, and for three weeks his
life hung in the balance.   It was a frightful time for his
mother, Madame Alexandre, who remained at his bedside,
no longer setting foot in the shop downstairs.   Moreover,
since the Simon affair she had gradually withdrawn from
it, leaving her sister-in-law, Madame Edouard, to conduct
the business in accordance with their joint interests.   As a
matter of fact, Madame Edouard, who was the man in their
partnership, was designated for the directorship by the triumph of the clerical party.   The custom of the secular
school was sufficiently insured by the presence of Madame
Alexandre behind her, and for her own part she intended
to increase her business among the devotees of the town
with the help of her son Victor, who had lately left the
Brothers' school.

He was now a big, squarely-built youth of seventeen,
with a large head, a harsh face, and fierce eyes.   He had
failed to secure an elementary certificate, having always
shown himself an execrable pupil; and he now dreamt of en-
listing and becoming a general as in the old days, when he
had played at war with his cousin Sébastien, taken him
prisoner, and pommelled him passionately.   Meantime, as
he was not old enough for soldiering, he lived in idleness,
making his escape from the shop as often as possible—for
he hated having to stand behind a counter and sell paper
and pens—and roaming through Maillebois in the company
of his old schoolfellow Polydor, the son of Souquet the road-
mender, and the nephew of Pélagie, Madame Duparque's
servant.

Polydor, a pale and artful youth, whose taste for idleness was extraordinary, desired to become an Ignorantine by way of flattering the inclinations of his aunt, from whom he thereby extracted little presents. Moreover, by embracing this religious calling he would not have to break stones on the roads as his father did, and, in particular, he would escape barrack-life, the thought of which quite horrified him. Though in other respects Victor and Polydor had different tastes, they were in full agreement as to the delight of roaming about from morn till night with their hands in their pockets, to say nothing of their goings on with the little hussies of the factory quarter of the town, whom they met in the fields near the Verpille. In this wise, Victor being always out and about, and Madame Alexandre remaining beside her son, Madame Edouard, since Sébastien had fallen so seriously ill, found herself quite without assistance in the shop, where she busied herself with her customers and gaily counted up her takings, which were often large.

Marc went every evening to ascertain the condition of his pupil, and thus he became a daily spectator of a heart-rending drama—the bitter grief of a mother who saw death taking her son a little further from her every hour. That gentle, fair, pale-faced Madame Alexandre, who had loved her husband passionately, had been leading a cloistered life, as it were, ever since his death, all her restrained passion going to that son of hers, who was fair and gentle like herself. Fondled, almost spoilt by that loving mother, Sébastien regarded her with a kind of filial idolatry, as if she were a divine mother whom he could never requite for all her delightful gifts. They were united by a strong, a powerful bond of tender affection, one of those infinite affections in which two beings mingle and blend to such a point that neither can quit the other without wrenching away his or her heart.

When Marc reached the little dark, close room over the stationery shop, he often found Madame Alexandre forcing back her tears and striving to smile at her son, who lay there already emaciated and burning with fever.

'Well, Sébastien, are you better to-day?' the master would ask.

'Oh! no, Monsieur Froment, I'm no better at all—no better at all.'

He could scarcely speak, his voice was faint, his breath came short. But the red-eyed, shuddering mother exclaimed gaily: 'Don't listen to him, Monsieur Froment, he is much better, we shall pull him through it.'

When, however, she had escorted the schoolmaster to the landing, and stood there with him after closing the door of the room, she broke down.

'Ah! God, he is lost, my poor child is lost! Is it not abominable, so strong and handsome as he was! His poor face is reduced to nothing; he has only his eyes left! Ah! God, God, I feel I shall die with him.'

But she stifled her cries, roughly wiped away her tears, and put on her smile once more before returning to the chamber of suffering where she spent hours and hours, without sleep, without help, ever fighting against death.

One evening Marc found her sobbing on her knees beside the bed, her face close pressed to the sheets. Her son could no longer hear or see her. Since the previous night he had been overpowered by his malady, seized with delirium. And now that he had neither ears to hear her nor eyes to see her, she abandoned herself to her frightful grief, and cried it aloud: 'My child, my child! What have I done that my child should be stolen from me? So good a son, who was all my heart as I was his! What can I have done then? What can I have done?'

She rose and, grasping Marc's hands, pressed them wildly. 'Tell me, monsieur, you who are just,' said she. 'Is it not impossible to suffer so much, to be stricken like this if one be free from all blame? . . . It would be monstrous to be punished when one has done no wrong. Is it not so? This, then, can only be an expiation, and if that were true, ah! if I knew, if I knew it were so! . . .'

She seemed a prey to some horrible struggle. For some days past anguish had been making her restless. Yet she did not speak out that evening; it was only on the morrow that, on Marc's arrival, she hastened towards him, as if carried away by an eager desire to have it all over. In the bed near her lay Sébastien, scarce able to breathe.

'Listen, Monsieur Froment,' said she, 'I must confess myself to you. The doctor has just left, my son is dying, only a prodigy can save him. . . . And now my fault stifles me. It seems to me that it is I who am killing my son—I who am punished by his death for having made him speak falsely long ago, and for having clung so stubbornly to that falsehood later on, in order to have peace and quietness in my home, when another, an innocent man, was suffering the worst torture. . . . Ah! for many, many days the struggle has been going on within me, lacerating my heart!'

Marc listened, amazed, not daring as yet to give a meaning to her words.

'You remember, Monsieur Froment,' she resumed, 'you remember that unhappy man Simon, the schoolmaster who was condemned for the murder of little Zéphirin. For more than eight years he has been in penal servitude, and you have often told me of all he suffered yonder, horrible things which made me feel quite ill. . . . I should have liked to speak out—yes, I swear it! I was often on the point of relieving my conscience, for remorse haunted me so dreadfully. . . . But cowardice came over me; I thought of my son's peace, of all the worries I should cause him. . . . Ah! how stupid, how foolish I was; I remained silent for the sake of his happiness, and now death is taking him from me—taking him, it's certain, because I wrongly remained silent!'

She paused, gesticulating wildly, as if Justice, the eternal, were falling on her like a thunderbolt.

'And so, Monsieur Froment, I must relieve my mind. Perhaps there is still time—perhaps Justice will take pity on me if I repair my fault. . . . You remember the writing slip, and the search which was made for another copy of it. On the day after the crime Sébastien told you that he had seen one in the hands of his cousin Victor, who had brought it from the Brothers' school; and that was true. But that same day we were frightened to such a point that my sister-in-law compelled my son to tell a falsehood by saying that he had made a mistake. . . . A long while afterwards I found that slip forgotten in an old copybook which Victor had given to Sébastien, and later Sébastien, who felt worried by his falsehood, acknowledged it to you. When he came home and told me of his confession, I was filled with alarm, and in my turn I lied—first of all to him, saying, in order to quiet his scruples, that the paper no longer existed, as I had destroyed it. And that assuredly is the wrong-doing for which I am punished. The paper still exists; I never dared to burn it; some remaining honesty restrained me. And here, here it is, Monsieur Froment! Rid me of it, rid me of that abominable paper, for it is that which has brought misfortune and death into the house!'

She hastened to a wardrobe, and from under a pile of linen she drew Victor's old copybook, in which the writing slip had been slumbering for eight years past. Marc looked at it, thunderstruck. At last, there was the document which he had believed to be destroyed, there was the 'new fact' which he had sought so long! The slip he held appeared to be in all respects similar to the one which had figured at the trial. There were the words '*Aimez vous les uns les autres*'; there was the illegible paraph recalling the one which the experts had pretended to identify with Simon's initials; and it was difficult to contend that the slip had not come from the Brothers' school, for Victor himself had copied it in his book, a whole page of which was filled with the words inscribed on it. But all at once Marc was dazed. There, in the left-hand corner of the slip—the corner missing in the copy which had been used in evidence at the trial —was an imprint, quite plain and quite intact, of the stamp with which the Brothers stamped everything belonging to their school. A sudden light was thus shed on the affair: somebody had torn away the corner of the copy found in Zéphirin's room in order to annihilate the stamp and put Justice off the scent.

Quivering with excitement, carried away by gratitude and sympathy, Marc grasped the poor mother's hands. 'Ah, madame,' he exclaimed, ' you have done a great and worthy action, and may death take pity and restore your son to you!'

At that moment they perceived that Sébastien, who had given no sign of consciousness since the previous evening, had just opened his eyes and was looking at them. They felt profoundly stirred. The ailing lad evidently recognised Marc, but he was not yet free from delirium. 'What beautiful sunshine, Monsieur Froment,' he stammered in a faint voice. 'I 'll get up and you 'll take me with you. I 'll help you to give lessons.'

His mother ran to him and kissed him wildly. 'Make haste to get well, make haste to get well, my boy! Neither of us must ever more tell a falsehood, we must be always good and just!'

As Marc quitted the room he found that Madame Edouard, hearing a noise, had come upstairs. The door having remained open she had witnessed the whole scene, and had seen him place her son's old copybook and the slip in the inner pocket of his coat. She followed him down the stairs in silence, but when they reached the shop she stopped him, saying, 'I am in despair, Monsieur Froment. You must not judge us severely; we are only two poor lone women, and find it difficult indeed to earn a little competence for our old age. . . . I don't ask you to give me that paper back. You are going to make use of it, and I cannot oppose you: I understand it fully. Only this is a real catastrophe for us. . . . And again, do not think me a bad woman if I try to save our little business.'

Indeed she was not a bad woman; it merely happened that she had no faith, no passion, apart from the prosperity of that humble stationery business. She had already reflected that if the secular school should gain the day, it would merely be necessary for her to retire into the background and allow Madame Alexandre to direct the shop. Nevertheless, this was hardly a pleasant prospect, given her business instincts and her fondness for domineering over others. So she strove to lighten the catastrophe as far as possible.

'You might content yourself with utilising the slip, without producing my son's copybook,' said she. 'Besides, it has just occurred to me that you might arrange a story and say, for instance, that I happened to find the slip and gave it to you. That would show us in a suitable *rôle*, and we could then openly pass over to your side, with the certainty that you would be victorious.'

In spite of his emotion Marc could not refrain from smiling. 'It is, I think, madame, easiest and most honourable to tell the truth,' said he. 'Your *rôle* will nevertheless remain praiseworthy.'

At this she seemed to feel somewhat reassured. 'Really,' she replied, 'you think so? Of course I ask nothing better than that the truth should become known if we do not have to suffer from it.'

Marc had complaisantly taken the copybook and the slip from his pocket in order to show her exactly what he was carrying away. And she was telling him that she fully recognised both book and slip when, all at once, her son Victor came in from some escapade, accompanied by his friend Polydor Souquet. While twisting about and laughing over some prank known to themselves alone, the two young fellows glanced at the copy-slip, and Polydor at once expressed the liveliest surprise.

'Hallo!' he exclaimed, 'the paper!'

But when Marc quickly raised his head, struck as he was by that exclamation, and divining that a little more of the truth lurked behind it, the youth reassumed his usual sleepy, hypocritical expression and tried to recall his words.

'What paper? Do you know it, then?' Marc asked him.

'I? No. . . . I said the paper because—because it is a paper.'

Marc could draw nothing further from him. As for Victor, he continued to sneer as if he were amused to find that old affair cropping up once more. Ah! yes, the copy-slip which he had brought home from school one day long ago, and which that little fool Sébastien had made such a fuss about! But Madame Edouard still felt ashamed, and when Marc withdrew she accompanied him outside to beg him to do all he could to spare them worry. She had just thought of General Jarousse, their cousin, who would certainly not be pleased if the affair were revived. He had formerly done them the great honour to call on them and explain that when one's country might suffer from the truth being made known it was infinitely preferable and far more glorious to tell a lie. And if General Jarousse should be angered, whatever would she do with her son Victor, who relied on his relative's protection to become a general in his turn?

That evening Marc was to dine at Madame Duparque's, whither he still repaired at times, as he was unwilling that Geneviève should always go alone. Polydor's exclamation still haunted him, for he felt that the truth lurked behind it; and it so happened that when he reached the ladies' house, with Geneviève and Louise, he caught sight of the young fellow whispering eagerly to his aunt Pélagie in the kitchen. Moreover, the ladies' greeting was so frigid that Marc divined in it some threat. During the last few years Madame Berthereau, Geneviève's mother, had been declining visibly, ever in an ailing state, full also of a kind of despairing sadness amid her resignation. But Madame Duparque, the grandmother, though she was now seventy-one, remained combative, terrible, implacable in her faith. In order that Marc might fully understand for what exceptional reasons she thought it right to receive him, she never invited anybody else when he dined at her house. By this course she hoped also to make him understand that his position was that of a pariah, and that it was impossible to ask honest folk to meet him.

That evening, then, as on previous occasions, silence and embarrassment reigned during the meal, and by the hostile demeanour of the others, and particularly by the brusqueness of Pélagie, who served at table, Marc became fully convinced that some storm was about to burst on him. Until the dessert was served, however, Madame Duparque restrained herself like a *bourgeoise* intent on playing her part as mistress of the house correctly. At last, when Pélagie came in with some apples and pears, she said to her: 'You may keep your nephew to dinner, I give you permission.'

The old servant in her scolding, aggressive voice replied: 'Ah! the poor boy needs to recruit himself after the violence that was done him this afternoon.'

At this Marc suddenly understood everything. The ladies had been made acquainted with his discovery of the copy-slip by Polydor, who, for some reason which remained obscure, had hastened to tell everything to his aunt.

'Oh, oh!' said Marc, who could not help laughing, 'who was it that wanted to do violence to Polydor? Was it I, by chance, when the dear boy ventured to bamboozle me so pleasantly by feigning stupidity at Mesdames Milhommes' this afternoon?'

Madame Duparque, however, would not allow such a serious matter to be treated in that ironical fashion. She proceeded to unbosom herself without any show of anger, but in that rigid, cutting manner of hers which suffered no reply. Was it possible that the husband of her dear Geneviève still thought of reviving the abominable affair of that man Simon, that vile assassin, who had been so justly condemned, who deserved no pity whatever, and who ought indeed to have been guillotined? True, there was a monstrous legend of his innocence which evil-minded folk hoped to make use of in order to shake religion and hand France over to the Jews. And now, after obstinately searching among all that filth, Marc pretended that he had found the proof, the famous new fact, which had been announced so many times already. A fine proof indeed, a strip of paper, which had come nobody knew whence nor how, the invention of a pack of children who either lied or were mistaken!

'Grandmother,' Marc quietly answered, 'it was agreed that we should not speak of those matters any more. I have not ventured to make the slightest allusion to them; it is you who begin again. But what good can a dispute do? My conviction is absolute.'

'And you know the real culprit, and you intend to denounce him to justice?' asked the old lady, quite beside herself.

'Certainly.'

At this Pélagie, who was beginning to clear away, could not restrain herself. 'In any case it is n't Brother Gorgias, I can answer for that!' she suddenly cried.

Marc, enlightened by these words, turned towards her. 'Why do you say that?' he asked.

'Because on the evening of the crime Brother Gorgias accompanied my nephew Polydor to his father's, on the road to Jonville, and got back to the school before eleven o'clock. Polydor and other witnesses testified to that at the trial.'

Marc was still gazing fixedly at the old woman, but his mind was busy at work. That which he had long suspected was becoming a moral certainty. He could picture the Brother accompanying Polydor, then returning homeward, pausing before Zéphirin's open window, and talking to the boy. At last he climbed over the low window bar, the better perhaps to see the pictures which the lad had set out on his table. Then, however, came the horrid impulse, abominable madness . . . and, the child strangled, the murderer fled by the window, which he still left wide open. It was from his own pocket that he had taken that copy of *Le Petit Beaumontais* to use it as a gag, never noticing in his perturbation that the copy-slip was with the newspaper. And on the morrow, when the crime was discovered, it was Father Philibin, who, finding himself unable to destroy the slip, as Mignot had seen it, had been obliged to content himself with tearing away the corner on which the stamp was impressed, thus at all events removing all positive proof of the place whence the slip had come.

Slowly and gravely Marc answered Pélagie: 'Brother Gorgias is the culprit, everything proves it, and I swear it is so!'

Indignant protests arose around the table. Madame Duparque was stifling with indignation. Madame Berthereau, whose mournful eyes went from her daughter to her son-in-law, whose rupture she sorely dreaded, made a gesture of supreme despair. And while little Louise, who paid great attention to her father's words, remained there quietly, never stirring, Geneviève sprang to her feet and quitted the table, saying:

'You would do better to hold your tongue! It will soon be quite impossible for me to remain near you: you will end by making me hate you!'

Later that same evening, when Louise had gone to sleep and the husband and the wife also lay in bed, there came a moment of profound silence in their dark room. Since dinner neither had spoken to the other. But Marc was always the first to try to make friends, for he could not bear the suffering which their quarrels brought him. Now, however, when he gently sought to embrace Geneviève, she nervously pushed him away, quivering as if with repulsion.

'No: let me be!'

Hurt by her manner, he did not insist. And the silence fell heavily again. At last she resumed: 'There is one thing I have not yet told you. . . . I believe that I am *enceinte*.'

At this, full of happy emotion, her husband drew near to her again, anxious to press her to his heart. 'Oh! my dear, dear wife, what good news! Now we shall indeed belong to each other once more.'

But she freed herself from his clasp with even more impatience than before, as if his presence near her brought her real suffering. 'No, no, let me be,' she repeated; 'I am not well. I sha'n't be able to sleep; it fidgets me to feel you stirring near me. . . . It will be better to have two beds if things go on like this.'

Not another word passed between them. They lapsed into silence, speaking neither of the Simon affair nor of the tidings which Geneviève had so abruptly announced. Only the sound of their heavy breathing was to be heard in the dark and lifeless room. Neither was asleep, but neither could penetrate the other's anxious, painful thoughts; it was as if they inhabited two different worlds, parted by a distance of many thousand leagues. And vague sobs seemed to come from far away, from the very depths of the black and dolorous night, bewailing the death of their love.

IV

AFTER a few days' reflection Marc made up his mind and requested David to meet him one evening at the Lehmanns' in the Rue du Trou.

For nearly ten years the Lehmanns had been living in their dim and damp little house, amid public execration. When, as sometimes happened, bands of clericals and anti-Semites came down and threatened the shop, they hastily put up the shutters and continued working by the smoky light of two lamps. All their Maillebois customers, even their co-religionists, having forsaken them, they were dependent on the piece-work they did for Paris clothiers dealing in ready-made goods. And that hard and ill-paid work kept old Lehmann and his mournful wife bent on their board for fourteen hours a day, and yielded scarcely enough money to provide food for themselves, Rachel, and her children, all of whom were huddled there in dismal distress, without a joy or a hope in life. Even now, after so many years, passing pedestrians spat on their doorstep to show how fully they loathed and hated that filthy den, whither, so the legend ran, Simon the murderer had brought Zéphirin's blood, while it was still warm, to use it in some vile deed of witchcraft. And nowadays to that abode of intense wretchedness and deep, cloistered grief came Simon's letters, briefer and more infrequent than formerly, yet still and ever telling the tale of the innocent man's long agony.

Those letters alone had the power of stirring Rachel into life, of drawing her from the torpor and resignation in which she spent most of her days. Her once beautiful countenance was now but a ruin, ravaged by her tears. She lived only for her children: Sarah, whom she still kept beside her, fearing to expose her to the insults of the malicious, and Joseph, whom Marc defended at the school. The dreadful story of their father's fate had long been hidden from them, but it had been necessary to tell them the truth at last,

partly in order to spare them much painful doubt and cogi-
tation. Nowadays, whenever a letter arrived from the
penal settlement yonder, it was read in their presence; and
those bitter trials inculcated virility of nature in them, and
helped to ripen their budding minds. After each perusal
their mother took them in her arms, repeating that nowhere
under the skies was there a more honest, a more noble, a
loftier-minded man than their father. She swore to them
that he was innocent, she told them of the awful martyrdom
he endured, she prophesied to them that he would some
day be freed, rehabilitated, and acclaimed; and she asked
them to love and revere him when that day should dawn,
to encompass him with a worship whose sweetness might
enable him to forget his many years of torture.

And yet would the unhappy man live until that day of
truth and justice? It was a miracle that he had not succumbed already, among the brutes who crucified him. To
survive, he had needed an extraordinary amount of moral
energy, the frigid power of resistance, the well-balanced
logical temperament with which nature had fortunately endowed him. Still, his last letters gave cause for increasing
anxiety, he was evidently at the end of his strength, quite
overcome. And Rachel's fears reached such a point that,
without pausing to consult anybody, she, usually so lan-
guid, repaired one morning to La Désirade to see Baron
Nathan, who was then staying there with the Sanglebœufs.
She took with her the last letter she had received from her
husband in order to show it to the Baron, meaning to beg
him—triumphant Jew that he was, one of the gold-kings of
the world—to exert his great influence in order to obtain a
little pity for the poor, wretched, crucified Jew who was
suffering yonder. And she came home in tears, shuddering, as if she had just left some dazzling and fearsome place.
She could hardly remember what had happened. The
Baron, the bloated renegade, had received her with a stern
countenance, as if angered by her audacity. Perhaps it
was his daughter, a white-faced, frigid lady, whom she had
found with him. She could not tell exactly how they had
got rid of her, but it was with words of refusal, such as
might have been addressed to a beggar. Then she had
found herself outside again, half-blinded by the wealth ac-
cumulated at that splendid abode of La Désirade, with its
sumptuous reception-rooms, its running waters, and its
white statues. And since that fruitless attempt she had

relapsed into the mournful, waiting attitude of former days, ever garbed in black, like a living statue of mutely protesting grief in the midst of persecution.

The only person on whom Marc relied in that home of wretchedness and suffering was David, whose mind was so clear, whose heart was so upright and so firm.   Ever since the condemnation of Simon Marc had seen him striving, evincing neither impatience, nor weakness, nor despair, despite all the difficulties of his task.   Indeed, David's faith remained entire; he was convinced of his brother's innocence, and felt certain that he would some day prove it. He had understood at the outset that he would need some money to achieve his task, and he had arranged his life accordingly.   He outwardly resumed the direction of the sand and gravel pits, which he had leased from Baron Nathan, in such wise that everybody believed that he conducted the business personally; but in reality the chief responsibility fell upon his foreman, who was devoted to him.   And the profits, being handled prudently, sufficed for David's other work, his real mission, the investigations which he carried on so discreetly.   Some people, who believed him to be a miser, accused him of earning large sums of money, and yet giving no help to his sister-in-law, who shared the wretched home of the Lehmanns, where incessant toil led only to a life of privations.   At one moment also an attempt was made to dispossess David of his sand and gravel pits, the Sanglebœufs threatening him with an action-at-law, which was evidently prompted by Father Crabot.   The Jesuit, indeed, was conscious of the stealthy, underhand efforts which that silent but active man was making, and would have liked to drive him from the district, or at least to cripple his resources.   But David fortunately held a thirty years' lease from Baron Nathan, and thus he was still able to carry on the business which ensured him the money he needed.

His principal efforts had been long concentrated on the illegal communication which President Gragnon was said to have made to the jurors in their retiring room, when the proceedings in Simon's trial were over.   After interminable inquiries David had collected enough information to picture the scene in its broad lines: the jurors, assailed by certain scruples, had sent for the presiding judge in order to question him about the penalties their verdict might entail; and the judge, in order to silence their scruples, had shown them an old letter of Simon's, which had been placed in his hands a moment previously. This letter, an insignificant note to a friend, acquired importance from the fact that it was followed by a postscript, signed with a paraph identical with the one which figured on the incriminating copy-slip. This singular document, produced at the last moment without the knowledge of the prisoner or his counsel, had assuredly led to the verdict of 'Guilty.' But how was David to establish all this? How could he induce one of the jurors to testify to the facts, the revelation of which would have brought about an immediate revision of the proceedings, particularly if—as David felt convinced—the postscriptum of the letter and its initialling were forgeries? He had long endeavoured to act, through others, on the foreman of the jury, Architect Jacquin, a devout and very upright Catholic; and he believed that he had lately disturbed that man's conscience by acquainting him with the illegality of the judge's communication under the circumstances. If, in addition, he could prove that the postscriptum and the paraph had been forged, Jacquin would speak out.

When Marc repaired to the Rue du Trou to keep the appointment he had made with David, he found the little shop shut, the house quite dark and lifeless. The family had prudently taken refuge in the back parlour, where Lehmann and his wife were working by lamplight; and it was there that the stirring scene took place in the presence of the quivering Rachel and her children, whose eyes were all ablaze.

Before speaking out, however, Marc wished to ascertain what point David had now reached in his investigations.

'Oh! things are moving, but still very, very slowly,' the other answered. 'Jacquin is one of those fair-minded Christians who worship a Deity of love and equity. At one moment I felt alarmed, for I discovered that Father Crabot was bringing the greatest pressure to bear on him through every possible intermediary. But I am now easy on that point—Jacquin will act only as his conscience may direct. . . . The difficulty is to get at the document in order that it may be examined by experts.'

'But did not Gragnon destroy it?' Marc inquired.

'It seems not. Having shown it to the jurors he did not dare to do so, but simply placed it with the papers in the case, among which it must still be. At least, such is the conviction of Delbos, based on certain information he has obtained. Thus the question is to exhume it from among the records, and it is not easy to devise a plausible motive for doing so. . . . Nevertheless, we are making progress.' And after a pause David added: 'And you, my friend, have you any good news?'

'Yes, good and great news.'

Then Marc slowly recounted all that had happened: Sébastien's illness, Madame Alexandre's despair, followed by her remorse and terror, which had prompted her to hand him the long-sought duplicate of the copy-slip, on which duplicate one found both the stamp of the Brothers' school and a paraph which undoubtedly represented Brother Gorgias's initials. 'Here it is,' said Marc. 'There, you see, is the stamp, in the very corner which was torn away from the copy found near little Zéphirin's body. We fancied that it might have been bitten off by the victim, but Father Philibin at least had time to tear it off; on that point the recollections of Mignot, my assistant, are precise. . . . Now, look at the paraph. It is identical with the other which figured at the trial, but it is more legible, and one can fully distinguish Brother Gorgias's initials,[1] that is an F and a G interlaced, which the experts, Masters Badoche and Trabut, with extraordinary aberration, persisted in declaring to be an L and an S, otherwise your brother's initials. . . . My conviction is now absolute: the culprit is Brother Gorgias, and none other.'

With passionate eagerness they all stared at the narrow yellow strip of paper produced by Marc, and scrutinised it in the pale lamplight. The old Lehmanns quitted their sewing and thrust their faces forward as if reviving to life. Rachel had emerged from her torpor, and stood there quivering, while the two children, Joseph and Sarah, their eyes aflame, pushed one another in order that they might see the better. Finally David, amid the deep silence of that mourning home, took the paper from Marc and examined it.

'Yes, yes,' he said, 'my conviction is the same as yours. What was suspected has now become certain. Brother Gorgias is the guilty man!'

A long discussion followed; all the facts were recalled in succession, and united in one sheaf. They threw light on each other, and all tended to the same conclusion. Apart

---

[1] Brother Gorgias = Frère Gorgias.

from the material proofs which were beginning to come in, there was a moral certainty, the demonstration as it were of a mathematical problem, which reasoning sufficed to solve. No doubt obscurity still hung around a few points, such as the presence of the copy-slip in the Brother's pocket, and the fate of the corner on which the stamp had been impressed. But all the rest seemed certain: Gorgias returning home on the night of the crime, chance bringing him before Zéphirin's open and lighted window, temptation, and afterwards murder; then, on the morrow, chance likewise bringing Father Philibin and Brother Fulgence on the scene in such wise that they became mixed up in the tragedy and were forced to act in order to save one of their fellows. And how plainly did the mutilation of the copy-slip designate the culprit, whose name was virtually proclaimed also by the fierce campaign which had ensued, the great efforts which the Church had made in order to shield him, and cause an innocent man to be sentenced in his stead. Moreover, each day now brought fresh light, and before long the whole huge edifice of falsehood would crumble.

'So that is the end of our wretchedness!' exclaimed old Lehmann, becoming quite gay. 'It will only be necessary to show that paper and Simon will be restored to us.'

The two children were already dancing with delight, repeating in blissful accents: 'Oh! papa will come back! papa will come back!'

But David and Marc remained grave. They knew how difficult and dangerous the situation still was. Questions of the greatest weight and gravity had to be settled: how were they to make use of that newly-discovered document, what course was to be followed in applying for a revision of the trial? Thus Marc answered softly: 'One must think it over, one must wait a little longer.'

At this Rachel, relapsing into tears, stammered amid her sobs: 'Wait! wait for what? For the poor man to die yonder, amid the torture of which he complains?'

Once more the dark little house sank into mourning. All felt that their unhappiness was not yet over. After their keen momentary delight came frightful anxiety as to what the morrow might bring forth.

'Delbos alone can guide us,' said David by way of conclusion. 'If you are willing, Marc, we will go to see him on Thursday.'

'Quite so: call for me on Thursday.'

In ten years Advocate Delbos had risen to a remarkable position at Maillebois. The Simon affair, that compromising case, the brief in which had been prudently declined by all his colleagues and bravely accepted by himself, had decided his future. At that time he had been merely a peasant's son, imbued with some democratic instincts and gifted with eloquence. But, while studying the affair and gradually becoming the impassioned defender of the truth, he had found himself in presence of all the *bourgeois* forces coalescing in favour of falsehood and the maintenance of every social iniquity. And this had ended by making him a militant Socialist, one who felt convinced that the salvation of the country could come solely from the masses. By degrees the whole revolutionary party of the town had grouped itself around him, and at the last elections he had forced a second ballot on the radical Lemarrois, who had been deputy for twenty years. And if Delbos still suffered in his immediate interests from the circumstance that he had defended a Jew charged with every crime, he was gradually rising to a lofty position by the firmness of his faith and the quiet valour of his actions, going forward to victory with gay and virile confidence.

As soon as Marc had shown him the copy-slip obtained from Madame Alexandre, the advocate raised a loud cry of delight: 'At last we hold them!' And turning towards David he added: 'This gives us a second new fact. The first is the letter—a forgery, no doubt—which was illegally communicated to the jury. . . . We must try to find it among the papers of the case. . . . And the second is this copy-slip, bearing the stamp of the Brothers' school, and a paraph which is evidently that of Brother Gorgias. It will, I think, be easier and more effective to use this second proof.'

'Then what do you advise me to do?' asked David. 'My idea is to write a letter to the Minister of Justice on behalf of my sister-in-law, a letter formally denouncing Brother Gorgias as the perpetrator of the crime, and applying for the revision of my brother's case.'

Delbos had become thoughtful again. 'That would undoubtedly be the correct course,' said he, 'but it is a delicate matter, and we must not act too hastily. . . . Let us return for a moment to the illegal communication of that letter, which it will be so difficult for us to prove as long as we cannot induce Architect Jacquin to relieve his conscience. You remember Father Philibin's evidence—his vague allusion to a paper signed by your brother with a flourish, similar to that on the incriminating copy-slip—a paper about which he would give no precise information—being bound, said he, by confessional secrecy? Well, I am convinced that he was then alluding to the very letter which was placed in Judge Gragnon's hands at the last moment, for which reason, like you, I suspect it to be forged. But these are only suppositions, theories; and we need proofs. Now, if we drop that matter, and, for the time at all events, content ourselves with this duplicate copy of the writing slip, on which the school stamp appears, and on which the initialling is much plainer, we still find ourselves face to face with some puzzling, obscure points. Without lingering too much over the question how it happened that such a slip was in the Brother's pocket at the moment of the crime —a point which it is rather difficult to explain—I am very worried by the disappearance of the corner on which the school stamp must have been impressed; and I should like to find that corner before acting, for I can foresee all sorts of objections which will be raised in opposition to us, in order to throw the affair into a muddle.'

Marc looked at him in astonishment. 'What! find that corner? It would be a wonderful chance if we should do so! We even admitted that it might have been torn away by the victim's teeth.'

'Oh! that is not credible,' Delbos answered. 'Besides, in that case the fragment would have been found on the floor. Nothing was found, so the corner was intentionally torn off. Besides, we here detect the intervention of Father Philibin, for, as you have told me, your assistant Mignot remembers that at his first glance the copy-slip appeared to him to be intact, and that he felt surprised when, after losing sight of it for a moment, he saw it still in Father Philibin's hands and mutilated. So there is no doubt on the point; the corner was torn away by Father Philibin. Throughout the campaign it was he, always he who turned up at decisive moments to save the culprit! And this is why I should like to have complete proof—that is to say, the little fragment of paper which he carried away with him.'

At this David in his turn expressed his surprise: 'You think that he kept it?'

'Certainly I think so. At all events he may have kept it. Philibin is a taciturn man, extremely dexterous, however

coarse and heavy he may look. He must have preserved
that fragment as a weapon for his own defence, as a means
of keeping a hold over his accomplices. I nowadays suspect that, influenced by some motive which remains obscure,
he was the great artisan of the iniquity. Perhaps he was
merely guided by a spirit of fidelity towards his chief, Father
Crabot; perhaps there has been some skeleton between
them since that suspicious affair of the donation of Valmarie;
perhaps too Philibin was actuated simply by militant faith
and a desire to promote the triumph of the Church. At all
events he's a terrible fellow, a man of determination and
action, by the side of whom that noisy, empty Brother
Fulgence is merely a vain fool.'

Marc had begun to ponder. 'Father Philibin, Father
Philibin. . . . Yes, I was altogether mistaken about
him. Even after the trial I still thought him a worthy man,
a man of upright nature, even if warped by his surroundings. . . . Yes, yes, he was the great culprit, the artisan
of forgery and falsehood.'

But David again turned to Delbos: 'Suppose,' said he,
'that Philibin should have kept the corner which he tore
from the slip, you surely don't expect that he will give it to
you, if you ask him for it—do you?'

'Oh! no,' the advocate answered with a laugh. 'But
before attempting anything decisive I should like to reflect,
and ascertain if there is no means of securing the irrefutable
proof. Moreover, a demand for the revision of a case is a
very serious matter, and nothing ought to be left to chance.
. . . Let me complete our case if I can; give me a few
days—two or three weeks if necessary—and then we will
act.'

On the morrow Marc understood by his wife's manner
that her grandmother had spoken out and that the Congregations, from Father Crabot to the humblest of the Ignorantines, were duly warned. The affair suddenly burst into
life again, there came increasing agitation and alarm. Informed as they were of the discovery of the duplicate copy-
slip, conscious that the innocent man's family were now on
the road to the truth, hourly expecting to see Brother
Gorgias denounced, the guilty ones, Brother Fulgence,
Father Philibin, and Father Crabot, returned to the fray,
striving to hide their former crime by committing fresh
ones. They divined that the masterpiece of iniquity which
they had reared so laboriously, and defended so fiercely,

was now in great peril, and, yielding to that fatality whereby
one lie inevitably leads to endless others, they were ready
for the worst deeds in order to save their work from destruction.   Besides, it was no mere question of protecting.
themselves, the salvation of the Church would depend on
the battle.   If the infamous structure of falsehood should
collapse, would not the Congregations be buried beneath it?
The Brothers' school would be ruined, closed, while the
secular school triumphed; the Capuchins' business would
be seriously damaged, customers would desert them, their
shrine of St. Antony of Padua would be reduced to paltry
profits; the college of Valmarie likewise would be threatened, the Jesuits would be forced to quit the region which
they now educated under various disguises; and all religious
influence would decline, the breach in the flanks of the
Church would be enlarged, and free thought would clear
the highway to the future.   How desperate therefore was
the resistance, how fiercely did the whole clerical army
arise in order that it might not be compelled to cede aught
of the wretched region of error and dolour, which, for ages,
it had steeped in night!

Before Brother Gorgias was even denounced, his superiors
felt it necessary to defend him, to cover him at all costs, to
forestall the threatened attack, by concocting a story which
might prove his innocence.   At the first moment, however,
there was terrible confusion; the Brother was seen hurrying
wildly, on his long thin legs, along the streets of Maillebois
and the roads of the neighbourhood.   With his eagle beak
set between his projecting cheek-bones, his deep black eyes,
with their thick brows, and his grimacing mouth, he resembled a fierce, scoffing bird of prey.   In the course of one
day he was seen on the road to Valmarie, then quitting the
residence of Philis, the Mayor of Maillebois, then alighting
from a train which had brought him from Beaumont.
Moreover, both in the town and the surrounding country
many cassocks and frocks were encountered hurrying hither
and thither, thus testifying to a perfect panic.   It was only
on the morrow that the meaning of the agitation was made
evident by an article in *Le Petit Beaumontais*, announcing
in violent language that the whole Simon affair was to be
revived by the friends of the ignoble Jew, who were about
to agitate the region by denouncing a worthy member of one
of the religious Orders, the holiest of men.

Brother Gorgias was not yet named, but from that mo-

ment a fresh article appeared every day, and by degrees the
version of the affair which the Brother's superiors had con-
cocted was set out in opposition to the version which, it was
foreseen, would be given by David, though the latter had
revealed it to nobody.   However, the desire of the clericals
was to wreck it beforehand.   Everything was flatly denied.
It was impossible that Brother Gorgias could have paused
before Zéphirin's window on the night of the crime, for witnesses had proved that he had already returned to the
school at half-past ten o'clock.   Besides, the initialling on
the copy-slip was not his, for the experts had fully recognised Simon's handwriting.   And everything could be
easily explained.   Simon, having procured a writing slip,
had imitated the Brother's paraph, which he had found in
one of Zéphirin's copybooks.   Then, as he knew that the
slips were stamped at the Brothers' school, he had torn off
one corner with diabolical cunning, in order to create a
belief in some precaution taken by the murderer; his infernal object being to cast the responsibility of his own
crime on some servant of God, and thereby gratify the
hatred of the Church which possessed him—Jew that he
was, fated to everlasting damnation.   And this extravagant
story, repeated every day, soon became the *credo* of the
readers whom the newspaper debased and poisoned with its
falsehoods.

It should be mentioned, however, that at the first moment
there was a little uncertainty and hesitation, for other explanations had been circulated, and Brother Gorgias himself
appeared to have made some curious statements.   Formerly
hidden away in the background, now suddenly thrust into
full light, this Brother Gorgias was an extraordinary character.   The Countess de Quédeville, the former owner of
Valmarie, had endeavoured to transform his father, Jean
Plumet, a poacher, into a kind of gamekeeper.   He, the
son, had never known his mother, a hussy who rambled
about the woods, for she had disappeared soon after his
birth.   Then his father had been shot one night by an old
fellow poacher, and the boy, at that time twelve years old,
had remained at Valmarie, protected by the Countess, and
becoming the playfellow of her grandson Gaston, with the
exact circumstances of whose death, while walking out with
Father Philibin, he was doubtless well acquainted, as well
as with all that had ensued when the last of the Quédevilles
died and bequeathed the estate to Father Crabot.   The two

Jesuits had never ceased to take an interest in him, and it
was thanks to them that he had become an Ignorantine, in
spite, it was said, of serious circumstances which tended to
prevent it.   For these reasons certain evil-minded folk suspected the existence of some corpse between the two Jesuit
fathers and their compromising inferior.

At the same time Brother Gorgias was cited as an admirable member of his cloth, one truly imbued with the
Holy Spirit.   He possessed faith, that sombre, savage faith
which pictures man as a weakling, a prey to perpetual sin,
ruled by an absolute master, a Deity of wrath and punishment.   That Deity alone reigned; it was for the Church to
visit His wrath upon the masses, whose duty it became to
bow their heads in servile submission until the day of resur-
rection dawned amid the delights of the heavenly kingdom.
He, Brother Gorgias, often sinned himself, but he invariably
confessed his transgression with a vehement show of repentance, striking his breast with both fists, and humbling
himself in the mud.   Then he rose again, absolved, at rest,
displaying the provoking serenity of a pure conscience.
He had paid his debt, and he would owe nothing more
until the weakness of his flesh should cast him into sin
again.   As a lad he had roamed the woods, growing up
amid poaching and thieving, and hiding himself away with
the little hussies of the district.   Later, after joining the Ignorantines, he had displayed the keenest appetites, showing
himself a big eater, a hard drinker, with inclinations towards
lubricity and violence.   But, as he said in that strangely-
compounded, humble, scoffing, threatening way of his to
Fathers Philibin and Crabot, whenever they reproached
him for some too serious prank: did not everybody sin? did
not everybody need forgiveness?   Half amusing, half alarm-
ing them, he won their pardon, so sincere and stupendous
did his remorse appear—remorse which sometimes impelled
him to fast for a week at a stretch, and to wear hair-cloths,
studded with small sharp nails, next to his skin.   It was
indeed on this account that he had been always well noted
by his superiors, who recognised that he possessed the genuine religious spirit — the spirit which, when his monkish
vices ran riot, atoned for them with the avenging flagellation
of penitence.

Now, on the revival of the Simon case, Brother Gorgias
made the mistake of saying too much in the course of his
first confidential chats with the writers of *Le Petit Beau-*

montais. No doubt his superiors had not yet expressly imposed their own version on him, and he was too intelligent to be blind to its exceeding absurdity. As another copy of the writing slip, one bearing his paraph, had been discovered, it must have seemed to him ridiculous to deny that this paraph was his writing. All the experts in the world would never prevent full light from being thrown on that point. Thus he gave some inkling of a version of his own, one which was more reasonable than that of his superiors, and in which a part of the truth appeared. For instance, he allowed it to be supposed that he had indeed halted for a moment outside Zéphirin's open window on the night of the crime, that he had engaged in a friendly chat with the little hunchback, and that he had scolded him on seeing on his table a copy-slip which he had taken from the school without permission. Next, however, had come falsehood. He, Gorgias, had gone off, the child had closed his window, then Simon must have come and have committed the horrid crime, Satan suddenly inspiring him to make use of the copy-slip, after which he had opened the window afresh, in order to let it appear that the murderer had fled that way.

But, although this version of the affair was at the first moment given by the newspaper, which declared that it emanated from a most reliable source, it was on the morrow contradicted energetically, even by Brother Gorgias himself, who repaired expressly to the newspaper office to enter his protest. He then swore on the gospel that he had gone straight home on the evening of the crime, and that the initialling on the copy-slip was a forgery in Simon's handwriting, even as the experts had demonstrated. As a matter of fact he was compelled to accept the concoction of his superiors in order that he might be backed up and saved by them. He grumbled over it, and shrugged his shoulders impatiently, for it seemed to him an extremely stupid version; but at the same time he bowed to the decision of the others, even though he foresaw that their system of defence must eventually crumble to pieces.

At this moment Brother Gorgias, with his scoffing impudence and his heroic mendacity, was really superb. But, then, was not the Deity behind him? Was he not lying in order to save Holy Church, knowing too that absolution would wash away his sin? He even dreamt of the palms of martyrdom; each pious act of infamy that he perpetrated would entitle him to another joy in heaven! From that moment, then, he became merely a docile instrument in the hands of Brother Fulgence, behind whom Father Philibin was secretly acting under the discreet orders of Father Crabot. Their tactics were to deny everything, even what was self-evident, for fear lest the smallest breach in the sacred wall of the Congregations should prove the beginning of inevitable ruin; and although their absurd version of the affair might seem idiotic to people possessed of logical minds, it would none the less long remain the only truth accepted by the mass of the faithful, with whom they could presume to do anything, knowing as they did their boundless, fathomless credulity.

The clericals, then, having assumed the offensive without waiting for Gorgias to be denounced, Brother Fulgence in particular displayed the most intemperate zeal. At times of great emotion, his father, the mad doctor who had died in an asylum, seemed to revive in him. With his brain all fogged, unhinged by vanity and ambition, he yielded to the first impulse that came to him, ever dreaming of doing some mighty service to the Church, which would raise him to the head of his Order. Thus, in the earlier stages of the Simon affair, he had lost the little common-sense which he had previously shown, for he had hoped that the case would yield him the glory he coveted; and now that it was revived he once more became delirious. He was constantly to be seen hurrying along the streets of Maillebois, little, dark, and lean, with the folds of his gown flying about him as if a gale were carrying him away. Whenever he entered into conversation he defended his school with passionate eagerness, calling on heaven to witness the angelic purity of his assistants. As for the abominable rumours which had been circulated long ago respecting some Brothers who had been so horribly compromised that it had been necessary to conjure them away with the greatest speed—all those infamous tales were inventions of the devil.

In this respect, perhaps, however contrary to the truth his vehement declarations might be, Brother Fulgence, in the first instance, made them in all good faith, for he lived very much in another world, far from mere reason. But he soon found himself caught beneath the millstone of falsehood; it became necessary that he should lie knowingly and deliberately, and he did so at last with a kind of devout rage, for the very love of God. Was he not, himself, chaste? Had he not always wrestled against temptation? That was so;

and he therefore made it his duty to guarantee the absolute
chastity of his entire Order; he answered for the Brothers
who stumbled by the way, he denied to laymen the right of
judging them, for the laymen belonged merely to the flock,
they knew nought of the temple.   If, then, Brother Gorgias
had sinned, he owed account of it to God only, not to man.
As a member of a religious Order he had ceased to be liable
to human justice.   In this way, consumed by his craving to
thrust himself forward, Brother Fulgence went on and on,
impelled by skilful and discreet hands which piled all re-
sponsibilities upon his shoulders.

It was not difficult to divine that Father Philibin stood
behind him in the gloom — Father Philibin, who, in his
turn, was the instrument of Father Crabot.   But how
supple and how powerful a one, retaining his personality
even amidst his obedience!   He willingly exaggerated the
characteristics of his peasant origin, affecting the heavy *bonhomie* of some rough-hewed son of the soil; yet he was full
of the shrewdest craft, endowed with the patience needed
for long enterprises, which he conducted with wonderful
dexterity.   He was always striving to attain some mysterious
object, but he made no stir, he showed no personal ambition; the only joy he coveted was that of seeing his work
prosper.   Supposing him to be possessed of faith, it must
have been a desire to serve his superiors and the Church
that impelled him to fight on like an unknown unscrupulous
soldier.   As Prefect of the Studies at Valmarie he there
kept a watch over everything, busied himself with everything; for, however massive his build, he was very active.
Mingling with the pupils of the college, playing with them,
watching them, studying them, diving to the very depths of
their souls, ascertaining everything he could about their
relatives and their friends, he possessed the master's all-
seeing eye, the mind which stripped the brains and hearts
of others.

At times, it was said, he shut himself up with Father
Crabot, the Rector, who affected to direct the establishment
from on high, never attending personally to the education
of the boys; and to him Father Philibin communicated his
notes, his reports, his many documents containing the most
complete and secret particulars about each pupil.   It was
asserted that Father Crabot, who prudently made it a principle to keep no papers whatever, did not approve of Philibin's practice of collecting and cataloguing documents.

Yet, in recognition of his great services, he let him do so, regarding himself meantime as the directing hand, the superior mind which made use of the other. Indeed, did he not reign from his austere little cell over all the fine folk of the department? Did not the ladies whom he confessed, the families whose children were educated at Valmarie, belong to him by virtue of the might of his sacred ministry? He flattered himself that it was he who wove and disposed the huge net in which he hoped to capture one and all, when in reality it was more frequently Father Philibin who covertly prepared the various campaigns and ensured victory. In the Simon case, in particular, the latter seemed to have been the hidden artisan who recoiled from no task, however dark and base it might be, the politic man whom nothing could disgust, who had remained the friend of that vicious but well-informed youth, Georges Plumet,—nowadays the terrible Brother Gorgias,—following him through life, protecting him because he was as dangerous as useful, and doing all that could be done to extricate him from that frightful affair, the murder of little Zéphirin, in order no doubt that he, Philibin himself, might not come to grief in it, in the company of his superior, Father Crabot, that glory of the Church.

Now, once again, Maillebois became impassioned, though as yet there were only rumours of the criminal devices which the Jews were preparing in order to set the devoted Brother Gorgias, that holy man, revered by the entire district, in the place of that infamous scoundrel Simon. Extraordinary efforts were made to induce the school children's parents— even those whose children attended the secular school—to condemn the revival of the affair. People talked as if the streets had been mined by some hidden band of scoundrels, the enemies of God and France, who had resolved to blow up the town as soon as a certain signal should reach them from abroad. At a sitting of the Municipal Council, Mayor Philis ventured to allude to a vague danger threatening the locality, and denounced the Jews who were secretly piling up millions for the diabolical work. Then, becoming more precise, he condemned the impious doings of the schoolmaster, that Marc Froment, of whom he had hitherto failed to rid the town. But he was still watching him, and this time he hoped that he would compel the Academy Inspector to show exemplary severity.

The successive versions which *Le Petit Beaumontais* had

given of Marc's share in the revival of the affair had cast
confusion into the minds of many folk.   There was certainly a question of a document found at the house of Mesdames Milhomme, the stationers; but some people spoke
also of another abominable forgery perpetrated by Simon, and
others of a crushing document which proved the complicity
of Father Crabot.   The only certain thing was that General Jarousse had paid another visit to his cousin, Madame
Edouard, that poor relation whose existence he so willingly
forgot.   One morning he had been seen arriving and rushing into the little shop, whence he had emerged half an hour
later, looking extremely red.   And the result of his tempestuous intervention was that Madame Alexandre, and her
son Sébastien, now convalescent, started on the morrow for
the South of France, while Madame Edouard continued to
manage the shop to the complete satisfaction of the clerical
customers.   She ascribed the absence of her sister-in-law to
the latter's maternal anxiety, for only a sojourn in a warm
climate would restore Sébastien to health; but as a matter
of fact she was quite ready to recall Madame Alexandre in
the interests of their business, should the secular school
prove victorious in the coming contest.

Amid the rumbling of the great storm which was rising,
Marc endeavoured to discharge his duties as schoolmaster
with all correctitude.   The affair was now in David's hands,
and in that respect he, Marc, merely had to wait until he
could assist him with his evidence.   Thus never had he devoted himself more entirely to his pupils, striving to inspire
them with reason and kindliness, for his active share in the
reparation of one of the most monstrous iniquities of the age
had filled him with greater fervour than ever for the cause
of human solidarity.   With Geneviève he showed himself
very affectionate, endeavouring to avoid all subjects on
which they disagreed, attentive only, it seemed, to those
little trifles which are yet of great importance in one's daily
life.   But whenever his wife returned from a visit to her relations he divined that she was nervous, impatient, more
and more exasperated with him, her mind being full of
stories which she had heard from his enemies.   Thus he
could not always avoid quarrels, which gradually became
more and more venomous and deadly.

One evening hostilities broke out on the subject of that
unhappy man Férou.   Tragic tidings had reached Marc
during the day: a sergeant, to whom Férou had behaved

rebelliously, had shot him dead with a revolver. Marc, on going to see the widow, had found her in her wretched home, weeping and begging death to take her also, together with her younger daughters, even as it had compassionately taken the eldest one already. Marc felt that Férou's frightful fate was the logical *dénouement* of his career: the poor schoolmaster, scorned, embittered to the point of rebellion, driven from his post, deserting in order that he might not have to pay to the barracks the debt which he had already paid in part to the school, then conquered by hunger, forcibly incorporated in the army when he returned to succour his despairing wife and children, and ending like a mad dog, yonder, under the flaming sky, amid the torturing life of a disciplinary company. At the same time, in presence of the sobbing wife and her stupefied daughters, in presence of those poor ragged waifs whom the iniquity of the social system cast into the last agony, Marc's brotherly and humane nature was stirred to furious protest. Even in the evening he had not calmed down, and forgot himself so far as to speak of the affair to Geneviève, while she was still moving about their bedroom before withdrawing to a small adjoining chamber, where, of recent times, she had slept by herself.

'Do you know the news?' said he. 'A sergeant has blown poor Férou's brains out, in some mutiny, in Algeria.'

'Ah!'

'Yes, I saw Madame Férou this afternoon; she is quite out of her mind. . . . It was really deliberate, premeditated murder. I don't know if General Jarousse, who showed himself so harsh in Férou's case, will sleep at ease to-night. In any case some of the blood of that poor madman, who was turned into a wild beast, will cling to his hands.'

'It would be very foolish of the general not to sleep!' Geneviève quickly retorted, interpreting Marc's words as an attack on her principles.

He made a gesture of mingled sorrow and indignation. But, recollecting the position, he regretted that he had named the general, for the latter was one of Father Crabot's dearest penitents, and at one moment there had been some thought of using him for a military *coup d'état*. A Bonapartist by repute, with a decorative, corpulent figure, he was very severe with his men, though jovial at bottom, and fond of the table and wenches. Of course there was no

harm in that; but, after some negotiations, the clericals
found that he was decidedly too big a fool for their purpose;
and so he remained a mere possible makeshift for their
party, though they still treated him with some consideration.

'When we first knew the Férou family at Le Moreux,'
Marc gently resumed, 'they were already so poor, so burdened with work and worries in their wretched school, that
I cannot think of that unhappy man, that master, tracked
and destroyed like a wolf, without a feeling of anguish and
compassion.'

At this Geneviève, thoroughly upset, her earlier displeasure turning into a kind of nervous exasperation, burst
into tears. 'Yes, yes! I understand you perfectly—I am
a heartless creature, eh? You began by thinking me a fool,
and now you believe I have an evil heart. How is it possible for us to continue loving one another if you treat me as
though I were a stupid and malicious woman?'

Astonished and grieved at having provoked such an outburst Marc wished to pacify his wife. But she became quite
wild. 'No, no! it is all over between us. As you hate me
more and more each day, it is best that we should separate
at once, without waiting till unworthy things happen!'

Then she rushed into the little room where she now slept,
and locked the door with no gentle hand. He, when he
saw it thus shut upon him, remained in despair, with tears
welling to his eyes. Hitherto that door had always been
left open, and, though the husband and wife had no longer
shared the same bed, they had remained in a degree together, able to converse with one another. But now came
total separation: henceforth they would live as strangers.

On the following evenings Geneviève in the same manner
locked herself in her room. Then, having acquired that
habit, she never showed herself to Marc until she was fully
dressed. As the time approached for the birth of the child
she expected, she displayed increasing repugnance for the
slightest caress, the merest touch, even, on the part of her
husband. He had ascribed this at first to her state of
health; but he became surprised as her repulsion developed
more and more into hatred, for it seemed to him that the
advent of another child ought to have drawn them more
closely together. And his anxiety augmented; for if, on
the one hand, he was aware that as long as man and woman are united by love no rupture is possible, for the bitterest quarrels evaporate amid their kisses, on the other he

knew that, as soon as virtual divorce is agreed upon, the
slightest conflict may prove deadly, beyond possibility of
reconciliation; indeed, it often happens when homes are
seen collapsing in a seemingly inexplicable manner, that
everything can be traced back to the severance of the carnal
bond, the tie of passion. As long as Geneviève had hung
about his neck Marc had not feared the attempts which
were made to take her from him. He knew that she was
his, he knew that no power in the world could conquer love.
But if she ceased to regard him with love and passion, would
not the fierce efforts of his enemies at last wrest her from
him? And, as day by day he saw her become colder and
colder, his heart was wrung by increasing, intolerable
anxiety.

At one moment some little enlightenment came to him
with respect to the change in his wife's manner. He learnt
that she had quitted Abbé Quandieu to take as her confessor Father Théodose, the Superior of the Capuchins, who
stage-managed so cleverly the miracles of St. Antony of
Padua. The reason given for this change was the discomfort, the unappeased hungry state in which she was left by
the ministrations of the priest of St. Martin's. He was now
too lukewarm for her ardent faith; whereas handsome Father
Théodose, whose fervour was so lofty, would nourish her
with the wholemeal bread of mysticism, which she needed
to satisfy her. In reality, it was Father Crabot, now sovereign lord at Madame Duparque's house, who had decided
on this change, doubtless in order to hasten victory after
proceeding with such artful slowness.

It never occurred to Marc to suspect Geneviève of any
base intrigue with the Capuchin, that superbly-built man,
Christlike in features but of dark complexion, whose large
glowing eyes and frizzy beard sent his penitents into raptures. Marc knew his wife to be possessed of too much
loyalty and too much dignity, both of mind and body—a
dignity that had never forsaken her even in moments of the
most passionate rapture. But without carrying matters as
far as that, was it not admissible that the growing influence
of Father Théodose was in part the domination of a handsome man over a woman who was still young—a man, too,
godlike in appearance, and godlike claiming obedience?
After her pious conversations with Father Théodose, after
the long hours she spent in the confessional, Geneviève returned to her husband quivering, distracted, such as he had

never seen her when she retuned from her visits to Abbé
Quandieu.   In her intercourse with her new confessor she
was certainly forming some mystical passion, finding some
new food for her craving nature.   Perhaps, too, the monk
availed himself of her perturbed state of health to terrorise
her.   Indeed, was not the father of the child she bore one of
the damned? She repeatedly spoke of that child in a despairing way, as if seized with a kind of terror, like one of those
mothers who dread lest they should give birth to a monster.
And if that happily should not come to pass, how would she
protect the child from surrounding sin, whither might she
carry her babe to save it from the contamination of its
father's sacrilegious home?   All this threw a little light on
Geneviève's rupture with Marc—a rupture in which there
might well be remorse at the thought that her child was also
the child of an unbeliever; then a vow that she would never
more be the mother of that unbeliever's children; and,
finally, a perversion and exasperation of love, which dreamt
of finding satisfaction henceforth in the *au-delà* of desire.
Yet how much still remained obscure, and how cruelly did
Marc suffer as he saw himself forsaken by that adored wife,
whom the Church was wrenching from his arms, in order
that by torturing him it might annihilate him and his work
of human liberation!

One day, on returning home after one of her long conferences with Father Théodose, Geneviève, who looked
both excited and exhausted, said to Louise, who at that
moment came in from school: ' To-morrow at five o'clock
you will have to go to confession at the Capuchins'.   If you
do not confess, you will no longer be received at the Catechism class.'

But Marc resolutely intervened.   While allowing Louise
to follow the Catechism class, he had hitherto strongly opposed her attendance at confession.   ' Louise will not go to
the Capuchins',' he said, firmly.   ' You know, my dear,
that I have given way on every other point, but I will not
allow the child to go to confession.'

' Why not? ' exclaimed Geneviève, still restraining herself.

' I cannot repeat my reasons before the child.   But you
know them, and I will not allow my daughter's mind to be
soiled, under the pretext of absolving her of trivial faults,
which her parents alone need know and correct.'

An explanation, indeed, had taken place between Marc
and Geneviève on this subject.   In his opinion it was most

loathsome and abominable that a little girl should be initiated to the passions of the flesh by a man who, by his very
vow of chastity, might be led to every curiosity and every
sexual aberration.   For ten priests who might be prudent,
it was sufficient there should be one of unbalanced mind,
and then confession became filth, to which risk Marc refused
to expose his daughter Louise.   Besides, in that disturbing
promiscuity, that secret colloquy amid the mystical, ener-
vating atmosphere and gloom of a chapel, there was not
merely the possibility of demoralisation for a girl only
twelve years old,—an anxious age, when the senses begin to
quicken,—there was also a seizure of her mind and person;
for whatever she might become later, girl, wife, and mother,
she would always remain the initiate of that minister, who
by his very questions had violated her modesty, and thereby
affianced her to his jealous Deity.   From that time forward,
indeed, woman, by her avowals, belonged to her confessor,
became his trembling, obedient thing, ever ready to do his
behests, to serve, in his hands, as an instrument of investigation and enthralment.

'If our daughter should be guilty of any fault,' Marc resumed, 'she shall confess it to you or me, whenever she
feels a need to do so.   That will be more logical and
cleaner.'

Geneviève shrugged her shoulders, like one who deemed
that solution to be both blasphemous and grotesque.   'I
won't discuss the matter any further with you,' she said.
'But just tell me this—if you prevent Louise from going to
confession, how will she be able to go to her first Communion?'

'Her first Communion?   But is it not settled that she will
wait till her twentieth birthday in order to decide that question herself?   I have let her go to the Catechism class, even
as she goes to her *cours* of history and sciences—that is, in
order that she may form an opinion and decide later on.'

At this Geneviève's anger mastered her.   She turned
towards her daughter: 'And you, Louise, what do you
think; what do you desire?'

The child, whose usually gay face had become quite
grave, had listened to her father and mother in silence.
Whenever such quarrels arose, she endeavoured to remain
neutral from a fear of embittering matters.   Her intelligent
eyes glanced from one to the other of her parents as if begging that they would not make themselves unhappy on her

account, for she was grieved indeed to find that she was so constantly the cause of their disputes. But, though she showed great deference and affection for her mother, the latter felt that she inclined towards her father, whom indeed she worshipped, and whose firm sense and passion for truth and equity she had inherited.

For a moment Louise remained as if undecided, looking at her parents in her usual affectionate way. Then she gently said: 'What I think, what I wish, mamma? Why, I should much like it to be whatever you and papa might agree upon. But does papa's desire seem to you so very unreasonable? Why not wait a little?'

The mother, quite beside herself, refused to listen any further. 'That is not an answer, my girl,' she cried. 'Remain with your father since you can no longer show me either respect or obedience! You will end, between you, by driving me from the house!'

Then she rushed away and shut herself up in her little room, as she always did nowadays whenever she encountered the slightest opposition. This was her method of ending their quarrels, and on each occasion she seemed to draw farther and farther away from her husband and her child, to set more and more space between herself and the dearly-loved family fireside of other days.

Her belief that attempts were being made to influence her daughter in order that the child might cast off her authority was strengthened by a fresh incident. After long and skilful manœuvring, Mademoiselle Rouzaire had at last secured the post of first assistant teacher at Beaumont, which post she had coveted for years. Inspector Le Barazer had yielded in the matter to the pressing applications of the clerical deputies and senators, at the head of whom Count Hector de Sanglebœuf marched with the noisy bustling gait of a great captain. But to compensate politically for this step, Le Barazer, with his usual maliciousness, had caused the vacant post at Maillebois to be assigned to Mademoiselle Mazeline, the schoolmistress at Jonville, whose good sense Marc so greatly admired. Perhaps, also, the Academy Inspector, who still covertly supported Marc, had desired to place a friend beside him, one whose object would be the same as his own, who would not try to thwart him at every step, as Mademoiselle Rouzaire had done. At all events, when Mayor Philis, in the name of the Municipal Council, complained to Le Barazer of this appointment, which, said

he, would place the little girls of Maillebois in the hands
of an unbelieving woman, the Academy Inspector affected
great astonishment.   What! had he not acted in accordance
with Count Hector de Sanglebœuf's pressing application?
Was it his fault if, owing to promotions among the school
staff, a most meritorious person, of whom no parents had
ever complained, had become entitled in due order to the
post at Maillebois?

As a matter of fact, Mademoiselle Mazeline's *début* in the
town proved very successful.   People were struck by her
gay serenity, the maternal manner in which from the very
first day she gained the affection of her pupils.   All gentleness and zeal, she directed her efforts in such wise that her
daughters, as she called them, might become worthy women,
wives, and mothers.   But she did not take them to Mass,
and she suppressed processions, prayers, and Catechism
lessons.   Before long, therefore, a few other mothers, who
belonged to the clerical faction, like Geneviève, began to
protest.   Indeed, though she had no cause to congratulate
herself on her intercourse with Mademoiselle Rouzaire,
whose intrigues had disturbed her home, she now seemed to
regret her, and spoke of the new schoolmistress as a most
suspicious character, who was capable of the blackest
enterprises.

'You hear me, Louise,' she said one day; 'if Mademoiselle Mazeline should say anything wrong to you, you must
tell me.   I won't allow my daughter's soul to be stolen from
me!'

Marc could not refrain from intervening.   'Mademoiselle
Mazeline stealing souls!' said he; 'that's foolish!   When
we were at Jonville you used to admire her, as I did.   No
woman has a loftier mind or a more tender heart.'

'Oh! naturally you back her up,' Geneviève replied;
'you are well fitted to understand each other.   Go and join
her, hand our daughter over to her, since I am no longer of
any account!'

Then, once again, Geneviève hastened to her room, where
little Louise had to join her, weep with her, and entreat her
for hours before she could be induced to attend to the home
again.

All at once some almost incredible news reached Maillebois, throwing the town into no little emotion.   Advocate
Delbos, who had gone to Paris and addressed himself to
some of the Government departments, laying before the

officials the famous duplicate copy-slip furnished by Madame Alexandre, had prevailed on them—by what high influence nobody knew—to order a perquisition in Father Philibin's rooms at Valmarie. The extraordinary part of the affair was the lightning-like speed with which this perquisition was made, the Commissary of Police arriving at the College quite unexpectedly, then at once examining the collection of documents formed by the Prefect of the Studies, and, in the second portfolio he opened, discovering an envelope, already yellow with age, which contained the fragment of the copy-slip torn off so long ago. There was no question of denying its authenticity, for when placed in position at the corner of the mutilated slip it fitted exactly.

It was added that Father Philibin, whom Father Crabot—utterly upset by the affair—immediately interrogated, had made a frank confession, explaining his conduct by a kind of instinctive impulse, his hand having acted before his mind had time to think, so great had been his anxiety on seeing the stamp of the Brother's school upon the copy-slip, when he found the latter in Zéphirin's room. If he had remained silent afterwards, this was because a careful study of the affair had convinced him that Simon was indeed the culprit, and had intentionally made use of what was evidently a gross forgery in order to injure religion. Thus Father Philibin gloried in his act, for by tearing off that corner and afterwards preserving silence, he had behaved like a hero who set Holy Church high above the justice of men. Would not a vulgar accomplice have destroyed the fragment? As the reverend Father had preserved it, could one not understand that it had been his intention to re-establish all the facts whenever it might become advisable to do so? Such was the language held by some of his partisans, but there were folk who attributed the preservation of the fragment to his mania for keeping even the smallest scraps of paper, and who thought also that he had wished to remain in possession of a weapon which might prove useful against others.

It was said that Father Crabot, who for his part destroyed even the cards which visitors left for him, was exasperated with his colleague, and that in his surprise and fury at the first moment he had cried: 'What! I gave him orders to burn everything, and he kept that!' In any case, on the evening of the day when the discovery was made by the Commissary, Father Philibin, against whom as yet no warrant had been issued, disappeared. When pious souls anxiously inquired what had become of him, they were told that Father Poirier, the Provincial of Beaumont, had decided to send him to a convent in Italy to observe a retreat; and there, as if engulfed, he was at once buried in eternal silence.

The revision of Simon's case now appeared to be inevitable. Delbos sent for David and Marc, in order to decide in what form the necessary application to the Minister of Justice should be made. The discovery of the long-missing corner of the copy-slip would alone suffice for the sentence of the Court of Beaumont to be quashed, and the advocate was of opinion that they ought to content themselves with this discovery, and, for the time at all events, leave on one side the illegal communication which Judge Gragnon had made to the jurors. Moreover, the circumstances of that communication, now difficult of proof, would be brought to light during the new investigations which must ensue. Meantime, as the truth in the matter of the copy-slip was manifest, as the report of the handwriting experts was entirely upset, the origin of the stamped and initialled slip constituting such a damaging element in the case that Father Philibin had practised dissimulation and falsehood to conceal it, the advocate considered it best to assail Brother Gorgias without more ado. When Marc and David quitted Delbos that decision had been adopted; and on the morrow David addressed to the Minister a letter in which he formally accused Brother Gorgias of having committed a heinous offence on little Zéphirin, and murdered him, for which crimes his, David's, brother Simon had been in penal servitude for ten years.

Emotion then reached a climax. On the day after the discovery of the corner of the copy-slip among Father Philibin's papers, there had come an hour of lassitude and discomfiture among the most ardent supporters of the Church. This time the battle really seemed to be lost, and *Le Petit Beaumontais* even printed an article in which the conduct of the reverend Jesuit was roundly blamed. But two days later the faction had recovered its self-possession, and the very same newspaper proceeded to canonise theft and falsehood. St. Philibin, hero and martyr, was portrayed amid a setting of palms, and with a halo about his head. A legend likewise arose, showing the reverend Father in a remote convent of the Apennines, surrounded by wild forests. There, wearing a hair-cloth next his skin, he prayed devoutly both by day and by night, and offered himself in sacrifice for the sins of the world. And on the back of the pious little pictures which circulated, showing him on his knees, there was a prayer by repeating which the faithful might gain indulgences.

The resounding accusation launched against Brother Gorgias fully restored to the clericals their rageful determination to attack and conquer, convinced as they were that the victory of the Jew would shake the Congregations in a terrible fashion and leave a gaping breach in the very heart of the Church. All the anti-Simonists of former days rose up again, more uncompromising than ever, eager to conquer or to die. And the old battle began afresh on every side; on one hand all the free-minded men who believed in truth and equity and looked to the future, on the other all the reactionaries, the believers in authority, who clung to the past with its God of wrath, and based salvation on priests and soldiers. The Municipal Council of Maillebois again quarrelled about schoolmaster Froment, families were rent asunder, the Brothers' pupils and Marc's stoned one another on the Place de la République after lessons. Then, too, the fine society of Beaumont was utterly upset, such was the feverish anxiety of all who had participated in any way in Simon's trial.

For one man, such as Salvan, who rejoiced with Marc at each successive interview, how many there were who no longer slept o' nights at the thought that all the iniquity which had been buried was about to be exhumed! Fresh elections were impending, and the politicians feared lest they should be unseated. Lemarrois, the Radical, the ex-Mayor of Beaumont, once the town's indispensable man, was terrified by the rise of Delbos's popularity; Marcilly, the amiable *arriviste*, ever anxious to be on the winning side, floundered in uncertainty, no longer knowing which party to support; the reactionary senators and deputies, headed by the fierce Hector de Sanglebœuf, resisted desperately as they saw the storm, which might sweep them away, rising all round. In the government world and the university world the anxiety was no less keen; Prefect Hennebise lamented that he could not stifle the affair; Rector Forbes, losing his depth, cast everything upon the shoulders of Academy Inspector Le Barazer, who alone remained calm and smiling amid the tempest, while Depinvilliers, the

Director of the Lycée, took his daughters to Mass despairingly, even as one may throw oneself into a river, and Inspector Mauraisin, in anguish and astonishment at the turn
which things were taking, wondered if the time had not
come to go over to the Freemasons.[1]

But the emotion was particularly keen in the judicial
world, for did not a revision of the former trial mean a new
trial directed against the judges who had conducted the first
proceedings? and if the papers in the case should be exhumed and examined would not terrible revelations ensue?
Investigating Magistrate Daix, that unlucky honest man,
who was haunted by remorse for having yielded to his wife's
covetous ambition, looked livid when he repaired in silence
each morning to his office at the Palace of Justice.   And
if Raoul de La Bissonnière, the dapper Public Prosecutor,
made, on the contrary, an excessive show of good humour
and ease of mind, one could divine that he did so from a
torturing desire to prevent his fears from being seen.   As
for Presiding Judge Gragnon, who was the most compromised of all, he seemed to have aged quite suddenly; his
face had become heavy, his shoulders bent beneath some
invisible weight, and he dragged his big body about with
shuffling steps, unless he noticed that he was being watched,
when, with a suspicious glance, he made an effort to draw
himself erect.   Meantime the gentlemen's ladies had once
more transformed their *salons* into hotbeds of intrigue,
barter, and propaganda.   And from the *bourgeois* to their
servants, from the servants to the tradespeople, from the
tradespeople to the working classes, the whole population
followed on, becoming more and more crazed amid the
tempest which cast men and things into general dementia.

The sudden self-effacement of Father Crabot, whose tall
and elegant figure and whose handsome gowns of fine cloth
were so well known at the reception hour in the Avenue des
Jaffres, was much remarked.   He ceased to show himself
there, and a proof of excellent taste and profound piety was
detected in his desire for retreat and meditation, of which
his friends spoke with devout emotion.   As Father Philibin
also had disappeared, the only one of the superior ecclesi-
astics who remained in the front rank was Brother Fulgence,
who somehow always contrived to act in a compromising

---

[1] The French Freemasons are largely identified with Republican and
anti-Catholic views.— *Trans.*

way, bestirring himself too much, showing indeed such
clumsiness at each step he took that nasty rumours began
to circulate among the clericals, in accordance, no doubt,
with some order from Valmarie to sacrifice the Brother.

But the hero, the extraordinary figure of the time, one
that became more and more amazing every day, was Brother
Gorgias, who met the accusation brought against him with
prodigious audacity.   On the very evening of the day when
David's letter denouncing him was made public, he hastened
to the office of *Le Petit Beaumontais* to answer it, insulting
the Jews, inventing extraordinary stories, clothing true facts
with falsehoods of genius, fit to disturb the soundest minds.
He scoffed, too, asking if schoolmasters were in the habit
of walking about with copy-slips in their pockets; and he
denied everything, both paraph and stamp, explaining that
Simon, who had imitated his handwriting, might very well
have procured a stamp from the Brothers' school, or even
have had one made.   It was idiotic; but he nevertheless
proclaimed this version in such a thundering voice and with
such violent gestures that it was accepted, and became
official truth.   From that moment *Le Petit Beaumontais*
showed no hesitation; it adopted the story of the forged
stamp as it had adopted that of the forged paraph, the
whole theory of abominable premeditation on the part of
Simon, who, in committing his crime, had sought with infernal cunning to cast it upon a holy man, in order to soil
the Church!   And this imbecile invention impassioned all
the folk who were brutified by centuries of Catechism and
bondage.   Brother Gorgias rose to be a martyr of the Faith,
like Father Philibin.

He could no longer show himself without being acclaimed,
women kissed the hem of his frock, children asked him to
bless them, while he, impudent and triumphant, harangued
the crowds, and indulged in the most extravagant mum-
mery, like a popular idol, a mountebank before a booth,
certain of applause.   Yet, behind all that assurance, those
who were warned, who knew the truth, detected the anxious
distress of that wretched man who was forced to play a
part, the folly and fragility of which he was the first to
recognise.   And it was evident that in him one simply had
an actor on the stage, a tragic puppet whose strings were
pulled by invisible hands.   Though Father Crabot had
hidden himself away, humbly cloistered himself in his bare,
cold cell at Valmarie, his black shadow still passed across

the scene, and one could divine that his were the dexterous hands which pulled the strings, pushed the puppets forward, and toiled for the triumph of the Congregations.

Amid the greatest commotion, and despite the opposition of all the coalesced reactionary forces, the Minister of Justice was obliged to lay the application for revision, drawn up by David on behalf of Madame Simon and her children, before the Court of Cassation. This was truth's first victory, and for a moment the clerical faction seemed to be overwhelmed. But on the morrow the struggle began afresh. Even the Court of Cassation was cast into the mud, insulted every morning, accused of having sold itself to the Jews. *Le Petit Beaumontais* enumerated the amounts which had been paid, libelled the presiding judge, the general prosecutor, and the counsellors by relating all sorts of abominable stories about their private lives, which stories were inventions from beginning to end. During the two months occupied by the preparation of the case the river of filth never ceased to flow; no manœuvre, however iniquitous, no lie, even no crime, was left untried to stay the march of inexorable justice. At last, after memorable discussions, during which several judges gave a high example of healthy common-sense and courageous equity, superior to all passion, the Court gave its decision, which, although foreseen, burst on its slanderers like a thunder-clap. It retained the cause, declared that there was ground for revision, and recognised the necessity of an investigation, which it decided to conduct itself.

That evening Marc, when afternoon lessons were over, found himself alone in his little garden, in the warm twilight of springtime. Louise had not yet come in from school, for Mademoiselle Mazeline, whose favourite pupil she had become, sometimes kept her with her. As for Geneviève, ever since *déjeuner*, she had been absent at her grandmother's, where, indeed, she now spent nearly all her time. And, despite the fresh perfume which the lilacs shed in the warm air, Marc, as he paced the garden paths, was pursued by bitter, torturing thoughts of his devastated home. He had not given way on the subject of Confession—indeed, his daughter had lately quitted the Catechism class, the priest having refused to receive her any longer if she did not come to him by way of the Confessional. But, morning and evening alike, Marc had to contend against the attacks of his wife, who was exasperated, maddened, by the idea

that Louise would be damned, and that she herself would
be virtually an accomplice in it as she could not find the
strength to take the girl in her arms and carry her to the
tribunal of penitence.   She remembered her own adorable
first Communion, the loveliest day of her life, with her white
gown, the incense, the candles, the gentle Jesus to whom
she had so sweetly affianced herself, and who had remained
her only real spouse, the spouse of a divine love, the delights of which—she vowed it—were the only ones which she
would taste henceforth.   But was her daughter to be robbed
of such felicity, degraded, reduced to the level of the beasts
of the field, which knew no religion?   She could not bear
such a thought, but sought every possible opportunity to
wring a consent from her husband, changing the family
hearth into a battlefield, where the most futile incidents
gave rise to endless bickering.

The night was falling, slowly and peacefully; and Marc,
on whom for the moment a feeling of great lassitude had
come, felt astonished that he should be able to resist his
wife with a courage which was cruel for her, himself, and
their daughter.   All his old spirit of tolerance came back;
he had allowed his daughter to be baptised, so might he not
also allow her to make her first Communion?   The reasons
which his wife urged, reasons to which he had long bowed
—respect of individual liberty, the rights of a mother, the
rights of conscience—were not without weight.   In a home
the mother necessarily became the educator and initiator,
particularly when girls were in question.   To take no account of her ideas, to oppose the desires of her mind and
heart, meant surely the wrecking of the home.   Nought
was left of the bond of agreement which a home requires to
flourish, all happiness was destroyed, the parents and their
child lapsed into horrible warfare—that warfare from which
Marc's own home, once so united and so sweet, now suffered.
And thus, while pacing the narrow paths of his little garden,
across which the shadows were spreading, Marc asked himself whether and in what manner he might give way again
in order to restore a little peace and happiness.

A feeling of remorse tortured him; for was not his misfortune due to himself?   His share of responsibility had become manifest to him more than once, and he had asked
himself why, on the morrow of his marriage, he had not
endeavoured to win Geneviève over to his own belief.   At
that time, amid the first revelation of love, she had indeed

belonged to him, she had cast herself into his arms with all confidence, ready to mingle with him, in such wise that they might be of one flesh and one mind. He alone, at that unique hour of life, might have had the power to wrest the woman from the priest, and turn the child of the ages, bending beneath the dread of hell, into the conscious companion of his own existence, a companion whose mind would be freed, opened to truth and equity.

At the time of their earliest quarrels Geneviève herself had cried it to him: ' If you suffer because we do not think the same, it is your own fault! You should have taught me. I am such as I was made, and the misfortune is that you did not know how to make me anew!'

She had got far beyond that point now; she did not allow that he could possibly influence her, such had become the unshakable pride of her faith. Nevertheless, he bitterly recalled his lost opportunity, and deplored his egotistical adoration during the delightful springtime of their married life, when he had never ceased to admire her beauty, without a thought of diving into her conscience and enlightening her. True, he had not then imagined that he would become an artisan of truth such as he was to-day; he had accepted certain compromises, imagining that he was strong enough to remain the master. Indeed, all his present torture arose from his whilom masculine vanity, the blind weakness of his early love.

He knew that now, and as he paused before a lilac bush, whose flowers, open since the previous day, were shedding a penetrating perfume around, a sudden flame, a renewed desire to fight and conquer, arose within him. Even if he had formerly failed in his duty, was that a reason for him to fail in it now, by allowing his daughter to wreck her life in the same way as her mother had wrecked hers? Such remissness on his part would be the more unpardonable as he had taken on himself the task of saving the children of others from the falsehoods of the centuries. Perhaps it might be allowable for some obscurely situated man to put up with the doings of a bigot wife, who was intent on crazing her daughter with foolish and dangerous practices; but how could he accept such a position—he who had removed the crucifix from his classroom, he whose teaching was strictly secular, he who openly proclaimed the necessity of saving woman from the Church if one desired to build the Happy City. Would not his acceptance of such a position be the fullest possible confession of impotence? It would be the denial and the annihilation of his mission. He would lose all power, all authority to ask others to do that which he could or would not do himself in his own home. And what an example of hypocrisy and egotistical weakness would he not give to his daughter, who was acquainted with his ideas, and knew him to be opposed to Confession and Communion. Would she not wonder why he tolerated at home the actions which he condemned when their neigh-bours were in question? Would it not seem to her that he thought one way and acted another? Ah! no, no, tolerance had become impossible; he could no longer give way unless he desired to see his work of deliverance crumble beneath universal contempt.

Once more Marc began to walk to and fro under the paling sky, where the first stars were beginning to twinkle. One of the triumphs of the Church was that freethinking parents did not remove their children from its control, bound as they were by social usages, and fearful of scandal. There was an apprehension among them that they might fail to start their sons in life, or find husbands for their daughters, if the children did not at least pass through the formal routine of the sacraments. So who would begin, who would set the example? No doubt it would be neces-sary to wait a very long time for a general change, the time which science might require to destroy dogma as a matter of usage, even as it had already destroyed it as a matter of sense. Yet it was the duty of brave minds to set the first examples, examples which the Church dreaded, and which nowadays impelled it to make so many efforts to retain the support and favour of women, whom it had so long brutal-ised, treated as daughters of the devil, responsible for all the sins of the world.

It seemed to Marc that the Jesuits, who by a stroke of genius had resolved to adapt the Deity to the requirements of human passions, were the real artisans of the great move-ment which had placed women as instruments of political and social conquest in the hands of the priests. The Church had cursed human love, and now it employed it. It had treated woman as a monster of lewdness, from whom it was the duty of the Saints to flee; yet now it caressed her, loaded her with flattery, made her the ornament and mainstay of the sanctuary, having resolved to exploit her power over man.

Indeed sexuality flames among the candles of the altars, the priests nowadays accept it as a means of grace, use it as a trap in which they hope to recapture and master man. Does not all the disunion, the painful quarrel of contemporary society, spring from the divorce existing between man and woman, the former half freed, the latter still a serf, a petted, hallucinated slave of expiring Catholicism? The problem lies in that; we men should not leave the Church to profit by the mystical rapture in which it steeps our daughters and our wives, we should wrest from it the merit of the spurious deliverance it brings to them, we should deliver them really from all their fancies, and take them from the Church to ourselves, since indeed they are ours, even as we are theirs.

Marc reflected that there were three forces in presence: man, woman, and the Church, and instead of woman and the Church being arrayed against man, it was necessary that man and woman should be arrayed against the Church. Besides, were not man and wife one? Neither could act without the other, whereas united in flesh and in mind they became invincible, the very force of life, the very embodiment of happiness in the midst of conquered nature. And the one, sole, true solution suddenly became manifest to Marc: woman must be taught, enlightened, she must be set in her rightful place as our equal and our companion, for only the freed woman can free man.

At the moment when, calmed and comforted, Marc was regaining the courage he needed to continue fighting, he heard Geneviève come in, and went to join her in the classroom where a little vague light still lingered. He found her standing there, and though the birth of the child she expected was now near at hand, she carried herself so upright, in such an aggressive posture, with such brilliant eyes, that he felt a supreme storm to be imminent.

'Well, are you pleased?' she asked him curtly.

'Pleased with what, my darling?'

'Ah! you don't know then. . . . So I shall have the pleasure of being the first to give you the great news. . . . Your heroic efforts have been successful, the news has just arrived by telegraph. The Court of Cassation has decided in favour of the revision of the affair.'

Marc raised a cry of intense joy, unwilling to notice the tone of furious irony in which Geneviève had announced the triumph: 'At last! So there are some real judges after

all! The innocent man will suffer no longer. . . . But
is the news quite certain?'

'Yes, yes, quite certain, I had it from honourable people
to whom it was telegraphed. Yes, the abomination is complete and you may well rejoice.'

In Geneviève's quivering bitterness there was an echo of
the violent scene which, doubtless, she had just witnessed
at her grandmother's house, whither some priest or monk,
some friend of Father Crabot's, had hastened to impart the
tidings of the catastrophe which imperilled religion.

But Marc, as if determined not to understand, opened his
arms to his wife, saying: 'Thank you; I could not have
had a better-loved messenger. Kiss me!'

Geneviève brushed him aside with a gesture of hatred.
'Kiss you!' she cried. 'Why? Because you have been
the artisan of an infamous deed; because this criminal victory over religion rejoices you? It is your country, your
family, yourself, that you cast into the mire in order to save
that filthy Jew, the greatest scoundrel in all the world!'

'Do not say such things,' replied Marc in a gentle, entreating way, seeking to pacify her. 'How can you repeat
such monstrous words, you who used to be so intelligent
and so kind-hearted? Is it true, then, that error is so contagious that it may obscure the soundest minds? Just think
a little. You know all; Simon is innocent; and to leave
him still in penal servitude would be frightful iniquity—a
source of social rottenness which would end by destroying
the nation.'

'No, no!' she cried, with a kind of mystical exaltation;
'Simon is guilty—men of recognised holiness accused him,
and accuse him still; and to regard him as innocent it would
be necessary to discard all faith in religion, to believe God
Himself capable of error! No, no! he must stay at the
galleys, for on the day of his release nothing divine, nothing
that one may revere, would be left on earth!'

Marc was becoming impatient. 'I cannot understand,'
said he, 'how we can disagree on so clear a question of truth
and justice. Heaven has nothing to do with this.'

'It has. There is no truth or justice outside heaven!'

'Ah! that is the gist of it all—that explains our disagreement and torture! You would still think as I do if you had
not set heaven between us! And you will come back to me
on the day when you consent to live on earth and show a
healthy mind and a sisterly heart. There is only one truth,

one justice, such as science establishes under the control
of human certainty and solidarity!'

Geneviève was becoming exasperated: 'Let us come to
the point once and for all,' she retorted. 'It is my religion
that you wish to destroy!'

'Yes,' he cried; 'it is against your Roman Catholicism
that I fight — against the imbecility of its teaching, the
hypocrisy of its practices, the perversion of its worship, its
deadly action on children and women, and its social in-
juriousness. The Roman Catholic Church — that is the
enemy of whom we must first clear the path. Before the
social question, before the political question, comes the religious question, which bars everything. We shall never be
able to take a single forward step unless we begin by striking down that Church, which corrupts, and poisons, and
murders. And, understand me fully, that is the reason why
I am resolved not to allow our Louise to confess and communicate. I should feel that I was not doing my duty,
that I was placing myself in contradiction with all my principles and lessons, if I were to allow such things. And on
the morrow I should have to leave this school and cease to
teach the children of others, for lack of having both the
loyalty and the strength to guide my own child towards
truth, the only real and only good truth. Thus I shall not
yield on the matter; our daughter herself will come to a
decision when she is twenty!'

Geneviève, now quite beside herself, was on the point of
replying, when Louise came in, followed by Mademoiselle
Mazeline, who, having detained her after lessons, wished
to explain that she had been teaching her a difficult crochet
stitch. Short and slight, possessed of no beauty, but extremely charming with her broad face, her large, loving
mouth, and her fine black eyes glowing with ardent sympathy, the schoolmistress called from the threshold: 'Why,
have you no light? I want to show you the clever work of
a good little girl.'

But Geneviève, without listening, sternly called the child
to her. 'Ah! so it 's you, Louise. Come here a moment.
Your father is again torturing me about you. He is now
positively opposed to your making your first Communion.
Well, I insist on your doing so this year. You are twelve
years old, you can delay the matter no longer without causing a scandal. But before deciding on my course, I wish
to know what your own views are.'

Tall as she was already, Louise looked almost a little woman, showing a very intelligent face, in which her mother's refined features seemed to mingle in an expression of quiet good sense, which she had inherited from her father. With an air of affectionate deference she answered: 'My views! Oh, mamma, I can have none. Only I thought it was all settled, as papa's only desire is that I should wait till my majority. Then I will tell you my views!'

'Is that how you answer me, unhappy child?' cried her mother, whose irritation was increasing. 'Wait! still wait! when your father's horrible lessons are evidently corrupting you, and robbing me more and more of your heart!'

At this moment Mademoiselle Mazeline made the mistake of intervening, but she did so like a good soul who was grieved by this quarrel in a home whose happiness in former days had greatly touched her. 'Oh, my dear Madame Froment!' she said, 'your Louise is very fond of you, and what she said just now was very reasonable.'

Geneviève turned violently towards the schoolmistress: 'Attend to your own affairs, mademoiselle. I won't inquire into your share in all this; but you would do well to teach your pupils to respect God and their parents! . . . This is not your home, remember!'

Then, as the schoolmistress withdrew, heavy at heart and saying nothing for fear lest she might embitter the quarrel, the mother again turned to the girl:

'Listen to me, Louise . . . and you, Marc, listen to me also. . . . I have had enough of it, I swear to you that I have had enough of it, that what has occurred this evening, what has just been said, has filled the cup to over-flowing. . . . You no longer have any love for me, you torture me in my faith, and you try to drive me from the house.'

Her daughter, full of distress and agitation, was weeping in a corner of the large, dim room, and the heart of her husband, who stood there motionless, bled as he heard those supreme, rending words. Both he and the child raised the same protest: 'Drive you from the house!'

'Yes, you do all you can to render it unbearable! . . . Indeed, it is impossible for me to remain longer in a spot where all is scandal, error, and impiety, where every word and every gesture wound and shock me. I have been told twenty times that it was not a fit place for me, and I will not damn myself with you, so I am going away, returning whence I came!'

She cried those last words aloud with extraordinary vehemence.

'To your grandmother's, eh?' exclaimed Marc.

'To my grandmother's, yes! That is an asylum, a refuge full of sovereign peace. They at least know how to understand and love me there! I ought never to have quitted that pious home of my youth. Good-bye! There is nothing here to detain either my body or my soul!'

She went towards the door, with a fierce, set face, but, owing to her condition, with somewhat unsteady steps. Louise was still sobbing violently. But Marc, making a last effort, resolutely strove to bar the way.

'In my turn,' he said, 'I beg you to listen to me. You wish to return whence you came, and I am not surprised at it, for I know that every effort has been made there to wrest you from me. It is a house of mourning and vengeance. . . . But you are not alone, remember; there is the child you bear, and you cannot take it from me in that way to hand it over to others.'

Geneviève was standing before her husband, who, on his side, leant against the door. She seemed to increase in stature, to become yet more resolute and stubborn as she cast in his face these words: 'I am going away expressly in order to take that child from you, and place it beyond the reach of your abominable influence. I will not have you make a pagan of that child and ruin it in mind and heart as you have ruined this unhappy girl here. It is my child, I suppose, and you surely don't mean to beat me under pretence of keeping it? Come, get away from that door, and let me go!'

He did not answer, he was making a superhuman effort to abstain from force, such as anger suggested. For a moment they looked at one another in the last faint gleam of the expiring light.

'Get away from that door!' she repeated harshly. 'Understand that I have quite made up my mind. You do not desire a scandal, do you? You would have nothing to gain by it; you would be dismissed and prevented from continuing what you call your great work—the teaching of those children, whom you have preferred to me, and whom you will turn into brigands with your fine lessons. . . . Yes, be prudent, take care of yourself for the sake of your school, a school of the damned, and let me return to my God, who, some day, will chastise you!'

'Ah! my poor wife,' he murmured in a faint voice, for her words had wounded him to the heart. 'Fortunately it is not you yourself who speak; it is those wretched people who are making use of you as a deadly weapon against me. I recognise their words, the hope of a drama, the desire to see me dismissed, my school closed, my work destroyed. It is still because I am a witness, a friend of Simon, whose innocence I shall soon help to establish, that they wish to strike me down, is it not? And you are right, I do not desire a scandal which would please so many people.'

'Then let me go,' she repeated stubbornly.

'Yes, by and by. Before then I wish you to know that I still love you, love you even more than ever, because you are a poor sick child, attacked by one of those contagious fevers, which it takes so much time to cure. But I do not despair, for at bottom you are a good and healthy creature, sensible and loving when you choose, and some day you will awaken from your nightmare. . . . Besides, we have lived together for nearly fourteen years, I made you wife and mother, and even though I neglected to re-mould you entirely, the many things which have come to you from me will continue to assert themselves. . . . You will come back to me, Geneviève.'

She laughed with an air of bravado. 'I do not think so,' she said.

'You will come back to me,' he repeated, in a voice instinct with conviction. 'When you know and understand the truth, the love you have borne me will do the rest; and you have a tender heart, you are not capable of long injustice. . . . I have never done you violence, I have constantly respected your wishes, and now, as you wish it, go to your folly, follow it till it is exhausted, as there is no other means of curing you of it.'

He drew aside from the door to make way for her, and she for a moment seemed to hesitate amid the quivering gloom which was enshrouding that dear and grief-stricken home. It had become so dark that Marc could no longer see her face, which had contracted while she listened to him. But all at once she made up her mind, exclaiming in a choking voice: 'Good-bye!'

Then Louise, lost amid the darkness, sprang forward in her turn, wishing to prevent her mother's departure: 'Oh!

mamma, mamma, you cannot go away like this! We, who love you so well—we, who only want you to be happy——'

But the door had closed, and the only response was a last, distant cry, half stifled by a sound of rapid footsteps: 'Good-bye! good-bye!'

Then, sobbing and staggering, Louise fell into her father's arms; and, sinking together upon one of the forms of the classroom, they long remained there, weeping together. Night had completely fallen now, nothing but the faint sound of their sobs was to be heard in the large dark room. The deep silence of abandonment and mourning filled the empty house. The wife, the mother, had gone, stolen from the husband and the child, in order that they might be tortured, cast into despair. Before Marc's tearful eyes there rose the whole machination, the hypocritical, underhand efforts of years, which now wrenched from him the wife whom he adored, in order to weaken him and goad him into some sudden rebellion which would sweep both his work and himself away. His heart bled, but he had found the strength to accept his torture, and none would ever know his distress, for none could see him sobbing with his daughter in the darkness of his deserted home, like a poor man who had nought left him save that child, and who was seized with terror at the thought that she likewise might be wrested from him, some day.

A little later that same evening, as Marc had to conduct a course of evening lessons for adults, the four gas jets of the classroom were lighted, and students flocked in. Several of his former pupils, artisans and young men of modest commercial pursuits, assiduously followed these courses of history, geography, physical and natural science. And for an hour and a half Marc, installed at his desk, spoke on very clearly, contending with error and conveying a little truth to the minds of the humble. But all the time frightful grief was consuming him, his home was pillaged, destroyed, his love bewailed the lost wife whom he would find no longer overhead, in the room once warm with tender love, and now so cold.

Nevertheless, like the obscure hero he was, he bravely pursued his work.

BOOK III

I

DIRECTLY the Court of Cassation started on its inquiry, David and Marc, meeting one evening in the Lehmanns' dark little shop, decided that it would be best to abstain from all agitation, and remain in the background. Now that the idea of a revision of the case was accepted, the family's great joy and hope had restored its courage. If the inquiry should be loyally conducted by the Court, Simon's innocence would surely be recognised, and acquittal would become certain. So it would suffice to remain wakeful and watchful of the march of the affair, without exhibiting any doubt of the conscientiousness and equity of the highest judges in the land.

There was only one thing which prevented the joy of those poor people from becoming perfect. The news of Simon's health was still far from good; and might he not succumb over yonder before the triumph? The Court had declared that there were no grounds for bringing him back to France before its final judgment, and it seemed likely that the inquiry might last several months. In spite of all this, however, David remained full of superb confidence, relying on the wonderful strength of resistance which his brother had hitherto displayed. He knew him, and he tranquillised the others, even made them laugh, by telling stories of Simon's youth, anecdotes which showed him retiring within himself with singular force of will, thoughtful both of his dignity and of the happiness of those near to him. So the interview between Marc, David, and the Lehmanns ended, and they separated, resolved to show neither anxiety nor impatience, but to behave as if the victory were already won.

From that time, then, Marc shut himself up in his school, attending to his pupils from morn till night, giving himself to them with an abnegation, a devotion, which seemed to increase in the midst of obstacles and suffering. While he

was busy with them in the classroom, while he acted as
their big brother, striving to apportion the bread of knowledge among them, he forgot some of his torture, he suffered
less from the ever-bleeding wound in his heart.   But in the
evenings, when he found himself alone in the home whence
love had fled, he relapsed into frightful despair, and wondered how it would be possible for him to continue living
in dark and chilly widowerhood.   Some little relief came to
him on the return of Louise from Mademoiselle Mazeline's;
and yet, when the lamp had been lighted for the evening
meal, what long spells of silence fell between the father and
the daughter, each plunged into inconsolable wretchedness
by the departure of the wife, the mother, whose desertion
haunted them!   They tried to escape from their pursuing
thoughts by talking of the petty incidents of the day.   But
everything brought them back to her; they ended by talking of her alone, drawing their chairs together, and taking
each other's hands, as if to warm each other in their solitude.   And all their evenings ended in that fashion, the
daughter seated on her father's lap with one arm around his
neck, and both sobbing and quivering beside the smoky
lamp.   The home was dead; the absent one had carried
away its life, its warmth, its light.

Yet Marc did nothing to compel Geneviève to return to
him.   Indeed, he did not wish to be indebted in any way
to such rights as it might be possible for him to enforce.
The idea of a scandal, a public dispute, was odious to him;
and not only had he resolved that he would not fall into the
trap set by those who had induced Geneviève to forsake
him, relying in this connection on some conjugal drama
which would bring about his revocation, but he also set all
his hope in the sole force of love.   Geneviève would surely
reflect and return home.   In particular, it seemed impossible that she would keep her expected child for herself
alone.   As soon as possible after its birth she would bring
it to him, since it belonged to both of them.   Even if the
Church had succeeded in perverting her as a loving woman,
surely it would be unable to kill her motherly feelings.
And as a mother she would come back, and remain with the
child.   The latter's birth was near at hand, so there would
not be more than a month to wait.

By degrees, after hoping for this *dénouement*, by way of
consoling himself, Marc began to regard it as a certainty.
And, like a good fellow, who did not wish to part mother

and daughter, he sent Louise to spend Thursday and Sunday afternoons with Geneviève at Madame Duparque's, although that dark, dank, pious house had already brought him so much suffering. Perhaps he unknowingly found some last, melancholy satisfaction in this indirect intercourse, as well as a means of maintaining a tie between himself and the absent one. Whenever Louise came home after spending several hours with her mother, she brought a little of Geneviève with her; and on those evenings her father kept her longer than usual on his knees, and questioned her eagerly, longing for tidings, even though they might make him suffer.

'How did you find her to-day, my dear?' he would ask. 'Does she laugh a little? Does she seem pleased? Did she play with you?'

'No, no, father. . . . You know very well that she has long ceased to play. But she still had a little gaiety when she was here, and now she looks sad and ill.'

'Ill!'

'Oh! not ill enough to remain in bed. On the contrary, she cannot keep from moving about, and her hands are burning hot, as if she had the fever.'

'And what did you do, my dear?'

'We went to Vespers, as we do every Sunday. Then we returned to grandmamma's for some refreshment. There was a monk there, whom I did not know, some missionary, who told us stories of savages.'

Then Marc remained silent for a moment, full of great bitterness of spirit, but unwilling to judge the mother in the daughter's presence, or to give the latter an order to disobey her by refusing to accompany her to church. At last he resumed gently: 'And did she speak to you of me, my dear?'

'No, no, father. . . . Nobody there speaks to me of you, and as you told me never to speak first about you, it is just as if you did not exist.'

'All the same, grandmother is not angry with you?'

'Grandmamma Duparque hardly looks at me, and I prefer that; for she has such eyes that she frightens me when she scolds. . . . But Grandmamma Berthereau is very kind, especially when there is nobody there to see her. She gives me sweets, and takes me in her arms and kisses me ever so much.'

'Grandmamma Berthereau!'

'Why, yes. One day even she told me that I ought to love you very much. She is the only one who has ever spoken to me of you.'

Marc again relapsed into silence, for he did not wish his daughter to be initiated too soon into the wretchedness of life. He had always suspected that the doleful, silent Madame Berthereau, once so well loved by her husband, now led a life of agony beneath the bigoted rule of her mother, that harsh Madame Duparque. And he felt that he might possibly have an ally in the younger woman, though, unfortunately, one whose spirit was so broken that she might never find the courage to speak or act.

'You must be very affectionate with Grandmamma Berthereau,' said Marc to Louise, by way of conclusion. 'Though she may not say it, I think she is grieved as we are. . . . And mind you kiss your mother for both of us, she will feel that I have joined in your caress.'

'Yes, father.'

Thus did the long evening pass away, bitter but quiet, in the wrecked home. Whenever, on a Sunday, the daughter returned with some bad tidings—speaking, for instance, of a sick headache or some affection of the nerves from which the mother now suffered—the father remained full of anxiety until the ensuing Thursday. That nervous affection did not surprise him, he trembled lest his poor wife should be consumed in the perverse and imbecile flames of mysticism. But if on the following Thursday his daughter told him that mamma had smiled, and inquired about the little cat she had left at home, he revived to hope, and laughed with satisfaction and relief. Then, once again, he composed himself to await the return of the dear absent one, who would surely come back with her new-born babe at her breast.

Since Geneviève's departure Mademoiselle Mazeline, by the force of things, had become a *confidente*, an intimate for Marc and Louise. She brought the child home almost every evening, after lessons, and rendered little services in that disorganised home where there was no longer any housewife. The dwellings of the schoolmaster and the schoolmistress almost touched one another; there was only a little yard to be crossed, while in the rear a gate facilitated communication between the two gardens. Thus the intercourse became closer, particularly as Marc felt great sympathy for Mademoiselle Mazeline, whom he regarded as a most courageous and excellent woman. He had learnt to esteem her at Jonville in former times on finding that she was quite free from superstition, and strove to endow her pupils with solid minds and loving hearts. And now at Maillebois he felt intense friendship for her, so well did she realise his ideal of the educating, initiating woman, the only one capable of liberating future society. Marc was now thoroughly convinced that no serious progress would ever be effected if woman did not accompany man, and even precede him, on the road to the Happy City. And how comforting it was to meet at least one of those pioneers, one who was both very intelligent and very kind-hearted, all simplicity too, accomplishing her work of salvation as if it were one of the natural functions of her being! Thus Mademoiselle Mazeline became for Marc, amid his torture, a friend prized for her serenity and gaiety, one who imparted consolation and hope.

He was profoundly touched by the schoolmistress's sympathy and obligingness. She frequently spoke of Geneviève with anxious affection, devising excuses for her, explaining her case like a sensible woman who regarded lack of sense in others with sympathetic compassion. And she particularly begged of Marc that he would not be violent, that he would not behave like an egotistical and jealous master, one of those for whom a wife is a slave, a thing handed over to them by the laws. Without doubt Mademoiselle Mazeline had much to do with the prudence which Marc evinced in striving to remain patient and relying on sense and love to convince Geneviève and bring her back to him. Finally, the schoolmistress endeavoured with so much delicacy to replace the absent mother with Louise that she became, as it were, the light of that mournful home, where father and daughter shivered at the thought of their abandonment.

During those first fine days of the year Mademoiselle Mazeline frequently found herself of an evening with Marc and Louise in their little garden behind the school. The schoolmistress had merely to open the gate of communication, whose bolts were drawn back on either side, and neighbourly intercourse followed. Indeed she somewhat neglected her own garden for the schoolmaster's, where a table and a few chairs were set out under some lilac bushes. They jestingly called this spot 'the wood,' as if they had sought shelter under some large oaks on a patch of forest land. Then the scanty lawn was likened to a great meadow, the two flower borders became royal *parterres ;*

and after the day's hard work it was pleasant indeed to chat there, amid the quietude of twilight.

One evening, Louise, who had been reflecting with all a big girl's gravity, suddenly inquired: 'Mademoiselle, why have you never married?'

At this the schoolmistress laughed good naturedly. 'Oh, my darling, have you never looked at me!' she answered. 'A husband is not easily found when one has such a big nose as mine, and no figure.'

The girl looked at her mistress with astonishment, for never had she thought her ugly. True enough, Mademoiselle Mazeline did not possess a fine figure, and her nose was too large, her face a broad one, with a bumpy forehead and projecting cheek bones. But her admirable eyes smiled so tenderly that her whole countenance became resplendent with charm.

'You are very pretty,' declared Louise in a tone of conviction. 'If I were a man I should like to marry you.'

Marc felt very much amused, while Mademoiselle Mazeline gave signs of restrained emotion, tinged somewhat with melancholy. 'It would seem that the men have n't the same taste as you, my dear,' said she, as she recovered her quiet gaiety. 'When I was between twenty and twenty-five I would willingly have married, but I met nobody who wished for me. And I should not think of marrying now, when I am six and thirty.'

'Why not?' Marc inquired.

'Oh! because the time has passed. . . . An humble elementary teacher, born of poor parents, hardly tempts the marrying men. Where can one be found willing to burden himself with a wife who earns little, who is tied to heavy duties, and compelled to live in the depths of some out of the way region? If she is not lucky enough to marry a schoolmaster, and share her poverty with his, she inevitably becomes an old maid. . . . I long since gave up all idea of marriage, and I am happy all the same.'

But she quickly added: 'Of course marriage is necessary; a woman ought to marry, for she does not live, she does not fulfil her natural destiny, unless she becomes wife and mother. No real health or happiness exists for any human creature apart from his or her complete florescence. And in teaching my girls I never forget that they are destined to have husbands and children some day. . . . Only, when one is forgotten, sacrificed as it were, one has to

arrange for oneself some little corner of content. Thus, I
have cut out for myself my share of work, and I don't complain so much, for, in spite of everything, I have succeeded
in becoming a mother. All the children of others, all the
dear little girls with whom I busy myself from morning till
evening, belong to me. I am not alone, I have a very large
family.'

She laughed as she thus referred to her admirable devotion in the simple way of one who seemed to feel that she
was under obligations to all the pupils who consented to
become the children of her mind and heart.

'Yes,' said Marc by way of conclusion, 'when life shows
itself harsh to any of us the disinherited one must behave
kindly to life. That is the only way to prevent misfortune.'

On most occasions when Marc and Mademoiselle Mazeline
met in the little garden, over which the twilight stole, their
talk was of Geneviève. This was particularly the case on
those evenings when Louise, after spending the afternoon
at Madame Duparque's, returned with news of her mother.
One day she came back in a state of much emotion, for her
mother, whom she had accompanied to the Capuchin Chapel
to witness some great ceremony in honour of St. Antony of
Padua, had fainted away there, and had been carried to
Madame Duparque's in a disquieting condition.

'They will end by killing her!' cried Marc despairingly.

But Mademoiselle Mazeline, wishing to comfort him,
evinced stubborn optimism.

'No, no, when all is said your Geneviève has only an ailing mind, she is physically healthy and strong. Some day,
you 'll see, my friend, her intelligence, helped by her heart,
will win the victory. . . . And what could you expect ?
She is paying for her mystical education and training in one
of those convents whence, as long as they remain unclosed,
the evils which assail women, and the disasters of married
life, will always come. You must forgive her, she is not the
real culprit. She suffers from the long heredity bequeathed
to her by her forerunners, possessed, terrorised, and stupefied by the Church.'

Overcome by sadness, Marc, though his daughter was
present, could not restrain a low plaint, a spontaneous
avowal: 'Ah, for her sake and mine it would have been
better if we had never married! She could not become my
helpmate, my other self!'

'But whom would you have married, then ?' the school-

mistress inquired. 'Where would you have found a girl of
the middle class who had not been brought up under
Catholic rule, possessed with error and falsehoods? The
wife you needed, my poor friend, with your free mind—an
artisan of the future as you are—still remains to be created.
Perhaps just a few specimens exist, but even they are tainted
by atavism and faulty education.'

Then, with a laugh, she added in her gentle yet resolute
way: 'But you know that I am trying to form such companions as may be needed by the men who have freed
themselves from dogmas, and who thirst for truth and
equity. Yes, I am trying to provide wives for the young
fellows whom you, on your side, are training. . . . As
for yourself, my friend, you were merely born too soon.'

Thus conversing, the schoolmaster and the schoolmistress,
those humble pioneers of the future social system, forgot in
some measure the presence of the big girl of thirteen who
listened to them in silence, but with her ears wide open.
Marc had discreetly refrained from giving any direct lessons
to his daughter. He contented himself with setting her an
example, and she loved him dearly because he showed so
much goodness of heart, sincerity, and equity. The mind
of that big girl was slowly awakening to reason, but she did
not dare to intervene as yet in the conversation of her
father and mademoiselle; though assuredly she derived
profit from it, even if, like other children, when their elders
forget themselves so far as to speak before them of things
regarded as being above their intelligence, she appeared
neither to hear nor to understand. With her glance wandering away into the falling night, her lips scarcely stirred
by a faint quiver, she was always learning, classifying in her
little head all the ideas that emanated from those two persons whom, with her mother, were the ones she loved best
in the world. And one day, after a conversation of the
kind, a remark, which escaped her as she emerged from one
of her deep reveries, showed that she had perfectly understood.

'When I marry,' said she, 'I shall want a husband whose
ideas are like papa's, so that we may discuss things and
come to an agreement. And if we both think alike, it will
all go well.'

This manner of resolving the problem greatly amused
Mademoiselle Mazeline. Marc on his side was moved, for
he felt that some of his own passion for truth, his clear firm

mind, was appearing in his daughter. Doubtless, while a child's brain is yet dimly developing, it is difficult to fore-tell what will be the woman's mature intellect. Yet Marc thought he had grounds for believing that Louise would prove sensible and healthy, free from many errors. And this probability was very sweet to him, as if indeed he awaited from his daughter the help, the loving mediation, which by bringing the absent one back to the home would re-establish all the ties so tragically severed.

However, the news which Louise brought from the Place des Capucins grew worse and worse. As the time for her child's birth drew near, Geneviève became more and more gloomy, more and more capricious and bad tempered, in such wise that at times she even rejected her daughter's caresses. She had had several more fainting fits, and was giving way, it seemed, to increasing religious exaltation, after the fashion of those patients who, disappointed by the inefficacy of certain drugs, double and double the dose until at last they poison themselves. Thus, one delightful even-ing, while Mademoiselle Mazeline sat with the others in the flowery garden, the news which Louise communicated rendered the schoolmistress so anxious that she made a proposal to Marc.

'Shall I go to see your wife, my friend?' she asked. 'She showed some affection for me in former times, and perhaps she might listen to me if I were to talk sense to her.'

'But what would you say to her?' Marc replied.

'Why, that her place is beside you, that she still loves you though she knows it not; that her sufferings are all due to a frightful misunderstanding; and that she will only be cured when she returns to you with that dear child, the thought of whom is stifling her like remorse.'

Tears had risen to the eyes of Marc, who felt quite upset by the schoolmistress's words. But Louise quickly inter-vened: 'Oh, no, mademoiselle,' she said, 'don't go to see mamma; I advise you not to.'

'Why not, my darling?'

The girl blushed, and became greatly embarrassed. She knew not how to explain in what contemptuous and hateful terms the schoolmistress was spoken of at the little house on the Place des Capucins. But Mademoiselle Mazeline under-stood, and, like a woman accustomed to misrepresentation, she gently asked: 'Does your mamma no longer like me, then? Do you fear she might receive me badly?'

'Oh! mamma does not say much,' Louise ended by confessing; 'it is the others.'

Then Marc, overcoming his emotion, resumed, 'The child is right, my friend. Your visit might become painful, and it would probably have no effect. None the less, I thank you for your kindness; I know how warm your heart is.'

A long spell of silence ensued. The sky overhead was beautifully clear, and quietude descended from the vast vault of azure, where the sun was expiring in a roseate flush. A few carnations, a few wallflowers, in the little garden borders perfumed the mild air. And nothing more was said that evening by Marc and his friend as they lingered, steeped in melancholy, amid the delightful close of a fine day.

The inevitable had duly come to pass. A week had not elapsed after Geneviève's departure from her home before all Maillebois was talking of a scandalous intrigue carried on publicly by the schoolmaster and the schoolmistress. In the daytime, it was said, they constantly left their classrooms to join one another, and they spent their evenings together in the garden of the boys' school, where they could be plainly distinguished from certain neighbouring windows. And the abominable thing was the constant presence of little Louise, who mingled with it all. The vilest reports speedily began to circulate. Passers-by pretended that they had heard Marc and Mademoiselle Mazeline singing, and laughing over, filthy songs. Then a legend sprang up, it being plainly established that if Geneviève had quitted her home it was in a spirit of legitimate revolt and disgust, and in order to avoid association with that other woman, that godless creature who depraved the little girls confided to her care. Thus there was not merely a question of restoring Louise to her mother; in order to save the children of Maillebois from perdition, the schoolmaster and the schoolmistress must be stoned and driven away.

Some of these rumours reached Marc's ears; but he, realising by their imbecile violence whence they emanated, merely shrugged his shoulders. As the Congregations had not managed to secure a scandal in connection with Geneviève's departure, they were resuming their underhand work of slander, striving to embitter the new state of things. They had failed to bring about Marc's revocation by taking his wife from him, but perhaps they might succeed by accusing him of keeping a mistress. Moreover, this would cast a slur on the secular schools, and was dirty work well suited to clerics who do not shrink from any lies to ensure the triumph of religion. Since the revival of the Simon case, Father Crabot, no doubt, had been leading a cloistered life, and, besides, he seemed to occupy too high a position to stoop to such abominable inventions; but all the cassocks and frocks of Maillebois were astir, Brothers and Capuchins ever winging their flight, like a covey of black gowns, over the road to Valmarie. They returned, looking very busy; and then, in all the confessional boxes of the region, in quiet corners of the chapels, and in the parlours of the convents, came endless whispering with excited female devotees, who grew terribly indignant at all the horrors they heard. Thence those horrors spread in undertones and hints to families, tradespeople, and dependents. Yet if Marc felt angry, it was only at the thought that ignoble tales were surely being whispered to Geneviève herself, in order to make their separation irrevocable.

A month elapsed, and it seemed to Marc that the birth of the expected child must be imminent. After counting the days with feverish longing he felt astonished at receiving no news, when one Thursday morning Pélagie presented herself at the school and drily requested that Mademoiselle Louise might not be sent to see her mamma that afternoon. Then, as Marc, recognising her voice, hastened to the door and demanded an explanation, the servant ended by informing him that Madame's accouchement had taken place on the Monday evening, and that she was not at all in a favourable state of health. That said, Pélagie took to her heels, feeling worried that she had spoken, for she had been told to say nothing. Marc, on his side, remained confounded. What! his wife's relations acted as if he did not exist. A child was born to him, and nobody informed him of it! And such rebellion, such a need of protest, arose within him that he at once put on his hat and repaired to the ladies' house.

When Pélagie opened the door she almost choked, thunderstruck, as she was, by his audacity. But with a wave of the arm he brushed her aside, and without a word walked into the little drawing-room where, according to their wont, Madame Duparque was knitting beside the window, while Madame Berthereau, seated a little in the rear, slowly continued some embroidery. The little room, which smelt as

usual of dampness and mouldiness, seemed to be slumbering amid the deep silence and the dismal light coming from
the square.

But the grandmother, amazed and indignant at the sight
of Marc, sprang abruptly to her feet: 'What! you take such
a liberty as this, sir! What do you want? Why have you
come here?' she cried.

The incredible violence of this greeting, when Marc himself was swayed by such legitimate anger, restored his calmness.

'I have come to see my child,' he answered; 'why was I
not warned?'

The old lady, who had remained rigidly erect, seemed to
understand on her side also that passion might place her in
a position of inferiority.

'I had no reason to warn you,' she replied; 'I was waiting
for Geneviève to request me to do so.'

'And she did not ask you?'

'No.'

All at once Marc fancied that he understood the position.
In the person of his wife the Church had not only striven to
kill the loving woman, it had wished to kill the mother also.
If Geneviève, on the eve of her delivery, had not returned
to him in accordance with his hopes, if she had hidden
herself away as if she were ashamed, the reason must be
that her child had been imputed to her as a crime. In
order to keep her in that house they must have filled her
mind with fear and horror, as if she were guilty of some sin,
for which she would never obtain absolution unless she
severed every tie that had united her to Satan.

'Is the baby a boy?' Marc asked.

'Yes, a boy.'

'Where is he? I wish to see and kiss him.'

'He is no longer here.'

'No longer here!'

'No, he was baptised yesterday under the name of the
blessed Saint Clément, and has gone away to be nursed.'

'But that is a crime!' Marc cried, with a pang of grief.
'It is not right to baptise a child without its father's consent, or to send it away, abduct it in that fashion! What!
Geneviève, Geneviève, who nursed Louise with such
motherly delight, is not to nurse her little Clément!'

Madame Duparque, still fully retaining her composure,
gave a little grunt of satisfaction, pleased as she was in her

rancour to see him suffer. 'A Catholic mother,' she answered, 'always has the right to have her child baptised, particularly when she has reason to suspect that its salvation may be imperilled by its father's atheism. And as for keeping the child here, there could be no thought of such a thing; it would have done neither the child itself, nor anybody, any good.'

Things were indeed such as Marc had fancied. The child had been regarded as the progeny of the devil, its birth had been awaited like that of Antichrist, and it had been necessary to baptise it, and send it away with all speed in order to avert the greatest misfortunes. Later, it might be taken back, an attempt might be made to consecrate it to the Deity and make a priest of it, in order to appease the divine anger. In this wise the pious little home of the Place des Capucins would not undergo the shame of sheltering that child, its father would not soil the house by coming to kiss it, and as it would not be constantly before its mother's eyes the latter would be delivered from remorseful thoughts.

Marc, however, having by an effort calmed himself, exclaimed firmly: 'I wish to see Geneviève.'

With equal decision Madame Duparque replied: 'You cannot see her.'

'I wish to see Geneviève,' he repeated. 'Where is she? Upstairs in her old room? I shall know how to find her.'

He was already walking towards the door when the grandmother barred his passage. 'You cannot see her, it is impossible,' said she. 'You do not wish to kill her, do you? The sight of you would give her the most terrible shock. She nearly died during her accouchement. For two days past she has been pale as death, unable to speak. At the least feverishness she loses her senses, the child had to be taken away without letting her see it. . . . Ah! you may be proud of your work; Heaven chastises all whom you have contaminated!'

Then Marc, no longer restraining himself, relieved his heart in low and quivering words: 'You evil woman! you have grown old in practising the dark cruelty of your Deity, and now you seek to annihilate your posterity. . . . You will pursue the work of withering your race as long as it retains in its flesh one drop of blood, one spark of human kindness. Ever since her widowhood you have banished your daughter here from life and its sweetness, you have deprived her of even the strength to speak and complain.

And if your granddaughter is dying upstairs, as the result
of having been wrenched from her husband and her child,
it is also because you agreed to it, for you alone served as
the instrument of the abominable authors of this crime.
. . . Ah! yes, my poor, my adored Geneviève, how
many lies, how many frightful impostures were needed to
take her from me! And here she has been so stupefied, so
perverted by black bigotry and senseless practices that she
is no longer woman, nor wife, nor mother. Her husband
is the devil, whom she may never see again lest she should
fall into hell; her babe is the offspring of sin, and she would
be in peril of damnation should she give it her breast.
. . . Well, listen, such crimes will not be carried out to
the very end. Life always regains the upper hand, it drives
away the darkness and its delirious nightmares at each fresh
dawn. You will be vanquished, I am convinced of it, and
I even feel less horror than pity for you, wretched old
woman that you are, without either mind or heart!'

Madame Duparque had listened, preserving her usual
expression of haughty severity, and not even attempting to
interrupt. 'Is that all!' she now inquired. 'I am aware
that you have no feelings of respect. As you deny God,
how could one expect you to show any deference for a
grandmother's white hair? Nevertheless, in order to show
you how mistaken you are in accusing me of cloistering
Geneviève, I will let you pass. . . . Go upstairs to
her, kill her at your ease, you alone will be responsible for
the fearful agony into which the sight of you will cast her.'

As she finished the old lady moved away from the door,
and, returning to her seat near the window, resumed her
knitting without the slightest sign of emotion, such as might
have made another's hands tremble.

Marc on his side for a moment remained motionless, bewildered, at a loss what to do. Was it possible for him to
see Geneviève, talk to her, strive to convince her and win
her back at such a time as this? He realised how inopportune, how perilous even, such an effort would be. So
without a word of adieu he slowly went towards the door.
But a sudden thought made him turn.

'Since the child is no longer here, give me the address of
the nurse,' he said.

Madame Duparque returned no answer, but continued to
manipulate her knitting needles with her long, withered
fingers in the same regular fashion as before.

'You won't give me the nurse's address ?' Marc repeated.

There came a fresh pause, and at last the old woman ended by saying: 'It is not my business to give it you. Go and ask Geneviève for it, since your idea is to kill the poor child.'

Fury then overcame Marc. He sprang to the window and shouted in the grandmother's impassive face: 'You must give me the nurse's address this moment, at once!'

She, however, was still silently braving him with her clear eyes fixed upon his face when Madame Berthereau, now utterly distracted, intervened. At the outset of the dispute she had stubbornly kept her head bent over her embroidery, like one who was resigned to everything, who had become cowardly, and wished to avoid compromising herself for fear of great personal worries. But when Marc, while reproaching Madame Duparque with her harsh and fanatical tyranny, had alluded to all that she herself had suffered since her widowhood in that bigoted home, she had yielded to increasing emotion, to the tears which, long forced back, again rose from her heart and almost choked her. She forgot some of her silent timidity; after long years she raised her head once more, and became impassioned. And when she heard her mother refuse to give that poor, robbed, tortured man the address of his child's nurse, she at last rebelled, and cried the address aloud:

'The nurse is a Madame Delorme, at Dherbecourt, near Valmarie!'

At this, suddenly roused from her rigidity, Madame Duparque sprang to her feet with the nimbleness of a young woman, waving her arm the while as if to strike down the audacious creature whom she still treated as a child, though she was more than fifty years old.

'Who allowed you to speak, my girl? Are you going to relapse into your past weakness?' she cried. 'Are years of penitence powerless to efface the fault of a wicked marriage? Take care! Sin is still within you, I feel it is so, in spite of all your apparent resignation. Why did you speak without my orders?'

For a moment Madame Berthereau, who still quivered with love and pity, was able to resist. 'I spoke,' said she, 'because my heart bleeds and protests. We have no right to refuse Marc the nurse's address. . . . Yes, yes, what we have done is abominable!'

'Be quiet!' cried her mother furiously.

'I say that it was abominable to separate the wife from the husband, and then to separate the child from both. . . . Never would Berthereau, my poor dead husband, who loved me so much, never would he have allowed love to be slain like that, had he been alive.'

'Be quiet! Be quiet!'

Erect, looking taller than ever in the vigorous leanness of her three and seventy years, the old woman repeated that cry in such an imperious voice that her white-haired daughter, seized with terror, surrendered, and again bent her head over her embroidery. And heavy silence fell while she shook with a slight convulsive tremor, and tears coursed slowly down her withered cheeks, which so many other tears, shed secretly, had ravaged.

Marc had been thunderstruck by the sudden outburst of that poignant family drama, the existence of which he hitherto had merely suspected. He felt intense sympathy for that sad widow who, for more than ten years past, had been hebetated, crushed down by maternal despotism, exercised in the name of a jealous and revengeful God. And if the poor woman had not defended his Geneviève, if she had abandoned her and him to the dark fury of the terrible grandmother, he forgave her for her shuddering cowardice on seeing how greatly she suffered herself.

But Madame Duparque had again recovered her quiet composure. 'You see, sir,' she said, 'your presence here brings scandal and violence. Everything you touch becomes corrupt, your breath suffices to taint the atmosphere of the spot where you are. Here is my daughter, who had never ventured to raise her voice against me, but as soon as you enter the house she lapses into disobedience and insult. . . . Go, sir, go to your dirty work! Leave honest folk alone, and work for your filthy Jew, though he will end by rotting where he is, it is I who predict it, for God will never suffer his venerable servants to be defeated.'

In spite of the emotion which made him quiver, Marc could not refrain from smiling as he heard those last words. 'Ah! you have come to the point,' he said, gently. 'The affair, alone, is at the bottom of all this, is it not so? And it is the friend, the defender of Simon who must be annihilated by dint of persecution and moral torture. Well, take heed of this, make no mistake; sooner or later truth and justice will win the victory, Simon will some day leave his prison, and the real culprits, the liars, the workers of darkness and death, will some day be swept away with their temples whence for ages past they have terrorised and stupefied mankind!'

Then, turning towards Madame Berthereau, who had sunk once more into silent prostration, he added yet more gently: 'And I shall wait for Geneviève. Tell her when she is able to understand you that I am waiting for her. I shall wait as long as she is not restored to me. Even if it be only after years, she will come back to me, I know it. . . . Suffering does not count; it is necessary to suffer a great deal to win the day, and to enjoy, at last, a little happiness.'

Then, with his heart lacerated, swollen with bitterness, yet retaining its courage, he withdrew. Madame Duparque had resumed her everlasting knitting, and it seemed to Marc that the little house he quitted sank once more into the cold gloom which came to it from the neighbouring church.

A month slipped away. Mark learnt that Geneviève was slowly recovering. One Sunday Pélagie came for Louise, who in the evening told her father that she had found her mother looking very thin and broken, but able to go down-stairs and seat herself at table, with the others, in the little dining-room. Fresh hope then came to Marc, the hope of seeing Geneviève return to him as soon as she should be able to walk from the Place des Capucins to the school. Assuredly she must have reflected, her heart must have awakened during her sufferings. Thus he started at the slightest sound he heard, imagining it was she. But the weeks went by, and the invisible hands which had taken her from him were doubtless barricading the doors and windows in order to detain her yonder. He then sank into deep sadness, though without losing his invincible faith, his conviction that he would yet conquer by force of truth and love. He found consolation during those dark days in going, as often as possible, to see his little son Clément, at the nurse's, in that pretty village of Dherbecourt, which looked so fresh and bright amid the meadows of the Ver-pille, among the poplar and willow trees. He there spent a delightfully comforting hour, hoping perhaps that some happy chance would lead to a meeting with Geneviève be-side the dear baby's cradle. But she was said to be still too weak to go to see her son, whom the nurse took to her on appointed days.

From that time Marc remained waiting. Nearly a year had elapsed since the Court of Cassation had begun its inquiry, which had been retarded by all sorts of complications, impeded by many obstacles, which were incessantly arising, thanks to the subterranean craft of the evil powers. At the Lehmanns' house, after the keen delight which had welcomed the first judgment ordering the inquiry, despair was reappearing now that things moved so slowly and the news of Simon was so bad. The Court, while deeming it useless to have him brought back to France immediately, had caused him to be informed that it was considering the revision of his case. But in what state would he return? Would he not succumb to his long sufferings before that constantly adjourned return could be effected? Even David, who was so firm and brave, now felt frightened. And the whole region suffered from that long wait full of anguish; it ravaged Maillebois like an exhausting crisis, the prolongation of which kept all social life in suspense. And it began to turn to the advantage of the anti-Simonists, who had recovered from the effects of the terrible discovery made at Father Philibin's. By degrees, availing themselves of the slowness of the proceedings and the false news prompted by the very secrecy of the inquiry, they again made a show of triumphing, and prophesied the certain and crushing overthrow of the Simonists. The lies and insults of great occasions again found place in the infamous articles of *Le Petit Beaumontais.* Then, at a ceremony in honour of St. Antony of Padua, Father Théodose, speaking from the pulpit, ventured to allude to God's approaching triumph over the accursed race of Judas. Brother Fulgence, also, was again seen rushing like a whirlwind along the streets and across the squares, seemingly very busy and exultant, as if indeed he were dragging the chariot of the Church behind him in some triumphal procession.

As for Brother Gorgias, whom the Congregations began to consider a very compromising personage, attempts were made to cloister him as much as possible, though his friends did not yet dare to conjure him away into some safe retreat, like Father Philibin. In this matter, as it happened, Brother Gorgias was not an easy customer to deal with, he delighted to show himself and astonish people by playing the part of a holy man who negotiated his salvation direct with Heaven. On two occasions he created a scandal by boxing the ears of some children who did not preserve a

sufficiently sanctimonious demeanour on quitting the
Brothers' school. Thus Mayor Philis, who, being a punctilious formalist, was scared by the other's extraordinary
and violent piety, thought it his duty to intervene in the
very interests of religion. The question came before the
Municipal Council, where, by the way, Darras, still in a
minority, was now evincing the more prudence as he did
not despair of becoming Mayor again, with a larger majority than formerly, should the Simon case only turn out well.
Meantime he avoided all occasions of speaking of it, keeping his lips sealed, feeling very anxious whenever he saw
the monks and the priests again taking the side of the wall
in Maillebois, as if it were for ever their conquered possession.

But bad though the news might be, Marc forced himself
to remain hopeful. He was very much encouraged by the
brave fidelity of his assistant, Mignot, who each day took a
larger share in his life of devotion and battle. A singular
moral phenomenon had manifested itself in this transformation in which one observed the slowly increasing influence
of a master over a disciple, who at first had rebelled, then
had been won back and gradually absorbed. In former
times nobody would have suspected there was such heroic
stuff in Mignot as now began to appear. In the affair he had
behaved in a most equivocal manner, helping on the charges
against Simon, and particularly endeavouring to avoid
everything compromising. It had seemed as if his only
thoughts were of his own advancement. Neither good nor
bad, he had been liable at that time to turn out well or ill,
according to circumstances and associates. And Marc had
come, and had proved to be the man of intellect and will
who was to decide the fate of that conscience, embellish it,
and raise it to a perception of truth and justice. The lesson shone forth, luminous and positive; example, the teaching of a hero, sufficed to make other heroes arise from
among the vague dim masses of average folk. On two
occasions during the last ten years there had been a desire
to appoint Mignot as headmaster in a neighbouring little
village, but he had declined the offer, preferring to remain
by the side of Marc, whose influence over him had become
so great that he spoke of never leaving him, of remaining
to the end his faithful disciple, resolutely sharing his victory
or defeat. In the same way, after postponing in a spirit of
expectant prudence the question whether he would marry

or not, he had decided to remain a bachelor, saying that it was too late for him to seek a wife, and that his pupils had now become his family. Besides, did he not take his meals at Marc's, where he was greeted as a brother, making that home his own, and enjoying all the delights of the nearest ties, those which are drawn closer and closer as, by degrees, one thinks and feels the same as one's fellow ?

Thus the slow sundering of Marc and Geneviève had proved extremely painful to Mignot, and since Geneviève's departure he was in despair. He now again took his meals at a neighbouring eating house in order not to increase the embarrassment of that stricken home where no housewife was left. But he gave proof of respectful affection for his principal, and endeavoured to console him. If he did not join him and keep him company every evening after dinner, it was from a delicate feeling of discretion, an unwillingness to obtrude himself when Marc was alone with his daughter. He held back also when Mademoiselle Mazeline was there, feeling that she would prove more useful to the forsaken husband, more expert, with her sisterly hands, in assuaging the pain of his wounds. And when he saw Marc plunging into the deepest melancholy, ready to surrender to his sufferings, he as yet knew of only one way of bringing joy and hope to his face again, which was to reproach himself with his testimony at Simon's former trial, and vow that at the coming one he would publicly relieve his conscience and cry the truth aloud! Ah! yes, he would swear that Simon was innocent, he was convinced of it now that a stream of light had illumined his memory.

However, the slow progress made by the Court of Cassation continued to encourage the anti-Simonists in their desperate campaign, and the onslaught of slander directed against Marc became fiercer than ever. One morning a rumour spread through Maillebois that he and Mademoiselle Mazeline had been seen under circumstances which left no doubt whatever of their guilt. And ignoble particulars were given, the inventions, evidently, of overheated pious minds. At the same time the story remained unreal, for it was impossible to find a single witness, and different versions began to circulate, contradictory in character though tending to make the affair appear yet more horrible. It was Mignot who, feeling very anxious, ventured to warn Marc of the gravity of the scandal; and this time it was not sufficient for the schoolmaster to meet the ignominious charges of

his enemies with the haughty silence of disdain.   He spent
a frightful day, wrestling with his feelings, his heart rent by
the fresh sacrifice which his work demanded of him.   When
twilight came, however, he had made up his mind; and,
according to habit, he repaired to the little garden where
he spent such a pleasant and comforting hour every evening
in the company of Mademoiselle Mazeline.   And as she
was already there, also looking very thoughtful and sad as
she sat under the lilac bushes, he took a seat in front of her.
For a moment he looked at her without speaking; then he
said:

'My dear friend, something has happened which grieves
me very much, and I wish to relieve my heart before Louise
joins us.   .   .   .   We cannot continue meeting every day,
as we have done.   I even think we should do well if we
abstained in future from all intercourse.   .   .   .   It is a
question of real farewell; it is necessary we should part, my
friend.'

She had listened without giving any sign of surprise; it
was as if she had known beforehand what he wished to say.
Indeed, in a sad but courageous voice she answered: 'Yes,
my friend, it was for that very farewell that I came here this
evening.   There is no necessity for you to urge me to it,
for, like you, I feel that it is a painful necessity.   .   .   .
Somebody has told me everything.   In presence of such infamy our only weapons are abnegation and renouncement.'

A long interval of silence fell under the broad, calm sky,
where the daylight was slowly dying.   A penetrating odour
came from the wallflowers, while a little freshness returned
to the grass, warmed by the sunshine.   And Marc resumed,
in an undertone: 'Those unfortunate men who live outside
the pale of simple nature and good sense can in no wise deal
with man and woman without imputing to them the filth
harboured by their own minds, which the idea of sin has
perverted.   For them woman is but a she-devil, whose contact corrupts everything—tenderness, affection, friendship.
.   .   .   I had foreseen what has happened, but I turned a
deaf ear to it all, unwilling as I was to give them the satisfaction of seeing that I heeded their slanders.   But if I
myself can afford to shrug my shoulders, there is the question of you, my friend, and that of Louise, who, so I heard
to-day, is likewise being assailed with this mud.   .   .   .
Thus they are again victorious, and will rejoice at having
added another great grief to all the others.'

'For me it will be the hardest of all,' Mademoiselle Mazeline answered, with much emotion.   'I shall not merely lose
the pleasure of our evening conversations; I shall have the
sorrow of feeling that I am of no further use to you, and
have left you yet more lonely and unhappy.   Forgive me
for that vain thought, my friend; but it made me so happy
to help you in your work, and to fancy I gave you some
comfort and support!   And now I shall never think of you
without picturing you forsaken, alone — even friendless.
. . . Ah! there are certainly some very detestable people
in the world.'

Marc made a trembling gesture, which betrayed his grief.
' It was what they wished to do,' said he; 'yes, they wished
to isolate me and reduce me by turning every affection
around me into a void.   And I will admit to you that this
is the only wound which really makes me suffer.   All the
rest, the attacks, the insults, the threats, spur me on, intoxi-
cate me with a desire to become heroic.   But to be struck
in the person of those who belong to me, to see them soiled,
poisoned, cast as victims among the cruelty and shame of
the struggle—that is a frightful thing, which tortures me
and makes me cowardly. . . . They have taken my
poor wife, now they are separating you from me, and—I
quite expect it—they will end by carrying off my daughter.'

Mademoiselle Mazeline, whose eyes were filling with
tears, endeavoured to silence him.   'Take care, my
friend,' she said; 'here is Louise coming.'

But he quickly retorted: ' I need not take care.   I was
waiting for her.   She must be told what has been decided.'
And as the smiling girl came forward and seated herself between them, he added: 'My darling, in a moment you
must make a little nosegay for Mademoiselle.   I want her
to have a few of our flowers before I bolt the door between
the two gardens.'

' Bolt the door—why, father?'

' Because Mademoiselle must not come here again.   Our
friend is being taken from us, as your mother was taken.'

Louise remained thoughtful and grave during the deep
silence which followed.   After looking at her father, she
looked at Mademoiselle Mazeline.   But she asked for no
explanations; she seemed to understand, all sorts of precocious thoughts passed like faint shadows over the pure
and lofty brow which she had inherited from her father,
while loving distress softened her eyes.

'I will go and make the nosegay,' she said at last, 'and you shall give it to Mademoiselle, father.'

Then, while the girl went seeking the freshest flowers along the borders, the others spent a few sad yet sweet minutes together. They no longer spoke, but their thoughts mingled in brotherly, sisterly fashion, thoughts which dwelt only on the happiness of others, the reconciliation of the sexes, the education and liberation of woman, who in her turn would liberate man. And this was human solidarity in all its broadness, with all the binding and absolute ties which friendship can set between two creatures, man and woman, apart from love. He was her brother, she was his sister. Thus did they ponder; and the night, which was falling more and more swiftly over the balmy garden, brought them a restful freshness amid their sorrow.

'Here is the nosegay, father,' said Louise, approaching; 'I have tied it with a bit of grass.'

Then Mademoiselle Mazeline stood up, and Marc gave her the nosegay. All three next went towards the door. When they reached it, they remained standing there, still saying nothing, but simply feeling happy at delaying their parting for a moment. At last Marc set the door wide open, and Mademoiselle Mazeline, after passing into her own garden, turned round and, for the last time, looked at Marc, whose daughter had cast her arms about him while resting her head against his shoulder.

'Good-bye, my friend.'

'Good-bye, my friend.'

That was all, the door was slowly closed; and on either side the bolts were gently pushed forward. But they had become rusty, and raised a little plaintive cry, which seemed very sad. Everything was over, blind hatred had slain something that was good and consoling.

Another month elapsed. Marc now had only his daughter beside him, and he felt his abandonment and solitude increasing. Louise, of course, still attended Mademoiselle Mazeline's school, and under the inquisitive eyes of the girls the mistress tried to evince no preference for her, but to treat her exactly as she treated the others. The child no longer lingered behind after class-time, but hastened home to prepare her lessons beside her father. And if the schoolmaster and the schoolmistress happened to meet, they merely bowed to each other, refraining from any exchange of words, apart from such as might be necessitated by their duties.

This attitude was very much remarked and discussed in Maillebois. Reasonable people were pleased to see they did their best to put an end to the horrid reports which had been circulated: but the others sneered, saying that it was all very well to save appearances, but this did not prevent the lovers from meeting secretly. Thus infamous reports again began to circulate. When Marc heard of them from Mignot he sank into bitter discouragement. There came hours when, his courage failing, he asked of what use it was for him to wreck his life and renounce every happiness, if no sacrifice was to be held in account by the malicious. Never had his solitude been so bitter, so hard to bear. As soon as at nightfall he found himself alone with Louise in the cold, deserted house, despair came over him at the thought that if he should some day lose his child nobody would be left to love him and warm his heart.

The girl lighted the lamp and seated herself at her little table, saying: 'Papa, I am going to write my history exercise, before I go to bed.'

'That's right, my darling, work,' he answered.

Then, amid the deep silence of the empty house, anguish came upon him. He could no longer continue correcting his pupils' exercises, but rose and walked heavily up and down the room. In this wise he long went on tramping to and fro in the gloom beyond the circle of light which fell from the lamp-shade. And, at times, as he passed behind his daughter he leant over her, and brusquely kissed her hair, tears gathering the while in his eyes.

'Oh! what is the matter, papa?' asked Louise. 'You are distressing yourself again.'

A hot tear had fallen on her brow. Then, turning round, she took hold of her father with her caressing arms and compelled him to sit down near her. 'It is not reasonable of you, papa, to distress yourself like that when we are alone,' she said. 'You are so brave in the daytime, but one would think you felt frightened in the evening, just as I used to do when I did not like to remain without a light. . . . But as you have work to do, you ought to work.'

He tried to laugh. 'So it is you who are now the sensible grown-up person, my darling,' said he. 'But you are right, certainly; I will get to work again.'

Then, however, as he continued looking at her, his eyes again clouded, and he once more began to kiss her hair, wildly, distractedly.

'What is the matter? What is the matter?' she stammered, deeply stirred, and, in her turn, shedding tears. 'Why do you kiss me like that, papa?'

In quivering accents he then confessed his terror, acknowledged how menacing he found all the surrounding gloom: 'Ah, if at least you remain with me, my child, if at least they do not rob me of you as well.'

She could find no answer to that plaint, but she caressed him, and they wept together. At last, having succeeded in inducing him to turn to his pupils' exercises, she herself reverted to her history lesson. But when a few minutes had elapsed anxiety came on Marc again, he was compelled to rise from his chair, and walk, walk, without a pause. One might have thought he was pursuing his lost happiness athwart all the silence and darkness of his wrecked home.

Louise had lately completed her thirteenth year, so that the time when the first Communion is usually made had quite come; and all the devotees of Maillebois were indignant to see such a big girl remaining religionless, refusing to go to confession, and no longer even attending Mass. And naturally she was compassionately called a victim, crushed down beneath the brutal authority of her father, who by way of sacrilege, it was said, made her spit on the crucifix every morning and evening. Moreover, Mademoiselle Mazeline assuredly gave her lessons of diabolical depravity. But was it not a crime to leave that poor girl's soul in a state of perdition, in the power of two of the damned, whose notorious misconduct horrified every conscience? Thus, there was talk of energetic action, of organising demonstrations to compel that unnatural father to restore the daughter to her mother, the pious woman whom he had driven away by the loathsome baseness of his life.

Accustomed as Marc was to insults, he only felt anxious when he thought of the violent scenes to which Louise must be subjected at the ladies' house. Her mother, still in an ailing state, was content to treat her coldly, with silent sadness, leaving Madame Duparque to thunder in the name of her angry Deity, and quicken the infernal flames under Satan's cauldrons. Ought not a big girl, already in her fourteenth year, to feel ashamed of living like a savage, like one of those dogs, who know nothing of religion and are driven from the churches? Was she not frightened by the thought of the eternal chastisement which would fall on her,

the boiling oil, the iron forks, the red hot hooks, the prospect of being lacerated, boiled, and roasted during thousands after thousands of centuries? When Louise, on
returning home in the evening, told Marc of those threats,
he shuddered to think that such attempts should be made to
capture her conscience by fright, and tried to read her eyes
in order to ascertain if she were shaken.

She at times seemed moved, but then things which were
really too abominable were told her. And in her quiet,
sensible way she would remark: ' It is really droll, papa,
that the good God should be so spiteful! Grandmamma
said to-day that if I once missed going to Mass the devil
would cut my feet into little pieces through all eternity.
. . . It would be very unjust; besides, it seems to me
hardly possible.'

After such remarks her father felt a little easier in mind.
Unwilling as he was to do any violence to his daughter's
growing intelligence, he entered into no direct discussion of
the strange lessons which she received at the ladies' house;
he contented himself with some general teaching, based on
reason, and appealing to the child's sense of truth, justice,
and kindness. He was delighted by the precocious wakening of good sense which he noticed in her, a craving for
logic and certainty which she must have inherited from
him. It was with joy that he saw a woman with a clear,
strong mind and a tender heart already emerging from the
weak girl, who still retained in many respects the childishness of her years. And if he felt anxious, it was from a fear
lest the promise of a beautiful harvest should be destroyed.
He only recovered his calmness when the girl astonished
him by reasoning things as if she were already a grown
woman full of sense.

' Oh! I am very polite, you know, with grandmamma,'
she said one day. ' I tell her that if I do not go to confession or make my first Communion, it is because I am waiting
till I am twenty years old, as you asked me to do. . . .
That seems to me very reasonable. And, by keeping to
that, I am very strong; for when one has reason on one's
side one is always very strong, is it not so?'

At times, too, in spite of her affection and deference for
her mother, she said with a smile, in a gentle, jesting way:
' You remember, papa, that mamma said she would explain
the Catechism to me, and I answered her, " Yes, mamma,
you shall hear me my lessons. You know that I try my

best to understand." Well, as I never understood anything at the Catechism class, mamma wished to explain
matters to me. But, unfortunately, I still understand
nothing whatever of it. . . . It puts me into great embarrassment. I feel afraid I may grieve her, and all I can
do is to pretend that I suddenly understand something.
But I must look very stupid, for she always interrupts the
lesson as if she were angry, and calls me foolish. . . .
The other day, when she was talking of the mystery of the
Incarnation, she repeated that it was not a question of
understanding but of believing; and as I unluckily told her
that I could not believe without understanding, she said
that was one of your phrases, papa, and that the devil would
take both of us. . . . Oh, I cried, I cried!'

She smiled, however, as she spoke of it, and added in a
lower tone: 'Instead of making me think more as mamma
does, the Catechism has rather taken me away from her
ideas. There are too many things in it that worry my
mind. It is wrong of mamma to try to force them into my
head.'

Her father could have kissed her. Was he to have the
joy of finding in his daughter an exception, one of those
well-balanced little minds that ripen early, in which sense
seems to grow as in some propitious soil? Other girls, at
that troublous hour of maidenhood, are still so childish and
so greatly disturbed by the quiver which comes upon them
that they easily fall a prey to fairy tales and mystical reveries.
How rare would be his luck if his own girl should escape
the fate of her companions, whom the Church seized and
conquered at a disturbing hour of life. Tall, strong, and
very healthy, she was already a young woman, though there
were days when she became quite childish once more,
amusing herself with trifles, saying silly things, returning
to her doll, with which she held extraordinary conversations. And on those days anxiety came back to her father;
he trembled as he observed that there was still so much
puerility in her nature, and wondered if the others might
not yet steal her from him, and end by obscuring her mind,
whose dawn was so limpid and so fresh.

'Ah, yes, papa, what my doll said just now was very
silly! But what can you expect? She's not very sensible
yet.'

'And do you hope to make her sensible, my darling?'

'I scarcely know. Her head is so hard. With Bible

history she does fairly well; she can recite that by heart. But with grammar and arithmetic she is a real blockhead.'

Then she laughed. That sorry home might be empty and icy cold, she none the less filled it with childish gaiety, as sonorous as April's trumpet-wind. But the days went by, and with the lapse of time Louise became more serious and thoughtful. On returning from her Thursday and Sunday visits to her mother she sank into long, silent reveries. Of an evening, while she was working beside the lamp, she paused at times to give her father a long look, full of sorrowful affection. And at last came that which was bound to come.

It was a warm evening, and a storm was threatening, the heavens were heavy with a mass of inky clouds. The father and the daughter, according to their habit, sat working in the little circular patch of light which fell from the lamp-shade; and through the window, set wide open upon the dark and slumbering town, some moths flew in, they alone disturbing the profound silence with the slight quiver of their wings. Louise, who had spent the afternoon at the house on the Place des Capucins, seemed very tired. It was as if her brow was laden with some weighty thought. Leaning over her exercise paper, she ceased writing and reflected. And, at last, making up her mind to set down her pen, she spoke out amid the deep, mournful quietude of the house.

'Papa, I want to tell you something which grieves me very much. I shall certainly cause you very great, great sorrow; and that is why I did not have the courage to tell you of it before. But I have made up my mind now not to go to bed before telling you of what I want to do—for it seems to me so reasonable and necessary.'

Marc had immediately looked up, a pang, a feeling of terror coming to his heart, for by the girl's tremulous voice he guessed that the supreme disaster was at hand. 'What is it, my darling?' he asked.

'Well, papa, I have been turning the matter over in my head all day, and it seems to me that, if you think as I do, I ought to go and live with mamma at grandmother's.'

Marc, thoroughly upset, began by protesting violently: 'What, think as you do! No, no, I won't allow it! I mean to keep you here, I will prevent you from forsaking me.'

'Oh! papa,' she murmured distressfully, 'think it over, only just a little, and you will see that I am right.'

But he did not listen, he had risen and was walking
wildly about the dim room. 'I have only you left me, and
you think of going away! My wife has been taken from
me, and now my daughter is to be taken, and I am to remain alone, stripped, forsaken, without an affection left!
Ah! I felt that this *coup de grâce* was coming, I foresaw that
those abominable hands, working in the darkness, would
tear away the last shred of my heart. . . . But no! no!
this is too much, never will I consent to such a separation!'

And stopping short before his daughter, he continued
roughly: 'Have you also had your mind and heart spoilt
that you no longer love me? . . . At each of your
visits to your grandmother's I am put on trial—is it not so?
—and infamous things are said about me in order to detach
you from me. It is a question—eh?—of saving you from
the damned and restoring you to the good friends of those
ladies, who will turn you into a hypocrite and a lunatic.
. . . And you listen to my enemies, and yield to their
constant obsession by forsaking me.'

Louise, in despair, her eyes full of tears, raised her hands
entreatingly. 'Papa, papa, calm yourself!' she cried. 'I
assure you that you are mistaken, mamma has never allowed
anything evil to be said about you before me. Grandmother, no doubt, does not like you, and she would often
do well to keep quiet when I am there. It would be telling
a falsehood to say that she does not do all she can to get me
to join mamma and live with her. But I swear to you that
neither she nor any of the others has anything to do with what
I propose. . . . You know very well that I never tell
you stories. It is I myself who have thought it all over, and
come to the conclusion that our separation would be a good
and sensible thing.'

'A good thing—that you should forsake me! Why, it
would kill me!'

'No, you will understand—and you are so brave! . . .
Sit down and listen to me.'

She gently compelled him to seat himself again in front
of her. And, taking his hands in hers caressingly, she
reasoned with him like a shrewd little woman.

'Everybody at grandmother's,' said she, 'is convinced
that you alone turn me away from religion. You weigh on
me, it is said, you impose your ideas on me, and if I could
only escape from you I should go to confession to-morrow
and make my first Communion. . . . So why should I

not prove to them that they are mistaken ?   To-morrow I
will go and live at grandmother's, and then they will see for
themselves, they will have to admit how mistaken they have
been, for nothing will prevent me from giving them always
the same answer: "I have promised not to make my first
Communion before I am twenty, in order that the full responsibility of such an action may be mine only, and I shall
keep my promise, I shall wait." '

Marc made a gesture of doubt.   'My poor child,' said
he, 'you don't know them, they will have broken down
your resistance and have conquered you in a few weeks'
time.   You are still only a little girl.'

In her turn Louise rebelled.   'Ah! it is not nice of you,
papa, to think there is so little seriousness in me!   I am a
little girl, it is true, but your little girl, and proud of it!'

She spoke those words with such childish bravery that he
could not help smiling.   That darling daughter, in whom
he every now and again recognised himself, in whom he
found thoughtfulness and logic blended with passionate
earnestness, warmed his heart.   He looked at her, and
found her very pretty and very sensible, with a face which
was both firm and proud, and bright eyes, whose frankness
was admirable.   And he continued listening while she,
keeping his hands in her own, set forth the reasons which
prompted her to join her mother in the devout little house
of the Place des Capucins.   Without any reference to the
frightful slanders which were current, she let him understand that it would be well for them not to brave public
opinion.   As people said on all sides that her right place
was at the ladies' house, she was willing to repair thither;
and though she was only thirteen years of age, she would
certainly be its most sensible inmate, folk would see if the
work she did there did not prove the best.

'No matter, my child,' Marc said at last with an air of
great lassitude, 'you will never convince me of the necessity of a rupture between you and me.'

She felt that he was weakening.   'But it is not a rupture
papa,' she exclaimed; 'I have gone to see mamma twice a
week, and I shall come to see you, more often than that,
too.   .   .   .   Besides, don't you understand ?   Perhaps
mamma will listen to me a little when I am beside her.   I
shall speak to her of you, I shall tell her how much you still
love her, how you weep for her.   And—who knows ?—she
will reflect, and perhaps I shall bring her back to you.'

Then the tears of both began to flow. They gave way to their emotion in each other's arms. The father was upset by the deep charm of that daughter in whom so much puerility still mingled with so much sense, goodness, and hopefulness. And the girl yielded to her heart, like one ripened before her time by things of which she was vaguely conscious, but which she would have been unable to explain.

'Do, then, as you please,' Marc ended by stammering amid his tears. 'But if I yield, don't think that I approve, for my whole being rebels and protests.'

That was the last evening they spent together. The warm night remained of an inky blackness. There seemed to be not a breath of air. And not a sound came through the open window from the resting town. Only the silent moths flew in, scorching themselves by contact with the lamp. The storm did not burst, and until very late the father and the daughter, speaking no further, remained, one in front of the other, seated at their table, as if busy with their work, but simply happy at being together yet a little longer, amid the far-spreading peaceful quietude.

How frightful, however, did the following evening prove for Marc! His daughter had left him, and he was absolutely alone in that empty and dismal dwelling. After the wife, the child—he had nobody to love him now, all his heart had been torn from him, bit by bit. Moreover, in order that he might not even have the consolation of friendship, he had been compelled, by base slanders, to cease all intercourse with the one woman whose lofty sisterly mind might have sustained him. The complete wrecking of his life, of the approach of which he had long been conscious, was now effected; the stealthy work of destruction, performed by hateful, invisible hands bent on undermining him and throwing him down on the ruins of his own work, was accomplished. And now, no doubt, the others believed they held him, bleeding from a hundred wounds, tortured and forsaken, strengthless in his blasted dwelling, that soiled and deserted home, where he was left in agony. And, indeed, on that first evening of solitude he was really a beaten man, and his enemies might well have thought him at their mercy had they been able to see him coming and going in the pale twilight with a staggering gait, like some wretched stricken beast seeking a shadowy nook there to lie down and die.

The times were, in truth, frightful. The worst possible news was current respecting the inquiry of the Court of

Cassation, whose slowness seemed to hide a desire to bury the affair. In vain had Marc hitherto compelled himself to hope: each day his dread increased lest he should hear of Simon's death before the revision of the case should be an accomplished fact. During that mournful time he pictured everything as lost, revision rejected, his long efforts proving useless, truth and justice finally slain—an execrable social crime, a shameful catastrophe, which would engulf the whole country. The thought of it filled him with a kind of pious horror, sent a chilling shudder of dread through his veins. And, besides that public disaster, there was the disaster of his own life, which weighed upon him more and more. Now that Louise was no longer there, moving his heart with her charming ways, inspiriting him with her precocious sense and courage, he asked himself how he could have been mad enough to let her go to the ladies' house. She was but a child, she would be conquered in a few weeks by the all-powerful Church, which for ages past had been victorious over woman. She had been taken from him; she would never be restored to him, indeed he would never see her more. And it was he who had sent that still defenceless victim to error. His work, he himself, and those who belonged to him, were all annihilated; and at the thought of it he sank into heartrending despair.

Eight o'clock struck, and Marc had not yet found the strength to seat himself and dine alone in that room, which now had become quite dim, when he heard a timid knock at the door. And great was his astonishment when in came Mignot, who at first found it difficult to explain himself.

'You see, Monsieur Froment,' he began, 'as you announced to me this morning the departure of your little Louise, an idea came to me, and I 've been turning it over in my mind all day. . . . So, this evening, before going to dine at the eating house——'

He paused, seeking his words.

'What, have n't you dined yet, Mignot!' Marc exclaimed.

'Why, no, Monsieur Froment. . . . You see, my idea was to come and dine with you, to keep you company a little. But I hesitated and lost time. . . . If it would please you, however, now that you are alone, I might board with you again. Two men can always agree. We could do the cooking, and surely get through the housework together. Are you agreeable? It would please me very much.'

A little joy had returned to Marc's heart; and, with a
smile tinged with emotion, he replied: 'I am quite willing.
. . . You are a good fellow, Mignot. . . . There,
sit down, we will begin by dining together.'

And they dined, face to face, the master relapsing the
while into his bitterness of spirit, the assistant rising every
now and then very quietly to fetch a plate or a piece of
bread, amid the melancholy calm of evening.

II

THEN, during the months and months that the inquiry of the Court of Cassation lasted, Marc again had to shut himself up in his school, and devote himself, body and soul, to his task of instructing the humble, and rendering them more capable of truth and justice.

Among the hopes and the despairs which continued to enfever him, according as the news he heard proved good or bad, there was one thought that haunted him more and more. Long previously, at the very outset of the affair, he had wondered why France, all France, did not rise to exact the release of the innocent prisoner. One of his dearest illusions had been his belief in a generous France, a magnanimous and just France, which many times already had passionately espoused the cause of equity, and which would surely prove its goodness of heart yet once again by striving its utmost to repair the most execrable of judicial errors. And the painful surprise he had experienced on finding the country so stolid and indifferent after the trial at Beaumont now increased daily, became more and more torturing; for in the earlier stages of the affair he had been able to excuse it, realising that people were ignorant of the true facts and poisoned with lies. But now, when so much light had been cast on the affair, so much truth made manifest, he could find no possible explanation for such prolonged and such shameful slumber in iniquity. Had France been changed, then? Was it no longer the liberator? Since it now knew the truth, why did it not rise *en masse*, instead of remaining an obstacle, a blind, deaf multitude barring the road?

And Marc always returned in thought to his starting-point, when the necessity of his humble work as a schoolmaster had become apparent to him. If France still slept the heavy sleep of conscienceless matter, it was because France did not yet know enough. A shudder came upon him: how many generations, how many centuries would be needed for a people, nourished with truth, to become

capable of equity?　For nearly fifteen years he had been
endeavouring to train up just men, a generation had already
passed through his hands, and he asked himself what was
really the progress that had been effected.　Whenever he
met any of his old pupils he chatted with them, and compared them both with their parents, who were less freed
from the original clay, and with the boys who nowadays
attended his school, and whom he hoped to free yet more
than their forerunners.　Therein lay his great task, the
mission he had undertaken at a decisive hour of his life,
and prosecuted throughout all his sufferings, doubting its
efficacy in occasional moments of weariness, but on the
morrow always taking it up again with renewed faith.

One bright August evening, having strolled along the
road to Valmarie as far as Bongard's farm, Marc perceived
Fernand, his former pupil, who was returning home with a
scythe on his shoulder.　Fernand had lately married Lucile,
the daughter of Doloir, the mason; he now being five-and-
twenty, and she nineteen years of age.　They had long
been friends, having played together in the old days on
leaving school; and that evening the young wife, a little
blonde, with a gentle, smiling demeanour, was also there,
seated in the yard and mending some linen.

'Well, Fernand, are you satisfied?　Is there a good crop
of wheat this year?' Marc inquired.

Fernand still had a heavy face with a hard and narrow
brow, and his words came slowly as in his childish days.
'Oh! Monsieur Froment,' he replied, 'one can never be
satisfied; there's too much worry with this wretched land,
it takes more than it gives.'

As his father, though barely fifty years of age, was already
heavy of limb, tortured by rheumatic pains, Fernand, on
finishing his term of military service, had resolved to help
him, instead of seeking employment elsewhere.　And the
struggle at the farm was the same bitter one as of old, the
family living from father to son on the fields whence it
seemed to have sprung, and toiling and moiling blindly in
its stubborn ignorance and neglect of progress.

'Ah! no, one is never satisfied,' Fernand slowly resumed;
'even you are not over-pleased with things, Monsieur Froment, in spite of all you know.'

Marc detected in those words some of the jeering contempt for knowledge which was to be expected from a hard-
headed, sleepy dunce who in his school-days had found it

difficult to remember a single lesson. Moreover, Fernand's remark embodied a prudent allusion to the events which were upsetting the whole region, and Marc availed himself of this circumstance to inquire into his former pupil's views.

'Oh! I am always pleased when my boys learn their lessons fairly well, and don't tell too many stories,' he said gaily. 'You know that very well; just remember. . . . Besides, I received to-day some good news about the affair to which I have been attending so long. Yes, the innocence of my poor friend Simon is about to be recognised for good.'

At this Fernand manifested great embarrassment, his countenance became heavier, and the light in his eyes died away. 'But that 's not what some folk say,' he remarked.

'What do they say, then ? '

'They say that the judges have found out more things about the old schoolmaster.'

'What things are those ? '

'Oh, all sorts, it seems.'

At last Fernand consented to explain himself, and started on a ridiculous yarn. The Jews, said he, had given a big sum of money, five millions of francs, to their co-religionist Simon in order that he might get a Brother of the Christian Doctrine guillotined. Simon having failed in his plan, the five millions were lying in a hiding-place, and the Jews were now striving to get Brother Gorgias sent to the galleys —even if in doing so they should drown France in blood— in order that Simon might return and dig up the treasure, the hiding-place of which was known only to himself.

'Come, my lad,' Marc answered, quite aghast, ' surely you don't believe such absurdity!'

'Well, why not ? ' rejoined the young peasant, who looked only half awake.

'Why, because your good sense ought to rebel against it. You know how to read, you know how to write, and I flattered myself also that I had in some degree awakened your mind and taught you how to distinguish between truth and falsehood. . . . Come, come, have n't you remembered anything of what you learnt when you were with me ? '

Fernand waved his hand in a tired, careless way. 'If one had to remember everything, Monsieur Froment, one would have one's head too full,' he said. 'I have only told you what I hear people saying everywhere. Folks who are far cleverer than I am give their word of honour that it 's true.

. . . Besides, I read something like it in *Le Petit Beau-montais* the day before yesterday. And since it's in print there must surely be some truth in it.'

Marc made a gesture of despair. What! he had not overcome ignorance more than that after all his years of striving! That young fellow remained the easiest prey for error and falsehood, he blindly accepted the most stupid inventions, he possessed neither the freedom of mind nor the sense of logic necessary to enable him to weigh the fables which he read in his newspaper. So great indeed was his credulity that it seemed to disturb even his wife, the blonde Lucile.

'Oh!' said she, raising her eyes from her work, 'a treasure of five millions, that is a great deal of money.'

Though Lucile had failed to secure a certificate, she had been one of Mademoiselle Rouzaire's passable pupils, and her mind now seemed to have awakened. It was said she was pious. In former days the schoolmistress had somewhat proudly cited her as an example, on account of the glib manner in which she recited the long Gospel narrative of the Passion without making a single mistake. But since her marriage, though one still found in her the sly submissiveness and the hypocritical restrictions of a woman on whom the Church had set its mark, she had ceased to follow the usual observances. And she even discussed things a little.

'Five millions in a hiding-place,' Marc repeated, 'five millions slumbering there, pending the return of my poor Simon—it's madness! But what of all the new documents that have been discovered, all the proofs against Brother Gorgias?'

Lucile was becoming bolder. With a pretty laugh she exclaimed: 'Oh! Brother Gorgias isn't worth much. He may well have a weight on his conscience, though all the same it would be as well to leave him quiet on account of religion. . . . But I've also read the newspapers, and they've made me reflect.'

'Ah! well,' concluded Fernand, 'one would never finish if one had to reflect after reading. It's far better to remain quiet in one's corner.'

Marc was again about to protest when a sound of footsteps made him turn his head, and he perceived old Bongard and his wife, who also had just returned from the fields, with their daughter, Angèle. Bongard, who had heard his

son's last words, at once addressed himself to the schoolmaster.

' What the lad says is quite true, Monsieur Froment.
It 's best not to worry one's mind with reading so much
stuff. . . . In my time we did not read the papers at
all, and we were no worse off. Is n't that so, wife ? '

' Sure it is! ' declared La Bongard energetically.

But Angèle, who, in spite of her hard nut, had won a
certificate at Mademoiselle Rouzaire's by force of stubbornness, smiled in a knowing manner. An inner light, fighting
its way through dense matter, occasionally illumined the
whole of her face, which with its short nose and large
mouth remained at other moments so dull and heavy. In
a few weeks' time Angèle was to marry Auguste Doloir, her
sister-in-law Lucile's brother, a big strapping fellow, following, like his father, the calling of a mason, and the girl
already indulged in ambitious dreams for him, some start in
business on his own account when she should be beside him
to guide his steps.

In response to her father's words she quietly remarked:
' Well, for my part I much prefer to know things. One can
never succeed unless one does. Everybody deceives and
robs one. . . . You yourself, mamma, would have
given three *sous* too many to the tinker yesterday if I had
not run through his bill.'

They all jogged their heads; and then Marc, in a
thoughtful mood, resumed his walk. That farmyard,
where he had just lingered for a few minutes, had not
changed since the now far-distant day of Simon's arrest,
when he had entered it seeking for favourable evidence.
The Bongards had remained the same, full of crass, suspicious, silent ignorance, like poor beings scarce raised from
the soil, who ever trembled lest they should be devoured
by others bigger and stronger than themselves. And the
only new element was that supplied by the children, whose
progress, however, was of the slightest; for if they knew a
little more than their parents they had been weakened by
the incompleteness of their education, and had fallen into
other imbecilities. Yet, after all, they had taken a step
forward, and the slightest step forward on mankind's long
road must tend to hope.

A few days later Marc repaired to Doloir's, in order to
speak to him of an idea which he had at heart. Auguste
and Charles, the mason's elder sons, had formerly belonged

to his school, and their younger brother, Léon,[1] had lately achieved great success there, having won his certificate already in his twelfth year.   For that very reason, however, he was about to quit the school, and his departure worried Marc, for, desirous as the latter was of securing good recruits for the elementary education staff, of which Salvan spoke to him at times so anxiously, he dreamt of making the lad a schoolmaster.

On reaching the flat over the wineshop in the Rue Plaisir, where the mason still dwelt, Marc found Madame Doloir alone for the moment with Léon, though the men would soon be home from work.   She listened to the schoolmaster very attentively in her serious and somewhat narrow-minded way, like a good housewife who only thought of the family interests; and then she answered: 'Oh, Monsieur Froment, I don't think it possible.   We shall have need of Léon: we mean to apprentice him at once.   Where could we find the money to enable him to continue his studies ?   Things like that cost too much even when they cost nothing.'   And turning to the boy she added: 'Isn't that so ?   A carpenter's trade suits you best.   My own father was a carpenter.'

But Léon, whose eyes glittered, was bold enough to declare his preference.   'Oh no, mamma,' said he, 'I should be so pleased if I could continue learning.'

Marc was backing up the boy when Doloir came in, accompanied by his elder sons.   Auguste worked for the same master as his father, and on their way home they had called for Charles, who was employed by a neighbouring locksmith.   On learning what was afoot Doloir quickly sided with his wife, who was regarded as the clever one of the home, the maintainer of sound traditions.   True, she was an honest and a worthy woman, but one who clung stubbornly to routine and who showed much narrow egotism. And her husband, though he put on airs of bravado, like an old soldier whose ideas had been broadened by regimental life, invariably bowed to her decisions.

---

[1] In the author's proofs of the earlier part of *Vérité*, Doloir the mason is said to have a young son named Léon ; Savin, the clerk, having one called Jules (see *ante*, p. 60).   Some confusion seems to have arisen subsequently in M. Zola's mind with respect to these boys, for in later passages of the French original the name of Jules is given to Doloir's child, and that of Léon to Savin's.   This error would undoubtedly have been rectified but for M. Zola's sudden death.   In the present translation Jules has been changed to Léon, and Léon to Jules, wherever necessary.— *Trans.*

'No, no, Monsieur Froment,' he said, 'I don't think it possible.'

'Come, let us reason a little,' Marc answered patiently; 'I will undertake to prepare Léon for the Training School. There we shall obtain a scholarship for him; so it will cost you absolutely nothing.'

'But what of his food all that time?' the mother asked.

'Well, just one more when there are several at table does not mean a great expense. . . . One may well risk a little for a child when he gives one such bright hopes.'

At this the two elder brothers began to laugh, like good-natured fellows who felt amused by the proud yet anxious bearing of their junior.

'I say, youngster, so you are to be the great man of the family, eh?' exclaimed Auguste. 'But don't put on too much side, for we won our certificates also. That sufficed for us; we had enough and to spare of all the things that one finds in books. . . . For my own part I much prefer to temper my mortar.' And, addressing the schoolmaster, Auguste continued gaily: 'Ah! did n't I worry you, Monsieur Froment! I could never keep still; there were days, I remember, when I revolutionised the whole class. Fortunately Charles was a little more reasonable.'

'No doubt,' said Charles, smiling in his turn, 'only I always ended by following you, for I did n't wish to be thought timid or stupid.'

'Stupid! no, no,' responded Auguste by way of conclusion: 'we were only wrong-headed and idle. . . . And nowadays we offer you every apology, Monsieur Froment. And I agree with you: I think that if Léon has a taste that way he ought to be helped on. Dash it all! one must be on the side of progress!'

Those words gave much pleasure to Marc, who thought it as well to rest content with them that day, and to postpone the task of finally prevailing over the parents. However, continuing his conversation with Auguste for a moment, he told him that he had lately seen his betrothed, Angèle Bongard, a shrewd little person who seemed determined to make her way in life. Then, seeing the young man laugh again and look very much flattered, Marc thought of pursuing his investigations and ascertaining what might be the views of his former pupil on the question which interested him so deeply.

'I also saw Fernand Bongard, your brother-in-law,' he

said ; 'you remember when he was at school with you——'

The brothers again became hilarious. 'Fernand ? Oh! he had a hard nut and no mistake,' said Auguste.

'Yes, and do you know, in that unfortunate Simon affair, Fernand believes that a treasure of five millions of francs, given by the Jews, is hidden away somewhere in readiness for the unhappy prisoner whenever one may succeed in bringing him back from the galleys, and setting a Brother of the Christian Doctrine in his place.'

As these words fell from Marc's lips Madame Doloir became very grave, drawing her little figure together, and then remaining motionless; while her husband on his side made a gesture of annoyance, and muttered between his teeth: 'That's another matter which my wife rightly enough does not wish us to meddle with.'

But Auguste, who seemed very much amused, exclaimed: 'Yes, I know, the story of the treasure which appeared in *Le Petit Beaumontais*. I'm not surprised at Fernand swallowing that yarn. . . . Five millions hidden in the ground—it's nonsense!'

At this his father looked vexed, and emerged from his reserve. 'A treasure,' said he, 'why not ? You are not so clever as you fancy, youngster. You don't know what the Jews are capable of. I knew a corporal in my regiment, who had been a servant to a Jewish banker. Well, every Saturday he saw that banker send casks full of gold to Germany—all the gold of France, as he used to say. . . . We are sold, that's quite certain.'

But Auguste, who never showed any great respect for anybody, retorted: 'Ah! no, father, you must not dish up the old stories of your regiment. I've just come back from barracks, you know; and it's all too stupid. . . . You'll soon see that for yourself, my poor Charles.'

Auguste, indeed, had lately finished his term of military service, and Charles in his turn would have to join the colours in October.

'And for my part,' Auguste continued, 'I can't swallow that absurd yarn of five millions buried at the foot of a tree, and waiting to be dug up on some moonlight night. . . . At the same time that does not prevent me from thinking that one would do well to leave that man Simon yonder, without troubling one's brains any more about his innocence.'

Marc, who had felt pleased by the intelligent things said by his former pupil, was painfully surprised by that sudden conclusion. 'How is that?' he inquired. 'If Simon is innocent, just think of the torture he has undergone! We should never be able to offer him sufficient reparation.'

'Oh! innocent—that remains to be proved. Though I often read what is printed, my mind only gets the more fogged by it.'

'That is because you only read falsehoods,' said Marc. 'Remember, it is now known that the copy-slip came from the Brothers' school. The corner which was torn off, and which was found at Father Philibin's, is the proof of it; and the ridiculous blunder which the experts made is demonstrated, for the paraph is certainly in the handwriting of Brother Gorgias.'

'Ah! I don't know all that,' Auguste answered. 'How can I read everything that is printed? As I said just now, the more people try to explain the affair to me, the less I understand of it. But, after all, as the experts and the Court formerly ascribed the copy-slip to the prisoner, the simplest thing is to believe that it was really his.'

From that opinion Auguste would not retreat in spite of all the efforts of Marc, who, after imagining for a moment that the young fellow possessed a free mind, was pained to discover that he had such narrow views, and such a faint perception of truth.

'Well, that is sufficient,' at last said Madame Doloir, in the authoritative manner of a prudent woman. 'You must excuse me, Monsieur Froment, if I ask you to talk no more of that affair here. You do as you please on your side, and I have nothing to say against it. Only, for poor folk like ourselves it is best that we should not meddle with what does not concern us.'

'But it would concern you, madame, if one of your sons should be taken and sent to the galleys in spite of his innocence. And we are fighting, remember, to prevent such monstrous injustice from ever being repeated.'

'Perhaps so, Monsieur Froment; but one of my sons won't be taken, for, as it happens, I try to get on well with everybody, even the priests. The priests are very strong, you see, and I would rather not have them after me.'

Thereupon Doloir was moved to intervene in a patriotic way: 'Oh! I don't care a curse about the priests,' he exclaimed. 'It's a question of defending the country,

and the Government allows us to be humiliated by the
English!'

'You also will please to keep quiet,' his wife immediately
retorted.   'It is best to leave both the Government and the
priests alone.   Let 's try to get bread to eat—that will be
far better.'

Then Doloir had to bend his head in spite of the circumstance that among his mates he posed as being a Socialist,
though he hardly knew the meaning of the word.   As for
Auguste and Charles, though they belonged to a better-
taught generation, they sided with their mother, almost
spoilt as they were by their ill-digested semi-education, too
ignorant as yet to recognise the law of human solidarity
which demands that the happiness of each should be compounded of the happiness of all.   Only little Léon, with his
ardent thirst for knowledge, remained impassioned, full of
anxiety also as to the turn which things were taking.

Marc, who was sorely grieved, felt that further discussion
would be useless.   So, taking his departure, he contented
himself with saying: 'Well, madame, I will see you again,
and I hope to persuade you to allow Léon to continue his
studies so that he may become a schoolmaster.'

'Quite so, Monsieur Froment,' the mother answered;
'but remember it must not cost us a *sou*, for in any case we
shall be sadly out of pocket.'

Some bitter thoughts came over Marc as he returned
home.   As in the case of the Bongards he was reminded
of the visit he had made to the Doloirs on the day of Simon's
arrest.   Those sorry folk, who were condemned to a life of
excessive toil and who imagined they defended themselves
by remaining in darkness and taking no interest in what
went on around them, had in no way changed.   They were
determined that they would know nothing, for fear lest
knowledge should bring them increase of wretchedness.
The sons, no doubt, were rather more enlightened than the
parents, but not enough to engage in any work of truth.
And if they had begun to reason, and no longer believed in
idiotic fables, how much ground there still remained for
their children to cover before their minds should be freed
completely from error!   It was grievous indeed that the
march of progress should be so slow; and yet it was necessary to remain content, if one desired to retain enough courage to pursue the arduous task of teaching and delivering
the humble.

On another occasion, a little later, Marc happened to
meet Savin the clerk, with whom he had had some unpleasant quarrels at the time when that embittered man's twin
sons, Achille and Philippe, had attended the school.
Savin had then thought it good policy to serve the Church,
although he publicly pretended to have nothing to do with
it, for he was continually dreading lest he should offend his
superiors. However, two catastrophes, which fell upon
him in rapid succession, steeped him in irremediable bitterness. First of all, things took a very bad turn with his pretty
daughter, Hortense — that model pupil, in whose ardent
fervour at her first Communion Mademoiselle Rouzaire had
gloried, but who in reality was full of precocious hypocrisy.
Savin, recognising the girl's beauty, had dreamt of marrying
her to the son of one of his superiors, but, instead of that,
he was compelled to marry her to a milkman's assistant,
who led her astray. Then, to complete the clerk's mortification and despair, he discovered that his wife, the refined
and tender-hearted Marguerite, had become unfaithful to
him. In spite of her repugnance he had long compelled
her to go to confession and Communion, holding that religion was a needful curb for feminine depravity; but, as it
happened, her frequent attendance at the chapel of the
Capuchins, whose superior, Father Théodose, was her confessor, led to her downfall, for that same holy man became
her lover. The facts were never exactly known, for no
scandal was raised by Savin, who, however great his rage,
was overcome by the irony of things. It was he himself,
indeed, who, by his imbecile jealousy, had turned his previously faithful wife into the path of infidelity. But if he
raised no great outcry, people declared that he revenged
himself terribly on the unhappy woman in the abominable
hell which their home had now become.

Having cause to hate the priests and the monks, Savin
had drawn a trifle nearer to Marc. On the day when they
met in the street the clerk had just quitted his office, and
was walking along with a sour and sleepy face, like some
old circus horse half stupefied by his never-varying round
of duties. On perceiving the schoolmaster he seemed to
wake up: 'Ah! I am pleased to meet you, Monsieur Froment,' he said. 'It would be very kind of you to come as
far as my rooms, for my son Philippe is causing me great
anxiety by his idleness, and you are the only person who
knows how to lecture him.'

'Willingly,' replied Marc, who was always desirous of seeing and judging things.

On reaching the dismal little lodging in the Rue Fauche they found Madame Savin—who still looked charming in spite of her four- and- forty years—engaged on some bead flowers which had to be delivered that same evening. Since his misfortune the clerk was no longer ashamed of letting people see his wife toil as if she were a mere work-woman. Perhaps, indeed, he hoped it would be thought that she was expiating her transgression. In former times he had evinced much pride in her when she went out wearing a lady's bonnet, but now she might well put on an apron and contribute to the support of the family. He himself also neglected his appearance, and had given up wearing frock coats.

No sooner did he enter the flat than he became brutal: 'You 've taken possession of the whole room as usual!' he shouted. 'Where can I ask Monsieur Froment to sit down?'

Gentle, timid, and somewhat red of face, his wife hastened to gather up her reels and boxes. 'But when I work, my friend,' she said, 'I need some room. Besides, I did not expect you home so soon.'

'Yes, yes, I know, you never expect *me!*''

Those words, in which, perhaps, there was some cruel allusion to what had happened, quite upset the unfortunate woman. One thing which her husband did not forgive her was her lover's handsomeness, particularly as he knew that he himself was so puny and sickly; and nothing enraged himself more than to read his wife's excuse in her clear eyes. However, she now bent her head, and made herself as small as possible, while she resumed her work.

'Sit down, Monsieur Froment,' said Savin. 'As I was telling you just now, that big fellow yonder drives me to despair. He is now nearly two- and- twenty, he has already tried two or three trades, and all he seems to be good for is to watch his mother work and pass her the beads she may require.'

Young Philippe, indeed, was sitting in a corner of the room, silent and motionless, like one who strove to keep in the background. Madame Savin, amidst her humiliation, had given him a tender glance, to which he had responded by a slight smile as if by way of consolation. One could detect that he and his mother were linked together by some bond of suffering. Pale, and of poor health, the sly, cowardly, and mendacious schoolboy of former times had become a sorry young fellow, quite destitute, it seemed, of energy, who sought a refuge in his mother's kindness of heart; she, still so young in appearance, looking like an elder sister, one who also suffered, and who therefore sympathised with him.

'Why did you not listen to me?' Marc exclaimed in answer to the clerk; 'we would have made a schoolmaster of him.'

But Savin protested: 'Ah! no, indeed. Rather than that I prefer to have him on my hands. To cram one's brains at school till one is over twenty, then start at a paltry salary of sixty francs a month, and work for more than ten years before earning a hundred—do you call that a profession? A schoolmaster, indeed! Nobody cares to become one nowadays; even the poorest peasants would rather break stones on the highways!'

'But I thought I had persuaded you to let your son Jules enter the Training College?' Marc rejoined. 'Don't you intend to make him an elementary teacher?'

'Oh, dear, no. I've put him with an artificial-manure merchant. He's barely sixteen, and he is already earning twenty francs a month. He will thank me for it later on.'

Marc made a gesture expressive of his regret. He remembered having seen Jules as a babe in swaddling clothes in his mother's arms. Later, the lad, from his seventh to his fourteenth year, had become one of his pupils—a pupil who evinced much higher intelligence than his elder brothers, and who inspired great hopes. Like the master, Madame Savin, no doubt, was worried that her youngest boy's studies had been cut short by his father; for, again raising her beautiful eyes, she glanced at Marc furtively and sadly.

'Come,' said her husband to the latter, 'what advice can you give me? And first of all can't you make that big idler feel ashamed of his sloth? As you were his master, perhaps he will listen to you.'

At that moment, however, Achille, the other son, came in, returning from the process-server's office where he was now employed. He had made a start there as an errand boy when he was fifteen, and though nearly seven years had elapsed he did not yet earn enough to keep himself. Paler and of even poorer blood than his brother Philippe, he had remained a beardless stripling, sly, pusillanimous, and distrustful as in his school-days, ever ready to denounce a comrade in order to escape personal punishment. He seemed surprised on seeing his former master, and, after bowing to him, he said, doubtless in a spirit of malice: 'I don't know what there can be in *Le Petit Beaumontais* to-day, but people are almost fighting for copies at Mesdames Milhomme's. It must certainly be something more about that beastly affair.'

Marc already knew that the paper contained a fresh recti-fication, brimful of extraordinary mendacious impudence, on the part of Brother Gorgias; and he decided to avail himself of this opportunity to sound the young men. 'Oh!' said he, 'whatever *Le Petit Beaumontais* may attempt with its stories of buried millions, and its superb denials of well-established facts, everybody is beginning to admit that Simon is innocent.'

At this the twins shrugged their shoulders, and Achille in his drawling way replied: 'Oh! only imbeciles believe in those buried millions, and it's true that they are lying too much: one can see it. But what does it all matter to us?'

'Eh? what does it matter to you?' the schoolmaster ex-claimed, surprised and failing to understand.

'Yes, what interest is there for us in that affair with which we have been plagued so long?'

Then Marc gradually became impassioned.

'My poor lads, I feel sorry for you,' he said; 'you admit Simon's innocence, do you not?'

'Well—yes. It is by no means clear, as yet; but when one has read things attentively it does seem that he may be innocent.'

'In that case, do not your feelings rebel at the idea that he is in prison?'

'Oh! it certainly isn't amusing for him,' Achille ad-mitted; 'but there are so many other innocent people in prison. Besides, the officials may release him for all I care. . . . One has quite enough worries of one's own, so why should one spoil one's life by meddling with the troubles of others?'

Then Philippe, in a more gentle voice, expressed his opinion, saying: 'I don't bother about that affair, for it would worry me too much. I can understand that it would be one's duty to act if one were the master. But when one can do nothing whatever, the best way is to ignore it all and keep quiet.'

In vain did Marc censure the indifference, the cowardly egotism, and desertion which those words implied. The great voice, the irresistible will of the people, said he, was compounded of individual protests, the protests of the humblest and the weakest. Nobody could claim exemption from his duty, the action of one single isolated individual might suffice to modify destiny. Besides, it was not true to say that only one person's fate was at stake in the struggle, all the members of the nation were jointly and severally interested, for each defended his own liberty by protecting that of his fellow. And then what a splendid opportunity it was to accomplish at one stroke the work of a century of slow political and social progress. On one side all the forces of reaction were leagued against an unhappy, innocent man for the sole purpose of keeping the old Catholic and monarchical scaffoldings erect; and on the other, all who were bent on ensuring the triumph of the future, all who believed in reason and liberty, had gathered together from the four points of the compass, and united in the name of truth and justice. And an effort on the part of the latter ought to suffice to throw the former beneath the remnants of those old, worm-eaten scaffoldings which were cracking on all sides. The scope of the affair had expanded: it was no longer merely the case of a poor innocent man who had been wrongly convicted; for that man had become the incarnation of the martyrdom of all mankind, which must be wrested from the prison of the ages. The release of Simon indeed would mean increase of freedom for the people of France and an acceleration of its march towards more dignity and happiness.

But Marc suddenly lapsed into silence, for he saw that Achille and Philippe were looking at him in bewilderment, their weak eyes blinking in their pale and sickly faces.

'Oh! Monsieur Froment, what 's all that ? When you put so many things into the affair we can't follow you, that 's certain. We know nothing of those things, we can do nothing.'

Savin for his part had listened, sneering and fidgeting, though unwilling to interrupt. Now, however, turning to the schoolmaster, he exploded. 'All that is humbug—excuse me for saying so, Monsieur Froment. Simon innocent —well, that 's a matter on which I have my doubts. I don't conceal it; I 'm of the same opinion as formerly, and I read nothing; I would rather let myself be killed than consent to swallow a line of all the trash that is published. And, mind, I don't say that because I like the priests. The dirty beasts—why, I wish a pestilence would sweep them all away! Only, when there is a religion, there is one. It's the same with the army. The army is the blood of France. I am a Republican, I am now a Freemason, I will go so far as to say that I am a Socialist, in the good sense of the word; but, before everything else, I am a Frenchman, and I won't have people setting their hands on what constitutes the grandeur of my country. Simon then is guilty; everything proves it: public sentiment, the proofs submitted to the Court, his condemnation, and the ignoble trafficking carried on by the Jews in order to save him. And if, by a miracle, he should not be guilty, the misfortune for the country would be too great; it would be absolutely necessary that he should be guilty all the same.'

Confronted by so much blindness, blended with so much folly, Marc could only bow. And he was about to withdraw when Savin's daughter Hortense made her appearance with her little girl Charlotte, now nearly seven years of age. Hortense was no longer the good-looking young person of former days; compelled to marry her seducer, the milkman's assistant, and lead with him a hard and toilsome life of poverty, she appeared faded and careworn. Savin, moreover, received her without cordiality, full of spite as he was, ashamed of that marriage which had mortified his pride. Only the grace and keen intelligence of little Charlotte assuaged, in some slight degree, his intensely bitter feelings.

'Good-morning, grandpapa; good-morning, grandmamma,' said the child. 'You know, I have been first in reading again, and Mademoiselle Mazeline has given me the medal.'[1]

She was a charming little girl, and Madame Savin, dropping her beads at once, took her on her lap, kissing her and feeling consoled and happy. But the child, turning towards Marc, with whom she was well acquainted, resumed: 'You know, I was the first, Monsieur Froment. It's fine—isn't it?—to be the first!'

[1] In French elementary schools the child who becomes first in his or her class is given a medal which is worn pinned to jacket or frock. Should the position be lost the medal has to be restored to the teacher, who then transfers it to the more successful pupil.— *Trans.*

'Yes, my dear,' said the master, 'it is very nice to be first. And I know that you are always very good. Mind, you must always listen to Mademoiselle Mazeline, because she will make a very clever and sensible little woman of you—one who will be very happy and who will give a deal of happiness to all her family around her.'

At this Savin again began to growl: Happiness to all her family, indeed! Well, that would be something new, for neither the grandmother nor the mother had given any happiness to him. And if Mademoiselle Mazeline should perform such a miracle as to turn a girl into something decent and useful, he would go to tell Mademoiselle Rouzaire of it. Then, annoyed at seeing his wife laugh, brightened as she was, rejuvenated, so to say, by the companionship of the child, he bade her get on with her work, speaking in so rough a voice that, as the unhappy woman again lowered her head over her bead flowers, her eyes filled with tears.

But Marc had now risen, and the clerk thereupon reverted to the matter he had at heart: 'So you can give me no advice about my big idler, Philippe ? . . . Don't you think that, through Monsieur Salvan, who is the friend of Monsieur Le Barazer, you might get him some petty situation at the Préfecture ?'

'Yes, certainly, I might try. I will speak to Monsieur Salvan about it, I promise you.'

Marc then withdrew, and, on reaching the street, walked slowly, his head bent, while he summed up the results of his visits to the parents of his former pupils. No doubt he had found Achille and Philippe possessed of riper and broader minds than Auguste and Charles, the sons of Doloir the mason, even as he had found the latter freed from the low credulity of Fernand, the son of the peasant Bongard. But at the Savins' he had once again observed the blind obstinacy of the father, who had learnt nothing, forgotten nothing, but still lingered in the same old rut of error; whilst even the evolution of the sons towards more reason and logic remained a very slight one. Just a little step had been taken, no more, and with that Marc had to remain content. He felt sad indeed when he compared all his efforts during a period of nearly fifteen years with the little amelioration which had resulted from them. And he shuddered as he thought of the vast amount of labour, devotion, and faith which would be required throughout the humble

world of the elementary teachers, before they would succeed in transforming the brutified, soiled, enthralled, lowly
ones and suffering ones into free and conscious men.   Generations indeed would be necessary for that to be effected.

The thought of poor Simon haunted Marc amid the grief
he felt at having failed to raise a people of truth and justice,
such as would have the strength of mind to rebel against the
old iniquity and repair it.   The nation still refused to be
the noble, generous, and equitable nation, in which he had
believed so long; and both his mind and his heart were
pained, for he could not accustom himself to the idea of a
France steeped in idiotic fanaticism.   Then, however, a
bright vision flitted before his eyes; he again saw little
Charlotte, so wide-awake and so delighted at being the first
of her class, and he began to hope once more.   The future
belonged to the children; and might not some of those
charming little ones take giant steps when firm and upright minds should direct them towards the light ?

However, as Marc drew near to the school, another
meeting brought a pang to his heart.   He encountered
Madame Férou carrying a bundle—some work which she
was taking home with her.   Having lost her eldest children,
who had succumbed more to want than to disease, she now
lived with her remaining girl in a frightful hovel, where they
worked themselves almost to death, without ever earning
enough to satisfy their hunger.   As she glided along the
street with downcast eyes, as if ashamed of her poverty,
Marc stopped her.   She was no longer the plump and
pleasant-looking blonde, with fleshy lips and large, bright,
prominent eyes, whom he had known in past years, but a
poor, squat, careworn woman, aged before her time.   'Well,
Madame Férou,' he inquired, 'does the sewing prosper a
little ? '

She began to stammer, then at last regained some confidence: 'Oh! things never prosper, Monsieur Froment,' she
said; 'we may tire our eyes out, but we are lucky when we
manage to earn twenty-five *sous* a day between us.'

'And what about the application for relief which you
sent to the Préfecture, as a schoolmaster's widow ? '

'Oh, they never answered me, and when I ventured to
call there in person, I really thought I should be arrested.
A big dark man with a fine beard asked me what I meant
by daring to recall the memory of my husband, the deserter
and Anarchist, who was condemned by court-martial, and

then shot like a mad dog. And he frightened me so much that I still tremble when I think of it.'

Then, as Marc, who was quivering, remained silent, the unhappy woman, growing bolder and bolder, resumed: 'Good heavens! My poor Férou a mad dog! You knew him when we were at Le Moreux. At first he only dreamt of devotion, fraternity, truth, and justice; and it was by dint of wretchedness, persecution, and iniquity that they ended by maddening him. When he left me, never to return, he said to me: "France is done for; it has been completely rotted by the priests, poisoned by a filthy press, plunged into such a morass of ignorance and credulity that one will never be able to extricate it!" . . . And you see, Monsieur Froment, he was right!'

'No, no! He was n't right, Madame Férou; one must never despair of one's country.'

But her blood was now up, and she retorted: 'I tell you that he *was* right! Have n't you any eyes to see? Are not affairs shameful at Le Moreux, where that man Chagnat, the creature of the priests, does nothing but debase and stupefy the children—to such a point, indeed, that for years past not a single one of them has been able to obtain a certificate of elementary studies? And then Monsieur Jauffre, your successor, does some fine work at Joinville in order to please Abbé Cognasse. At the rate they are all going, France will have forgotten how to read and write before ten years are over!'

She drew herself up as she spoke, and, consumed by hatred and rancour, the rancour of a poor downtrodden woman overcome by social injustice, she went on to prophesy: 'You hear me, Monsieur Froment. I tell you that France is done for! Nothing good nor just will ever come from her again; she will sink to the level of all those dead nations on whom Catholicism has preyed like vermin and rottenness!'

Then, still quivering with the excitement which had prompted that outburst, and trembling at having dared to say so much, she glided away with humble and anxious mien, returning to the den of suffering where her pale and silent daughter awaited her.

Marc remained confounded; it was as if he had heard Férou himself calling from his grave, crying aloud the bitter pessimism, the savage protest, dictated by the cruel sufferings of his life. And, making all allowance for rancorous exaggeration, there was great truth in the widow's words. Chagnat, indeed, was still brutifying Le Moreux, and Jauffre, under the stubborn and narrow-minded sway of Abbé Cognasse, was completing his deadly work at Joinville, in spite of the covert rage he experienced at finding that his services remained so long unrecognised, when, by rights, he ought to have been appointed at once to the headmastership of a school at Beaumont. And the great work of elementary education scarcely made more progress in any part of the region. Nearly all the schools of Beaumont were still in the power of timid masters and mistresses who, thinking of their advancement, wished to remain on good terms with the Church. Mademoiselle Rouzaire achieved great success by her devout zeal, while Doutrequin, that Republican of the early days, whom patriotic alarm had gradually cast into reaction, remained, though he was now on the retired list, a personage of great influence, one whose lofty character was cited to newcomers by way of example. How could young teachers believe in the innocence of Simon, and fight against the Congregational schools, when such a man, a combatant of 1870, a friend of the founder of the Republic, set himself on the side of the Congregations in the name of the country threatened by the Jews? For one Mademoiselle Mazeline, who ever firmly inculcated sense and kindliness, for one Mignot, won by example to the good cause, how many cowards and traitors there were, and how very slowly did the teaching staff progress in breadth of mind, generosity, and devotion, in spite of the reinforcements which came to it every year from the training schools! Yet Salvan persevered in his work of regeneration, full of ardent faith, convinced that the humble schoolmaster alone would save the country from being annihilated by the Clericals, when he himself should at last possess a free mind and the capacity to teach truth and justice. As Salvan ever repeated, the worth of the nation depended on the worth of the schoolmasters. And if the march of progress was so slow, it was because the work of evolution by which good masters might be produced had to be spread over several generations, even as several generations of pupils would be needed before a just nation, freed from error and falsehood, could spring into being.

Having reached that conclusion as the result of his inquiries and the despairing call which seemed to have come to him from Férou's grave, Marc only retained a feverish eagerness to continue the battle and increase his efforts. For some time past he had been busying himself with what were called ' after-school ' enterprises, established in order to maintain a link between the masters and their former pupils, whom the laws took from them at thirteen years of age. Friendly societies were being founded on all sides, and some of the organisers dreamt of federating all those of the same *arrondissement*, then those of the same department, and finally all similar societies in France. Moreover, there were patronage societies, mutual relief and pension funds; but Marc, with the object he had in view, attached most importance to the classes for adults which he held of an evening at his school. Mademoiselle Mazeline, on her side also, had set an excellent example and won very great success by giving occasional evening lessons in cookery, family hygiene, and home nursing to those of her former pupils who were now big girls. And such numbers of young people applied to her that she ended by sacrificing her Sunday afternoons in order to instruct those who could not conveniently attend of an evening. It made her so happy, she said, to help her girls to become good wives and mothers, able to keep house and shed gaiety, health, and happiness around them.

Marc, in the same way, opened his school on three evenings every week, summoned back the boys who had left him, and endeavoured to complete their education with respect to all the practical questions of life. He sowed good seed in those young brains unsparingly, saying to himself that he would be well rewarded for his pains if but one grain out of every hundred should germinate and bear fruit. And he interested himself particularly in the few pupils whom he induced to enter the teaching profession, keeping them near him, and preparing them right zealously for the preliminary examinations at the Training College. On his side, indeed, he devoted his Sunday afternoons to those private lessons, and when evening came he was as delighted as if he had been indulging in the greatest amusement.

One of Marc's victories at this juncture was to prevail on Madame Doloir to allow him to continue educating little Léon, in order that the boy might enter the Training College in due course. The dearest of all Marc's former pupils, Sébastien Milhomme, was there already; and Sébas-

tien's mother, Madame Alexandre, had on her side returned
to the stationery shop, though she discreetly remained in
the background, for fear lest she might scare away the
clerical customers. And Salvan, like Marc, had now become very much attached to Sébastien, regarding him as
one of those future missionaries of good tidings, whom he
desired to disseminate through the country districts. Recently also, at the beginning of a new term, Marc had
experienced the satisfaction of confiding to his old friend
yet another pupil, none other than Joseph Simon, the innocent man's son, who, in spite of every painful obstacle, had
resolved to become a schoolmaster like his father, hoping
to conquer on the very field where the dear stricken prisoner had fought with so tragical a result. Thus Sébastien
and Joseph had met again, each inspired with the same
zeal, the same faith, their old bond of friendship tightened
by yet closer sympathy than before. And what pleasant
hours they spent whenever an afternoon's holiday enabled
them to go to Maillebois, together, to shake hands with
their former master!

While things were thus slowly moving, Marc, with respect to his home troubles, remained in suspense, one day
despairing and the morrow reviving to hope. In vain had
he relied on Geneviève returning to him, enlightened at last
and saved from the poison; at present he set his only consolation in the quiet firmness of his daughter Louise. She,
as she had promised to do, came to see him every Thursday
and Sunday, invariably gay and full of gentle resolution.
He dared not question her about her mother, respecting
whom she seldom volunteered any information, for having
no good news to give she doubtless regarded the subject
as painful. Louise would now soon be sixteen, and with
increase of age she became the better able to understand
the cause of their sufferings. She would have been pleased
indeed could she have become the mediator, the healer, the
one to place the parents she loved so well in each other's
arms once more. On the days when she detected extreme
impatient anguish in her father's glance, she referred discreetly to the frightful situation which haunted them.

'Mamma is still very poorly,' she would say; 'it is necessary to be very careful, and I dare not as yet talk to her as
to a friend. But I have hopes. There are times when she
takes me in her arms, and presses me to her so tightly that
I nearly suffocate, while her eyes fill with tears. At other

times, it is true, she becomes harsh and unjust—accuses me
of not loving her—complains, indeed, that nobody has ever
loved her. . . . You see, father, one must be very kind
to her, for she must suffer frightfully, thinking as she does
that she will never more be able to content her heart.'

Then Marc, in his excitement, cried: ' But why does she
not come back here ? I still love her to distraction, and if
she still loved me, we might be so happy.'

But Louise, in a sorrowful, gentle, caressing way, placed
her hand over his mouth: ' No, no, papa, do not let us talk
of that! I did wrong to begin—it can only make us grieve
the more. We must wait. . . . I am now beside
mamma; and some day she will surely see that only we two
love her. She will listen to me and follow me.'

At other times the girl arrived at her father's with glittering eyes and a determined bearing, as if she had just
emerged from some contest. Marc noticed it, and said to
her: ' You have been disputing with your grandmother
again!'

'Ah! you can see it ? Well, it 's true, she kept me for a
good hour this morning trying to shame and terrify me
about my first Communion. She speaks to me as if I were
the vilest of creatures, describes to me all the abominable
tortures of hell, and seems quite stupefied and scandalised
by what she calls my inconceivable obstinacy.'

At this Marc brightened up, feeling somewhat reassured.
He had so greatly feared that his daughter might prove as
weak as other girls, and was happy to find that she remained
so firm and strong-minded even when he was no longer
present to support her. But emotion came upon him when
he pictured her in the midst of persistent attacks, scoldings,
and scenes, which left her no peace.

' My poor child!' said he, ' how much courage you need!
Those constant quarrels must be very painful to you.'

But she, having now quite recovered her composure,
answered, smiling: ' Quarrels? Oh! no, papa. I am too
respectful with grandmamma to quarrel with her. It is she
who is always getting angry and threatening me. I listen
to her very deferentially, without ever making the slightest
interruption. And when she has quite finished, after beginning two or three times afresh, I content myself with saying
very gently: " But how can I help it, grandmamma? I
promised papa that I would wait until I was twenty before
deciding whether I would make my first Communion or

not; and as I swore it, I will keep my word." You see, I never depart from that answer. I know it by heart, and repeat it without changing a word. That makes me invincible. And I sometimes begin to pity poor grandmamma, for she flies into such a temper, banging the door in my face as soon as ever I begin that phrase!'

In the depths of her heart Louise suffered from that perpetual warfare; but on observing her father's delight, she prettily cast her arms around his neck, and added, ' You see, you may be quite easy, I am really your daughter. Nobody will ever make me do anything when I have decided that I won't do it!'

The girl also had to carry on a battle with her grandmother in order to continue her studies, resolved as she was to devote herself to the teaching profession. In this respect she fortunately had the support of her mother, who regarded the future as being very uncertain by reason of the increasing avarice which Madame Duparque displayed towards her family. The old lady preferred to devote her little fortune to pious works; and since giving an asylum to Geneviève and her daughter she had insisted upon their paying for their board, in this respect wishing to annoy Marc, who consequently had to make his wife a considerable allowance out of his meagre salary. Perhaps Madame Duparque—advised in this matter as in others by her good friends, those masters of intrigue, whose unseen hands pulled every string—had hoped that Marc would respond by a refusal, and that a scandal would ensue. But he could live on very little, and he consented immediately, as if indeed he were well pleased to remain the paterfamilias, the worker, and supporter of those who belonged to him. And although straitened circumstances aggravated his solitude, the meals he shared with Mignot becoming extremely frugal, he did not suffer, for it was sufficient for him to know that Geneviève had appeared moved by his willingness to provide for her, and that she found in this pecuniary question a motive to approve of Louise's resolution to pursue her studies in order to ensure her future. Thus the girl, who had already obtained her elementary certificate, continued to take lessons from Mademoiselle Mazeline, preparing herself for the superior certificate examination, which circumstance gave rise to further disputes with Madame Duparque, who was exasperated by all the science which it had become the fashion to impart to young girls, when, in her opinion, the catechism ought to have sufficed them. And as Louise always answered every protest in her extremely deferential manner: ' Yes, grandmamma; certainly, grandmamma,' the old lady grew more exasperated than ever, and ended by picking quarrels with Geneviève, who, losing patience, occasionally answered back.

One day while Marc was listening to the news his daughter gave him, he became quite astonished. ' Does mamma quarrel with grandmother then? ' he inquired.

' Oh, yes, papa. This was even the second or third time. And mamma, you know, does not beat about the bush. She loses her temper at once, answers back in a loud voice, and then goes to sulk in her room as she used to do here before she left.'

Marc listened, unwilling to give utterance to the secret delight, the hope, which was rising within him.

' And does Madame Berthereau take part in these discussions? ' he resumed.

' Oh, grandmamma Berthereau never says anything. She sides with mamma and me, I think; but she does not dare to support us openly for fear of worries. . . . She looks very sad and very ailing.'

However, months went by, and Marc saw none of his hopes fulfilled. It must be said that he observed great discretion in questioning his daughter, for it was repugnant to him to turn her into a kind of spy for the purpose of keeping himself informed of everything that occurred in the dismal little house on the Place des Capucins. For weeks at a time when Louise ceased to speak of her own accord, Marc relapsed into anxious ignorance, again losing all hope of Geneviève's return. His only consolation then lay in his daughter's presence beside him for a few hours on Thursdays and Sundays. On those days also it occasionally happened that the two chums of the Beaumont Training College, Joseph Simon and Sébastien Milhomme, arrived at the Maillebois school about three o'clock, and remained there until six, happy to meet their friend Louise, who like themselves was all aglow with youth and courage and faith. Their long chats were enlivened by merry laughter, which left some gaiety in the mournful home throughout the ensuing week. Marc, who felt comforted by these meetings, at times requested Joseph to bring his sister Sarah from the Lehmanns', and likewise told Sébastien that he would be happy to see his mother, Madame Alexandre, accompany

him.   The schoolmaster would have been delighted to
gather a number of worthy folk, all the forces of the future,
around him.   At those affectionate meetings the sympathies
of former times revived, acquiring a strength full of gentleness and gaiety, drawing Sébastien and Sarah, Joseph and
Louise together; while the master, smiling and content to
await victory at the hands of those who represented to-
morrow, allowed good Mother Nature, beneficent love, to
do their work.

All at once, amidst the disheartening delays of the Court
of Cassation, at a moment when courage was forsaking
David and Marc, they received a letter from Delbos acquainting them with some great news and requesting them
to call on him.   They did so in all haste.   The great news
—destined to burst on Beaumont like a thunderclap—was
that, after a long and cruel struggle, Jacquin, the diocesan
architect and foreman of the jury which had convicted
Simon, had at last felt it absolutely necessary to relieve his
conscience.   Very pious, attending confession and Communion, strict in his faith, and in all respects an upright
man, Jacquin had ended by feeling anxious with respect to
his salvation, asking himself whether, as he was in possession of the truth, it was possible for him to keep silent any
longer without incurring the risk of damnation.   It was
said that his confessor, feeling extremely perplexed, not
daring to decide the question himself, had advised him to
consult Father Crabot, and that if the architect had remained silent several months longer it was on account of
the great pressure brought to bear on him by the Jesuit,
who, in the name of the Church's political interests, had
prevented him from speaking out.   If, however, Jacquin
was unable to keep his terrible secret any longer, it was
precisely by reason of the anguish he felt as a Christian, one
who believed that the Christ had descended upon earth to
ensure the triumph of truth and justice.   And the knowledge
which consumed him was that of Judge Gragnon's illegal
communication to the jury in the Simon case of a document
unknown either to the prisoner or to his counsel.   Summoned to the retiring room to enlighten the jurymen respecting the penalty which might attach to their verdict, the
judge had shown them a letter received by him a moment
previously, a letter from Simon to a friend, followed by a
postcript and a paraph, which last was similar to the one
on the copy-slip tendered as evidence.   It was to this same

letter and this paraph that Father Philibin had alluded in his sensational evidence; and now it had been established that if the body of the letter was indeed in Simon's handwriting, the postcript and the paraph were assuredly impudent forgeries, in fact gross ones, by which a child even would hardly have been deceived.

Thus David and Marc found Delbos triumphant: 'Ah! did n't I tell you so?' he exclaimed. 'That illegal communication is now proved! Jacquin has written to the President of the Court of Cassation, confessing the truth, and asking to be heard. . . . I knew that the letter was among the papers of the case, for Gragnon had not dared to destroy it. But how difficult it was to have it produced and submitted to the examination of experts! I scented a forgery; I felt that we were confronted by some more of the handiwork of that terrible Father Philibin! Ah! that man, how heavy and common he looked! But the more I fathom the affair the greater do his talents, his suppleness, artfulness, and audacity appear. He was not content with tearing off the stamped corner of the copyslip, he also falsified one of Simon's letters, so arranging matters that this letter might prevail over the jury at the last moment. Yes, assuredly that forgery was his work!'

However, David, who had met with so many deceptions, retained some fears. 'But are you sure,' he asked, 'that Jacquin, who is the diocesan architect and at the mercy of the priests, will remain firm to the end?'

'Quite sure. You don't know Jacquin. He is not at the mercy of the priests; he is one of the few Christians who are governed solely by their consciences. Some extraordinary things have been told me respecting his interviews with Father Crabot. At first the Jesuit spoke in a domineering way, in the name of his imperative Deity, who forgives and even glorifies the worst deeds when the salvation of the Church is in question. But Jacquin answered back in the name of a good and equitable God, the God of the innocent and the just, who tolerates neither error, nor falsehood, nor crime. I wish I had been present; that battle between the mere believer and the political agent of a crumbling religion must have been a fine spectacle. However, I have been told that it was the Jesuit who ended by humbling himself, and entreating Jacquin, though he failed to prevent him from doing his duty——'

'All the same,' Marc interrupted, 'it took Jacquin a very long time to relieve his conscience.'

'Oh! no doubt; I don't say that his duty became manifest to him at once. For years, however, he did not know that President Gragnon's communication was illegal. Almost all jurors are similarly situated; they know nothing of the law, and take as correct whatever the chief magistrates may say to them. When Jacquin learnt the truth he hesitated evidently, and for years and years went about with a burden on his conscience, saying nothing, however, for fear of scandal. We shall never know the sufferings and the struggles of that man, who went regularly to confession and Communion, ever terrified by the thought that he was perhaps damning himself for all eternity. However, I can assure you that when he became certain that the document was a forgery, he no longer hesitated; he resolved to speak out, even if by doing so he should cause the cathedral of Saint Maxence to fall, for on no account was he disposed to disregard what he deemed to be his duty towards God.'

Then Delbos, like a man who, after long efforts, was at last reaching his goal, gaily summed up the situation, and David and Marc went off radiant with hope.

But how great was the commotion in Beaumont when Jacquin's letter to the Court of Cassation, his confession and his offer of evidence became known. Judge Gragnon hastily closed his doors, refusing to answer the journalists who applied to him, wrapping himself, as it were, in haughty silence. He was no longer a jovial, sarcastic sportsman and pursuer of pretty girls. People said that he was quite overwhelmed by the blow which had thus fallen on him on the eve of his retirement from the bench, at the moment when he was expecting to receive the collar of a Commandership in the Legion of Honour. Of recent years his wife, the once beautiful Madame Gragnon, having passed the age for reading poetry with General Jarousse's young officers, had decided to occupy herself in converting him, pointing out to him no doubt all the advantages of a pious old age; and he followed her to confession and Communion, giving a lofty example of fervent Catholicism, which explained the passionate zeal with which Father Crabot had tried to prevent Jacquin from relieving his conscience. The Jesuit, indeed, wished to save Gragnon, a believer of great importance and influence, of whom the Church was very proud.

Moreover, the whole judicial world of Beaumont sided
with the presiding judge, defending the conviction and condemnation of Simon as its own work, its masterpiece, which
none might touch without committing high treason against
the country. Behind that fine assumption of indignation,
however, there was base, shivering dread—dread of the galleys, dread lest the gendarmes should set their heavy hands
some evening on the black or red robes, furred with ermine,
whose wearers had imagined themselves to be above the
laws. The handsome Raoul de La Bissonnière was no longer
public prosecutor at Beaumont, he had been transferred to
the neighbouring Appeal Court of Mornay, where he was
growing embittered by his failure to secure a post in Paris,
in spite of all his suppleness and skill under every succeeding government. On the other hand, Investigating Magistrate Daix had not quitted the town, where he had been
promoted to the rank of counsellor; but he was still tortured
by his terrible wife, whose ambition and craving for luxury
made his home a hell. It was said that Daix, seized with
remorse like Jacquin, was on the point of throwing off his
wife's acrimonious authority, and relating how he had
cowardly yielded to her representations, and sent Simon
for trial, at the very moment when, from lack of proof, he
was about to stay further proceedings. Thus the Palais de
Justice was all agog, swept by gusts of fear and anger,
pending the advent of the cataclysm which would at last
annihilate the ancient worm-eaten framework of so-called
human justice.

The political world of Beaumont was no less shaken, no
less distracted. Lemarrois, the Deputy and Mayor, felt
that the Radical Republican views he had long professed
were losing their hold on the electorate, and that he might
be swept away in this supreme crisis which was bringing
the living strength of the people forward. Thus, in the
much-frequented *salon* of his intelligent wife, the evolution
towards reactionary courses became more pronounced.
Among those now often seen there was Marcilly, once the
representative of the intellectual young men, the hope of
the French mind, but now reduced to a kind of political
paralysis, bewildered by his inability to detect in which
direction lay his personal interests, and forced to inaction
by the haunting fear that if he should act in any particular
way he might not be re-elected. Then another visitor was
General Jarousse, who, though a mere cipher, now showed

himself aggressive, spurred on, it seemed, by the perpetual
nagging of his little, dusky, withered wife. And Prefect
Hennebise also called at times, accompanied by the placid
Madame Hennebise, each desiring to live at peace with
everybody, such being indeed the wish of the government,
whose motto was: 'No difficulties, only handshakes and
smiles.' There was great fear of 'bad' elections, as the
department was so enfevered by the revival of the Simon
affair; and Marcilly and even Lemarrois, though they did
not own it, had resolved to ally themselves secretly with
Hector de Sanglebœuf and their other reactionary colleagues
in order to overcome the Socialist candidates, particularly
Delbos, whose success would become certain should he
succeed in his efforts on behalf of the innocent prisoner.

All this tended to the confusion which broke out directly
people heard of the intervention of Jacquin, by which the
revision of the case was rendered inevitable. The Simonists
triumphed, and for a few days the anti-Simonists seemed
crushed. Nothing else was talked about on the aristocratic
promenade of Les Jaffres; and though *Le Petit Beaumontais*,
in order to inspirit its readers, declared every morning that
the revision of the case would be refused by a majority of
two to one, the friends of the Church remained plunged in
desolation, for private estimates indicated quite a different
result.

Meantime the delight shown among the University men
was very temperate. Nearly all of them were Simonists,
but they had hoped in vain so often that they now scarcely
dared to rejoice. Rector Forbes was relieved to think that
he would soon be rid of the case of that Maillebois schoolmaster, Marc Froment, about whom he was so frequently
assailed by the reactionary forces. In spite of his desire to
meddle with nothing, Forbes had been obliged to confer
with Le Barazer respecting the necessity of an execution;
and Le Barazer, whose own powers of resistance were exhausted, foresaw the moment when policy would compel
him to sacrifice Marc. He had even mentioned it to Salvan, who had shown deep grief at the announcement.
When, however, Marc came to him with the great news
that made revision certain, the kind-hearted man revived to
gaiety and gave his friend quite a triumphal greeting. He
embraced him and then told him of the threatening danger
from which the favourable decision of the Court of Cassation
alone would save him.

'If revision should not be granted, my dear fellow,' he said, 'you would certainly be revoked, for this time you are deeply involved in the affair, and all the reactionaries demand your head. . . . However, the news you bring pleases me, for you are at last victorious, and our secular schools triumph.'

'They need to do so,' Marc replied; 'our conquests over error and ignorance are still so slight in spite of all your efforts to endow the region with good masters.'

'Certainly a good many lives will be needed; but, no matter, we are marching on, and we shall reach the goal,' Salvan responded with his usual gesture expressive of unshakable hope.

Perhaps the best proof that Marc was really victorious was found by him in the eager manner with which handsome Mauraisin, the Elementary Inspector, rushed towards him, that same day, just as he had quitted Salvan.

'Ah! my dear Monsieur Froment, I am very pleased to meet you,' the Inspector exclaimed. 'We see each other so seldom apart from the requirements of our duties.'

Since the revival of the affair, mortal anxiety had taken possession of Mauraisin, who at an earlier stage had openly sided with the anti-Simonists, convinced as he then was that the priests never allowed themselves to be beaten. But now, if they should lose the game, how would he be able to save himself? The idea of not being on the winning side distressed him greatly.

Though nobody was passing in the street, he leant towards Marc to whisper in his ear: 'For my part, you know, my dear Froment, I never doubted Simon's innocence. I was convinced of it at bottom. Only it is so necessary for public men like ourselves to remain prudent—is that not so?'

For a long time past Mauraisin had been keeping his eye on Salvan's post, hoping to secure it in due course; and in view of a possible triumph of the Simonists he felt it would be as well to side with them on the eve of victory. But as that victory was not yet quite certain he did not wish to exhibit himself in their company. So he speedily took leave of Marc, whispering, as he pressed his hand for the last time, 'Simon's triumph will be a triumph for all of us.'

On returning to Maillebois Marc preceived a change there also. Darras, the ex-Mayor, whom he chanced to meet, did not rest content with bowing to him discreetly, according to his wont, but stopped him in the middle of the high

street, and talked and laughed with him for more than ten
minutes.   He, Darras, had been a Simonist at the outset,
but since he had lost his position as Mayor he had put his
flag in his pocket, and made it a habit to bolt his door before divulging what he thought.   If, therefore, he now
openly chatted with Marc, it must have been because
Simon's acquittal seemed to him a certainty.   As it happened, Philis, the new Mayor, went by at that moment,
gliding swiftly over the pavement with his head bent and
his eyes darting furtive glances around him.   This amused
Darras, who with a knowing look at Marc exclaimed: 'What
pleases some displeases others, is it not so, Monsieur Froment?   We all have our turns!'

Indeed a great change in public opinion gradually became
manifest.   Day by day for several weeks Marc observed the
increasing favour of the cause he defended.   However, the
decisive importance of the success already achieved became
most manifest to him when he received a letter from Baron
Nathan, who was again staying at La Désirade, and who
asked him to call there with respect to a prize for the Communal School, which he, the Baron, desired to found.   Although Nathan, on two or three occasions previously, had
given a hundred francs or so to be distributed in savings-
bank deposits among the best pupils, Marc felt that the offer
of a prize at that juncture was only a pretext.   So he repaired to La Désirade full of wonder and curiosity.

He had not returned thither since the now distant day
when he had accompanied David on his attempt to interest
the all-powerful Baron in the cause of his accused and im-
prisoned brother.   Marc remembered the most trifling details of that visit, the skilful manner in which the triumphant
Jew, a king of finance and the father-in-law of a Sanglebœuf,
had shaken off the poor Jew, on whom public execration
had fallen.   And now, on returning to La Désirade, Marc
found that its majesty and beauty had increased.   Recently
a million of francs had been spent on new terraces and new
fountains, which imparted an aspect of sovereign grandeur
to the parterres in front of the château.   Encompassed by
plashing waters and a galaxy of marble nymphs, he ended
by reaching the steps, where two tall lackeys, in liveries of
green and gold, were waiting.   On one of them conducting
him to a little drawing-room, where he was requested to wait,
he remained alone for a moment, and heard a confused
murmur of voices in some neighbouring room.   Then two

doors were shut, all became quiet, and finally Baron Nathan
entered with outstretched hand.

'' Excuse me for having disturbed you, my dear Monsieur
Froment,' he said, 'but I know how devoted you are to
your pupils, and I wish to double the sum which I have
been giving you of recent years. You are aware that my
ideas are broad, that I desire to reward merit wherever it
may be found, apart from all political and religious questions. . . . Yes, I make no difference between the
congregational and the secular schools; I am for all
France.'

Short and somewhat bent, with a yellow face, a bald
cranium, and a large nose resembling the beak of a bird of
prey, Nathan went on talking, while Marc gazed at him.
The schoolmaster knew that of recent times the Baron had
still further enriched himself by stealing a hundred millions
of francs in a colonial affair, a deed of rapine, the huge
booty of which he had been obliged to share with a Catholic
bank. And he had now plunged into fierce reaction, for as
new millions were added to his former ones he became more
and more convinced that priests and soldiers were needed
to enable him to retain his ill-gotten wealth. He was no
longer content with having wormed his way, through his
daughter, into the ancient family of the Sanglebœufs: he
now absolutely denied his race, openly displaying a ferocious
anti-Semitism, showing himself a monarchist, a militarist, a
respectful friend of those who in olden time had burnt the
Jews. Nevertheless—and this astonished Marc—Nathan,
whatever his wealth, still retained much of his racial humility. A dread of the persecutions which had fallen on
his ancestors appeared in his anxious eyes as they glanced
at the doors as if he wished to be ready to slip under a table
at the slightest sign of danger.

'So it is settled,' he said, after all sorts of involved explanations, 'and you will dispose of these two hundred
francs yourself, as you please, for I have perfect confidence
in your sagacity.'

Marc thanked him, but still failed to understand the
meaning of it all. Even a politic desire to remain on good
terms with everybody, a wish to be among the Simonists if
they should win the battle, did not explain that flattering
and useless appointment, that over-cordial reception at La
Désirade. However, just as the schoolmaster was retiring,
there came an explanation.

Baron Nathan, having accompanied him to the drawing-room door, detained him there, and with a keen smile, which seemed prompted by a sudden inspiration, exclaimed: 'My dear Monsieur Froment, I am going to be very indiscreet. . . . When I was informed of your arrival just now, I happened to be with somebody, an important personage, who exclaimed, "Monsieur Froment! Oh! I should be so pleased to have a moment's conversation with him!" A cry from the heart in fact.'

The Baron paused, waiting a few seconds in the hope that he would be questioned. Then, as Marc remained silent, he laughed and said in a jesting way: 'You would be greatly surprised if I told you who the personage was.' And as the schoolmaster still looked grave, remaining on the defensive, Nathan blurted out everything: 'It was Father Crabot. You did not expect that, eh? . . . But he came to lunch here this morning. As you may know, he honours my daughter with his affection, and is a frequent visitor here. Well, he expressed to me a desire to have some conversation with you. Setting aside all matters of opinion, he is a man of the rarest merit. Why should you refuse to see him?'

To this Marc, who at last understood the object of the appointment given him, and whose curiosity was more and more aroused, quietly responded: 'But I don't refuse to see Father Crabot. If he has anything to say to me I will listen to him willingly.'

'Very good, very good!' exclaimed the Baron, delighted with the success of his diplomacy. 'I will go to tell him.'

Again the two doors opened, one after the other, and a confused murmur of voices once more reached the little drawing-room. Then all relapsed into silence, and Marc was left waiting for some time. Having at last drawn near to the window he saw the persons, whose voices he had heard, step on to the adjoining terrace. And he recognised Hector de Sanglebœuf and his wife, the still beautiful Léa, accompanied by their good friend, the Marchioness de Boise, who, though her fifty-seventh birthday was now past, remained a buxom blonde, the ruins of whose beauty were magnificent. Nathan likewise appeared, and one could also divine that Father Crabot was standing at the glass door of the grand drawing-room, still talking to his hosts, who left him in possession of the apartment in order that he might receive the visitor as if he were at home.

The Marchioness de Boise seemed particularly amused by

the incident.   Though she had originally resolved to disappear as soon as she should be fifty, unwilling as she was to
impose too old a mistress on Hector, she had ended by
making the château her permanent home.   Besides, people
said that she was still adorable, so why should she not continue to ensure the happiness of the husband whose marriage
she had so wisely negotiated, and of the wife whose tender
friend she was?   Thus age might come but happiness still
reigned at La Désirade, amid its luxurious appointments
and Father Crabot's discreet smiles and pious benisons.

As Marc looked out of the window and observed the terrible Sanglebœuf waving his arms and shaking his carroty
head, it seemed to him that this clerical champion with the
heavy face and the narrow, stubborn brow was deploring the
practice of so much diplomacy, the honour which Father
Crabot accorded to a petty anarchical schoolmaster by thus
receiving him.   Sanglebœuf had never once fought in his
cuirassier days, but he always talked of sabring people.
Although the Marchioness, after securing his election as a
deputy, had made him rally to the Republic—in accordance
with the Pope's express commands—he still and ever prated
about his regiment, and flew into a passion whenever there
was any question of the flag.   Indeed, he would have committed blunder upon blunder had it not been for that intelligent Marchioness, and this was one of the reasons she
gave for remaining near him.   Again, on this occasion, she
had to intervene and lead him and his wife away, walking
slowly between them, in the direction of the park, and
showing the while much gaiety of mien, and motherliness
of manner towards both.

Baron Nathan, however, had quickly returned to the
grand drawing-room, the glass door of which he closed; and
almost immediately afterwards Marc heard himself called:

'Kindly follow me, my dear Monsieur Froment.'

The Baron led him through a billiard-room; then, having
opened the drawing-room door, drew back and ushered him
in, delighted, it seemed, with the strange part he was playing, his body bowed in a posture which again showed racial
humility reviving in the triumphant king of finance.

'Please enter—you are awaited.'

Nathan himself did not enter, but discreetly closed the
door and disappeared; while Marc, amazed, found himself
in the presence of Father Crabot, who stood, in his long
black gown, in the centre of the spacious and sumptuous

room, hung with crimson and gold. A moment's silence followed.

The Jesuit, whose noble mien, whose lofty and elegant carriage Marc well remembered, seemed to him to have greatly aged. His hair had whitened, and his countenance was ravaged by all the terrible anxiety he had experienced for some time past. But the caressing charm of his voice, its grave and captivating modulations, had remained.

'As circumstances have brought us both to this friendly house, monsieur,' said he, ' you will perhaps excuse me for having prompted an interview which I have long desired. I am aware of your merits, I can render homage to all convictions, when they are sincere, loyal, and courageous.'

He went on speaking in this strain for some minutes, heaping praises on his adversary as if to daze him and win him over. But the device was too familiar and too childish to influence Marc, who, after bowing politely, quietly awaited the rest, striving even to conceal his curiosity, for only some very grave reason could have induced such a man as Father Crabot to run the risk of such an interview.

' How deplorable it is,' the Jesuit at last exclaimed, 'that the misfortunes of the times should separate minds so fit to understand each other! Some of the victims of our dissensions are really to be pitied. For instance, there is President Gragnon——'

Then, as a hasty gesture escaped the schoolmaster, he broke off in order to interpolate a brief explanation. ' I name him,' he said, ' because I know him well. He is a penitent of mine—a friend. A loftier soul, a more upright and loyal heart could be found nowhere. You are aware of the frightful position in which he finds himself—that charge of prevarication,[1] which means the collapse of his entire judicial career. He no longer sleeps; you would pity him if you were to witness his sufferings.'

At last Marc understood everything. They wished to save Gragnon, who only yesterday had been an all-powerful son of the Church, which felt it would be grievously maimed if he should be struck down.

' I can understand his torment,' Marc finally answered, ' but he is paying the penalty of his transgression. A judge

---

[1] The word ' Prevarication ' is used in a legal sense, as signifying the betrayal of the interests of one party in a lawsuit by collusion with the other party. The French call this *forfaiture.—Trans.*

must know the laws, and the illegal communication of which he was guilty had frightful consequences.'

'No, no, I assure you, he acted in all simplicity,' the Jesuit exclaimed. 'That letter which he received at the last moment seemed to him without importance. He still had it in his hand when he was summoned to the jurymen's retiring room, and he no longer remembers how it happened that he showed it to them.'

Marc gave a little shrug of the shoulders. 'Well,' he responded, 'he will only have to tell that to the new judges, if there should be a new trial. . . . In any case I hardly understand your intervention with me. I can do nothing.'

'Oh! do not say that, monsieur! We know how great your power is, however modest your position may seem to be. And that is why I thought of applying to you. Throughout this affair all thought and action and will-power have been centred in you. You are the friend of the Simon family, which will do whatever you advise. So, come, will you not spare an unfortunate man, whose ruin is by no means indispensable for your cause?'

Father Crabot joined his hands and entreated his adversary so fervently that the latter, again all astonishment, wondered what could be the real reason of such a desperate appeal, such clumsy and impolitic insistence. Did the Jesuit feel that the cause he defended was lost? Did he possess private information which made him regard revision as a certainty? In any case, matters had come to such a pass that he was now ready to leave something to the fire in order to save the rest. He abandoned his former creatures, who were now too deeply compromised. That poor Brother Fulgence had a befogged, unbalanced mind, spoilt by excessive pride; disastrous consequences had attended his actions. That unfortunate Father Philibin had always been full of faith, no doubt; but then there were many gaps in his nature. He was deplorably deficient in moral sense. As for the disastrous Brother Gorgias, Father Crabot cast him off entirely; he was one of those adventurous, erring sons of the Church, who become its curse. And if the Jesuit did not go so far as to admit the possible innocence of Simon, he was, at least, not far from believing Brother Gorgias capable of every crime.

'You see, my dear sir,' he said, 'I do not deceive myself; but there are other men whom it would be really cruel to

visit too severely for mere errors.   Help us to save them,
and we will requite the service by ceasing to contend with
you in other matters.'

Never had Marc so plainly realised his strength, the very
strength of truth.   He answered, engaging in quite a long
discussion, desirous as he was of forming a final opinion
with respect to the merits of Father Crabot.   And his
stupefaction increased as he fathomed the extraordinary
poverty of argument, the arrant clumsiness too, which accompanied the vanity of this man, accustomed never to be
contradicted.   Was this, then, the profound diplomatist
whose crafty genius was feared by everybody, and the
presence of whose hand was suspected in every incident, as
if, indeed, he ruled the world?   In this interview, which
had been prepared so clumsily, he showed himself a poor
bewildered individual, committing himself far more than was
necessary, even incompetent to defend his faith against one
who was merely possessed of sense and logic.   A mediocrity
—that was what he was—a mediocrity, with a *façade* of
social gifts, which imposed on the man in the street.   His
real strength lay in the stupidity of his flock, the submissiveness with which the faithful bent low before his statements,
which they regarded as being beyond discussion.   And Marc
ended by understanding that he was confronted by a mere
show Jesuit, one of those who for decorative purposes were
allowed by their Order to thrust themselves forward, shine,
and charm, while, in the rear, other Jesuits—such, for instance, as Father Poirier, the Provincial installed at Rozan,
whose name was never mentioned—directed everything like
unknown sovereign rulers hidden away in distant places of
retreat.

Father Crabot, however, was shrewd enough to understand at last that he was taking the wrong course with Marc,
and he thereupon did what he could to recover his lost
ground.   The whole ended by an exchange of frigid courte-
sies.   Then Baron Nathan, who must have remained
listening outside the door, reappeared, looking also very
discomfited, with only one remaining anxiety, which was to
rid La Désirade as soon as possible of the presence of that
petty schoolmaster, who was such a fool that he could not
even understand his own interests.   He escorted him to the
terrace and watched his departure.   And Marc, as he went
his way among the parterres, the plashing waters, and the
marble nymphs, again caught a glimpse of the Marchioness

de Boise, laughing affectionately with her good friends
Hector and Léa, as all three strolled slowly under the far-
spreading foliage.

On the evening of that same day Marc repaired to the
Rue du Trou, having given David an appointment at the
Lehmanns'. He found them all in a state of delirious joy,
for a telegram from a friend in Paris had just informed them
that the Court of Cassation had at last pronounced an unanimous judgment, quashing the proceedings of Beaumont,
and sending Simon before the Assize Court of Rozan. For
Marc this news was like a flash of light, and what he had
regarded as Father Crabot's folly seemed to him more ex-
cusable than before. The Jesuit had evidently been well
informed; that judgment had been known to him; and, revision becoming a certainty, he had simply wished to save
those whom he thought might still be saved. And now, at
the Lehmanns', all were weeping with joy, for the long
calamity was over. Wildly did Joseph and Sarah kiss
Rachel, their poor, aged, and exhausted mother. Both
children and wife were intoxicated by the thought of the
return of the father, the husband, for whom they had
mourned and longed so much. Outrage and torture were
all forgotten, for acquittal was now certain; nobody doubted
it either at Maillebois or at Beaumont. And David and
Marc, those two brave workers in the cause of justice, also
embraced each other, drawn together by a great impulse of
affection and hope.

But, as the days went by, anxiety arose once more. At
the penal settlement yonder Simon had fallen so dangerously ill that for a long time yet it would be impossible to
bring him back to France. Months and months might
elapse before the new trial would begin at Rozan. And
thus all necessary time was given to the spirit of injustice to
revive and spread once more in the midst of mendacity and
the multitude's cowardly ignorance.

III

DURING the year which followed, a year full of anxiety, uneasiness, and contention, the Church made a supreme effort to regain her power. Never had her position been more critical, more threatened, than during that desperate battle, by which the duration of her empire might be prolonged for a century, or perhaps two centuries, should she win it. In order to do so it was necessary she should continue to educate and train the youth of France, retain her sway over children and women, and avail herself of the ignorance of the humble in such wise as to mould them and make them all error, credulity, and submissiveness, even as she needed them to be in order to reign. The day when she might be forbidden to teach, when her schools would be closed, and disappear, would prove for her the beginning of the end, when she would be annihilated amidst a new and free people, which would have grown up outside the pale of her falsehoods, cultivating an ideal of reason and humanity. And the hour was a grave one. That Simon affair, with the expected return and triumph of the innocent prisoner, might deal a most terrible blow to the Congregational schools by glorifying the secular ones. Meantime Father Crabot, who wished to save Judge Gragnon, was so compromised himself that he had disappeared from society and hidden himself, pale and trembling, in his lonely cell. Father Philibin, who had been consigned to an Italian convent, was spending the remainder of his days in penitence, unless indeed he were already dead. Brother Fulgence, removed by his superiors in punishment for the discredit which had fallen on his school, a third of whose pupils had already quitted it, was said to have fallen dangerously ill in the distant department whither he had been sent. Finally, Brother Gorgias had fled, fearing that he might be arrested, and feeling that his principals were forsaking him, willing to sacrifice him as an expiatory victim. And this flight had increased the anxiety

378

of the defenders of the Church, who lived only with the
thought of fighting a last and merciless battle when the
Simon affair should come before the Rozan Assize Court.

Marc also, while lamenting Simon's ill health, which delayed his return to France, was preparing for that same
battle, fully realising its decisive importance. Almost every
Thursday, sometimes with David, sometimes alone, he repaired to Beaumont, calling first on Delbos, to whom he
made suggestions, and whom he questioned about the
slightest incidents of the week. And afterwards he went
to see Salvan, who kept him informed of the state of public
opinion, every fluctuation of which set all classes in the
town agog. In this wise, then, one Thursday, Marc paid a
visit to the Training College, and on quitting it went down
the Avenue des Jaffres, where, close to the cathedral of St.
Maxence, he was upset by a most unexpected meeting.

On one of the deserted sidewalks of the avenue, at a spot
where scarcely anybody was ever seen after four o'clock,
he perceived Geneviève seated on a bench, and looking
very downcast, weary, and lonely in the cold shadow falling
from the cathedral, whose proximity encouraged the moss
to grow on the trunks of the old elms.

For a moment Marc remained motionless, quite thunderstruck. He had met his wife in Maillebois at long intervals,
but invariably in the company of Madame Duparque; and
on those occasions she had passed through the streets with
absent-minded eyes, on her way, no doubt, to some de-
votional exercise. This time, however, they found themselves face to face, in perfect solitude, parted by none.
Geneviève had seen him, and was looking at him with an
expression in which he fancied he could detect great suffering, and an unacknowledged craving for help. Thus he
went forward, and even ventured to seat himself on the
same bench, though at some little distance from her, for fear
lest he should frighten her and drive her away.

Deep silence reigned. It was June, and the sun, descending towards the horizon in a vast stretch of limpid sky,
transpierced the surrounding foliage with slender golden
darts; while little wandering zephyrs already began to cool
the warm afternoon atmosphere. And Marc still looked
at his wife, saying nothing, but feeling deeply moved as he
noticed that she had grown thinner and paler, as if after a
serious illness. Her face, crowned by splendid fair hair,
and with large eyes which once had been all passion and

gaiety, had not only become emaciated, but had acquired an expression of ardent anxiety, the torment of a parching thirst, which nothing could assuage. Her eyelids quivered, and two tears, which she vainly tried to force back, coursed down her cheeks. Then Marc began to speak—in such a way that it seemed as if he had quitted her only the previous day, such indeed was his desire to reassure her.

'Is our little Clément well?' he asked.

She did not answer immediately, for she feared, no doubt, that she might reveal the emotion which was choking her. The little boy, who had lately completed his fourth year, was no longer at Dherbecourt. Having removed him from his nurse, Geneviève now kept him with her in spite of all her grandmother's scoldings.

'He is quite well,' she said at last in a slightly tremulous voice, though on her side also she strove to affect a kind of indifferent quietude.

'And our Louise,' Marc resumed, 'are you satisfied with her?'

'Yes: she does not comply with my desires; you have remained the master of her mind; but she is well behaved, she studies, and I do not complain of her.'

Silence fell again, embarrassment once more stayed their tongues. That allusion to their daughter's first Communion, and the terrible quarrel which had parted them, had been sufficient. Yet the virulence of that quarrel was necessarily abating day by day, the girl herself having assumed all responsibility by her quiet resolve to await her twentieth year before making any formal confession of religious faith. In her gentle way she had exhausted her mother's resolution; and indeed a gesture of lassitude had escaped the latter when speaking of her, as if she had referred to some long-desired happiness, all hope of which had fled. A few moments went by, and then Marc gently ventured to put another question to her: 'And you, my friend, you have been so ill: how are you now?'

She shrugged her shoulders in a hopeless way, and was again obliged to force back her tears. 'I? Oh, I have long ceased to know how I am! But no matter, I resign myself to live since God gives me the strength to do so.'

So great was Marc's distress, so deeply was his whole being stirred by a quiver of loving compassion at the sight of such great suffering, that a cry of intense anxiety sprang from his lips: 'Geneviève, my Geneviève, what ails you?

what is your torment? Tell me! Ah, if I could only console you, and cure you!'

Thus speaking, he came nearer to her on the bench, near
enough indeed to touch the folds of her gown, but she
hastily drew back. 'No, no, we have nothing more in common,' she exclaimed. 'You can no longer do anything for
me, my friend, for we belong to different worlds. . . .
Ah! if I were to tell you! But of what use would it be?
You would not understand me!'

Nevertheless, she went on speaking; and in short and
feverish sentences, never noticing that she was confessing
herself, she told him of her torture, her daily increasing
anguish, for she had reached one of those distressful hours
when the heart instinctively opens and overflows. She
related how, unknown to Madame Duparque, she had
escaped that afternoon from Maillebois, in order to speak
with a famous missionary, Father Athanase, whose pious
counsels were at that time revolutionising the pious folk of
Beaumont. The missionary was merely sojourning there
for a short time, but it was said that he had already worked
some marvellous cures—a blessing, a prayer, from his lips
having restored angelic calmness to the unappeasable souls
of women who were racked by their yearning for Jesus.
And Geneviève had just left the neighbouring cathedral,
where for two hours she had remained in prayer, after confessing to that holy man her unquenchable thirst for divine
happiness. But he had merely absolved her for what he
called excess of pride and human passion, and by way of
penitence had told her to occupy her mind with humble
duties, such as the care of the poor and the sick. In vain
afterwards had she striven to humble, annihilate herself, in
the darkest, the loneliest chapel of St. Maxence; she had
not found peace, she had not satisfied her hunger; she still
glowed with the same craving—a return for the gift of her
whole being to the Deity, that gift which she had tendered
again and again, though never once had it brought real
peace and happiness to her flesh and her heart.

As Marc listened to what she said, he began to suspect
the truth, and whatever might be his sadness at seeing his
Geneviève so wretched, a quiver of hope arose within him.
Plainly enough, neither Abbé Quandieu nor even Father
Théodose had satisfied the intense need of love that existed
in her nature. She had known love, and she must still love
the man, the husband, whom she had quitted, and who

adored her. Mere mystical delights had left her unsatisfied
and irritated. She was now but the proud, stubborn
daughter of Catholicism, who turns desperately to harsher
and more frantic religious practices, as to stronger stupefacients, in order to numb the bitterness and rebellion induced by increasing disillusion. Everything pointed to it:
the revival of motherliness in her nature, for she had taken
little Clément back, and busied herself with him, and she
even found some consolation in Louise, who exercised a
gentle healing influence over her, leading her back a little
more each day towards the father, the husband. Then, also,
there were her dissensions with her terrible grandmother,
and her dawning dislike for the little house on the Place
des Capucins, where she at last felt she could no longer live,
for its coldness, silence, and gloom were deathly. And,
after failing with Abbé Quandieu and Father Théodose, her
sufferings had led her to make a supreme attempt with that
powerful missionary, to whom she had transferred her faith,
that miracle-working confessor, whom she had hastened to
consult in secret for fear lest she might be prevented, and
who, by way of relief, had only been able to prescribe practices which, in the circumstances, were childish.

'But, my Geneviève,' Marc cried again, carried away,
losing all thought of prudence, 'if you are thus beset, thus
tortured, it is because you lack our home! You are too
unhappy: come back, come back, I entreat you!'

Her pride bristled up, however, and she answered: 'No,
no, I shall never go back to you. I am not unhappy: it is
untrue. I am punished for having loved you, for having
been part of you, for having had a share in your crime.
Grandmother does right to remind me of it when I am so
weak as to complain. I expiate your sin, God strikes me
to punish you, and it is your poison which burns me beyond
hope of relief.'

'But, my poor wife, all that is monstrous. They are
driving you mad! If it is true that I set a new harvest in
you, it is precisely on that harvest that I rely to ensure our
happiness some day. Yes, we became so blended one with
the other that we can never be wholly parted. And you
will end by returning to me: our children will bring you
back. The pretended poison which your foolish grandmother talks about is our love itself; it is working in your
heart, and it will bring you back.'

'Never! . . . God would strike us down, both of

us,' she retorted. 'You drove me from our home by your
blasphemy. If you had really loved me, you would not
have taken my daughter from me, by refusing to let her
make her first Communion. How can I return to a home
of impiety where it would not even be allowable for me to
pray? Ah! how wretched I am; nobody, nobody loves me,
and heaven itself will not open!'

She burst into sobs. Filled with despair by that frightful
cry of distress Marc felt that it would be useless and cruel
to torture her further. The hour for reunion had not yet
come. Silence fell between them once more, while in the
distance, on the Avenue des Jaffres, the cries of some children at play rose into the limpid evening atmosphere.

During their impassioned converse they had at last drawn
nearer to each other on the lonely bench; and now, seated
side by side, they seemed to be reflecting, their glances
wandering away amid the golden dust of the sunset. At
last Marc spoke again, as if finishing his thoughts aloud:
'I do not think, my friend, that you gave for a moment any
credit to the abominable charges with which certain people
wished to besmirch me *à propos* of my brotherly intercourse
with Mademoiselle Mazeline.'

'Oh! no,' Geneviève answered quickly, 'I know you,
and I know her. Do not imagine that I have become so
foolish as to believe all that has been said to me.'

Then with some slight embarrassment she continued: 'It
is the same with me. Some people, I know it, have set me
among the flock which Father Théodose is said to have
turned into a kind of *cour galante*. In the first place I do
not admit that anything of the kind exists. Father Théodose is, perhaps, rather too proud of his person, but I believe his faith to be sincere. Besides, I should have known
how to defend myself—you do not doubt it, I hope?'

In spite of his sorrow Marc could not help smiling
slightly. Geneviève's evident embarrassment indicated that
there had been some audacity on the part of the Capuchin,
and that she had checked it. Assuming this to be the case
Marc felt the better able to understand why she was so
perturbed and embittered.

'I certainly do not doubt it,' he responded. 'I know
you, as you know me, and I am aware that you are incapable of wrongdoing. I have no anxiety respecting Father
Théodose on your account, whatever another husband of
my acquaintance may have to say. . . . Yet all the same

I regret that you were so badly advised as to quit worthy
Abbé Quandieu for that handsome monk.'

A fugitive blush which appeared on Geneviève's cheeks
while her husband was speaking told him that he had
guessed aright. It was not without a profound knowledge
of woman in her earlier years, when an *amorosa* may exist
within the penitent, that Father Crabot had advised Madame
Duparque to remove her daughter from the charge of old
Abbé Quandieu and place her in that of handsome Father
Théodose. The Catholic doctors are well aware that love
alone can kill love, and that a woman who loves apart from
Christ never wholly belongs to Christ. The return of
Geneviève to her husband and her sin was fatal unless she
should cease to love, or rather unless she should love elsewhere. But, as it happened, Father Théodose was not expert
in analysing human nature, he had blundered with respect
to the passionate yet loyal penitent confided to his hands,
and had thus precipitated the crisis, provoking repugnance
and rebellion in that distracted, suffering woman, who,
without as yet returning to sober reason, saw the glorious,
mystical stage-scenery of the religion of her childhood collapse around her.

Well pleased with the symptoms which he fancied he
could detect, Marc asked somewhat maliciously: 'And so
Father Théodose is no longer your confessor?'

Geneviève turned her clear eyes upon him, and answered
plainly: 'No, Father Théodose does not suit me, and I have
gone back to Abbé Quandieu, who, as grandmother rightly
says, lacks warmth, but who quiets me at times, for he is
very kind.'

For a moment she seemed to ponder. Then, in an undertone, she allowed another avowal to cross her lips: 'All the
same, the dear man does not know how greatly he has increased the torment in which I live by what he said to me
about that abominable affair ——'

She stopped short, and Marc, guessing the truth, becoming quite impassioned now that this subject was broached,
continued: 'The Simon affair, eh? Abbé Quandieu believes
Simon to be innocent, does he not?'

Geneviève had cast her eyes towards the ground. For a
moment she remained silent; then said, very faintly: 'Yes,
he believes in his innocence; he told me so with great mystery in the choir of his church, at the foot of the altar, before our Lord who heard him.'

'And you yourself, Geneviève, tell me, do you now believe in Simon's innocence?'

'No, I do not, I cannot. You must remember that I should never have left you had I believed him innocent, for his innocence would have meant the guilt of the defenders of God. You, by defending him, charged God with error and falsehood.'

Marc well remembered the circumstances. He again saw his wife bring him the news of the revision, growing exasperated at the sight of his delight, exclaiming that there was no truth or justice outside heaven, and at last fleeing from the house where her faith was outraged. And now that she seemed to him to be shaken he desired more ardently than ever to convince her of the truth, for he felt that he would win her back as soon as with the triumph of truth her mind should awaken to the necessity of justice.

'But once more, Geneviève, my Geneviève, it is impossible that you, who are so upright and so sincere, whose mind is so clear when the superstitions of your childhood do not cloud it—it is impossible that you should believe such gross falsehoods. Inform yourself, read the documents.'

'But I am fully informed, I assure you, my friend; I have read everything.'

'You have read all the documents which have been published? All the inquiry of the Court of Cassation?'

'Why, yes! I have read everything that has appeared in *Le Petit Beaumontais.* You know very well that grandmother takes that paper every morning.'

With a violent gesture Marc gave expression to his disgust and indignation. 'Ah well, my darling, you are, indeed, fully informed! The vile print you speak of is a sewer of poison, which disseminates only filth and falsehood. Documents are falsified in it, texts are mutilated, and the poor credulous minds of the poor and the lowly are gorged with stupid fables.[1] . . . You are simply poisoned like many other worthy folk.'

---

[1] This is exactly what happened in the Dreyfus case. If, apart from all those who, hating Dreyfus as a Jew, were resolved *a priori* to regard him as guilty whatever might be the evidence, there are still millions of Frenchmen who honestly retain a belief in his culpability, this is because scores of French newspapers—those owned or patronised by the Nationalist party and the Roman Catholic Church—deliberately falsified and mutilated documents and evidence, serving to their readers only

She herself, no doubt, was conscious that the folly and impudence of *Le Petit Beaumontais* were excessive, for again she cast down her eyes, and looked distressed.

'Listen!' Marc resumed. 'Let me send you the complete verbatim report of the Court's inquiry, with the documents annexed to it; and promise me that you will read everything attentively and straightforwardly.'

But at this suggestion she vivaciously raised her head: 'No, no; send me nothing. I do not wish it.'

'Why?'

'Because it is useless. There is no need for me to read anything.'

He looked at her, again feeling discouraged and grieved.

'Say rather that you won't read.'

'Well, yes, if you prefer it that way, I won't read anything. As grandmother says: "What is the use of it?" Ought one not always to distrust one's reason?'

'You won't read anything because you fear you might be convinced, because you already doubt the things which, only yesterday, you regarded as certainties.'

She interrupted him with a gesture of fatigue and unconcern, but he continued: 'And the words of Abbé Quandieu pursue you; you ask yourself with terror how a holy priest can believe in an innocence which, if recognised, would compel you to curse all the years of error with which you have tortured our poor home.'

This time she did not even make a gesture, but it was apparent that she had resolved to listen no further. For a moment her glance remained fixed on the ground. Then she slowly said: 'Do not amuse yourself by increasing my sorrow. Our life has been shattered. It is all over. I should deem myself still more guilty than now if I were to go back to you. And what personal relief could it give you to imagine that I made a mistake, and that I have not found my grandmother's house to be the home of peace and faith in which I thought I was taking refuge? My sufferings would not cure yours.'

This, as Marc felt, was almost a confession—an acknow-

---

such particulars as tended to indicate the prisoner's guilt. It is hardly too much to say that half of France is still ignorant of the real facts of the Dreyfus case. We are often told that the press has much power for good : never was its power for evil more strikingly exemplified than in that lamentable affair, from the effects of which France is still suffering. —*Trans.*

ledgment of her secret regret at having quitted him, and of
the anxious doubts into which she had sunk. Once more,
therefore, he exclaimed: 'But if you are unhappy, say it!
And come back; bring the children with you; the house
still awaits you! It would be great joy, great happiness.'

But she stood up and repeated, like one who obstinately
remains blind and deaf: 'I am not unhappy. I am being
punished, and I will endure my punishment to the end.
And if you have any pity for me, remain here; do not try
to follow me. Should you meet me again, too, turn your
head away, for all is ended, all must be ended, between
us.'

Then she went off along the deserted avenue, amid the
paling gold of the sunset, her figure quite sombre, tall, and
slim; and all that Marc could still see of her beauty was her
splendid fair hair, which a last sunbeam irradiated. He
obediently refrained from moving, but, hoping for a last
glance of farewell, he watched her as she walked away.
She did not turn, however; she disappeared from view
among the trees, while the evening wind, now rising, passed
with a chilling quiver beneath the foliage.

When Marc painfully rose to his feet, he was amazed to
see his good friend Salvan standing before him, with a happy
smile on his lips. 'Ah! my fine lover, so this is how I catch
you giving assignations in lonely corners! I saw you already
some time ago, but remained watching, for I did not wish
to disturb you. . . . So this is why you remained with
me such a short time when you called at the college this
afternoon, Master Slyboots!'

Sadly shaking his head, Marc walked away beside his old
friend. 'No, no,' he said, 'we merely met by chance, and
my heart is quite lacerated.'

Then he recounted the meeting, and the long conversation from which he had just emerged feeling more convinced
than ever that the rupture was definitive. Salvan, who had
never consoled himself for having promoted a marriage
which, however happy at the outset, was ending so badly,
and who recognised that he had acted with great imprudence
in wedding free thought to the Church, listened attentively,
ceasing to smile, yet looking fairly satisfied.

'But that is not so bad,' he said at last. 'You surely
did not expect that our poor Geneviève would throw herself
at your head, and entreat you to take her back? When a
woman leaves her husband to give herself to God, as your

wife did, her pride prevents her from acknowledging in that
way the distress she now feels at having failed to find the
contentment she anticipated. None the less, in my opinion,
Geneviève is passing through a frightful crisis, which may
bring her back to you at any moment.   .   .   .   If truth
should enlighten her, she will act at once. She has retained
too much sense to be unjust.'

And again becoming gay and animated, Salvan went on:
' I never told you, my friend, of the attempts I made with
Madame Duparque of recent years. As they resulted in
nothing, there was no occasion for me to vaunt them to you.
However, when your wife acted so inconsiderately, when
she left you, I thought of giving her a little lecture, for I
was an old friend of her father's, and, besides, I had been
her own guardian. That circumstance naturally gave me
admittance to the dismal little house on the Place des
Capucins. But you can have no idea of the ferocious manner in which the terrible old grandmother received me.
She would not leave me alone with Geneviève for a moment,
and she interrupted every conciliatory phrase of mine with
imprecations intended to fall on you. Nevertheless, I think
I managed to say what I wished to say. True, the poor
child was in no fit state to listen to me. When Catholic
training revives, the ravages which religious exaltation may
cause in a woman's brain are frightful. Geneviève, for her
part, appeared well-balanced and healthy when you married
her; but that unfortunate Simon affair sufficed to shatter all
equilibrium. She would not even listen to me; her answers
were so wild and foolish as to make one's reason stagger.
Briefly, I was beaten. I was not exactly turned out of
doors, but, after two subsequent attempts made at long intervals, I lost all hope of introducing a little reasonableness
into that abode of insanity, where poor Madame Berthereau,
in spite of her sufferings, seemed the only person who retained a little good sense.'

' You see very well that there is no hope,' responded
Marc, who remained very gloomy. ' One cannot reclaim
people when they so stubbornly persist in refusing to make
themselves acquainted with the truth.'

' Why not? ' asked Salvan. ' I 'm done for, that 's true.
It would be useless for me to make any fresh attempt; they
would stop up their eyes and ears beforehand in order to
see and hear nothing. But remember that you have the
most powerful of helpers, the best of advocates, the shrewd-

est of diplomatists, the most skilful of captains, and in fact
the most triumphant of conquerors at work in that house!'

He laughed, and, growing quite excited, resumed: 'Yes,
yes, your charming Louise, whom I 'm very fond of, and
whom I regard as a prodigy of good sense and grace.   The
firm and yet gentle behaviour of that young girl, ever since
her twelfth year, has been that of a heroine.   I know of no
loftier or more touching example.   Seldom does one meet
with such precocious sense and courage.   And she is all
deference and affection, even when she refuses to do what
her mother desires, by reason of her promise to you respecting her first Communion.   Now that she has acquired
the right to keep that promise, you should see how prettily,
how sedately, she manœuvres to effect the conquest of that
house where everybody is against her.   Even her grandmother becomes tired of scolding.   But her dexterity is
most marvellous with her mother, whom she encompasses
with an active worship, with all sorts of attentions, as if
dealing with some convalescent patient whose physical and
moral strength must first of all be restored, in order that she
may afterwards return to ordinary life.   She seldom speaks
to her mother of you, but she accustoms her to live in an
atmosphere which is full of you, full of your thoughts and
your love.   She is there like your other self, never pausing
in her endeavours to bring about the return of the wife and
mother, by reconnecting the severed bond with her own
caressing hands.   And if your wife returns to you, my
friend, it will be the child who will bring her back, the all-
powerful child, whose presence ensures health and peace in
one's home.'

Marc listened, feeling deeply moved, and reviving to
hope.   'Ah! may it be true,' said he; 'nevertheless my
poor Geneviève is still very ill.'

'Let your little healer do her work,' Salvan responded:
'the kiss she gives her mother every morning brings life with
it.   .   .   .   If Geneviève suffers such torture it is because
life is struggling within her, and wresting her a little more
each day from the deadly crisis in which you nearly lost her.
As soon as good Mother Nature triumphs over mystical imbecility, she and your children will be in your arms.   .   .   .
Come, my friend, be brave.   It would be hard indeed if,
after restoring poor Simon to his family, your own domestic
happiness should not be assured by the triumph of truth and
justice.'

They shook hands in brotherly fashion, and Marc, who returned to Maillebois somewhat comforted, found himself on the morrow in the thick of the fight again. The flight of Brother Gorgias had had a disastrous effect in the little town, and the great days of the affair were now beginning afresh. There was not a house whose inmates did not quarrel and fight over the possible guilt of that terrible Christian Brother, who, in disappearing from the scene, had impudently written to *Le Petit Beaumontais* to explain that, as his cowardly superiors had decided to abandon him to his enemies, he was about to place himself in safety, in order that he might be free to defend himself when and how he pleased.

A much more important feature of this letter was, however, a revised statement which Gorgias made in it to account for the presence of the famous copy-slip in the paper gag found near Zéphirin's body. No doubt the complicated story of a forgery, invented by his leaders, who were unwilling even to admit that the copy-slip had come from the Brothers' school, had always been regarded by Gorgias as idiotic. He must have thought it stupid to deny the origin of the slip and the authenticity of the initialling. Although every expert in the world might ascribe that initialling to Simon, it would remain his, Gorgias's, handiwork in the estimation of all honest and sensible folk. However, as his superiors had threatened to abandon him to his own resources if he did not accept their version of the affair, he had resigned himself and relinquished his own. It was to the latter that he now reverted, for since the missing corner bearing the school stamp had been found at Father Philibin's, he regarded his superiors' version as utterly ridiculous. It seemed to him absurd to pretend, as the Congregations did, that Simon had procured a stamp, or had caused one to be made, with the deliberate intention of ruining the Brothers' school. Now, therefore, realising that his supporters were on the point of forsaking and sacrificing him, Gorgias left them of his own accord, and by way of intimidation revealed a part of the truth. His new version, which upset all the credulous readers of *Le Petit Beaumontais*, was that the copy-slip had really come from the Brothers', and had been initialled by himself, but that Zéphirin had assuredly taken it home with him from the school, even as Victor Milhomme had taken a similar slip, in spite of all prohibitions; and that Simon had thus

found it on the table in his victim's room on the night of
the abominable crime.

A fortnight after the appearance of this version the newspaper published a fresh letter from Brother Gorgias. He
had taken refuge in Italy, he said; but he abstained from
supplying his exact address, though he offered to return
and give evidence at the approaching trial at Rozan if he
received a formal guarantee that his liberty would not be
interfered with. In this second letter he still called Simon
a loathsome Jew, and declared that he possessed overwhelming proof of his guilt, which proof, however, he would
only divulge to the jury at the Assize Court. At the same
time this did not prevent him from referring to his superiors,
notably Father Crabot, in aggressive and outrageous terms
fraught with all the bitter violence of an accomplice once
willingly accepted but now cast off and sacrificed. How
idiotic, said he, was their story of a forged school stamp!
What a wretched falsehood, when the truth might well be
told! They were fools and cowards, cowards especially, for
had they not acted with the vilest cowardice in abandoning
him, Gorgias, the faithful servant of God, after sacrificing
both the heroic Father Philibin and the unhappy Brother
Fulgence? Of the latter he only spoke in terms of indulgent
contempt; Fulgence, said he, had been a sorry individual,
unhinged, and full of vanity; and the others, after allowing
him all freedom to compromise himself, had got rid of him
by sending him to some distant spot under the pretext that
he was ill. As for Father Philibin, Gorgias set him on a
pinnacle, called him his friend, a hero of dutifulness, one
who displayed passive obedience to his chiefs, who on their
side employed him for the dirtiest work, and struck him
down as soon as it was to their interest to close his mouth.
And this hero, who was now suffering untold agony in a
convent among the Apennines, was depicted by Gorgias as
a martyr of the faith, even as he had been depicted in
print, with a palm and a halo, by some of the ardent anti-
Simonists.

From this point Gorgias proceeded to glorify himself with
extrardinaory vehemence, wild and splendid impudence.
He became superb; he displayed such a mixture of frankness and falsehood, energy and duplicity, that, if the
fates had been propitious, this base rascal might assuredly
have become a great man. Even as his superiors were
still pleased to admit, he remained a model cleric, full of

admirable, exclusive, militant faith, one who assigned to the
Church the royalty both of heaven and of earth, and who
regarded himself as the Church's soldier, privileged to do
everything in her defence.   At the head of the Church was
the Deity, then came his superiors and himself, and when
he had given an account of his actions to his superiors and
the Deity, the only thing left for the rest of the world was
submission.   Moreover, his superiors were of no account
when he deemed them to be unworthy.   In that case he remained alone in the presence of heaven.   Thus, on days of
confession, when God had absolved him, he regarded himself as the unique, the one pure man, who owed no account
of his actions to anybody, and who was above all human
laws.   Was not this indeed the essential Catholic doctrine,
according to which the ministers of the faith are rightly
amenable to the divine authority alone?   And was it not
only a Father Crabot, full of social cowardice, who could
trouble himself about imbecile human justice, and the stupid
opinions of the multitude?

   In this second letter, moreover, Brother Gorgias admitted,
with a serene lack of shame, that he himself occasionally
sinned.   He then beat his breast, cried aloud that he was
but a wolf and a hog, and humbly cast himself in the dust
at the feet of God.   Having thus made atonement, he became tranquil and continued to serve the Church in all
holiness until the clay of creation cast him into sin again,
whereupon fresh absolution became necessary.   But in any
case he was at least a loyal Catholic, he had the courage to
confess, and the strength to endure penitence, whereas all
those dignitaries of the Church, those Superiors of the Religious Orders, of whom he complained so bitterly, were
liars and poltroons, who trembled before the consequences
of their transgressions—who, like base hypocrites, concealed
them or else cast them upon others in their terror of the
judgment of men.

   At the outset Brother Gorgias's passionate recriminations
had seemed to be prompted merely by his anger at being
so brutally abandoned after serving as a docile instrument;
but at present veiled threats began to mingle with his reproaches.   If he himself had always paid for his transgressions like a good Christian, there were others, he said, who
had not done so.   Yet some day assuredly they would be
forced to make atonement, should they continue to try the
patience of heaven, which would well know how to set up

an avenger, a justiciary to proclaim the unconfessed, unpunished crimes.   In saying this Gorgias was evidently
alluding to Father Crabot and the mysterious story of the
acquisition of the Countess de Quédeville's immense fortune
—that splendid domain of Valmarie, where the Jesuit College had been subsequently established.

Several confused versions of that story had been current,
and certain particulars were now recalled: The old but still
beautiful Countess becoming extremely pious, and engaging
Father Philibin, then a young man, as tutor to her grandson, Gaston, the last of the Quédevilles, who was barely
nine years old.   Next, Father Crabot arriving at the
château and becoming the confessor, the friend, and some
even said the lover, of the still beautiful Countess.   Finally,
the accident, the death of little Gaston, who had been
drowned while walking out with his tutor, his death allowing his grandmother to bequeath the family estate and fortune to Father Crabot, through the medium of a clerical
banker of Beaumont.   And it was also remembered that
among little Gaston's playmates there had been a gamekeeper's son, a lad named Georges Plumet, whom the
Jesuits of Valmarie subsequently protected and assisted,
and who was none other than the present Brother Gorgias.

The latter's violent language and threatening manner recalled all those half-forgotten incidents, and revived the
old suspicion that some dark deed might link the gamekeeper's humble son to the powerful clerics who ruled the
region.   Would that not explain the protection which they
had so long given him, the audacious manner in which they
had shielded him, and at last even made his cause their
own?   Doubtless their first impulse had been to save the
Church, but a little later they had done their utmost to
make that terrible Ignorantine appear innocent; and if they
had now sacrificed him, it must be because they deemed it
impossible to defend him any longer.   Perhaps, too, Brother
Gorgias only wished to alarm them in order to wring from
them as much money as possible.   That he did alarm them
was certain; one could detect that they were greatly disturbed by the letters and articles of that dreadful chatterer,
who was ever ready to beat his breast and cry his sinfulness
and that of others aloud.   Moreover, in spite of the seem-
ing abandonment in which he was left, one could divine
that he was still protected, powerfully even if secretly;
while his sudden intervals of silence, which lasted at times

for weeks, plainly indicated that friendly messages and money had been sent to him.

His admissions and his threats quite upset the rank and file of the clerical faction. It was horrible! He profaned the temple, he exposed the secrets of the tabernacle to the unhealthy curiosity of unbelievers! Nevertheless, a good many devout folk remained attached to him, impressed by the uncompromising faith with which he bowed to God alone, and refused to recognise any of the so-called rights of human society. Besides, why should one not accept his version of the affair, his admission that he had really initialled the copy-slip, that it had been carried away by Zéphirin, and utilised by Simon for a diabolical purpose? This version was less ridiculous than that of his superiors: it even supplied an excuse for what Father Philibin had done, for one could picture the latter losing his head, and tearing off the stamped corner of the slip, in a moment of blind zeal for the safety of his holy mother, the Church.

To tell the truth, however, a far greater number of laymen, those who were faithful to Father Crabot, as well as nearly all the priests and other clerics clung stubbornly to the Jesuits' revised version of the incident—that of Simon forging the paraph, and using a false stamp. It was an absurd idea, but the readers of *Le Petit Beaumontais* became all the more impassioned over it, for the invention of a false stamp added yet another glaring improbability to the affair. Every morning the newspaper repeated imperturbably that material proofs existed of the making of that false stamp, and that the recondemnation of Simon by the Rozan Assize Court could no longer be a matter of doubt for anybody.

The rallying word had been passed round, and all 'right-minded' people made a show of believing that the Brothers' school would triumph as soon as the impious adversaries of the unfortunate Brother Gorgias should be confounded. The school greatly needed such a victory, for, discredited as it was by the semi-confessions and unpleasant discoveries of recent times, it had just lost two more of its pupils. Only the final overthrow of Simon and his return to the galleys could restore its lustre. Until then it was fit that Brother Fulgence's successor should remain patiently in the background, while Father Théodose, the Superior of the Capuchins,—who also triumphed, even when others were being ruined,—skilfully exploited the situation by urging his devotees to make little periodical offerings, such for instance

as two francs a month, to St. Antony of Padua, in order
that the saint might exert his influence to keep the good
Brothers' school at Maillebois.

However, the most serious incident of the turmoil in the
town was supplied by Abbé Quandieu, who had long been
regarded as a prudent Simonist. At that time it had been
said that Monseigneur Bergerot, the Bishop, was behind
him, even as Father Crabot was behind the Capuchins and
the Brothers of the Christian Doctrine. As usual, indeed,
the Seculars and the Regulars confronted each other, the
priests resenting the efforts which were made by the monks
to divert all worship and revenue to their own profit. And
in this instance, as in fact in all others, the better cause
was that of the priests, whose conception of the religion of
Christ was more equitable and human than that of the
monks. Nevertheless, Monseigneur Bergerot had been defeated, and by his advice Abbé Quandieu had submitted
and had done penance by attending an idolatrous ceremony
at the Capuchin Chapel.

But all the disastrous disclosures and occurrences of recent times—first Father Philibin shown guilty of perjury
and forgery, then Brother Fulgence spirited away after
compromising himself, then, too, Brother Gorgias abscond-
ing and almost confessing his guilt—had stirred the parish
priest of Maillebois to rebellion, and revived his former belief in Simon's innocence. Nevertheless he would probably
have remained silent, in a spirit of discipline, if Abbé Cognasse, the priest of Jonville, had not gone out of his way to
allude to him in a sermon, saying that an apostate priest, a
hireling of the Jews, a traitor to his God and his country,
was unhappily at the head of a neighbouring parish. On
hearing this, Abbé Quandieu's Christian ardour asserted
itself; he could no longer control the grief he felt at seeing
'the dealers of the Temple,' as he called them, betraying
the Saviour who was all truth and justice. Thus, in his
sermon on the following Sunday, he spoke of certain baleful
men who were slaying the Church by their abominable complicity with the perpetrators of the vilest crimes. One may
picture the scandal, the agitation, that ensued in the clerical
world, particularly as it was asserted that Monseigneur Bergerot was again behind Abbé Quandieu, and was determined
this time that fanatical and malignant sectarians should not
be allowed to compromise religion any further.

At last, while passion was thus running riot, the new trial

began before the Rozan Assize Court.　It had been possible
to bring Simon back to France, though he was still ailing,
imperfectly cured as yet of the exhausting fevers which had
delayed his return for nearly a year.　During the voyage it
had been feared that he would not be put ashore alive.
Moreover, for fear of disorder, violence, and outrage, it
had been necessary to practise dissimulation with respect to
the spot where he would land, and bring him to Rozan at
night time by roundabout ways which none suspected.　At
present he was in prison near the Palace of Justice, having
only a street to cross in order to appear before his judges.
And pending that event he was closely watched and guarded,
defended also, like the important and disquieting personage
he had become, one with whose fate that of the whole nation
was bound up.

The first person privileged to see him was Rachel his
wife, whom that reunion, after so many frightful years, cast
into wild emotion.　Ah! what an embrace they exchanged!
And how great was the grief she displayed after that visit,
so thin, so weak had she found him, so aged, too, with his
white hair!　And he had showed himself so strange, ignorant as he still was of the facts, for the brief communication
by which the Court of Cassation had informed him of the
approaching revision of his case had given no particulars.
It had not surprised him to hear of the revision, he had
always felt that it would some day take place; and this conviction, in spite of all his tortures, had lent him the strength
to live in order that he might once more see his children
and give them back a spotless name.　But how dark was
the anguish in which he had remained plunged, his mind
ever dwelling on the frightful enigma of his condemnation,
which he could not unravel!　His brother David and Advocate Delbos, who hastened to the prison, ended by
acquainting him with the whole monstrous affair, the terrible war which had been waged for years respecting his case,
between those perpetual foes, the men of authoritarian views
who defended the rotten edifice of the past, and the men
of free thought who went towards the future.　Then only
did Simon understand the truth and come to regard his
personal sufferings as mere incidents, whose only importance
arose from the fact that they had led to a splendid uprising
in the name of justice, which would benefit all mankind.
Moreover, he did not willingly speak of his torments; he
had suffered less from his companions, the thieves and

murderers around him, than from his keepers, those ferocious brutes who were left free to act as they pleased, and
who, like disciples of the Marquis de Sade, took a voluptu-
ous delight in torturing and killing with impunity. Had it
not been for the strength of resistance which Simon owed
to racial heredity, and his cold logical temperament, he
would twenty times have provoked his custodians to shoot
him dead. And at present he talked of all those things in
a quiet way, and evinced a naïve astonishment on being
told of the extraordinary complications of the drama of
which he was the victim.

Having secured a citation as a witness, Marc obtained
leave of absence, and, a few days before the trial began, he
took up his abode at Rozan, where he found David and
Delbos already in the thick of the supreme battle. He was
surprised by the nervousness and anxious thoughtfulness
of David, who was usually so brave and calm. And it
seemed to him that Delbos, as a rule so gaily valiant, was
likewise uneasy. As a matter of fact it was for the latter a
very big affair, in which he risked both his position as an
advocate and his increasing popularity as a Socialist leader.
If he should win the case he would doubtless end by beating
Lemarrois at Beaumont; but unfortunately all sorts of disquieting symptoms were becoming manifest. Indeed Marc
himself, after reaching Rozan full of hope, soon began to
feel alarmed amid his new surroundings.

Elsewhere, even at Maillebois, the acquittal of Simon appeared certain to everybody possessed of any sense. Father
Crabot's clients, in their private converse, did not conceal
the fact that they felt their cause to be greatly endangered.
The best news also came from Paris, where the Ministers
regarded a just *dénouement* as certain, lulled into confidence
as they were by their agents' reports respecting the Court
and the jury. But the atmosphere was very different at
Rozan, where an odour of falsehood and treachery pervaded the streets, and found its way into the depths of
men's souls. This town, once the capital of a province,
and now greatly fallen from its former importance, had retained all its monarchical and religious faith, all the antiquated fanaticism of a past age, which elsewhere had
disappeared.[1] Thus it supplied an excellent battle-ground

---

[1] If proof were wanted to show that by Rozan M. Zola means Rennes,
the fanatical ex-capital of Brittany, it would be found in the passage
given above.— *Trans.*

for the Congregations, which absolutely needed a decisive
victory if they were to retain their teaching privileges and
control the future.   And never had Marc more fully
realised how deeply Rome was interested in winning that
battle; never had he more plainly detected that behind the
slightest incidents of that interminable and monstrous affair
there was papal Rome, clinging stubbornly to its dream of
universal domination—Rome which, at every step over the
paving-stones of Rozan, he found at work there, whispering,
striving, and conquering.

Delbos and David advised him to observe extreme prudence.   They themselves were guarded by detectives for
fear of some ambush; and he, on the very morrow of his
arrival, found shadowy forms hovering around him.   Was
he not Simon's successor, the secular schoolmaster, the
enemy of which the Church must rid itself if it desired to
triumph?   And the stealthy hatred by which Marc felt
himself to be encompassed, the menace of an evil blow in
some dark corner, sufficed to show him that the battle
had sunk to the very lowest level, and that his adversaries
were indeed those men of blind, bigoted violence, who
through the ages had tortured, burnt, and murdered their
fellow-beings in their mad dream of staying the march of
mankind!

That much established, Marc understood the terror
weighing on the town, the dismal aspect of its houses,
whose shutters remained closed, as if an epidemic were
raging.   As a rule, there is little animation in Rozan during
the summer, and at that moment the town seemed emptier
than ever.   Pedestrians hastened their steps, glancing
anxiously around them as they went their way in the broad
sunshine; shopkeepers stood at their windows, inspecting
the streets as if they feared some massacre.   The selection
of the jury particularly upset those trembling folk; there
was much melancholy jogging of heads when the names of
the chosen jurors were made public.   It was evidently considered a disaster to have one among one's relatives.

Churchgoers abounded among the petty *rentiers*, manufacturers, and tradespeople of that clerical centre, where
lack of religion was regarded as a shameful blot, and proved
extremely prejudicial to one's pecuniary interests.   Frantic
was the pressure exercised by mothers and wives, led by all
the priests, abbés, and monks of the six parish churches and
the thirty convents, whose bells were always ringing.   At

Beaumont, in former times, the Church had been obliged
to work with some discretion, for it had found itself in the
presence of both an old Voltairean *bourgeoisie* and of revolutionary *faubourgs*. But there was no need for it to beat
about the bush in that sleepy city of Rozan, whose traditions were entirely pious. The workmen's wives went to
Mass, the women of the middle class formed all sorts of religious associations; and thus a holy crusade began; none
refused to help in defeating Simon. A week before the
trial the whole town had become a battlefield; there was
not a house that did not witness some combat waged for the
good cause. The wretched jurors shut themselves up, no
longer daring to go out, for strangers accosted them in the
streets, terrified them with evil glances or passing words, in
which there lurked a threat to punish them in their pockets
or their persons if they did not behave as good Catholics,
and re-condemn the dirty Jew.

Marc was rendered yet more anxious by some information
he received respecting Counsellor Guybaraud, who was to
preside over the Assize Court, and Procureur Pacart, who
was to conduct the prosecution. The first had been a pupil
of the Valmarie Jesuits, to whom he owed his rapid promotion, and had married a very wealthy and very pious hunch-
backed girl, whom he had received from their hands. The
latter, an ex-demagogue, had been vaguely compromised in
some gambling affair, and, becoming a frantic anti-semite,
had rallied to the Church, from which he expected a post
in Paris. Marc felt particularly distrustful of Pacart on
observing how insidiously the anti-Simonists affected anxiety
respecting his attitude, as if indeed they feared some revival
of his revolutionary past. While they never ceased praising
the lofty conscientiousness of Guybaraud, they spoke of
Pacart with all sorts of reservations, in order, no doubt, to
enable him to play the heroic part of an honest man, overcome by the force of truth, on the day when he would have
to ask the jury for Simon's head. The very circumstance
that the clericals went about Rozan dolefully repeating that
Pacart was not on their side made Marc distrustful, for information from a good source had acquainted him with the
undoubted venality of this man, who was ready for the
vilest bargaining in his eager desire to regain a semblance of
honour in some high position.

However, the desperate and deadly battle became at Rozan
a subterranean one. The affair was not lightly prosecuted

in drawing-rooms among the smiles of ladies, as at Beaumont. Nor was there any question of a liberal prelate like Monseigneur Bergerot resisting the Congregations from a dread lest the Church should be submerged and swept away by the rising tide of base superstition. This time the contest was carried on in the darkness in which great social crimes take their course; all that appeared on the surface was some turbid ebullition, a kind of terror sweeping through the streets as through a city stricken with a pestilence. And Marc's anguish arose particularly from that circumstance. Instead of again witnessing the resounding clash of Simonists and anti-Simonists, as at Beaumont, he was confronted by the stealthy preparations for a dark crime, for which a Guybaraud and a Pacart were doubtless the necessary chosen instruments.

Every evening David and Delbos repaired to the large room which Marc had rented in a lonely street, and ardent friends of all classes surrounded them. These formed the little sacred phalanx; each visitor brought some news, contributed suggestions and courage. They were determined that they would not despair. Indeed, after an evening spent together they felt inspirited, ready for fresh encounters. And they were aware that their enemies met in a neighbouring street, at the house of a brother-in-law of Judge Gragnon, who, having been summoned as a witness by the defence, was staying there, receiving all the militant anti-Simonists of the town—a procession of frocks and gowns that slipped into the house as soon as night had fallen. Father Crabot had slept there twice, it was said, and had then returned to Valmarie, where with a great display of humility he had cloistered himself in penitence.

Suspicious characters prowled about that sparsely populated district; the streets were not safe; and, accordingly, when David and Delbos quitted Marc at night, their friends accompanied them home in a band. One night a shot was fired; but the detectives, though always on the watch, could find nobody to arrest. But the favourite weapon of the priests is venomous slander, moral murder, perpetrated in a cowardly fashion in the dark. And Delbos became the chosen victim. On the very day when the trial was to begin, the number of *Le Petit Beaumontais* which reached Rozan contained an abominable disclosure, full of mendacity, a shamefully travestied story, half a century old, about the advocate's father. The elder Delbos, though of peasant stock, had become a goldsmith, in a small way, in the neighbourhood of the Bishop's residence at Beaumont; and the newspaper charged him with having made away with certain sacred vessels which had been entrusted to him for repair. The truth was that the goldsmith, robbed by a woman whom he was unwilling to denounce, had found himself obliged to pay the value of the stolen goods. There had been no prosecution; the affair had remained obscure; but one had to read that filthy print to realise to what depths of malevolence and ignominy certain men could descend. That painful, forgotten, buried misfortune of the father's was cast in the face of the son with an abundance of spurious particulars, vile imaginings, set forth in language which was all outrage and mire. And the desecrator of the grave, the murderously-minded libeller who wrote those things, had plainly obtained the documents he published from the very hands of Father Crabot, to whom they had been communicated, no doubt, by some priestly archivist. It was hoped that this unexpected bludgeon-blow would strike Delbos full in the heart, assassinate him morally, discredit him as an advocate, annihilate him to such a point that he would have neither the strength to speak nor the authority to gain a hearing in the defence of Simon.

However, the trial began one Monday, a hot day in July. Apart from Gragnon, whom it was intended to confront with Jacquin, the foreman of the first jury, several witnesses had been cited for the defence. Mignot, Mlle. Rouzaire, Daix, Mauraisin, Salvan, Sébastien and Victor Milhomme, Polydor Souquet, the younger Bongards, Doloirs, and Savins were all on the list. Fathers Crabot and Philibin, Brothers Fulgence and Gorgias had also been cited, though it was known that the last three would not appear. On the other side the Procureur de la République had contented himself with recalling the witnesses for the prosecution who had given evidence at the first trial. And the streets of Rozan had at last become animated with witnesses, journalists, and inquisitive folk, arriving in fresh batches by each succeeding train. Already at six o'clock in the morning a crowd assembled near the Palace of Justice eager to catch a glimpse of Simon. But a considerable military force had been set on foot, the street was cleared, and Simon crossed it between two rows of soldiers, set so closely together that none of the onlookers could distinguish his features. It was then eight o'clock. That early hour had been chosen in order to

avoid the oppressive heat of the afterpart of the day when
one would have stifled in the court-room.

The scene was very different from that presented by the
brand new assize-hall of Beaumont, where a profusion of
gilding had glittered in the crude light that streamed in by
the lofty windows. At Rozan the assizes were held in an
ancient feudal castle; the hall was small and low, panelled
with old oak, and scarcely lighted by the windows of a few
deep bays. One might have thought the place to be one of
those dark chapels where the Inquisition pronounced sentence. Only a few ladies could possibly be admitted, and
all of them, moreover, wore sombre garb. Most of the
seats were occupied by the witnesses, and even the little
standing-room usually allowed to the public had to be curtailed. The audience, packed since seven o'clock in that
stern and mournful room, preserved a relative silence,
through which swept a stealthy quiver. If the eyes of the
onlookers remained ardent their gestures were restrained;
they had come there for a subterranean execution, a work
of suppression which had to be accomplished far from the
light, with the least noise possible.

As soon as Marc was seated beside David, who went in
with the witnesses, he experienced a feeling of anguish, a
stifling sensation, as if the walls were about to crumble and
bury them. He had seen all eyes turn in their direction.
David, particularly, aroused great curiosity. Then Marc
felt moved, for Delbos had just come in, looking pale but
resolute amid the evil glances of most of the spectators, who
were eager to ascertain if he had been upset by the infamous
article which had appeared that morning. However, the
advocate, as if arrayed in an armour of valour and contempt, remained for some time standing there, displaying
only smiling strength and indifference.

Marc then interested himself in the jurors, scrutinising
them as they entered, one by one, anxious as he was to
ascertain to what kind of men the great task of reparation
was confided. And he perceived the insignificant faces of
various petty tradespeople, petty *bourgeois*, with a chemist,
a veterinary surgeon, and two retired captains. On all
those faces one found an expression of mournful disquietude,
the signs of a desire to hide internal perturbation. The
worries which had assailed those men since their names had
become known had pursued them to that hall. Several
had the wan countenances of devotees, of shaven, canting

beadles, while others, red and corpulent, looked as if they had doubled their usual ration of brandy that morning in order to instil a little courage into their paunches. Behind them one could divine the entirety of that old priestly and military city with its convents and its barracks; and one shuddered to think that those men, whose minds and consciences had been deformed, stifled, by their surroundings, should be entrusted with such a work of justice.

But a buzzing spread through the hall, and all at once Marc experienced the most poignant thrill of emotion he had ever known. He had not seen Simon since his return, and now he suddenly perceived him, standing behind Delbos. And terrible was the apparition of that bent and emaciated little man, with ravaged features and bald cranium, on which only a few scanty white locks remained. What! that wreck, that puny remnant of a man was his old comrade, whom he had known so vivacious and refined! If Simon had never possessed any great physical gifts, if his voice had been weak, his gestures inelegant, at least a brazier of youth and faith had glowed within him. And the galleys had only given back that poor, broken, crushed being, a mere shred of humanity, in whom nought of the past subsisted save two flaming eyes, which alone proclaimed the invincible will and courage he preserved. One recognised him only by those eyes; and they, too, explained how he had been able for so many years to resist suffering, for their expression told of the world of fancy, of pure ideality, in which he had always lived. Every glance was turned upon him, but he did not seem conscious of it, such was the power he possessed of isolating himself. He gazed at the assembly in an absent-minded way until at last a smile of infinite tenderness came over his face as he perceived his brother David. Marc, who sat beside the latter, then felt him tremble in every limb.

It was a quarter past eight o'clock when the usher's call rang out, and the Court entered. The assembly arose and then sat down again. Marc, who remembered the violence of the spectators at Beaumont, who from growls had passed to vociferations, was astonished by the heavy quietude preserved by the present onlookers, though he divined that they were swayed by the same passions, and remained mutely eager for slaughter, as if they were lying in ambush in some sombre nook. The sight of the prisoner had scarcely wrung a low murmur from them; and now while the judges took

their seats, they relapsed into their attitude of dark expectancy. Again, compared with the rough and jovial
Gragnon, the new presiding judge, Guybaraud, surprised
one by his perfect courtesy, his unctuous gestures, his insinuating speech. He was a little man, whose manner was
all smiles and gentleness, but an odour of the sacristies
seemed to emanate from his person, and his grey eyes were
as cold and as cutting as steel. Nor was the difference
less remarkable between the former Procureur de la République, the brilliant Raoul de La Bissonnière, and Pacart,
the present one, who was very long, slender, and lean, with
a yellow, baked face, as if he were consumed by a desire to
efface his equivocal past and make a rapid fortune.

After the first formalities, when the jury had been em-
panelled, an usher called the names of the witnesses, who,
one by one, withdrew. Marc, like the others, had to leave
the hall. Then, in a leisurely way, President Guybaraud
began to interrogate Simon, putting his questions in a tone
of voice that suggested the coldness of a blade, handled
with deadly skill and precision. That interminable examination, which lingered over the slightest incidents of the
old affair, and insisted on the charge which the inquiry of
the Court of Cassation had destroyed, proved quite a surprise. Some clearing of the ground, an examination on the
questions set by the supreme jurisdiction, was all that had
been expected; but it at once became evident that the
Assize Court of Rozan did not intend to take any account
of the facts established by that jurisdiction, and that the
presiding judge meant to avail himself of his discretionary
powers to deal with the entire case from the very beginning.
Soon, indeed, by the questions which he asked, one understood that nothing of the old indictment had been relinquished. It was again alleged that Simon had returned
from Beaumont by rail, that he had reached Maillebois at
twenty minutes to eleven o'clock, and that soon afterwards
he had committed the crime. At this point, however, the
new version of the Jesuits—necessitated by the discovery at
Father Philibin's—was interpolated, and the prisoner was
accused of having procured a copy-slip, of having caused a
false stamp to be made, and of having forged on the slip the
initials of Brother Gorgias. Thus that childish story, which
Gorgias himself had deemed so idiotic that he had admitted
the authenticity of the slip and the paraph, was retained.
While nothing was abandoned of the original charges, a

gross invention was brought forward in support of them; and everything was again based on the famous report of the experts, Masters Badoche and Trabut, who clung to their original statements in spite of Brother Gorgias's formal admissions. And the Procureur de la République, as if to leave no doubt of his own views, intervened in order to extract precise statements from the prisoner with respect to his denials on the question of the false stamp.

Simon's demeanour during that long examination was regarded as pitiful. Many of his partisans had dreamt of him as a justiciar, armed with the thunderbolts of heaven, and rising like an avenger from the grave into which he had been thrust by iniquitous hands. And as he answered politely in a voice which still quivered feverishly, and with none of the outbursts that had been anticipated, the disappointment was extreme. His enemies once more began to say that he virtually confessed his crime, the ignominy of which they found stamped upon his unprepossessing countenance. Only at one moment did he become excited, display any passionate fervour. This was when the judge spoke to him of the false stamp of which he heard for the first time. It should be added that no proof was supplied respecting that stamp; the prosecution contented itself with relating that an unknown workman had confided to a woman that he had secretly done a curious job for the schoolmaster of Maillebois. Confronted, however, by the sudden violence of Simon, the judge did not insist on the point, particularly as Delbos had risen, prepared to raise an ' incident.' And the public prosecutor merely added that, though they had failed to find the unknown workman, he reserved to himself the right of insisting on the serious probability of the alleged occurrence.

In the evening, when David related what had occurred at that first sitting, Marc, who divined some fresh iniquity, felt a pang at the heart. Assuredly the greatest crime of all was now in preparation. He was not astonished by the calm and unobtrusive bearing of Simon, who was confident in the strength of his innocence, and incapable of an outward show of emotion.[1] But he perfectly understood the

[1] This was a marked characteristic of the unfortunate Captain Dreyfus, whose demeanour at the trial at Rennes produced such an unfavourable impression on sundry foolish English ' special correspondents,' that they veered round and began to regard the prisoner as guilty, quite irrespective of the evidence. As one who has witnessed many criminal trials,

bad effect which had been produced; while, from the aggressive coldness of the presiding judge, and the importance the latter gave to the most trivial matters, already elucidated, he derived a disastrous impression, a quasi-certainty that a fresh conviction was impending.   On hearing him, David, from whom he thought it wrong to hide his anxiety, could only with difficulty restrain his tears, for he also had quitted the Palace of Justice in despair, full of a dreadful presentiment.

However, the following days, which were entirely devoted to the hearing of evidence, brought back some courage and illusion.   The former witnesses for the prosecution were first examined, and one again beheld a procession of railway employés and *octroi* officials, who contradicted one another on the question whether Simon, on the night of the crime, had returned to Maillebois by train or on foot.   Marc, who wished to follow the case, had asked Delbos to have him called as soon as possible, and this being done he gave evidence respecting the discovery of poor little Zéphirin's body. He was then able to seat himself once more beside David, who still occupied a corner of the small space allotted to the witnesses.   And thus Marc was present at the first 'incident' raised by the counsel for the defence, who had retained all his bravery and self-possession in spite of the cruel blow which had lately struck him in the heart.

He rose to demand the attendance of Father Philibin and Brothers Fulgence and Gorgias, who, said he, had been duly cited.   But the presiding judge briefly explained that the citations had reached neither Father Philibin nor Brother Gorgias, both of whom, no doubt, were abroad, though their exact whereabouts was not known.   As for Brother Fulgence, he was seriously ill, and had sent a medical certificate to that effect.   Delbos insisted, however, with respect to Brother Fulgence, and ended by obtaining a promise that he should be visited by a sworn medical man. Then, also, the advocate was unwilling to content himself with a letter in which Father Crabot, while urging his occupations, his confessional duties, as an excuse for absence, declared that he knew nothing whatever of the affair; and, in spite of the acrimonious intervention of the Procureur

who has been a juror and the foreman of a jury, I feel that everything that has been written to my knowledge in English literature respecting the 'proper' demeanour of an innocent man is nonsense and nothing else.— *Trans.*

de la République, Delbos again carried his point—that the Court should insist on the attendance of the Rector of Valmarie. However, this first collision fomented anger, and from that moment conflicts continually arose between the judge and the advocate.

The day's sitting ended amidst an outburst of emotion, occasioned by the unexpected character of the evidence given by assistant-teacher Mignot. Mademoiselle Rouzaire, as bitter and as positive as ever, had just reaffirmed that, at about twenty minutes to eleven o'clock, she had heard the footsteps and the voice of Simon coming in and speaking with Zéphirin—which evidence had weighed so heavily on the prisoner at the previous trial—when Mignot, following her at the bar, retracted the whole of his former statements in a tone of wondrous frankness and emotion. He had heard nothing; he was now convinced of Simon's innocence, and adduced the weightiest reasons. Mademoiselle Rouzaire was then recalled, and there came a dramatic confrontation, in which the schoolmistress ended by losing ground, becoming embarrassed in her estimate of the hour, and finding nothing to answer when Mignot pointed out that it was impossible to hear from her room anything that took place in little Zéphirin's. Marc was recalled to confirm Mignot's demonstration, and at the bar he found himself for a moment beside Inspector Mauraisin, who, being asked for his opinion respecting the prisoner and the witnesses, endeavoured to get out of his difficulty by indulging in extravagant praise of Mademoiselle Rouzaire's merits, while saying nothing particular against Mignot or Marc, or even Simon, at a loss as he was to tell what turn the case might take.

The next two sittings of the Court proved even better for the defence. The question of hearing a part of the evidence *in camera*, which had impassioned people at the first trial, was not even put, for the presiding judge did not dare to raise it. It was in public that he interrogated Simon's former pupils, boys at the time of the crime but now grown men, for the most part married. Fernand Bongard, Auguste and Charles Doloir, Achille and Philippe Savin came in succession to relate the little they remembered, and their statements were favourable to the prisoner rather than the reverse. Thus ended the abominable legend built up by the help of the former proceedings *in camera*, the legend of horrible charges with which, it had been said, one could not possibly soil the ears of an audience composed partially of women.

However, the sensational evidence of the sitting was that given by Sébastien and Victor Milhomme. In accents of emotion Sébastien, now two and twenty years of age, explained the falsehood of his childhood, the alarm of his mother, the suppression of the truth, which he and she had expiated after prolonged torture. And he stated the facts such as they really were, how he had seen a copy-slip in the hands of his cousin Victor, how that slip had disappeared, how it had been found again, and given up when his mother, grief-stricken beside his bed of sickness, had deemed herself punished for her bad action. As for Victor, when his turn came to testify, in order to please his mother, who did not wish to compromise the stationery business any further, he feigned total forgetfulness, the obtuseness of a big fellow who had no memory. No doubt he must have brought the copy-slip from the Brothers' school, as it had been found, but he knew nothing, he could say nothing further.

Finally, another of the Brothers' former pupils, Polydor Souquet, now a servant in a Beaumont convent, appeared at the bar, and was questioned very pressingly by Delbos respecting the manner in which Brother Gorgias had escorted him home on the night of the crime, the incidents which had occurred on the road, the words that had been exchanged, and the hour. But all that Delbos could extract from Polydor were some evasive answers, and malicious glances promptly tempered by an affectation of stupidity. How could one remember after so many years? the witness asked. The excuse was too convenient, and the Procureur de la République began to show signs of anxious impatience, while the onlookers, though they failed to understand why the advocate insisted so much with an apparently insignificant witness, felt as it were a quiver of the truth passing through the atmosphere — the truth suspected, but once more taking flight.

People were stirred again at the next sitting of the Court, though it began with the interminable demonstrations of the experts, Masters Badoche and Trabut, who, disregarding even the admissions of Brother Gorgias himself, obstinately refused to recognise his initials, an F and a G, in the incriminated paraph, in which they alone recognised those of Simon, an E and an S interlaced, but, it was true, illegible. For more than three hours these men piled argument upon

argument, demonstration on demonstration, calmly persevering in their lunacy. And the marvel was that the presiding judge allowed them to go on, and listened to them
with manifest complacency, while the Procureur made a
show of taking notes, and asked the experts for precise information on certain points, as if the prosecution still
adopted their system. In presence of this *mise-en-scène*,
even reasonable people in the hall began to hesitate. And,
after all, why not? For in matters of handwriting one could
never tell.

But at the close of the sitting an incident, which did not
last ten minutes, upset everybody. Clad in black from
head to foot, ex-Investigating Magistrate Daix, who had
been cited by the defence, appeared at the bar. He was
scarcely fifty-six years old, but he looked seventy; thin and
bent, his hair quite white, his face so emaciated that little
of it, save the slender, blade-like nose, seemed to remain.
He had lately lost his wife, and people talked of the torturing life which that ugly, coquettish, ambitious woman had
led him in her despair that nothing ever raised them from
their narrow circumstances, not even the condemnation of
that Jew Simon, on which she had insisted and from which
she had hoped to derive so much. And now that his wife
was no longer beside him, Daix, timid and anxious, pains-
taking in his profession, an honest man at heart, had come
there to relieve his conscience, distracted as he was by the
deeds which had been wrung from his weakness, his craving
to have peace at home. He did not positively speak of all
those things, he did not even admit that after his investigations he had felt that the only possible decision was an order
to stay further proceedings. But he allowed Delbos to
question him, and when his present opinion was asked, he
replied plainly that the inquiry of the Court of Cassation
had destroyed his work, the original indictment, and that
for his own part he now regarded Simon as innocent. Then
he withdrew amidst the silent stupefaction of the onlookers.
The apparition of that man in mourning garb, the admissions
made by him in slow and sorrowful accents, had stirred
every heart.

That evening, in Marc's large room, where Simon's
friends met after every sitting of the Court in order to discuss matters, Delbos and David expressed keen satisfaction,
a conviction that success was almost certain now, so great,
apparently, was the impression which Daix's evidence had

produced on the jury. Nevertheless, Marc remained
anxious. He told the others of certain rumours which were
circulating concerning the stealthy doings of ex-President
Gragnon, who had been carrying on a subterranean campaign ever since his arrival at Rozan. Marc was aware
that, even as the friends of the defence met in his own
room, in like way mysterious meetings took place every
night at Gragnon's in an adjoining street. And there the
partisans of the prosecution certainly decided on the line
they would pursue on the morrow, invented the answers
which it would be best to give, planned the incidents which
they felt ought to be raised, in particular preparing the evidence in accordance with the result of the day's sitting.
For instance, whenever that sitting was regarded as unfavourable to the prosecution, one might be sure that there
would be some surprise detrimental to the prisoner, at the
outset of the sitting on the morrow. Moreover, Father
Crabot had been again seen slipping into Gragnon's house.
Several people also declared that they had seen young
Polydor Souquet leaving it. And others alleged that at a
very late hour they had met in the street a lady and a
gentleman who looked extremely like Mademoiselle Rouzaire and Inspector Mauraisin. But the worst was some
mysterious work, which centred round those jurors who
were notoriously on the side of the Church, and of which
Marc obtained an inkling, though his informant could not
give him full particulars. Gragnon did not commit such
a blunder as to ask those men to call at his house, nor
did he, indeed, address himself to them personally; but he
made others call on them, and show them, so it was said,
an irrefutable proof of Simon's guilt, a terrible document,
which the most serious reasons prevented him from making
public, though he was resolved to employ it, all the same,
should the defence drive him to extremities. And this information made Marc feel anxious, for he scented some
fresh abomination in it. Thus, on the evening of the day
when Daix had dealt the prosecution such a severe blow,
he predicted to his friends some deed of retaliation on the
enemy's part, some sample of the thunder which Gragnon,
according to his own account, had in his pocket.

The following sitting of the Court was, indeed, one of the
gravest and most exciting. Jacquin, the foreman of the
first jury, in his turn came forward to relieve his conscience.
In simple language he related how President Gragnon, on

being summoned by the jurors, who had wished to consult him respecting the penalty attaching to their verdict, had entered their room carrying a letter, and looking very much disturbed. And he had shown them that letter, which bore Simon's signature, followed by a postscriptum and a paraph, which last was identical with the one on the copy-slip tendered as evidence. Several jurymen, who had hesitated previously, then declared themselves convinced of the prisoner's guilt. He, Jacquin, had retained no further doubts; and for the peace of his conscience he had been well pleased at thus acquiring certainty. At that time he had not known that such a communication was illegal. It was only later that he had discovered such to be the case, and had experienced great distress of mind until, at last, the postscriptum and the paraph being recognised as forgeries, he had resolved, like a good Christian, to make amends for his involuntary error. A shudder of awe sped through those who heard him, when in his quiet way he added a last detail: He had heard the very voice of Jesus telling him to speak out, one evening when, tortured by remorse, he was kneeling in a dim chapel of St. Maxence.

Then Gragnon was summoned to the bar, and at first tried the effect of the rough frankness which he had so often assumed in his browbeating judicial days. He was still fat, though his fears had made him pale; and, striving to hide his prolonged anguish beneath the impudence of a *bon vivant*, he pretended that he no longer remembered petty details. And well—yes, he believed he had gone into the jurors' room carrying the letter which he had just received. He had been upset by it, and had shown it to the others in a moment of emotion, scarcely realising the nature of his action, and being only desirous of establishing the truth. He had never regretted that communication, so fully was he convinced of the authenticity of the postscript and the paraph. In his opinion the assertion that they were forgeries remained to be proved. Then, as he formally charged Jacquin with having read the letter aloud to the other jurors, and of having commented on it, the ex-foreman was recalled, and a sharp dispute ensued. At last Gragnon convicted the architect of some error or forgetfulness respecting the perusal of the letter; and thereupon he triumphed while the spectators began to hiss the honest witness, who from that moment was suspected of having sold himself to the Jews.

In vain did Delbos repeatedly intervene, striving to exasperate Gragnon and unmask him, by forcing him to an
explosion, the production of the famous document which it
was said would clench everything.   The ex-judge, who retained all his self-possession, and who was satisfied with
having escaped immediate danger by casting a doubt on his
adversary's veracity, relapsed into evasive answers.   It was
noticed, however, that one of the jurors caused a question
to be put to him—a question which nobody understood, but
which was whether he did not possess some knowledge of
another document bearing on the authenticity of the copy-
slip.   Gragnon answered enigmatically, that he abided by
his previous declarations, and was unwilling to enter into
other matters, however certain they might be.   And thus
that sitting of the Court, which, at the outset, had seemed
likely to ruin the prosecution, ended to its advantage.   In
Marc's room in the evening, Simon's friends again began to
despair.

The examination of the witnesses dragged on during a
few more sittings.   The doctor appointed to visit Brother
Fulgence had returned with a report that the Brother's condition was very serious, and that it was impossible to bring
him to Rozan.   In like manner Father Crabot avoided the
embarrassment of attendance by feigning a sudden accident
—a severe sprain.   In vain did Delbos make an application
for his evidence to be taken by commission.   President
Guybaraud, who at the outset had shown himself so phleg-
matic, now sabred everybody and everything in his eagerness to bring the case to an end.   He treated Simon
harshly, as if, indeed, he were already a condemned man;
being emboldened to this course by the singular calmness
of the prisoner, who still listened to the witnesses with
curiosity and stupefaction, as if the extraordinary adventures
of somebody else were being recounted to him.   Only on
two or three occasions did some extremely mendacious
testimony prompt him to a little rebellion; for the most
part he contented himself with smiling and shrugging his
shoulders.

At last Pacart, the Procureur de la République, addressed
the Court.   Tall and thin, he was addicted to long, nervous
gestures, and affected an unadorned, mathematically precise
kind of eloquence.   In presence of the plainly-worded judgment of the Court of Cassation, his task was not easy.   But
his tactics were very simple, he took no account of that

judgment, he did not once allude to the long inquiry which had ended in a decision to send the affair for trial by another Assize Court. He quietly reverted to the old indictment, based himself on the report of the experts, and accepted the revised account of the copy-slip, holding that the school-stamp as well as the initialling had been forged. He even spoke of that stamp in a positive way, as if he held a proof that it had been forged but could not produce it. As for Brother Gorgias, he regarded him simply as an unfortunate man, perhaps mentally unhinged, assuredly in need, and of a passionate nature—one who, after proving an undisciplined and compromising son of the Church, had quitted it and sold himself to the Jews. And Pacart concluded by asking the jurors to put an end to this affair, which was so disastrous for the peace of the country, by saying once more on which side the culprit really was, whether among the Anarchists and the Cosmopolites—who sought to destroy all belief in God and country—or among the men upholding faith, respect, and tradition, to whom, for ages past, France had owed her grandeur.

Then Delbos spoke during two sittings. Eager and nervous, endowed with passionate eloquence, he also dealt with the affair from the very beginning. But he did so in order to destroy the allegations in the old indictment, with the help of the arguments supplied by the Court of Cassation's inquiry. Not one of those allegations was worth anything. It was proved that Simon had returned home on foot on the night of the crime; that he had reached Maillebois at twenty minutes to twelve o'clock, an hour after the crime had been committed. Again, there was proof that the copy-slip had been stamped at the Brothers' school and initialled by Brother Gorgias, whose admissions on the subject were not even necessary, for counter experts, in a memorable report addressed to the Court of Cassation, had destroyed the extraordinary farrago of Masters Badoche and Trabut. Then Delbos turned to the new story of the forged stamp. No proof of this had been supplied. Nevertheless, he insisted on the subject; for he divined that some supreme abomination lurked beneath all that stealthy manœuvring compounded of mere allegation and reticence. A sick workman, it was said, had told a woman a vague story about a stamp which he had made for the Maillebois schoolmaster. Where was that woman? Who was she? What was her calling? As nobody would or could reply, he (Delbos) had a right to conclude that this story was one of those absurd lies such as *Le Petit Beaumontais* was in the habit of retailing. However, if he was able to picture the whole crime as it must have taken place—Brother Gorgias returning after he had escorted Polydor home, pausing before Zéphirin's open window, finally entering the room, and at last succumbing to his ungovernable passions—he admitted that there was a gap in his narrative. Where had Gorgias found the copy-slip? For the rascal was right when he jeeringly inquired if schoolmasters usually walked about in the evening with copy-slips in their pockets. Undoubtedly the number of *Le Petit Beaumontais* had been in the pocket of his own cassock, whence he had taken it in order to gag his victim. And the slip must have been there also. But how had that happened? Delbos suspected the truth, and if he had questioned Polydor Souquet so pressingly it was in order to extract it from him. He had failed in that endeavour, the witness having met him with an assumption of hypocritical stupidity. But, after all, what did that obscure point matter? Was not Gorgias's guilt absolutely manifest? His alleged alibi was based solely on a series of false statements. Everything proved his guilt—his flight, his semi-confessions, the criminal efforts made to save him, and the dispersal of his accomplices—Father Philibin hiding himself in some Italian convent; Brother Fulgence seeking refuge at a distance, and shielding himself with a diplomatic illness; and Father Crabot withdrawing to his cell, where Providence had visited him with a very salutary sprain. Was it not also in order to save Gorgias that President Gragnon had illegally communicated a forgery to the first jurors, as had been proved by the evidence of architect Jacquin? Amidst the accumulation of crimes, that one alone ought to have sufficed to open the eyes of the most prejudiced. And Delbos ended by depicting the frightful sufferings experienced by Simon, the fifteen years of transportation which he had endured amidst the most cruel physical and moral tortures, while ever stubbornly raising his cry of innocence. The advocate added that, like the Procureur de la République, he also desired to have the affair ended, but ended by an act of justice which would redound to the honour of France; for if the innocent man should be struck down again, the shame of France would be indescribable, and a future full of incalculable evils would lie before her.

There was no reply from the prosecution, the case was closed, and the jury at once withdrew to its retiring-room.[1] It was about eleven o'clock in the morning, and for more than an hour the spectators remained waiting, silent and anxious, in no wise resembling the audience at Beaumont, which had been so tumultuous and violent. The hall was very hot, and the atmosphere seemed as heavy as lead. There was little conversation, though occasionally the Simonists and the anti-Simonists glanced askance at one another. One might have fancied oneself in some funeral chamber where the life or death of a nation, the whole dolorous question of its future, was being decided. At last the jury reappeared, the judges came in, and amidst lugubrious silence the foreman arose. He was a little grey, lean man, a goldsmith, enjoying the custom of the local clergy. His shrill voice was distinctly heard. On the question of guilt the verdict was ' Yes,' by a majority; while ' extenuating circumstances ' were unanimously granted. At Beaumont the jury had been unanimous with respect to guilt, and only a small majority had favoured the admission of extenuating circumstances. And now, after expediting the formalities, President Guybaraud hastily pronounced a sentence of ten years' solitary confinement. That done, he withdrew, and Pacart, the Procureur de la République, followed him, after bowing to the jury as if to thank them.

Marc, meantime, had glanced at Simon, on whose face he only detected a kind of faint smile, a painful contraction of the lips. Delbos, beside himself, was clenching his fists. David, whose emotion was too intense, had not returned into Court, but was awaiting the decision outside. The thunderbolt had fallen, and Marc felt a deadly chill in every vein. It was a frigid horror: the supreme iniquity, in which just minds had refused to believe, the crime of crimes, which had seemed impossible a few hours earlier, which reason had rejected, had suddenly become a monstrous reality. And there were no ferocious cries of joy, there was no onslaught like that of cannibals rushing to a feast of blood, as at Beaumont. Though the hall was full of rabid anti-Simonists, the frightful silence continued, such was the horror which froze one and all to their very bones.

[1] At French criminal trials the judges no longer sum up the evidence before the verdict is given. That privilege was taken from them by a special law several years ago, in consequence of their scandalous abuse of it.—*Trans.*

Only a long shudder, a stifled groan, sped through the throng. And they went out without a word, without a push, in a dark stream like some funeral assembly choking with emotion, stricken with fear. And outside Marc found David sobbing.

So the Church was victorious—the Brothers' school would revive to life, while the secular school would again become the ante-room of hell, the satanic den where children were corrupted both in mind and body. The desperate and gigantic effort made by the Congregations and by almost all the clergy had again retarded their defeat, which was certain in the future. For years, however, one would again see the young generations stupefied by error, rotted by lies. The forward march of mankind would be hampered afresh until the day when free thought—invincible and still pursuing its course in spite of everything—should at last deliver the people by science, which alone could render it capable of truth and equity.

On the following evening, when Marc returned to Maillebois, exhausted by fatigue and quite heart-broken, he found a letter of three lines awaiting him: 'I have read the whole of the inquiry, I have followed the trial. The most monstrous of crimes has been committed. Simon is innocent. —*Geneviève.*'

IV

ON the morrow, a Thursday, Marc, who had scarcely slept that night, had just risen when he received an early visit from his daughter Louise. She, having heard of his return, had escaped for a moment from her grandmother's house. And, throwing her arms wildly about her father's neck, she exclaimed: 'Oh! father, father, what a deal of sorrow you must have had, and how pleased I am to be able to kiss you!'

A big girl nowadays, Louise was fully acquainted with the Simon affair, and shared all the faith, all the passion for justice displayed by that dearly-loved father, the master whose lofty mind was her guide. Thus her cry was instinct with the revolt and despair into which she had been cast by the monstrous proceedings at Rozan.

But, on thus seeing her before him and feeling her embrace, Marc thought of Geneviève's letter, to which his sleeplessness that night had been largely due. 'And your mother,' he asked, 'do you know that she has written to me, and that she is now on our side?'

'Yes, yes, father, I know it. She spoke of it to me. . . . Ah! if I were to tell you of all the quarrels there were when grandmother saw mamma beginning to read everything, procuring documents which had never been in the house before, and going out every morning to buy the full report of the new trial. Grandmother wanted to burn everything, so mamma shut herself up in her own room and spent all her time there. . . . And I also read everything; mamma allowed me to do so. Oh! papa, what a dreadful affair—that poor man, that poor innocent, overwhelmed by so many cruel people! If I could, I should love you all the more for having loved and defended him!'

She again threw her arms about her father's neck and kissed him with heartfelt fervour. And he, in spite of his sufferings, began to smile as if some delicious balm had somewhat calmed the smarting of his wounds. And while

he smiled he pictured his wife and his daughter reading
together, learning the truth, and at last returning to him.
' Her letter, her dear letter,' he said in an undertone, ' what
consolation and hope it gave me!   Will not joy return after
so many misfortunes ? '

Then he anxiously questioned Louise: ' So your mother
spoke to you of me ?   Does she understand, does she regret
our torments ?   I always felt that she would come back to
me when she knew the truth.'

But the girl prettily raised a finger to her lips.   She, in
her turn, was smiling.   ' Oh! papa,' she said, ' don't try to
make me say what I can't say yet.   I should be telling a
falsehood if I spoke positively.   Our affairs are in a good
way, that is all.   .   .   .   Remain patient a little longer,
remain confident in your daughter, who tries to be as
reasonable and affectionate as you are.'

Then she gave him some bad news about Madame Berthereau.   For several years the latter had been suffering
from a heart complaint, which recent events seemed to have
suddenly aggravated.   Madame Duparque's fits of anger,
the outbursts with which she made the dark, dismal little
house shake at all hours of the day, proved very prejudicial
to the sick woman, for they brought on shuddering and
stifling fits, which she could hardly overcome.   At present,
in order to escape those nervous frights, she no longer went
down into the little sitting-room, but remained on a couch
in her bed-chamber, gazing from morn till night at the deserted Place des Capucins, with those poor, melancholy eyes
of hers, in which one read such keen regret for the joys she
had lost so long ago.

' Oh! we don't amuse ourselves at all now,' Louise continued.   ' Mamma remains in her room, grandmamma Berthereau in hers, and grandmamma Duparque goes up and
down, bangs the doors, and quarrels with Pélagie when she
finds nobody to scold.   .   .   .   But I don't complain, for
I shut myself up as well, and work.   Mamma has agreed to
it, you know; I shall go up for admission to the training
school in six months' time, and I hope to get in.'

Just at that moment, Sébastien Milhomme, who was free
that day, arrived from Beaumont, all anxiety to embrace
his former master, of whose return he had heard.   And
almost immediately afterwards came Joseph and Sarah,
who, on behalf of their mother and the Lehmanns, whom
the reconviction of Simon had overwhelmed, wished to

thank Marc for his heroic if vain efforts. The brother and sister related what a thunderbolt had fallen on the wretched shop in the Rue du Trou on the previous evening, when David had telegraphed the frightful tidings. Madame Simon had preferred to await them there with her parents and her children, such great hostility had she encountered in that clerical town of Rozan, where, moreover, her modest means did not allow her to live. And the mournful house was again in tears, acquainted only with the iniquitous verdict and ignorant of what might now happen, all decision as to the future being postponed until the return of David, who, for the time, had remained near his brother.

The eyes of Joseph and Sarah were still red and swollen, for they had spent a tearful, feverish night without a moment's quiet rest; and as, while speaking of their father, they again began to sob, Sébastien, carried away by his feelings, kissed his good friend Sarah, while Louise, taking hold of Joseph's hands, and likewise shedding tears, naïvely sought to console him somewhat by speaking of her great affection for him. She was seventeen and he twenty. Sébastien was a year or two older, and Sarah was eighteen. Marc felt moved as he saw those young folk there before him, quivering with youth, intelligence, and kindliness. And a thought, which had occurred to him and brought him a delightful hope already in the days when he had seen them playing as children, now returned. Might they not, indeed, be predestined consorts, such as would produce the happy harvest of the future, who would bring broader hearts and more liberal minds to the great work of to-morrow?

But although his daughter's visit gave Marc no little comfort for the time, he became very downcast on the ensuing days, so distressful was the spectacle which his poor poisoned and dishonoured country now presented. The crime of crimes had been committed, and France did not rise against it! During the long struggle for revision Marc had already failed to recognise in her the generous, magnanimous, liberating, and justice-dealing country to which he had dedicated such lofty and passionate love. But never had he thought it possible that she would sink to that base level, and become a deaf, harsh, sleepy, and cowardly France, making her bed in shame and iniquity!

How many years and generations would be needed to arouse her from that abominable somnolence? For a moment Marc despaired; he deemed his country lost; it was as if he could hear Férou's maledictions arising from the grave: 'France doomed, completely rotted by the priests, poisoned by a filthy press, sunk in such a morass of ignorance and credulity that never would one be able to extricate her.' On the morrow of the monstrous verdict of Rozan he had still imagined an awakening to be possible, he had awaited a rising of upright consciences and healthy minds; but none had stirred, the bravest seemed to hide themselves away in their corners, and the supreme ignominy took its course, thanks to the universal imbecility and cowardice.

As he went about Maillebois, Marc caught sight of Darras, who now pulled a very long face, though he was simply in despair at the mayoralty again escaping him, owing to the triumph of the clerical party. Then, on meeting Fernand Bongard, the Doloirs and the Savins, his former pupils, Marc felt greatly distressed, for he now realised, decisively, that he had been able to impart to them little if any social equity and civic courage. Fernand shrugged his shoulders, bent on knowing nothing. The Doloirs had again begun to doubt Simon's innocence; while as for the twin Savins, if they remained convinced of it, they argued that they could not effect a revolution by themselves, and that, after all, one Jew more or less was a matter of no importance. Terror reigned, people hurried home, resolved to compromise themselves no further. Things were even worse at Beaumont, whither Marc repaired to see if he could not arouse some influential people and persuade them to attempt a last effort to have the infamous verdict set aside. Lemarrois, to whom he thus ventured to apply, seemed to take him for a madman; and discarding his usual courteous kindliness, he plainly, almost roughly, told him that the affair was ended, and that any attempt to revise it would be insane, for the country was utterly sick and weary of the whole business. It had become most hurtful as a basis for political action, and if the clerical reactionaries were allowed an opportunity to exploit it any further, the Republic would certainly be undone at the approaching elections. The elections indeed! That was again the great argument. The only policy was to bury the supreme iniquity in even deeper silence than after the first trial. There was no need of any understanding to that effect. The deputies, the senators, the prefect, the officials, all sank instinctively into perfect silence, in the dread they felt at the thought of the twice

condemned but innocent man. And once again former
Republicans and Voltaireans like Lemarrois drew yet nearer
to the Church, whose help they thought they might require
to resist the rising tide of Socialism. Lemarrois, personally,
had been pleased to see his adversary Delbos defeated at
Rozan, and in resorting to a cowardly policy of silence he
was largely influenced by a desire to let Simon's compromised champions drown themselves. Amid that general
débâcle only Marcilly retained his amiable smile. He had
already held the portfolio of Public Instruction in a Radical
ministry, and felt certain of securing it again, some day, in
a Moderate one. And so convinced was he now of the
irresistible power of his suppleness and his freely-bestowed
hand-shakes that, alone amongst those to whom Marc applied, he gave him a cordial greeting; and, without making
any express promise, allowed him to hope for everything
should he (Marcilly) return to power.

For the moment the Congregations became triumphant.
What a relief it was to think that Father Crabot, his accomplices and his creatures, were saved! Ex-presiding Judge
Gragnon gave a grand dinner, followed by a reception, to
which flocked all the members of the judicial world, with
many functionaries and even university men. They smiled
and shook hands, well pleased at finding themselves alive
after incurring such serious danger. Every morning *Le
Petit Beaumontais* celebrated the victory of the valiant
soldiers of God and the country. Then, all at once, it became silent, in compliance no doubt with some hint received
from exalted spheres. The fact was that amid all the stir
of victory everybody began to detect moral defeat. Fear of
the morrow revived, and it was deemed prudent to divert
people's minds.

Moreover, the Rozan jurors had now made revelations; it
was known that they had convicted Simon merely by a majority of seven to five, and that on quitting the court they
had unanimously signed a recommendation for pardon.
They could not have confessed more plainly the mortal embarrassment in which they had been placed, the cruel necessity of confirming the former verdict of Beaumont, even
though they retained little doubt of the prisoner's innocence. And the extraordinary course taken by that jury,
which, in the most contradictory way, at one moment condemned Simon and at another absolved him, tended to
make his innocence manifest to everybody. A pardon was

felt to be so necessary and so inevitable that nobody was surprised when one was signed a few days later. *Le Petit Beaumontais* thought fit to insult the dirty Jew a last time, but even the managers of that unprincipled rag heaved a sigh of relief, glad to be at last delivered from the abominable part they had played for so many years.

David was beset by a final anguish, a frightful struggle of conscience, in connection with that pardon. His brother's strength was quite spent, fever consumed him, he was so exhausted, both physically and morally, that, doubtless, he would merely return to prison to die there. And, on the other hand, a weeping wife and children awaited him, still hoping that they might save him by dint of care and love. Nevertheless, David at first rejected the idea of a pardon, and, before everything else, wished to consult Marc, Delbos, and the other valiant defenders of the innocent prisoner; for he well understood that, even if the pardon would not deprive Simon of the right of some day establishing his innocence, it would rob the others of their most powerful means of prosecuting that cause of justice to which they had given their lives. But, however grieved they might be, all bowed to the suggestion of a pardon, and David then accepted it. At the same time it was felt by Marc and Delbos that the Congregations had good reason to be triumphant, for, humanly, the Simon affair was ended by that pardon, in consequence of which it would no longer stir the multitude to a sense of equity and generosity.

The question of Simon's future was speedily settled. It was impossible to take him back to Maillebois, where Madame Simon had decided to remain a little longer with her children, Joseph and Sarah, who were awaiting the reopening of the neighbouring training schools. David once more took everything on himself. He had long previously formed his plans, which were to dispose of his sand and gravel pits, and acquire a marble quarry in a lonely valley of the Pyrenees—an excellent affair, which a friend had recommended to him and which he had carefully studied. He meant to remove Simon thither, taking him as a partner, and assuredly the mountain air and the delight of active life would restore his health within six months' time. As soon as the installation should be effected Madame Simon might rejoin her husband, and even the children might end the vacation in their father's company. All this was carried into effect with remarkable precision and despatch. Simon was conjured away from Rozan, which was still in an agitated state, and for a time nobody even suspected that he had been removed. He travelled unrecognised, vanishing with David into that lonely valley, embosomed amid lofty peaks. It only became known by a newspaper article that his family had joined him. From that moment he altogether disappeared, and people even began to forget his existence.

On the very day when the Simon family found itself reunited in that Pyrenean solitude, Marc repaired to the Training College of Beaumont, whither an urgent letter from Salvan had summoned him. And as soon as they had shaken hands they began to talk of the Simons, evoking the sweet and touching scene which was being enacted far away—indeed at the other end of France.

'We must all take it as our reward,' said Salvan. 'If we have not yet managed to make the affair yield the great social lesson and the penalties that attach to it, we have at least brought this happiness to pass, we have restored the poor martyr to his wife and his children.'

'Yes,' said Marc, 'I have been thinking of it ever since this morning. I can picture them all together, smiling, in peace, under the broad blue sky. And, for that poor man so long fastened to his chain, what a delight it must be to be able to walk about freely, inhaling the freshness of the mountain springs, the pure odours of the plants and trees! The dear children, too, and the dear wife, how happy they must feel to see their dream realised, to have him beside them again, to take him about like a big child just recovering from a severe illness, and watch him reviving to health and strength! . . . You are right, it is our reward—the only one.'

He paused, then added in a lower voice with some of the bitterness of a combatant who laments that his weapon should have been broken in his hand: 'Our *rôle* is quite over. A pardon was inevitable, no doubt, but it has deprived us of all power of action. We can only wait for the crop of good grain we have sown—that is, if ever it will sprout up in the hard ground where we have scattered it.'

'Oh! it will rise, never fear, my friend,' Salvan exclaimed. 'We must never despair of our poor, great country. It may be deceived, it may deceive itself, but it always returns to truth and reason. Let us rest satisfied with our work, it will bear fruit in the future.' Then, after a pause, he continued in a thoughtful way: 'But I agree with you that our victory will not be immediate. The times are really execrable; never have we passed through a more troublous and threatening period. And, indeed, if I asked you to call to-day, it was in order to talk to you of the present disquieting situation.'

Then he acquainted Marc with what he had learnt. Since the trial at Rozan, all the recognised Simonists, all the brave men who had become compromised in the affair, had found themselves exposed to the vengeance of the Congregations, the hatred of the egotistical and cowardly multitude. Undoubtedly they would be made to pay heavily in their interests and their persons for the crime they had committed by supporting the cause of truth and justice.

'Have you heard that nobody now bows to Delbos at the Palace of Justice?' said Salvan. 'Half the cases confided to him have been withdrawn. Clients regard him as being altogether too compromising. He has to begin his career afresh; and at the next elections he will certainly be defeated again, for the affair has led to disruption even in the Socialist ranks. . . . For my own part, I shall probably be dismissed——'

'Dismissed? You!' interrupted Marc in accents of surprise and grief.

'Why, yes, my friend. You are not ignorant of the fact that Mauraisin has long coveted my post. He never manœuvred otherwise than in order to dislodge me. His prolonged flirtation with the Church party has been simply a matter of tactics in order to secure its support in the hour of victory. After the inquiry of the Court of Cassation he certainly felt frightened, and began to say that he had always regarded Simon as innocent. But, since Simon was reconvicted, Mauraisin has again been barking with the clerical pack, feeling convinced that Le Barazer will be compelled to dismiss me by the pressure brought to bear on him by all the victorious reactionary forces. It will astonish me very much if I am still here when the new term begins in October.'

Marc again began to express his grief; and, moreover, he refused to believe Salvan. He recalled all the services which the latter had rendered, and set forth the necessity of persevering with the great work of saving France from falsehood and credulity. 'You cannot leave before your task is accomplished,' he added; 'there remains so much for you to do.   Although Le Barazer has never spoken out plainly, he has been at heart on our side, and I am sure that he will never be guilty of such a bad action as to dismiss you.'

Salvan smiled somewhat sadly.   'In the first place,' he answered, 'nobody is indispensable; I may disappear, but others will rise to continue the good work we have begun. Mauraisin may take my place, but I am convinced that he will do no great harm, for he will not retain it long, and he will be forced to follow in my footsteps.   Some work, you see, when once it has been begun, is accomplished by the very force of human evolution, and remains independent of any particular, individual men.   .   .   .   But one might think by the way you talk that you did not know Le Barazer.   We are, personally, of little account in his intricate republican diplomacy.   He was on our side, that is certain; he would be with us still if we had won the battle.   But our defeat has placed him into the greatest possible embarrassment.   He really has but one desire, to save his work, the system of secular and compulsory education of which he was one of the creators.   Thus, as the Church has regained power for the moment and threatens his work, he will resign himself to necessary sacrifices and temporise until he is able to speak as a master in his turn.   Such is his nature, and we cannot alter him.'

Salvan continued in this strain, enumerating all the influences which were being brought to bear on Le Barazer. Rector Forbes, who was so desirous of quietude and who so greatly feared worries with the minister, had plainly told him that he must satisfy the demands of the opposition deputies.   These, at the head of whom Count Hector de Sanglebœuf distinguished himself by his violence, were making every effort to secure the dismissal of all the notorious Simonists belonging to the civil and the educational services.   And none of the Republican deputies, not even the radical Lemarrois, moved; indeed, they consented to that hecatomb in order to pacify public opinion, anxious as they were to lose as few electors as possible.   At present, also, professors and masters followed the example of Principal Depinvilliers, attending Mass with their wives and daughters every Sunday.   Then, at the Lycée of Beaumont, the chaplain reigned supreme; religious exercises were becoming compulsory; all pupils who refused attendance were badly noted, harassed and ill-treated until no resource was left them but to comply or quit. Father Crabot made his hand felt at that Lycée with the same reactionary authority that he displayed in the management of the College of Valmarie. And the increasing audacity of the Congregations was demonstrated by the fact that the Jesuit professors of Valmarie now openly acknowledged their standing, whereas previously, in order to defeat the laws, they had outwardly passed themselves off as secular priests.

' That is how we stand,' Salvan concluded. ' Thanks to the reconviction of Simon, they speak as masters, and wring whatever they please from the universal cowardice and imbecility. . . . It is already said that Mademoiselle Rouzaire is to be appointed head-mistress of the chief girls' school in Beaumont. Jauffre, now at Jonville, is also to be appointed here, it seems; for he has threatened to turn against Abbé Cognasse if there should be any further delay in rewarding his services. Finally, Doutrequin, once a Republican, who has rallied to the Church from a deplorable aberration of patriotism, has secured two suburban schools for his sons, who have made Nationalism and Anti-Semitism their chief dogmas, so that we are now once more in a period of acute reaction—the last we shall witness, I hope, pending the day when the country will spit out the poison which is killing it. . . . And if I am dismissed, my friend—you suspect it, do you not?—you will be dismissed also.'

Marc smiled. He now understood why Salvan had sent for him in all haste. ' So I am condemned ? ' he said.

' Yes, I am afraid so; and I wished to warn you of it immediately. . . . Oh! the thing is not settled yet; Le Barazer remains silent, biding his time, as it were, and saying nothing of his intentions. But you can have no idea of the assaults he has to withstand, particularly with respect to yourself. Naturally enough, it is your dismissal that is most urgently demanded. I was talking to you just now of that big simpleton Sanglebœuf, that puppet whose strings are pulled by the old Marchioness de Boise, whom he drives to despair, I hear, so clumsily does he execute the movements which she directs. Well, three times already Sanglebœuf has bounced up to the Prefecture to threaten Le Barazer with an interpellation in the Chamber of Deputies if he does not come to an understanding with Prefect Hennebise to annihilate you. You would be already

dead, I think, if it had not been for the arrogance of that
ultimatum. But it is n't possible for Le Barazer to resist
much longer, my poor friend. And you must n't bear him
any malice. Remember all the quiet obstinacy and diplomatic skill with which for many years he supported you.
He always found some means of saving you by granting
compensations to your adversaries. But now it is all over,
I have not even spoken to him about you. All efforts on
your behalf would be useless. You must let him act as he
pleases. Doubtless he is only delaying his decision in order
to devise something ingenious; for he himself does not like
to be defeated, and he will never relinquish his efforts on
behalf of his work, that system of secular and compulsory
education which alone can give us a new France.'

Marc smiled no longer; indeed, he had become very sad.
' It will be a great blow,' he answered. ' I shall leave the
best of myself behind me in that school of Maillebois,
among those dear lads whom I regard almost as my own
children. . . . Besides, what shall I do if my career is
thus brought to an end? I am not competent to take up
any other useful work, and how painful it will be to see the
work I have been doing interrupted, left unfinished at the
very moment when, more than ever, truth has need of sturdy
workers.'

But Salvan in his turn bravely smiled, and, taking hold
of Marc's hands, said to him: ' Come, don't lose your courage. We shall surely find something to do; we sha'n't
remain with our arms crossed.'

Then Marc, feeling comforted, replied: ' You are right!
When a man like you is struck, one can follow him into disgrace without thought of shame. The future, at all events,
belongs to us.'

A few more days went by. At Maillebois the victorious
Congregations were endeavouring to turn the situation to
pecuniary account. Great efforts were made to restore the
former prosperity of the Brothers' school, several families
were won over, and it seemed likely that at the new term
the school would gain a dozen fresh pupils. Meantime
the Capuchins showed extraordinary audacity. Was it
not, after all, the glorious St. Antony of Padua who had
managed everything, obtained everything from the benevo-
lence of heaven? Indeed, it could not be denied. It was
to him that one owed the reconviction of Simon, thanks to
the franc and two-franc pieces which so many pious souls

had dropped into the saint's collection-boxes while asking
him to bring about the annihilation of the Jew.   Thus a
fresh miracle had been performed.   Never before had the
saint's power been manifested in so lofty a manner, and as
a natural result offerings poured in from all sides.   Moreover, Father Théodose, encouraged, inspired by this success, conceived a masterly plan to reap another large harvest
of money by the saint's aid.   He launched an extraordinary
financial affair with mortgage bonds on Paradise, each bond
being of five francs' value.   The district was flooded with
circulars and prospectuses explaining the ingenious working
of these investments in celestial felicity.   Each bond comprised ten coupons of half a franc, representing good works,
prayers, and masses payable as interest here below, and re-
deemable in heaven at the cashier's office of the miracle-
working St. Antony.   Premiums were also offered in order
to attract subscribers.   Twenty bonds gave one a right to a
coloured statuette of the saint, and a hundred ensured one
an annual Mass.   Finally, the prospectus explained that
the name of St. Antony's Bonds was given to this scrip,
because it was the saint who would redeem it a hundred-
fold in the next world.   And the announcement ended
with these words: 'Such supernatural guarantees make
these bonds absolutely safe.   No financial catastrophe can
threaten them.   Even the destruction of the world, at the
end of time, would leave them in force, or rather would at
once place the holders in the enjoyment of the full capital-
ised interest.'[1]

The success was enormous.   In a few weeks' time thousands of bonds had been sold.   Those devotees who were
too poor to buy a whole one clubbed together, and then
divided the coupons.   Credulous and suffering souls eagerly
risked their money in this new lottery, whose great prize
was to be the realisation of a fondly dreamt-of eternity of
happy life.   It was certainly rumoured that Monseigneur
Bergerot intended to prohibit this impudent speculation
which scandalised the more reasonable Catholics; but in
the unpleasant position in which the prelate had been
placed by the defeat of the Simonists, whom he was accused
of having stealthily supported, he was doubtless afraid to
do so.   Though it greatly distressed him to abandon the

---

[1] As some readers might think this an invention on M. Zola's part, it
is as well to mention that the prospectus referred to was actually issued
by a French religious community.— *Trans.*

Church to the rising tide of superstition, he had found that
he could place little reliance on his clergy, and thus he had
never had the courage to resist the all-powerful Congregations. Aged as he now was, he had become weaker still,
only retaining enough strength to kneel and beg God's forgiveness for thus suffering the merchants to invade the
temple. But Abbé Quandieu, the priest of St. Martin's,
could not bear that desecration any longer. All his Christian resignation forsook him when the so-called Bonds of
St. Antony made their appearance. Such trafficking was
too outrageous, and he gave expression in the pulpit to his
revolt as a minister of Christ, his grief at beholding the
base downfall of that great Christianity which had renewed
the world, and which so many illustrious minds had raised
to the purest summits of ideality. Then he paid a last visit
to his Bishop and friend, Monseigneur Bergerot, and finding him unable to continue the struggle, feeling too that he
himself was vanquished and paralysed, he resigned his cure
and withdrew to a little house in the outskirts of Maillebois,
intending to dwell there on a scanty income, outside that
Church whose policy of hatred and whose basely superstitious worship he could no longer serve.

The Capuchins deemed the opportunity favourable for a
fresh triumph in celebration of what Father Théodose styled
the flight of their former adversary. By careful manœuvring the Bishop had been induced to appoint a young curate
of the *arriviste* school, a creature of Father Crabot's, to the
parish of Maillebois, and the idea was to bear a superb
statue of St. Antony, all red and gold, in solemn procession from the Capuchin Chapel to St. Martin's, where it
would be set up in great pomp. This would be the crown-
ing consecration of the victory which had been achieved,
the conquest of the parish by the Congregation, the monks
becoming its sovereign masters, able to disseminate on
every side the idolatrous worship, by which they hoped to
bleed and abase the community, and turn it into the ignorant flock of the days of servitude. The procession, which
took place one warm day in September, with the co-opera-
tion of all the clergy of the district, proved magnificent, and
was attended by a great concourse of people who repaired
to Maillebois from all points of the department. Only the
Place des Capucins and a short lane really separated the
chapel from the church, but a roundabout line of route
was selected; they crossed the Place de la République and

marched along the whole high street, in this wise promenading St. Antony from one to the other end of the town. Mayor Philis, surrounded by the clerical majority of the Municipal Council, followed the painted statue, which was borne on a platform draped with red velvet. Although it was holiday time, the whole of the Brothers' school had been mobilised, boys had been specially recruited, dressed, and provided with candles. Behind them came the Daughters of Mary and numerous pious brotherhoods, sisterhoods, and other associations, an interminable string of devotees, to say nothing of all the nuns brought expressly from the Beaumont convents. Only Monseigneur Bergerot was wanting. As it happened he had sent a letter of regret, having fallen ill two days previously.

Never before had Maillebois been possessed by such religious fever. People knelt on the foot pavements, men shed tears, three girls fell to the ground in hysterical fits, and had to be carried to a chemist's shop. In the evening the benediction at St. Martin's amid the pealing of the bells was quite dazzling. And not a doubt remained; surely the town was now redeemed and forgiven; by that grandiose ceremony Providence signified its willingness to wipe out for ever the vile memory of Simon the Jew.

It so happened that Salvan came to Maillebois that day in order to see Madame Berthereau, respecting whom he had received some extremely disquieting news. And he had just quitted the little house in the Place des Capucins when he caught sight of Marc, who, on his way home after a visit to the Lehmanns, had found his progress barred by the interminable procession. They shook hands in silence; then for some time were compelled to remain waiting. When the last of the monks had gone by behind the idol all ablaze with gilding and red paint, they just exchanged a glance and took a few steps in silence.

'I was going to call on you,' said Salvan at last.

Marc fancied that he had brought him news of his dismissal. 'Is it signed then?' he inquired. 'Am I to pack my trunks?'

'No, no, my friend; Le Barazer has given no signs of life as yet. He is preparing something. . . . But our dismissal is certain, you must take a little patience.' Then, ceasing to jest, he added with an expression of grief: 'The fact is, I heard that Madame Berthereau was at the last stage and I desired to see her. . . . I have just left her, and her end is certainly very near.'

'Louise came to warn me of it yesterday evening,' Marc replied. 'I should have liked to call at once, as you have done. But Madame Duparque has signified that she will immediately quit the house if I should dare to set foot in it on any pretext. And though Madame Berthereau, as I know, would like to see me, she is afraid to give expression to her desire, for fear of some scandal beside her death-bed. . . . Ah! my friend, one can never overcome the hatred of a bigot.'

They walked on, again preserving silence. At last Salvan resumed: 'Yes, Madame Duparque keeps good guard, and for a moment I thought that she would not let me go up-stairs. At all events she did not quit me; she kept a watch on everything I said, either to the patient or your wife. . . . She is certainly afraid that something may result from the blow which is about to fall on the house. Yes, Madame Berthereau, her daughter, is about to escape from her by death, and she fears, perhaps, that Geneviève, her granddaughter, may also free herself.'

Marc halted, and, giving his friend a keen glance, inquired: 'Did you notice any sign of that?'

'Well, yes; but I did not wish to mention it to you, for it would distress me to give you any false hope. . . . But it was in connection with that procession, that bare-faced idolatry which we witnessed just now. It appears that your wife absolutely refused to attend it. And that is why I found Madame Duparque at home. She, of course, was very desirous of displaying her piety in the front rank of all the devotees, but she feared that if she should absent herself for a single moment, you or some other soul-snatcher might get into the house and rob her of her daughter and granddaughter. So she remained at home, and you can imagine with what cold fury she received me, trying to transpierce me with those eyes of hers, which are like rapiers.'

Marc was becoming excited: 'Ah! so Geneviève refused to attend that procession! She understood its hurtfulness, its baseness and folly, then; and she is returning in some degree to the healthy commonsense she used to show?'

'No doubt,' Salvan answered. 'I believe that she felt particularly hurt by those ridiculous mortgage bonds on Paradise. . . . Ah! what a master-stroke, my friend!

Never before was human imbecility exploited to such a
degree by religious impudence.'

While conversing the friends had slowly directed their
steps towards the railway station, where Salvan intended to
take the train in order to return to Beaumont.   He did so,
and Marc, on quitting him, felt once again full of hope.

As Salvan had indeed suggested, Geneviève—in that little
house of the Place des Capucins, which had become yet
more mournful and frigid now that death hovered over it so
threateningly — was assailed by another crisis which was
gradually transforming her.   At first she had been thunderstruck by the revelation of the truth, the certainty of Simon's
innocence, which the perusal of all the documents had
brought her—that terrible light whose blaze had revealed to
her the infamy of the holy men whom she had hitherto accepted as the directors of her conscience and her heart.
All came from that, doubt penetrated into her mind, faith
took flight, she could not do otherwise than reflect, examine
and judge everything.   A feeling of disquietude had already
come upon her at the time when she quitted Father Théodose; and the latter's Bonds of St. Antony, that base
attempt to exploit the credulity of the public, had suddenly
shown her his venality and disgusted her with him.   Moreover, not only did the monk's character decline in her estimation to the lowest level, but the worship he represented
—that religion which had cast her into transports of mystical
desire likewise lost its semblance of holiness.   What! must
she accept that unworthy trafficking, that idolatrous superstition, if she desired to remain a practising Catholic, stead-
fast in her faith?   She had long bowed to beliefs and
mysteries, even when her natural good sense had covertly
protested against them; but there were limits to everything.
She could not countenance that flotation of shares in heaven;
she refused to walk behind that St. Antony, bedaubed
with red and gold and carried about like a guy or an adver-
tisement, to increase the multitude of subscribers.   And the
revolt of her reason gathered additional strength when she
thought of the retirement of Abbé Quandieu, the gentle
and paternal confessor, to whom she had returned when the
suspicious ardour of Father Théodose had alarmed her.   If
such a man as the Abbé felt unable to abide in the Church,
such as it had been made by the clerical policy of hatred
and domination, was it not certain that all upright souls
would henceforth find it difficult to remain in it?

Doubtless, however, Geneviève's evolution would not have been so rapid if certain preparatory work had not been already effected in her, slowly and without her knowledge. In order that one might fully understand those first causes, it was necessary to recall the whole of her story. Inheriting much of her father's nature—tender, gay, and amorous—she had fallen in love with Marc, carried away by such ardent passion that, in order to have that modest schoolmaster as her husband, she was willing to dwell with him almost in poverty, in the depths of a lonely village. Weary, too, in her eighteenth year, of the mournful life she had led beside Madame Duparque, the idea of liberty had attracted her; and for a moment it had seemed as if she had cast aside all her pious training, for with her husband she had displayed such youthful enchantment that he had been able to think she was wholly his. Moreover, if any fears lurked within him, he had dismissed them, setting himself to worship her, imagining he would be powerful enough to recast her in his own image, and so carried away by the happiness of the hour that he deferred that moral conquest till some other time.

But her past had revived, and again he had shown weakness, delaying action under the pretext of respecting the freedom of her conscience, and allowing her to return to religious observances. All her childhood then came back, the mystical poison which had not been eliminated from her system asserted itself, and the crisis which fatally assails the souls of women nourished on errors and falsehoods arrived, her case being aggravated by her frequentation of that bigoted and domineering woman, her grandmother. Then a whole series of incidents—the Simon case, the postponement of Louise's first Communion—had precipitated the rupture between husband and wife. In Geneviève there glowed a desire for the *au-delà* of passion, a hope of finding in heaven the divine and boundless bliss promised to her formerly in her girlish days; and her love for Marc had simply become dimmed amid her dream of the ecstasies which the canticles celebrate, an ever loftier and ever deceptive delight. But in vain had others excited her, lied to her, set her against her husband, by promising to raise her to the highest truth, the most perfect felicity. The failure, the defeat she ever encountered, sprang from her abandonment of the only natural and possible human happiness; for never since that time had she been able to content her

longings.   She had lived, indeed, amid increasing distress
without either repose or joy, however stubbornly she might
declare that she had found felicity in her deceptive and
empty chimeras.

Even now she did not confess in what a void she had
ever remained after her long prayers on the old flagstones
of chapels, her useless Communions, when she had vainly
hoped to feel the flesh and blood of Jesus mingling with
her own in a union of eternal rapture.   But good Mother
Nature each day was winning her back, restoring her a little
more to health and human love; while the old poison of
mysticism became in an increasing degree eliminated at
each successive defeat of religious imposture.   Cast for
a time into great perturbation, she strove to divert her
thoughts, to stupefy herself, by stern and painful religious
practices in order that she might not be compelled to understand that her love for Marc had reawakened, that she
craved for rest in his embrace, in the one, sole, eternal
certainty which makes of husband and wife the emblems of
health and happiness.

But quarrels had broken out between Madame Duparque
and Geneviève, and had grown more and more frequent
and bitter.   The grandmother felt that her granddaughter
was escaping from her.   She watched her closely, made
her almost a prisoner; but, whenever a dispute arose, Geneviève always had the resource of shutting herself up in her
own room.   There she could dwell upon her thoughts, and
she did not answer even when the terrible old woman came
up and hammered at the door.   In this way she secluded
herself on two successive Sundays, refusing to accompany
her grandmother to vespers, in spite of both entreaties and
threats.

Madame Duparque, now seventy-eight years old, had become a most uncompromising bigot, fashioned in that sense
by a long life of absolute servitude to the Church.   Reared
by a rigid mother, she had found no affection in her husband,
whose mind had been set on his business.   For nearly five
and twenty years they had kept a draper's shop in front of
the Cathedral of St. Maxence at Beaumont, a shop whose
custom came chiefly from the convents and the parsonages.
And it was towards her thirtieth year that Madame Duparque, neglected by her husband and too upright to take a
lover, had begun to devote herself more and more to religious observances.   She checked her passions, she quieted

them amid the ceremonies of the ritual, the smell of the
incense, the fervour of the prayers, the mystical assignations
she made with the fair-haired Jesus depicted in pious prints.
Having never known the transports of love, she found sufficient consolation in the society of priests. And not only
did she derive happiness from the unctuous gestures and
caressing words of her confessor, but even his occasional
rigour, his threats of hell and all its torments, sent a delightful quiver coursing through her veins. In blind belief and
strict adherence to the most rigid practices, she found, too,
not only satisfaction for her deadened senses, but the support and governance she needed in her weakness as a
daughter of the ages. The Church knows it well; it does
not conquer woman only by the sensuality of its worship, it
makes her its own by brutalising and terrorising her. It
treats her as a slave habituated to harsh treatment for centuries, a slave who ends by feeling a bitter delight in her very
servitude.

Thus Madame Duparque, broken to obedience from her
cradle days, was one of the subjugated daughters of the
Church, one of those creatures whom it distrusts, strikes,
and disciplines, turning them into docile instruments, which
enable it to attack men and conquer them in their turn.
When, after losing her husband and liquidating her business,
Madame Duparque had installed herself at Maillebois, her
one occupation, her one passion had become the practice
of that authoritarian piety, by which she strove to remedy
the spoiling of her life, and obtain compensation for all the
natural joys, all the human forms of happiness, which she
had never known. And the roughness with which she tried
to impose her narrow, chilling faith upon her granddaughter
Geneviève was due, in some degree certainly, to the regret
she felt at having never experienced the felicity of love,
which she would have liked to forbid her grandchild, as if
it were indeed some unknown and perchance delightful hell,
where she herself would never set foot.

But between the grandmother and the granddaughter
there was the doleful Madame Berthereau. She likewise
seemed to be only a devotee bent beneath the rule of the
Church, which had taken possession of her from the moment
of her birth. Never for a single day had she ceased to follow its observances. With loving weakness her husband,
Berthereau the freethinker, had accompanied her to Mass.
But she had also known his love, the ardent passion with

which he had always encompassed her, and the recollection
of it possessed her for ever. Though many years had
elapsed since his death, she still belonged to him; she lived
on that one memory, ending her days in solitude, in the
arms of that dear shade. This explained her long spells of
silence, the resigned, retiring manner she preserved in the
mournful little house to which, as to a convent, she had
withdrawn with her daughter Geneviève. She had never
thought of marrying again; she had become a second
Madame Duparque, rigidly and meticulously pious, clad
invariably in black, and showing a waxen countenance, a
cowed and crushed demeanour under the rough hand which
weighed so heavily on the house. At the utmost a faint
twinge of bitterness appeared on her tired lips, and a fugitive gleam of rebellion shone in her submissive eyes when
at times the memory of her dead husband, awakening
within her, filled her amid the frigid empty life of religious
observances in which she agonised with bitter regret for
all the old happiness of love. And of recent times only
the sight of her daughter Geneviève's frightful torment,
that struggle of a woman for whom priest and husband were
contending, had been able to draw her from the shrinking
self-surrender of a recluse taking no interest in the cares of
worldly life, and lend her enough courage to face her terrible mother.

And now Madame Berthereau was near her death, well
pleased, personally, by the prospect of that deliverance.
Nevertheless, as her strength ebbed away, day by day, she
felt more and more grieved at having to leave Geneviève
struggling in torture, and at the mercy of Madame Duparque.
When she herself was gone, what would become of her poor
daughter in that abode of agony, where she had suffered so
dreadfully already? To the poor dying woman the thought
of going off like that, without doing anything, saying anything that might save her daughter, and help her to recover
a little health and happiness, became intolerable. It haunted
her, and one evening, when it was still possible for her to
speak gently and very slowly, she mustered sufficient courage to satisfy her heart.

It was an evening in September—a mild and rainy one.
Night was at hand, and the little room, which, with its few
old pieces of walnut furniture, had an aspect of conventual
simplicity, was gradually growing dim. As the sick woman
could not lie down, for she then at once began to stifle, she

remained in a sitting posture, propped up by pillows, on a
couch. Although she was only fifty-six, her long sad face,
crowned by snowy hair, looked very aged indeed, worn and
blanched by the emptiness of her life. Geneviève sat near
her in an armchair, and Louise had just come upstairs with
a cup of milk, the only nourishment which the ailing woman
could still take. A heavy silence was lulling the house to
sleep, the last clang of the bells of the Capuchin Chapel
having just died away in the lifeless atmosphere of the little
deserted square.

' My daughter,' at last said Madame Berthereau in accents
which came from her lips very faintly and slowly, 'as we are
alone, I beg you to listen to me, for I have various things
to tell you, and it is quite time I should do so.'

Geneviève, surprised, and anxious as to the effect which
this supreme effort might have on her mother, wished her
to remain silent. But Madame Berthereau made such a
resolute gesture that the young woman merely inquired:
' Do you wish to speak to me alone, mother? Would you
like Louise to go away?'

For a moment Madame Berthereau preserved silence.
She had turned her face towards the girl, who, tall and
charming, with a lofty brow and frank eyes, gazed at her in
affectionate distress. And the old lady ended by murmur-
ing: ' I prefer Louise to remain. She is seventeen, she also
ought to know. . . . Come and sit here, close beside
me, my darling.'

Then, the girl having seated herself on a chair by the
side of the couch, Madame Berthereau took hold of her
hands. ' I know how sensible and brave you are,' she said,
' and if I have sometimes blamed you, I none the less
acknowledge how frank you are. . . . To-day, do you
know, now that I am near my last hour, I believe in nothing
save kindness.'

Again she paused for a moment, reflecting, and turning
her eyes towards the open window, towards the paling sky,
as if she were seeking her long life of dejection and resignation in the farewell gleam of the sun. Then her eyes came
back to her daughter, at whom for a while she remained
gazing with an expression of indescribable compassion.

' It grieves me extremely, my Geneviève, to leave you so
unhappy,' she said. 'Ah! do not say no. I sometimes
hear you sobbing overhead, at night, when you are unable
to sleep. And I can picture your wretchedness, the battle

which rends your heart. . . .   For years now you have
been suffering, and I have not had even enough bravery to
succour you.'

Hot tears gathered suddenly in Geneviève's eyes.   The
evocation of her sufferings at that tragic hour quite upset
her. 'Mother, I beg you, do not think of me,' she stammered; 'my only grief will be that of losing you.'

'No, no, my girl; each has to go in turn, satisfied or in
despair, according to the life which he or she has chosen.
But those who remain behind ought not to persevere obstinately in useless suffering when they may still be happy.'
And joining her hands, and raising them with a gesture of
ardent entreaty, Madame Berthereau added: 'Oh! my girl,
I beg you, do not remain a day longer in this house.   Make
haste, take your children, and go back to your husband.'

Geneviève did not even have time to answer.   A tall
black form was before her, for Madame Duparque had
slipped noiselessly into the room.   Always prowling about
the house, haunted by an everlasting suspicion of sin, she
began to worry herself directly she was at a loss to tell
where Geneviève and Louise might be.   If they had hidden
themselves did it not follow that they must be doing something evil ?   Moreover, the old woman never liked to leave
them long with Madame Berthereau for fear lest something
forbidden should be said.   That evening, therefore, she
had crept up the stairs as quietly as possible, with her ears
on the alert; and, hearing certain words, she had gently
opened the door, thus catching the others *in flagrante delicto*.

'What is that you say, my daughter ? ' she demanded, her
rasping voice ringing with angry imperiousness.

The sick woman, pale already, became quite ghastly at
that sudden intervention, while Geneviève and Louise
remained thunderstruck, alarmed also as to what might
now happen.

'What is that you say, my daughter ? ' Madame Duparque
repeated.   'Are you not aware that God can hear you ? '

Madame Berthereau had sunk back on her pillows, closing
her eyes as if to collect her courage.   She had so greatly
hoped that she might be able to speak to Geneviève alone,
and avoid a battle with her redoubtable mother.   All her life
long she had avoided any such collision, any such struggle,
feeling that she would be beaten in it.   But now she had
only a few hours left her to be good and brave; and so she
opened her eyes, and dared—at last—to speak out.

'May God indeed hear me, mother! I am doing my duty,' she said. 'I have told my daughter to take her children and return to her husband, for she will only find real health and happiness in the home which she quitted so imprudently.'

Madame Duparque, who waved her arms violently, had been minded to interrupt her at the first word she spoke. But awed, perhaps, by the majesty of death, which was already gathering in the room, embarrassed too by the heartfelt cry of that poor enslaved creature, whose reason and whose love were at last freeing themselves from their shackles, the terrible old lady allowed her daughter to finish her sentence. A pause, fraught with infinite anguish, then followed between those four women who were thus gathered together, and who represented four generations of their line.

There was a certain family resemblance between them; they were all tall, they had long faces and somewhat prominent noses. But Madame Duparque, now eight and seventy, and displaying a harsh jaw and rigidly wrinkled cheeks, had grown lean and sallow in the practice of narrow piety; whereas Madame Berthereau, who had reached her fifty-sixth year, showed more flesh and suppleness, in spite of her malady, and still retained on her livid face the gentleness bequeathed by the brief love which she had tasted, and which she had ever mourned. From those two solemn women, dark-haired in their younger days, had sprung Geneviève, fair and gay, refined by paternal heredity, loving and lovable, and still very charming at seven and thirty years of age. And Louise, the last, who would soon be in her eighteenth year, was in her turn a brunette, with hair of a deep gilded brown, inherited from her father, Marc, who had also bestowed on her his broad forehead, and his large bright eyes, glowing with passion for truth.

In like way one detected among those four women the progress of moral evolution. First there was the great-grandmother, a serf of the Church, one whose flesh and mind had been absolutely subjugated, who had become a passive instrument of error and domination; next there was the daughter, who had remained a practising and conquered Catholic, but who was disturbed, tortured by her brief experience of human happiness; then came the struggling granddaughter, in whose poor heart and mind Catholicism was fighting its last battle, who was almost rent atwain between the mendacious nothingness of her mystical education, and the living reality of her wifely love and motherly tenderness, who needed, too, all her strength to free herself; and finally there was the great-granddaughter, who was at last freed, who had escaped the clutch which the priest sets upon women and children, and who, all youth and health, had reverted to happy nature, to the glorious beneficence of the sunlight.

But in faint, slow accents Madame Berthereau was repeating: 'Listen, my Geneviève! Do not remain here any longer. As soon as I am gone, go away—go as speedily as you can. . . . My misfortunes began on the day when I lost your father. He adored me. The only hours that I ever really lived were those that I spent beside him; and I have often reproached myself for not having then appreciated them more, for in my stupidity I was ignorant of their value, and I only understood how delightful, how unique they had been, when I came here, a widow, loveless, for ever cut off from the world. . . . Ah! the icy cold of this house, how often has it made me shiver! Ah! the silence and the gloom in which I have gone on dying for years, not even daring to open a window to inhale a little life, so foolish and so cowardly I was!'

Erect and motionless, Madame Duparque still refrained from interrupting her daughter; but on hearing that cry of dolorous rebellion she could not restrain a gesture of protest. 'I will not prevent you from speaking, my daughter,' she said when the other paused, 'though if you have a confession to make it would be better to send for Father Théodose. . . . But since you were not wholly God's, why did you seek refuge in this house? You knew very well that here you would find none but God.'

'I have confessed,' the dying woman answered gently. 'I shall not go off without receiving extreme unction, for I belong to God entirely, I can only belong to Him now. . . . And even if I suffered so much from the loss of my husband, I never regretted having come here. Where else could I have gone? I had no other refuge. I was too closely linked to religion to attempt to seek other happiness, even for an instant. Thus I have lived the life I was bound to live. . . . But my daughter, in her turn, is suffering too cruelly, and I will not have her begin my sorry story over again, and fade away in the void in which I have agonised for so many years, for she is free, and she still has

a husband who adores her. . . . You hear me, you
hear me, do you not, my daughter ? '

With a gesture of tender entreaty, she held out her poor
waxen hands, and Geneviève fell upon her knees beside
her, with big tears rolling down her cheeks, so deeply was
she stirred by that extraordinary scene, that poignant
awakening of love at the very hour of death.

' Mother, I beg you, mother,' she said, ' do not continue
to grieve about my sufferings. You rend my heart by
thinking only of me when we are all here, with the one desire to give you a little comfort, whereas you, it seems, wish
to go off in despair.'

Increasing excitement had now gained possession of
Madame Berthereau. Taking Geneviève's head between
her hands, she gazed into her eyes and answered, ' No, no,
listen to me. There is only one thing that can make me
happy before I leave you, and that is a certainty that you
will not lead a life of sacrifice and torture as I have done.
Give me that last consolation, do not let me go without your
promise. . . . I shall repeat what I have said as long
as I have strength to do so. Leave this house of error and
death, return to your home, your husband. Give him back
his children, love each other with all your strength. Life
lies in that, and truth, aye, and happiness also. . . . I
beg you, my girl, promise me, swear to me that you will
comply with my last desire.'

Then, as Geneviève, utterly upset, choking with sobs,
gave her no answer, Madame Berthereau turned towards
Louise, who, likewise distracted, was now kneeling at the
other side of the couch. ' Help me, my dear granddaughter,' she said, 'I know what your views are. I have noticed
your efforts to lead your mother home. You are a little
fairy, a very sensible little person, and you have done a
great deal to give a little quietness to all four of us.
. . . Your mother must make me a promise, is it not
so ? Tell her that she will make me very joyful indeed by
promising me to be happy.'

Louise had caught hold of the poor woman's hands, and
kissing them she stammered: ' Oh! grandmother, grandmother, how good you are, and how I love you! . . .
Mother will remember your last wishes, she will reflect, and
act as her heart bids her, you may be sure of it.'

Madame Duparque meanwhile had not for a moment
departed from her rigidity. Her eyes alone seemed to be

alive in her frigid, wrinkled face. And furious anger blazed
in them while she strove to restrain herself from any brutal
action. At last she growled huskily: 'Be quiet, all three
of you! You are unhappy infidels, rebelling against God,
who will punish you with the flames of hell. . . . Be
quiet, I tell you, don't let me hear another word! Am I no
longer mistress here? You, my daughter, your illness has
impaired your mind, I am willing to grant it. You, my
granddaughter, have Satan in you, and I excuse you for
having failed as yet to drive him out, in spite of your penitence. And you, my great-granddaughter, I still hope that
when I am free to correct you I shall prevent you from
going to damnation. . . . Be quiet, my children, I tell
you. If it were not for me you would not exist! It is I
who command here, and you would be guilty of yet another
mortal sin if you should not obey me!'

Her stature seemed to have increased, and her voice had
risen while, with fierce gestures, she thus spoke in the name
of her Deity of anger and vengeance. But, in spite of her
commands, her daughter, who already felt freed from her
domination by the approach of death, was bold enough to
continue: 'I have been obeying for more than twenty years,
mother, I have preserved silence for more than twenty
years; and if my last hour were not at hand, perhaps I
should be so cowardly as to obey and keep silent now.
. . . But I have gone through too much. All that has
tortured me, all that I have left unsaid would choke me in
my grave, and even there the cry I have stifled so long
would rise from my lips. . . . Oh! my daughter,
promise me, promise me what I ask!'

Then Madame Duparque, beside herself, exclaimed in a
rougher voice: 'Geneviève, I, your grandmother, forbid
you to speak!'

It was Louise who, seeing that her mother was still sobbing, waging a most frightful battle, with her face close
pressed to the blanket spread over the couch, took upon
herself to answer in her resolute yet deferential way:
'Grandmother, one must be kind to grandmother who is
so ill. Mother also is very ailing, and it is cruel to upset
her like this. Is it not right that each should act according
to her conscience?'

Thereupon, without giving Madame Duparque time to intervene again, Geneviève, whose heart melted, touched as
it was by her daughter's courageous gentleness, raised her

head, and kissed the dying woman with intense emotion:
'Mother, mother, you may sleep in peace, I will not let you
carry away any bitter thought on my account. . . .
Yes, I promise you I will remember your desire, I promise
you I will do all that my love for you may advise me to do.
. . . Yes, yes, there is only kindness, there is only love:
therein lies the only truth.'

Then, as Madame Berthereau, exhausted, but with a
divine smile brightening her face, pressed her daughter to
her bosom, Madame Duparque made a last threatening
gesture. The twilight had now fallen, and only the pale
gleam of the broad, cloudless sky, where the first stars were
shining, lighted up the room; while the open window admitted the deep silence that rose from the deserted square,
broken only by the laugh of a child. And as everything
thus sank into a quiescence through which swept the august
breath of coming death, the old woman, who in her obstinacy would neither see nor hear, added these words: 'You
belong to me no more, neither daughter, nor granddaughter, nor great-granddaughter. One impelling the other,
you are, all three of you, on the road to eternal damnation!
Go, go! God casts you off, and I cast you off also!'

Then she departed, shutting the door roughly behind her.
In the dim quiet room the mother remained agonising between her daughter and her granddaughter, all three united
in the same embrace. And for a long, long while they continued weeping, their tears full of delightful comfort as well
as bitter grief.

Two days later Madame Berthereau died, in a very
Catholic spirit, after receiving extreme unction, as she had
desired. At the church the stern demeanour of Madame
Duparque, clad in the deepest mourning, was much remarked. Only Louise accompanied her. Geneviève had
been obliged to take to her bed again, overcome by such a
nervous shock that she seemed no longer able to see or hear.
For three days longer she thus remained in bed with her
face turned to the wall, unwilling to answer anybody, even
her daughter. She must have suffered terribly; distressful
moans escaped her, fits of weeping shook her from head to
foot. When the grandmother went up to her, obstinately
remaining there, lecturing her, and pointing out the necessity of appeasing the divine anger, the attacks became yet
more violent, there were convulsions and shrieks. And
Louise, who wished her mother to be spared any such

aggravation of her torment, in the supreme struggle which was almost rending her asunder, ended by bolting the door, and remaining there as a sentinel, forbidding access to everybody.

On the fourth day came the *dénouement*. Pélagie alone managed to force an occasional entry in order to attend to certain work. Sixty years of age, with a sullen face, a large nose, and thin lips, the servant had become not only very thin, almost withered, but also insufferable in manner. Ever mumbling sour words, she actually overruled her terrible mistress, and often turned the workgirls, whom the latter engaged to help her, into the street. Madame Duparque kept her, however, for she was an old retainer, an old instrument who had always been ready at hand. Indeed, her mistress could hardly have lived if she had not had that underling, that serf beside her to extend, as it were, her domination over all around. She employed her as a spy, as the executor of base designs, and in return she herself belonged to her, having to put up with all the bad temper, all the additional worry and dolefulness with which the other filled the house.

On the morning of the fourth day, after the first breakfast, Pélagie, having gone upstairs to fetch the cups and plates, hastened down again, quite scared, and said to her mistress: 'Does madame know what is going on up there? They are packing their trunks!'

'The mother and daughter?'

'Yes, madame. Oh! they are making no secret of it. The girl goes from one room to the other, carrying armfuls of linen. . . . If madame cares to go up, the door is wide open.'

Frigidly, without answering, Madame Duparque went up. And she indeed found Geneviève and Louise actively engaged in packing two trunks, as if for immediate departure, while little Clément, who was scarcely six years old, sat very quietly on a chair, watching the preparations. The mother and daughter just raised their heads when the old lady entered, then went on with their work again.

A moment of silence followed; finally, Madame Duparque, not a muscle of whose face stirred, but who seemed to become yet more frigid and stern, inquired: 'Do you feel better, then, Geneviève?'

'Yes, grandmother. I have still some fever, but I shall never get well if I remain shut up here.'

'So you have decided to go elsewhere, I see. Where are you going?'

A quiver came over Geneviève, who once more raised her head, showing her eyes, which were still red with weeping: 'I am going where I promised my mother I would go. For four days past the struggle has been killing me.'

Another pause ensued. 'Your promise did not seem to me a formal one; I regarded your words as mere words of consolation,' said Madame Duparque at last. 'So you are going back to that man? You can have very little pride!'

'Pride! Ah, yes, I know, it is by pride that you have kept me here so long. . . . But I have had plenty of pride. Many a time, though I have wept all night long, I have refused to admit my error. . . . But now I understand the stupidity of my pride, the wretchedness into which I have sunk is too great.'

'You unhappy creature! Has neither prayer nor penitence been able to rid you of the poison, then? That poison is mastering you again, and it will end by casting you into eternal punishment should you relapse into your abominable sin.'

'What poison are you talking of, grandmother? My husband loves me, and, in spite of everything, I love him still. Is that poison? I have struggled for five years; I wished to give myself entirely to God; why did not God fill the aching void of my being, in which I desired to receive Him alone? Religion has satisfied me neither as to wifely happiness nor as to motherly tenderness, and if I am now going back to that happiness and tenderness, it is because of the downfall of that heaven in which I have found only deception and falsehood.'

'You are blaspheming, my girl, and you will be punished for it by the most cruel sufferings. . . . If the poison which has tortured you did not come from Satan, it follows that it must have come from God. Faith is forsaking you; you are on the high road to negation, to absolute perdition.'

'That is true; for months now I have believed a little less each day. I did not dare to confess it to myself, but amid all my bitterness of feeling something was slowly destroying the beliefs of my childhood and youth. . . . How strange it was! All my childhood full of chimeras, all my pious youth had revived within me, with all the fine mysteries and ceremonies of worship, when I first sought refuge here. But when I again endeavoured to plunge into the

au delà of the mysteries, when I strove to give myself to
Jesus amid the chants and the flowers, those dreams gradually faded, became mere deceptive fancies, in which nought
of my being found contentment. . . . Yes, the poison
must have been my training, the errors in which I grew up,
which brought me so much suffering when they revived,
and of which I shall only be cured when the evil ferment
is completely eliminated. . . . Shall I ever be cured?
I hardly know. There is still such strife within me!'

Madame Duparque was restraining herself, for she well
understood that violence on her part would seal her rupture
with the young woman and the girl, who, with the little boy,
seated on his chair, listening attentively without understanding, were all that remained of her race. Thus she was
minded to make a last effort, and addressing herself to
Louise, she said: 'You, my poor child, are the most to be
pitied, and I shudder when I think of the pit of abomination into which you are casting yourself. . . . If you
had made your first Communion all these sorrows would
have been spared us. God is punishing us for having
failed to overcome your impious resistance. Yet there is
still time, and what favours would you not obtain from His
infinite mercy if you would only submit, and approach the
Holy Table as a humble handmaiden of Jesus!'

But the girl responded gently: 'Why revert to that,
grandmother? You know very well what promise I gave
my father. I cannot vary in my answer; I will come to a
decision when I am twenty; I shall then see if I have faith.'

'But, you unhappy, obstinate child, if you go back to that
man, who has wrecked both your mother's life and your
own, your decision can be told in advance! You will remain without any belief, any religion at all, like a mere
beast of the fields!'

Then, as the daughter and mother deferentially preserved
silence, and even resumed their packing in order to curtail
a useless and painful discussion, the old lady gave expression to a last desire: 'Well, if you have both resolved to go,
at least leave me the little boy—leave me Clément. He will
redeem your folly, I will bring him up in the love of God,
I will make a holy priest of him, and at least I shall not be
alone; there will be two of us to pray that the divine anger
may not fall upon you on the terrible Day of Judgment.'

But Geneviève had sprung to her feet. 'Leave Clément!'
she exclaimed; 'why, it is largely on his account that I am

going. I no longer know how to bring him up; I wish to
restore him to his father, in order that we may come to an
understanding and endeavour to make a man of him. . . .
No, no, I am taking him with me!'

Then Louise, who also stepped forward, added very
gently and respectfully: 'Why do you say that you will remain alone, grandmother? We do not wish to forsake you,
we will often come to see you, every day if you will allow
us. And we will love you well, and try to show you how
much we desire to make you happy.'

Madame Duparque could restrain herself no longer. The
flood of anger which she had found it so difficult to check
flowed over and carried her away with a rush of furious
words: 'That's enough! Keep quiet! I will listen to you
no longer! But you are quite right, pack your boxes and
be off! Be off, all three of you, I cast you out! Go and
join that cursed man, that bandit who spat on God and His
ministers to endeavour to save that filthy Jew, who has been
twice condemned!'

'Simon is innocent!' cried Geneviève, in her turn losing
all restraint; 'and those who caused him to be condemned
are liars and forgers!'

'Yes, yes, I know; it is that affair which has ruined you
and is separating us. You imagine the Jew to be innocent;
you can no longer believe in God. But your imbecile
justice is the negation of divine authority. And for that
reason all is quite over between us. . . . Go, go as
quickly as possible with your children! Don't soil this
house any longer, don't bring any more thunderbolts upon
it! You are the sole cause of its misfortunes. . . .
And, mind, don't set foot here again; I cast you off, I cast
you off for ever! When once you have crossed the threshold you need never knock at the door, it will not be opened
to you. I have no children left, I am alone in the world,
and I will live and die alone!'

As she spoke, the old woman, nearly in her eightieth
year, drew up her lofty figure with a fierce energy. Her
voice was still strong, her gestures were commanding ones.
She cursed, she punished, she exterminated after the fashion
of her Deity of wrath and death. And afterwards she descended the stairs with a pitiless tread, and shut herself in
her room, waiting there till the last children of her flesh
should be gone for ever.

It so happened that Marc, that very same day, received

a visit from Salvan, who found him in the large classroom, which was quite bright with the glow of the September sunshine. The vacation would come to an end in another ten days, and, though Marc hourly expected to be informed of his dismissal, he was consulting his books and notes as if preparing for the new school year. However, by Salvan's grave if smiling demeanour, he at once understood the truth.

'This time it's done, is it not?' he exclaimed.

'*Mon Dieu*, yes, it's done, my friend. Quite a long list of changes, appointments, and promotions, prepared by Le Barazer, has been signed. . . . Jauffre will leave Jonville and come to Beaumont, which is fine advancement for him. That clerical Chagnat goes from Le Moreux to Dherbecourt, which is scandalous when one remembers what a brute the fellow is. . . . For my part, I am simply pensioned off to make room for Mauraisin, who triumphs. . . . And you, my friend——'

'I am dismissed, eh?'

'No, no, you have simply fallen into disgrace. You are sent back to Jonville in the place of Jauffre, and Mignot, your assistant, who is compromised with you, is to take Chagnat's post at Le Moreux.'

Marc raised a cry of happy surprise: 'But I am delighted!'

Salvan, who had come expressly to acquaint him with the news, indulged in a hearty laugh. 'That is Le Barazer's diplomacy, you see! That is what he was preparing, when, according to his habit, he endeavoured to gain time. He has ended by satisfying that terrible Sanglebœuf and all the other reactionaries by appointing Mauraisin to succeed me, and promoting Jauffre and Chagnat. And this has enabled him to retain your services and those of Mignot. Outwardly he seems to blame you, but he does not intend to disown you entirely. Besides, he is leaving Mademoiselle Mazeline here, and in your place is appointing Joulic, one of my best pupils, a man of free and healthy mind. Thus Maillebois, Jonville, and Le Moreux will be henceforth provided with excellent masters, ardent missionaries of the future. . . . That is the position, and, I tell you once again, nobody can alter Le Barazer; one must take him as he is and feel pleased, even when what he does is only half of what one would like to see.'

'I am delighted,' Marc repeated. 'It was more particularly the prospect of having to quit the profession altogether that grieved me. Thinking of the new term I felt sorrowful all this morning. Where could I have gone, what could I have done? It will certainly pain me to leave the boys here, for I am very fond of them. But my consolation will be to find others yonder, to whom I shall also become attached. And as for the humbleness of the school, what does that matter if I am able to continue my life-work and still sow the seed which alone can yield the harvest of truth and equity? Ah! yes, I shall go back to Jonville right willingly, and with fresh hope.'

Then he strode gaily about the bright, sunshiny classroom as if again taking on himself that teaching mission, the relinquishment of which would have been so hard to bear. And at last, with juvenile ardour and delight, he flung his arms about Salvan and embraced him. At that same moment Mignot, who, also expecting dismissal, had been seeking a situation for some days past, came in, worried at having encountered another refusal on the part of the manager of a neighbouring factory. But when he learnt that he was appointed to Le Moreux, he likewise gave expression to his joy. 'Le Moreux! Le Moreux! a real land of savages!' said he. 'No matter, one will try to civilise them a little. And we sha'n't be separated, the distance is less than three miles. That, you know, is what pleases me most of all!'

But Marc had now calmed down, and, indeed, sorrow was reviving in him, dimming his eyes once more. Silence fell, and the others could feel a quiver pass—the quiver of hope deferred, of a heart-pang which was ever keen. How hard would be the battle that Marc still had before him, how many more tears must he shed before he regained his lost happiness! At that thought he, and the others also, preserved silence; and Salvan, unable to give his friends any further comfort, sank into a sorrowful reverie as he stood gazing through the large sunlit window which faced the square outside.

But all at once he exclaimed: 'Why, are you expecting somebody?'

'Expecting somebody?' rejoined Marc, at a loss to understand.

'Yes, here comes a little hand-cart with some trunks on it.'

At that same moment the door opened, and they turned round. It was Geneviève who came in, holding little Clément by the hand, and having Louise also beside her. The surprise and the emotion were so great that at first nobody spoke. Marc was trembling. But Geneviève, in a halting voice, began at last: 'My dear Marc, I have brought you back your son. Yes, I give him back to you —he belongs to you—he belongs to us both. Let us try to make a man of him.'

The boy had stretched out his little arms, and the father caught him up wildly, and pressed him to his heart, while the mother, the wife, continued: 'And I have come back to you with him, my good Marc. You told me that I should bring him back, and come back myself. . . . It was truth that first conquered me; then all that you had set in me germinated, no doubt, and I have no pride left. . . . And here I am, for I still love you. . . . I vainly sought other happiness, but only your love exists. Apart from us and our children there is only unreason and wretchedness. . . . Take me back, my good Marc! I give myself to you as you give yourself to me.'

Thus speaking, she had slowly drawn near to her husband, and she was about to cast her arms around his neck when Louise's gay voice was heard: 'And I, and I, father! I must share in it too, you know. You must not forget me.'

'Yes, indeed, she must share in it, the dear girl!' said Geneviève. 'She strove so much to bring about this happiness, she showed such gentleness and skill.'

Then she caught Louise also in her embrace, and kissed both her and Marc, who was already holding Clément to his heart. All four were at last re-united, held in the same bond of flesh and love, having but one heart, one breath between them. And what a quiver of deep humanity, of fruitful and healthy joy now filled that large classroom, which looked so bare and empty, pending the return of the boys for the new term! Big tears welled into the eyes of Salvan and Mignot, whom emotion quite upset.

At last Marc was able to speak, and his whole heart rose to his lips: 'Ah! my dear wife, as you return to me you must at last be cured. I knew it would be so. You turned to more and more rigid religious practices as to stronger and stronger stupefacients for the purpose of sending your nature to sleep; but, in spite of everything, nature was bound to eliminate the poison when at last you again felt that you were a wife and a mother. . . . Yes, yes, you are right: love has delivered you; you are won from that religion of error and death, from which human society has suffered for eighteen centuries past.'

But Geneviève quivered again, becoming anxious and disturbed. 'Ah! no, no, my good Marc, do not say that! Who can tell if I am really cured? Never, perhaps, shall I be cured completely. . . . Our Louise will be entirely free, but the mark set on me is ineffaceable, I shall always be afraid of relapsing into those mystical dreams. . . . And if I have come back, it is to seek a refuge in your embrace, and to enable you to complete the work that has begun. Keep me, perfect me, try to prevent anything from ever separating us again!'

They caught each other in a tighter clasp: it was as if they were but one. Even as Geneviève had said, was not that the great work which needed to be accomplished—the work of taking woman from the Church, and setting her in her true place as companion and mother, by the side of man? For only the freed woman can free man: her slavery is ours.

But all at once Louise, who a moment previously had disappeared, opened the door again, bringing with her Mademoiselle Mazeline, who entered breathless and smiling. 'Mamma,' said the girl, 'mademoiselle must have a share in our happiness. If you only knew how she has loved me, and how kind and useful she was here!'

Geneviève stepped forward and embraced the schoolmistress affectionately. 'I knew it,' she said. 'Thank you, my friend, for all you did for us during our long worries.'

The good woman laughed, with tears in her eyes. 'Oh! don't thank me, my dear. It is I who am grateful to you for all the happiness you give me to-day.'

Salvan and Mignot were also laughing now. More handshakes were exchanged. And as Salvan, amid the babel of voices which burst forth, informed the schoolmistress of the appointments signed the previous day, Geneviève raised a cry of joy.

'What! we are going back to Jonville? Is it really true? . . . Ah! Jonville, that charming, lonely village where we loved each other so well, where we first lived together so happily! What a good omen it is that we are going back there, to begin our life afresh in affection and quietude! Maillebois made me feel nervous, but Jonville is hope and certainty.'

Renewed courage and infinite confidence in the future were now upbuoying Marc, filling him with superb enthusiasm. 'Love has returned to us,' said he; 'henceforth we are all-powerful. And even though falsehood, iniquity, and crime triumphed to-day, eternal victory will to-morrow be ours.'

BOOK IV

I

WHEN October arrived, Marc with joyous serenity repaired to Jonville, to take the modest post of village schoolmaster which he had formerly occupied there. Great quietude had now fallen on him, new courage and hope had followed the despair and weariness by which he had been prostrated after the monstrous trial of Rozan.

The whole of one's ideal is never realised, and Marc almost reproached himself for having relied on a splendid triumph. Human affairs do not progress by superb leaps and bounds, glorious *coups-de-théâtre*. It was chimerical to imagine that justice would be acclaimed by millions of lips, that the innocent prisoner would return amid a great national festival, transforming the country into a nation of brothers. All progress, the very slightest, the most legitimate, has been won by centuries of battling. Each forward step taken by mankind has demanded torrents of blood and tears, hecatombs of victims, sacrificing themselves for the good of future generations. Thus, in the eternal battle with the evil powers, it was unreasonable to expect a decisive victory, a supreme triumph, such as would fulfil all one's hopes, all one's dream of fraternity and equity among mankind.

Besides, Marc had ended by perceiving what a considerable step had been taken, after all, along that road of progress, which is so rough and deadly. While one is still in the thick of the fight, exposed to taunts and wounds, one does not always notice what ground one gains. One may even think oneself defeated when one has really made much progress and drawn very near to the goal. In this way, if the second condemnation of Simon had at first sight seemed a frightful defeat, it soon became apparent that the moral victory of his defenders was a great one. And there were all sorts of gains, a grouping of free minds and generous hearts, a broadening of human solidarity from one to the other end of the world, a sowing of truth and justice, which would end by sprouting up, even if the good grain should require many long winters to germinate in the furrows. And, again, it was only with the greatest difficulty that the reactionary castes, by dint of falsehoods and crimes, had for a time saved the rotten fabric of the past from utter collapse. It was none the less cracking on all sides; the blow dealt to it had rent it from top to bottom, and the blows of the future would complete its destruction and cast it down in a litter of wretched remnants.

Thus the only regret which Marc now experienced was that he had not been able to utilise that prodigious Simon affair as an admirable lesson of things which would have instructed the masses, enlightened them like a blaze of lightning. Never again, perhaps, would there be so complete and decisive a case. There was the complicity of all the powerful and all the oppressors banding themselves together to crush a poor innocent man, whose innocence imperilled the compact of human exploitation which the great ones of the world had signed together. There were all the averred crimes of the priests, soldiers, magistrates, and ministers, who, to continue deceiving the people, had piled the most extraordinary infamies one on another, and who had all been caught lying and assassinating, with no resource left them but to sink in an ocean of mud; and finally there had been the division of the country into two camps—on one hand the old authoritarian, antiquated, and condemned social order, on the other the young society of the future, free in mind already and ever tending towards increase of truth, equity, and peace. If Simon's innocence had been recognised, the reactionary past would have been struck down at one blow, and the joyous future would have appeared to the simplest, whose eyes, at last, would have been opened. Never before would the revolutionary axe have sunk so deeply into the old worm-eaten social edifice. Irresistible enthusiasm would have carried the nation towards the future city. In a few months the Simon affair would have done more for the emancipation of the masses and the reign of justice than a hundred years of ardent politics. And grief that things should have become so spoilt, and should have shattered the admirable work in

their hands, was destined to abide in the hearts of the combatants as long as they might live.

But life continued, and it was necessary to fight again,
fight on for ever. A step had been taken forward, and
other steps remained to be taken. Duty demanded that,
day by day, whatever the bitterness and often the obscurity
of life, one should again give one's blood and one's tears,
satisfied with gaining ground inch by inch, without even the
reward of ever beholding the victory. Marc accepted that
sacrifice, no longer hoping to see Simon's innocence recognised legally, definitively, and triumphantly by the whole
people. He felt it was impossible to revive the affair amid
the passions of the moment, for the innocent man's enemies
would begin their atrocious campaign again, helped on by
the cowardice of the multitude. It would be necessary,
no doubt, to wait for the death of the personages involved
in the case, for some transformation of parties, some new
phase of politics, before the Government would be bold
enough to apply once more to the Court of Cassation and
ask it to efface that abominable page from the history of
France. Such seemed to be the conviction of even David
and Simon, who, while leading a sequestered life, busy with
their Pyrenean enterprise, watched for favourable incidents
and circumstances, but felt that the situation tied their
hands, and that it was necessary to remain waiting, unless
indeed they wished to stir up another useless and dangerous
onslaught.

Marc, being thus compelled to live in patience, reverted
to his mission, to the one work on which he set his hopes—
the instruction of the humble, the dissemination of truth
by knowledge which alone could render a nation capable of
equity. Great serenity had come to him, and he accepted
the fact that generations of pupils would be necessary to
rouse France from her numbness, deliver her from the
poisons with which she had been gorged, and fill her with
new blood which would transform her into the France of
his old dreams—a generous, freedom-giving, and justice-
dealing nation.

Never had Marc loved truth so passionately as he did
now. In former times he had needed it, even as one needs
the air one breathes; he had felt unable to live without it,
sinking into intolerable anguish whenever it escaped him.
At present, after seeing it attacked so furiously, denied,
and hidden away in the depths of lies, like a corpse which

would never revive, he believed in it still more; he felt that
it was irresistible, possessed of sufficient power to blow up
the world should men again try to bury it underground. It
followed its road without ever taking an hour's rest; it
marched on to its goal of light, and nothing would ever stop
it. Marc shrugged his shoulders with ironical contempt
when he beheld guilty men imagining that they had annihilated truth, that it lay beneath their feet as if it had ceased
to exist. When the right moment came, truth would ex-
plode, scatter them like dust, and shine forth serenely and
radiantly. And it was the certainty that truth, ever victorious, even after the lapse of ages, was upon his side, that
lent Marc all necessary strength and composure to return
to his work, and wait cheerfully for truth's triumph, even
though it might only come after his own lifetime.

Moreover, the Simon case had imparted solidity to his
convictions, breadth to his faith. He had previously passed
condemnation on the *bourgeoisie*, which was exhausted by
the abuse of its usurped power, which, from being a liberal
class, had become a reactionary one, passing from free
thought to the basest clericalism as it had felt the Church
to be its natural ally in its career of rapine and enjoyment.
And now he had seen the French *bourgeoisie* at work, he had
seen it full of cowardice and falsehood, weak but tyrannical,
denying all justice to the innocent, ready for every crime in
order that it might not have to part with any of its millions,
terrified as it was by the gradual awakening of the masses
who claimed their due. And finding that *bourgeoisie* to be
even more rotten, more stricken, than he had imagined, he
held that it must promptly disappear if the nation did not
desire to perish of incurable infection. Henceforth salvation was only to be found in the masses, in that new force—
that inexhaustible reservoir of men, work, and energy.
Marc felt that the masses were ever rising, like a new, rejuvenated race, bringing to social life more power for truth,
justice, and happiness. And this confirmed him in the
mission he had assumed, that seemingly modest mission of
a village schoolmaster, which was in reality the apostolate
of modern times, the only important work that could fashion
the society of to-morrow. There was no loftier duty than
that of striking down the errors and impostures of the
Church and setting in their place truth as proclaimed by
science, and human peace, based upon knowledge and solidarity. The France of the future was growing up in the

rural districts, in the humblest, loneliest hamlets, and it was there that one must work and conquer.

Marc speedily set to work. He had to repair all the harm which Jauffre had caused by abandoning Jonville to Abbé Cognasse. But during the earlier days, while Marc and Geneviève were settling down, how delightful it was for them —reconciled as they were and renewing the love of youthful times—to find themselves again in the poor little nest of long ago! Sixteen years had passed, yet nothing seemed to be changed; the little school was just the same, with its tiny lodging and its strip of garden. The walls had merely been whitewashed, but the place seemed fairly clean, thanks to a good scouring which Geneviève superintended. She was never weary of summoning Marc to remind him of one thing and another, laughing happily at all that recalled the past.

'Oh! come and look at the picture of Useful Insects which you hung up in the classroom! It is still there. . . . I myself put up those pegs for the boys' hats. . . . In the cupboard yonder, you 'll find the collection of solid bodies, which you cut out of beechwood.'

Marc hastened to her and joined in her laughter. And in his turn he summoned her to him: 'Come upstairs—make haste! Do you see that date cut with a knife in the wall of the alcove? Don't you remember that I did that the day Louise was born? . . . And just recollect, when we were in bed, we used to look at that crack in the ceiling, and jest about it, saying that the stars were watching and smiling at us.'

Then, as they went through the little garden, they burst into exclamations: 'Why, look at the old fig tree! It has n't changed a bit; we might have left it only yesterday. . . . Ah! we had a border of strawberries in the place of that sorrel; we shall have to plant one again. . . . The pump has been changed—that 's a blessing! Perhaps we shall be able to get water with this one. . . . Why, there 's our seat, our seat under the creeper! We must sit down and kiss each other—all the young kisses of long ago in a good kiss of to-day.'

They felt moved to tears, and for an instant they lingered embracing, amid that delightful renewal of their happiness. Great courage came to them from the sight of those friendly surroundings, where they had never shed a tear. Everything they saw drew them more closely together, and seemed to promise them victory.

With respect to their daughter Louise, a separation had become necessary at the very outset. She had been obliged to leave them for the Training School of Fontenay, to which she had secured admission. Her tastes and her love for her father had made her desirous of becoming a mere schoolmistress, even as he was a mere village schoolmaster. And Marc and Geneviève, remaining alone with little Clément, saddened by their daughter's departure, though they knew it to be necessary, drew yet closer together, in order to deaden their sense of that sudden void. True, Clément remained with them, and gave them occupation. He was now becoming quite a little man, and it was with affectionate solicitude that they watched over the awakening of his faculties.

Besides, Marc prevailed on Geneviève to undertake the management of the adjoining girls' school—that is after requesting Salvan to intervene with Le Barazer with a view to her appointment to the post. It will be remembered that immediately after her convent days she had obtained the necessary certificates, and that if she had not taken charge of the girls' school when her husband was first appointed to Jonville, it had been because Mademoiselle Mazeline had then held the post. But the advancement now given to Jauffre and his wife had left both posts vacant, and it seemed best that the two schools should be confided to Marc and Geneviève, the husband taking the boys and the wife the girls—this indeed being an arrangement which the authorities always preferred.

Marc, for his part, perceived all sorts of advantages in it: the teaching would proceed on the same lines in both schools; he would have a devoted collaborator who would help instead of trying to thwart him in his advance towards the future. And, again, though Geneviève had given him no cause for anxiety since her return, she would find occupation for her mind; she would be compelled to recover and exert her reason in acting as a teacher, a guardian of the little maids who would be the wives and mothers of to-morrow. Besides, would not their union be perfected? would they not be blended for ever, if, with all faith and all affection, they should share the same blessed work of teaching the poor and lowly, from whom the felicity of the future would spring? When a notification of the appointment arrived, fresh joy came to them; it was as if they now had but one heart and one brain.

But in what a ruinous and uneasy state did Marc now
find that village of Jonville which he had loved so well!
He remembered his first struggles with the terrible Abbé
Cognasse, and how he had triumphed by securing the support of Mayor Martineau, that well-to-do, illiterate but
sensible peasant, who retained all a peasant's racial antipathy for the priests—those lazy fellows, who lived well and
did nothing. Between them, Marc and Martineau had
begun to secularise the parish; the schoolmaster no longer
sang in the choir, no longer rang the bell for Mass, no
longer conducted his pupils to the Catechism classes; while
the Mayor and the parish council escaped from routine and
favoured the evolution which gave the school precedence
over the Church. Thanks to the action Marc brought to
bear on his boys and their parents, and the influence he
exercised at the parish offices, where he held the post of
secretary, he had seen great prosperity set in around him.
But as soon as he had been transferred to Maillebois, Martineau, falling into the hands of Jauffre, the man of the
Congregations, had speedily weakened. Indeed, he was
incapable of action when he did not feel himself supported
by a resolute will. Racial prudence deterred him from expressing an opinion of his own; he sided with the priest or
with the schoolmaster according as one or the other proved
to be the stronger. Thus, while Jauffre, thinking merely of his
own advancement, chanted the litanies, rang the bell, and attended the Communion, Abbé Cognasse gradually became
master of the parish, setting the Mayor and the council beneath his heel, to the secret delight of the beautiful Madame
Martineau, who, though not piously inclined, was very fond
of displaying new gowns at High Mass on days of festival.
Never had there been a plainer demonstration of the axiom,
'According to the worth of the schoolmaster, such is the
worth of the school; and according to the worth of the
school, such is the worth of the parish.' In very few years,
indeed, the prosperity which had declared itself in Jonville,
the ground which had been gained, thanks to Marc, was
lost. The village retrograded, its life died away in increasing torpor after Jauffre had delivered Martineau and his
fellow-parishioners into the hands of the triumphant
Cognasse.

In this way sixteen years elapsed, bringing disaster. All
moral and intellectual decline leads inevitably to material
misery. There is no country where the Roman Church has

reigned as absolute sovereign that is not now a dead
country. Ignorance, error, and base credulity render men
powerless. And what can be the use of exercising one's
will, acting and progressing, if one be a mere toy in the
hands of a Deity who plays with one according to his
fancy? That Deity suffices, supplies the place of everything. At the end of such a religion of terrestrial and
human nothingness, there is but stupidity, inertia, surrender into the hands of Providence, mere routine in the
avocations of life, idleness, and want. Jauffre let his boys
gorge themselves with Bible history and Catechism, while
in their peasant families all ideas of any improved system
of cultivating the land were regarded with increasing suspicion. They knew nothing of those matters, they would
not learn. Fields remained unproductive, crops were lost
for want of intelligent care. Then effort seemed excessive
and useless, and the countryside became impoverished,
deserted, though above it there still shone the all-powerful
and fructifying sun—that ignored, insulted god of life.

The decline of Jonville had become yet more marked
after Abbé Cognasse had prevailed on the weak Martineau
to allow the parish to be dedicated to the Sacred Heart in a
pompous and well-remembered ceremony. The peasants
were still waiting for that Sacred Heart to bring them the
wondrous promised harvests by dispelling the hailstorms
and granting rain and fine weather in due season. By way
of result one only found more imbecility weighing on the
parish, a sleepy waiting for divine intervention, the slow
agony of fanatical believers, in whom all power of initiative
has been destroyed, and who, if their Deity did not nourish
them, would let themselves starve rather than raise an arm.

During the first days that followed his return, Marc, on
taking a few country walks with Geneviève, felt quite distressed by all the incompetency and neglect he beheld.
The fields were ill-kept, the roads scarcely passable. One
morning they went as far as Le Moreux, where they found
Mignot installing himself in his wretched school, and feeling
as grieved as they were that the district should have fallen
into such a deplorable state.

'You have no idea, my friends,' said he, ' of the ravages
of that terrible Cognasse. He exercises some little restraint
at Jonville; but here, in this lonely village, whose inhabitants are too miserly to pay for a priest of their own, he
terrorises and sabres everybody. Of late years, he and his

creature Chagnat, while reigning here, virtually suppressed
the Mayor, Saleur, who felt flattered at being re-elected
every time, but who turned all the worries of his office over
to his secretary, Chagnat, and by way of exhibiting his
person, let himself be taken to Mass, though at heart he
scarcely cared for the priests. . . . Ah! how well I
now understand the torments of poor Férou, his exasperation, and the fit of lunacy which led to his martyrdom.'

With a quivering gesture Marc indicated that he was
haunted by the thought of that unhappy man, struck down
by a revolver-shot yonder, under the burning sun. 'When
I came in just now, he seemed to rise before me. Famished,
having only his scanty pay to provide for himself, his wife,
and his children, he endured untold agony at feeling that
he was the only intelligent, the only educated, man among
all those ignorant dolts living at their ease, who disdained
him for his poverty and feared him for his attainments,
which humiliated them. . . . That explains, too, the
power acquired by Chagnat over the Mayor, the latter's
one desire being to live in peace on his income, in the
somnolent state of a man whose appetite is satisfied.'

'But the whole parish is like that,' Mignot replied.
'There are no poor, and each peasant remains content with
what he harvests, not in a spirit of wisdom, but from a kind
of egotism, ignorance, and laziness. If they are perpetually
quarrelling with the priest, it is because they accuse him of
slighting them, of not giving them the Masses and other
ceremonies to which they consider themselves entitled.
Thanks to Chagnat, in his time something like an understanding was arrived at, and, indeed, all that was said and
done here in honour of St. Antony of Padua can hardly be
pictured. . . . But the result of Chagnat's *régime* is
deplorable; I found the school as dirty as a cowshed; one
might have thought that the Chagnats had lodged all the
cattle of the district in it, and I had to engage a woman to
help me to scour and scrape everything.'

Geneviève, meantime, had become dreamy; her glance
seemed to wander away to far-off memories. 'Ah! poor
Férou!' she murmured, 'I was not always kind to him and
his family. That is one of my regrets. But how can one
remedy so much suffering and disaster? We have so little
power, we are still so few. There are times when I despair.'
Then, suddenly waking up, as it were, and smiling, she
nestled close to her husband and resumed: 'There, there,

don't scold me, my dear, I did wrong to speak like that. But you must allow me enough time to become fearless and reproachless as you yourself are. . . . Come, it's understood, we are going to set to work, and we shall conquer.'

Thereupon they all became merry, and Mignot, who wished to escort his friends a little way, ended by accompanying them almost to Jonville. There, at the roadside, stood a large square building, a kind of factory, the branch establishment of the Good Shepherd of Beaumont, which had been promised at the time of the consecration of the parish to the Sacred Heart, and which had now been working for several years. The fine clerical folk had made a great noise about the prosperity which such an establishment would bring with it: all the daughters of the peasants would find employment and become skilful workwomen, there would be a great improvement in their morality, drones and gadabouts would be duly corrected, and the business might end by endowing the district with quite an industry.

The specialty of the Good Shepherd establishments was to provide the big drapery shops of Paris with petticoats, knickers, and chemises—the finest, most ornamental, and most delicate feminine body linen. At Jonville, under the superintendence of some ten sisters, two hundred girls worked from morning till night, trying their eyes over all that rich and fashionable underwear, which was often destined for strange festivities. And those two hundred little *lingères* constituted but a tiny fraction of all the poor hirelings who were thus exploited, for the Order had establishments from one to the other end of France; nearly fifty thousand girls toiled in its workshops, scantily paid, ill-treated, and ill-fed, while they earned for it millions of francs. At Jonville, there had been speedy disenchantment, none of the fine promises had been fulfilled, the establishment seemed a gulf which swallowed up the last energies of the region. The farms were raided and their women folk carried off, the peasants could no longer keep their daughters with them,—the girls all dreamt of becoming young ladies, of spending their days on chairs, engaged in light work. But they soon repented of their folly, for what with the long hours of enforced immobility, the exhausting strain of unremitting application, never was there more frightful drudgery; the stomach remained empty, the head became heavy, there was no time for sleep in summer, and there

was no fire in winter.   The place was a prison-house, where,
under the pretext of practising charity, of promoting morality, woman was exploited in the most frightful manner,
sweated in her flesh, stupefied in her intelligence, turned
into a beast of burden, from whom the greatest gain possible
was extracted.   And scandals burst forth at Jonville; one
girl nearly perished of cold and starvation, another became
half mad, while another, turned out of doors penniless after
years of crushing toil, rebelled, and threatened the good
sisters with a sensational lawsuit.[1]

Marc, stopping short on the road, looked at the big factory, silent like a prison, deathly like a cloister, where so
many young lives were wearing themselves away, nothing
carolling, meanwhile, the happiness of fruitful work.

'One source of the Church's strength,' said he, ' a very
simple matter in practice, is that she stoops to present-day
requirements and borrows our own weapons to fight us.
She manufactures and she trades; there is no object or
article of daily consumption that she does not produce or
sell, from clothes to *liqueurs*.   Several Orders are merely
industrial associations, which undersell other people, as
they secure labour for next to nothing, and thus compete
disloyally with our smaller producers.   The millions of
francs they gain go into the cash-boxes of the Black Band,
supplying sinews for the war of extermination which is
waged against us, swelling the thousands of millions which
the Congregations possess already, and which may render
them so redoubtable.'

Geneviève and Mignot had listened thoughtfully.   And
a moment of anxious silence now followed amid the evening
quietude, while the sunset cast a great pink glow on the
closed and mournful factory of the Good Shepherd.

'Why, I myself seem to be despairing now!' Marc resumed gaily.   'They are still very powerful, it is certain.
But we have a book on our side, the little book of elementary knowledge, which brings truth with it, and which will
end by for ever overcoming the falsehoods they have circulated for so many centuries.   All our strength is in that,
Mignot.   They may accumulate ruins here, they may lead

[1] In the above account of the Good Shepherd establishments, M.
Zola has made use of numerous incidents brought to light by proceedings in the French law courts, and also by the action of the Bishop of
Nancy, who, in attempting to put a stop to abominable practices, incurred the odium of all the money-grubbing Congregations.—*Trans.*

poor ignorant folk backward, and destroy the little good done by us formerly; but it will suffice for us to resume our efforts to bring about progress by knowledge, and we shall regain the lost ground, and continue to advance until we at last reach the City of solidarity and peace. Their prison-house of the Good Shepherd will crumble like all others, their Sacred Heart will go whither all the gross fetiches of the dead religions have gone. You hear me, Mignot; each pupil in whom you instil a little truth will be another helper in the cause of justice. So to work, to work! Victory is certain, whatever difficulties and sufferings may be encountered on the road!'

That cry of faith and everlasting hope rang out across the quiet countryside amid the calm setting of the planet which foretold a bright to-morrow. And Mignot bravely returned to his task at Le Moreux, while Marc and Geneviève went homeward to begin their work at Jonville.

Arduous work it was, requiring much will and patience, for it was necessary to free Mayor Martineau, the parish council, and indeed the whole village from the hands of the priest, who was determined not to relax his hold. On hearing of Marc's appointment, Abbé Cognasse, instead of evincing any anger or fear of the redoubtable adversary who was being sent to face him, had contented himself with shrugging his shoulders and affecting extreme contempt. He said on all sides that this beaten man, this disgraced mediocrity, who had lost all honour by his complicity in the Simon case, would not remain six months at Jonville. His superiors had merely sent him there in order to finish him off, not wishing to execute him at one blow. In reality, no doubt, Abbé Cognasse scarcely felt at ease, for he knew the man he had to deal with—a man all calmness and strength, derived from his reliance on truth. And that the priest plainly scented danger was shown by the prudence and *sangfroid* which he himself strove to preserve, for fear of spoiling everything if he should yield to some of his customary fits of passion. Thus the unexpected spectacle of a superbly diplomatic Abbé Cognasse, who left to Providence the duty of striking down the enemy, was presented to the village. As his servant Palmyre, who with increasing age had become quite terrible, did not possess sufficient self-restraint to imitate his silent contempt, he scolded her in public when she ventured to declare that the new school-master had stolen some consecrated wafers from the church

at Maillebois for the purpose of profaning them in the presence of his pupils. That was not proved, said the Abbé,
nor was there any proof of the story that hell had lent Marc
a devil, who, on being summoned, stepped out of the wall
and helped him with his class-work. Indoors, however,
all was agreement between the priest and the servant, who
both displayed extraordinary greed and avarice, the former
picking up as many Masses as possible, the latter keeping
the accounts, and growling angrily when money did not
come in. With reference to Marc, then, there ensued, on
the Abbé's part, a stealthy and venomous campaign, with
the object of destroying both the master and his school, in
order that he, Cognasse, might continue to reign over the
parish.

Marc, on his side, behaved as if the Church and the priest
did not exist. To win back Martineau, the council, and the
inhabitants, he contented himself with teaching the truth,
with promoting the triumph of reason over ridiculous dogmas, limiting himself strictly to his duties as a master, convinced as he was that the true and the good would prove
victorious when he should have fashioned hearts and minds
capable of will and understanding. He had necessarily
resumed the duties of secretary at the parish office, but he
there contented himself with discreetly advising Martineau,
who at heart was well pleased by his return. The Mayor
had already had a quarrel with his wife respecting the
chanting of Mass, which chanting Abbé Cognasse had done
away with now that Jauffre was no longer there. And
there was also the ancient and everlasting quarrel about the
church clock, which would not work. The first thing
which showed that a change had taken place at Jonville
was the vote of a sum of three hundred francs by the council for the purchase of a new clock which was fixed to the
pediment of the parish offices. This seemed a very bold
step to take, but it met with the approval of the villagers.
They would at last know the correct time, which the rusty,
old, worn-out clock of the church no longer gave. However, Marc avoided any semblance of triumph; he knew
that years would be needed to regain all the lost ground.
Each day would bring a little progress, and he patiently
sowed the future, convinced that those peasants would
come over to his side when they found in truth the one sole
source of health, prosperity, and peace.

And now, for Marc and Geneviève, came fruitful years

of work and happiness. He, in particular, had never felt
so courageous and strong. The loving return of his wife,
and the complete union which had followed it, brought him
fresh power, for his life now accorded with his work. In
former times he had greatly suffered at finding that, while
he claimed to teach truth to others, he could not convince
the companion of his life, the wife he loved, the mother of
his children; and he had felt hampered in his task of wresting
others from error when, from weakness or powerlessness, he
tolerated error in his own home. But now he possessed
irresistible strength, all the authority which comes to one
from example, from the realisation of happiness at the
family hearth through perfect agreement and a common
faith. And what healthy delight there was in the prosecution of the same work by the husband and the wife, acting
in conjunction one with the other, and yet freely, each retaining the exercise of his or her individuality! Moments
of weakness still came occasionally to Geneviève, but
Marc scarcely intervened; he preferred to let her regret
and repair the errors arising from the past, of her own accord.

Every evening, when the boys and girls had gone home,
the master and the mistress found themselves together in
their little lodging, and talked of the children confided to
them, taking account of the day's work, and coming to an
understanding respecting the work of the morrow, though
without binding themselves to identical programmes.
Geneviève, being sentimentally inclined, endeavoured the
more particularly to make sincere and happy creatures of
her girls, trying to free them from the ancient slavery less
by knowledge than by sense and love, for fear of casting
them into pride and solitude. Marc, perhaps, would have
gone further, and have fed both boys and girls on the same
knowledge, leaving life to indicate the social *rôle* of each
sex. Before long the great regret experienced by himself
and his wife was that they did not direct a mixed school,
like Mignot's at Le Moreux, whose population of little
more than two hundred souls supplied scarcely a dozen
boys and as many girls. At Jonville, which numbered
nearly eight hundred inhabitants, the master had some thirty
boys under him, and the mistress some thirty girls. Had
they been united, what a fine class there would have been
—Marc acting as director, and Geneviève as his assistant!
Such indeed was their idea; had they been in authority

they would no longer have separated the girls from the boys; they would have entrusted all those little folk to a married couple, a father and a mother, who would have educated and reared them one with the other as if they all belonged to their own family. They held that all sorts of advantages would result from such a course, a more logical apprenticeship of life, excellent emulation, more frank and gentle manners. In particular, the adjunction of the wife to the husband as an assistant seemed likely to prove fruitful in good results. Briefly, they would have liked to pull down the wall which separated their pupils from one another, in such wise as to have had but one school, a little miniature world in which he would have set his virility, she her tenderness, and what good work would they not then have accomplished, devoting themselves entirely to those little couples of the future!

But the regulations had to be observed, and Marc, on resuming his work, pursued the methods that he had followed at Maillebois for fifteen years.. His class was smaller than it had been there, and his resources were more limited; but he had the satisfaction of being almost *en famille*, and his action became more direct and efficacious. After all, what did it matter if the number of pupils whom he fashioned into men was only a score or so? Had each schoolmaster in all the little villages followed Marc's example, so as to endow the nation with twenty just and sensible men, the result would have sufficed to make France the emancipator of the world. Another source of contentment for Marc was that he secured almost complete liberty of action from Mauraisin's successor, the new Elementary Inspector, M. Mauroy, to whom Le Barazer, whose friend he was, had discreetly given special instructions. The village was so small that Marc's doings could not attract much attention, and thus he was able to pursue his methods without any great interference. As a first step, he again got rid of all religious emblems, all pictures, copybooks, and books in which the supernatural was shown triumphant, and in which war, massacre, and rapine appeared as ideals of power and beauty. He considered that it was a crime to poison a lad's brain with a belief in miracles, and to set brute force, assassination, and theft in the front rank as manly and patriotic duties. Such teaching could only produce imbecile inertia, sudden criminal frenzy, iniquity, and wretchedness. Marc's dream, on the contrary, was to set pictures of work

and peace before his pupils, to show sovereign reason ruling
the world, justice establishing brotherliness among men, the
ancient violence of warlike ages being condemned, and
giving place to agreement among all nations, in order that
they might arrive at the greatest possible happiness.   And
having rid his class of the poisonous ferments of the past,
Marc particularly instructed his pupils in civic morality,
striving to make each a citizen well informed about his
country, and able to serve and love it, without setting it
apart from the rest of mankind.   Marc held that France
ought no longer to dream of conquering the world by arms,
but rather by the irresistible force of ideas, and by setting
an example of so much freedom, truth, and equity, that
she would deliver all other countries and enjoy the glory of
founding with them the great confederation of free and
brotherly nations.

For the rest, Marc tried to conform to the school programmes, though, as they were very heavy, he occasionally
set them aside.   Experience had taught him that learning
was nothing if one did not understand what one learnt and
if one could not put it to use.   Accordingly, without ex-
cluding books, he gave great development to oral lessons,
and, once again, he strove to rejuvenate himself, to share
the pastimes of his pupils, and descend, as it were, to their
mental level, in such wise that, like them, he seemed to be
learning, seeking truth, and making discoveries.   It was in
the fields also that he explained to them how the soil
ought to be cultivated, and he took them to carpenters,
locksmiths, and masons in order that they might acquire
correct ideas of manual work.   In his opinion, moreover,
it was fit that gymnastics should partake of the character of
amusement, and thus playtime was largely devoted to bodily
exercise.   Again, Marc took on himself the office of a
judge; he requested his boys to lay all their little differences before him, and he strove to make his decisions
acceptable to all parties; for not only did he possess absolute faith in the beneficent power of truth upon young
minds, but he was also convinced of the necessity of equity
to content and ripen them.   By truth and justice towards
love: such was his motto.   A boy to whom one never tells
a falsehood, whom one treats invariably with justice, becomes a friendly, sensible, intelligent, and healthy man.
And this was why Marc kept such a careful watch over the
books which the curriculum compelled him to place in the

hands of his pupils; for he well knew that the best of them, written with the most excellent intentions, were still full of ancient falsehoods, the great iniquities consecrated by history. If he distrusted phrases and words, the sense of which seemed likely to escape his little peasants, and endeavoured to interpret them in clear and simple language, he feared yet more the dangerous legends, the errors of articles of faith, the abominable notions set forth in the name of a mendacious religion and a false patriotism. There was often no difference between the books written by clerics for the Brothers' schools and those which university men prepared for the secular ones. The intentional errors contained in the former were reproduced in the latter, and it was impossible for Marc to refrain from intervening and refuting those errors by verbal explanations, since it was essentially his task to fight the Congregational system of teaching, that source of all falsehood and all misery.

For four years Marc and Geneviève worked on, modestly but efficaciously, silently accomplishing as much good as was possible in their little sphere. Generations of children followed one another; and to the master and the mistress it seemed that fifty years would have sufficed to rejuvenate the world, if each child, on reaching maturity, had contributed to it a little more truth and justice. Four years of effort had certainly not yielded a marked result, but many good symptoms were manifest; the future was already rising from the fruitful soil, sown so perseveringly.

Salvan, after being pensioned off, had ended by taking up his abode at Jonville, in a little house left him by a cousin. He lived there like a sage, with just enough money to provide for his wants and indulge in the cultivation of a few flowers. In his garden, under an arbour of roses and clematis, there was a large stone table, round which on Sundays he liked to assemble a few friends, former pupils of the Training College, who chatted, fraternised, and indulged together in fine dreams. Salvan was the patriarch of the gathering, which Marc joined every Sunday, his satisfaction being complete whenever he there met Joulic, his successor at Maillebois, from whom he obtained information about his old school. Joulic was a tall, slim, fair young man, gentle yet energetic, who had taken to the teaching profession by taste, and in order to escape the brutifying office life from which his father, a petty clerk, had suffered. One of Salvan's best pupils, he brought to his work a mind liberated from all absurd dogmas, won over entirely to experimental methods. And thanks to a great deal of shrewdness and quiet firmness, which had enabled him to avoid the traps set for him by the Congregations, he proved very successful at Maillebois. He had lately married a schoolmaster's daughter, a fair little creature, gentle like himself, and this had helped to make his school an abode of gaiety and peace.

One Sunday, when Marc reached Salvan's, he found Joulic already chatting with the master of the house at the stone table in the flowery arbour, and they, at the sight of him, at once made merry.

'Come on, my friend!' cried Salvan; 'here's Joulic telling me that some more boys have left the Brothers' school at Maillebois. People say that we are beaten, but we work on quietly, and our action spreads and triumphs more and more each year!'

'Yes,' Joulic added, 'everything is progressing at Maillebois, which once seemed to be the rotten borough of clericalism. . . . Brother Joachim, Fulgence's successor, is certainly a very clever man, as artful and as prudent as the other was wild and rough, but he cannot overcome the distrust of the families of the town—the turn which public opinion has taken against the Congregational schools, where the studies are indifferent and the morals doubtful. Simon may have been reconvicted, but, all the same, the ghost of Gorgias returns to the spot which he polluted, and his very defenders are haunted by the memory of his crime. And thus I recruit each boy who leaves the Ignorantines.'

Marc, who had now seated himself, laughed and thanked his young colleague. 'You don't know how much your news pleases me, my dear Joulic,' he replied. 'When I quitted Maillebois I left a part of my heart there, and I felt worried as to what might become of the work which I had been pursuing for fifteen years; but I have long ceased to feel any anxiety, knowing my old school to be in such capable hands as yours. Yes, if some of the poison which infected Maillebois has been eliminated, it is because the pupils who quit you, year by year, become men of sense and equity. . . . Ask your old master, Salvan, what he thinks of you.'

But Joulic with a gesture curtailed Marc's praises. 'No, no,' said he, 'I am only a pawn in the great battle. If I am worth anything I owe it to my training, so that the chief

merit belongs to our master.   Besides, I am not alone at
Maillebois; I derive the most precious help, I will even say
the greatest support, from Mademoiselle Mazeline.   She
has often consoled and encouraged me.   You cannot
imagine how much moral energy that gentle and sensible
woman possesses.   A large part of our success is due to
her, for it is she who has gradually won family people over
to our cause by turning out so many good wives and
mothers.   .   .   .   When a woman personifies truth, justice, and love, she becomes the greatest power in the
world——'

Joulic paused, for at that moment Mignot made his appearance.   Those Sunday meetings brought delightful relaxation to Marc's former assistant, who cheerfully walked
the two and a half miles which separated Le Moreux from
Jonville.   Having caught Joulic's last words, he at once
exclaimed: 'Ah! Mademoiselle Mazeline — do you know
that I wanted to marry her?   I never mentioned it, but I
may admit it now.   .   .   .   It is all very well to say that
she is plain; but at Maillebois, on seeing how good and
sensible, how admirable she was, I dreamt of her.   And
one day I told her of my idea.   You should have seen how
moved she was—grave, yet smiling, quite sisterly!   She
explained her position to me, saying that she was too old—
already five and thirty, just my own age.   Besides, she
added, her girls had become her family, and she had long
renounced all idea of living for herself.   .   .   .   Yet I
fancy that my proposal stirred up some old regrets.   .   .   .
Briefly, we continued good friends, and I decided to remain
a bachelor, though this occasionally embarrasses me at Le
Moreux, on account of my girl pupils, who would be better
cared for by a woman.'

Then he, also, gave some good news of the state of feeling in his parish.   All the crass ignorance and error, which
Chagnat had voluntarily allowed to accumulate there, were
beginning to disappear.   Saleur, the Mayor, had experienced great trouble with his son, Honoré, whom he had
sent to the Lycée of Beaumont, where he had been stuffed
by the chaplain with as much religious knowledge as he
would have acquired in a seminary—in such wise that,
after being appointed to the management of a little Catholic
bank in Paris, he had come to grief there by practices
which had nearly landed him in a criminal court.   Since
then his father, the ex-grazier, who at heart had never

liked the priests, never wearied of denouncing what he called the Black Band, exasperated as he was by the downfall of his son, which had quite upset his comfortable life as an enriched peasant. And thus, at each fresh quarrel with Abbé Cognasse, he sided with schoolmaster Mignot, carrying the parish council with him, and threatening to have nothing more to do with the Church if the priest should still treat the inhabitants as a subjugated flock. Indeed, never before had that lonely sluggish village of Le Moreux so freely granted admittance to the new ideas. In part this was due to the better position which the schoolmasters had secured of recent years. Various laws had been passed improving their circumstances, and the lowest annual salaries were now fixed at twelve hundred francs without any deductions.[1] It had not been necessary to wait long for the result of this change. If Férou, ill-paid, ragged, and wretched, had formerly incurred the contempt of the peasantry on being compared by them with Abbé Cognasse, who waxed fat on surplice-fees and presents, and was therefore honoured and feared, Mignot, on the contrary, being able to live in a dignified way, had risen to his proper position—that is the first. Indeed, in that century-old struggle between the Church and the school, the whole region was now favouring the latter, whose victory appeared to be certain.

'My peasants are still very ignorant,' Mignot continued. 'You cannot imagine what a sluggish spot Le Moreux is, all numbness and routine. The peasants have lands of their own, they have never lacked bread, and they would submit to be fleeced as in former times rather than turn to anything novel and strange. . . . But there is some change all the same; I can see it by the way they take off their hats to me, and the more and more preponderating position which the school assumes in their estimation. And,

[1] It is true that such laws have been passed, but in various respects they are merely of a permissive character, and the financial circumstances of the French Government have hitherto prevented the realisation of provisions favoured by the Legislature. Several publications issued in the autumn of 1902, since M. Zola's death, have shown this to be the case. M. Zola, however, in this last section of 'Truth,' anticipates rather than follows events, as will plainly appear in the final chapters ; and, as a strong movement in favour of the secular schoolmasters is now following the suppression of the Congregational schools, considerable improvement in the former's position will probably take place before long.— *Trans.*

by the way, this morning, when Abbé Cognasse came over
to say Mass, there were just three women and a boy in the
church.   When the Abbé went off he banged the vestry
door behind him, threatening that he would n't come back
any more, as it was useless for him to walk all that distance
for nobody.'

Marc began to laugh.   'Yes,' said he, 'I 've heard that
the Abbé is getting surly again at Le Moreux.   Here he
still restrains himself, and strives to win the battle by diplomatic artfulness, particularly with the women, for his
superiors have taught him, no doubt, that one is never
beaten so long as one has the women on one's side.   I
have been told that he frequently goes to Valmarie to see
Father Crabot, and it is surely there that he acquires that
unctuous, caressing way with the ladies which surprises
one so much in a rough, brutal man of his stamp.   When
he again loses his temper, as he will some day, it will be all
over.   .   .   .   Besides, things are quite satisfactory at
Jonville.   We gain a little ground every year; the parish
is regaining prosperity and health.   In consequence of the
recent scandals the peasants no longer allow their daughters
to work at the factory of the Good Shepherd.   And it seems
that the parish council—Martineau at the head of it—
greatly regrets its imbecility in having allowed Abbé Cognasse and Jauffre to dedicate Jonville to the Sacred Heart.
I am on the lookout for an opportunity to efface that remembrance, and I shall end by finding one.'

There came a short pause.   Then Salvan, who had
listened complacently, said, by way of conclusion, in his
quiet, cheerful manner: 'All that is very encouraging.
Maillebois, Jonville, and Le Moreux are advancing towards
those better times for which we have battled.   The others
thought they would conquer us, exterminate us for ever,
and indeed, for months, it seemed as if we were dead; but
now comes the slow awakening, the seed has germinated in
the ground; it was sufficient for us to resume our work in
silence, and the good grain grows and flowers once more.
And now nothing will hinder the future harvest.   The fact
is that we have been on the side of truth, which nothing can
destroy, nothing arrest in its splendour.   .   .   .   No
doubt, things are not quite satisfactory at Beaumont.   The
sons of Doutrequin, that old Republican of the heroic times
who lapsed into clericalism, have obtained advancement,
and Mademoiselle Rouzaire still gorges her girls with Bible

history and Catechism. But even public feeling at Beaumont is beginning to change. Moreover, Mauraisin has
not succeeded at the Training College. Some of the
students have told me jocularly that my ghost appears to
him there, and paralyses him with fear. The fact is that
the impulse had been given, and he has found it impossible
to stop the emancipation of the schoolmaster. I even hope
that we shall soon be rid of him. . . . And a very
hopeful symptom is that, behind Maillebois, Jonville, and
Le Moreux, there are other small towns and villages, nearly
all in fact, where the schoolmaster is defeating the priest,
and setting the secular school erect on the ruins of the
Congregational school. Reason is triumphing, and justice
and truth are slowly increasing their sphere of conquest
at Dherbecourt, Juilleroy, Rouville, and Les Bordes. It is
a general awakening, an irresistible movement, carrying
France towards her liberating mission.'

'But it is your work!' cried Marc with sudden enthusiasm. 'There is a pupil of yours in each of the localities
you have named. They are the children of your heart and
mind; it was you who sent them as missionaries into lonely
country districts to diffuse the new gospel of truth and
justice. If people are at last awaking, returning to manly
dignity, becoming an equitable, free, and healthy democracy, it is because a generation of your pupils is now installed
in our classrooms, instructing the young, and making true
citizens of them. You are the good workman; you realised
that no progress is possible save by reason and knowledge.'

Then Joulic and Mignot seconded Marc with similar enthusiasm: 'Yes, yes, you have been the father, we are your
children! The country will only be worth what the schoolmasters may make it, and the schoolmasters themselves can
only be worth what the training colleges have made them.'

Salvan, who seemed very moved, protested with modest
bonhomie. 'Men like me, my friends? Why, there are
some everywhere; there will be plenty when they are allowed
to act. Le Barazer helped me a great deal by keeping me
at my post, and not tying me down too much. What I did?
Why, Mauraisin himself is almost obliged to do the same,
for the evolution carries him on; the work, once begun,
never stops. And you 'll see, Mauraisin's successor will
turn out even better masters than those who passed through
my hands. . . . One thing which delights me, and
which you have not mentioned, is that nowadays students

are recruited much more easily for the training colleges.
What made me most anxious in former times was the distrust, the contempt into which the teaching profession had
fallen, ill-paid, unhonoured as it was. But since the salaries
have been inceased, now that real honour attaches to the
humblest members of the profession, candidates arrive from
all quarters, so that one is able to pick and choose, and form
an excellent staff. . . . And if I have rendered any services you may be sure that, on seeing my work continued and
fulfilled, I feel rewarded beyond all my hopes. At present
I desire to remain a mere spectator of things; I applaud
your efforts, and live happily in my little garden, delighted to
be forgotten by everybody—excepting you, my lads.'

He ceased speaking, and a thrill of feeling passed
through the others as they sat there at the large stone table
in the arbour, balmy with the perfume of the roses, while
from the verdant garden, from the whole stretch of country
around them, infinite serenity was wafted.

Every year since her parents had removed to Jonville,
Louise had spent the vacation with them. Her brother
Clément would now soon be ten years old, and Marc still
kept him in his school, giving him that elementary education which he would have liked to have seen generalised,
applied to all the children of the nation to whatever class
they might belong, in order that one might have based upon
it, in accordance with the tastes and talents of the pupils, a
system of general and gratuitous secondary education. If
his own tastes should be shared by his son, he intended to
prepare him for the Training College of Beaumont, for the
great national work of salvation would lie in the humble
village schools for many years longer. Louise also had
disinterestedly set her ambition upon becoming an elementary teacher. And, indeed, on quitting the school of
Fontenay with the necessary certificates, she was, to her
great delight, appointed assistant to her former and well-
loved mistress, Mademoiselle Mazeline, at Maillebois.

At that time Louise was nineteen years of age. Salvan
had intervened with Le Barazer to secure her appointment,
which passed virtually unnoticed. The times were changing
more and more; the period of delirium—when the mere
names of Simon and Froment had sufficed to raise a tempest
—was quite over. And this emboldened Le Barazer, six
months later, to appoint Simon's son Joseph as assistant to
Joulic. Joseph, it should be said, had made his *début* at

Dherbecourt after quitting the Training College two years previously with an excellent record. As advancement his transfer to Maillebois was of little account, but it was a somewhat bold action to place him in a school where his presence implied at least some preliminary rehabilitation of his father. For a moment there was a slight outcry, the Congregations tried to stir up the parents of the town; but the new assistant soon won their favour, for he behaved very discreetly, gently, yet firmly, in all his intercourse with the children.

One incident which at that time plainly indicated the change in public opinion was the little revolution that took place at the Milhommes' stationery shop. One day Madame Edouard, so long the absolute mistress of the establishment, disappeared into the back shop, where Madame Alexandre had remained so many years. And Madame Alexandre took her place at the counter and served the customers. Nobody mistook the meaning of that revolution,—the customers were changing, the secular school was triumphing over its Congregational rival, and thus, in the interests of the business, Madame Edouard, like a good trader, made way for her sister-in-law. It must be said, too, that Madame Edouard now had some great worries with her son Victor, who, entering the army after his departure from the Brothers' school, and reaching the rank of sergeant, had lately been compromised in a very unpleasant affair; whereas Madame Alexandre had every right to be proud of her son Sébastien, who had been one of Simon's and Marc's best pupils, then Joseph's companion at the Training College, and was now, for three years past, assistant-master at Rouville. Indeed, all those young folk, Sébastien, Joseph, and Louise, after growing up together, had at last reached active life, bringing with them broad minds, ripened early in the midst of tears, to continue the bitterly-contested work of their elders.

A year went by. Louise was now twenty, and, repairing to Jonville every Sunday, spent the day with her parents. She then often met Joseph and Sébastien, who had remained great friends and were very fond of visiting their former masters, Marc and Salvan. It also frequently happened that Joseph was accompanied by his sister Sarah, who was well pleased to spend a day in the open air among her best friends. For three years past she had been residing with her grandparents, the Lehmanns, displaying so much activity and skill that a little prosperity had returned to the dismal shop in the Rue du Trou. Customers had returned to it, and Sarah, retaining the connection formed with some of the large Paris clothiers, had recruited several work girls and banded them together in a kind of co-operative group. Madame Lehmann had lately died, however, and her husband, now seventy-five years old, lingered on with only one regret, which was that his age deprived him of all hope of ever witnessing Simon's rehabilitation. Every year he spent a week or two with Simon, David, and Rachel among the Pyrenees, and returned home well pleased to have found them working quietly in their lonely retreat, but also very sad when he realized that they would know no real happiness as long as the monstrous proceedings of Rozan should remain unrevised. Sarah had tried to induce the old man to stay with the others in the south, but he obstinately returned to the Rue du Trou, under the pretence of making himself useful there by superintending the workroom. And, as it happened, this circumstance enabled the girl to take an occasional holiday when, on accompanying her brother Joseph to Jonville, she chanced to feel somewhat tired.

The reunion of the young people at Jonville, the days they spent there so gaily, brought about the long-foreseen marriages. At first it was a question of Sébastien marrying Sarah, which surprised nobody; though it was regarded as an indication of the changing times that young Milhomme should marry Simon's daughter not only with the consent of his mother but also with the approval of Madame Edouard, his aunt. A little later, when the wedding was postponed for a few months in order that it might coincide with that of Louise and Joseph, a little excitement arose at Maillebois, for this time the proposed union was one between the condemned man's son and the daughter of his most valiant defender. But the idyl of their love, which was the outcome of the old bitter battle and all the heroism that had been displayed in it, touched many a heart, and even tended to pacify the onlookers, though all were curious to learn how Louise's marriage would be regarded by her great-grandmother, Madame Duparque, who, for three years past, had not quitted her little house on the Place des Capucins. And, indeed, the marriage was postponed for another month in order that Madame Duparque might come to some decision respecting it.

Though Louise was now twenty years old, she had not made her first Communion, and it had been settled that only the civil ceremony should be performed at her wedding with Joseph, as at that of Sébastien with Sarah. Anxious as she was for an interview with Madame Duparque, the girl wrote her an entreating letter; but all in vain, for she did not even receive an answer. The old lady's door had not been opened to Geneviève and her children since they had returned to Marc. For nearly five years now the great-grandmother had clung to her fierce oath that she would cast off all her relatives and live cloistered, alone with God. Geneviève, touched by the thought of that woman of fourscore years leading in solitude a life of gloom and silence, had made a few attempts at a *rapprochement*, but they had been savagely, obstinately repulsed. Nevertheless, Louise desired to make a last attempt, distressed as she was at not having the approval of all her kinsfolk in her happiness.

One evening, then, at sunset, she repaired to the little house, which was already steeped in the dimness of twilight. But, to her astonishment, on pulling the bell-knob, she heard no sound; it seemed as if somebody had cut the wire. Gathering courage, she then ventured to knock, at first lightly, and then loudly; and at last she heard a slight noise, the board of a little judas cut in the door, as in the door of a convent, having been pulled aside.

'Is it you, Pélagie?' Louise inquired. 'Is it you? Answer me!'

It was only with difficulty, after placing her ear close to the judas, that she at last heard the servant's deadened and almost unrecognisable voice: 'Go away, go away,' Pélagie answered; 'madame says that you are to go away at once!'

'Well, no, Pélagie, I won't go away,' Louise promptly retorted. 'Go back and tell grandmother that I shall not leave the door until she has come and answered me herself.'

The girl remained waiting for ten minutes, or perhaps a quarter of an hour. From time to time she knocked again —not angrily, but with respectful, solicitous persistence. And all at once the judas was re-opened, but this time in a tempestuous fashion, and a rough, subterranean voice called to her: 'What have you come here for? . . . You wrote to me about a fresh abomination, a marriage, the very shame of which might well suffice to kill me! What is the use of speaking of it? Are you even fit to

marry ?   Have you made your first Communion ?   No, eh ?
You amused yourself with me, you were to have made it
when you were twenty years old; but to-day, no doubt, you
have decided that you will never do so.   .   .   .   So it is
useless for you to come here.   Be off, I tell you, I am dead
to you! '

Louise, quite upset, shuddering as if she had felt an icy
breath from the grave sweeping across her cheek, had
barely time to cry: ' Grandmother, I will wait a little longer;
I will come back in a month's time! '   Then the judas was
shut violently, and the little dim and silent house became
quite deathly in the darkness, which had now gathered all
around.

During the previous five years Madame Duparque had
gradually relinquished all intercourse with the world.   At
first, on the morrow of Madame Berthereau's death and
Geneviève's departure, she had contented herself with
ceasing to receive her relations, restricting herself to the
society of a few pious friends of her own sex, and of the
priests and other clerics whom she had made her familiars.
Among these was Abbé Coquard, who had succeeded Abbé
Quandieu at St. Martin's.   He was a rigid man, full of a
sombre faith, and it delighted Madame Duparque to hear
the threats which he addressed to the wicked—threats of
hell with its consuming flames, its red forks, and its boiling
oil.   Thus, morning and evening she was seen repairing
now to the parish church, now to the Capuchin Chapel, in
order to attend the various offices and ceremonies.   But
as time went by she went out less and less, and at last a
day came when she ceased to cross her threshold.   It was
as if she were gradually sinking into gloom and silence,
burying herself by slow degrees.   One day even the shutters of her house, which had still been opened every morning
and closed at night, remained closed, the façade becoming
blind, as it were, the house dead, neither a glimmer nor a
breath of life emanating from it any more.   One might have
thought that it was abandoned, uninhabited, if sundry
frocks and gowns had not been seen slipping through the
doorway at nightfall.   They were the gowns of Abbé
Coquard, Father Théodose, and at times—so people said—
Father Crabot, who thus paid the old lady friendly visits.
Her little fortune, now a matter of two or three thousand
francs a year, which she had arranged to leave, one half to
the College of Valmarie, the other to the Capuchin Chapel,

hardly sufficed to explain the fidelity of her clerical friends.
Their visits must also have been due in part to her exacting
and despotic nature, which overcame the most powerful,
and in part to their apprehensions of some deed of mystical
madness, of which they knew her to be capable. It was
said, too, that she had obtained an authorisation to hear
Mass and take the Communion at home; and this, no
doubt, explained why she no longer set foot out of doors.
By the force of her piety she had compelled even the Deity
to come to her house, in order that she might be spared the
affliction of going to His; for the idea of seeing the streets
and the people in them, of again setting her eyes on that
abominable age in which Holy Church was agonising, had
become such torture to her that she had caused her shutters
to be nailed in position, and every chink in the woodwork
to be stopped up, in order that no sound or gleam of the
world might again reach her.

This was the supreme crisis. She spent her days in
prayer. She was not content with having broken off all
intercourse with her impious and accursed relations, she
asked herself if her own salvation were not in danger
through having incurred, perhaps, some responsibility in
the damnation of her kinsfolk. She was haunted by a recollection of Madame Berthereau's sacrilegious revolt on
her death-bed, and believed that unhappy woman to be not
merely in purgatory, but in hell. Then, too, came the
thought of Geneviève, whom the demon had assailed so
terribly, and who had gone back to her errors like a dog to
his vomit. And, finally, there was Louise, the pagan, the
godless creature, who had rejected even the gift of the
Divine Body of Jesus. Those two—Geneviève and Louise
—belonged, both in body and in spirit, to the devil; and if
Madame Duparque caused Masses to be said and candles
burnt for the repose of her dead daughter's soul, she had
abandoned those who still lived to the just wrath of her
God of anger and punishment. But, at the same time, her
anguish remained extreme; she wondered why Heaven had
thus stricken her in her posterity, and strove to interpret
this visitation as a terrible trial, whence her own holiness
would emerge dazzling and triumphant. The confined,
claustral life she led, entirely devoted to religious practices,
seemed to her to be necessary reparation, for which she
would be rewarded by an eternity of delight. In this wise
she expiated the monstrous sinfulness of her descendants,

those women guilty of free thought, who, in three generations, had escaped from the Church and ended madly by
putting their belief in a religion of human solidarity.   Thus,
wishing to redeem the apostasy of her grandchildren,
Madame Duparque set all her pride in humbling herself,
in living for God alone, in seeking to slay what little
womanliness still lingered in her; for it was from that
womanliness that her condemned descendants had sprung.

So stern and sombre was her ardour that she wearied the
few clerics who alone now linked her to the world.   She
was conscious of the decline of the Church; she could detect the collapse of Catholicism under the efforts of those
diabolical times from which she had withdrawn by way of
protest against Satan's victory—as if, indeed, she denied
that victory by not beholding it.   And in her opinion her
renunciation, her fancied martyrdom, might perhaps impart new vigour to the soldiers of religion.   She would
have liked to have seen them as ardent, as resolute, as fierce
as she herself was, encasing themselves in the rigidity of
dogmas, carrying fire and sword into the midst of the unbelievers, and aiding the great Exterminator to conquer His
people by dint of thunderbolts.   She never felt satisfied;
she found Father Crabot, Father Théodose, even the sombre
Abbé Coquard, altogether too lukewarm.   She accused
them of compounding with the hateful worldly spirit of the
times, and of completing the ruin of the Church with their
own hands by adapting religion to the tastes of the day.
She dictated their duty to them, preached a campaign of
frankness and violence, unhinged as she was, thrown into
extreme exaltation by her lonely life, and ever athirst with
some supreme longings in spite of all the penitence heaped
upon her.

Father Crabot was the first to grow tired of that strange
penitent, who, at eighty-three years of age, treated herself
so harshly, and bore herself like a despairing prophetess,
whose uncompromising Catholicism was really a condemnation of the long efforts made by his own Order to humanise
the terrible Deity of the stakes and the massacres.   Thus
the Jesuit allowed long intervals to elapse between his discreet visits, and, finally, he altogether ceased to call, being
of opinion, no doubt, that the legacy he had hoped to receive for Valmarie would not be sufficient compensation
for the dangers he might incur with a woman whose soul
was ever in a tempest.   A few months later Abbé Coquard

likewise withdrew, not because he had any cowardly fears
of being compromised, but because each of his discussions with the old lady degenerated into a horrible battle.
Eager and despotic like herself, the Abbé was bent on
retaining all his power and authority as a priest; and one
day, when Madame Duparque began to thunder in the name
of God, reproaching him with inaction, in such wise that
he appeared to be a mere transgressing sinner, he became
quite angry, for he declined to accept such a reversal of
their respective positions.   Then, for nearly another year,
only Father Théodose's frock was to be seen slipping into
the little, silent, closed house of the Place des Capucins.

Father Théodose, no doubt, regarded Madame Duparque's little fortune as worth taking, for the times were hard
with poor St. Antony of Padua.   In vain did the Capuchin
scatter prospectuses broadcast; money did not now flow
into the collection boxes as it had done in the happy days
when, by a stroke of genius, he had induced Monseigneur
Bergerot to bless one of the saint's bones.   In those days
the miracle lottery had put people into quite a fever; the
sick, the idle, and the poor had all dreamt of winning happiness from heaven in return for an investment of twenty
sous; whereas, now that a little sense and truth were
spreading through the district, thanks to the secular
schools, the base commerce of the Capuchin Chapel stood
revealed in all its shameful imbecility.

For a time, it is true, another stroke of genius on the
part of Father Théodose, the creation of some wonderful
mortgage bonds on heaven, had again stirred the souls of
the humble and the suffering, who, as life below proved so
cruel to them, hungered for felicity beyond the grave.
Then, during several months, the money of dupes had
flowed in; all the savings hidden in old stockings had been
brought forth by believers anxious to secure the chance of
a little peace in the Unknown.   But finally, being confronted by growing incredulity, Father Théodose had found
it difficult to place his remaining bonds, and had thereupon
planned a third stroke of genius—this time the invention of
some private, reserved gardens in the ever-flowery Fields of
the Blessed.   According to him there were to be some delightful little nooks in Eternity, garnished with roses and
lilies of the very best varieties, under foliage set out to
please the eyes, and near springs which would be particularly pure and fresh.   And thanks once more to the decisive

intervention of St. Antony of Padua, one might book those
little nooks in advance, thereby ensuring to oneself the
eternal enjoyment of them.   Naturally, the booking was
very expensive if one desired something spacious and comfortable, though there were indeed gardens at all prices,
which varied in accordance with site, charm, and proximity
to the abodes of the angels.   Two old ladies, it appeared,
had already bequeathed their fortunes to the Capuchins in
order that the miracle-working saint might reserve for them
two of the best gardens that were still vacant, one being in
the style of an old French park, whereas the other was
more of the ' romantic ' type, with a maze and a waterfall.
And it was also said that Madame Duparque had in a like
way made her choice, this being a golden grotto on the
slope of an azure mount, among clumps of myrtle bushes
and oleanders.

Father Théodose, then, alone continued to visit the old
lady, putting up with her fits of temper, and returning to
the house even after she had driven him from it in exasperation at finding him so lukewarm and resigned to the triumph
of the Church's enemies.   And the Capuchin had actually
ended by securing a latch-key in order that he might enter
the house whenever he pleased, instead of having to ring
the bell again and again, for poor Pélagie had become extremely deaf.   It was also at this same moment that the two
women, the two recluses as they may be called, cut the bell
wire; for of what use was it to retain that connecting link
with the outer world?   The only living being whom they
now received had a key to admit himself, and by cutting
the wire they were spared the nervous starts that came upon
them whenever they heard that jangling bell which they
did not wish to answer.   Pélagie, indeed, had become as
fierce and as maniacal as her mistress.   She had begun by
curtailing her chats in the tradespeople's shops, scarcely
speaking to anybody when she went out, but gliding swiftly
past the houses like a shadow.   Next, she had decided to
go shopping twice a week only, in this wise condemning
her mistress and herself to live on stale bread and a few
vegetables—such fare as might have suited a pair of hermits
in the desert.   And now the few tradespeople came themselves to the house at nightfall on Saturday evenings, and
left their goods at the doorway in a basket, which they
found waiting for them on the ensuing Saturday, with the
money due to them wrapped in a scrap of newspaper.

At the same time Pélagie had one great worry — her nephew Polydor, who had entered a Beaumont monastery in a menial capacity, and who came and made frightful scenes with her whenever he wished to extort money. He alarmed the old woman to such a degree that she did not even dare to leave him at the door, for she felt sure that on some pretext or other he would collect a crowd and force his way in. And when she had admitted him, she trembled still more; for she knew that he was a man to deal her a nasty blow should she refuse to give him a ten-franc piece. For many long years she had caressed the dream of employing all her savings—some ten thousand francs, scraped together copper by copper—to procure some happiness in the other world; and if the little treasure was still carefully hidden away inside her palliasse, this was because she hesitated as to the best, the most efficacious mode of investment. Should she found a perpetual Mass for the repose of her soul, or should she book one of Father Théodose's reserved gardens, a modest little nook in heaven, by the side of her mistress's lordly grotto ? And she was still hesitating in this respect when misfortune fell upon her.

One night, when she had been obliged to admit Polydor, the rascal did not murder her, but rushed in turn upon every article of furniture in her garret, finally ripping up the palliasse and fleeing with the ten thousand francs, while Pélagie, whom he had thrust aside and who had fallen beside the bed, groaned with despair at seeing that bandit—who was of her own flesh and blood—make off with the blessed money which St. Antony of Padua was to have given her back in eternal delight. Would she be damned, then, as she no longer possessed the wherewithal to speculate in the miraculous lottery ? Such was the shock the old woman experienced that two days later she died; and it was Father Théodose who found her, already stark and cold, in her bare and dirty garret, to which he climbed in his surprise and anxiety at discovering her nowhere else. He was obliged to attend to everything—declare the death, make arrangements for the funeral, and busy himself as to how the last remaining inmate of the little house would live now that she had nobody left to serve her.

For several weeks past Madame Duparque, whose legs had become too feeble to support her weight, had taken to her bed, in which, however, she remained in a sitting posture, erect and tall, though withered. Little breath was

left her, yet she still seemed to reign despotically over that
silent, dark, and empty house, whence she had driven all
her kith and kin, and where the only creature, the domestic
animal, whom she had been willing to tolerate, had just
died. When Father Théodose, on returning from Pélagie's
funeral, tried to ascertain Madame Duparque's intentions
with respect to her future mode of life, he could not even
extract an answer from her. Greatly embarrassed, he insisted, and offered to send her a sister, pointing out that it
was impossible for her to attend to any household duties as
she could not even leave her bed. But she at once flew
into a temper, growled like some mighty animal stricken
unto death and unwilling to be disturbed in its final hour.
Vague charges gurgled in her throat; they were all cowards,
all traitors to their God, all egotists who abandoned the
Church in order that the vaults might not fall upon their
heads! Thereupon Father Théodose, in his turn growing
exasperated, left her, deciding that he would return the
following morning to see if she had become more reasonable.

A night and a day elapsed, for the Superior of the Capuchins was only able to return at dusk, four and twenty hours
later. During that night and day, then, Madame Duparque
remained alone, absolutely alone, behind the nailed shutters,
the carefully closed doors and windows of her dark room,
where neither a sound nor a ray of light from the outer
world penetrated. She herself had willed it thus, severing
all carnal ties with her relations, withdrawing from the
world in protest against the hateful society of the times in
which sin had proved triumphant. And, after giving herself wholly to the Church, she had gradually become disgusted with its ministers — those priests who lacked all
militant faith, those monks who had no heroic bravery, but
who were all worldly men bent on personal enjoyment.
Thus she had dismissed them also, and now she remained
alone with her Deity—an implacable and stubborn Deity,
who ruled with absolute, exterminating, and vengeful power.
All light and all life had departed from that cold, dismal,
fast-closed, and tomb-like house, where there only remained
a feeble octogenarian woman, sitting up in bed, gazing into
the black darkness, and waiting for her jealous God to carry
her away, in order that lukewarm souls might have an example of a really pious end. And when Father Théodose
presented himself at the house at dusk he found, to his in-

tense surprise, that the door would not open, that it resisted all his efforts. The key turned readily enough in the lock, and it seemed, therefore, that the door must have been bolted. But who could have bolted it? There was nobody inside except the ailing woman, who could not leave her bed. The Capuchin then made fresh attempts, but in vain; and at last, feeling frightened, unwilling to incur any further responsibility, he hastened to the Town Hall to explain the matter to the authorities. A messenger was at once sent to Mademoiselle Mazeline's for Louise; and, as it happened, Marc and Geneviève were there, having come over from Jonville as the news of Pélagie's death had made them feel anxious.

A tragical business followed. The whole family repaired to the Place des Capucins. As the door would not yield, a locksmith was sent for, but he declared he could do nothing, for assuredly the bolts were fastened. It therefore became necessary to send for a mason, who, with his pick, unsealed the door hinges set in the stone work. At each blow the silent house re-echoed like a closed vault. And when the door had been torn down it was with a quiver that Marc and Geneviève, followed by Louise, re-entered that family abode whence they had been banished. An icy dampness reigned there; it was only with difficulty that they managed to light a candle. And upstairs, in the bed, they found Madame Duparque, still in a sitting posture, propped up by pillows, but quite dead, with a large crucifix between her long, thin, shrivelled hands.

In a superhuman effort she had assuredly found the supreme energy to leave her bed, crawl down the stairs, and shoot the bolts in order that no living soul, not even a priest, might disturb her in her last communion with God. And then she had crawled upstairs again, and had died there. When Father Théodose saw her he fell on his knees, shuddering, and stammering a prayer. He was distraught, for he detected in that death not merely the end of a terrible old woman, raised to a fierce grandeur, as it were, by her uncompromising faith, but also the end of all superstitious and mendacious religion. And Marc, in whose arms Geneviève and Louise had sought a refuge, seemed to feel a great gust sweeping by, as though eternal life were springing from that death.

When the family, after leaving the funeral arrangements to Abbé Coquard, made a search in the old lady's drawers, they found nothing—neither will nor securities of any kind. It could not be said that Father Théodose had purloined any property, for he had not returned to the house. Was it to be assumed, then, that the old lady had previously handed her securities to him or to another? Or had she destroyed them, unwilling that her relatives should benefit by her fortune? The mystery was never solved, not a copper was ever found. Only the little house remained, and it was sold, the proceeds being given to the poor at the request of Geneviève, who said that in taking that course she was certainly doing what her grandmother would have desired.

In the evening, after returning from the funeral, Geneviève cast her arms round her husband's neck, and made him a frank confession: 'If you only knew!' said she. 'I was beset again when I heard that grandmother was all alone, so bravely and loftily adhering to her stubborn faith. . . . Yes, I asked myself if my place were not beside her, and if I had done right in leaving her. . . . But what can you expect, dear? I shall never be quite cured. In the depths of my being I shall always retain a little of my old belief. . . . Yet, what a frightful death that was! And how right you are in asking that people should live as they ought to; that women should be liberated, set in their right position as the equals and companions of men, and that life should partake of all that is good and true and just!'

A month later the two long-deferred weddings at last took place. Louise was married to Joseph, Sarah to Sébastien; and in those espousals Marc perceived a beginning of victory. The good crop, sown with so much difficulty in the midst of persecution and outrage, was germinating and growing already.

II

YEARS went by, and Marc continued his work, sturdy
yet at sixty years of age, and as passionately attached
to truth and justice as he had been at the outset of
the great struggle. And one day, when he happened to go
to Beaumont to call on Delbos, the latter suddenly said to
him: 'By the way, my dear fellow, I have had a strange
encounter. . . . The other evening, at dusk, while I
was returning home I noticed a man of about your age,
looking wretched and ravaged, walking ahead of me along
the Avenue des Jaffres. . . . And, all at once, in the
blaze of light coming from the confectioner's shop at the
corner of the Rue Gambetta, it seemed to me that I recognised our Gorgias.'

' Eh, our Gorgias ? '

' Why, yes, Brother Gorgias, not wearing an Ignorantine's
cassock, but a greasy frock-coat, and slipping alongside the
walls, with the suspicious gait of an emaciated old wolf.
. . . He must have come back secretly, and must be
living in some dark nook or other, still trying to frighten
and exploit his old accomplices.'

Marc, whom the announcement had greatly surprised,
remained full of doubt. 'You must have been mistaken,'
said he; 'Gorgias attaches too much value to his skin to
return to Beaumont and run the risk of being sent to the
galleys—that is whenever the discovery of a new fact may
enable us to apply for the quashing of the Rozan judgment.'

' It is you who are mistaken, my friend,' Delbos answered.
' Our man has nothing more to fear. According to our law
of limitation there can be no public action in a criminal
matter after the expiration of ten years, and so, even nowadays, little Zéphirin's murderer can walk the streets in the
daylight without any fear of arrest. . . . However, I
may have been deceived by a mere resemblance; and in
any case the return of Gorgias can have no interest for us,
for you agree with me, do you not, that we can derive
nothing useful from him ? '

' No, nothing whatever. He lied so much at the time
of the affair that if he should say anything now he would
certainly lie again. . . . The long-sought truth can
never come to us from him.'

In this wise, at long intervals, Marc called upon Delbos
in order to chat with him about that everlasting Simon
case, which, after the lapse of so many years, still remained
like a cancer gnawing at the heart of the country. People
might deny its existence, believe it to be dead, cease to
speak of it, but nevertheless it still stealthily prosecuted
its ravages, like some secret venom poisoning life. Twice
a year David quitted his lonely retreat in the Pyrenees
and came to Beaumont in order to confer with Delbos and
Marc; for, in spite of the pardon granted to his brother,
he had not for an hour relinquished his hope of eventual
acquittal and rehabilitation They, David, Delbos, and
Marc, were convinced that the monstrous verdict would be
some day set aside, and that the affair would end by the
victory of the innocent. But, even as in previous years,
after the judgment of the Court of Cassation, they found
themselves struggling amidst an intricate network of falsehoods. After hesitating for a time as to which scent they
might best follow, they had decided to investigate a second
crime committed by ex-President Gragnon, a crime which
they had already suspected at Rozan, and of which they
were now convinced.

Gragnon, at the time of the Rozan proceedings, had repeated his illegal communication trick. On this second
occasion, however, he had availed himself, not of one of
Simon's letters with a forged postscript and paraph, but of
a confession alleged to have been written by the workman
who was said to have made a false stamp for the Maillebois
schoolmaster—this confession having been handed, it was
alleged, to one of the nuns of the Beaumont hospital by the
workman in question when he was near his death. Assuredly Gragnon had walked about Beaumont with that
confession in his pocket, speaking of it as a thunderbolt
which he would hurl at the Simonists if they drove him to
extremities, showing it also, or causing it to be shown, to
certain members of the jury, those who were pious and
weak-minded, but at the same time affecting a keen desire
to save the holy nun to whom the confession had been
given from being publicly mixed up in such a scandal. And
this explained everything. The abominable behaviour of

the jury in reconvicting the innocent prisoner became ex-
cusable. Those men of average intelligence and honesty
had been deceived like the jurors of Beaumont, and had
yielded to motives which had remained secret. Marc and
David well remembered that they had heard some juryman
ask certain questions which had then seemed to them
ridiculous. But they now understood that this juryman
had referred to the terrible document which Gragnon had
stealthily hawked about, and of which it was not prudent to
speak plainly. Delbos therefore busied himself with that
new fact, that second criminal communication, which, if
proved, would entail the immediate annulment of the proceedings at Rozan. But, unfortunately, nothing could be
more difficult to prove, and for years Delbos and his friends
had striven vainly. Only one hope remained to them: a
juror, a retired medical man, named Beauchamp, had
acquired a certainty that the workman's alleged confession
was simply a gross forgery. In a measure things repeated
themselves, as is not infrequently the case in real life,
Beauchamp being assailed by remorse like his predecessor,
architect Jacquin. He himself, it is true, was not a clerical,
but he had an extremely devout wife and did not wish to
plunge her into desolation by relieving his conscience.
Thus it was necessary to wait.[1]

However, as the years went by, circumstances became
more favourable. Thanks to the spread of secular education the social evolution was being hastened and giving
great results. All France was being renewed, a new nation
was coming from its thousands of parish schools, whose influence was to be found beneath each fresh reform that was
effected, each fresh step that was taken toward solidarity
and peace. Things which had seemed impossible in former
times were easily accomplished now that the nation was delivered from error and falsehood, endowed with knowledge
and force of will.

Thus, at the general elections which took place in May

[1] It may be held that M. Zola has perpetrated an artistic blunder by
introducing into his narrative a repetition, so to say, of the Jacquin epi-
sode; but it should be remembered that the Simon affair is based on
the Dreyfus case, in which there were several repetitions of that character. Among those who sat in judgment on Dreyfus, Esterhazy, and
Picquart, there were repeated instances of belated conscientious scruples,
some indeed known to the initiated but never made public. Thus, if
M. Zola is inartistic in making two characters of his story adopt virtually
the same course, he is at least true to life.—*Trans.*

that year, Delbos at last defeated Lemarrois, who had been
Mayor of Beaumont for so long a period. At one time it
had seemed as if the latter would never lose his seat, per-
sonifying as he did the great mass of average public opinion.
But the *bourgeoisie* had denied its revolutionary past, and
allied itself with the Church in order that it might not have
to abandon any of its usurped power. It clung to the privileges it had acquired, and, rather than share its royalty or
its wealth with the masses, it preferred to make use of all
the old reactionary forces in order to thrust the now awakened and enlightened people into servitude once more.
Lemarrois was a typical example of the *bourgeois* Republican, who, wishing to defend his class, sank into a kind of
involuntary reaction, and was therefore condemned and
swept away in the inevitable *débâcle* of that *bourgeoisie* which
a hundred years of trafficking and enjoyment had sufficed
to rot. It was inevitable that the people should ascend to
power as soon as it became conscious of its strength, of the
inexhaustible reserve of energy, intelligence, and will slumbering within it; and it was sufficient that it should be
emancipated, roused from the heavy sleep of ignorance by
the schools in order that it might take its due place and rejuvenate the nation. The *bourgeoisie* was now at the point
of death, and the people would necessarily become the great
liberating, justice-dealing France of to-morrow. And there
was, so to say, an annunciation of all those things in the
victory achieved at Beaumont by Delbos, the man who had
been Simon's counsel, who had been denied and insulted
so long, at first securing only a few Socialist votes, which by
degrees had become an overwhelming majority.

Another proof of the people's accession to power was to be
found in the complete change which had come over Marcilly.
He had formerly figured in a Radical ministry; then, after the
reconviction of Simon, he had entered a Moderate administration; and now he affected extreme Socialist principles;
and, by harnessing himself to Delbos's triumphal car, had
managed to get re-elected. It is true that the popular victory was not complete throughout the department, for Count
Hector de Sanglebœuf had also been re-elected, this time
as an uncompromising reactionary; for the usual phenomenon of troublous times had appeared, only plain, frank, extreme opinions finding support. The party vanquished for
ever was the old Liberal *bourgeoisie*, which had become
Conservative from egotism and fright, and which, lacking

all strength and logic, was ripe for its fall. And the ascending class, the great mass of those who only the day before had been called the disinherited, would naturally take the place of the *bourgeoisie* after sweeping away the few stubborn defenders that remained to the Church.

But the election of Delbos was particularly notable as being the first great success achieved by one of those rascals without God or country, one of those traitors who had publicly declared Simon to be innocent. After the monstrous proceedings of Rozan all the notable Simonists had suffered in their persons or their pockets for having dared to desire truth and justice. Insult, persecution, summary dismissal had been heaped upon them. There was Delbos, to whom no client had dared to confide his interests; there was Salvan dismissed, compulsorily retired; there was Marc disgraced, sent to a little village; and behind the leaders how many others there were, relations and friends, who for merely behaving in an upright manner were assailed with worries, and at times even ruined!

Full of mute grief at the sight of such aberration, well understanding that all rebellion was useless, the friends of truth had simply turned to their work, awaiting the inevitable hour when reason and equity would triumph. And that hour seemed to be approaching; for now Delbos, one of the most deeply involved in the affair, had defeated Lemarrois, who had long pursued a pusillanimous policy, refusing to take sides either for or against Simon. Was not this a proof that opinion had changed, that a great advance had been effected? Moreover, Salvan secured consolation, for one of his old pupils was appointed to the directorship of the Training College after Mauraisin had been virtually dismissed for incapacity. Great was the delight of the sage when those tidings reached him, not because it pleased him to crow over his vanquished adversary, but because he at last saw the continuation of his work entrusted to one who was brave and faithful. And, finally, a day came when Le Barazer, who now felt strong enough to repair former injustice, sent for Marc and offered him the head mastership of a school at Beaumont. Such an offer, on the part of that prudent diplomatist, the Academy Inspector, was extremely significant, and Marc was pleased indeed; nevertheless he declined it, for he did not wish to leave Jonville, where his task was not yet finished.

There were also other precursory signs of the great

impending change in the country.   Prefect Hennebise had been replaced by a very energetic and sensible functionary who had immediately demanded the revocation of Depinvilliers, under whose management the Lycée of Beaumont had become a kind of seminary.   Rector Forbes had been compelled to rouse himself from the study of ancient history, in order to dismiss the chaplains, rid the classrooms of the religious emblems placed in them, and secularise secondary as well as elementary education.   Then General Jarousse, having been placed on the retired list, had decided to quit Beaumont; for, though his wife owned a house there, he was exasperated with the new spirit which reigned in the town, and did not wish to come into contact with his successor, a Republican general, whom some people even declared to be a Socialist.   Moreover, ex-investigating Magistrate Daix had met a wretched death, haunted as he was by spectres, in spite of his belated confession at Rozan; while the former Procureur de la République, Raoul de La Bissonnière, after having a fine career in Paris, seemed likely to come to grief there amidst the collapse of a colossal swindle[1] which he had in some way befriended.   And, as a last and excellent symptom of the times, nobody now saluted Gragnon, the ex-presiding judge, when, thin and yellow, he anxiously threaded the Avenue des Jaffres, hanging his head but glancing nervously to right and left as if he feared that somebody might spit upon him as he passed.

The happy effects of free and secular education, which brought light and health in its train, were also manifest at Maillebois, whither Marc often repaired to see his daughter Louise, who, with Joseph her husband, lived in the little lodging which Mignot had so long occupied at the Communal school.   Maillebois, indeed, was no longer that intensely clerical little town, where the Congregations had succeeded in raising their creature Philis to the mayoralty. In former times the eight hundred working men of the *faubourg*, being divided among themselves, could return only a few Republicans to the Municipal Council, in which they were reduced to inaction.   But at the recent elections the whole Republican and Socialist list had passed, by a large majority, in such wise that Darras, defeating his rival Philis, had now again become Mayor.   And his delight at returning to that office, whence the priests had driven him, was

---

[1] All newspaper readers know that various judicial personages have been compromised in recent French swindles.— *Trans.*

the keener as he was now supported by a compact majority which would enable him to act frankly instead of being continually reduced to compromises.

Marc met Darras one day and found him quite radiant. 'Yes, I remember,' said he, 'you did not think me very brave in former times. That poor Simon! I was convinced of his innocence, yet I refused to act when you came to me at the municipal offices. But how could I help it? I had a bare majority of two, the council constantly escaped my control, and the proof is that it ended by overthrowing me. . . . Ah! if I had then only had the majority we now possess! We are the masters at last, and things will move quickly, I promise you.'

Marc smiled and asked him what had become of Philis, his defeated adversary.

'Philis—oh! he has been greatly tried. A certain person —you know whom I mean—died recently, and so he has had to resign himself to living alone with his daughter Octavie, a very pious young woman who does not care to marry. His son Raymond, being a naval officer, is always far away, and the house cannot be very cheerful, unless indeed Philis is already seeking consolation, which may be the case, for I saw a new servant there the other day—yes, quite a sturdy, fresh-looking girl!'

Darras burst into a loud laugh. For his own part, having retired from business with a handsome fortune, he was living his last years in perfect union with his wife, their only regret being that they had no children.

'Well,' Marc resumed, 'Joulic may now feel certain that he will not be worried any more. . . . It is he, you know, who, in spite of all difficulties, transformed the town with his school, and made your election possible.'

'Oh! you were the first great worker,' Darras exclaimed. 'I don't forget the immense services which you rendered. . . . But you may be quite easy, Joulic is now safe from all vexations, and I will help him as much as I can in his efforts to make Maillebois free and intelligent. . . . Besides, your daughter Louise and Simon's son Joseph are now, in their turn, continuing the work of liberation. You are a knot of brave but modest workers, to whom we shall all feel very grateful hereafter.'

Then, for a moment, they chatted about the now distant times when Marc had been first appointed to the Maillebois school. More than thirty years had elapsed! And how

many were the events that had occurred, and how many
were the children who had passed through the schoolroom
and carried some of the new spirit into the district around
them! Marc recalled some of his old, his first, pupils.
Fernand Bongard, the little peasant with the hard nut, who
had married Lucille Doloir, an intelligent girl, whom Mademoiselle Rouzaire had tried to rear in sanctimonious fashion, was now the father of a girl eleven years of age, named
Claire, whom Mademoiselle Mazeline was freeing somewhat
from clerical servitude. Then Auguste Doloir, the mason's
undisciplined son, who had married Angèle Bongard, an
obstinate young woman of narrow ambition, had a son of
fifteen, Adrien, a remarkably intelligent youth whom Joulic,
his master, greatly praised. Charles Doloir, the locksmith,
who had been as bad a pupil as his brother, but who had
improved somewhat since his marriage with his master's
daughter, Marthe Dupuis, also had a son, Marcel, who was
now thirteen, and had left the school with excellent certificates. There was also Léon Doloir, who, thanks to Marc,
had taken to the teaching profession, and after becoming
one of Salvan's best students, now directed the school at
Les Bordes, assisted by his wife, Juliette Hochard, who had
quitted the Training School at Fontenay with 'No. 1'
against her name. That young couple was all health and
good sense, and their life was brightened by the presence
of a little four-year-old urchin, Edmond, who was sharp for
his age, already knowing his letters thoroughly. Then
came the twin Savins: first Achille, so sly, so addicted to
falsehoods as a boy, then placed with a process-server,
dulled like his father by years of office work, and married
to a colleague's sister, Virginie Deschamps, a lean and insignificant *blonde*, by whom he had a charming little girl,
Léontine, who at eleven years of age had just secured her
certificate, and was one of Mademoiselle Mazeline's favourite pupils. Then came Philippe Savin, who, long remaining
without employment, had been rendered better by a life of
hardship, and was now still a bachelor, and manager of a
model farm, being associated in that enterprise with his
younger brother Jules, the most intelligent of the two,
who had given himself to the soil and married a peasant
girl, Rosalie Bonin—their firstborn, Pierre, now six years
old, having lately entered Joulic's school. Thus generation followed generation, each going towards increase of
knowledge, reason, truth, and justice, and it was assuredly

from that constant evolution which education produced, that the happiness of the communities of the future would spring.

But Marc was more particularly interested in the home of Louise and Joseph, and in that of his dearest pupil, Sébastien Milhomme, who had married Sarah. That day, on quitting Darras, he repaired to the Communal school in order to see his daughter. Mademoiselle Mazeline, now more than sixty years of age, with a record of forty years spent in elementary teaching, had, like Salvan, lately retired to Jonville, where she now dwelt in a very modest little house near his beautiful garden. She might still have rendered some services in her profession had not her eyesight failed her. Indeed, she was nearly blind. In retiring, however, she at least had the consolation of handing her duties over to her well-loved assistant Louise, who was appointed head mistress in her stead. Moreover, a headmastership at Beaumont was now being spoken of for Joulic, in such wise that his assistant Joseph might succeed him at Maillebois; and thus the young couple would share the school which still re-echoed the names of Simon and Marc, whose good work they would continue. Louise, who was now two and thirty, had presented her husband with a son, François, who at twelve years of age was already wonderfully like his grandfather Marc. And the ambition of that big bright-eyed boy with the lofty brow was to enter the Training College like his forerunners, for he also wished to become an elementary teacher.

It was a Thursday—half-holiday day—and Marc found Louise just quitting a house-work class which she held once a week outside the regulation hours. Joseph, with his son and some other boys, had gone on a geological and botanical ramble along the banks of the Verpille. But Sarah happened to be with Louise, for she was very much attached to her sister-in-law, and always visited her when she came over from Rouville, where her husband Sébastien was now headmaster.

They had a charming little girl, Thérèse, in whom all the beauty of her grandmother Rachel had reappeared. And three times a week Sarah came from Rouville to Maillebois —the journey by rail lasting barely ten minutes—in order to superintend the tailoring business which was still carried on at old Lehmann's in the Rue du Trou. He was now very old indeed, more than eighty, and as it had become difficult for Sarah to superintend the establishment she thought of disposing of it.

As soon as Marc had kissed Louise he pressed both of Sarah's hands. 'And how is my faithful Sébastien?' he asked. 'How is your big girl Thérèse, and how are you yourself, my dear?'

'Everybody is in the best of health,' Sarah answered gaily. 'Even grandfather Lehmann is as strong as an oak-tree in spite of his advanced years. . . . And I have had good news from yonder, you know. Uncle David has written to say that my father has got over the attacks of fever which have been troubling him occasionally.'

Marc jogged his head gently. 'Yes, yes, his wound is not altogether healed. To restore him completely to health one needs that long-desired rehabilitation which it is so difficult to obtain. We are advancing towards it, however; I am still full of hope, for glorious times are coming. . . . Remind Sébastien that each boy he makes a man of will be another worker in the cause of truth and justice.'

Then Marc chatted a while with Louise, giving her news of Mademoiselle Mazeline, who lived a very retired life at Jonville in the company of birds and flowers. And he made his daughter promise to send her son François to spend the Sunday there, for it was a great delight for his grandmother to have the boy with her occasionally. 'And why not come yourself?' he added. 'Tell Joseph to come as well; we will all call on Salvan, who will be well pleased to see such a gathering of teachers, whose father in a measure he is. . . . And you, Sarah, you ought to come with Sébastien and your daughter Thérèse. Let it be a general outing and our pleasure will be complete. . . . Come, it is understood, eh? Till Sunday, then!'

He kissed the two young women and hurried away, for he wished to catch the six-o'clock train. But he nearly missed it by reason of a strange encounter which for a moment delayed him. He was turning out of the High Street into the avenue leading to the railway station, when he espied two individuals who were disputing violently behind a clump of spindle trees. One of them, who seemed to be a man of forty, attracted Marc's attention by his long, livid, and doltish face. Where was it that he had previously seen that stupid, vicious countenance? All at once he remembered: that man was certainly Polydor, Pélagie's nephew. For more than twenty years Marc had not met him, but he

was aware that he had been dismissed, long ago, from the
Beaumont convent which he had entered as a servant, and
that he led a chance existence among the knaves of dis-
reputable neighbourhoods.   However, Polydor, noticing
and probably recognising the bystander who was looking at
him so attentively, hastened to lead his companion away.
And then, as Marc glanced at the other man, he started
with surprise.   Clad in a dirty frock-coat, looking both
wretched and fierce, Polydor's companion had the haggard
countenance of an old bird of prey.   Surely he was Brother
Gorgias!   Marc at once remembered what Delbos had told
him; and thereupon, wishing to arrive at a certainty, he
started after the two men, who had already turned into a
little side street.   But though he gave the street a good
look, he could see nobody.   Polydor and the other had disappeared into one of the houses of suspicious aspect which
lined it.   Then Marc again began to doubt.   Was it really
Gorgias whom he had seen?   He was not prepared to swear
it; he feared that he had perhaps yielded to some fancy.

At present Marc triumphed at Jonville.   By degrees, as
healthy and reasonable men had emerged from his school,
the mentality of the region had improved, and not only was
there increase of knowledge, logic, frankness, and brotherliness, but great material prosperity was appearing, for a
land's fortune and happiness depend solely upon the mental
culture and the civic morality of its inhabitants.   Again,
then, was abundance returning to clean and well-kept
homes; the fields, thanks to newly adopted methods of
culture, displayed magnificent crops; the country-side was
once more becoming a joy for the eyes in the bright summer
sunshine.   And thus a happy stretch of land was at last
advancing towards that perpetual peace which for centuries
had been so ardently desired.

Martineau the Mayor, followed by the whole parish council, now acted in agreement with Marc.   A series of incidents had hastened that good understanding by which all
desirable reforms were accelerated.   Abbé Cognasse, after
for some time restraining himself, in accordance with the
advice given him at Valmarie, which was to retain his influence over the women,—for whoever possesses their support
proves invincible,—had relapsed into his wonted violence,
incapable as he was of long remaining patient, and enraged,
too, at seeing the women gradually escape from him, owing
to the ill grace with which he sought to detain them.   At

last, like the vengeful minister of a ravaging and exterminating Deity, he became absolutely brutal, distributing outrageous punishment in his wrath at the slightest offences. One day, for instance, he rubbed little Moulin's ears till they positively bled, merely because the lad had playfully pulled the skirts of the terrible Palmyre, who, in her time, had administered smacks and whippings so freely. Another day the Abbé boxed young Catherine's ears in church because she laughed during Mass on seeing him blow his nose at the altar. And finally, one Sunday, quite beside himself at finding that the district was escaping from his control, he actually launched a kick at Madame Martineau the mayoress, imagining that she defied him because she did not make room for him to pass as quickly as he desired. This time it was held that his behaviour exceeded all bounds, and Martineau, quite enraged, cited him before the Tribunal of Correctional Police, with the result that the battle became a furious one, Cognasse retaliating with fresh acts of violence, and gathering quite a quantity of lawsuits around him.

Marc meanwhile, anxious to complete his work in the village, had been nursing an idea, which he was at last able to carry into effect. In consequence of some new laws enacted by the Legislature, the Sisters of the Good Shepherd, who carried on the factory in which two hundred work-girls were sweated and starved, had been obliged to quit Jonville. And it was a good riddance for the district, a plague-spot, a shame the less. Marc, however, persuaded the parish council to purchase the large factory buildings, when they were offered for sale by auction; his idea being to modify and turn them into a Common House, in which recreation and dancing rooms, a library, a museum, and even some free baths might be gradually installed as by degrees the resources of the parish increased. In this wise he dreamt of setting, in full view of the church, a kind of civic palace, which would become a meeting and recreation place for the hard-working community. If the women for years past had only continued to go to Mass in order to show their new gowns and see those of their acquaintances, they would yet more willingly repair to that cheerful palace of solidarity, where a little healthy amusement would await them. Thus, the recreation rooms were the first inaugurated, and the ceremony gave rise to a great popular demonstration.

The desire of the inhabitants was to efface and redeem that former consecration of the parish to the Sacred Heart, which had filled the mayor and the council with keen remorse ever since they had recovered their senses. Martineau, for his part, accounted for that proceeding by accusing Jauffre of having abandoned him to Abbé Cognasse, after disturbing his mind by threatening both the parish and himself with all sorts of misfortunes if he did not submit to the Church, which would always be the most powerful of the social forces. Martineau, who now perceived that this was not correct, for the Church was already being beaten, and the more the district drew away from it the more prosperous it became, was very desirous of setting himself on the winning side, like a practical peasant, one who talked little but who always kept his eye fixed on the main chance. He would therefore have liked some kind of abjuration, some ceremony such as might allow him to come forward at the head of the council, and restore the parish to the worship of reason and truth, in order to wipe out that former ceremony when it had dedicated itself to dementia and falsehood. And it was this desire which Marc thought of fulfilling by arranging that the mayor and the council should in a fitting manner inaugurate the recreation rooms of the new Common House, in which it was proposed that the inhabitants of the district should meet every Sunday to take part in suitable civic festivities.

Great preparations were made. It was arranged that the pupils of Marc and Geneviève should act a little play, dance, and sing. An orchestra was soon recruited among the young men of the region. Maidens clad in white were also to sing and dance in honour of the work of the fields and the joys of life. Indeed it was particularly life, lived healthily and fully, overflowing with duties and felicities, that was to be celebrated as the universal source of strength and certainty. And the various games and recreations which had been provided, games of skill and energy, gymnastic appliances, with running tracks and lawns set out in the adjoining grounds, were to be handed over to the young folk who would meet there every week, while shady nooks would be reserved for wives and mothers, who would be drawn together and enlivened by having a *salon*, a meeting place, assigned to them. For the inaugural ceremony, the rooms were decorated with flowers and foliage, and already at an early hour the inhabitants of Jonville, clad in their Sunday best, filled the village streets with their mirth.

By Marc's desire, and with the consent of the parents, Mignot, that Sunday, brought his pupils over from Le Moreux in order that they might participate in the festivity. He was met by Marc near the church just as old Palmyre double-locked the door of the edifice in a violent, wrathful fashion. That morning Abbé Cognasse had said Mass to empty benches, and it was he who, in a fit of furious anger, had ordered his servant to close the church. Nobody should enter it again, said he, as those impious people were bent on offering sacrifices to the idols of human bestiality. He himself had disappeared, hiding away in the parsonage whose garden wall bordered the road leading to the new Common House.

'This is the second Sunday that he has not gone to Le Moreux,' Mignot said to Marc. 'He declares with some truth that it is not worth his while to trudge so many miles to say Mass in the presence of two old women and three little girls. The whole village has rebelled against him, you know, since he brutally spanked little Eugénie Louvard for having put out her tongue to him; though that is only one of the acts of violence in which he has indulged since he has felt himself to be defeated. Curiously enough, it is I who am obliged to defend him now for fear lest the indignant villagers should do him an injury.'

Mignot laughed and, on being questioned, gave further particulars. 'Yes, Saleur, our mayor, has talked of bringing an action against him and writing to his bishop. As a matter of fact, if I at first had some difficulty in extricating Le Moreux from the ignorance and credulity in which it was steeped by my predecessor Chagnat, at present I simply have to let events follow their course. The whole population is rallying around me, the school will soon reign without a rival, for, as the church is being shut up, the battle is virtually over.'

'Oh! we have not got to that point yet,' Marc answered. 'Here, at Jonville, Cognasse will resist till the last moment —that is, as long as he is paid by the State and imposed on us by Rome. But I have often thought that the lonely little hamlets like Le Moreux, particularly when life is easy there, would be the first to free themselves from the priests, because the latter's departure would make virtually no alteration in their social life. When people don't like their priest, when they go to church less and less, the disappearance of the priest is witnessed without regret.'

However, Marc and Mignot could not linger chatting any longer, for the ceremony would soon begin. So they repaired to the Common House, where their pupils had now assembled. They there found Geneviève with Salvan and Mademoiselle Mazeline, both the latter having emerged from their retirement to attend that festival which was, so to say, their work, the celebration of their teaching. And everything passed off in a very simple, fraternal, and joyous manner. The authorities, Martineau wearing his scarf of office at the head of the council, took possession of that little Palace of the People in the name of the parish. Then the schoolchildren acted, played, and sang, inaugurating, as it were, the future of happy peace and beneficent work with their healthy and innocent hands. It was, indeed, ever-reviving youth, it was the children, who would overcome the last obstacles on the road to the future city of perfect solidarity. That which the child of to-day had been unable to do would be done by the child of to-morrow. And when the little ones had raised their cry of hope, the youths and the maidens came forward, displaying the promise of early fruitfulness. One found, too, maturity and harvest in all the assembled fathers and mothers, behind whom were the old folk typifying the happy evening which attends life when it has been lived as it should be lived. And all were now acquiring a true consciousness of things, setting their ideal no longer in any mysticism, but in the proper regulation of human life, which needed to be all reason, truth, and justice in order that mankind might dwell together in peace, brotherliness, and happiness. Henceforth Jonville would have a meeting hall in that fraternal house where joy and health would take the place of threat and punishment, where enlightenment would gladden the hearts of one and all. No heart nor mind would be disturbed there by mystical impostures, no shares in any false paradise would be offered for sale. Those who came forth from that building would be cheerful citizens, happy to live for the sake of the joy of life. And all the cruel and grotesque absurdity of dogmas would crumble in the presence of that simple gaiety, that beneficent light.

The dancing lasted until the evening. Never had the comely peasant women of Jonville participated in such a festival. Everybody noticed the radiant countenance of

Madame Martineau, who had remained one of Abbé Cognasse's last worshippers, though, in reality, she had only gone to church in order to show off her new gowns. She wore a new gown that day, and was delighted at being able to display it without any fear that it might become soiled by trailing over damp and dirty flagstones. Again, she knew that she ran no risk of being kicked if she did not get soon enough out of somebody's way. Briefly, in that Common House Jonville would at last have a fitting *salon* where one and all might freely meet and chat, and even indulge in a little harmless coquetry.

But it so happened that an extraordinary incident marked the close of that great day. Marc and Geneviève were escorting their pupils homeward, with Mignot, who also had marshalled his children together; and Salvan and Mademoiselle Mazeline likewise figured in the party, which was all gaiety, jest, and laughter. Near by, too, there was Madame Martineau, accompanied by a group of women, to whom she recounted the result of the legal proceedings which her husband had brought against the priest for kicking her. Fifteen witnesses had given evidence before the Court, and after some uproarious proceedings Abbé Cognasse had been sentenced to a fine of five and twenty francs, this being the chief cause of the fury which he had displayed for several days past. And, all at once, as Madame Martineau—finishing her narrative as she passed the parsonage garden—remarked that the fine was no more than the priest deserved, Abbé Cognasse in person popped his head over the garden wall and began to vociferate insults.

'Ah! you vain hussy!' he cried, 'you lying thing! how dare you spit on God? I'll force your serpent tongue back into your throat!'

How was it that the priest happened to be there at that particular moment? Nobody could tell. Perhaps he had been waiting behind the wall for the return of the villagers. Perhaps he had set a ladder in readiness in order that he might climb and look over. At all events, when he perceived La Martineau in her new gown, surrounded by a number of other sprucely dressed women, who had deserted the church to attend an impious ceremony in the devil's house, he completely lost his head.

'You shameless creatures, you make the very angels weep!' he shouted. 'You cursed creatures, you poison the whole district with your filth! But wait, wait a moment, I

will settle your accounts for you without waiting for Satan
to come and take you!'

And forthwith, exasperated as he was at no longer having
even the women with him,—those unhappy, feared, and exe-
crated women whom the Church captures and employs as
its instruments,—he tore some stones from the ruined coping
of the wall and flung them with his lean dark hands at
Madame Martineau and her companions.

'That's one for you, La Mathurine!' he shouted. 'I
know of your goings on with your husband's farm hands!
. . . That's one for you, La Durande! You robbed
your sister of her share of your father's property. . . .
And here's for you, La Désirée! You have n't yet paid
for the three Masses which I said for the repose of your
child's soul! . . . And as for you, you, La Martineau,
who got the judges to condemn God and me, here's one
stone, and two, and three! Yes, wait a moment, you
shall have a stone for every one of those five and twenty
francs!'

The scandal was tremendous; two women were struck,
and the rural guard, who had now come up, at once began
to scribble an official report. Amidst the shouting and
hooting Abbé Cognasse suddenly recovered his senses.
Like some deity threatening the world with destruction he
made a last fierce gesture, then sprang down his ladder, and
disappeared like a Jack into his box. He had just set another fine lawsuit on his shoulders, which bent already beneath a pile of citations.

On the following Thursday Marc repaired to Maillebois,
and a fancy which had been haunting him for some time
past was then suddenly changed into certainty. While
crossing the little Place des Capucins, his attention was attracted by a wretched-looking man, who stood in front of
the Brothers' school gazing fixedly at the dilapidated walls.
And Marc immediately recognised this man to be the one
whom he had perceived with Polydor, in the avenue leading
to the railway station, a month previously. This time he
had no cause for hesitation. He was able to examine the
man at his ease, in the broad sunlight, and he saw that he
was, indeed, Brother Gorgias—Gorgias, in old and greasy
clothing, with hollow cheeks and bent limbs, but still easily
recognisable by the large, fierce beak which jutted out from
between his projecting cheek-bones. Thus Delbos had not
been mistaken; Gorgias had really returned, and, doubtless,

had been prowling about the region for a good many months
already.

The Ignorantine, amid the reverie into which he had sunk
as he stood on that sleepy and almost invariably deserted
little square, must have become conscious of the scrutinising
gaze which was being directed upon him.   He slowly turned
round, and his eyes then met those of the man who stood
only a few steps away.   And he, on his side, assuredly
recognised Marc.   Instead, however, of evincing any alarm,
instead of taking to his heels as he had done on the first occasion, he lingered there, and his old sneer, that involuntary
twitching of the lips which disclosed some of his wolfish
teeth in a manner suggesting both contempt and cruelty,
appeared upon his face.   Then, pointing to the tumble-
down walls of the Brothers' school, he said quietly: ' That
sight must please you every time you pass this way—eh,
Monsieur Froment ?   .   .   .   It angers me; I 'd like to set
fire to the shanty, and burn the last of those cowards in it! '

Then, as Marc shuddered without replying, thunderstruck
as he was by the bandit's audacity in addressing him,
Gorgias again grinned in his silent, evil way, and added:
' Are you astonished that I should confess myself to you?
You, no doubt, were my worst enemy.   But, after all, why
should I bear you malice?   You owed me nothing, you
were fighting for your own opinions.   .   .   .   The men I
hate and whom I mean to pursue until my last breath are
my superiors, my brothers in Jesus Christ, all those whose
duty it was to cover and save me, but who flung me into
the streets, hoping I should die of shame and starvation.
.   .   .   I myself, it may be allowed, am but a poor and
erring creature, but it was God whom those wretched
cowards betrayed and sold, for it is their fault, the fault of
their imbecile weakness if the Church is now near to defeat,
and if that poor school yonder is already falling to pieces.
.   .   .   Ah! when one remembers what a position it held
in my time!   We were the victors then; we had reduced
your secular schools to next to nothing.   But now they are
triumphing, and will soon be the only ones left.   The
thought of it fills me with regret and anger! '

Then, as two old women crossed the square and a Capuchin came out of the neighbouring chapel, Gorgias, after
glancing anxiously about him, added swiftly in an undertone: ' Listen to me, Monsieur Froment; for a long time
past I have wished to have a chat with you.   If you are

willing I will call on you at Jonville some day, after night-fall.'

Then he hurried off, disappearing before Marc could say a word. The schoolmaster, who was quite upset by that meeting, spoke of it to nobody excepting his wife, who felt alarmed when she heard of it. They agreed that they would not admit that man if he should venture to call on them, for the visit he announced might well prove to be some machination of treachery and falsehood. Gorgias had always lied, and he would lie again; so it was absurd to expect from him any useful new fact such as had been sought so long. However, some months elapsed and the other made no sign; in such wise that Marc who, at the outset, had remained watchful with a view of keeping his door shut, gradually grew astonished and impatient. He wondered what might be the things which Gorgias had wished to tell him; and a desire to know them worried him more and more. After all, why should he not receive the scamp? Even if he learnt nothing useful from him, he would have an opportunity of fathoming his nature. And having come to that conclusion, Marc lived on in suspense, waiting for the visit which was so long deferred.

At last, one winter evening, when the rain was pouring in torrents, Brother Gorgias presented himself, clad in an old cloak, streaming with mud and water. As soon as he had rid himself of that rag, Marc showed him into his classroom, which was still warm, for the fire in the faïence stove was only just dying out. A little oil lamp alone cast some light over a portion of that large and silent room around which big shadows had gathered. And Geneviève, trembling slightly with a vague fear of some possible attempt upon her husband, remained listening behind a door.

As for Brother Gorgias, he, without any ado, resumed the conversation interrupted on the Place des Capucins, as if it had taken place that very afternoon.

'You know, Monsieur Froment,' he began, 'the Church is dying because she no longer possesses any priests resolute enough to support her by fire and steel, if need be. Not one of the poor fools, the whimpering clowns of the present day, loves or even knows the real God—He who at once exterminated the nations that dared to disobey Him, and who reigned over the bodies and souls of men like an absolute master, ever armed with resistless thunderbolts. . . . How can you expect the world to be different from what it

is, if the Deity now merely has poltroons and fools to speak
in His name?'

Then Gorgias enumerated his superiors, his brothers in
Christ, as he called them, one by one, and a perfect massacre
ensued.   Monseigneur Bergerot, who had lately died at the
advanced age of eighty-seven, had never been aught than
a poor, timid, incoherent creature, lacking the necessary
courage to secede from Rome and establish that famous
liberal and rationalist Church of France which he had
dreamt of, and which would have been little else than a
new Protestant sect.   Those lettered Bishops gifted with
inquiring minds, but destitute of all sturdiness of faith,
suffered the incredulous masses to desert the altars instead
of flagellating them mercilessly with the dread of hell.   But
Gorgias's most intense hatred was directed against Abbé
Quandieu, who still survived though his eightieth year was
past.   For the Ignorantine the ex-priest of St. Martin's was
a perjurer, an apostate, a bad priest who had spat upon his
own religion by openly upholding God's enemies at the time
of the Simon case.   Moreover, he had abandoned his ministry, and gone to dwell in a little house in a lonely neighbourhood, impudently saying that he was disgusted with
the base superstition of the last believers, and carrying his
audacity so far as to pretend that the monks, whom he
called the traders of the Temple, were demolishers who un-
consciously hastened the downfall of the Church.   But if
there was a demolisher it was he himself, for his desertion
had served as an argument to the enemies of Catholicism.
Surely indeed it was an abominable example that he had
set—forswearing all his past life, breaking his vows, and
preferring a sleek and shameful old age to martyrdom.   As
for that big, lean, stern Abbé Coquart, his successor at St.
Martin's, however imposing the newcomer might look he
was in reality only a fool.

Marc had, for a while, listened in silence, determined to
offer no interruption.   But his feelings rebelled when he
heard Gorgias's violent attack upon Abbé Quandieu.   'You
do not know that priest,' he said quietly.   'Your judgment
is that of an enemy, blinded by spite. . . . As a matter
of fact, Abbé Quandieu was the only priest of this region
who, at the outset, understood what frightful harm the
Church would do herself by openly and passionately defy-
ing truth and justice.   She claims to represent a Deity of
certainty and equity, kindness and innocence; she was

founded to exalt the suffering and the meek, and yet, all at
once, in order to retain temporal authority, she makes common cause with oppressors and liars and forgers! It was
certain that the consequences would be terrible for her as
soon as Simon's innocence should become manifest. Such
conduct was suicide on the Church's part. With her own
hands she prepared her condemnation, showing the world
that she was no longer the abode of the true and the just,
of everlasting purity and goodness! And her expiation is
only just beginning; she will slowly die of that denial of
justice which she took upon herself and which has become
a devouring sore. . . . Abbé Quandieu foresaw it and
said it. It is not true that he fled from the Church in any
spirit of cowardice; he quitted his ministry bleeding and
weeping, and it is in grief that he is ending a life of misery
and bitterness.'

By a rough gesture Gorgias signified that he did not intend to argue. With his glowing eyes gazing far away into
the galling memories of his personal experiences, he scarcely
listened to Marc, impatient as he was to continue his own
rageful diatribe.

'Good, good, I say what I think,' he resumed, 'but I
don't prevent you from thinking whatever you please.
. . . There are, at all events, other imbeciles and
cowards whom you won't defend, for instance, that rascal
Father Théodose, the mirror of the devotees, the thieving
cashier of heaven!'

Thereupon Gorgias assailed the superior of the Capuchins
with murderous fury. He did not blame the worship of St.
Antony of Padua. On the contrary he praised it; he set
all his hopes in miracles, he would have liked to have seen
the whole world bringing money to the shrine of the Saint
in order that the latter might persuade the Deity to hurl His
thunderbolts upon the cities of sin. But Father Théodose was a mere conscienceless mountebank, who amassed
money for himself alone, and gave no assistance whatever
to the afflicted servants of God. Though hundreds of thousands of francs had formerly overflowed from his collection
boxes, he had not devoted even an occasional five-franc
piece to render life a little less hard than it was to the poor
Brothers of the Christian Doctrine, his neighbours. And
now that the gifts he received were dwindling year by year
his avarice was even greater. He had refused the smallest
alms to him, Brother Gorgias, at a time when he was in the

most desperate circumstances, when, indeed, a ten-franc
piece might have saved his life.

They all abandoned him, yes, all—not only that lecherous
money-mongering Father Théodose, but even the other, the
great chief, the great culprit, who was as big a fool as he
was a rascal. Then Gorgias blurted out the name of Father
Crabot which had been burning his lips. Ah! Father Crabot, Father Crabot, he had worshipped him in former times,
he had served him on his knees in respectful silence, ready
to carry his devotion to the point of crime. He had then
regarded him as an all-powerful, able, and valiant master,
favoured by Jesus, who had promised him eternal victory
in this world. By Father Crabot's side he, Gorgias, had
thought himself protected from the wicked, assured of success in every enterprise, even the most dangerous. And
yet that venerated master to whom he had dedicated his
life, that glorious Father Crabot, now denied him and left
him without shelter and without a crust. He did worse
indeed; he cast him upon the waters as if he were a trouble-
some accomplice, whose disappearance was desired. Besides, had he not always displayed the most monstrous
egotism? Had he not previously sacrificed poor Father
Philibin, who had lately died in the Italian convent where
he had lingered, virtually dead, for many years already?
Father Philibin had been a hero, a victim, who had invariably obeyed his superior, who had carried devotion so
far as to take upon his shoulders all the punishment for the
deeds which had been commanded of him and which he
had done in silence. Yet another victim was that hallucinated Brother Fulgence, a perfect nincompoop with his
excitable sparrow's brain, but who, none the less, had not
deserved to be swept away into the nothingness in which,
somewhere or other, he was dying. What good purpose
had been served by all that villainy and ingratitude? Had
it not been as stupid as it was cruel on Father Crabot's part
to abandon in that fashion all his old friends, all the instruments of his fortune? Had not his own position been
shaken by his conduct in allowing the others to be struck
down? And had he never thought that one of them might
at last grow weary of it all, and rise up and cast terrible
truths in his face?

'Beneath all Crabot's grand manners,' cried Brother
Gorgias excitedly, 'beneath all his reputation for cleverness
and diplomatic skill, there is rank stupidity. He must be

quite a fool to treat me in the way he does. But let him
take care, let him take care, or else one of these days, before long, I shall speak out!'

At this, Marc, who had been listening with passionate
interest, made an effort to hasten the other's revelations:
'Speak out? What have you to say then?' he inquired.

'Nothing, nothing, there are only some matters between
him and me—I shall tell them to God alone, in a confession.' Then, reverting to his bitter catalogue of accusations, Gorgias exclaimed: 'And, to finish, there 's that
Brother Joachim, whom they have set at the head of our
school at Maillebois in Brother Fulgence's place. Joachim
is another of Father Crabot's creatures, a hypocrite, chosen
on account of his supposed skill and artfulness—one who
imagines himself to be a great man because he does not pull
the ears of the little vermin entrusted to him. You know
the result—the school will soon have to be closed for lack
of pupils! If the wretched offspring of men are to grow up
fairly well, they must be trained by kicks and blows, as God
requires. . . . And—if you want my opinion—there is
only one priest imbued with the right spirit in the whole
region, and that is your Abbé Cognasse. He, too, went to
seek advice at Valmarie, and they nearly rotted him as they
rotted the others, by advising him to be supple and crafty.
But he fortunately regained possession of himself; it is with
stones that he now pursues the enemies of the Church!
That is the right course for the real saints to follow, that is
the way in which God, when He chooses to interfere, will
end by reconquering the world!'

Thus speaking, Gorgias raised his clenched fists and
brandished them wildly, vehemently, in that usually quiet
classroom where the little lamp shed but a faint glimmer of
light. Then, for a moment, came deep silence, amid which
one only heard the pouring rain pattering on the window-
panes.

'Well, at all events,' said Marc with a touch of irony,
'God seems to have forsaken and sacrificed you even as
your superiors have done.'

Brother Gorgias glanced at his wretched clothes and
emaciated hands which testified to his sufferings. 'It is
true,' he answered, 'God has chastised me severely for my
transgressions and for those of others. I bow to His will,
He is working my salvation. But I do not forget, I do not
forgive the others for having aggravated my misery. Ah,

the bandits! Have they not condemned me to the most
frightful existence ever since they compelled me to quit
Maillebois? It is in misery that I have had to come back
here to endeavour to wring from them the crust of bread
which is my due!'

He was unwilling to say more on that subject, but his
tragic story could be well divined by the shudder that came
over him—the shudder of a wild beast driven from the
woods by hunger. The Order, no doubt, had sent him
from community to community, the poorest, the most obscure, until at last it had finally cast him out altogether as
being by far too compromising. And then he had quitted
his gown and rolled along the roads, carrying with him the
stigma attaching to a disfrocked cleric. One would never
know through what distant lands he had roamed, what a life
of privation and chance he had led, what unacknowledgeable adventures he had met with, what shameful vices he had
indulged in: one could only read a little of all that on the
tanned skin of his eager face, in the depths of his eyes
which glowed with suffering and hatred. The greater part
of his resources must certainly have come from his former
confederates, who had wished to purchase his silence and
keep him at a distance. Every now and again, when he
had written letter upon letter, when he had furiously threatened crushing revelations, some small sum had been sent to
him, and then for a few months he had been able to prolong
the wretched life he led as a waif whom all rejected.

But at last a time had come when he had no longer received any answer to his applications, when his letters and
his threats had remained without any effect; for his former
superiors had grown weary of his voracious demands, and
regarded him, perhaps, as being no longer dangerous after
the lapse of so many years. He himself was intelligent
enough to understand that his confessions could no longer
have any very serious consequences for his accomplices, but
might even deprive him of his last chance of extracting
money from them. Nevertheless he had resolved to return
and prowl around Maillebois. He knew the Code, he was
aware that the law of limitation covered him. And thus for
long months he had been living, in some dark nook, on the
five-franc pieces which he wrung from the fears of Simon's
accusers, who still trembled at the thought of their shameful
victory at Rozan. Yet they must again have been growing
weary of his persecution, for his bitterness was too great;

he would never have heaped so many insults upon them if they had let him dip his hands in their purses, the previous day, by way of once more purchasing his silence.

Marc readily understood the position. Brother Gorgias only sprang out of the suspicious darkness in which he concealed himself when he had spent his money in crapulous debauchery. And if he had come to Jonville that winter night, in the pouring rain, it was assuredly because his pockets were empty and because he expected to derive some profit from that visit. But what profit could it be? What motive lurked beneath his long and furious denunciation of the men of whom, according to his own account, he had only been a docile instrument?

'So you are living at Maillebois?' inquired Marc, whose curiosity was fully awakened.

'No, no, not at Maillebois. . . . I live where I can.'

'But I thought I had already seen you there before meeting you on the Place des Capucins. . . . You were with one of your former pupils—Polydor, I fancy.'

A faint smile appeared on Brother Gorgias's ravaged face. 'Polydor,' said he, 'yes, yes, I was always very fond of him. He was a pious and discreet lad. Like myself he has suffered from the maliciousness of men. He has been accused of all sorts of crimes, cast out unjustly by people who did not understand his nature. And I was glad to meet him when I returned here; we set our wretchedness together, and consoled each other, abandoning ourselves to the divine arms of our Lord. . . . But Polydor is young, and he will end by treating me as the others have done. For a month past I have been looking for him: he has disappeared. Ah! everything is going wrong, there must be an end to it all!'

A raucous sigh escaped him, and Marc shuddered, for Gorgias's manner and tone as he referred to Polydor afforded a glimpse of yet another hell. But there was no time for reflection. Drawing nearer to the schoolmaster the disfrocked brother resumed: 'Now, listen to me, Monsieur Froment; I have had enough of it, I have come to tell you everything. . . . Yes, if you will promise to listen to me as a priest would listen, I will tell you the truth, the real truth. You are the only man to whom I can make such a confession without doing violence to my dignity or pride, for you alone have always been a disinterested and loyal enemy. . . . So receive my confession, on the one understanding that you will keep it secret until I authorise you to divulge it.'

But Marc hastily interrupted him: 'No, no, I will not enter into such a compact. I have done nothing to provoke any revelations on your part; you have come here of your own accord, and you say what you please. Should you really place the truth in my hands, I mean to remain at liberty to make use of it according as my conscience may bid me.'

Brother Gorgias scarcely hesitated. 'Well, let it be so; it is in your conscience that I will confide,' said he.

Nevertheless he did not immediately speak out. Silence fell once more. The rain was still streaming down the window panes, and gusts of wind howled along the deserted streets, while the flame of the little lamp began to flare amid the vague shadows which hovered about the quiet room. Marc, gradually growing uncomfortable, suffering from all the abominable memories which that man's presence aroused, glanced anxiously at the door behind which Geneviève must have remained. Had she heard what had been said? If so how uncomfortable must the stirring up of all that old mud have made her feel also!

At last, after long remaining silent as if to impart yet more solemnity to his confession, Brother Gorgias raised his hand towards the ceiling in a dramatic manner, and after a fresh interval said slowly, in a rough voice: 'It is true, I confess it before God, I entered little Zéphirin's room on the night of the crime!'

At this, although Marc awaited the promised confession with a good deal of scepticism, expecting to hear merely some more falsehoods, he was unable to overcome a great shudder, a feeling of horror, which made him spring to his feet. But Gorgias quietly motioned him to his chair again.

'I entered the room,' said he, 'or rather I leant from outside on the window-bar at about twenty minutes past ten o'clock, before the crime. And that is what I wished to tell you, in order to relieve my conscience. . . . On leaving the Capuchin Chapel that night I undertook to escort little Polydor to the cottage of his father, the road-mender, on the way to Jonville, for fear of any mishap befalling the lad. We left the chapel at ten o'clock, and if I took ten minutes to escort Polydor home and ten minutes to return, it must, you see, have been about twenty minutes past ten when I again passed before the school. As I crossed the little deserted square I was surprised to see Zéphirin's window lighted up and wide open. I drew near, and I saw the dear child in his nightdress, setting out some religious prints, which some of his companions at the first Communion had given him. And I scolded him for not having closed his window, for the first passer-by might easily have sprung into his room. But he laughed in his pretty way, and complained of feeling very hot. It was, as you must remember, a close and stormy night. . . . Well, I was making him promise that he would do as I told him, and go to bed as soon as possible, when, among the religious pictures set out on his table, I saw a copy-slip which had come from my class, and which was stamped and initialled by me. It made me angry to see it there, and I reminded Zéphirin that the boys were forbidden to take away anything belonging to the school. He turned very red, and tried to excuse himself, saying that he had taken the slip home in order to finish an exercise. And he asked me to leave the slip with him, promising to bring it back the next morning, and restore it to me. . . . Then he closed his window, and I went off. That is the truth, the whole truth, I swear it before God!'

Marc, who had now recovered his calmness, gazed at Gorgias fixedly, endeavouring to conceal his impressions. ' You are quite sure that the boy shut his window when you went away?' he asked.

' He shut it, and I heard him putting up the shutter-bar.'

' Then you still assert that Simon was guilty, for nobody could have got in from outside; and you hold that Simon, after the crime, opened the shutters again in order to cast suspicion on some unknown prowler?'

'Yes, it is still my opinion that Simon was the culprit. But there is also this chance, that Zéphirin, oppressed by the heat, may have opened the window again after I had gone.'

Marc was not deceived by that supposition, which was offered him as a guide that might lead to a new fact. He even shrugged his shoulders, feeling that as Gorgias still accused another of his crime, his pretended confession had little value. At the same time, however, that medley of fact and fiction cast just a little more light on the affair, and this Marc desired to establish.

' Why did you not relate at the Assizes what you have now stated ?' he inquired. 'A great act of injustice might then have been avoided.'

'Why I did not relate it?' Gorgias replied. 'Why, because I should have compromised myself to no good purpose! My own innocence would have been doubted, and
besides, I was then already convinced of Simon's guilt even
as I am now; and thus my silence was quite natural. . . .
Moreover, I repeat it, I had seen the copy-slip lying on the
table.'

'Yes, only you now admit that it came from your school
and that you had stamped and initialled it yourself. You
did not always say that, remember.'

'Oh! those fools, Father Crabot and the others, imposed
a ridiculous story on me; and to prop up their senseless
theory with the help of their grotesque experts they afterwards invented the still more foolish idea of a forged stamp.
. . . For my part, I at once desired to admit the authenticity of the copy-slip, which was self-evident. But I
had to bow to their authority, accept their ridiculous inventions, under penalty of being abandoned and sacrificed.
. . . You saw how furious they became before the trial
at Rozan, when I ended by acknowledging that the paraph
was mine. They wanted to save that unfortunate Philibin;
they fancied they were clever enough to spare the Church
even the shadow of a suspicion, and for that very reason
they do not even now forgive me for having ceased to repeat their lies!'

Then Marc, noticing that Gorgias was gradually becoming exasperated, said, as if thinking aloud and by way of
spurring him on: 'All the same, it is very strange that the
copy-slip should have been on the child's table.'

'Strange! why? It often happened that one of the boys
took a slip away with him. Little Victor Milhomme had
taken one, and it was that very circumstance that made you
suspect the truth as to the origin of the slip. . . . But
do you still accuse me of being the murderer? Do you still
believe that I walked about with that slip in my pocket?
Come, is it reasonable—eh?'

Gorgias spoke with such jeering, aggressive violence, his
lips twitching the while with that rictus which disclosed his
wolfish teeth, that Marc slightly lost countenance. In spite
of his conviction of the brother's guilt, that slip, which had
come nobody knew whence, had always seemed to him a
very obscure feature of the affair. Even as the Ignorantine
constantly repeated, it was scarcely likely that he had carried the paper in his pocket that evening on quitting the

ceremony at the Capuchin Chapel. Whence had it come
then? How was it that Gorgias had found it mingled with
a copy of *Le Petit Beaumontais?* Marc felt that if he had
been able to penetrate that mystery the whole affair would
have been perfectly clear. To conceal his perplexity he
tried an argument: 'It was n't necessary for you to have
the slip in your pocket,' said he, 'for you have said that
you saw it lying on the table.'

But Brother Gorgias had now risen, either yielding to his
usual vehemence or playing some comedy in order to end
the interview, which was not taking the course he desired.
Black and bent, he walked up and down the shadowy room,
gesticulating wildly.

'On the table, yes, of course I saw it on the table! If I
say that, it is because I have nothing to fear from such an
admission. You suppose me to be guilty, but in that case
do you imagine I should give you a weapon by telling you
where I took the slip! . . . We say it was on the table,
eh? So it would follow that I took it up, and took a newspaper also out of my pocket, and crumpled it up with the
slip, in order to turn both into a gag. What an operation
—eh?—at such a moment, how logical and simple it would
have been! . . . But no, no! If the newspaper was
in my pocket the slip must have been there also. Prove
that it was; for otherwise you have nothing substantial and
decisive to go upon. And it was n't in my pocket, for I
saw it on the table, I swear it again before God!'

Wildly, savagely, he drew near to Marc and cast in his
face those words in which one detected a kind of audacious
provocation, compounded of scraps of truth, impudently
set forth in the shape of suppositions, falsehoods that barely
masked the frightful scene which he must have lived afresh
with a frightful, demoniacal delight.

But Marc, cast into disturbing perplexity, feeling that he
would learn nothing useful from his visitor, had also decided to end the interview. 'Listen,' said he, 'why should
I believe you? You come here and you tell me a tale which
is the third version you have given of the affair. . . .
At the outset you agreed with the prosecution; the slip,
you said, belonged to the secular school; you did not initial
it; it was Simon who had done so in order to cast his crime
on you. Then, on the discovery of the stamped corner
torn off by Father Philibin, you felt it impossible to shelter
yourself any longer behind the stupid report of the experts;

you admitted that the initialling was your work, and that the slip had come from you. At present, with what motive I do not know, you make a fresh confession to me; you assert that you saw little Zéphirin in his room a few minutes before the crime, that the copy-slip was then lying on his table, that you scolded him, and that he closed his shutters. . . . Well, think it over; there is no reason why I should regard this version as final. I shall wait to hear the plain truth, if indeed it ever pleases you to tell it.'

Pausing in his stormy perambulations, Brother Gorgias drew up his gaunt and tragic figure. His eyes were blazing, an evil laugh distorted his face once more. For a moment he remained silent. Then in a jeering way he said: ' As you choose, Monsieur Froment! I came here in a friendly spirit to give you some particulars about the affair, which still interests you as you have not renounced the hope of getting Simon rehabilitated. You can make use of those particulars; I authorise you to make them known. And I ask you for no thanks, for I no longer expect any gratitude from men.'

Then he wrapped himself in his ragged cloak, and went off as he had come, opening the doors himself, and giving never a glance behind. Outside the icy rain was coming down in furious squalls, the wind filled the street with its howls, and Gorgias vanished like a ghost into the depths of the lugubrious darkness.

Geneviève had now opened the door behind which she had remained listening. Stupefied by all she had heard she let her arms drop, and for a moment remained gazing at Marc, who likewise stood there motionless, at a loss whether to laugh or to feel angry.

' He is mad, my friend,' said Geneviève. ' If I had been in your place I should not have had the patience to listen to him so long; he lies as he has always lied!' Then, as Marc seemed inclined to take things gaily, she continued: ' No, no, it is not at all amusing. The revival of all those horrid things has made me feel quite ill and anxious also, for I do not understand what can have been his purpose in coming here. Why did he make that pretended confession? Why did he select you to hear it?'

' Oh! I think I know, my dear,' Marc answered. ' In all probability Father Crabot and the others no longer give him a copper, that is, apart from some petty monthly allowance which they may have arranged to make him. And as the rascal has a huge appetite he tries to terrify them from time to time, in order to extract some big sum from them. I have had information; they have done their utmost to induce him to leave the region. Twice already, by filling his pockets they have prevailed on him to do so; but as soon as his pockets were empty he came back. They dare not employ the police in the affair, otherwise the gendarmes would have rid them of him long ago. And so, once again, as they have refused to let him have more money, he wishes to give them a good fright by threatening to tell me everything. And he has told me just a little truth mixed with a great deal of falsehood, in the hope that I may speak of it, and that the others in their fright may pay him well to prevent him from telling me all the rest.'

This logical explanation restored the calmness of Geneviève, who merely added: 'The rest—the full, plain truth —he will never tell it!'

'Who knows?' Marc retorted. 'His craving for money is great, but there is yet more hatred in his heart. And he is courageous; he would willingly risk his skin to revenge himself on those old accomplices who have cowardly forsaken him. Moreover, in spite of all his crimes, he really belongs to his Deity of extermination; he glows with a sombre, devouring faith, which would prompt him to martyrdom if he only thought that he might thereby win salvation and cast his enemies into the torments of hell.'

'Shall you try to make any use of what he told you?' Geneviève inquired.

'No, I think not. I shall talk it over with Delbos; but he, I know, has resolved that he will only move when he has a certainty to act upon. . . . Ah! poor Simon, I despair of ever seeing him rehabilitated; I have become so old!'

All at once, however, the new fact, awaited for so many years, became manifest, and Marc then beheld the realisation of the most ardent desire of his life. Delbos, who placed no faith in any help from Brother Gorgias, had set all his hopes on the Rozan medical man, that Dr. Beauchamp, a juror at the second trial, to whom Judge Gragnon was said to have made his second illegal communication, and who was reported to be tortured by remorse. This scent Delbos followed with infinite patience, having a watch kept upon the doctor, who preserved silence in compliance with the entreaties of his wife, a very pious and also sickly

woman, whose death would probably have been hastened
by any scandal. All at once indeed she died, and Delbos
then no longer doubted the success of his enterprise. It
took him another six months to perfect his arrangements;
he managed to enter into direct relations with Beauchamp,
whom he found all anxiety and indecision, assailed by a
variety of scruples. But at last the doctor made up his
mind to hand the advocate a signed statement in which he
related how one day a friend, acting on behalf of Gragnon,
had shown him the pretended confession which a workman,
dying at the Beaumont hospital, was said to have made to
one of the sisters—a confession in which this man acknowledged that he had engraved a false stamp for Simon, the
Maillebois schoolmaster. And Beauchamp added that this
secret communication alone had convinced him of the guilt
of Simon, whom previously he had been disposed to acquit
for lack of all serious proof.

Having secured this decisive statement Delbos did not
act precipitately. He waited a little longer. He gathered
together other documents, which showed that Gragnon had
communicated his extravagant forgery to other jurors, men
of the most amazing credulity. Equally extraordinary was
it to find that the ex-presiding judge had dared to repeat
the trick of Beaumont, carrying a gross forgery in his pocket,
circulating it secretly through Rozan, exploiting human imbecility with the most sovereign contempt. And twice had
the trick succeeded, Gragnon on the second occasion saving
himself from the galleys by sheer criminal audacity. He
was now beyond the reach of punishment, for he had lately
died, perishing miserably, quite withered away, his features
furrowed, it seemed, by invisible claws. And it was certainly his death which had induced Dr. Beauchamp to speak
out.

Marc and David had long thought that the Simon affair
would be quite settled when the personages compromised
in it should have disappeared. At present ex-investigating
Magistrate Daix was also dead, while the former Procureur
de la République, Raoul de La Bissonnière, had lately been
retired with the grant of a Commandership of the Legion of
Honour. Then Counsellor Guybaraud, who had presided
at the Assizes at Rozan, having been stricken with hemi-
plegia, was passing away between his confessor and a
servant-mistress; whereas Pacard, the ex-demagogue who
in spite of a nasty story of cheating at cards had managed

to become a public prosecutor, had quitted the magistracy to take up somewhat mysterious duties at Rome as legal adviser to some of the congregations. Again, at Beaumont there were great changes in the political, administrative, clerical, and teaching worlds. Other men had succeeded Lemarrois, Marcilly, Hennebise, Bergerot, Forbes, and Mauraisin. Of the direct accomplices in the crime, Father Philibin had died far away, Brother Fulgence had disappeared, being also dead perhaps, in such wise that there only remained Father Crabot, the great chief. But even he had withdrawn from among the living, cloistered, it was alleged, in some lonely cell, where he was spending his last years in great penitence.

And thus there was quite a new social atmosphere; politics had altogether changed, men's passions were no longer the same when Delbos, having at last collected the weapons he desired, brought the affair forward once more with masterly energy. Of recent years he had risen to a position of influence in the Chamber of Deputies, so he took his documents straight to the Minister of Justice and speedily prevailed on him to lay the new fact before the Court of Cassation. It is true that a debate on the subject ensued the very next day, but the Minister contented himself with stating that the matter was purely and simply a legal one, and that the Government could not allow it to be turned once more into a political question. And then, amid the indifference with which this old Simon affair was now regarded, a vote of confidence in the Government was passed by a considerable majority. As for the Court of Cassation, which still smarted from the smack it had received at Rozan, it tried the case with extraordinary despatch, purely and simply annulling the Rozan verdict without sending Simon before any other tribunal. It was all, so to say, a mere formality; in three phrases everything was effaced, and justice was done at last.

Thus, then, in all simplicity, the innocence of Simon was recognised and proclaimed amid the pure glow of truth triumphant after so many years of falsehood and of crime.

ON the morrow of the court's judgment there came an
extraordinary revival of emotion at Maillebois.
There was no surprise, for those who now believed
in Simon's innocence were very numerous; but the material
fact of that decisive legal rehabilitation upset everybody.
And the same thought came to men of the most varied views.
They approached one another, and they said:

'What! can no possible reparation be offered to that unfortunate man who suffered so dreadfully? Doubtless
neither money nor honours of any kind could indemnify
him for his horrible martyrdom. But when a whole people
has been guilty of such an abominable error, when it has
turned a fellow-being into such a pitiable, suffering creature,
it would be good that it should acknowledge its fault, and
confer some triumph on that man by a great act of frankness, in which truth and justice would find recognition.'

From that moment, indeed, the idea that reparation was
necessary gained ground, spreading by degrees through the
entire region. One circumstance touched every heart.
While the Court of Cassation was examining the documents
respecting the illegal communication made at Rozan, old
Lehmann, the tailor, who had reached his ninetieth year,
lay dying in that wretched house of the Rue du Trou which
had been saddened by so many tears and so much mourning. His daughter Rachel had hastened from her Pyrenean
retreat in order that she might be beside him at the last
hour. But every morning, by some effort of will, the old
man seemed to revive; being unwilling to die, said he, so
long as justice should not have been done to the honour of
his son-in-law and his grandchildren. And, indeed, it was
only on the night of the day when the news of the acquittal
reached him that he at last expired, radiant with supreme
joy.

After the funeral Rachel immediately rejoined Simon and
David in their solitude, where they intended to remain for

another four or five years, when perhaps they might sell
their marble quarry and liquidate their little fortune.   And
it so happened that the old house of the Rue du Trou was
now demolished, a happy inspiration coming to the Municipal
Council of Maillebois to purify that sordid district of the
town by carrying a broad thoroughfare through it, and laying out a small recreation-ground for the working-class
children.   Sarah, whose husband Sébastien had now been
appointed headmaster of one of the Beaumont schools, had
sold the tailoring business to a Madame Savin, a relative of
those Savins who in former times had pelted her brother
Joseph and herself with stones; and thus no trace remained
of the spot where the Simon family had wept so bitterly in
the distant days, when each letter arriving from the innocent
prisoner in the penal settlement yonder had brought them
fresh torture.   Trees now grew there in the sunshine, flowers
shed their perfume beside the lawns, and it seemed as if it
were from that health-bringing spot that spread the covert
remorse of Maillebois, its desire to repair the frightful iniquity of the past.

Nevertheless, things slumbered for a long time yet.   A
period of four years went by, during which only individual
suggestions were made, no general agreement being arrived
at.   But generation was following generation; after the
children had come the grandchildren, and then the great-
grandchildren of those who had persecuted Simon, in such
wise that quite a new population ended by dwelling in
Maillebois.   Yet it was necessary for the great evolution
towards other social conditions to be entirely accomplished,
in order that the seed which had been sown should yield a
harvest of citizens freed from error and falsehood, to whom
one might look for a great manifestation of equity.

Meantime life continued, and the valiant workers whose
task was completed made way for their children.   Marc
and Geneviève, now nearly seventy years old, retired, and
the Jonville schools were entrusted to their son Clément and
his wife Charlotte, Hortense Savin's daughter, who, like himself, had adopted the teaching profession.   Mignot, on his
side, had quitted Le Moreux and retired to Jonville, in order
to be near Marc and Geneviève, who dwelt in a small house
near their old school.   Thus the village held quite a little
colony of the first participators in the great enterprise, for
Salvan and Mademoiselle Mazeline were still alive, enjoying
a smiling and kindly old age.   Then, at Maillebois, the

boys' school was in the hands of Joseph, and the girls' school in those of his wife Louise. He was now forty-four, she two years younger; and they had a big son, François, who, in his twenty-second year, had married his cousin Thérèse, the daughter of Sébastien and Sarah, by whom he had a beautiful baby-girl named Rose, now barely a twelve-month old. Joseph and Louise were bent on never quitting Maillebois, and they gently chaffed Sébastien and Sarah respecting the honours which awaited them; for there was now a question of appointing Sébastien to the directorship of the Training College where Salvan had worked so well. As for François and Thérèse, who by hereditary vocation had also adopted the scholastic profession, they now dwelt at Dherbecourt, where both had become assistant teachers. And what a swarming of the sowers of truth there was on certain Sundays when the whole family assembled at Jonville round the grandparents, Marc and Geneviève! And what fine, bright health was brought from Beaumont by Sébastien and Sarah, from Maillebois by Joseph and Louise, from Dherbecourt by François and Thérèse, who came carrying their little Rose; while at Jonville they were met by Clément and Charlotte, who also had a daughter, Lucienne, now a big girl, nearly seven years of age! And, again, what a table had to be laid for that gathering of the four generations, particularly when their good friends Salvan, Mignot, and Mademoiselle Mazeline were willing to join them to drink to the defeat of Ignorance, the parent of every evil and every form of servitude!

The times of human liberation, which had been so long in coming, which had been awaited so feverishly, were now being brought to pass by sudden evolutions. A terrible blow had been dealt to the Church, for the last Legislature had voted the complete separation of Church and State,[1] and the millions formerly given to the priests, who had employed them to perpetuate among the people both hatred of the Republic and such abasement as was suited to a flock kept merely to be sheared, would now be better employed in doubling the salaries of the elementary schoolmasters. Thus the situation was entirely changed: the schoolmaster ceased to be the poor devil, the ill-paid varlet, whom the

[1] It will be understood that in the above passage M. Zola anticipates events; but it may be remarked that the separation of Church and State in France within a few years has never appeared more likely than it does now (1902-3). — *Trans.*

peasant regarded with so much contempt when he thought of the well-paid priest, who waxed fat on surplice fees and the presents of the devout.   The priest ceased to be a functionary, drawing pay from the State revenue, supported both by the prefect and by the bishop; and thus he lost the respect of the country-folk.   They no longer feared him; he was but a kind of chance sacristan, dependent on a few remaining believers, who from time to time paid him for a Mass.   Again, the churches ceased to be State institutions, and became theatres run on commercial lines, subsisting on the payments made by the spectators, the last admirers of the ceremonies performed in them.   It was certain, too, that before long many would have to close their doors, business already being so bad with some that they were threatened with bankruptcy.   And nothing could be more typical than the position of that terrible Abbé Cognasse, whose outbursts of passion had so long upset Le Moreux and Jonville.   His numerous lawsuits had remained famous; one could no longer count the number of times he had been fined for pulling boys' ears, kicking women, and flinging stones from his garden wall upon those passers who declined to make the sign of the Cross.   Nevertheless, he had retained his office amid all the worries brought upon him by the citations he received, for he was virtually irremovable and exercised a paid State function.   When, however, in consequence of the separation of Church and State, he suddenly became merely the representative of an opinion, a belief, when he ceased to receive State pay to impose that belief on others, he lapsed into such nothingness that people no longer bowed to him.   In a few months' time he found himself almost alone in his church with his old servant Palmyre, for, however much the latter might pull the bell-rope with her shrivelled arms, only some five or six women still came to Mass.   A little later there were but three, and finally only one came.   She, fortunately, persevered, and the Abbé was pleased to be able to celebrate the offices in her presence, for he feared lest he should have the same deplorable experience at Jonville as he had encountered at Le Moreux.   During a period of three months he had gone every Sunday to the latter village in order to say Mass without even being able to get a child as server, so that he had been obliged to take his little clerk with him from Jonville.   And during those three months nobody had come to worship; he had officiated in solitude in the dank, dark,

empty church. Naturally, he had ended by no longer returning thither, and at present the closed church was rotting
away and falling into ruins. When, indeed, one of the
functions of social life disappears, the building and the man
associated with it become useless and likewise disappear.
And in spite of the violent demeanour which Abbé Cognasse
still preserved, his great dread was that he might see his last
parishioner forsake him and his church closed, crumbling
away amidst an invading growth of brambles.

At Maillebois the separation of Church and State had
dealt a last blow to the once prosperous School of the Christian Brothers. Victorious over the secular school at the
time of the Simon case, it had fallen into increasing dis-
favour as the truth had gradually become manifest. But
with true clerical obstinacy it had been kept in existence
even when only four and five pupils could be recruited for
it; and the new laws and the dispersion of the community
had been needed to close its doors. The Church was now
driven from the national educational service. Henceforth
to the sixteen hundred thousand children whom year by year
the Congregations had poisoned, a system of purely secular
instruction was to be applied. And the reform had spread
from the primary to the secondary establishments. Even
the celebrated College of Valmarie, already weakened by
the expulsion of the Jesuits, was stricken unto death by the
great work of renovation which was in progress. The principle of integral and gratuitous instruction for all citizens
was beginning to prevail. Why should there be two
Frances? Why should there be a lower class doomed to
ignorance, and an upper class alone endowed with instruction and culture? Was not this nonsense? Was it not a
fault, a danger in a democracy, all of whose children should
be called upon to increase the nation's sum of intelligence
and strength? In the near future all the children of France,
united in a bond of brotherliness, would begin their education in the primary schools, and would thence pass into the
secondary and the superior schools, according to their aptitudes, their choice, and their tastes. This was an urgent
reform, a great work of salvation and glory, the necessity of
which was plainly indicated by the great contemporary
social movement, that downfall of the exhausted *bourgeoisie*
and the irresistible rise of the masses, in whom quivered the
energies of to-morrow. Henceforth it was on them one
would have to draw; and among them, as in some huge

reservoir of accumulated force, one would find the men of
sense, truth, and equity, who, in the name of happiness and
peace, would build the city of the future.   But, as a first
step, the bestowal of gratuitous national education on all
the children would finish killing off those pretended free
and voluntary schools, those hotbeds of clerical infection,
where the only work accomplished was a work of servitude
and death.   And after the Brothers' school of Maillebois,
now empty and long since virtually dead, after the College
of Valmarie, whose buildings and grounds were shortly to
be sold, the last religious communities would soon disappear, together with all their teaching establishments, their
factories of divers kinds, and their princely domains, which
represented millions of money filched from human imbecility
and expended to maintain the human flock in subjection
under the slaughterer's knife.

Nevertheless, near the dismal Brothers' school of Maillebois, where the shutters were closed and where spiders spun
their webs in the deserted classrooms, the Capuchin community maintained its chapel dedicated to St. Antony,
whose painted and gilded statue still stood there erect in a
place of honour.   But in vain did Father Théodose, now
very aged, exert himself to invent some more extraordinary
financial devices.   The zeal of the masses was exhausted,
and only a few old devotees occasionally slipped half-franc
pieces into the dusty collection-boxes.   It was rumoured,
indeed, that the saint had lost his power.   He could no
longer even find lost things.   One day, too, an old woman
actually climbed upon a chair in the chapel and slapped the
cheeks of his statue because, instead of healing her sick
goat, he had allowed the animal to die.   Briefly, thanks to
public good sense, aroused at last by the acquirement of a
little knowledge, one of the basest of superstitions was
dying.

Meantime, at the ancient and venerable parish church of
St. Martin's, Abbé Coquard, encountering much the same
experience as Abbé Cognasse at Jonville, found himself
more and more forsaken, in such wise that it seemed as if
he would soon officiate in the solitude and darkness of a
necropolis.   Unlike Cognasse, however, he evinced no violence.   Rigid, gloomy, and silent, he seemed to be leading
religion to the grave, preserving the while a sombre stubbornness, refusing to concede anything whatever to the impious men of the age.   In his distress he more particularly

sought refuge in the worship of the Sacred Heart, decorating his church with all the flags which the neighbouring
parishes refused to keep—large red, white, and blue flags,
on which huge gory hearts were embroidered in silk and
gold.   One of his altars, too, was covered with other hearts
—of metal, porcelain, goffered leather, and painted mill-
board.   Of all sizes were these, and one might have thought
them just plucked from some bosom, for they seemed to be
still warm, to palpitate and shed tears of blood, in such wise
that the altar looked like some butcher's gory stall.   But
that gross re-incarnation no longer touched the masses,
which had learnt that a people stricken by disaster raises
itself afresh by work and reason, and not by penitence at
the feet of monstrous idols.   As religions grow old and sink
into carnal and base idolatries they seem to rot and fritter
away in mouldiness.   If the Roman Church, however, was
thus at the last gasp, it was, as Abbé Quandieu had said,
because it had virtually committed suicide on the day when
it had become an upholder of iniquity and falsehood.   How
was it that it had not foreseen that by siding with liars and
forgers it must disappear with them, and share the shame
of their infamy on the inevitable day when the innocent and
the just would triumph in the full sunlight?   Its real master
was no longer the Jesus of innocence, of gentleness and
charity; it had openly denied Him, driven Him from His
temple; and all it retained was that heart of flesh, that
barbarous fetish with which it hoped to influence the
sick nerves of the poor in spirit.   Laden with years and
bitterness, Abbé Quandieu had lately passed away repeating: 'They have for the second time condemned and
crucified the Lord—the Church will die of it.'   And dying
it was.

Moreover, it was not passing away alone; the aristocratic
and *bourgeois* classes, on which it had vainly sought to lean,
were collapsing also.   All the ancient noble and military
forces, even the financial powers, were collapsing, stricken
with madness and impotence, since the reorganisation of
the conditions of work had been leading to an equitable
distribution of the national wealth.   Some characteristic
incidents which occurred at La Désirade showed what a
wretched fate fell on the whilom rich and powerful, whose
millions flowed away like water.   Hector de Sanglebœuf
lost his seat in the Chamber when the electorate, enlightened and moralised by the new schools, at last rid itself of

all reactionary and violent representatives. But a greater
misfortune was the death of the Marchioness de Boise, that
intelligent and broad-minded woman who had so long promoted prosperity and peace at La Désirade. When she was
gone the vain and foolish Sanglebœuf went altogether wrong,
becoming a gambler, losing huge sums at play, and descending to ignoble amours; with the result that he was one day
brought home beaten unmercifully—so battered, indeed,
that three days later he died; no complaint, however, being
lodged with the authorities, for fear of all the mud which
would soil his memory if the real facts of his death were
brought to light.

His wife, the once beautiful and indolent Léa, the pious
and ever sleepy Marie of later times, then remained alone
amid the splendours of that large estate. When her father,
Baron Nathan, the millionaire Jew banker, suddenly died
after being confined by paralysis to his sumptuous mansion
in the Champs Elysées, he had long ceased to see her; and
he left her as little as possible of his fortune, slices of which
had already gone to all sorts of aristocratic charitable enterprises, and even to certain ladies of society who, during the
final years of his life, had procured him the illusion of
imagining that he had become really one of their set, and
was quite cleansed of all his Jewry. However, his supine
and indolent daughter, who had never known a passion in
her life, not even one for money, paid due honour to his
memory, even ordering Masses to be said for his soul, by
way of compelling heaven to admit him within its precincts;
for, as she often repeated, he had rendered quite enough
services to Catholicism to be entitled to a place on the
Deity's right hand. And now, having no children, Léa led
a lonely life at La Désirade, which remained empty and
deathly, enclosed on every side by walls and railings, which
shut out the public as if it were some forbidden paradise.
Yet there were rumours to the effect that, on the closing of
the College of Valmarie, the Countess had granted an asylum
to her old friend Father Crabot, who had now reached a
very great age. His removal to La Désirade was said by
some to be a mere change of cell, for in an ascetic spirit he
was content to occupy a little garret formerly assigned to a
servant, and furnished with merely an iron bedstead, a deal
table, and a rush-seated chair. But he none the less reigned
over the estate, as if he were its sovereign master; the only
visitors being a few priests and other clerics, who came to

take counsel of him, and whose gowns might be seen occasionally gliding between the clumps of verdure or past the
marble basins and their plashing waters.   Though his ninetieth year was past, Crabot, ever a conqueror of women, a
bewitcher of pious souls, repeated the triumphant stroke of
his earlier days.   He had lost Valmarie, that royal gift,
which he had owed to the love of the Countess de Quédeville, but he won La Désirade from the good grace of that
ever-beautiful Léa, whom he so fervently called 'my sister
Marie in Jesus Christ.'   As manager and almoner he set
his hands on her fortune, financing all sorts of religious
enterprises, and subscribing lavishly to the funds which the
reactionary parties established for the purpose of carrying
on their desperate campaign against the Republic and its
institutions.   And thus, when the Countess was found dead
on her couch one evening, looking as if in her indolence she
had just fallen asleep, she was ruined; her millions had all
passed into the cash-boxes of the Black Band, and there
only remained the estate of La Désirade, which was willed
to Father Crabot on the one condition that he should there
establish some such Christian enterprise as he might choose
to select.

But these were merely the last convulsions of an expiring
world.   All Maillebois was now passing into the hands of
those Socialists whom the pious dames of other times had
pictured as bandits, cut-throats, and footpads.   That whilom
clerical centre had now gone so completely over to the cause
of reason that not a single reactionary member remained in
its Municipal Council.   Both Philis, once the priests' mayor,
and Darras, the so-called traitors' mayor, were dead, and
the latter, who was remembered as a man of weak, timorous,
hesitating mind, had been replaced by a mayor of great good
sense and industrous energy; this being Jules Savin, the
younger brother of the twins, those mediocrities, Achille
and Philippe.   Jules, after marrying a peasant girl named
Rosalie Bonin, had worked most courageously, in fifteen
years establishing an admirable model farm, which had
revolutionised the agricultural methods of the region and
greatly increased its wealth.   He was now barely more than
forty years old, and rather stubborn by nature, for he only
yielded to substantial arguments which tended to the general good.   And it was under his presidency that the
Municipal Council at last found itself called upon to examine a scheme for offering some public reparation to

Simon—that idea which had slumbered for a few years, and which now awoke once more.

The subject had frequently been mentioned to Marc, who, indeed, could never come to Maillebois without encountering somebody who spoke to him about it. In this respect he was particularly moved one day when he happened to meet Adrien Doloir, a son of his former pupil Auguste by his wife Angèle. Adrien, after studying successfully under Joulic, had become an architect of great merit, and though barely eight and twenty years of age, had been lately elected to the Municipal Council; of which, indeed, he was the youngest member, one whose schemes were said to be somewhat bold, though none the less practical.

'Ah! my dear Monsieur Froment, how pleased I am to meet you!' he exclaimed as he accosted Marc. 'It so happens that I wished to go over to Jonville to speak to you.'

Like all the young men of the new generation, who loved and venerated Marc as a patriarch, as one of the great workers of the heroic times, Adrien addressed him most deferentially, standing uncovered, with his hat in his hand. Personally, he had only been a pupil of Marc for a very brief period, when he was very young indeed; but his brother and his uncles had all grown up in the old master's class.

'What do you desire of me, my dear lad?' inquired Marc, who felt both brightened and moved whenever he met any of his former boys or their children.

'Well, it is like this. Can you tell me if it is true that the Simon family will soon return to Maillebois? It is said that Simon and his brother David have decided to quit the Pyrenees and settle here again. . . . Is it true? You must be well acquainted with their views.'

'Such is certainly their intention,' Marc responded with his pleasant smile. 'But I do not think one can expect them till next year; for, though they have found a purchaser for their marble quarry, they are to carry it on for another twelvemonth. Besides, a variety of matters will have to be settled, and they themselves cannot yet tell exactly how and when they will install themselves here.'

'But if we have only a year before us,' exclaimed Adrien with sudden excitement, 'we shall barely have the necessary time for the realisation of a plan I have formed. . . .

I wish to submit it to you before doing anything decisive.
What day would be convenient for me to call on you at
Jonville ? '

Marc, who intended to spend the day at Maillebois with
his daughter Louise, pointed out that it would be preferable
to profit by this opportunity, and Adrien assenting, it was
eventually arranged that he should call at the latter's house
in the afternoon. This house was a pleasant dwelling,
built by Adrien himself on one of the fields of the farm
which had belonged to the old Bongards, in the outskirts of
Maillebois. They had long been dead, and the property
had remained in the hands of Fernand, the father of Claire,
to whom Adrien was married. Thus many memories arose
in Marc's mind when, with a still firm and brave step, he
walked past the old farm-buildings on his way to the architect's little house. Had he not repaired to that same spot
forty years previously—on the very day, indeed, of Simon's
arrest — with the object of collecting information in his
friend's favour ? In imagination Marc again accosted Bongard, the stoutly built and narrow-minded peasant, and his
bony and suspicious wife, and found them both stubbornly
determined to say nothing, for fear lest they might compromise themselves. He well remembered that he had
been unable to extract anything from them, incapable as
they were of any act of justice, since they knew nothing and
would learn nothing, being, so to say, only so much brute
matter steeped in a thick layer of ignorance.

With a sigh, Marc passed on and rang at the gate of
Adrien's house. The young architect was awaiting him
under an old apple tree, whose strong branches, laden with
fruit, sheltered a few garden chairs and a table. 'Ah, master!' Adrien exclaimed, 'what an honour you do me by
coming to sit here for a little while! But I have another
favour to ask of you. You must kiss my little Georgette,
for it will bring her good luck! '

Beside Adrien was Claire, his wife, a smiling blonde,
scarcely in her twenty-fourth year, with a limpid face and
eyes all intelligence and kindness. It was she who presented the little girl, a pretty child, fair like her mother,
and already very knowing for her five years.

'You must remember, my treasure, that Monsieur Froment has kissed you, for it will make you glorious all your
life! '

'Oh, I know, mamma! I often hear you talk of him,'

said Georgette. 'It is as if a little of the sun came down to see me.'

At this the others began to laugh; but all at once Claire's father and mother, Fernand Bongard and his wife Lucille, made their appearance, having heard that the old school-master intended to call, and wishing to show him some politeness. Although Fernand, with his hard nut, had been anything but a satisfactory pupil in bygone years, Marc was pleased to see him once more. The farmer, now near his fiftieth year, still looked very dull and heavy, as if he were scarcely awake, and his manner remained an uneasy one.

'Well, Fernand,' Marc said to him, 'you ought to be pleased; this has been a good year for the grain crops.'

'Yes, Monsieur Froment, there's some truth in that. But the year's never a really good one. When things go well in one respect they go badly in another. And, besides, I never had any luck, you know.'

His wife, whose mind was sharper than his, thereupon ventured to intervene. 'He says that, Monsieur Froment, because he always used to be the last of his class, and because he imagines that a spell was cast on him by some gipsy when he was quite a little child. A spell, indeed! As if there were any sense in such an idea! It would be different if he believed in the devil, for there is a devil sure enough. Mademoiselle Rouzaire, whose best pupil I was, showed him to me one day, a short time before my first Communion.'

Then, as Claire made merry over this statement, and even little Georgette laughed very irreverently at the idea of there being any such thing as a devil, Lucille continued: 'Oh! I know that you believe in nothing. None of the young folks of nowadays have any religious principles left. Mademoiselle Mazeline made strong-minded women of you all. Nevertheless, one evening, as I well remember, Mademoiselle Rouzaire showed us a shadow passing over the wall, and told us it was the devil. And it was, indeed!'

Adrien, somewhat embarrassed by his mother-in-law's chatter, now interrupted her, and addressed Marc on the subject of his visit. They had all seated themselves, Claire taking Georgette on her lap, while her father and mother kept a little apart from the others, the former smoking his pipe and the latter knitting a stocking.

'Well, master, this is the question,' said Adrien. 'Many

young people of the district feel that great dishonour will
rest on the name of Maillebois as long as the town has not
repaired, as well as it can, the frightful iniquity which it
allowed, and in which, indeed, it became an accomplice,
when Simon was condemned.　His legal acquittal does not
suffice; for us—the children and grandchildren of the persecutors—it is a duty to confess and efface the transgression
of our forerunners.　Yesterday evening, at my father's
house, on seeing my grandfather and my uncles there, I
again asked them: " How was it that you ever allowed such
stupid and monstrous iniquity, when the exercise of a little
reason ought to have sufficed to prevent it ? "　And, as
usual, they made vague gestures and answered that they
did not know, that they could not know.'

Silence fell, and all eyes turned towards Fernand, who
belonged to the incriminated generations.　But he likewise
rid himself of the question by taking his pipe from his
mouth and gesticulating in an embarrassed way, while he
remarked: 'Well, to be sure, we did n't know—how could
we have known ?　My father and mother could scarcely sign
their names, and they were not so imprudent as to meddle
in their neighbours' affairs, for they might have got punished for it.　And though I had learnt rather more than
they had, I was n't learned by any means; and so I distrusted the whole business, for a man does not care to risk
his skin and his money when he feels he is ignorant.
.　.　.　To you young men nowadays it seems very easy to
be brave and wise, because you 've been well taught.　But
I should have liked to have seen you as we were—with no
means of telling right from wrong, with our minds at sea
amid a lot of affairs in which nobody could distinguish
anything certain.'

'That 's true,' said Lucille.　'I never thought myself a
fool, but all the same I could not understand much of that
business, and I tried not to think of it, for my mother was
always repeating that poor folk ought not to meddle with
the affairs of the rich, unless they wanted to get poorer still.'

Marc had listened with silent gravity.　All the past came
back: he heard old Bongard and his wife refuse to answer
him, like the illiterate peasants they were, whose one desire
was to continue toiling and moiling in quietude; and he
also remembered Fernand's demeanour on the morrow of
the trial at Rozan, when he had still shrugged his shoulders,
still persisted in his desire to know nothing.　How many

years and what prolonged teaching of human reason and civic courage had been needed before a new generation had at last opened its eyes to truth, dared to recognise and admit it! And as Marc looked at Fernand he began to nod, as if to say that he thought the farmer's excuses good ones; for he was already inclined to forgive those persecutors whose ignorance had been the chief cause of their crime. And he ended by smiling at Georgette, in whom, on the other hand, the future seemed to be flowering, as she sat there with her beautiful eyes wide open and her keen ears on the alert, waiting, one might have thought, for some fine story.

'And so, master,' Adrien resumed, 'my plan is a very simple one. As you are aware, some great improvements have been effected at Maillebois lately, with the view of rendering the old quarter of the town more salubrious. An avenue has replaced those sewers, the Rue Plaisir and the Rue Fauche, while on the site of the filthy Rue du Trou is a recreation-ground, which the children of the neighbourhood fill with their play and their laughter. Well, among the building land in front of that square is the very spot on which stood old Lehmann's wretched house, that house of mourning, which our forerunners used to stone. It is my idea, then, to propose to the Municipal Council the erection of a new house on that site—not a palace, but a modest, bright, cheerful dwelling, which might be offered to Simon, so that he might end his days in it encompassed by the respect and affection of everybody. The gift would have no great pecuniary value—it would simply represent delicate and brotherly homage.'

Tears had risen to the eyes of Marc, who was greatly touched by the kind thought thus bestowed on his old friend, the persecuted, innocent man.

'Do you approve of my idea?' inquired Adrien, who on his side was stirred by the sight of Marc's emotion.

The old schoolmaster rose and embraced him: 'Yes, my lad, I approve of it, and I owe you one of the greatest joys of my life.'

'Thank you, master. But that is not everything. Wait a moment. I wish to show you a plan of the house, which I have already prepared, for I should like to direct the work gratuitously, and I feel certain that I should find contractors and men prepared to undertake the building at very low rates.'

He withdrew for a moment, and on returning with the plan he spread it out upon the garden-table, under the old apple tree. And everybody approached and leant over to examine it. The house, such as it had been depicted, was, indeed, a very simple but also a very pleasant one, two storeys high, with a white frontage, and a garden enclosed by some iron railings. Above the entrance a marble slab was figured.

'Is there to be an inscription, then?' Marc inquired.

'Certainly; the house is intended for one. This is what I shall suggest to the Council: "Presented by the Town of Maillebois to Schoolmaster Simon, in the name of Truth and Justice, and in reparation for the torture inflicted on him." And the whole will be signed: "The Grandchildren of his Persecutors."'

With gestures of protest and anxiety Fernand and Lucille glanced at their daughter Claire. Surely that was going too far! She must not let her husband compromise himself to such a point! But Claire, who was leaning lovingly against Adrien's shoulder, smiled, and responded to the consternation of her parents by saying: 'I helped to prepare the inscription, Monsieur Froment; I should like that to be known.'

'Oh! I will make it known, you may depend on it,' Marc answered gaily. 'But the inscription must be accepted, and, first of all, there is the question of the house.'

'Quite so,' replied Adrien. 'I wished to show you my plan with the view of securing your approval and help. The question of the expense will hardly affect the Council. I am more apprehensive of certain scruples, some last attempts at resistance, inspired by the old spirit. Though the members of the Council are nowadays all convinced of Simon's innocence, some of them are timid men, who will only yield to the force of public opinion. And our Mayor, Jules Savin, has said to me, truly enough, that it is essential the scheme should be voted unanimously on the day it is brought forward.'

Then, as a fresh idea occurred to him, Adrien added: 'Do you know, master, as you have been good enough to come so far, you ought to cap your kindness by accompanying me to Jules Savin's at once. He was a pupil of yours, and I feel certain that our cause would make great progress if you would only have a short chat with him.'

' I will do so willingly,' Marc answered. ' Let us start; I will go wherever you like.'

Fernand and Lucille protested no longer. She had returned to her knitting, while he, pulling at his pipe, relapsed into the indifference of a dullard unable to understand the new times. Claire, however, suddenly had to defend the plan from the enterprising hands of little Georgette, who wished to appropriate ' the pretty picture.' Then, as Marc and Adrien made ready to go, there came more embraces, handshakes, and laughter.

The farm of Les Amettes, where Jules Savin resided, was on the other side of Maillebois, and in order to reach it Marc and the young architect had to pass the new recreation-ground. For a moment, therefore, they paused before the plot of land on which the architect proposed to build the projected house.

' You see,' said he, ' all the requirements for a house will be found united here——'

But he broke off on seeing a stout and smiling man approach him. ' Why, here 's uncle Charles!' he exclaimed. ' I say, uncle, when we build the house for Simon the martyr, which I have told you about, you will undertake to provide all the locksmith's work at cost price, will you not ? '

' Well, I don't mind, my boy, if it pleases you,' said Charles Doloir. ' And I 'll do it also for your sake, Monsieur Froment, for it pains me at times to think of how I used to worry you.'

Charles, after marrying Marthe Dupuis, his employer's daughter, had for a long time been managing the business. He had a son named Marcel, who was about the same age as Adrien, and who, having married a carpenter's daughter, Laure Dumont, had become a contractor for house carpentry.

' I am going to your father's,' Charles resumed, addressing his nephew; ' I have an appointment with Marcel about some work. Come with me, for if you build this house you will have some work to give them as well. . . . And you will come also, Monsieur Froment ? It will please you, perhaps, to meet some more of your old pupils.'

' Yes, indeed it will,' Marc answered gaily. ' Besides, we shall be able to settle the specifications.'

' The specifications! Oh! we have not got to that point yet,' Adrien retorted. ' Moreover, my father is n't an enthusiast. . . . But no matter; I 'll go to see him.'

Auguste Doloir, thanks to the friendly protection of
Darras, the former mayor, had become a building contractor in a small way.   After his father's death he had taken
his mother to live with him, and since the demolition of the
Rue Plaisir he had been residing in the new avenue, where
he occupied a ground floor flanked by a large yard, in which
he stored some of his materials.   The lodging was very
clean, very healthy, and full of sunlight.

When Marc found himself in the bright dining-room,
face to face with Madame Doilor the elder, some more
memories of the past returned to him.   The old woman,
now sixty-nine years old, had retained the demeanour of a
good and prudent housewife, one who was instinctively conservative, and allowed neither her husband nor her children
to compromise themselves by dabbling in politics. Marc also
recalled her husband, Doloir the mason, that big, fair, ignorant fellow, good-natured in his way, but spoilt by barrack
life, haunted as he was by idiotic notions of the army being
disorganised by those who knew no country, and of France
being sold to the foreigners by the Jews.   One day, unfortunately, he had been brought home dead on a stretcher,
after falling from a scaffolding; and it seemed as if he had
been drinking previously, though Madame Doloir would
not acknowledge it, for she was one of those who never
admit the existence of family failings.

On perceiving Marc she at once said to him: 'Ah! monsieur, we are no longer young; we are very old acquaintances indeed.   Auguste and Charles were not more than
eight and six years old when I first saw you.'

'Quite so, madame; I well remember it.   I called on
you, on behalf of my colleague Simon, to ask you to let
your boys tell the truth if they should be questioned.'

At this, though the case was now such a very old one,
Madame Doloir became grave and suspicious.   'That affair
was no concern of ours,' she answered, 'and I acted rightly
in refusing to let it enter our home, for it did great harm to
many people.'

Charles, however, perceiving his brother Auguste in the
yard with Marcel, ready for the appointment, now called
him into the room: 'Come here a moment; I've brought
somebody to see you.   Besides, your son Adrien is here,
and wants to give us an order.'

Auguste, who was as tall and sturdy as his father had
been, pressed Marc's hand vigorously. 'Ah, Monsieur

Froment,' said he, 'we often talk about you—Charles and
I—when we remember our school-days! I was a very bad
pupil, and I 've regretted it at times. Yet I hope I have n't
disgraced you too much; and, in any case, my son Adrien
is becoming a man after your own heart.' Then he added,
laughing: 'I know what Adrien's order is! Yes, indeed,
the house which he wants to build for your friend Simon!
. . . All the same, a house is perhaps a good deal to
give to an ex-convict.'

In spite of the bantering *bonhomie* of Auguste's tone, Marc
felt grieved by that last remark. 'Do you still think Simon
guilty?' he inquired. 'At one time you became convinced
of his innocence. But you began to doubt it again after
that monstrous trial at Rozan.'

'Well, of course, Monsieur Froment, one feels impressed
when a man is found guilty by two juries in succession.
. . . But no! I no longer say that he was the culprit.
And besides, at bottom it is all one to us. We are even
quite willing that a present should be made to him, if by
that means the affair can be brought to an end once and
for all, so that we shall never have it dinned into our ears
again. Is n't that so, brother?'

'That 's correct,' responded Charles. 'If those big fellows were listened to, we ourselves should be the only real
criminals, on the ground that we tolerated the injustice.
It vexes me. There must be an end to it all!'

The two cousins, Adrien and Marcel, who took an equally
passionate interest in the affair, laughed triumphantly. 'So
it is settled!' exclaimed Marcel, as he tapped his father on
the shoulder. 'You will take charge of the locksmith's
work, uncle Auguste of the masonry, and I of the timber
work. In that way your share in the crime, as you put it,
will be repaired. And we will never mention the matter to
you again, we swear it!'

Adrien was laughing and nodding his approval when old
Madame Doloir, who had remained standing there, stiff and
silent, intervened in her obstinate way. 'Auguste and
Charles,' said she, 'have nothing to repair. It will never
be known whether Schoolmaster Simon was guilty or not.
We little folk ought never to poke our noses into affairs
which only concern the Government. And I pity you boys
—yes, both of you, Adrien and Marcel—if you imagine that
you are strong enough to change things. You fancy that
you now know everything, whereas you know nothing at

all. . . . For instance, my poor dead husband, your grandfather, knew that a general meeting of all the Jew millionaires was held in Paris, in a subterranean gallery near the fortifications, every Saturday, when it was decided what sums should be paid to the traitors who betrayed France to Germany. And he knew the story to be a true one, for it had been told him by his own captain, who vouched for it on his honour.'

Marc gazed at the old woman in wonderment, for it was as if he had been carried forty years back. He recognised in her tale one of those extraordinary stories which Doloir the mason had picked up while he was soldiering. For their part, Auguste and Charles had listened to the anecdote in quite a serious way, without any sign of embarrassment, for it was amid similar imbecilities that they had spent their childhood. But neither Adrien nor Marcel could refrain from smiling, however great might be their affectionate deference for their grandmother.

'The Jew syndicate in a cellar! Ah, what an idea, grandmother!' said Adrien softly. 'There are no more Jews, for there will soon be no more Catholics. . . . The disappearance of the Churches means the end of all religious warfare.'

Then, as his mother now came into the room, he went to kiss her. Angèle Bongard, who had married Auguste Doloir when a shrewd young peasant girl, had largely contributed to her husband's success, though she had no very exceptional gifts. She now at once asked for news of her brother Fernand, her sister-in-law Lucille, and their daughter Claire, who had married her son. Then the whole family became interested in the latest addition to its number, this being a baby-boy named Célestin, to whom Marcel's wife had given birth a fortnight previously.

'You see, Monsieur Froment,' remarked old Madame Doloir, 'I have become a great-grandmother for the second time; after Georgette has come this little fellow, Célestin. My younger son, Léon, also has a big boy, Edmond, now twelve years old; but he is only my grandson, so with him I don't seem to be quite so old.'

The old woman was becoming amiable — anxious, it seemed, to efface the recollection of her former stiffness, for she continued: 'And, by the way, Monsieur Froment, we never seem to agree; but there is one thing for which I really have to thank you, and that is for having almost compelled me to make Léon a schoolmaster. I did n't care for that profession, for it seemed to me hardly a tempting one; but you took all sorts of pains; you gave lessons to Léon, and now, though he's not yet forty, he already has a good position.'

She had become, indeed, very proud of her youngest son, Léon, who had lately succeeded Sébastien Milhomme in the headmastership of a school at Beaumont, Sébastien having been appointed director of the Training College. The schoolmistress whom Léon had married, Juliette Hochard, had also been transferred to Beaumont, there taking the former post of Mademoiselle Rouzaire; and their eldest son, Edmond, now a pupil at the Lycée, was studying brilliantly.

Well pleased at seeing his grandmother so amiable with Marc, Adrien kissed her, and then said jestingly: ' That's very nice of you, grandmother; you are now on Monsieur Froment's side. And, do you know, on the day when Simon returns we will choose you to offer him a bouquet at the railway station.'

But she again became grave and suspicious. 'Ah, no; not that; certainly not! I don't want to get myself into trouble. You young men are mad with your new ideas!'

After a merry leave-taking, Adrien and Marc at last retired in order to make their way to Jules Savin's. The model farm of Les Amettes spread over some two hundred and fifty acres in the outskirts of Maillebois, just beyond the new district. Jules, after his mother's death, had given a home to his father, the former petty clerk, who was now seventy-one years old; and he had been obliged to do the same for his elder brother, Achille, one of the twins, who, after being for many years a clerk like his father, had been suddenly stricken with paralysis. Philippe, the other twin, and at one time the partner of Jules, was now dead.

It so happened that Marc had become a connection of this family by reason of the marriage of his son Clément with Charlotte, the daughter of Hortense Savin, who had died some years previously. But the marriage had taken place somewhat against Marc's desires, and thus, while allowing Clément all latitude to follow the dictates of his heart, he had preferred personally to hold aloof. He was too broad-minded to make Charlotte responsible for the flighty conduct of her mother, who, after being led astray in her sixteenth year and marrying her seducer, had ended by eloping with another lover, meeting at last with a wretched

death in some other part of France. And thus, while imputing nothing to her daughter, Marc harboured certain
prejudices against the Savin family generally, and, whatever alacrity he had professed, it had been necessary for
him to do violence to his feelings when Adrien had begged
him to go to Les Amettes.

As it happened Jules was not at home, but his return was
expected every moment. In the meantime the visitors
found themselves in the presence of Savin senior, who was
watching over his son Achille in a little sitting-room, where
the paralysed man now spent his life in an armchair placed
near the window. Directly Savin senior caught sight of
Marc he raised a cry of surprise: 'Ah! Monsieur Froment,'
said he, 'I thought you were angry with me. Well, it is
kind of you to call.'

He was still as thin and as puny as ever, still racked, too,
by a dreadful cough, yet he had contrived to survive his
fresh, pretty, and plump wife, whom, indeed, he had killed
by dint of daily vexations inspired by his bitter jealousy.

'Angry?' Marc quietly responded. 'Why should I be
angry with you, Monsieur Savin?'

'Oh! because our ideas have never been the same,' said
the ex-clerk. 'Your son may have married my granddaughter, but that does not suffice to reconcile our opinions.
. . . For instance, you and your friends are now driving
away all the priests and monks, which I regard as very unfortunate, for it will only lead to an increase of immorality.
Heaven knows that I don't like those gentry, for I am an
old Republican, a Socialist—yes, a Socialist, Monsieur Froment! But then, women and children need the threats of
religion to check them from evil courses, as I have never
grown tired of saying.'

An involuntary smile escaped Marc as he listened. 'Religion a police service!' said he; 'I know your theory.
But how can religion exercise any power when people no
longer believe, and there is no longer any reason to fear the
priests?'

'No longer a reason to fear them!' cried Savin. 'Good
Heavens! you are much mistaken. I myself have always
been one of their victims. If I had sided with them, do
you think that I should have vegetated all my life in a little
office, and now be a charge on my son Jules, after losing
my wife, who was killed by all sorts of privations? And
my son Achille, whom you see here, so grievously afflicted

—he again is a victim of the priests. I ought to have sent him to a seminary, and he would now be a prefect or a judge, instead of having contracted all sorts of aches and pains in a horrible office, which he left unable to use either his legs or his arms, so that now he cannot even take a basin of soup unassisted. . . . The priests are dirty scamps; is it not so, Achille? But all the same, it is better to have them on one's side than against one.'

The cripple, who had greeted his old master with a friendly nod, now remarked slowly, his speech being already impeded by paralysis: 'The priests long controlled the weather, no doubt; nevertheless, one is beginning to do without them very well.' Then, with something like a sneer, he added: 'And so it has become easy enough to settle their account, and play the judge.'

As he spoke he looked at Adrien, for whom that uncomplimentary allusion was doubtless intended. Achille's unfortunate position, the death of his wife, and a quarrel which had arisen between him and his daughter Léontine, who was married to a Beaumont ironmonger, had embittered his nature. And deeming his allusion insufficient, wishing to be more precise, he continued: 'You will remember, Monsieur Froment, that I told you I was still convinced of Simon's innocence at the time when he was recondemned at Rozan. But what could I do? Could I have made a revolution by myself? No, of course not; so it was best to remain silent. . . . Nevertheless, I now see a number of young gentlemen calling us cowards, and trying to give us a lesson by raising triumphal arches to the martyr. It is brave work indeed!'

On being challenged in this fashion Adrien immediately understood that Jules Savin must have spoken of the great plan. And instead of losing his temper he strove to be very amiable and conciliatory: 'Oh! everybody is brave on becoming just,' he replied. 'I know very well, monsieur, that you were always among the reasonable folk, and I confess that some members of my own family showed even greater blindness and obstinacy than others. But to-day the general desire ought to be to unite, so that all may mingle in the same flame of solidarity and justice.'

Savin senior, who had been listening with an air of stupefaction, now suddenly understood why Marc and Adrien were there, awaiting the return of his son Jules. At the outset he had attributed their visit to politeness only. 'Ah!

of course, you have come about that stupid scheme for offering reparation,' said he. 'Well, like those relatives you speak of, I have nothing to do with that business! No, indeed! My son Jules will act as he pleases, of course; but that will not prevent me from keeping my own opinion. . . . The Jews, monsieur, the Jews, always the Jews!'

Adrien looked at him, in his turn full of stupefaction. The Jews, indeed! Why did he speak of the Jews! Anti-Semitism was dead—to such a degree, indeed, that the new generation failed to understand what was meant when people accused the Jews of every crime. As Adrien had said to his grandmother, Madame Doloir, there were no Jews left, since only citizens, freed from the tyranny of dogmas, remained. It was essentially the Roman Church which had exploited anti-Semitism, in the hope of thereby winning back the incredulous masses; and anti-Semitism had disappeared when that Church sank into the darkness of expiring religions.

Marc had followed the scene with great interest, comparing the past with the present, recalling the incidents and the words of forty years ago, the better to discern the moral of those of to-day. However, Jules Savin at last came in, accompanied by his son Robert, a tall youth of sixteen, whom he was already initiating into the farmwork. And directly he learnt the purpose of his visitors he appeared to be much touched, and addressing Marc with great deference, exclaimed:

'Monsieur Froment, you cannot doubt my desire to be agreeable to you. We all regard you nowadays as a just and venerable master. Besides, as my friend Adrien must have told you, I am in no sense opposed to his plan. On the contrary, I will employ all the authority I possess to second it, for I am entirely of his opinion. Maillebois will only regain its honour when it has offered reparation for its fault. . . . Only, I repeat it, there must be absolute unanimity in the Municipal Council. I am working in that sense, and I beg you to do the same.'

Then, as his father began to sneer, Jules said to him, smiling: 'Come, don't pretend to be so hard-headed; you admitted Simon's innocence to me the other day.'

'His innocence? Oh! I don't dispute that. I also am innocent, but nobody builds me a house.'

'You have mine,' Jules retorted somewhat roughly.

At bottom it was precisely that circumstance which hurt Savin's feelings. The hospitality he received at his son's house, the fate that had befallen him of ending his days peacefully, in the home of one who had succeeded by dint of great personal efforts, gave the lie to his everlasting recriminations, the regret he was always expressing at not having sided with the priests in spite of the hatred with which he regarded them. Thus, losing his temper, he cried: ' Well, if you choose you can build a cathedral for your Simon! It won't matter to me, for I shall stay at home.'

Then Achille, who, tortured by the pains in his legs, had just raised a pitiful moan, exclaimed: 'Alas! I shall stay at home as well.   But if I were not nailed to this armchair I would willingly go with you, my dear Jules, for I belong to the generation which did not, perhaps, do all its duty, but which was not ignorant of it, and is ready to do it now.'

After those words Marc and Adrien withdrew, delighted, feeling certain of success.   And when Marc found himself alone again, returning to his daughter Louise by way of the broad thoroughfares of the new district, he summed up all he had just seen and heard; the far-off memories, which at the same time returned to him, enabling him to gauge the distance which had been travelled during the last forty years.   The whole story of his life, his efforts and his triumph, was spread out, and he felt that he had been right in former days, when he had said that if France did not protest and rise to do justice in the Simon case, it was because she was steeped in too much ignorance, because she was debased and poisoned by religious imbecility and malice, because she was kept in childish superstitions and notions by a Press given over to lucre, scandal, and blackmailing.   And, in the same way, a clear intuition had come to him of the only possible remedy—instruction, education, which would liberate one and all, endow them with solidarity and the intelligent bravery of life, by killing falsehood, destroying error, sweeping away the senseless dogmas of the Church, with its hell, its heaven, and its doctrines of social death.   That was what Marc had desired, and that, indeed, was the work which was being accomplished—the liberation of the people by the primary schools, the rescue of all citizens from the state of iniquity in which they had been plunged, in order that they might at last become capable of truth and justice.

But it was particularly a feeling of appeasement which now came over Marc. Only forgiveness, tolerance, and kindliness surged from his heart. In former times he had greatly suffered, and he had often felt passionately angry with men on seeing with what stupid cruelty they behaved, and how obstinately they persisted in evil. At present, however, he could not forget the words spoken by Fernand Bongard and Achille Savin. They had tolerated injustice, no doubt; but as they now said, this was because they had not known, and because they had not felt strong enough to contend with that injustice. The slumber of their intelligence could not be imputed to the disinherited scions of ignorance as a crime. And Marc willingly forgave one and all; he no longer harboured any rancour even against the obstinate ones, who refused to open their minds to facts; he would simply have liked the festival planned for Simon's return to become a festival of general reconciliation, one in which the whole of Maillebois would embrace and mingle in brotherly concord, resolving to work henceforth for the happiness of all.

On reaching Louise's quarters at the school, where Geneviève had awaited him, and where they were to dine in company with Clément, Charlotte, and Lucienne, Marc was pleased to find that Sébastien and Sarah were also there, having just arrived from Beaumont to share the meal. Indeed, it was a general family gathering, and several leaves had to be added to the table. There were Marc and Geneviève; then Clément and Charlotte, with their daughter Lucienne, who was already seven years old; then Joseph Simon and Louise; then Sébastien Milhomme and Sarah; then François Simon, Joseph's son, and Thérèse Milhomme, Sarah's daughter, two cousins who had married, and who were already the parents of a little two-year-old named Rose. Altogether they made a dozen, full of health and appetite.

Acclamations arose when Marc recounted his afternoon, describing Adrien's plan and expressing his belief in its success. Joseph alone felt doubtful, for he was not convinced, he said, of the Mayor's favourable disposition. But Charlotte immediately intervened. 'You are mistaken,' she exclaimed; 'my uncle Jules is altogether on our side. . . . We can rely on him. He is the only one of the family who ever showed me any kindness.'

Charlotte, it should be said, had become dependent on

her grandfather, Savin senior, at the time when her mother had eloped, for it had become necessary to place her father in an asylum on account of the alcoholism to which he had given way. The girl had then experienced much suffering, being often cuffed and sparsely fed. Savin, who seemed oblivious of the deplorable result of the pious hypocrisy in which his daughter Hortense had been reared by Mademoiselle Rouzaire, accused his grandchild of being an atheist, a rebel, full of deplorable ways, which were due to the teaching of Mademoiselle Mazeline. As a matter of fact, however, Charlotte was delightful, free from all false prudery, and gifted with healthy uprightness, sense, and tenderness. And Clément having married her in spite of all obstacles, they had since lived together in the happiest and the closest of unions.

'Charlotte is right,' said Marc, who also desired to defend Jules Savin; 'the Mayor is on our side. But the best of all is that, among the contractors for the house which it is proposed to present to Simon, there will be the two Doloirs, Auguste the mason and Charles the locksmith; besides which, by their ties of relationship, even Fernand Bongard and Achille Savin will be indirectly concerned in it. . . . Ah! Sébastien, my friend, who would have thought that would come to pass in the days when you and those fine fellows attended my school?'

At this sally Sébastien Milhomme began to laugh; though his mood was scarcely a cheerful one, for a recent family loss, a very tragical affair, had affected him painfully. During the previous spring his aunt, Madame Edouard, had died, leaving the stationery business to her sister-in-law, Madame Alexandre. Her son Victor having disappeared, she had of recent years seemed to waste away, no longer attending to the business, in which she had once taken such a passionate interest, and feeling, indeed, quite at sea amidst those new times, which she altogether failed to understand. Madame Alexandre on remaining alone had continued carrying on the business, for she did not wish to inconvenience her son Sébastien, though the latter's position was becoming extremely good. One evening, however, Victor suddenly reappeared, emerging hungry and sordid from the depths in which he had been leading a crapulous life. He had heard of his mother's death, and he instantly demanded that the business should be put up for sale and the old partnership liquidated, in order that he might carry off his share of the proceeds. Such, then, was the end of the little shop in the Rue Courte, where many generations of schoolboys had purchased their copybooks and their pens. For a short time Victor showed himself here and there in Maillebois, leading a merry life, almost invariably in the company of his old chum, Polydor Souquet, who had fallen to the gutter. One evening Marc, having to cross a street of ill-repute, caught sight of them with another man, whose black figure strikingly resembled that of Brother Gorgias. And finally, barely a week before the family dinner given by Louise, the police had found a man lying dead, with his skull split, outside a haunt of debauchery. The dead man was Victor. There had evidently been some dim, ignoble tragedy, which the interested parties endeavoured to hush up.

'Yes, yes,' said Sébastien in reply to Marc, 'I remember my schoolfellows. With a few unfortunate exceptions they have not turned out so badly. But in life one is at times exposed to certain poisons, which prove pitiless.'

The others did not insist. They preferred to inquire after his mother, whom he had now taken to live with him at the Beaumont Training College, and who still enjoyed good health in spite of her great age. Sébastien's new position gave him a great deal of occupation, particularly as he desired to perfect the work of his venerated master, Salvan. 'Ah!' he exclaimed, 'that public reparation offered to Simon, that glorification of a schoolmaster, will be a great joy for all of us. I want my pupils to participate in it, and for that purpose I shall endeavour to obtain a day's holiday for them.'

Marc, who had rejoiced at Sébastien's appointment as if it were a personal triumph, at once signified his approval. 'Quite so,' said he, 'and we will bring the old ones as well —Salvan, Mademoiselle Mazeline, and Mignot. Besides, speaking of school-teachers, there is already a fine battalion here present.'

The others began to laugh. With the exception of the two children they were, indeed, all teachers. Clément and Charlotte still carried on the Jonville schools, Joseph and Louise had decided that they would never quit Maillebois, Sébastien and Sarah relied on remaining at the Beaumont Training College until the former reached the age limit; while as for the younger couple, François and Thérèse, they had not long been appointed to the Dherbecourt schools, where their parents had previously made their *débuts.*

François, in whom one traced a likeness to his parents, Joseph and Louise, also resembled his grandfather Marc, for he had much the same lofty brow and bright eyes, though the latter in his case glowed with what seemed to be a flame of insatiable desire. In Thérèse, on the other hand, one found the great beauty of her mother Sarah softened, quieted, as it were, by the intellectual refinement which she had inherited from her father, Sébastien. And Rose, the young couple's little girl, the last born of the family, and as such worshipped by one and all, seemed to personify the budding future.

The dinner proved delightfully gay. How joyful for Joseph and Sarah, the children of the innocent martyr, tortured for so many years, was the thought of the festival of reparation which was now being planned! Their own children and their grandchild—all that had come from their blood mingled with that of Marc, the martyr's most heroic defender — would participate in that glorification. Four generations, indeed, would be present to celebrate the truth, and the *cortège* would be formed of all the good workers who, having suffered for its sake, were entitled to share its triumph.

Laughter, and again laughter, arose. They all drank to the return of Simon, and even when ten o'clock struck the happy family continued to give expression to its delight, quite forgetful of the trains by which some of its members were to return to Beaumont and others to Jonville.

From that day forward things moved with unexpected rapidity. Adrien's scheme on being laid before the Municipal Council was voted unanimously, as Jules Savin, the Mayor, had desired. Nobody even thought of opposing the suggested inscription. None of the applications and pleadings, which the promoters of the scheme had imagined necessary, were required, for the idea to which they gave expression already existed, in embryo, in the minds of all. There was remorse for the past, uneasiness at the thought of the unhealed iniquity, and a craving to repair it for the sake of the town's honour. Everybody now felt that it was impossible to be happy outside the pale of civic solidarity, for durable happiness can only come to a people when it is just. And so in a few weeks' time the subscription lists were filled. As the amount required was a comparatively small one, being no more than thirty thousand francs,[1]—for

---

[1] $6000.

the site of the house was given by the municipality,—people
contented themselves with subscribing two, three, or at the
utmost five francs, in order that a larger number of subscribers might participate.   The workmen of the *faubourg*
and the peasants of the environs contributed their half-francs
and their francs; and at the end of March the building was
put in hand, for it was desired that everything should be in
readiness, the last woodwork in position, and the last paint
dry, by mid-September, the date which Simon had ended
by fixing for his return.

In September, then, the simple but cheerful house stood
completed in its pleasant garden, which was faced by a
railing on the side of the square.   Its affectionately-awaited
owner might come to take possession of it when he pleased,
for nothing was lacking.   True, a drapery hung before the
marble slab bearing an inscription over the doorway; but
this inscription, so far as Simon was concerned, was to
be the great surprise, and would only be uncovered at
the last moment.   Adrien repaired to the Pyrenees to plan
the final arrangements with Simon and David, and it was
then decided that the former's wife, who was in a very
weak state of health, should in the first instance install
herself in the house, with the help of her children, Joseph
and Sarah.   Then, on the appointed day, Simon would
arrive with his brother David.   There would be an official
reception at the railway station, and afterwards he would
be conducted in triumph to his new home, the gift of
his fellow-townsmen, where his wife and children would
await him.

At last, on the Twentieth of September, a Sunday, the
solemnity was enacted amid radiant sunshine and a warm
and pure atmosphere.   The streets of Maillebois were
decorated with flags, the last flowers of the season were
scattered along the procession's line of route.   And early
in the morning—although the train would only arrive at
three o'clock in the afternoon—the population assembled
out of doors, gathering together in a happy, singing, laughing multitude, whose numbers were swollen by all the
visitors who flocked in from neighbouring parishes.   At
noon one could no longer circulate outside the house on
the large new square, whose recreation-ground was invaded
by the working-class families of the neighbourhood.   There
were people, too, at all the windows, and the very roadways
were blocked by waves of spectators eager to see and to cry

their passion for justice.   Nothing could have been grander
or more inspiring.

Marc and Geneviève had arrived from Jonville, with
Clément, Charlotte, and little Lucienne, early in the day.
It was arranged that they should await Simon in the garden
of the house, grouped around Madame Simon, her children,
Joseph and Sarah, her grandchildren, François and Thérèse,
and her great-granddaughter, little Rose.   Louise, of course,
was there, beside her husband Joseph, and Sébastien beside
his wife Sarah.   These constituted the three generations
which had sprung from the blood of the innocent man
mingled with that of his champions.   Then, also, places
had been reserved for the first defenders, the survivors of
the heroic days,— Salvan, Mademoiselle Mazeline, and
Mignot,—as well as for the fervent artisans of the work of
reparation, the now conquered and enthusiastic members
of the Bongard, Doloir, and Savin families.   It was rumoured
that Delbos, the ex-advocate, the hero of the two trials,
who for four years recently had held the office of Minister
of the Interior, had gone to join Simon and David, in order
to reach the town in their company.   Only the Mayor and
a deputation of the Municipal Council were to meet the
brothers at the railway station and conduct them to the
house, decked with banners and garlands, where the ceremony of presentation would take place.   And there, in
accordance with this programme, Marc remained waiting
with the rest of the family, in spite of all his joyous eagerness to embrace the triumpher.

Two o'clock struck; there was still an hour to be spent
patiently.   Meanwhile the crowd steadily increased.   Marc,
having left the garden to mingle with the groups and hear
what was being said, found that the one subject of conversation was that extraordinary story emerging from the
past, that condemnation of an innocent man, which had
become both abominable and inexplicable in the eyes of the
new generations.   From the younger folk a long cry of indignant amazement arose; while the old people, those who
had witnessed the iniquity, tried to defend themselves with
vague gestures and shamefaced explanations.   Now that
the truth had become manifest in the full sunlight, endowed
with all the force of invincible certainty, the children and
the grandchildren could not understand how their parents
and grandparents had carried blindness and egotism so far
as to fail to fathom so simple an affair.   And doubtless

many of the older folk shared the astonishment of the younger ones, and were at a loss to account for the credulity into which they had fallen. That, indeed, was their best answer to the reproaches they heard; it was necessary to have lived in those times to understand the power of false-hood over ignorance. One old man penitently confessed his error; another related how he had hissed Simon on the day of his arrest, and how he had now been waiting two hours in order to acclaim him, anxious as he was not to die with his bad action upon his conscience. And a youth, his grandson, thereupon threw himself on the old man's neck and kissed him, laughing, with tears in his eyes. Marc was delightfully touched by the scene, and continued to walk about, looking and listening.

But all at once he stopped short. He had just recognised Polydor Souquet, clad in rags, with a ravaged countenance, as if still under the effects of a night of intoxication. And Marc was thunderstruck when by the side of Polydor he perceived Brother Gorgias, clad as usual in black, without a sign of linen, his greasy old frock-coat clinging fast to his dark hide. He, Gorgias, was not drunk. Silent and fierce of aspect, erect in all his tragic leanness, he darted fiery glances at the crowd. And Marc could hear that Polydor, with a drunkard's stupid obstinacy, was deriding him re-specting the affair, of which everybody was talking around them. Slabbering and stammering, the scamp went on:

'I say, old man, the copy-slip—you remember, eh? The copy-slip! It was I who sneaked it. I had it in my pocket, and I was stupid enough to give it you back while you were seeing me home. . . . Ah, yes! that wretched copy-slip.'

A sudden flash of light illumined Marc's mind. He now knew the whole truth. The one gap in the affair, which had still worried him occasionally, was now filled. Poly-dor had given the slip to Gorgias, and that explained how it had chanced to be in his pocket, and how it had become mingled with a copy of *Le Petit Beaumontais* when, terrified by his victim's cries, he had hastily sought a handkerchief, a stopper of any kind, to use as a gag.

'But you know, old man,' stammered Polydor, 'we liked each other very much, and we did n't tell our business to other folk. And yet, if I *had* chattered, what a rumpus there would have been! Ah! what a face my Aunt Pélagie would have pulled!'

Half-fuddled, in an ignoble state, the rascal went on
jeering, unconscious, it seemed, of the presence of the
people around him. And Gorgias, who from time to time
gave him a contemptuous glance, must suddenly have
understood that Marc had heard the drunkard's involuntary
confession, for in a low voice he growled: ' Be quiet, you
wine-bag! Be quiet, you rotten cur! You stink of your
sin and mine; you have damned me again by your ignominy!
Be quiet, you filthy thing; it is I who will speak! Yes, I
will confess my fault, in order that God may pardon
me! '

Then, addressing himself to Marc, who was still lost in
silent amazement, he went on: ' You heard him, Monsieur Froment, did n't you ? Well, it 's necessary that all
should hear. I have been consumed long enough by a desire to confess myself to men, even as I have confessed to
God, in order that my salvation may be the more glorious.
And, besides, all these people exasperate me! They know
absolutely nothing; they keep on repeating my name with
execration, as if I were the only culprit! But wait a moment; they will see it is not so, for I will tell them everything! '

Then, though he was over seventy years old, he contrived to spring upon the low wall supporting the garden
railing of the house where Simon, the innocent man, was
soon to be received in triumph. And clinging with one
hand to that railing, he turned and faced his mighty audience. During the hour he had spent roaming through the
groups, he had heard his name fall from every tongue as a
name of infamy. And he had gradually been fired by a
sombre fever, the bravery of a fine bandit, who denies none
of his actions, but is ready to cast them in the teeth of men,
full of a mad pride that he should have dared to commit
them. What caused him most suffering, however, was that
he alone should be named, that all the weight of the general
execration should be cast upon his shoulders, for the others,
his accomplices, seemed to be quite forgotten. Only the
previous day, his resources again being exhausted, he had
attempted to force himself upon Father Crabot, who was
shut up at the estate of La Désirade, and he had been flung
out with the alms of a twenty-franc piece, the very last that
would be given him, so he had been told. And now, amid
all the insulting words that were levelled at him, nobody
shouted the name of Father Crabot. Why, as he was ready

to expiate his transgression, why should not Father Crabot
expiate his also ?   No doubt he, Gorgias, would extract no
more twenty-franc pieces from that coward if he were to
reveal everything; but his hatred was now dearer to him
than money, and it would be blissful to cast his enemy into
the flames of hell, while he himself ascended to the delights
of paradise by virtue of the penance of a public confession,
the idea of which had long haunted him.

Thus an unexpected, an extraordinary scene began.
With a violent, sweeping gesture, Gorgias sought to gather
the crowd together and attract its attention.   And in a
shrill but still powerful voice he called: ' Listen to me!
listen to me!   I will tell you everything! '

But at first he was not heard, and he had to raise the
same cry twice, thrice, a dozen times, with increasing, un-
wearying energy.   By degrees he was noticed and people
became attentive; and when some of the old folk had recognised him, when his name had flown from mouth to mouth
amid a quiver of horror, a death-like silence at last fell
from one to the other end of the great square.

' Listen to me! listen to me!   I will tell you everything! '

Raised above the heads of all the others, with the broad
sunlight streaming on him, he clung with one hand to the
iron railing, while with the other he went on making vehement gesticulations as if he were sabring the air.   His
threadbare frock-coat hung closely to his withered, knotty
frame, and with his dusky face, from which jutted the big
beak of a bird of prey, he looked quite terrible, like some
phantom of the past, whose eyes glowed with the flames of
all the abominable passions of long ago.

' You speak of truth and justice,' he cried.   ' But you
know nothing, and you are not just!   . . .   You all fall
upon me, you treat me as if I were the only culprit, whereas
others sinned more even than I did.   I may have been a
criminal, but others accepted my crime, hid it, and continued it.   . . .   Wait a little while; you will see by-
and-by that I don't lack the courage to confess my sin.
But why am I the only one ready to confess ?   Why is n't
my master, my chief, the all-powerful Father Crabot, here
also, ready to humiliate himself and tell everything ?   Let
him come!   Go and fetch him from his hiding-place, and let
him confess his sins before you and do penitence beside
me.   Otherwise I shall speak out; I shall proclaim his
crime with mine, for though I be the most humble, the

most miserable of sinners, God is in me, and it is God who demands expiation of him as of me.'

Then, in the bitterest language, he declared that all his superiors, Father Crabot at the head of them, were but degenerate Catholics, poltroons, and enjoyers of life. The Church was dying by reason of their cowardice, their compromises with the weaknesses and the vanities of the world. It was, indeed, his favourite theory that all true religious spirit had departed from those monks, those priests, and those bishops, who ought to have ensured the reign of Jesus by fire and sword. Earth and mankind belonged to God alone, and God had given them to His Church, the sovereign delegate of His power. The Church therefore possessed everything, and held absolute dominion over everybody and everything. To her belonged the disposal of wealth; none could be wealthy save by her permission. To her belonged even the disposal of life, for every living man was her subject, whom she allowed to live or suppressed according to the interests of Heaven. Such was the doctrine from which the true saints had never departed. He, a mere humble Ignorantine, had always practised and exalted that doctrine, and his superiors, though they had wronged him in other respects, had always recognised in him the rare merit of possessing the true, absolute religious spirit; whereas they themselves—the Crabots, the Philibins, and the Fulgences—had ruined religion by their compromises, their trickery with the Freethinkers, the Jews, the Protestants, and the Freemasons. Like opportunists, anxious to please, they had gradually abandoned dogmas and concealed the asperity of doctrines, whereas they ought to have fought openly against impiety, and have slaughtered and burnt all heretics. He himself dreamt of seeing a huge sacrificial pyre set up in the midst of Paris, on which he would have cast the whole guilty nation, in order that the flames and the stench from all those millions of bodies might have ascended to the glowing skies to rejoice and appease the Deity.

And he next exclaimed: 'As soon as a sinner confesses and does penance, he is no longer guilty, he again recovers the grace of his Sovereign Master. What man is there who never sins? All who are made of flesh are liable to err. Even like the layman, he who is in holy orders and whom the beast, which is in all men, precipitates into crime has but one obligation cast upon him—that of confession; and if he receives absolution, if he expiates his sin with firm repentance, he redeems himself, he becomes again as white as snow, worthy to enter into Heaven, among the roses and lilies of Mary. . . . I confessed my sin to Father Théodose, who absolved me, and I owed nothing more to anybody, since God, who ordains and knows all things, had pardoned me by the sacrament of one of His ministers. And in the same way, from that day forward, each time that I lied, each time that my superiors compelled me to lie, I went back to the confessional, and I washed my soul clean of all the impurities with which human fragility had soiled it. Alas! I have often and I have greatly sinned, for God, in order no doubt to try me, has allowed the devil to assail me with all the fires of hell. But I have battered my chest with my fists, I have made my knees bleed by dragging them over the flagstones of chapels—I have paid, and I repeat that I owe nothing whatever. A flight of archangels would bear me straight to Paradise if I should die by-and-by, ere lapsing again into the original mire, whence in common with all men I have sprung. And in particular I owe nothing to men; I have never owed them anything; my crime lies between God and me, His servant. But He has forgiven me, and so, if I speak here to-day, it is because I choose to do so, because I desire to couple with the Divine mercy the martyrdom of a last humiliation, in order that I may enter Paradise in triumph—a celestial joy which, whatever my abjection, I shall assuredly taste, thanks to my penitence; whereas you will never taste it—race of unbelievers and blasphemers that you are, destined, one and all, to the flames of hell!'

Amid his sombre fury, that transport of savage faith which had raised him there, alone and impudent, face to face with the multitude, Gorgias again began to jeer. And there came to him that habitual twitching of the lips, which disclosed some of his teeth in a grimace suggestive of both scorn and cruelty. Polydor, who for a moment had seemed quite scared, and had gazed at him with dilated eyes, blurred by his drunkenness, had now fallen beside the railing, overcome by sleepiness and already snoring. The crowd, in horrified expectancy of the promised confession, had hitherto preserved death-like silence. But it was now growing weary of that long oration, in which it found all the unconquerable pride and insolence of the Churchman who deems himself all-powerful and inviolate. What did

the scamp mean by that speech ?   Why did he not content
himself with stating the facts ?   What was the use of such
a long preamble when a dozen words would have sufficed ?
Thus a growl arose, and a rush would have swept Gorgias
away if Marc, now very attentive and fully master of himself, had not stepped forward and with a gesture calmed the
growing impatience and anger.   Moreover, Gorgias remained imperturbable.   Despite all interruptions, he went
on repeating in the same shrill voice that he alone was
brave, that he alone was really upon God's side, and that
the other sinners, the cowards, would after all have to pay
for their transgressions, since God had set him there to
make public confession on their behalf as well as his own,
this being a supreme expiation, whence the Church, compromised by her unworthy leaders, would emerge rejuvenated and for ever victorious.

Then all at once, as if he were a prey to the wildest
remorse, he beat his chest violently with both fists, and
cried in distressful, tearful accents: ' I have sinned, O God!
O God, do Thou forgive me! Release me from the claws
of the devil, O God, that I may yet bless Thy holy name!
.   .   .   Yes, God wills it!   Listen to me, listen to me; I
will tell you everything! '

Then he laid himself bare, as it were, before the assembled throng.   He spoke plainly of his gross appetites;
he set forth that he had been a big eater, a deep drinker,
and that vice had dogged him from his childhood.   In
spite of all his intelligence he had then refused to study; he
had preferred to play the truant, to roam the fields, and hide
in the woods with little hussies.   His father, Jean Plumet,
after being a poacher, had been turned into a gamekeeper
by the Countess de Quédeville.   His mother, a hussy, had
disappeared after giving him birth.   He could still picture
his father as he had appeared to him lying on a stretcher in
the courtyard at Valmarie, whither he had been brought
dead, after two bullets had been lodged in his chest by one
of his former companions, a poacher.   And subsequently
he, Gorgias, had been brought up with the Countess's
grandson, Gaston, an unmanageable lad, who also refused
to study, preferring to hide himself away with little hussies,
climb poplar trees for magpies' nests, and wade the rivers
in search of crawfish.   At that time he, Gorgias, had become acquainted with Father Philibin, Gaston's tutor, and
Father Crabot, who was then in all his manly prime, adored

by the old Countess, and already the real master of Valmarie. Then, with sudden abruptness, plainly and brutally,
Gorgias related how Gaston, the grandson and heir, had
come by his death—a death which he had witnessed from
a distance, and of which he had kept the terrible secret for
so many years. The boy had been deliberately pushed into
the river and drowned there, the misfortune being attributed
to an accident, in such wise that a few months later the old
Countess finally bestowed her property upon Father Crabot.

Striking his breast with increasing fury, beside himself
with contrition, Gorgias continued amid his sobs: 'I have
sinned, I have sinned, O God! And my superiors have
sinned still more frightfully than I, for it was they, O God!
who ever set me an evil example! . . . But since I am
here to expiate their sins as well as mine by confessing
everything, O God, perchance Thou wilt pardon them in
Thine infinite mercy, even as Thou wilt assuredly pardon
me also!'

But a quiver of indignant revolt now sped through the
crowd. Fists were raised and voices demanded vengeance;
while Gorgias, resuming his narrative, related that from
that time forward Fathers Crabot and Philibin had never
abandoned him, linked to him as they were by a bond of
blood, relying on him as he relied on them. This was the
old pact which Marc had long suspected—Gorgias being
admitted to the Church and becoming an Ignorantine, an
enfant terrible of the Deity, one who both alarmed and enraptured his superiors by the wonderful religious spirit
which glowed in his guilty flesh. Again the wretched man
sobbed aloud, and all at once he passed to the horrid crime
of which Simon had been accused.

'The little angel was there, O God! . . . It is the
truth. I had just taken the other boy home, and I was
passing across the dark square, when I saw the little angel
in his room, which was lighted up. . . . Thou God
knowest that I approached him without evil intention,
simply out of curiosity, and in a fatherly spirit, in order to
scold him for leaving his window open. And Thou knowest also that for a while I talked to him as a friend, asking
him to show me the pictures on his table, sweet and pious
pictures, which were still perfumed by the incense of the
first Communion. But why, O God, why didst Thou then
allow the devil to tempt me? Why didst Thou abandon
me to the tempter, who impelled me to spring over the

window-bar under the pretence of taking a closer look at the pictures, though, alas! the flames of hell were already burning within me ? Ah! why didst Thou suffer it, O God ? Ah! verily, my God, Thy ways are mysterious and terrible!'

The throng had now again relapsed into deathly silence amid the frightful anguish which wrung every breast as the ignoble confession at last took its course. Not a breath was heard; horror spread over all those motionless folk, terrified by the thought of what was coming. And Marc, who was very white, quite scared at seeing the truth rise before him at last, after so many lies, gazed fixedly at the wretched culprit, who was gesticulating frantically amid the sobs which choked him.

'The little child—he was so pretty. Thou hadst given him, O God! the fair and curly head of a little angel. Like the cherubs of pious paintings, he seemed, indeed, to have but that angelic head with two wings. . . . Kill him, O God! Did I have any such horrible thought? Speak! Thou canst read my heart! I was so fond of him, I would not have plucked a hair from his head. . . But it is true the fire of hell had come upon me; Satan transported me, blinded me, and the boy became alarmed; he began to call out, to call out, to call out. . . . O God, those calls, those calls! I hear them always, always, and they madden me!'

It seemed, indeed, as if Gorgias were now a prey to some supreme paroxysm; his eyes glowed like coals of fire in his convulsed countenance, a little foam appeared upon his twisted lips, while his lean, bent frame quivered from head to foot with spasmodic shocks. And at last a great access of rage transported him. Like one of the damned whom the devil turns with his fork over the infernal brazier, he howled: 'No, no, that's not the plain truth; that again is arranged and embellished. . . . I must tell all, I will tell all; it is at that price only that I shall taste the eternal delights of Paradise!'

What followed was full of horror. He related everything in plain, crude, abominable language, and when he again came to his victim's cries he recounted his cowardly terror, his eager desire to conceal his crime, for his buzzing ears already seemed to re-echo the gallop of the gendarmes pursuing him. In wild despair he had sought for something; he had searched his pocket, and finding some papers in it, he had stuffed them without foresight or method into his victim's mouth, all eagerness as he was to hear those terrible cries no more.   But they had begun again, and he told how he had then murdered, strangled, the boy, pressing his strong, bony, hairy fingers, like iron bands, around the child's delicate neck, and marking it with deep, dark furrows.

'O God!' he cried, 'I am a hog, I am a murderous brute, my limbs are stained with mire and blood!   .   .   . And I fled like a wretched coward, without an idea in my head, quite brutified and senseless, leaving the window open, and thereby showing my stupidity and the innocence in which I should have remained but for the devil's unforeseen and victorious assault upon me.   .   .   .   And now that I have confessed everything to men, O God, I beg Thee, in reward for my penitence, open to me the doors of Heaven!'

But the horror-fraught patience of the crowd was now exhausted.   After the stupor which had kept it chilled and mute there came an outburst of extraordinary violence.   A loud roar of imprecations rolled from one to the other end of the square, a huge wave gathered and bounded towards the railings, towards the impudent wretch, the monstrous penitent, who in his religious dementia had thus dared to proclaim his crime in the full sunlight.   Shouts arose: 'To death with the scoundrel!   To death with the murderer! To death with the polluter and killer of children!'   And Marc then understood the terrible danger; he pictured the crowd lynching that wretched man in its craving for immediate justice; he beheld that festival of kindness and solidarity, that triumph of truth and equity, soiled, blackened by the summary execution of the culprit, whose limbs would be torn from him and cast to the four winds of heaven.   So in all haste he strove to remove Gorgias from the railings. But he had to contend with his resistance, for the obstinate, frantic scoundrel desired to say something more.   At last, helped by the vigorous arms of some of the bystanders, Marc managed to carry him into the garden, the gate of which was at once shut.   The rescue was effected none too soon, for the huge wave of the indignant crowd rolled up and burst against the railings, which fortunately checked its further progress, as they were new and strong.   Thus Gorgias was for the moment out of reach, sheltered by the very house which had been built for the innocent man, for whose tortures he was responsible.   And such was his obstinacy, that when those who had seized him released their hold, thinking him conquered, he picked himself up, and, rushing back to the railings, hung to them from inside. And there, protected by the iron bars, against which the furious, surging throng was sweeping, he began once more:

' Thou didst witness, O God! my first expiation, when my superiors, as foolish as they were cruel, abandoned me on the road to exile! Thou knowest to what unacknowledgeable callings they reduced me, what fresh and hateful transgressions they caused me to commit! Thou knowest their base avarice—how they refused me even a crust of bread, how they refuse it still, after being my counsellors and accomplices all my life long. . . . For thou wert always present, O God! Thou didst hear them bind themselves to me. Thou knowest that after my crime I did but obey them, and that if I aggravated it by other crimes it was only by and for them. Doubtless the desire was to save Thy Holy Church from scandal — and I, indeed, would have given my blood, my life. But they thought only of saving their own skins, and it is that which has enraged me and stirred me to tell everything. . . . And now, O God! that I have been Thy justiciary, that I have spoken the words of violence ordained by Thee, and have cried aloud their unknown and unpunished sins, it is for Thee to decide if Thou wilt pardon them or strike them down in Thy wrath, even before these swinish people, who pretend to forget Thy name, and for the roasting of whose sacrilegious limbs there will never be room enough in hell! '

Threatening hoots interrupted him at every word; stones, passing from hand to hand, began to fly around his head. The railings would not have resisted much longer; in fact, a last great onrush was about to throw them down when Marc and his assistants again managed to seize Gorgias and carry him to the end of the garden, behind the house. On that side there was a little gate conducting to a deserted lane, and the miscreant was soon led forth, and then driven away.

If, however, the growling, threatening crowd suddenly became calm, it was because cries of joy and glorification arose above the shouts of anger, drawing nearer every moment in sonorous waves along the sunlit avenue. Simon, having been received at the railway station by a deputation of the Municipal Council, was arriving in a large landau, he and David occupying the back seat, while in front of

them were Advocate Delbos and Jules Savin, the Mayor.
As the carriage slowly advanced between the serried crowd
there came an extraordinary ovation. Spurred to it by the
abominable scene which had left everybody quivering, they
acclaimed Simon with the wildest enthusiasm, for his innocence and his heroism seemed to have been rendered yet
more glorious by the public confession now made by the
real culprit, the savage and bestial Gorgias. Women wept
and raised their children to let them see the hero. Men
rushed to unharness the horses; and indeed they did unharness them, in such wise that the landau was dragged
to the house by a hundred brave arms. And all along the
flower-strewn line of route other flowers were flung from
the windows, where handkerchiefs as well as banners
waved. A very beautiful girl mounted the carriage step,
and remained there like a living statue of youth, contributing the splendour of her beauty to the martyr's triumph.
Kisses were wafted, words of affection and glorification fell
into the carriage with the bouquets which rained from
every side. Never had people been stirred by such intense
emotion—emotion wrung from their very vitals by the
thought of such a great iniquity—emotion which, seeking
to bestow some supreme compensation on the victim, found
it in the gift without reserve of the hearts and love of all.
Glory to the innocent man who had well-nigh perished by
the people's fault, and on whom the people would never be
able to bestow sufficient happiness! Glory to the martyr
who had suffered so greatly for unrecognised and strangled
truth, and whose victory was that of human reason freeing
itself from the bonds of error and falsehood! And glory to
the schoolmaster struck down in his functions, a victim of
his efforts to promote enlightenment, and now exalted the
more as he had suffered untold pain and grief for each and
every particle of truth that he had imparted to the ignorant
and the humble!

Marc, who stood on the threshold of the house, dizzy
with happiness, watching that triumph approach amid an
explosion of fraternity and affection, bethought himself of
the far-off day of Simon's arrest, the hateful day when a
vehicle had carried him away from Maillebois at the moment of little Zéphirin's funeral. A furious crowd had
rushed to seize him, roll him in the mud, and tear him to
pieces. A horrible clamour had arisen: 'To death, to
death with the assassin and sacrilegist! To death, to death

with the Jew!' And the crowd had pursued the rolling
wheels, unwilling to relinquish its prey, while Simon, pale
and frozen, responded with his ceaseless cry: 'I am innocent! I am innocent! I am innocent!' And now that
after long years that innocence was manifest, how striking
was the transformation! The crowd was rejuvenated,
transfigured; the children and the grandchildren of the
blind insulters of former days had grown up in knowledge
of truth, and become enthusiastic applauders, striving by
dint of sincerity and affection to redeem the crime of their
forerunners!

But the landau drew up before the garden gate, and the
emotion increased when Simon was seen to alight with the
help of his brother David, who had remained more nimble
and vigorous. Emaciated, reduced to a shadow, Simon had
white hair and a gentle countenance, softened by extreme
age. He smiled his thanks to David, and again there were
frantic acclamations at the sight of those two brothers,
bound together by long years of heroism. The cheers continued when, after the Mayor, Jules Savin, Delbos also
alighted—the great Delbos, as the crowd called him, the
hero of Beaumont and Rozan, who had not feared to speak
the truth aloud in the terrible days when it was perilous to
do so, and who ever since had worked for the advent of a
just society. Then, as Marc went forward to meet Simon
and David, whom Delbos had just joined, the four men
found themselves together for a moment on the very threshold of the house. And at that sight there came an increase
of enthusiasm. Cries were raised and arms were waved
deliriously as the three heroic defenders and the innocent
man, whom they had rescued from the worst of tortures,
were seen thus standing side by side.

Then Simon impulsively cast himself on the neck of
Marc, who returned his embrace. Both sobbed, and were
only able to stammer a few words—almost the same as they
had stammered long ago, on the abominable day when they
had been parted.

'Thank you, thank you, comrade. Like David, you
have been to me a brother—a second brother; you saved
my own and my children's honour.'

'Oh! I merely helped David, comrade; the victory was
won by truth alone. . . . And there are your children
—of their own accord they have grown up in strength and
reason.'

The whole family, indeed, was assembled amid the garden greenery; four generations awaited the venerable old man, who triumphed after so many years of suffering. Rachel, his wife, stood beside Geneviève, the wife of his dear, good friend. Then came those whose blood had mingled—Joseph and Louise, Sarah and Sébastien, accompanied by their children, François and Thérèse, who were followed by little Rose, the last born of the line. Clément and Charlotte were also present with Lucienne. And tears started from all eyes, and endless kisses were exchanged.

But a very fresh, sweet song arose. The children of the boys' and girls' schools, the pupils of Joseph and Louise, were singing a welcome to the former schoolmaster of Maillebois. Nothing could have been more simple and more touching than that childish strophe, instinct with tenderness and suggestive of the happy future. Then a lad stepped forward and offered Simon a bouquet in the name of the boys' school.

'Thank you, my little friend. How fine you look. . . . Who are you?'

'I am Edmond Doloir; my father is Léon Doloir, a schoolmaster; he is yonder, beside Monsieur Salvan.'

Then came the turn of a little girl, who, in like fashion, carried a bouquet offered by the girls' school.

'Oh! what a pretty little darling! Thank you, thank you. . . . And what is your name?'

'I am Georgette Doloir; I am the daughter of Adrien Doloir and Claire Bongard. You can see them there with my grandpapa and grandmamma, and my uncles and aunts.'

But there was yet another bouquet, and this was presented by Lucienne Froment on behalf of Rose Simon, the last-born of the family, whom she carried in her arms. And Lucienne recited: 'I am Lucienne Froment, the daughter of Clément Froment and Charlotte Savin. . . . And this is Rose Simon, the little daughter of your grandson François, and your own great-granddaughter, as she is also the great-granddaughter of your friend Marc Froment through her grandmother, Louise.'

With trembling hands Simon took the dear and bonnie babe in his arms. 'Ah! you dear little treasure, flesh of my flesh, you are like the ark of alliance. . . . Ah, how good and vigorous has life proved! how bravely it has worked in giving us so many strong, healthy, and handsome offspring! And how everything broadens at each fresh generation; what an increase of truth and justice and peace does life bring as it pursues its eternal task!'

They were now all pressing around him, introducing themselves, embracing him, and shaking his hands. There were the Savins, Jules and his son Robert, the former the Mayor who had so actively helped on the work of reparation, and who had received him at the railway station on behalf of the whole town. There were the Doloirs also— Auguste, who had built the house, Adrien, who had planned it, Charles, who had undertaken the locksmith's work, and Marcel, who had attended to the carpentry. There were likewise the Bongards—Fernand and his wife Lucille, and Claire their daughter. And all were mingled, connected by marriages, forming, as it were, but one great family, in such wise that Simon could hardly tell who was who. But his old pupils gave their names, and he traced on their aged faces some likeness to the boyish features of long ago, while embrace followed embrace amid ever-increasing emotion. And all at once, finding himself in presence of Salvan, now very old indeed, but still showing a smiling countenance, Simon fell into his arms, saying, 'Ah! my master, I owe everything to you; it is your work which now triumphs, thanks to the valiant artisans of truth whom you formed and sent out into the world!'

Then came the turn of Mademoiselle Mazeline, whom he kissed gaily on both cheeks, and next that of Mignot, who shed tears when Simon had embraced him.

' Have you forgiven me, Monsieur Simon ?' he asked.

' Forgiven you, my old friend Mignot! You have shown a valiant and noble heart! Ah! how delightful it is to meet again like this!'

The ceremony, so simple, yet so grand, was at last drawing to a close. The house offered to the innocent man, that bright-looking house standing on the site of the old den of the Rue du Trou, smiled right gaily in the sunlight with its decorative garlands of flowers and foliage. And all at once the drapery which still hung before the inscription above the door was pulled aside, and the marble slab appeared with its inscription in vivid letters of gold: ' Presented by the town of Maillebois to Schoolmaster Simon in the name of Truth and Justice, and as Reparation for the Torture inflicted on him.' Then came the signature, which seemed to show forth in a yet brighter blaze: ' The

Grandchildren of his Persecutors.' And at that sight, from all the great square, and from the neighbouring avenue, from every window and from every roof, there arose a last mighty acclamation, which rolled on like thunder—an acclamation in which all at last united, none henceforth daring to deny that truth and justice had triumphed.

On the morrow *Le Petit Beaumontais* published an enthusiastic account of the ceremony. That once filthy print had been quite transformed by the new spirit, which had raised its readers both morally and intellectually. Its offices, so long infected by poison, had been swept and purged. The Press will, indeed, become a most admirable instrument of education when it is no longer, as now, in the hands of political and financial bandits, bent on debasing and plundering their readers. And thus *Le Petit Beaumontais*, cleansed and rejuvenated, was beginning to render great services, contributing day by day to increase of enlightenment, reason, and brotherliness.

A few days later a terrible storm, one of those September storms which consume everything, destroyed the Capuchin chapel at Maillebois. That chapel was the last religious edifice of the district remaining open, and several bigots still attended it. At Jonville, Abbé Cognasse had lately been found dead in his sacristy, carried off by an apoplectic stroke, which had followed one of his violent fits of anger; and his church, long empty, was now definitively closed. At Maillebois, Abbé Coquard no longer even opened the doors of St. Martin's, but officiated alone at the altar, unable as he was to find a server for the Mass. Thus the little chapel of the Capuchins, which, with its big gilded and painted statue of St. Antony of Padua, standing amid candles and artificial flowers, retained to the end its reputation as a miracle-shop, sufficed for the few folk who still followed the observances of the Church.

That day, as it happened, they were celebrating there some festival connected with the saint,[1] a ceremony which had attracted about a hundred of the faithful. Yielding to the solicitations of Father Théodose, Father Crabot, who nowadays remained shut up at La Désirade, where he intended to install some pious enterprise, had decided to honour the solemnity with his presence. Thus both were there, one officiating, the other seated in a velvet arm-chair

---

[1] The real festival of St. Antony of Padua falls on June 13th.—*Trans.*

before the statue of the great saint, who was implored to show his miraculous power and obtain from God the grace of some dreadful cataclysm, such as would at once sweep away the infamous and sacrilegious society of the new times. And it was then that the storm burst forth. A great inky, terrifying cloud spread over Maillebois; there came flashes of lightning, which seemed to show the furnaces of hell blazing in the empyrean, and thunderclaps which suggested salvoes of some giant artillery bombarding the earth. Father Théodose had ordered the bells to be rung, and a loud and prolonged pealing arose from the chapel, as if to indicate to the Deity that this was His house and should be protected by Him. But in lieu thereof extermination came. A frightful clap resounded, the lightning struck the bells, descended by the rope, and burst forth in the nave with a detonation as if the very heavens were crumbling. Father Théodose, fired as he stood at the altar, flamed there like a torch. The sacerdotal vestments, the sacred vases, the very tabernacle, were melted, reduced to ashes. And the great St. Antony, shivered to pieces, fell upon the stricken Father Crabot, of whom only a bent and blackened skeleton remained beneath all the dust. And as if those two ministers of the Church were not sufficient sacrifice, five of the devotees present were also killed, while the others fled, howling with terror, eager to escape being crushed by the vaulted roof, which cracked, then crumbled in a pile of remnants, leaving nought of the cult intact.

The stupefaction was universal throughout Maillebois. How could the Deity of the Holy Roman and Apostolic Church have made such a mistake? The same question had often been asked in former times—each time, indeed, that a church had been struck and its steeple had fallen on the priest and the kneeling worshippers. Had God desired, then, the end of the religion which had taken His name? Or, more reasonably, was it that no Divine hand whatever guided the lightning, and that it was but a natural force, which would prove a source of happiness whenever mankind should have domesticated it? In any case, after the calamity, Brother Gorgias suddenly reappeared and was seen hurrying along the streets of Maillebois, crying aloud that God had made no mistake. It was to him, he said, that God had hearkened, resolving to strike down his imbecile and cowardly superiors, and thus give a lesson to the whole Church, which could only flourish anew by the

power of fire and steel. And a month later Gorgias himself was found, his skull split, his body soiled with filth,
outside the same suspicious house before which, some time
previously, a passer had already found the body of Victor
Milhomme.

IV

YEARS, and again years, elapsed, and, thanks to the
generosity of life,—which, as Marc had lived and
served it so well, wished, it seemed, to reward him
by keeping him and his adored Geneviève erect like triumphant spectators,—he, now over eighty, still tasted the
supreme joy of seeing his dreams fulfilled yet more and
more.

Generations continued to arise, each more freed, more
purified, more endowed with knowledge than its forerunners. In former days there had been two Frances, each
receiving a different education, remaining ignorant of the
other, hating it, and contending with it. For the multitude
of the nation, for the immense majority of the country folk,
there had only been what was called elementary instruction
—reading, writing, a little arithmetic, the rudiments which
raised man just a span above the level of the brute beast.
To the *bourgeoisie*, the petty minority of the elect, who
had seized all wealth and power, secondary education and
superior education, every means of learning and reigning,
lay open. Thus was perpetuated the most frightful of all
social iniquities. The poor and the humble were kept
down in their ignorance beneath a heavy tombstone. To
them it was forbidden to learn, to become men of knowledge, power, and mastery. At rare intervals one of them
escaped and raised himself to the highest rank. But that
was the exception, tolerated, and cited with canting hypocrisy as an example. All men were equal, it was said, and
might raise themselves by their own merits. But as a first
step, by way of preventing it, the necessary instruction, the
enlightenment due to each and every child of the nation,
was withheld from the great majority, so intense, indeed,
was the terror of the great movement of truth and justice
which would accrue from the diffusion of knowledge—a
movement which would sweep away the *bourgeoisie* and its
monstrous errors and compel disgorgement of the national

fortune, in order that by just labour the city of solidarity and peace might be at last established.

And now a France which soon would be all one was being constituted; there would soon be no upper class, no lower class; those who knew would cease to crush and exploit those who did not know in a stealthy, fratricidal warfare, whose paroxysms had often reddened the paving of the streets with blood. A system of integral education for one and all was already at work; all the children of France had to pass through the gratuitous, secular, compulsory primary schools, where experimental facts, in lieu of grammatical rules, were now the bases of all education. Moreover, the acquirement of knowledge did not suffice; it was necessary one should learn to love, for it was only by love that truth could prove fruitful. And a process of natural selection ensued according to the tastes, aptitudes, and faculties of the pupils, who from the primary schools passed to special schools, arranged in accordance with requirements, embracing all practical applications of knowledge and extending to the highest speculations of the human mind. The law was that no member of a nation was privileged; that each being born into the world was to be welcomed as a possible force, whose culture was demanded by the national interests. And in this there was not only equality and equity, but a wise employment of the common treasure, a practical desire to lose nought that might contribute to the power and grandeur of the country. And, indeed, what a mighty awakening there was of all the accumulated energy which had lain slumbering in the country districts and the industrial towns! Quite an intellectual florescence sprang up, a new generation, able to act and think, supplying the sap which had long been exhausted in the old governing classes, worn out by the abuse of power. Genius arose daily from the fertile popular soil; a great epoch, a renascence of mankind, was impending. Integral instruction, which the ruling *bourgeoisie* had so long opposed, because it felt that it would destroy the old social order, was, indeed, destroying it, but at the same time it was setting in its place the fresh and magnificent blossoming of all the intellectual and moral power which would make France the liberator, the emancipator of the world.

Thus disappeared the divided France of former times, the France in which there had been two classes, two hostile, ever-warring races, reared, it might have been thought, in different planets, as if they were destined never to meet, never to come to an agreement. The schoolmasters, also, were no longer herded in two unfriendly groups, the one full of humiliation, the other full of contempt—on one side the poor, imperfectly educated elementary teachers, scarcely cleansed of the loam of their native fields, and on the other the professors of the Lycées and the special schools, redolent of science and literature. The masters who now taught the pupils of the primary schools followed them through all the stages of their education. It was held that a man needed as much intelligence and training to be able to awaken a boy's mind, impart first principles, and set him on the right road, as to maintain him in it and develop his faculties subsequently. A rotatory service was organised, teachers were easily recruited, and worked right zealously now that the profession had become one of the first of the land, well paid, honoured, and glorified.

The nation had also understood it to be necessary that the integral instruction it imparted should be gratuitous at all stages, however great might be the cost, for its millions were not cast stupidly to the winds, to foster falsehood and slaughter—they helped to rear good artisans of prosperity and peace. No other harvest could be compared with that: each *sou* that was expended helped to give more intelligence and strength to the people, helped it to master to-morrow. And the inanity of the great reproach levelled at the general diffusion of knowledge, that of casting *déclassés*, rebels, across the narrow limits of old-time society, became plainly manifest now that those limits had crumbled as the new society came into being. The *bourgeoisie*, even as it feared, was bound to be swept away as soon as it no longer possessed a monopoly of knowledge. But if in former years each penniless and hungry peasant's or artisan's son who rose up by the acquirement of knowledge had become a source of embarrassment and danger by reason of his eagerness to carve for himself a share of enjoyment among that of those who enjoyed already, that danger had now disappeared. There could be no more *déclassés*, since the classes themselves had ceased to exist, and no more rebels either, since the normal condition of life was the ascent of one and all towards more and more culture, in order that the most useful civic action might ensue. Thus education had accomplished its revolutionary work, and it was now the very strength of the community, the power which had both

broadened and tightened the bond of brotherliness, all
being called upon to work for the happiness of all, the
energy of none remaining ignored and lost.

That complete education, the culture of the whole community, which now yielded such a magnificent harvest, had
only become possible on the day when the Church had been
deprived of her teaching privileges.   The separation of
Church and State, and the suppression of the budget of
Public Worship, had freed the country and enabled it to
dower its schools more liberally.   The priest ceased to be
a functionary, the Catholic faith no longer possessed the
force of a law; those who chose remained free to go to
church, even as to the theatre, by paying for their seats,
but, in the result, the churches gradually emptied.   And if
this occurred it was because they no longer manufactured
worshippers, poor stupefied beings, such as they needed to
fill their naves.   Long and terrible years had elapsed before
it had become possible to wrest the children from the teachers of the Church, those who had poisoned mankind through
the ages, who had reigned over it by falsehood and terror-
ism.   From the very first day the Church had realised that
she must kill truth if she did not wish it to kill her; and
what furious battles had followed, what a desperate resistance she had offered in order to delay her inevitable defeat,
the resplendent outpouring of Light, freed at last from
every hindrance!   Society would soon be reduced to treating her as one treated those malodorous fishwives whose
shops were closed by the police.   Yet she, the dogmatic
and authoritarian ruler — she who, imitating her Deity,
strove to impose her will on the world by thunderbolts, impudently dared to invoke and claim liberty, in order that
she might perpetuate her abominable work of debasement
and servitude.   Laws of social protection then proved necessary; it became imperative to deprive her legally of her
power, by refusing to her members, the monks and the
priests, the right of teaching.   And then again what an
uproar followed, what frantic attempts to plunge France
into civil war, credulous parents being banded together,
while the religious orders, thrust out by the doorways once
more, slipped into their dens by the windows, with the
obstinacy of folk who relied on the eternal credulity which
they fancied they had sown in the minds of men!   Did they
not represent error, superstition, and wretched human
cowardice, and did it not follow, therefore, that eternity

was theirs? But, for this to be, they had to retain their hold upon the children, and, by them, obscure the morrow; and it happened that the morrow and the children gradually escaped them, and that the time came when the Holy Roman Catholic Church lay agonising beneath the crumbling of her idiotic dogmas, pierced and destroyed by science. Truth had conquered, the schools given to all had formed men who knew, and who could exercise their will.

Thus hardly a day elapsed without Marc observing some fresh fortunate conquest, some increase of reason and comfort. He and his wife Geneviève alone remained erect of all the valiant generation which had fought and suffered so much. Good old Salvan had been the first to depart, then Mademoiselle Mazeline and Mignot had followed him. But of all the deaths the most painful for Marc had been those of Simon and David, the two brothers, carried off one after the other at an interval of only a few days, as if they had been still linked together by their heroic fraternity. Madame Simon had preceded them; all who had participated in the monstrous affair were now beneath the peaceful soil, lying there side by side, the good and the wicked, the heroes and the criminals, all plunged in eternal silence. Many of the children and grandchildren, moreover, had departed before their parents, for death never paused in his mysterious work, mowing down men as he listed in order to fertilise one or another field, whence other men would spring.

At last, quitting their retreat of Jonville, Marc and Geneviève had come to reside again at Maillebois, where they occupied the first floor of the house presented to Simon, and now belonging to his children, Joseph and Sarah. She and her husband Sébastien still resided at Beaumont, where the latter remained director of the Training College. But Joseph, afflicted in the legs, almost infirm, had been obliged to retire; and as his wife Louise had at the same time quitted the Maillebois school, they were now installed on the second floor of the paternal house, which the family shared in this fashion, well pleased to be together during the last gentle, declining days of life. And if they themselves had given up teaching, they at least had the joy of seeing the good work carried on by their descendants, for François and Thérèse had now been appointed to the Maillebois schools, in which, therefore, three generations of the family had succeeded one another.

The delight of living side by side, in close affection, had lasted two years, when quite a drama plunged the family into grief. One of those insensate passions which devastate a man came upon François, then in all the strength of his two and thirty years, and hitherto so tenderly attached to his wife Thérèse. He became enamoured of a young woman of eight and twenty years named Colette Roudille, whose mother, a very pious widow, had lately died. Colette's father was said to have been Théodose, the Capuchin, at one time her mother's confessor; and she certainly resembled him, having a splendid head, with blood-red lips and eyes of fire. The widow had lived on a little income, upon which, however, her son Faustin, twelve years older than his sister, had encroached to such a degree that the old woman had remained at last with barely enough money to buy bread. However, the little clerical group, all that remained of the once powerful faction which had ruled the district, took an interest in Faustin, and ended by obtaining a situation for him. For some months, then, he had been keeper of the estate of La Désirade, which since Father Crabot's death had become the subject of a number of lawsuits, and which some of the neighbouring localities proposed to purchase and turn into a people's palace and convalescent home, even as Valmarie had been turned into an asylum where young mothers recovered their strength. Thus Colette lived alone and in all freedom at Maillebois, almost in front of the school; and it was certain that the glow of her fine eyes and the smile of her red lips had largely helped on the passion which was maddening François.

But it happened that one day Thérèse surprised them, and dolorous anger came upon her, the more particularly as she was not the only one who might suffer from her husband's folly. Might it not, indeed, prove a disaster for their daughter Rose, who was now near her twelfth birthday? At one moment Thérèse appealed to her parents, Sébastien and Sarah, wishing to have their views respecting the course she ought to take. She spoke of a separation, offering to restore freedom to the husband who had ceased to love her and who told her lies. But she remained very calm, firm, and sensible in her trouble, and she soon understood that on this occasion it was wise and fit to forgive. Moreover, Marc and Geneviève, afflicted by the rupture, lectured their grandson François severely, and he evinced great sorrow, recognising that he was in the wrong, and accepting the most violent reproaches. But even while he confessed his fault, he unhappily remained disturbed, full of anguish, with an evident fear that his passion might again overcome him. Never had Marc so cruelly realised the fragility of human happiness. It was not sufficient, then, that one should instruct men and lead them towards justice by the paths of truth; it was also necessary that passion should not rend them and cast them one against the other like madmen. Marc had spent his life fighting in order that a little light might extricate the children from the dim gaol in which their fathers had groaned; and, in giving more happiness to others, he thought he had given it to his own family. Yet now, at the hearth of his grandson, who had seemed quite freed from error and very sensible, another form of suffering displayed itself—the suffering of love, with its eternal felicity and eternal torture! It was evident that one must not be proud of one's knowledge, that one must not set all one's strength in it. It was necessary that one should also be prepared to suffer in one's heart, and strive to make it valiant in order that it might bear up against a rending which always remained possible. And, again, it was wrong to think that it was sufficient to do good in order to be sheltered from the blows of evil. But though Marc said all those things to himself, placing a very modest estimate on the work he had accomplished, he still felt very sad as he saw mankind voluntarily leaving some of its flesh on all the briars of its path, and lingering there, as if unwilling to reach the happy city.

The holidays arrived, and all at once François disappeared. It seemed as if he had waited to be rid of his pupils in order to go off with Colette, the shutters of whose windows facing the High street remained closed. Wishing to stifle the scandal, the family related that, as François was in poor health, he had gone with a friend to take an air cure abroad during the holidays. A tacit understanding ensued in Maillebois—everybody pretended to accept that explanation out of regard for Thérèse, the forsaken wife, who was much liked and respected; but nobody really remained ignorant of the true cause of her husband's flight. She behaved admirably in those painful circumstances, hiding her tears, preserving perfect dignity in her home. In particular she bestowed increased tenderness on her daughter Rose, from whom, unfortunately, she could not

hide the facts, but in whom she inculcated a continuance
of respect for her father in spite of his bad conduct.

A month went by, and Marc, who was deeply grieved,
still visited Thérèse every day, when one evening there
came a dramatic, a horrible, occurrence. Rose having
gone to spend the afternoon with a little friend in the
neighbourhood, Marc had found Thérèse alone, sobbing in
silence, far away from all prying eyes. For a long while
he strove to comfort her and restore her to some hope.
Then, at nightfall, he was obliged to leave her without
having seen Rose, who had remained apparently with her
little friend. The evening was dark, the atmosphere heavy
with a threatening storm, and as Marc, eager to get home,
was crossing the small, dim square behind the school, into
which looked the window of the room once occupied by
little Zéphirin, he suddenly heard a confused noise of footsteps and calls.

'What is the matter?   What is the matter?' he exclaimed
as he went forward.

He felt a chill in his veins, though why it was he could
not tell. Apparently some gust of terror, coming from
afar, was sweeping by. And at last in the faint light Marc
perceived a man whom he recognised as a certain Marsouillier, a poor nephew of the deceased Philis, at one time
mayor of Maillebois. Marsouillier now acted as beadle at
St. Martin's, where, since the destruction of the Capuchin
Chapel, a small party of believers still supported a priest.

'What is the matter?' Marc repeated, surprised to see
that the other was gesticulating and mumbling to himself.

Marsouillier in his turn now recognised Marc. 'I don't
know, Monsieur Froment,' he stammered with a terrified
air. 'I was passing; I had come from the Place des
Capucins, when, all at once, I heard the cries of a child,
choking, it seemed, with fright. And as I hastened up I
just caught sight of a man running away, while yonder on
the ground lay that little body. . . .   Then I also began
to call.'

Marc himself now distinguished a pale and motionless
form lying on the ground. And a suspicion came to him,
Was it this man Marsouillier who had ill-used the child?
Perhaps so, for curiously enough he was holding something
white—a handkerchief.

'And that handkerchief?' Marc asked.

'Oh! I picked it up here just now. . . .   Perhaps the

man wanted to stifle the child's cries with it, and dropped it as he ran away.'

But Marc no longer listened; he was leaning over the little form upon the ground, and an exclamation of frantic grief suddenly escaped his lips: 'Rose! our little Rose!'

The victim was indeed the pretty little girl, who, as a babe, in the arms of her cousin Lucienne, had offered a bouquet to Simon on the occasion of his triumph ten years previously. She had grown up full of beauty and charm, with a bright, dimpled, smiling face amid a mass of fair and wavy tresses. And the scene could be easily pictured: the child returning home across that deserted square in the falling night, some bandit surprising her, ill-using her, and flinging her there upon the ground, whereupon, hearing a sound of footsteps, he had been seized with terror and had fled. The child did not stir; she lay there as if lifeless, in her little white frock figured with pink flowerets, a holiday frock which her mother had allowed her to wear for her visit to her friend.

'Rose! Rose!' called Marc, who was beside himself. 'Why do you not answer me, my darling? Speak, say only one word to me, only one word.'

He touched her gently, not daring as yet to raise her from the ground. And, talking to himself, he said, 'She has only fainted; I can tell that she is breathing. But I fear that something is broken. . . . Ah! misfortune dogs us; here again is grief indeed!'

Indescribable terror came upon him as all the frightful past suddenly arose before his mind's eye. There, under that tragic window, close to that room where the wretched Gorgias had killed little Zéphirin, he had now found his own great-granddaughter, his well-loved little Rose, who was assuredly hurt, and who in all probability only owed her salvation to the accidental arrival of a stranger. Who was it that had brought about that awful renewal of the past? What new and prolonged anguish was foreboded by that crime? As if by the glow of a great lightning flash, Marc, at that horrible moment, saw all his past life spread out, and lived all his battles and all his sufferings anew.

Marsouillier, however, had remained there with the handkerchief in his hand. He ended by slipping it into his pocket in an embarrassed way, like a man who had not said all he knew, and who devoutly wished that he had not crossed the square that evening.

'One ought not to leave her there, Monsieur Froment,' he said at last. 'You are not strong enough to pick her up; if you like I will take her in my arms and carry her to her mamma's, as it is close by.'

Marc was compelled to accept the offer, and followed the sturdy beadle, who took the child up very gently, without rousing her from her fainting fit. In this wise they reached the mother's door, and for her what a shock it was when she beheld her well-loved child, now her only joy and comfort, brought back to her insensible, as pale as death in her bright frock, and with her beautiful hair streaming loosely about her! The frock was in shreds, a lock of hair which had been torn off was caught in the lace collar. And the struggle must have been terrible, for the child's wrenched hands were all bruised, and her right arm hung down so limply that it was certainly broken.

Thérèse, distracted, beside herself, repeated amid her choking sobs: 'Rose, my little Rose! They have killed my Rose!'

In vain did Marc point out to her that the child was still breathing, and that not a drop of blood was to be seen; the mother still repeated that her child was dead. But Marsouillier carried the girl upstairs and laid her on a bed, where all at once she suddenly opened her eyes and gazed around her with indescribable terror. Then, shivering the while, she began to stammer: 'Oh, mamma, mamma, hide me, I am frightened!'

Thunderstruck by her revival to consciousness, Thérèse sank on the bed beside her, caught her in her arms and pressed her to her bosom, so overcome by emotion that she could no longer speak. Marc, however, begged the assistant teacher, who happened to be present, to go for a doctor; and then, quite upset by the mystery, endeavoured to fathom it at once.

'What happened to you, my darling?' he inquired; 'can you tell us?'

Rose looked at him for a moment as if to make sure who was speaking to her, and then, with haggard, wandering eyes, peered into all the dim corners of the room. 'I 'm afraid, I 'm afraid, grandfather,' she said.

He endeavoured to reassure her and inquired gently: 'Did nobody accompany you when you left your little friend's?'

'I did n't want anybody to come. The house is so near.

And we had played so long, I was afraid I would get home still later.'

'And so you came back running, my darling, eh? And somebody sprang on you; that is what happened, is it not?'

But the terrified child again began to tremble, and did not answer. Marc had to repeat his question. 'Yes, yes, somebody,' she stammered at last.

Marc waited till she became calmer, caressing her hair the while, and kissing her on the forehead. 'You see, you ought to tell us,' he resumed. 'You cried out, naturally, you struggled. The man wanted to close your mouth, did he not?'

'Oh, grandfather, it was all so quick! He took hold of my arms, and he twisted them round. He wanted to drive me out of my senses and carry me off on his back. It hurt me so dreadfully, I thought I should die, and I fell to the ground: that is all I remember.'

Marc felt greatly relieved; he was now convinced that nothing worse had happened, particularly as Marsouillier, on hearing the girl's cries, had hastened to the spot. And so he asked but one question more: 'And would you be able to recognise the man, my dear?'

Again Rose quivered, and her eyes became quite wild as if some terrible vision was rising before her. Then, covering her face with her hand, she relapsed into stubborn silence. As her glance had already fallen on Marsouillier and she had raised no exclamation on seeing him, Marc realised that he had been mistaken when he had suspected the beadle of the crime. Nevertheless he wished to question him also; for, even allowing that he had spoken the truth, it might be that he had not told the whole of it.

'You saw the man run away?' said Marc. 'Would you be able to recognise him?'

'Oh! I don't think so, Monsieur Froment. He passed me, but it was already dark. Besides, I was so disturbed.' And the beadle, who had not yet fully recovered his composure, let a further detail escape him: 'He said something as he passed, I fancy . . . he called "Imbecile!"'

'What! Imbecile?' retorted Marc, who was greatly surprised. 'Why should he have said that to you?'

But Marsouillier, deeply regretting that he had added that particular, for he understood the possible gravity of any admission on his part, endeavoured to recall his words. 'I can't be sure of anything,' he said, 'it was like a growl.

. . . And no, no, I should not be able to recognise him.'

Then, as Marc asked him for the handkerchief, he drew it from his pocket with some appearance of *ennui*, and laid it on a table. It was a very common kind of handkerchief, one of those which are embroidered by the gross with initials in red thread. This one was marked with the letter F, and the clue was a slight one, for dozens of similar handkerchiefs were sold in the shops.

Meantime Thérèse, who had again caught Rose in a gentle embrace, caressed her lovingly. 'The doctor is coming, my treasure,' she said. 'I won't touch you any more till he is here. It won't be anything. You are not in great pain, are you?'

'No, mother,' Rose replied, 'but my arm burns me and seems very heavy.'

Then, in an undertone, Thérèse, in her turn, tried to confess the girl, for the mysteriousness of the assault had left her very anxious. But at each fresh question Rose evinced yet greater alarm, and at last she closed her eyes and buried her head in the pillow, so as to see and hear nothing more. Every time her mother made a fresh attempt, begging her to say if she knew the man and would be able to recognise him, the child quivered dreadfully. But all at once, bursting into loud sobs, quite beside herself, almost delirious, she told everything in a loud, distressful voice, fancying, perhaps, that she was simply whispering her words in her mother's ear.

'Oh! mother, mother, I am so grieved! I recognised him—it was father who was waiting there, and who threw himself upon me!'

Thérèse sprang to her feet in stupefaction. 'Your father? What is it you say, you unhappy child?'

Marc and Marsouillier also had heard the girl. And the former drew near to her with a violent gesture of incredulity: 'Your father? It is impossible! . . . Come, come, my darling, you must have dreamt that.'

'No, no, father was waiting for me behind the school, and I recognised him by his beard and his hat. He tried to carry me away, and as I would not let him he twisted my arms and made me fall.'

She clung stubbornly to that account of the affair, though she could supply little proof of what she asserted, for the man had not spoken a word to her, and she had only noticed his beard and hat, remembering nothing else, not even his features, which had been hidden by the darkness. Nevertheless, that man was her father, she was sure of it; nothing could efface that impression, which, if incorrect, might be some haunting idea which had sprung from the grief in which she had seen her mother plunged since the departure of the unfaithful François.

'It is impossible; it is madness!' Marc repeated, for his reason rebelled and protested against such a notion. 'If François had wished to take Rose away he would not have hurt her—killed her almost!'

Thérèse also quietly displayed a feeling of perfect certainty. 'François is incapable of such an action,' said she. 'He has caused me a great deal of grief, but I know him, and will defend him if need be. . . . You were mistaken, my poor Rose.'

Nevertheless the unhappy woman went to look at the handkerchief which had remained on the table. And she could not restrain a nervous start, for it appeared to be one of a dozen marked with a similar letter F, which she had purchased for her husband of the sisters Landois, who kept a drapery shop in the High Street. On going to a chest of drawers Thérèse found ten similar handkerchiefs, and it was quite possible that François had taken two away with him at the time of his flight. However, the unhappy wife strove to overcome her uneasiness, and as firmly and as positively as before, she said: 'The handkerchief may belong to him. . . . But it was not he; never shall I think him guilty.'

The strange scene seemed to have stupefied Marsouillier. He had remained on one side, at a loss apparently as to how he might quit those sorrowing folk, and since he had heard the child's story his eyes had been all astonishment. The recognition of the handkerchief brought his dismay to a climax, and at last, profiting by the arrival of the doctor fetched by the assistant teacher, he managed to slip away. Marc, on his side, went into the dining-room to await the result of the medical examination. Rose's right arm was indeed broken, but there was nothing of a disquieting character about the fracture, and the wrenched wrists and a few bruises were the only other marks of violence which the doctor found. He, indeed, was most concerned respecting the result of the nervous shock which the girl had experienced, for it had been a violent one. And he only left her an hour later, when he had reduced the fracture and saw her overcome, as it were, plunged in a heavy sleep.

Marc, however, had meantime sent a message to his wife
and Louise, for he feared that they might be alarmed by
his failure to return home. And they hastened to the
school, terrified by this frightful business, which reminded
them also of the old and abominable affair. Thérèse having joined them, a kind of family council was held, the
door of the bedroom remaining open in order that they
might at once hear the injured girl if she should wake up.
Marc, who was quite feverish, expressed his views at length.
What possible reason could there have been for François to
commit such a deed ? He might have yielded to a transport of passion by running away with Colette, but he had
invariably shown himself to be a loving father, and his wife
did not even complain of his manner towards herself, for
it had remained outwardly dignified, almost deferential.
Thus, what motive could have prompted him if he were
guilty ? Hidden away with his mistress in some unknown
retreat, it could hardly be that he had experienced a sudden craving to have his daughter with him. What could
he have done with the child ? She would have been a burden on him in the life he must be leading. And even supposing that he had wished to strike a cruel blow at his wife,
and reduce her to solitude, without a consolation remaining
to her, it was incredible that he should have ill-used and
injured his daughter, have left her upon the ground senseless ! He would simply have taken her away with him.
Thus, in spite of Rose's statements, in spite of the handkerchief, François could not be guilty, the impossibilities were
too great. Nevertheless, faced as he was by this mysterious
problem, and the task of again seeking the truth, Marc felt
disturbed and anxious, for he was convinced that Marsouillier would relate what he had seen and heard, and that
all Maillebois would be discussing the drama on the morrow.
And as all the appearances were against François, would
public opinion denounce him, even as in former days it had
denounced his grandfather, Simon the Jew ? In that case,
how could he be defended ? what ought to be done to prevent a renewal of the monstrous iniquity of long ago ?

'The one thing that tends to tranquillise me,' said Marc
at last, 'is that the times have changed. We now have to
deal with people who have been freed and educated, and it
will greatly surprise me if they do not help us to unravel the
truth.'

Silence fell. At last, in spite of the little quiver which

she was unable to master, Thérèse exclaimed energetically,
'You are right, grandfather. Before everything else we
must establish the innocence of François, which I cannot
possibly doubt, whatever may be the accusations. . . .
He has made me suffer dreadfully, but I will forget it, and
you may rely on me, I will help you with all my strength.'

Geneviève and Louise nodded their assent. 'Ah!' muttered the latter, 'the unhappy lad! When he was seven
years old he used to throw his arms round me and say,
"Little mother, I love you very dearly!" He has a tender
and passionate nature, and thus one must forgive him a
great deal.'

'There is always some resource when one has to deal
with loving natures,' remarked Geneviève in her turn.
'Even if they become guilty of great transgressions, love
helps them to repair them.'

On the morrow, even as Marc had foreseen, all Maillebois
was in a hubbub. People talked of nothing but that assault, of the charge which the injured girl had brought
against her own father, of the handkerchief picked up by a
passer, and recognised by the wife. Marsouillier told the
story to all who were willing to listen to him, and he even
embellished it somewhat, making out that he had seen and
done everything in connection with the rescue. He was
not a malicious man, he was simply vain and inclined to
poltroonery in such wise that while it flattered his feelings
to become a personage he remained secretly apprehensive
of great personal worries if the affair should turn out badly.
He was, as already mentioned, a nephew of the pious
Philis, and he lived on his pay as a beadle, which pay was
extremely small now that only a few believers provided for
the expenses at St. Martin's. And it was said that he
himself was not a believer at all, that his views were really
very free ones, and that if he thus ate the bread of hypocrisy
it was simply because he was unable to earn any other.
However that might be, the few remaining worshippers who
paid his salary, the last Catholics of the district, who were
enraged by their defeat and the abandonment into which
the Church was sinking, at once seized upon his adventure
and resolved to exploit that scandal which had assuredly
been vouchsafed to them by Heaven. Never had they
dared to hope for such an opportunity to resume hostilities,
and they must profit by the divine favour to make a supreme
effort. Thus black skirts were again seen gliding along the

streets of Maillebois, old ladies were again heard telling the
most extraordinary stories. Some unknown person had related that she had seen François on the night of the crime
in the company of two masked men, who were Freemasons
undoubtedly. And, as everybody knew that the Freemasons needed the blood of a young girl for their Black
Mass, it followed that François, after some drawing of lots,
had been chosen to provide the blood of his daughter.
Did that not explain everything — the sectarian's savage
violence, his unnatural ferocity? But it happened that the
inventors of that idiotic fable could not find a single newspaper to print it, and thus they had to spread it by word of
mouth among the poorer folk. When evening came it had
already gone all round the town, and had even reached
Jonville, Le Moreux, and other neighbouring villages.
And the seed of falsehood being sown, the plotters only
had to wait for the poisonous crop which they hoped to see
arise from the popular ignorance.

But, as Marc had said, the times had changed. On all
sides people shrugged their shoulders when they heard that
foolish story. Such inventions had been all very well in
former times, when men were children and fell eagerly on
improbabilities. But nowadays people knew too much,
and a story of that kind was not accepted without due
examination. In the first place, it was immediately ascertained that François did not happen to be a Freemason.
Moreover, nobody had seen him in the town; and it seemed
certain that he was hidden away at a distance with that girl
Colette, who had disappeared from Maillebois at the same
time as himself. Again, there were all sorts of reasons for
thinking him innocent. Indeed the whole district pronounced the same opinion on him as his relatives had done.
He was a man of an amorous nature, who might yield to
a passionate transport, but he was also a loving father, and
as such incapable of ill-treating his own child. Excellent
testimony came in from all sides. His pupils and their
parents praised his gentleness; several neighbours related
that in spite of his errors he had remained affectionately
attached to his wife. Nevertheless, people were confronted
by the accusations of Rose, the disquieting clue of the
handkerchief, the scene repeatedly recounted by Marsouillier—the whole constituting an irritating mystery, a distressing problem for all who were competent to weigh and
judge facts. If, indeed, François were not guilty, however

much appearances might be against him, somebody else must be the culprit, and who could that be, and how was he to be discovered ?

Then, while the judicial authorities were inquiring into the matter, something quite new was seen—mere ordinary townsfolk came forward, quite voluntarily, to relate whatever they knew, whatever they had witnessed, felt, or surmised. Now that men's minds were cultivated there was a general desire for justice, a dread of any possible error. A Bongard came to say that on the evening of the assault, while he was passing the town hall, he had seen a man who looked somewhat scared, and who seemed to have run up from the direction of the Place des Capucins. And that man was not François. Then a Doloir brought a smoker's tinder-box, which he had found between two paving-stones behind the schools. And he pointed out that this box might have fallen from the culprit's pocket, and that François did not smoke. A Savin also recounted that he had overheard a conversation between two old ladies, from which he had drawn the conclusion that the culprit was to be sought among the acquaintances of Marsouillier, the latter having let his tongue wag while he was in the company of certain friendly devotees. But the most intelligent and active helpers were the sisters Landois, who kept the drapery shop in the High Street. They had been pupils of Mademoiselle Mazeline; and, indeed, all the workers in the cause of truth, all the voluntary witnesses, had passed through the hands of the secular teachers, Marc, Joulic, or Joseph. As for the sisters Landois, it had occurred to them to consult their books to ascertain the names of the persons to whom they had sold handkerchiefs similar to the one which the culprit had wished to employ as a gag. They readily found François' name; and below it, two days later, they perceived that of Faustin Roudille, the brother of the young woman Colette, with whom François had fled. That was the first clue, the first gleam of the light which was to spread and become decisive.

As it happened, this man Faustin had been without a situation for the last fortnight. After coming to an agreement with the surrounding localities, the town of Maillebois had at last purchased the magnificent estate of La Désirade, which it intended to transform into a People's Palace, a convalescent home, a public park, open to all the workers of the region. Instead of some congregation of black frocks being installed in that delightful spot, under that royal verdure, among those plashing waters and those gleaming marbles, swains and their lassies, young mothers and their babes, old folk desirous of repose, would flock thither to enjoy the sweetness and splendour of the scene. Thus Faustin, the ex-keeper, a creature of the last remaining clericalists, had quitted the estate, and was to be seen prowling about Maillebois, showing himself very bitter and aggressive, especially with respect to his sister Colette, whose escapade, said he, had dishonoured him. People were somewhat surprised by this sudden severity on his part, for nobody was ignorant of the good understanding which had previously reigned between the brother and the sister, and the frequency with which the former had borrowed money from the young woman when he knew her to be in funds. Had there been a rupture, then? Was Faustin exasperated with Colette because she had taken herself off just as he lost his situation? Or was he playing some comedy, still remaining in agreement with his sister, acquainted with her hiding-place, and secretly working on her behalf? These points remained obscure, but the discovery made by the sisters Landois directed general attention to Faustin, his actions, and his words. A week, then, sufficed for the inquiry to make considerable progress.

First of all, Bongard's evidence was confirmed; several people now remembered that on the evening of the assault they had met Faustin in the High Street, looking agitated, and turning round as if he wished to ascertain what might be taking place in the direction of the schools. And it was certainly he whom they had seen; they had positively recognised him. Then, too, the tinder-box found by Doloir seemed to belong to him—at least, folk asserted that they had seen a similar one in his hands. Finally, the conversation which Savin had overheard, and the hypothesis of an acquaintance between Marsouillier and the culprit received striking confirmation, for the beadle and the ex-keeper of La Désirade had been quite intimate. That seemed to be the decisive fact, the clue which would lead to full enlightenment, as Marc, who was following the inquiry with impassioned attention, immediately understood. Thus he took it upon himself to extract a confession from Marsouillier. He recalled the beadle's strange manner when he had found him near Rose after the culprit's flight. He remembered that he had seemed embarrassed and anxious, disturbed at having to give up the handkerchief; and he particularly recalled his stupefaction when Rose had accused her father, and Thérèse had produced some similar hand-kerchiefs from her chest of drawers. And he was greatly struck by that word 'Imbecile!' which the culprit had cast in the beadle's face, and which the latter in his perturbation had repeated. It was a significant word, it was like a re-proach hurled by a man at a blundering friend whose inopportune arrival on the scene had spoilt everything.

Thus Marc called upon Marsouillier. 'You know, my man,' he said to him, 'the gravest charges are being ac-cumulated against Faustin; he will certainly be arrested this evening. Are you not afraid of being compromised?'

Silent, with hanging head, the beadle listened to an enumeration of the proofs.

'Come, own that you recognised him!' Marc added.

'But how could I have recognised him, Monsieur Fro-ment?' said Marsouillier. 'Faustin has no beard, and he wears a cap; whereas the man I saw had a full beard and a felt hat.'

Those were points which Rose herself confirmed, and which as yet remained unelucidated.

'Oh! he might have got a hat somewhere, and have put on a false beard,' Marc suggested. 'But in any case he spoke; you yourself told me so. Surely you must have recognised his voice when he called you an imbecile!'

Marsouillier was already raising his hand to contradict himself, and swear that the man had not pronounced a single word. But Marc's bright eyes were fixed upon him, and as he met their gaze his strength failed him. And then, good-hearted man as he was at bottom, he grew dis-turbed, no longer having the courage to do a bad action in some stupid spirit of vanity.

'Naturally I have inquired into your connection with Faustin,' Marc resumed. 'I know that you and he often met, and that he readily cast that expression "imbecile" in your face when he found you more scrupulous than he liked.'

'That's true,' Marsouillier admitted; 'he called me an imbecile, and it ended by being hardly pleasant.'

Then, on being pressed, exhorted to relieve his conscience in his own interest, for the authorities might believe him to be an accomplice, he ended by yielding to his fears as much as to his respect for truth. 'Well, yes, Monsieur Froment,

I did recognise him. . . . Only he could have called me an imbecile in that voice. I can't be mistaken, he has given me that name too many times. And he must merely have worn a false beard, as you surmise, and have pulled it off as he ran away, for when some people saw him at the corner of the High Street he was wearing a hat, but he was shaven as usual, with no beard at all.'

Marc felt delighted, for this testimony would certainly prove decisive. Shaking hands with Marsouillier, he said to him: 'Ah! I knew it very well; you are a good fellow.'

'A good fellow, no doubt. . . . You see, Monsieur Froment, I am an old pupil of Monsieur Joulic, and when a master has taught one to love truth it never goes away. One may wish to tell a falsehood, but the whole of one's being rises up in protest. Besides, when one knows how to use one's reason a little, it becomes impossible to credit the foolish things which are put into circulation. I was very worried at heart about this unhappy affair. But then I 'm a very poor man; I have only my post as beadle as a means of livelihood, and my position compelled me to say the same as the old friends of my uncle Philis.'

Then Marsouillier paused, and, with a gesture of despair, big tears gathering the while in his eyes, he added: 'Ah! I 'm done for now. I shall be turned out of doors, and left to starve in the streets.'

But Marc reassured him by a positive promise to find him some employment. And then he hastened away, eager as he was to acquaint Thérèse with the result of the interview, that conclusive testimony by which François was completely cleared.

For a fortnight past Thérèse had remained nursing Rose, still feeling firmly convinced of her husband's innocence, but intensely hurt at receiving no news of him in spite of the stir occasioned by the affair, which all the newspapers had recounted. And since her daughter had been recovering, already able to get up, her arm healing in a satisfactory manner, Thérèse, mastered by increasing sorrow, had remained mute, quite overcome, in her deserted home. But that very evening, while Marc was gaily completing his account of his conversation with Marsouillier, she experienced a great shock, for François suddenly entered the room. And the scene was a poignant one, however simple might be the words that were exchanged.

' You did not think me guilty, Thérèse? '

'No, François, I assure you.'

'This morning, in the sad solitude in which I found my-self, I was still ignorant of everything. . . . But I happened to glance at an old newspaper, and then I hastened here. How is Rose?'

'She is much better. She is there, in the bedroom.'

François had not dared to kiss his wife. She stood be-fore him, erect and severe amid her emotion. But Marc, who had risen, caught hold of his grandson's hands, guess-ing by his pallor, his ravaged face, which still bore traces of his tears, that he had been involved in some tragic drama.

'Come, tell me everything, my poor lad.'

Then François, in a few quivering words and with all sincerity, recounted his folly—his sudden flight from Maille-bois on the arm of that Colette who had maddened him; their life of seclusion in a lonely district of Beaumont, where they had scarcely quitted their room; a fortnight's cloistered life, interspersed with furious storms, extrava-gant caprices on the part of that passionate gipsy, re-proaches, tears, and even blows; then, all at once, her flight nobody knew whither, after a last scene when she had flung the furniture at her lover's head. That had happened three weeks previously, and at first he had awaited her re-turn, then buried himself, as it were, in the seclusion of that lonely room, full of despair and remorse, no longer knowing how to return to Maillebois to his wife, whom he declared he had never ceased to love in spite of all his folly.

While he spoke, Thérèse, who was still standing there, had turned her head aside. And when he had finished she said, 'There is no occasion for me to know those things. . . . I merely understand that you have come back to answer the charges brought against you.'

'Oh!' Marc gently observed, 'those charges have now ceased to exist.'

'I have come back to see Rose,' François on his side de-clared, 'and I repeat that I would have been here the very next day if I had not remained ignorant of everything.'

'Very good,' Thérèse rejoined; 'I do not prevent you from seeing your daughter; she is there—you may go in.'

There ensued a very singular scene which Marc watched with impassioned interest. Rose was seated in an arm-chair, reading, her injured arm hanging in a sling. As the door opened she looked up and raised a quivering cry, instinct, it seemed, both with fear and with joy.

' Oh! papa! '

Then she rose, and all at once seemed stupefied. ' But it was n't you, papa—was it—the other evening ? ' she cried. ' The man was shorter and his beard was different! '

And she continued to scrutinise her father as if she found him otherwise than she had pictured him since his flight— since she had watched her forsaken mother weeping. Had she pictured him as a wicked man, then, squat of build and with an ogre's face ? She now recognised the father with the pleasant smile, whom she adored; and if he had come back it was surely in order that no more tears might be shed in their dear home. But all at once she began to tremble at the thought of the dreadful consequences of her error.

'And to think I accused you, papa — that I kept on saying that the man was you! No, no, it was n't you, I told a story; I will explain it to the gendarmes if they come to take you! '

She sank back in the arm-chair, weeping bitterly, and her father had to take her on his lap, kiss her, and vow to her that their sorrows were all over. He himself stammered with emotion as he spoke. Had he behaved so vilely, then, that he had appeared a very monster in the eyes of his daughter, and that she had thought him capable of ill-using her so dreadfully ?

Thérèse, meantime, while listening, had striven to remain impassive, saying never a word. François glanced at her anxiously, as if to ascertain whether she would again tolerate his presence in that home which he had ravaged. And Marc, noticing the severity of her demeanour, her unwillingness to forgive, preferred to take his grandson away with him and provide him with a lodging pending the advent of a calmer hour.

That very evening the officers of the law presented themselves at Faustin's dwelling, but they did not find the rascal there. The place was closed, the man had fled, and the search for him failed: he was never taken. People ended by believing that he had escaped to America. His sister Colette had perhaps accompanied him thither, for although she was sought she was never seen again, either at Maillebois or at Beaumont. And the whole affair remained very obscure; one was reduced to conjectures. Had the brother and sister been accomplices ? Had Colette co-operated in some plot when she had induced François to carry her off, or had Faustin merely wished to avail himself in some mysterious manner of the situation which the elopement had created ? But the chief point of all was whether there had been some superior behind him, some man of intelligence and will, who had planned and prepared everything in view of a supreme assault on the new order of things, by renewing, as it were, the old Simon affair. All those suppositions were allowable, given the facts; and in the end nobody doubted that there had really been some mysterious agreement and ambush.

Thus, how great was Marc's relief when the authorities, being convinced of Faustin's guilt and flight, set the affair aside. At the first moment that renewal of the old abominations, that last supreme attempt to besmirch the secular schools, had greatly disquieted Marc. But he was astonished at the rapidity with which the truth had been made manifest by public good sense. The appearances against François had been far greater than those against Simon in the old days. His own daughter had accused him; and, even if she had retracted her words, it would simply have been said that she had yielded to family pressure. In former times no witnesses, neither a Bongard, nor a Doloir, nor a Savin, would have dared to come forward and say what they had heard or seen, for fear of compromising themselves. In former times Marsouillier would not have relieved his conscience; firstly, because he would have felt no need of doing so, and secondly because a powerful faction would have immediately risen to support and glorify his original falsehood. The Congregations had then been ready at hand, poisoning everything, making a dogma, a cult, of error. Rome in her battle against free thought had made a savage use of political parties, maddening them, hurling them one upon the other, in the hope of some civil war which, by cutting the nation in halves, might render her mistress of the majority, the poor and ignorant. And now that Rome was vanquished, that the Congregations were disappearing, that not a Jesuit would soon be left to obscure men's thoughts and pervert their actions, human reason was working freely. The explanation of all the good sense and logic which Marc had lately observed was not to be sought elsewhere. The simple fact was that the people, being now educated and freed from the errors of centuries, were becoming capable of truth and justice.

But amid the delight of victory some anxiety lingered in

Marc's heart, anxiety at the rupture which had occurred between François and Thérèse, that question of the happiness of man and woman, which happiness can only spring from their perfect agreement. Marc did not entertain any wild hope of being able to kill the passions and prevent our poor humanity from bleeding beneath the spur of desire. There would always be broken hearts, tortured and jealous flesh. Only, might one not hope that woman, being freed and raised to equality with man, would render the sexual struggle less bitter, impart to it some calm dignity ? Already during the recent scandal women had shown themselves the friends of truth, employing all their energy to discover it. They were emancipated from the Church; they were no longer possessed by base superstition and the fear of hell; they no longer feigned a false humility before the priests; they were no longer the servants who prostrated themselves before men, the sex which seems to acknowledge its abjection and which revenges itself for its enforced humility by rotting and disorganising everything. They had ceased to act as snares of voluptuousness in accordance with the discreet advice of their confessors, seeking to entrap men in order to promote the triumph of religion. They had become normal wives and mothers since they had been wrested from that morbid falsehood of the divine spouse, which had unhinged so many poor minds. And now was it not their duty to complete the great work by exercising the rights they had regained with great wisdom and kindness ?

At last it occurred to Marc to assemble the whole family at the school, in that large classroom where he himself had taught, and where Joseph and François had taught after him. And there was a certain solemnity about that meeting, held one afternoon at the close of September, amid the sunshine which cast gentle beams on the master's desk, the boys' forms, the blackboards, and the pictures hanging from the walls. Sébastien and Sarah came from Beaumont; Clément and Charlotte arrived with their daughter Lucienne from Jonville. And Joseph, warned some days previously, had returned from a holiday tour feeling very much affected by all that had occurred in his absence. Finally, Marc himself and Geneviève, accompanied by Louise and Joseph, repaired to the rendezvous, taking François with them— Thérèse and Rose awaiting their arrival in the classroom. Altogether twelve members of the family attended the gathering, and at first deep silence prevailed.

' My dear Thérèse,' said Marc at last, ' we have no wish
to do violence to your feelings, we have only come here for
a family chat.   .   .   .   You have no doubt suffered in your
heart, but you have never known such a great rending as
when husband and wife have seemed to come from two different worlds, and have suddenly found themselves parted
by such an abyss as to suggest no likelihood of ever being
united again.   In former times woman, in the hands of the
Church, had become an instrument of torture for man,
who was already freed.   Ah! how many tears were shed in
those days, how many homes were broken up! '

Silence fell again; then Geneviève, who was deeply
moved, in her turn said: ' Yes, my dear Marc, I often
regarded you wrongly, I often tortured you in the old days,
and you do right to recall those evil years; your words cannot wound me now, since I have had strength enough to
overcome the poison.   But how many women remained
agonising in the old dungeon, how many homes perished in
grief ?   I myself have never been entirely cured; I have
always trembled with the dread of being mastered once
more by long heredity and the perverting influence of early
education.   And if I have managed to remain erect, it is
thanks to you, your sturdy good sense and active affection,
for all which I thank you, my good Marc.'

Happy tears had come into her eyes, and she continued
with increasing emotion: 'Ah! my poor grandmother, my
poor mother!   Yes, they were to be pitied!   They were so
wretched, assailed by destructive ferments, cast out of their
sex, as it were, by their voluntary martyrdom.   My poor
grandmother was a terrible woman; but then she had never
known a joy in life, she lived in perpetual nothingness—
and thus why should she not have dreamt of reducing
others to the same painful renunciation of everything which
she had imposed upon herself ?   And my poor mother, too,
what a long agony did she undergo from having tasted the
delight of being loved, and afterwards from having lapsed
for ever into that religion of falsehood and death which
denies all the powers and joys of life! '

While Geneviève spoke two shadowy forms seemed to
flit by — the vanished forms of Madame Duparque and
Madame Berthereau—those pitiable, disquieting devotees
of another age, one of whom had belonged entirely to the
ferocious, exterminating Church, while the other, of a gentler
nature, had died in despair at the thought that she had never

attempted to sever her chain.   Geneviève's eyes seemed to wander away after them both.   She herself had known the great battle, for it had been waged around her and within her; and it was happiness for her to think that she had one day felt free again, and had returned to life and to health. But her eyes at last fell upon her daughter Louise, who smiled at her very lovingly, and then leant forward to kiss her.

'Mother,' said Louise, 'you were the bravest and the most deserving, for it was you who fought and suffered.   It is to you we owe the victory, paid for with so many tears. I remember.   Coming as I did after you, it was no great merit for me to free myself from the past; and if never a quiver of error disturbed me, it was because I profited by the terrible lesson which at one time made all our hearts bleed in our poor mourning home.'

'Be quiet, you flatterer,' replied Geneviève, laughing and returning her kiss.   'You were the child who saved us, whose strong and skilful little mind intervened so lovingly and triumphed over every obstacle.   We owe our peace to you; you were the first free little woman with enough intelligence, will, and resolution to set happiness on earth.

Then Marc, turning towards Thérèse, explained: 'You were not born, my dear, at the time of all those things, and you are ignorant of them.   Having come after Louise, having never had anything to do with baptism or confession or communion, you find it easy and simple to live freely beyond the pale of religious imposture and social prejudice, with no other bonds about you than those of your own reason and conscience.   But, for things to be as they are, mothers and grandmothers passed through frightful crises, the worst follies, the worst torments. . . . As is the case with all the social questions, the one solution lay in education.   It was necessary to impart knowledge to woman before setting her in her legitimate place as the equal and companion of man.   That was the first thing necessary, the essential condition of human happiness, for woman could only free man after being freed herself.   As long as she remained the priest's servant and accomplice, an instrument of reaction, espionage, and warfare in the home, man himself remained in chains, incapable of all virile and decisive action.   The strength of the future will lie in the absolute agreement of man and wife. . . . And so, my dear, you see how sad it makes us that misfortune should again

have come into your home. There is no abyss created by
different beliefs between you and François. You are of
the same spheres, the same education. He is not your
master by law and custom, as he would have been in the
old days; you are not his servant, seeking an opportunity
to revenge yourself on him for his mastery. You have the
same rights as he has. You can dispose of your life as you
choose. Your joint peace and agreement are based solely
on reason, logic, and the dictates of life itself, which, to be
lived in health and all fulness, requires the mating of man
and woman. But, alas! we see your peace destroyed by
the eternal fragility of human nature, unless indeed kindness of heart should help you to win it back.'

Thérèse had listened, calm, dignified, and with an expression of great deference: 'I know all those things,
grandfather; you must not think I have forgotten them,'
said she. 'But why has François been living with you for
some days past? He might have remained here. There
are two lodgings, the schoolmaster's and the schoolmistress's, and I do not prevent him from taking possession
of the former while I occupy the other. In that fashion he
can resume his duties when the boys come back in a few
days' time. We are free, as you say, and I desire to remain
free.'

Her father and her mother, Sébastien and Sarah, then
tried to intervene affectionately; and Geneviève, Louise,
and Charlotte, indeed all the women present, smiled at her,
entreated her with their glances; but she would listen to
nothing, she rejected their suggestions resolutely, though
without any anger.

'François has wounded me cruelly,' she said. 'I thought
I had quite ceased to love him, and I should be telling you
a falsehood if I said that I am now certain I love him
still. . . . You cannot wish me to tell an untruth,
you cannot wish me to resume life in common with him,
when it would be cowardice and shame.'

At this a cry escaped François, who hitherto had remained silent, and visibly anxious. 'But I, Thérèse, I
still love you!' he exclaimed. 'I love you as I never loved
you before, and if you have suffered, I think that I now
suffer even more than you have done!'

She turned towards him, and said very gently: 'You
speak the truth, I am willing to believe it. . . . It is
quite possible that you still love, in spite of your folly, for

amid all our craving for reason, our poor human hearts will ever remain a source of dementia. And as you suffer so much, there are two of us who suffer . . . dreadfully. But I cannot be your wife again if I no longer love you, if I no longer wish you for my husband. It would be unworthy of us both, our ill, in lieu of healing, would be poisoned by it. The best course for us to follow is to live as good neighbours, good friends, and attending to our work, each free once more.'

'But I, mamma!' cried Rose, whose eyes were full of tears.

'You, my darling? You will love us both to-morrow as you loved us yesterday. . . . And don't be anxious, these are questions which one only understands when one is older than you are.'

With a caressing gesture Marc summoned the girl to him, and, having seated her on his knees, he was about to plead the cause of François once more when Thérèse hastily forestalled him.

'No, no, grandfather, do not insist, I beg you. It is your tender heart, not your reason, that now wishes to speak. If you prevailed over me you might have cause to repent it. Let me be wise and strong. . . . I know very well that you wish to spare us suffering. Ah! let us confess that suffering will be eternal. It is in us, no doubt, for one of the unknown purposes of life. Our poor hearts will always bleed, we shall always rend them in hours of exasperated passion, in spite of all the health and all the good sense that we may succeed in acquiring. And, perhaps, that is the necessary good for happiness!'

A slight chilling quiver seemed to dim the bright sunlight; through all there passed a consciousness of the sorrowful grandeur of that recognition of suffering.

'But what does it matter?' Thérèse continued. 'Have no fears, grandfather, we will be worthy and brave. It is nothing to suffer, it is only necessary that suffering should not make us blind and wicked. Nobody will know that we suffer, and we will even try to be the better for it, more gentle to others, more desirous of assuaging the causes of grief which exist in the world. . . . And, besides, grandfather, do not regret anything; say to yourself that you have done all you possibly could do, that you have carried out an admirable task which will give us all the happiness that reason can yield. As for the rest, as for sentimental life, each with his or her love will settle that according to personal circumstances, even if it be in tears. Leave us, François and me, leave us to live and suffer even, as we choose, for it only concerns ourselves. It is sufficient that you should have freed our minds, and made us conscious of a world of truth and justice. . . . And as you have brought us together here, grandfather, it shall not be for the purpose of preventing a rupture, of which only François and myself can be the judges, but it shall be to give us an opportunity to acclaim you, to express to you our adoration, and our gratitude for your work! '

At this they all clapped hands, transported with delight, and the splendour of the sun seemed to have returned and to stream in a sheet of gold through the lofty windows. Yes, yes, this was the grandfather's triumph in that very classroom where he had fought so bravely, where he had given the best of his heart and his mind to those who would become the people of the morrow. Children, grand-children, great-grandchildren, all were his pupils, and all surrounded him as if he were a very venerable and powerful patriarch, from whom the happy future had sprung. He had kept Rose, who represented the last generation in its flower, on his lap; and she had twined her arms about his neck, and was covering his face with kisses. His daughter Louise, his son Clément, had set themselves beside him with Joseph and Charlotte. And Sébastien and Sarah smiled at him and stretched out their clasped hands, while Thérèse and François, drawn nearer together, it seemed, by their affection for the august old man, seated themselves at his feet. At last Marc, deeply moved, almost stifled by the caresses heaped on him, said jestingly, with a pleasant laugh, ' My children, my children, you must not make a god of me! You know very well that the churches are being shut up. . . . I am only a hard worker who has finished his day. Besides, I don't want to triumph without my dear Geneviève beside me.'

He drew her near, taking her by the arm, and they all kissed her as they had kissed him, in such wise that the husband and wife, once parted, then reconciled and from that time commanding all possible happiness, were conjointly glorified in that elementary classroom, among those humble forms on which, again and again, the children's children, all the generations going towards the happy city, would take their seats.

And that was Marc's reward for all his years of courage and effort. He saw his work before him. Rome had lost the battle, France was saved from death, from the dust and ruin in which Catholic nations disappear, one after the other. She had been rid of the clerical faction which had chosen her territory as its battlefield, ravaging her fields, poisoning her people, striving to create darkness in order to dominate the world once more. She was no longer threatened with burial beneath the ashes of a dead religion; she had again become her own mistress; she could go forward to her destiny as a liberating and justice-dealing power. And if she had conquered it was solely by the means of that primary education which had extracted the humble, the lowly ones of her country districts, from the ignorance of slaves, from the deadly imbecility in which Roman Catholicism had maintained them for centuries. Some had dared to say, ' Happy the poor in spirit! ' and from that mortal error had sprung the misery of two thousand years. The legend of the benefits of ignorance now appeared like a prolonged social crime. Poverty, dirt, superstition, falsehood, tyranny, woman exploited and held in contempt, man stupefied and mastered, every physical and every moral ill, were the fruits of that ignorance which had been fostered intentionally, which had served as a system of state politics and religious police. Knowledge alone would slay mendacious dogmas, disperse those who traded and lived on them, and become the source of wealth, whether in respect to the harvests of the soil or the general florescence of the human mind. No! happiness had never had its abode in ignorance; it lay in knowledge, which will change the frightful field of material and moral wretchedness into a vast and fruitful expanse, whose wealth from year to year culture will increase tenfold.

Thus Marc, laden with years and glory, had enjoyed the great reward of living long enough to see his work's result. Justice resides in truth alone, and there is no happiness apart from justice. And after the creation of families, after the foundation of the cities of just work, the nation itself was constituted on the day when, by decreeing integral education for all its citizens, it showed itself capable of practising truth and equity.

THE END